T0296639

ERROR-CORRECTING CODES

SECOND EDITION

THE MIT PRESS
CAMBRIDGE, MASSACHUSETTS, AND LONDON, ENGLAND

ERROR-CORRECTING CODES

SECOND EDITION

THE MIT PRESS
CAMBRIDGE, MASSACHUSETTS, AND LONDON, ENGLAND

ERROR-CORRECTING CODES

SECOND EDITION

W. Wesley Peterson
E. J. Weldon, Jr.

Set in Monotype Times New Roman

ISBN 978-0-262-16039-1 (hc : alk. paper), 978-0-262-52731-6 (pb)

Library of Congress catalog card number: 76-122262

The MIT Press is pleased to keep this title available in print by manufacturing
single copies, on demand, via digital printing technology.

Preface

Since the publication of the first edition of this book, there has been considerable progress in coding theory, and error-correcting codes have been incorporated in numerous working communication and memory systems. There has been a need for a revision of the book for perhaps the past five years. In fact, so much new work on error-correcting codes has been published since the first edition that preparation of the second edition has been a much greater task than writing the original book. Even in the original edition there were several difficult decisions as to what material to include; the decisions this time were much more difficult and subjective, and we expect them in many cases to prove controversial.

Unquestionably the most serious omission from this book is the recent work done in Russia and Eastern Europe. Important works include a highly-regarded book, *Decoding of Error-Correcting Codes* (1958) by V. D. Kolesnik and E. T. Mironchikov, a considerable portion of which deals with majority-logic decoding. S. I. Samoylenko's fine book *Error-Protection Coding* (1966) emphasizes codes for which error correction is easily implemented by computer. V. G. Dadaev has a book *Arithmetic Error-Correcting Codes* (1969) and L. F. Borodin, in his book *Introduction to Error-Protection Coding* (1969), describes some decoding methods that use analog received signals. A further indication of the extent of Russian work is the extensive bibliography "A Survey of Progress in Coding Theory in the Soviet Union," compiled by W. H. Kautz and K. N. Levitt (*IEEE Trans.*, *IT-15*, No. 1, Part II), which references over 400 Russian papers on coding. In light of these publications, a more suitable title for the present book might have been "Error-Correcting Codes in the Western World."

This second edition contains essentially all of the material of the first. The major additions are Chapter 10 on Majority-Logic Codes, Chapter 12 on Synchronization, and Chapters 13 and 14 on Convolutional Codes. Much new material has also been added to Chapters 5 and 8.

We would like to thank our friend and colleague at the University of Hawaii, Shu Lin, for many helpful comments and discussions during the four years we spent writing this book. Other valuable inputs were provided by T. Kasami, C. L. Chen, and E. R. Berlekamp. Our typists Gayle Harimoto and Roberta Hakoda have also contributed importantly to the book.

Our work has been supported by the University of Hawaii, the U.S. Air Force Cambridge Research Laboratory, the NASA Electronics Research Center, and the National Science Foundation.

Chapter dependencies are approximately as follows: 1, 2, 3(1, 2), 4(3), 5(3), 6(2), 7(6), 8(3, 7), 9(8), 10(8), 11(8), 12(8), 13(3), 14(3), 15(6).

Honolulu, Hawaii W. W. PETERSON
February, 1971 E. J. WELDON, JR.

Contents

1 The Coding Problem

Several major developments have contributed to the rapid emergence of the field of error-correcting codes over the past two decades. Externally, the cost of solid-state electronic devices has decreased almost as dramatically as their size. This has stimulated the development of digital computers and peripheral devices and this, in turn, has caused a dramatic increase in the volume of data communicated between such machines. The intolerance of computing systems to error, and in some cases the inherently critical nature of the data demand the use of either error-free facilities or some type of error-detecting or correcting code in the terminal devices. In many cases the latter approach is the more economical.

There have also been significant accomplishments within the field of error-correcting codes itself. Several classes of long, powerful codes have been devised. In addition, decoding procedures which can be implemented with a modest amount of hardware have been devised for several of these classes of codes.

These and other developments have made the use of error-correcting codes quite practical today in data communications systems. In the near future the prospect is that the trends mentioned above will continue, and that error-correcting codes will become much more widely employed.

This chapter introduces the concept of a communication channel, describes the role of codes in communication, and defines block and tree codes and other fundamental concepts.

1.1 The Communication Channel

A block diagram of a digital communication system is shown in Figure 1.1. The same model can be used to describe an information storage system, if the storage medium is considered to be a channel. A typical transmission channel is a telephone line; a typical storage device is a magnetic-tape unit including writing and reading heads. The source information is usually composed of binary or decimal digits or alphabetic information in some form. The encoder transforms these messages into signals acceptable to the channel — typically electrical signals with some restrictions on power, bandwidth, and duration. These signals enter the channel and are perturbed by noise. The output enters the decoder, which makes a decision concerning which message was sent and delivers this message to the sink. The communication engineering problem is principally to design the encoder and the decoder, although it may also include improving the channel. Note that here the encoder performs what is usually called modulation and the decoder includes detection.

Analysis shows that many communication channels of the form of Figure 1.1 have a definite capacity for information transmission. Furthermore, if the rate of the source is less than this capacity, then it is possible to choose a set of signals such that the probability of erroneous decoding is arbitrarily small (Fano 1961; Feinstein 1958; Kelly 1960; Shannon 1949, 1957). This theory does not indicate precisely how these signals are to be constructed nor does it guarantee that such a system can be built in the real world.

The use of error-correcting codes is an attempt to circumvent these last two problems. A system that employs the type of coding described in this book is shown in Figure 1.2.

The converters in this system simply translate symbols in one alphabet to symbols in another. Usually both alphabets are rather small — a typical conversion might be from decimal to binary. The modulator accepts at its input a single channel symbol and produces at its output the corresponding channel waveform, that is, a pulse which is always

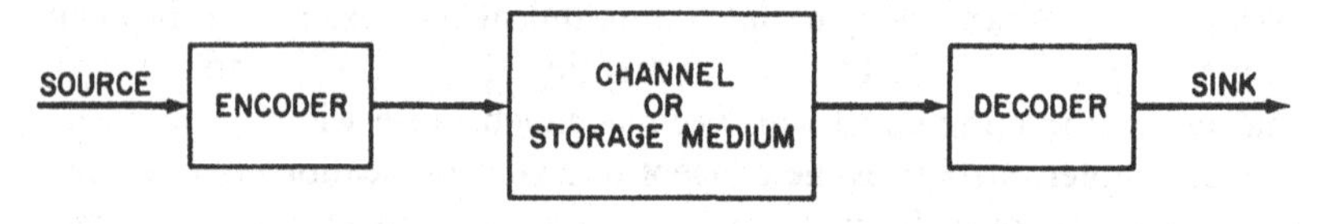

Figure 1.1. Block diagram of a general data communication or storage system.

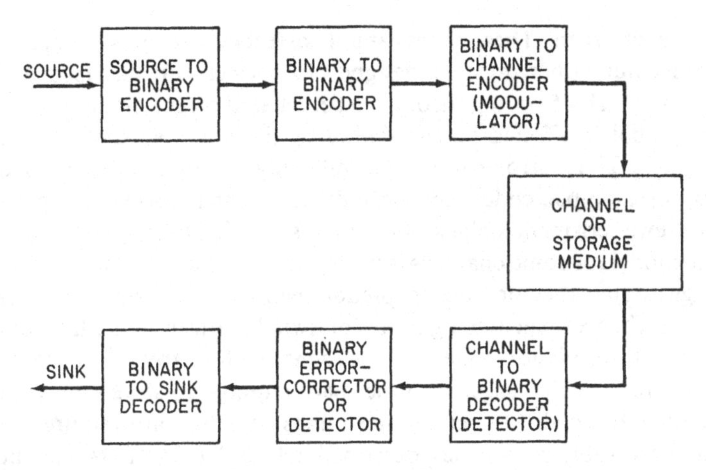

Figure 1.2. Block diagram of a typical data communication system employing an error-correcting code.

associated with that symbol. This handling of a single channel symbol at a time by the modulator is a restriction that definitely causes a loss in channel capacity. The demodulator performs the inverse operation of the modulator; it attempts to associate a channel symbol with the noise-corrupted received waveform. This independent demodulation of individual pulses results in a further loss in channel capacity. The encoder and decoder implement the channel symbol error-correcting code which is employed. The efficient design of these devices is the subject of this book.

Even though breaking the receiver into a demodulator and decoder and the transmitter into an encoder and modulator reduces the performance ultimately attainable with a data transmission system, it is still possible to attain an arbitrarily low probability of erroneous decoding with such a system, although the channel capacity is somewhat lower. In addition, and most important from a practical viewpoint, the use of coding makes it possible to design and actually construct highly effective data transmission and storage terminals.

1.2 Some General Remarks on Error-Detecting and Error-Correcting Codes

In an ideal system the symbol that comes out of the channel-symbol-to-sink-symbol converter should match the symbol that entered the source-symbol-to-channel-symbol converter. In a practical system there are occasional errors, and it is the purpose of codes to detect and perhaps correct such errors. These codes cannot correct every conceivable pattern of errors but rather must be designed to correct only the most likely patterns. Much of coding theory has been based on the assumption that each symbol is affected independently by the noise, so that the probability of a given error pattern depends only on the number of errors. Thus, for example, codes have been developed that correct any pattern of t or fewer errors in a block of n symbols. While this may be an appropriate model for some channels, on telephone lines and on magnetic-tape storage systems errors occur predominantly in bursts. Telephone-line disturbances, such as lightning or switching transients, last longer than the transmission time for one symbol. Similarly, magnetic-tape defects are typically larger than the space required to store one symbol. Consequently, codes for correcting bursts of errors are required, and some remarkably good codes, described in Chapters 11 and 14, have been developed for this purpose.

The communication channels shown in Figures 1.1 and 1.2 are strictly one-way channels. Very frequently communication systems employ two-way channels, a fact that must be considered in designing codes. With a two-way channel, for example, an error-detecting code can be used. When an error is detected at one terminal, a request for a repeat can be given, and thus errors can effectively be corrected.

There are true examples of one-way channels, in which error probabilities can be reduced with error-correcting codes but not by error detection and retransmission. With a magnetic-tape storage system, for example, it is too late to ask for a retransmission after the tape has been stored a week or a month, and errors are detected when the record is read. Encoding for error-correcting codes is no more complex than for error detection; it is the decoding that is likely to require complex equipment. For transmission from a space vehicle, for example, where the amount of equipment at the transmitter is much more important than the total amount of equipment, the encoding equipment for an error-correcting system is likely to be more practical than provision for remotely controlled retransmission. The complex error-correcting procedures can be performed on earth, where equipment limitations are not severe. Hence there are system problems that call for error-correcting codes requiring no feedback.

On the other hand, there are good reasons for using error detection and retransmission when possible in practical systems. Error detection is by its nature a much simpler task than error correction and requires much simpler decoding equipment. Also, error detection with retransmission is adaptive — transmission of redundant information is increased when errors occur. This makes it possible under certain circumstances to get better performance with a system of this kind than is theoretically possible on a one-way channel.

There is a definite limit to the efficiency of a system that uses simple error detection alone. Short error-detecting codes cannot detect errors efficiently, while if extremely long codes are used, retransmission must be done too frequently. It can be shown that a combination of correction of the most frequent error patterns and detection coupled with retransmission for less frequent error patterns is not subject to this limitation and, in fact, is often more efficient than either error correction or detection and retransmission alone. Although most present-day equipment uses error detection and retransmission only, several systems have been built that demonstrate clearly the potential of combined error correction and detection with feedback (Burton and Weldon, 1965; Lebow et al., 1963).

1.3 Types of Codes

The encoder of Figure 1.2 accepts at its input a continuous sequence of information digits. At its output it produces another sequence with somewhat more digits, which is fed to the modulator. Conversely, the decoder accepts a sequence of channel symbols from the demodulator and translates it into a somewhat shorter sequence of information digits. The rules under which the encoder and decoder operate are specified by the particular code that is employed.

There are two fundamentally different types of codes. The encoder for a *block code* breaks the continuous sequence of information digits into k-symbol sections or blocks. It then operates on these blocks independently according to the particular code to be employed. With each possible information block is associated an n-tuple of channel symbols, where $n > k$. The result, now called a *code word*, is transmitted, corrupted by noise, and decoded independently of all other code words. The quantity n is referred to as the *code length* or *block length*.

The other type of code, called a *tree code*, operates on the information sequence without breaking it up into independent blocks. Rather, the encoder for a tree code processes the information continuously and associates each long (perhaps semi-infinite) information sequence with a code sequence containing somewhat more digits. The encoder breaks its input sequence into k_0-symbol blocks, where k_0 is usually a small number. Then, on the basis of this k_0-tuple and the preceding information symbols, it emits an n_0-symbol section of the code sequence. The name "tree code" stems from the fact that the encoding rules for this type of code are most conveniently described by means of a tree graph. This point is explained in Section 1.5.

Of the two classes of codes, the older block codes have a considerably better developed theory. The reason for this seems to be that block codes are more closely related to established, relatively well-understood, mathematical structures. As a result, considerably more research has been done on them than on tree codes.

The class of *convolutional codes* forms a subset of the class of tree codes. These codes are important since they are simpler to implement than other types of tree codes. In this book only these convolutional tree codes are considered.

Block codes and convolutional codes have similar error-correcting capabilities and the same fundamental limitations. In particular, Shannon's fundamental theorem for the discrete noisy channel holds for both types of codes. This result states that a channel has a well-defined capacity and that by using suitable codes it is possible to transmit information at any rate less than channel capacity with arbitrarily small probability of decoding erroneously.

1.4 Block Codes

Let q denote the number of distinct symbols employed on the channel; here q is arbitrary, although in later chapters q will be assumed to be a power of a prime and the binary case ($q = 2$) will receive the greatest emphasis. A block code is a set of M sequences of channel symbols of length n. These q-ary n-tuples are called the *code words* of the code. In this book, as in all practical systems and most theoretical analyses, the number of code words is taken to be a power of q; that is, $M = q^k$.

At the receiver a decision is made, on the basis of the information in the received n-tuple, concerning the code word transmitted. This decision is a statistical decision; that is, it is of the nature of a best guess on the basis of available information and so is not infallible. With a good code, the probability of a wrong decision is usually much smaller than the probability that the original channel input symbols are reproduced without error at the channel output.

The decision process can be defined mathematically by a *decoding table*. The code words make up the first row of the table. If a code word is received, it is logical to assume the same code word was transmitted. The decision of the receiver for other possible received words is described by listing under each code word the received words that would be decoded into it. Thus every possible received word appears once and only once in the decoding table.

Example: Suppose that there are four possible messages, a, b, c, and d, and that a message is to be transmitted using a binary block code of length five. Then four code words must be chosen, say 1 1 0 0 0 for a, 0 0 1 1 0 for b, 1 0 0 1 1 for c, and 0 1 1 0 1 for d. The decision of the receiver must be described for each of the $2^5 = 32$ possible received words, or 5-tuples. An example of how this might be done is shown in Figure 1.3.

The code and decoding scheme shown in Figure 1.3 decode correctly if the received word has no more than one error, that is, no more than one altered symbol, since each of the five words that would result from a single error are listed below each code word. Certain other error patterns are decoded correctly, while still others result in errors. For example, if 1 1 0 0 0 is transmitted, and two errors occur, resulting in reception of 1 1 1 1 0, it will be decoded correctly, because 1 1 1 1 0 is in the column under 1 1 0 0 0 in Figure 1.3. However, if two errors result in 1 1 0 1 1, it will be decoded incorrectly into 1 0 0 1 1, because 1 1 0 1 1 is in the column under 1 0 0 1 1.

In some situations one might allow the decoder simply to state that an error is detected but not to guess which code word was transmitted. This might take the form of an error-detection system, in which the decoder signals detection but attempts no other decision if other than a code word is received. Also, as mentioned earlier, it might combine error detection and correction. For example, for the code shown in Figure 1.3, any received word above the dashed line might be decoded into the code word at the top of the column, but the decoder might merely signal "error detection" for received words below the dashed line. This would correspond to single-error correction with detection of some combinations of two or more errors.

In order to predict the performance of a code, it is necessary to have precise information about the channel. Though most real communica-

Code Words	1 1 0 0 0	0 0 1 1 0	1 0 0 1 1	0 1 1 0 1
Other Received Words	1 1 0 0 1	0 0 1 1 1	1 0 0 1 0	0 1 1 0 0
	1 1 0 1 0	0 0 1 0 0	1 0 0 0 1	0 1 1 1 1
	1 1 1 0 0	0 0 0 1 0	1 0 1 1 1	0 1 0 0 1
	1 0 0 0 0	0 1 1 1 0	1 1 0 1 1	0 0 1 0 1
	0 1 0 0 0	1 0 1 1 0	0 0 0 1 1	1 1 1 0 1
	- - - - -	- - - - -	- - - - -	- - - - -
	1 1 1 1 0	0 0 0 0 0	0 1 0 1 1	1 0 1 0 1
	0 1 0 1 0	1 0 1 0 0	1 1 1 1 1	0 0 0 0 1

Figure 1.3. Decoding table for a binary code with $q = k = 2$ and $n = 5$.

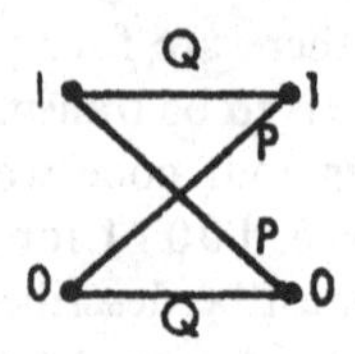

Figure 1.4. The binary symmetric channel.

tion channels are not accurately represented by the binary symmetric channel (BSC), shown in Figure 1.4, it has been studied extensively. For the binary symmetric channel, the probability is Q that the same symbol as transmitted will be received. It is assumed that $Q > P$ and that each symbol is independent of all others. (Such a channel is called "memoryless.") Note that this "channel" includes the modulator, channel, and demodulator of the typical system shown in Figure 1.2.

Another idealized channel that has been studied extensively is the binary erasure channel, shown in Figure 1.5. For this channel, the probability is Q that the same binary digit (bit) will be received as was transmitted. The probability is $P = 1 - Q$ that a transmitted symbol will be erased. (An erasure is indicated by an X.) The binary symbols are assumed to be affected independently. Note that with this channel the locations of perturbed symbols are known, and this fact makes correction of erasures easier than correction of errors. Generalizations of the erasure channel include a nonbinary erasure channel and a channel with both erasures and errors. The erasure channel is an idealization of a system in which the demodulator of Figure 1.2 is designed to deliver an erasure symbol rather than a 1 or 0 in doubtful cases.

Now if the binary symmetric channel is assumed, and if a particular binary code word is transmitted, the probability that no error will occur is Q^n. The probability that one error will occur in a specified position is PQ^{n-1}. The probability of a particular received word that differs from the transmitted word in i positions is P^iQ^{n-i}. Since $Q > P$, the received block with no errors is more likely than any other. Any received word

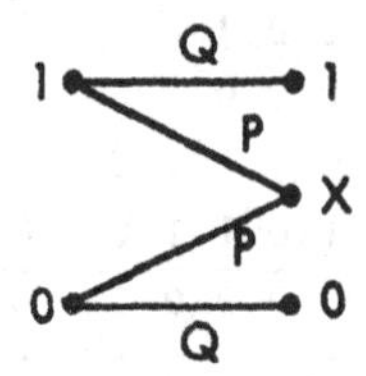

Figure 1.5. The binary erasure channel.

with one error is more likely than any with two or more errors, and so on. In this case, for an assumption that all the code words are equally likely to be transmitted, the best decision at the receiver would be always to decode into a code word that differs from the received word in the fewest positions. This *maximum-likelihood decoding*, as it is called, can be generalized to nonbinary memoryless channels.

Again for an assumption of the binary symmetric channel, the probability of correct decoding can be calculated in the following way for the code shown in Figure 1.3. Suppose that 1 1 0 0 0 is transmitted. It will be decoded correctly if any word in its column is received. One of these words differs in no positions, five differ in one position, and two differ in two positions. The probability of correct decoding is then

$$P(\text{correct decoding}) = 1P^0Q^5 + 5P^1Q^4 + 2P^2Q^3.$$

Similar calculations can be made for the other code words.

If this code is used only for error detection, the probability of correct reception is Q^5. The probability of an undetected error if 1 1 0 0 0 is transmitted is the probability that another code word is received when 1 1 0 0 0 is transmitted. Since one code word differs in four positions and the other two in three positions each,

$$P(\text{undetected error}) = 1P^4Q + 2P^3Q^2.$$

The concept of Hamming distance (Hamming 1950) is useful in discussing the error-correcting ability of codes. The *Hamming distance* between two words is defined to be the number of positions in which the words differ. Thus, a single error results in a Hamming distance 1 between transmitted word and received word. If a code is used only for error detection and must detect all patterns of $d - 1$ or fewer errors, it is necessary and sufficient for the minimum Hamming distance between code words to be d. For if the minimum distance is d, no pattern of $d - 1$ errors can change one code word into another, while if the minimum distance is $d - 1$ or less, there exists some pair of words at distance less than d apart and then there is a pattern of fewer than d errors which will carry one into the other.

Similarly, it is possible to decode in such a way as to correct all patterns of t or fewer errors if and only if the minimum distance between code words is at least $2t + 1$. Then any received word with $t' \leqq t$ errors differs from the transmitted code word in t' symbols but from every other code word in at least $2t + 1 - t' > t'$ symbols. On the other hand, if the minimum distance is less, there is at least one case where a t-fold error results in a received word at least as close to an incorrect code word as to the transmitted code word. Finally, by a similar argument, it can be seen that it is possible to decode in a way that corrects all combinations of t or fewer errors and simultaneously detects all combinations of d or fewer errors ($d \geq t$) if and only if the minimum distance between code words is $t + d + 1$.

In addition to their application to the communication problem, block codes have application in several other areas: They are the basis for the load-sharing switching matrix (Chien 1959; Constantine 1958; Marcus 1959; Takahashi and Goto 1959), which is not only more efficient than conventional memory addressing systems but does some automatic correction for component failures, and they are the same in mathematical structure as some statistical experiment designs (Bose 1939; Mann 1949; Lin 1968). They have also been proposed for use in document retrieval systems (Chien and Frazer 1966), for data compression (Berger 1970) and fault-tolerant computers.

1.5 Tree Codes

Unlike block codes, the codes of this section do not break the information sequence into blocks and handle them independently. Rather, a tree code associates a (possibly semi-infinite) code sequence with an information sequence. The rules for this association are most easily described by means of a tree graph. A particular binary tree is depicted in Figure 1.6. The vertical members are called *nodes*, the horizontal members, *branches*. In the general case every branch has an n_0-symbol q-ary sequence; from every node emanate q^{k_0} branches, where $k_0 < n_0$. (Trees in which the number of symbols per branch and number of branches per node are not constant can also be defined, but these are unimportant in coding theory.)

Now, given an information sequence, a tree is used to specify a code sequence in the following way: First, the q-ary information sequence is broken into k_0-symbol blocks. Then the first block is used to specify one of the branches at the first node according to some prearranged convention. Similarly, the second k_0-symbol information block employs the same convention to specify one of the branches emanating from the second node, and so forth. In this way a single path is traced through the tree. The set of n_0-tuples associated with the path forms the code sequence specified by the information sequence. The rate R of such a code is k_0/n_0. Figure 1.7 depicts a general encoder for a tree code.

Example: Let the information sequence to be encoded be 1 0 1 1 0 0 1 0... and assume that the binary code determined by the tree of Figure 1.6 is to be used. For this code, $q = 2$, $k_0 = 1$, $n_0 = 2$ and

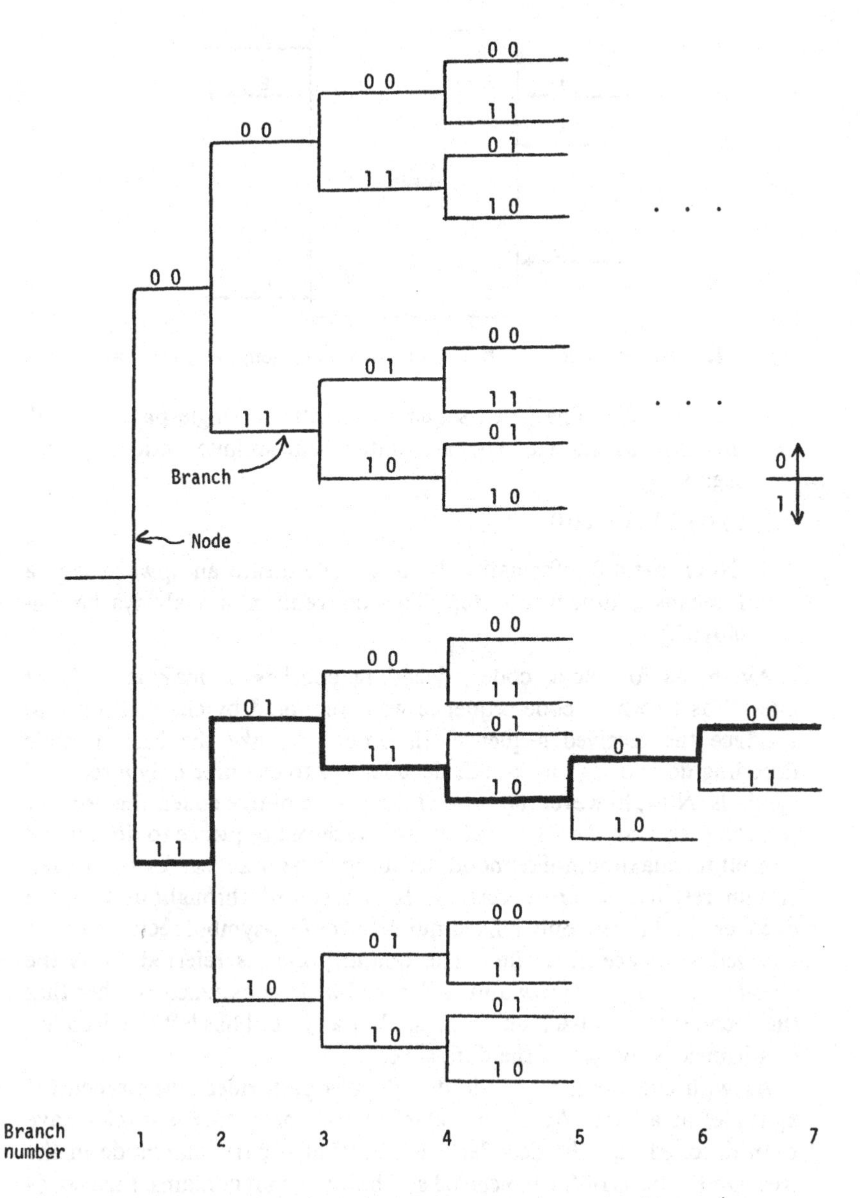

Figure 1.6. A section of a semi-infinite binary tree for a code with $R = \frac{1}{2}$. (The heavy-line path is for the information sequence 1 0 1 1 0 0 . . . .)

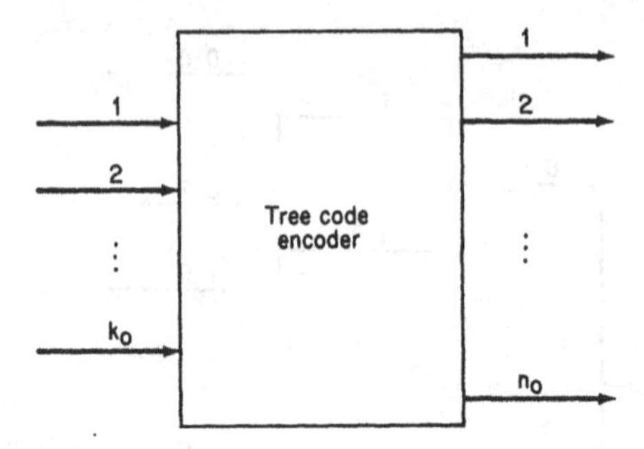

Figure 1.7. An encoder for a tree code with block length n_0 and rate k_0/n_0.

then $R = 0.5$. The given sequence specifies a single path through the tree, as shown. The associated semi-infinite code sequence begins

110111100100...

(Note that a 0 information bit at a node means an upward step, a 1 means a downward step. This convention will always be employed.)

Again, as for block codes, decoding consists of making a "best guess" as to which code sequence was corrupted by channel noise to produce the received sequence. In order to make the best possible decoding decision, a block-code decoder has to examine only n received symbols. Now, however, because of the nature of tree codes, the decoder may have to examine an extremely long received sequence to do this. As a result for maximum-likelihood decoding to be practical for tree codes, certain restrictions are necessary. It is assumed throughout that the decoder can process only a fixed number m of n_0-symbol sections of the received sequence at a time. The quantity mn_0 is referred to as the *decoding constraint length* and is denoted n. It is assumed further that the decoder cannot back up. That is, after a symbol has left the decoder, it is irretrievably lost to the data sink.

As with encoding, tree-code decoding is performed one branch (or n_0-tuple) at a time. At a particular time all preceding n_0-tuples have been decoded and the decoder finds itself at a particular node in the tree. On the basis of the n received symbols which it contains, the decoder must decide which of the q^{k_0} branches leading from that node is the correct one. It makes its choice, the k_0-symbol information block corresponding to the chosen branch is forwarded to the data sink, and another n_0-symbol section of the received sequence enters the decoder.

The rules that are employed in the decision process are determined, in large measure, by the channel. For instance, on the binary symmetric channel a well-designed decoder chooses the branch that leads to the path whose Hamming distance from the received sequence is smallest.

Example: Suppose the second digit of the received sequence of the previous example is in error. That is, let the received sequence be 1 0 0 1 1 1 .... The possible code sequences (paths) begin

0000..., 0011..., 1101..., 1110....

Clearly, the third path, which differs from the received sequence in but a single position, is the best choice. The information sequence for this path begins 1 0 .... Thus, the single error has been corrected.

Now suppose digits 2 and 3 were erroneously received. The closest path would be 0 0 1 1 ..., and the information sequence at the decoder output would be 0 1 ... rather than 1 0 ..., as it would in the absence of errors. Thus, the decoder would make an error.

In this example the decoder examined 4-bit sections of the received sequence. This was sufficient to correct a single error but not two errors. It is reasonable to guess that, had the decoding constraint length been larger, it would have been possible to correct more errors. For tree codes in general this may be true. In the present example it is not; double error patterns cannot be unambiguously corrected regardless of how large n is made. This is because of the repetitive nature of the particular tree employed. (See Problem 1.7.)

In this book a *code word* in a tree code is taken to mean an n-tuple associated with an m-branch path. With this definition the notions of the minimum distance between code words, the decoding table, etc., previously defined for block codes carry over to tree codes, although not without modification.

A tree code with rate $R = k_0/n_0$ which employs a decoder capable of processing m branches at a time has $q^{k_0 m} = q^k$ code words. Clearly, there are only $q^{mn_0} = q^n$ possible received words to consider. As before, the decoding table consists of this set of received words arranged in q^k columns with each column headed by a code word. Each column consists of the received words that are decoded into the code word at its head. With a tree code, however, there is no point in distinguishing between code words whose first n_0 digits are identical, for these q^{k_0} words result in exactly the same decoder output. Thus, it is natural to group the columns of the decoding table into q^{k_0} *subsets*, the first of which is referred to as the *correct subset*. (The other subsets form the *incorrect subset*.) It can easily be seen that each of these subsets contains exactly q^{k-k_0} columns. Then in decoding it is necessary to determine only in which subset the received word lies.

Example: The code of the preceding examples can be decoded with a 2-branch decoder. Thus $n = 4$. The table for decoding the first block is shown in Figure 1.8.

This table shows that if a single error occurs, correct decoding results because each of the four received words which could result from a single error is in the same subset as the transmitted code word, that is, the correct subset. It also shows that all double errors cause erroneous decoding. Some triple errors will be decoded correctly, however. For instance, if the code word 0000 is transmitted and the word 0111 is received, the decoder output is 0, as it should be. However, these errors will cause the decoder to err when it attempts to decode the second block, because in the absence of additional errors, and on assumption that the third transmitted block is also 00, the received word will be 1100. This word is closest to the code word 1110 and so causes the second decoder output to be a 1 rather than a 0.

The usefulness of a decoding table for tree codes appears to be somewhat limited, because, in general, a different table may be necessary for each node in the tree. The reader may notice that in Figure 1.6, for example, two apparently different tables are necessary. (See Problem 1.6.) Fortunately, for all tree codes discussed in later chapters, that is, convolutional or recurrent codes, this difference is unimportant and a single decoding table suffices.

The minimum Hamming distance, denoted d, of a tree code is defined as the minimum over the entire tree of the distances between code words in different subsets. For tree codes in general this is not a very useful concept. However, for the important subclass of convolu-

	Correct Subset		Incorrect Subset	
Code Words	0 0 0 0	0 0 1 1	1 1 0 1	1 1 1 0
Other Received Words	1 0 0 0	1 0 1 1	0 1 0 1	0 1 1 0
	0 1 0 0	0 1 1 1	1 0 0 1	1 0 1 0
	0 0 1 0	0 0 0 1	1 1 1 1	1 1 0 0
Decoder Output	0		1	

Figure 1.8. A decoding table for the binary tree code of Figure 1.6.

tional codes, all nodes have identical distance properties. Thus, for these codes d is simply the smallest distance between code words in different subsets of the decoding table. In any case, the code can correct all error sequences in which not more than t errors occur in any m adjacent n_0-symbol blocks if and only if $d \geqq 2t + 1$. Also, any error sequence which contains $d - 1$ or fewer errors in m consecutive blocks will be detected if and only if the code has minimum distance d.

The problem of determining the probability of correct decoding for tree codes is considerably more difficult than for block codes. On a binary symmetric channel, for example, successive decodings of block-code words are independent events, and it is not difficult, at least conceptually, to sum the probabilities of all correctable error patterns. With tree codes, on the contrary, successive decodings are highly dependent events even on a memoryless channel. For in this case a particular decoding involves exactly $(m - 1)n_0$ of the symbols employed in decoding the preceding word. Thus, if it is known that the preceding word was decoded incorrectly, the probability that the current word will also be incorrectly decoded is considerably higher than if nothing is known about the preceding word.

It is not possible, in most practical situations, to compute the conditional probability of correct decoding, given the results of all previous decodings; there are simply too many cases to consider. Because of this difficulty, it is customary to calculate the probability of a correct first decoding, that is, with information about preceding decodings ignored.

1.6 The Coding Problem

For codes to be very effective they must be long, so as to average the effects of noise over a large number of symbols. Such a code may have 10^{100} possible code words and many times this number of possible received words. While the code and decoding are still conceptually described by a table such as that shown in Figure 1.3, it becomes impossible to construct such a table, or even list the code words. Mathematical structure can enable us to determine the important properties of such codes, however. Even more important, such structure can make it feasible for the encoding and decoding operations to be implemented in electronic equipment.

Thus, there are three main aspects of the coding problems: (1) To find codes that have the required error-correcting ability. This usually demands that the codes be long. (2) To find a practical method of encoding. (3) To find a practical method of making the decision at the receiver, that is, a method of error correction. The typical attack on the problem has been to find codes that could be proved mathematically to satisfy the required error-correcting ability. These codes must have mathematical structure to make even this possible. This mathematical structure is then exploited to meet the other two requirements, ability to encode and to decode.

Notes

While the principal purpose of this book is to treat error-correcting codes, error detection, including combined error detection and error correction, is also discussed. The error-detecting ability of a code is closely related to its ability to correct errors, and it is only natural to consider both properties together.

Nearly all present-day equipment is binary, and therefore binary codes are of the greatest importance now. In most cases codes can be generalized to the case of q symbols, where q is any power of any prime number, with very minor changes in descriptions, derivations, and proofs. This more general case is important: In the first place a nonbinary code may be used with nonbinary information — decimal information can be represented quite efficiently in a $q = 11$ code, for example. Second, new binary codes can be constructed from nonbinary codes, especially those for which q is a power of 2. The general case is treated in this book wherever it does not encumber the presentation. The reader who is interested only in binary codes can merely replace q by 2 and the words "field element" by "binary symbol" as he reads.

Hamming distance (Hamming 1950) is emphasized in this book; however, at least one other distance function, Lee distance (Berlekamp 1968*a*; Lee 1958; Prange 1959; Ulrich 1957), has been used in coding theory. Lee distance and Hamming distance coincide in the binary case and for $q = 3$.

The emphasis in this book is on codes whose basic structure is algebraic. Most work in coding theory is in this area. Codes associated with other types of mathematical structures, such as finite geometries, are also considered.

Random codes, that is, codes selected at random and having no structure whatever, have also been studied. These are discussed briefly in this book; the reader is referred to Gallager 1963, 1968, Wozencraft 1957, Shannon and Weaver 1949, and to the numerous technical papers on random coding. Both block and tree random codes have been studied. Gallager (1963) has devised an effective decoding procedure for random block codes; Wozencraft (1957, 1961) and others (Fano 1963; Savage 1966*a*, 1966*b*; Wozencraft and Jacobs 1965) have devised a practical decoding procedure, known as sequential decoding, for random tree codes. It appears that in many situations these random codes are competitive with algebraic codes. Sequential decoding is discussed briefly in Chapter 13.

Almost invariably, for any result pertaining to an error channel (such as the binary symmetric channel), an analogous result exists for an erasure channel. Many of these are given as exercises. A few — notably the use of Bose-Chaudhuri-Hocquenghem (BCH) codes with a channel with errors and erasures — are presented in the text. Elias (1954) introduced the concept of an erasure channel, and many of the results presented in this book on erasure channels are directly or indirectly attributable to him. General decoding for the erasure channel has been studied by Epstein (1958). Convolutional codes originated with Elias (1954) and Wozencraft (1957).

In this book decoders are considered for channels with q inputs and outputs and for the binary erasure channel. Decoding for more general channels, in which the number of outputs exceeds the number of inputs, has also been studied. (Elias 1956 Fano 1961, Gallager 1968). For these channels the decoder can be said to receive some reliability information along with the sequence of symbols. The problem of using this information in decoding block codes has been considered by Gallager (1963), Massey (1963), and Forney (1966). The most important known decoding procedures for convolutional codes (Massey 1963, Wozencraft 1957, Viterbi 1967) can also make use of this reliability information.

Our present understanding of the more general problem of coding messages into continuous signals and thereby utilizing the full capacity of a continuous channel is comparable with our understanding fifteen years ago of the discrete channel (Kelly 1960; Shannon 1959; Slepian 1968). Some progress has also been made in the understanding of the use of a two-way channel (Berlekamp 1964*a*; Horstein 1960; Weldon 1963; Wozencraft 1960).

Gallager (1968) presents an excellent general treatment of information theory; this book contains many important results relating to coding theory that are otherwise available only in journal articles, if at all. Shannon's classic original paper (1949) is still a good reference.

Problems

1.1. Form a maximum-likelihood decoding table for the binary code consisting of the four code words 0000, 0011, 1100, and 1111,

a. Assuming the binary symmetric channel,
b. Assuming the binary erasure channel.

1.2. A "metric" function is defined as a real-valued function having the following three properties:

A: $d(x, y) = 0$ if and only if $x = y$	(reflexive)
B: $d(x, y) = d(y, x)$	(symmetric)
C: $d(x, y) \leqq d(y, z) + d(x, z)$	(triangle inequality)

Show that the Hamming distance is a metric function.

1.3. Suppose that the set of all received messages $x, y, \ldots$ is S, and that a metric function $d(x,y)$ is defined on this set S. Suppose that transmitted messages are in the same set. If x is transmitted and y received, an error of magnitude $d(x, y)$ is said to have occurred. A code C is a subset of S, the idea being that in using a code C, only messages $x_1, x_2, \ldots$ in C are transmitted.

a. Show that a code C is capable of detecting any error of magnitude d or less if and only if the distance between messages in the code C is greater than d.
b. Show that a code is capable of correcting any error of magnitude t if the minimum distance between code messages is greater than $2t$.

c. Show that a code can correct errors of magnitude t and simultaneously detect errors of magnitude $d \geqq t$ if the minimum distance between code messages is at least $t + d + 1$.

1.4. Show that if a code with minimum Hamming distance $e + 1$ between code blocks is used with an erasure channel, it is possible to decode in such a way as to correct all combinations of e or fewer erasures but not all combinations of $e + 1$ erasures.

1.5. Show that minimum Hamming distance at least $2t + e + 1$ between code blocks is necessary and sufficient for correcting all combinations of t errors and e erasures.

1.6. Construct a decoding table to correct all single errors for the second node of the tree code used in the examples. Assume that the first received block was 1 1.

1.7 The tree of Figure 1.6 is repetitive in an obvious way. Determine the weight of the lowest weight nonzero path through the entire tree. Use this information to show that regardless of how large n is allowed to be, not all double-error patterns can be corrected. (Weight equals number of 1s; see p. 41.)

1.8 Determine the probability of decoding the first block of the example code of Figure 1.6 erroneously when the code is used on a binary symmetric channel with crossover probability P.

1.9. Does the decoding rule specified in Figure 1.3 satisfy the conditions for maximum likelihood decoding? Assume that the channel is a BSC and only error correction is performed.

2 Introduction to Algebra

Structure is desirable in error-correcting codes for two reasons: It facilitates finding properties of a code, and even more important, it makes instrumentation of the codes practical. Algebraic structure has been the basis of the most important known codes.

This chapter consists of two parts. The first defines the most significant algebraic structures and gives a few examples of each. The rest of the chapter reviews some of the theory of vector spaces and matrices. Chapter 6 is also purely mathematical, dealing with the theory of rings and finite fields. These two chapters are in no sense complete mathematical presentations but rather barely minimum mathematical prerequisites for the discussion of codes.

Algebraic systems are systems that satisfy certain rules or laws, and for the most part, these are the same laws as apply to our ordinary number system. Thus a *group* is a system with one operation and its inverse, such as addition and its inverse, subtraction, or multiplication and its inverse, division. A *ring* has two operations, addition and multiplication, and the inverse operation, subtraction, for the first. A *field* has the two operations, both with inverses.

2.1 Groups

A group G is a set of objects, or elements, for which an operation is defined and for which Axioms G.1 to G.4 hold. Let $a, b, c, \dots$ be elements of the group. The operation is a single-valued function of two variables, and might well be denoted $f(a, b) = c$ but is customarily denoted $a + b = c$ or $ab = c$ and called addition or multiplication, even though it may not be the addition or multiplication of the arithmetic of ordinary numbers.

AXIOM G.1. (*Closure*). *The operation can be applied to any two group elements to give a third group element as a result.*

AXIOM G.2. (*Associative Law*). *For any three elements a, b, and c of the group, $(a + b) + c = a + (b + c)$ if the operation is written as addition, or $a(bc) = (ab)c$ if the operation is written as multiplication.*

The associative law means that the order of performing operations is immaterial, and so parentheses are unnecessary.

AXIOM G.3. *There is an identity element.*

If the operation is called addition, the identity element is called zero and written 0 and is defined by the equation $0 + a = a + 0 = a$ for every element of a of the group. If the operation is called multiplication, the identity is one, written 1, and is defined by the equation $1a = a1 = a$.

AXIOM G.4. *Every element of the group has an inverse element.*

If the operation is addition, the inverse element corresponding to a is denoted $-a$ and is defined by the equation $a + (-a) = (-a) + a = 0$. If the operation is multiplication, the inverse of a is denoted a^{-1} and is defined by the equation $aa^{-1} = a^{-1}a = 1$.

In addition to the above laws, a group may satisfy the commutative law; that is, $a + b = b + a$, or if the operation is multiplication, $ab = ba$. Such a group is called *Abelian* or *commutative*.

In developing a general theory of groups, the multiplicative notation is used in this book.

THEOREM 2.1. *The identity element in a group is unique, and the inverse of each group element is unique.*

Proof. The identity element is unique, for if there were two identity elements, 1 and 1′, $(1)(1') = 1 = 1'$. Similarly, inverses are unique, for if a group element g were to have two inverses g^{-1} and g_1^{-1}, then $g^{-1} = 1g^{-1} = g_1^{-1}gg^{-1} = g_1^{-1}1 = g_1^{-1}$, so that they must be equal. Q.E.D.

Note that the inverse of a product is the product of inverses *in reverse order,* for $(ab)(b^{-1}a^{-1}) = a(bb^{-1})a^{-1} = a1a^{-1} = aa^{-1} = 1$, and therefore $b^{-1}a^{-1} = (ab)^{-1}$.

Examples. The set of all real numbers is a group under the operation of ordinary addition. The set of all positive and negative integers and zero is also a group under addition. The set of all real numbers excluding zero is a group under the operation of ordinary multiplication. All these groups are Abelian. The set of all nonsingular $n \times n$ matrices is a non-Abelian group, under the operation matrix multiplication.

Many important groups are sets of transformations of some space, with the operation called multiplication, defined as follows: The transformation ab is the result of performing the transformation b followed by the transformation a. For example, the set of rotations of n-dimensional Euclidean space is a group. Note that the rotations of two-dimensional space form an Abelian group, while the rotations of three dimensional space are not commutative.

As a first example of a finite group, consider a transformation of a plane which maps a square onto itself. A transformation is completely determined if its effect on the four vertices is specified.

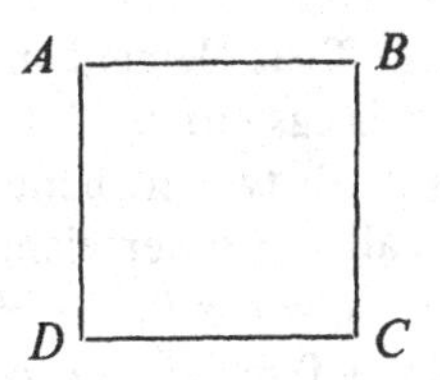

For example, one possible mapping is a 90° counterclockwise rotation of the square, which maps A onto D, B onto A, C onto B, and D onto C. It can be described in the notation sometimes used for permutations:

$$\begin{pmatrix} ABCD \\ DABC \end{pmatrix}.$$

There are eight such transformations in all:

$$1 = \begin{pmatrix} ABCD \\ ABCD \end{pmatrix}, \quad a = \begin{pmatrix} ABCD \\ DABC \end{pmatrix}, \quad b = \begin{pmatrix} ABCD \\ CDAB \end{pmatrix}, \quad c = \begin{pmatrix} ABCD \\ BCDA \end{pmatrix},$$

$$d = \begin{pmatrix} ABCD \\ BADC \end{pmatrix}, \quad e = \begin{pmatrix} ABCD \\ ADCB \end{pmatrix}, \quad f = \begin{pmatrix} ABCD \\ DCBA \end{pmatrix}, \quad g = \begin{pmatrix} ABCD \\ CBAD \end{pmatrix}.$$

The multiplication table is

	1	a	b	c	d	e	f	g
1	1	a	b	c	d	e	f	g
a	a	b	c	1	e	f	g	d
b	b	c	1	a	f	g	d	e
c	c	1	a	b	g	d	e	f
d	d	g	f	e	1	c	b	a
e	e	d	g	f	a	1	c	b
f	f	e	d	g	b	a	1	c
g	g	f	e	d	c	b	a	1

The fact that each element has an inverse can be easily seen from the multiplication table. Although the associative law could be verified from the multiplication table, this would be a very tedious job, but it should be clear from the definition of the group that the associative law does hold.

There is a group with only one element. That element must be the identity element by Axiom G.3, and it is easy to verify that the other axioms hold. There is also a group with two elements. One must be the identity element, 0. Let us call the other element a. Then a must have an inverse, and since $a + 0 = a \neq 0$, $-a \neq 0$, so $-a = a$. Thus the addition table *must be* $0 + 0 = 0$, $0 + a = a + 0 = a$, $a + a = 0$, and a set of two elements with addition defined in this way satisfies all the axioms G.1 to G.4. In fact, the only group with two elements is also Abelian.

2.2 Rings

A *ring* R is a set of elements for which two operations are defined. One is called addition and denoted $a + b$, and the other is called multiplication and denoted ab, even though these operations may not be ordinary addition or multiplication of numbers. In order for R to be a ring, the following axioms must be satisfied:

AXIOM R.1. *The set R is an Abelian group under addition.*

AXIOM R.2. (*Closure*). *For any two elements a and b of R, the product ab is defined and is an element of R.*

AXIOM R.3. (*Associative Law*). *For any three elements a, b, and c of R,* $a(bc) = (ab)c$.

AXIOM R.4. (*Distributive Law*). *For any three elements a, b, and c of R,* $a(b + c) = ab + ac$ *and* $(b + c)a = ba + ca$.

A ring is called *commutative* if its multiplication operation is commutative; that is, if for any two elements a and b, $ab = ba$.

THEOREM 2.2. *In any ring, for any elements a and b,* $a0 = 0a = 0$ *and* $a(-b) = (-a)b = -(ab)$.

Proof. In any ring, by Axiom R.4, for any a, $a(0 + 0) = a0 + a0$. But since $0 + 0 = 0$, $a0 = a0 + a0$. Next $a0$ must have an additive inverse, and adding this to both sides gives $0 = a0 + (-a0) = a0 + a0 + (-a0) = a0 + 0 = a0$, so in any ring $a0 = 0$. Similarly $0a = 0$. Then $0 = a0 = a(b + (-b)) = ab + a(-b)$, so $a(-b) = -(ab)$. Similarly $(-a)b = -(ab)$. Q.E.D.

Examples. The set of all real numbers is a ring under the operations of ordinary addition and multiplication. The set of all positive and negative integers and zero is also a ring under ordinary addition and multiplication. Both these rings are commutative. The set of all $n \times n$ matrices with either integer or real-number elements is a ring under the operations matrix addition and matrix multiplication, and this ring is noncommutative. The set of all polynomials in one indeterminant, or variable, with integer coefficients is a commutative ring.

A set consisting of a zero element only is a ring, with the rules $0 + 0 = 0$, $(0)(0) = 0$. There are two different rings with two elements. One element must be the additive identity 0. The other element a must satisfy $a + a = 0$. Since $(0)(0) = 0a = a0 = 0$ by Theorem 2.2, the only question is, what is the value of aa? It turns out that either $aa = a$ or $aa = 0$ satisfies both the distributive and associative laws, and thus either choice gives a ring, and clearly these two choices give rings of different structure.

2.3 Fields

A *field* is a commutative ring with a unit element (multiplicative identity) in which every nonzero element has a multiplicative inverse.

A noncommutative ring in which every nonzero element has an inverse is usually called a *division ring* or a *skew field.*

Note that the nonzero elements of a field satisfy all the axioms for a group and thus form a group under the operation multiplication.

Examples. The set of all real numbers form, a field, as do also the set of all rational numbers and the set of all complex numbers.

The minimum number of elements a field can have is two, for it must have both an additive identity 0 and a multiplicative identity 1. They have to satisfy the addition and multiplication tables given in Table 2.1, for there is only one possible addition table for a

Table 2.1. Addition and Multiplication Tables for the Field with Two Elements

+	0	1
0	0	1
1	1	0

.	0	1
0	0	0
1	0	1

group of two elements. Also, it was shown that for rings in general, $0a = 0$ for any a, and, since 1 is a unit element, $(1)(1) = 1$. It can be verified easily that the set 0 and 1 with the operations defined earlier satisfy all the axioms for a field.

It can be shown that for every number q that is a power of a prime number there is a field with q elements. The proof of this fits in better with the material of Chapter 6 and is presented there. However, it might be well to point out here that a field with p elements can be formed by taking the integers modulo p, provided p is a prime. *The integers modulo q do not form field if q is not a prime and the fields with $q = p^m$ elements ($m > 1$) are not formed by taking integers modulo q.* For use in examples, addition and multiplication tables for fields with three and four elements are given in Tables 2.2 and 2.3. The field of four elements described in Table 2.3 is *not* the integers modulo 4.

Table 2.2. Addition and Multiplication Table for the Field with Three Elements

+	0	1	2
0	0	1	2
1	1	2	0
2	2	0	1

.	0	1	2
0	0	0	0
1	0	1	2
2	0	2	1

Table 2.3. Addition and Multiplication Table for the Field with Four Elements

+	0	1	a	b
0	0	1	a	b
1	1	0	b	a
a	a	b	0	1
b	b	a	1	0

.	0	1	a	b
0	0	0	0	0
1	0	1	a	b
a	0	a	b	1
b	0	b	1	a

2.4 Subgroups and Factor Groups

A subset of elements of a group G is called a *subgroup* H if it satisfies all the axioms for the group itself with the same operation. To determine whether H is a subgroup, it is necessary to check only for closure (that is, if a and b are in H, then ab must be in H) and for inverses (that is, if a is in H, then a^{-1} must be also). If a set is closed under the group operation and the inverse is present, the identity must be present also, and the associative law must hold in the subgroup if it does in the group.

Example. In the group of eight transformations of a square given previously, the sets $(1, a, b, c)$ and $(1, d)$ are both subgroups.

In the group of all integers, the set of all integers that are even multiples of a given integer m is a subgroup for every m.

Suppose that the elements of a group G are $g_1, g_2, g_3, \ldots$, and the elements of a subgroup H are $h_1, h_2, h_3, \ldots$, and consider the array formed as follows: The first row is the subgroup, with the identity at the left and each other element appearing once and only once. The first element in the second row is any element not appearing in the first row, and the rest of the elements are obtained by multiplying each subgroup element by this first element on the left. Similarly a third, fourth, and fifth row are formed, each with a previously unused group element in the first column, until all the group elements appear somewhere in the array.

$$\begin{array}{llllll}
h_1 = 1, & h_2, & h_3, & h_4, & \ldots, & h_n \\
g_1 h_1 = g_1, & g_1 h_2, & g_1 h_3, & g_1 h_4, & \ldots, & g_1 h_n \\
g_2 h_1 = g_2, & g_2 h_2, & g_2 h_3, & g_2 h_4, & \ldots, & g_2 h_n \\
\vdots & \vdots & \vdots & \vdots & \vdots & \vdots \\
g_m h_1 = g_m, & g_m h_2, & g_m h_3, & g_m h_4, & \ldots, & g_m h_n
\end{array}$$

The set of elements in a row of this array is called a left *coset*, and the element appearing in the first column is called the *coset leader*. Right cosets could be similarly formed. The array itself is known as the *coset decomposition* of the group.

THEOREM 2.3. *Two elements g and g' of a group G are in the same left coset of a subgroup H of G if and only if $g^{-1}g'$ is an element of H.*

Proof. If g and g' belong to the coset whose leader is g_i, then $g = g_i h_j$ for some j, $g' = g_i h_k$ for some k, and $g^{-1}g' = (g_i h_j)^{-1} \cdot g_i h_k = h_j^{-1} g_i^{-1} g_i h_k = h_j^{-1} h_k$, which is in the subgroup. On the other hand, if $g = g_i h$, where g_i is the coset leader, and if $g^{-1}g' = h'$, then $g' = gh' = g_i hh'$, which is in the same coset, since hh' is in the subgroup.

Q.E.D.

THEOREM 2.4 *Every element of the group G is in one and only one coset of a subgroup H.*

Proof. Every element appears at least once, by the definition of the construction of the array. It must be shown that each element appears only once in the array. Suppose first that two elements in the same row, $g_i h_j$ and $g_i h_k$, are equal. Then multiplying each on the left by g_i^{-1} would give $h_j = h_k$, a result that is a contradiction, since each subgroup element was assumed to appear only once in the first row. Now suppose that two equal elements appear in different rows, $g_i h_j = g_k h_l$, and suppose that $i > k$. Then multiplying on the right by h_j^{-1} gives $g_i = g_k h_l h_j^{-1}$. Since $h_l h_j^{-1}$ is in the subgroup, this indicates that g_i is in the kth coset, a situation that contradicts the rule of construction that coset leaders should be previously unused.

Q.E.D.

The number of elements in a group is called the *order* of the group. The number of cosets of G with respect to a subgroup H is called the *index* of G over H. Clearly,

(Order of H) (index of G over H) = (order of G).

A subgroup H of a group G is called *normal* if, for any element h of H and any element g of G, $g^{-1}hg$ is in H. In general, left cosets may not be right cosets, and vice versa. However, every left coset of a normal subgroup is also a right coset, and vice versa. In an Abelian group, every left coset is trivially a right coset, and also all subgroups are trivially normal. In this book the only use made of normal subgroups will be for Abelian groups, and therefore the foregoing result will not be proved in general.

If a subgroup H of a group G is normal, it is possible to define an operation on cosets to form a new group for which the cosets are the elements. This group is called the *factor group* and denoted G/H. The coset containing g is denoted $\{g\}$. The definition of multiplication for cosets is

$$\{g_1\}\{g_2\} = \{g_1 g_2\}.$$

This is not a valid definition unless it happens that, no matter which element is chosen as a representive of each of the two cosets to be multiplied, the resulting coset is the same. In other words, it must be shown that if g_1 and g_1' are in the same coset, and g_2 and g_2' are in the same coset, then $g_1 g_2$ and $g_1' g_2'$ are also in the same coset. Assume that $g_1^{-1}g_1' = h_1$, $g_2^{-1}g_2' = h_2$, and then, since the subgroup is normal, $g_2'^{-1}h_1 g_2'$ must be an element of H, say h_3. Hence $(g_1 g_2)^{-1}g_1' g_2' = g_2^{-1}g_1^{-1}g_1' g_2' = g_2^{-1}h_1 g_2' = g_2^{-1}g_2' h_3 = h_2 h_3$, which is an element of H. Therefore $g_1 g_2$ and $g_1' g_2'$ are in the same coset, and the definition is consistent.

Now let us check that G/H is actually a group. The operation is clearly defined for all pairs of cosets, and therefore Axiom G.1 is satisfied. To check the associative law, note that

$$\begin{aligned}\{g_1\}(\{g_2\}\{g_3\}) = \{g_1\}\{g_2 g_3\} = \{g_1 g_2 g_3\} &= \{g_1 g_2\}\{g_3\} \\ &= (\{g_1\}\{g_2\})\{g_3\}.\end{aligned}$$

The identity element is the subgroup itself, $H = \{1\}$, since $\{1\}\{g\} = \{1g\} = \{g\}$ and $\{g\}\{1\} = \{g1\} = \{g\}$. Similarly the inverse coset of $\{g\}$ is the coset containing g^{-1}, $\{g^{-1}\}$, since $\{g\}\{g^{-1}\} = \{gg^{-1}\} = \{1\}$ and $\{g^{-1}\} \cdot \{g\} = \{g^{-1}g\} = \{1\}$. Also if the original group is Abelian, it is easily verified that the factor group is also.

Examples. Suppose that the group G is the group of eight transformations of the square, and H is the subgroup consisting of 1, a, b, c. Then the standard array of left cosets is, if d is chosen as the coset leader,

1	a	b	c
d	$da = g$	$db = f$	$dc = e$

There is only one coset consisting of all the elements of G except those in H, and so this must also be a right coset, and H must be normal. If the identity coset is called I and the other one D, then the multiplication table is $II = I$, $ID = \{1\}\{d\} = d = D$, $DI = D$, $DD = \{d\}\{d\} = \{dd\} = \{1\} = I$. This, of course, has the same structure as the only group of two elements.

As a more important example, let G be the group of all positive and negative integers and zero under addition, and let H be the subgroup that consists of all multiples of an integer n. All the numbers from zero to $n - 1$ inclusive are in different cosets, since for two elements a and b to be in the same coset, $(-a) + b$ must be in the subgroup and thus be a multiple of n. These can be taken as coset leaders, and it is easily seen that there are no other cosets. Since G is Abelian, addition of cosets can be defined, and the cosets form a group. For example, let $n = 3$. Then the cosets are

$$0,\ 3,\ -3,\ 6,\ -6,\ 9,\ -9,\ \ldots$$
$$1,\ 4,\ -2,\ 7,\ -5,\ 10,\ -8,\ \ldots$$
$$2,\ 5,\ -1,\ 8,\ -4,\ 11,\ -7,\ \ldots$$

If these are called {0},{1}, and {2}, respectively, the addition table is

+	{0}	{1}	{2}
{0}	{0}	{1}	{2}
{1}	{1}	{2}	{0}
{2}	{2}	{0}	{1}

This may be recognized as addition modulo 3.

2.5 Vector Spaces and Linear Algebras

A set V of elements is called a *vector space* over a field F if it satisfies the following axioms:

AXIOM V.1. *The set V is an Abelian group under addition.*

AXIOM V.2. *For any vector* **v** *in V and any field element c, a product c***v***, which is a vector in V, is defined. (Field elements are called scalars, elements of V are vectors.)*

AXIOM V.3. (*Distributive Law*). *If* **u** *and* **v** *are vectors in V and c is a scalar,* $c(\mathbf{u} + \mathbf{v}) = c\mathbf{u} + c\mathbf{v}$.

AXIOM V.4. (*Distributive Law*). *If* **v** *is a vector and c and d are scalars,* $(c + d)\mathbf{v} = c\mathbf{v} + d\mathbf{v}$.

AXIOM V.5. (*Associative Law*). *If* **v** *is a vector and c and d are scalars,* $(cd)\mathbf{v} = c(d\mathbf{v})$, *and* $1\mathbf{v} = \mathbf{v}$.

A set A of elements is called a *linear associative algebra* over a field F if it satisfies the following axioms:

AXIOM A.1. *The set A is a vector space over F.*

AXIOM A.2. *For any two elements* $\mathbf{u}$ *and* $\mathbf{v}$ *of A, there is a product* $\mathbf{uv}$ *defined that is in A.*

AXIOM A.3. *(Associative Law) For any three elements* $\mathbf{u}$, $\mathbf{v}$, *and* $\mathbf{w}$ *of A,* $(\mathbf{uv})\mathbf{w} = \mathbf{u}(\mathbf{vw})$.

AXIOM A.4. *(Bilinear Law) If c and d are scalars in F and* $\mathbf{u}$, $\mathbf{v}$, *and* $\mathbf{w}$ *are vectors in A, then*

$$\mathbf{u}(c\mathbf{v} + d\mathbf{w}) = c\mathbf{uv} + d\mathbf{uw} \text{ and } (c\mathbf{v} + d\mathbf{w})\mathbf{u} = c\mathbf{vu} + d\mathbf{wu}.$$

An *n-tuple* over a field is an ordered set of n field elements and is denoted $(a_1, a_2, a_3, \ldots, a_n)$, where each a_i is an element of the field. Addition of n-tuples is defined as follows:

$$(a_1, a_2, \ldots, a_n) + (b_1, b_2, \ldots, b_n) = (a_1 + b_1, a_2 + b_2, \ldots, a_n + b_n).$$

Multiplication of an n-tuple by a field element is defined as follows:

$$c(a_1, a_2, \ldots, a_n) = (ca_1, ca_2, \ldots, ca_n).$$

With these two definitions it can be verified easily that the set of all n-tuples over a field form a vector space, and such vector spaces play a central role in coding theory. They are the subject of the remainder of this chapter.

Multiplication of n-tuples can be defined as follows:

$$(a_1, a_2, \ldots, a_n)(b_1, b_2, \ldots, b_n) = (a_1 b_1, a_2 b_2, \ldots, a_n b_n);$$

with this definition the n-tuples form a linear algebra. This type of multiplication is occasionally useful. Another type of multiplication of n-tuples leading to a linear algebra is described in Chapter 6 and plays a more important role in coding theory.

The identity element of the vector space will be denoted $\mathbf{0}$; that is,

$$\mathbf{0} = (0, \ldots, 0).$$

It is clearly true for n-tuples and in fact easily shown for vector spaces in general that for any vector $\mathbf{v}$, $0\mathbf{v} = \mathbf{0}$, and for any scalar c, $c\mathbf{0} = \mathbf{0}$. Also, $(-\mathbf{v}) = (-1)\mathbf{v}$, for $\mathbf{v} + (-1)\mathbf{v} = 1\mathbf{v} + (-1)\mathbf{v} = [1 + (-1)]\mathbf{v} = 0\mathbf{v} = \mathbf{0}$.

A subset of a vector space is called a *subspace* if it satisfies the axioms for a vector space. In order to check whether a subset of a vector space is a subspace, it is necessary only to check for closure under addition and multiplication by scalars. Note that, since $-\mathbf{v} = (-1)\mathbf{v}$, closure under multiplication by scalars assures that the inverse of each element is in the subspace. Then closure under addition is sufficient to ensure that it is a subgroup, and the associative and distributive laws must hold in the subspace if they hold in the original vector space.

A *linear combination* of k vectors $\mathbf{v}_1, \ldots, \mathbf{v}_k$ is a sum of the form

$$\mathbf{u} = a_1\mathbf{v}_1 + a_2\mathbf{v}_2 + \cdots + a_k\mathbf{v}_k.$$

The a_i are scalars, that is, field elements.

THEOREM 2.5. *The set of all linear combinations of a set of vectors* $\mathbf{v}_1, \ldots, \mathbf{v}_k$ *of a vector space* V *is a subspace of* V.

Proof. Clearly every linear combination of vectors of V is also a vector of V. If the set of all linear combinations of $\mathbf{v}_1, \ldots, \mathbf{v}_k$ is called S, and $\mathbf{w} = b_1\mathbf{v}_1 + \cdots + b_k\mathbf{v}_k$ and $\mathbf{u} = c_1\mathbf{v}_1 + \cdots + c_k\mathbf{v}_k$ are any two elements of S, then $\mathbf{w} + \mathbf{u}$ is also in S, for $\mathbf{w} + \mathbf{u} = (b_1 + c_1)\mathbf{v}_1 + \cdots + (b_k + c_k)\mathbf{v}_k$ is in S. Also any scalar multiple of $\mathbf{w}$, $a\mathbf{w} = ab_1\mathbf{v}_1 + \cdots + ab_k\mathbf{v}_k$ is in S. Since S is closed under addition and multiplication by scalars, S is a subspace of V. Q.E.D.

A set of vectors $\mathbf{v}_1, \ldots, \mathbf{v}_k$ is *linearly dependent* if and only if there are scalars $c_1, \ldots, c_k$, not all zero, such that

$$c_1\mathbf{v}_1 + c_2\mathbf{v}_2 + \cdots + c_k\mathbf{v}_k = \mathbf{0}.$$

A set of vectors is *linearly independent* if it is not linearly dependent. A set of vectors is said to *span* a vector space if every vector in the vector space equals a linear combination of the vectors in the set.

THEOREM 2.6. *If a set of k vectors* $\mathbf{v}_1, \ldots, \mathbf{v}_k$ *spans a vector space that contains a set of m linearly independent vectors* $\mathbf{u}_1, \ldots, \mathbf{u}_m$, *then* $k \geq m$.

Proof. Since $\mathbf{v}_1, \ldots, \mathbf{v}_k$ span the space, $\mathbf{u}_1$ can be expressed as a linear combination of the $\mathbf{v}_i$. Therefore, this equation can be solved for some one of the $\mathbf{v}_i$, say $\mathbf{v}_j$, in terms of $\mathbf{u}_1$ and the rest of the $\mathbf{v}_i$. Consequently, the set consisting of $\mathbf{u}_1$ and the rest of the $\mathbf{v}_i$ spans the vector space, since any linear combination of the $\mathbf{v}_i$ becomes a linear combination of $\mathbf{u}_1$ and all the $\mathbf{v}_i$ except $\mathbf{v}_j$ when the expression for $\mathbf{v}_j$ in terms of $\mathbf{u}_1$ and the other $\mathbf{v}_i$ is used to eliminate $\mathbf{v}_j$. Then $\mathbf{u}_2$ can be expressed as a linear combination of $\mathbf{u}_1$ and all the $\mathbf{v}_i$ except $\mathbf{v}_j$. Since the $\mathbf{u}_i$ are linearly independent, some $\mathbf{v}_i$ must have a nonzero coefficient, and therefore this $\mathbf{v}_i$ can be expressed in terms of $\mathbf{u}_1$, $\mathbf{u}_2$, and the remaining $k-2$ vectors $\mathbf{v}_i$, and these k vectors span the space. The process can be continued until all m of the $\mathbf{u}_i$ vectors are used, and, since at each stage one $\mathbf{v}_i$ vector is replaced, the number of vectors $\mathbf{v}_i$ must have been at least as great as the number of vectors $\mathbf{u}_i$. Q.E.D.

THEOREM 2.7. *If two sets of linearly independent vectors span the same space, there are the same number of vectors in each set.*

Proof. If there are m vectors in one set and k in the other, then by Theorem 2.6, $m \geqq k$ and $k \geqq m$, and thus $m = k$. Q.E.D.

In any space, the number of linearly independent vectors that span the space is called the *dimension* of the space. A set of k linearly independent vectors spanning a k-dimensional vector space is called a *basis* of the space. It follows from Theorem 2.7 that every set of more than k vectors in a k-dimensional vector space is linearly dependent. It follows from Theorem 2.6 that no set of fewer than k vectors can span a k-dimensional space.

THEOREM 2.8. *If V is a k-dimensional vector space, any set of k linearly independent vectors in V is a basis for V.*

Proof. Let $\mathbf{v}_1, \mathbf{v}_2, \ldots, \mathbf{v}_k$ be a set of linearly independent vectors in V. If they do not span V, there must be some vector $\mathbf{v}$ in V that is not a linear combination of $\mathbf{v}_1, \mathbf{v}_2, \ldots, \mathbf{v}_k$. Then the set $\mathbf{v}, \mathbf{v}_1, \mathbf{v}_2, \ldots, \mathbf{v}_k$ of $k+1$ vectors in V is linearly independent. This contradicts Theorem 2.6, and therefore $\mathbf{v}_1, \mathbf{v}_2, \ldots, \mathbf{v}_k$ must span V. Q.E.D.

THEOREM 2.9. *If a vector space V_1 is contained in a vector space V_2 and they have the same dimension k, they are equal.*

Proof. A basis for V_1 is a set of k linearly independent vectors in V_2. Therefore, every vector in V_2 is also in V_1. Q.E.D.

An *inner product* or *dot product* of two n-tuples is a scalar and is defined as follows:

$$(a_1, \ldots, a_n) \cdot (b_1, \ldots, b_n) = a_1 b_1 + \cdots + a_n b_n.$$

It is easily verified that $\mathbf{u} \cdot \mathbf{v} = \mathbf{v} \cdot \mathbf{u}$ and that $\mathbf{w} \cdot (\mathbf{u} + \mathbf{v}) = \mathbf{w} \cdot \mathbf{u} + \mathbf{w} \cdot \mathbf{v}$. If the inner product of two vectors is zero, they are said to be *orthogonal.*

2.6 Matrices

The purpose of this section is to outline the parts of matrix theory that apply to the codes studied in the next three chapters. For the most part, proofs are given, but this can hardly serve as more than a review of the necessary parts of matrix theory.

An $n \times m$ matrix is an ordered set of nm elements in a rectangular array of n rows and m columns:

$$\begin{bmatrix} a_{11} & a_{12} & \cdots & a_{1m} \\ a_{21} & a_{22} & \cdots & a_{2m} \\ \vdots & \vdots & & \vdots \\ a_{n1} & a_{n2} & \cdots & a_{nm} \end{bmatrix} = [a_{ij}].$$

The elements of a matrix may in general be elements of any ring, but in this book only matrices with elements in a field find application. The n rows may be thought of as n m-tuples or vectors, and similarly, the m columns may be thought of as vectors. The set of elements a_{ii} for which the column number and row number are equal is called the main diagonal.

The *row space* of an $n \times m$ matrix $\mathbf{M}$ is the set of all linear combinations of row vectors of $\mathbf{M}$. They form a subspace of the vector space of m-tuples. The dimension of the row space is called the *row rank*. Similarly, the set of all linear combinations of column vectors of the matrix forms the *column space*, whose dimension is called the *column rank*. It can be shown that row rank equals column rank; this value is referred to as the *rank* of the matrix.

There is a set of *elementary row operations* defined for matrices:

1. Interchange of any two rows.
2. Multiplication of any row by a nonzero field element.
3. Addition of any multiple of one row to another.

The inverse of each elementary row operation is clearly an elementary row operation of the same kind.

THEOREM 2.10. *If one matrix is obtained from another by a succession of elementary operations, both matrices have the same row space.*

Proof. If the theorem is true for each elementary row operation, it will clearly be true for a succession. It is obviously true of row operations 1 and 2. Suppose that the matrix $\mathbf{M}'$ is obtained from the matrix $\mathbf{M}$ by a type 3 elementary row operation. Then, since the altered row of $\mathbf{M}'$ is a linear combination of two rows of $\mathbf{M}$, any linear combination of rows of **M**′ is also a linear combination of rows of **M**, so the row space of **M**′ is contained in the row space of **M**. But **M** can be obtained from **M**′ by the inverse operation, which is again an operation of type 3, so the row space of **M** must be contained in the row space of **M**′. Therefore they are equal. Q.E.D.

Elementary row operations can be used to simplify a matrix and put it in a standard form. The form, called *echelon canonical form*, is as follows:

1. Every leading term of a nonzero row is 1.
2. Every column containing such a leading term has all its other entries zero.
3. The leading term of any row is to the right of the leading term in every preceding row. All zero rows are below all nonzero rows.

The procedure is essentially the same as that used in solving linear equations by elimination of one variable at a time. It is best illustrated by an example. Consider the following matrix with real numbers as elements:

$$\begin{bmatrix} 0 & 0 & 2 & 2 & 0 & 2 \\ 2 & 2 & 6 & 8 & 4 & 8 \\ 1 & 1 & 5 & 6 & 2 & 5 \\ 1 & 1 & 3 & 4 & 2 & 7 \end{bmatrix}$$

To simplify the matrix, the first step would be to locate the first column with a nonzero element, interchange rows if necessary to place a nonzero element in the first row, and multiply the row by the inverse of that element to give a leading 1. Interchanging rows 1 and 2 and dividing by 2 give

$$\begin{bmatrix} 1 & 1 & 3 & 4 & 2 & 4 \\ 0 & 0 & 2 & 2 & 0 & 2 \\ 1 & 1 & 5 & 6 & 2 & 5 \\ 1 & 1 & 3 & 4 & 2 & 7 \end{bmatrix}$$

The next step is to subtract a multiple of the first row from each other row to make the rest of the column corresponding to the leading element in the first row 0:

$$\begin{bmatrix} 1 & 1 & 3 & 4 & 2 & 4 \\ 0 & 0 & 2 & 2 & 0 & 2 \\ 0 & 0 & 2 & 2 & 0 & 1 \\ 0 & 0 & 0 & 0 & 0 & 3 \end{bmatrix}$$

Then, disregarding the first row, again the first column with a nonzero element is located, and rows are interchanged if necessary to place a nonzero element in this column in the second row. The row is next multiplied by the inverse of its leading element to give a leading 1. This is accomplished in the above matrix by dividing the second row by 2. Then the appropriate multiple of this row is subtracted from each other row to make *all* the other entries 0 in the column of the leading element of the second row. This yields

$$\begin{bmatrix} 1 & 1 & 0 & 1 & 2 & 1 \\ 0 & 0 & 1 & 1 & 0 & 1 \\ 0 & 0 & 0 & 0 & 0 & -1 \\ 0 & 0 & 0 & 0 & 0 & 3 \end{bmatrix}$$

One more step in the process yields

$$\begin{bmatrix} 110120 \\ 001100 \\ 000001 \\ 000000 \end{bmatrix}$$

This process will always result in a matrix in echelon canonical form.

The nonzero rows of a matrix in echelon canonical form are linearly independent, and thus the number of nonzero rows is the dimension of the row space. It can be shown that there is only one matrix in echelon canonical form for any given row space.

If all the rows of an $n \times n$ matrix are linearly independent, the matrix is said to be nonsingular. When such a matrix is put in echelon canonical form, there must still be n linearly independent rows, and thus every row must contain a 1. This can occur only if it has 1's on the main diagonal and 0's elsewhere. Such a matrix is called an *identity matrix* and denoted $\mathbf{I}$. Thus any nonsingular matrix can be transformed into an identity matrix by elementary row operations.

The *transpose* of an $n \times m$ matrix $\mathbf{M}$ is an $m \times n$ matrix, denoted $\mathbf{M}^T$, whose rows are the columns of $\mathbf{M}$, and thus whose columns are the rows of $\mathbf{M}$. The transpose of $[a_{ij}]$ is $[a_{ji}]$.

Two $n \times m$ matrices can be added, element by element:

$$[a_{ij}] + [b_{ij}] = [a_{ij} + b_{ij}].$$

With this definition it is easily verified that matrices form an Abelian group under addition.

An $n \times k$ matrix $[a_{ij}]$ and a $k \times m$ matrix $[b_{ij}]$ can be multiplied to give an $n \times m$ product matrix $[c_{ij}]$ by the rule

$$c_{ij} = \sum_{l=1}^{k} a_{il} b_{lj}.$$

It can be verified by direct calculation that with this definition matrix multiplication satisfies the associative law, and multiplication and addition satisfy the distributive law.

The element c_{ij} of the product is the inner product of the ith row of $[a_{ij}]$ by the jth column of $[b_{ij}]$. Also the ith row vector of the product $[c_{ij}]$ is a linear combination of the row vectors of $[b_{ij}]$ with the coefficient a_{il} on the lth row. Similarly the columns of the product are linear combinations of the column vectors of $[a_{ij}]$.

Multiplying an $n \times m$ matrix $\mathbf{M}$ on the left by an $n \times n$ matrix $\mathbf{P}$ that has one 1 in each row and each column and all the rest of the elements 0 simply permutes the rows of the matrix $\mathbf{M}$, and any permutation of rows can be accomplished in this way. Thus the first elementary row operation can be accomplished by multiplying on the left by a permutation matrix. The second elementary row operation, multiplying the jth row of $\mathbf{M}$ by c, can be accomplished by multiplying $\mathbf{M}$ on the left by a matrix that has 0's off the main diagonal, c on the main diagonal in the jth row, and 1's on the rest of the main diagonal. Finally, the third elementary operation, adding c times the jth row to the kth row, can be accomplished by multiplying on the left by a matrix that has 1's on the main diagonal, c in the position that is in the jth column and kth row, and 0's elsewhere. These matrices are called *elementary matrices.*

THEOREM 2.11. *Every nonsingular matrix has a left inverse that is a product of elementary matrices.*

Proof. If a nonsingular $n \times n$ matrix $\mathbf{M}$ is transformed into echelon canonical form, it becomes an identity matrix. Since $\mathbf{M}$ can be put in echelon canonical form by elementary row operations, there is some set of elementary matrices $\mathbf{E}_1, \ldots, \mathbf{E}_k$ whose product with M is the identity matrix:

$$\mathbf{E}_k \mathbf{E}_{k-1} \cdots \mathbf{E}_1 \mathbf{M} = \mathbf{I}.$$

Then $\mathbf{E}_k \cdots \mathbf{E}_1$ is the left inverse of $\mathbf{M}$. Q.E.D.

It can be shown that the left inverse of a matrix is also a right inverse.

THEOREM 2.12. *If* $\mathbf{M}$ *is an* $n \times m$ *matrix and* $\mathbf{S}$ *is a nonsingular* $n \times n$ *matrix, then the product of* $\mathbf{S}$ *and* $\mathbf{M}$ *has the same row space as* $\mathbf{M}$ *has.*

Proof. The rows of $\mathbf{SM}$ are linear combinations of the rows of $\mathbf{M}$, and therefore the row space of $\mathbf{SM}$ is contained in the row space of $\mathbf{M}$. But $\mathbf{S}$ has a left inverse $\mathbf{S}^{-1}$, and the rows of $\mathbf{S}^{-1}\mathbf{SM} = \mathbf{M}$ are linear combinations of the rows of $\mathbf{SM}$, and hence the row space of $\mathbf{M}$ is contained in the row space of $\mathbf{SM}$. Therefore, they must be equal.

Q.E.D.

THEOREM 2.13. *The set of all n-tuples orthogonal to a subspace* V_1 *of n-tuples forms a subspace* V_2 *of n-tuples.*

Proof. Let V_1 be a subspace of the vector space of all n-tuples over a field. Let V_2 be the set of all vectors orthogonal to every vector in V_1. Let $\mathbf{v}$ be any vector in V_1 and $\mathbf{u}_1$ and $\mathbf{u}_2$ any vectors in V_2. Then $\mathbf{v} \cdot \mathbf{u}_1 = \mathbf{v} \cdot \mathbf{u}_2 = 0$, and $\mathbf{v} \cdot \mathbf{u}_1 + \mathbf{v} \cdot \mathbf{u}_2 = 0 = \mathbf{v} \cdot (\mathbf{u}_1 + \mathbf{u}_2)$. Therefore $\mathbf{u}_1 + \mathbf{u}_2$ is in V_2. Also $\mathbf{v} \cdot (c\mathbf{u}_1) = c(\mathbf{v} \cdot \mathbf{u}_1) = 0$, so $c\mathbf{u}_1$ is in V_2. Thus V_2 must be a subspace. Q.E.D.

The subspace V_2 in Theorem 2.13 is called the *null space* of V_1.

THEOREM 2.14. *If a vector is orthogonal to every vector of a set which spans* V_1, *it is in the null space of* V_1.

Proof. If $\mathbf{v}_1, \ldots, \mathbf{v}_k$ span V_1, then every vector in V_1 can be expressed in the form $\mathbf{v} = c_1\mathbf{v}_1 + \cdots + c_k\mathbf{v}_k$. Then

$$\mathbf{v} \cdot \mathbf{u} = (c_1\mathbf{v}_1 + \cdots + c_k\mathbf{v}_k) \cdot \mathbf{u} = c_1\mathbf{v}_1 \cdot \mathbf{u} + \cdots + c_k\mathbf{v}_k \cdot \mathbf{u}$$

and if $\mathbf{u}$ is orthogonal to each $\mathbf{v}_i$, it is orthogonal to $\mathbf{v}$. Q.E.D.

The null space of the row space of a matrix is called the null space of the matrix. A vector is in the null space of a matrix if it is orthogonal to each row of the matrix. If the n-tuple $\mathbf{v}$ is considered to be a $1 \times n$ matrix, $\mathbf{v}$ is in the null space of an $m \times n$ matrix $\mathbf{M}$ if and only if $\mathbf{vM}^T = \mathbf{0}$.

THEOREM 2.15. *If the dimension of a subspace of n-tuples is k, the dimension of the null space is* $n - k$.

The proof of this theorem will be omitted, because it requires some background otherwise unnecessary. One consequence of the theorem is

THEOREM 2.16. *If* V_2 *is a subspace of n-tuples and* V_1 *is the null space of* V_2, *then* V_2 *is the null space of* V_1.

Proof. If V_2 has dimension k, then V_1 has dimension $n - k$, and the null space of V_1 has dimension k. Since V_2 is contained in the null space of V_1 and has the same dimension, they are equal. Q.E.D.

If $\mathbf{M}_1$ and $\mathbf{M}_2$ are two matrices that have n columns, and if $\mathbf{M}_1 \mathbf{M}_2^T$ is a matrix of all 0's, then the row space of $\mathbf{M}_2$ is contained in the null space of $\mathbf{M}_1$, and vice versa. If the row rank of $\mathbf{M}_1$ and the row rank of $\mathbf{M}_2$ add to n, then the row space of $\mathbf{M}_2$ is the null space of $\mathbf{M}_1$, and vice versa.

Let $U \cap V$ be vector spaces and let $U \cap V$ denote the set of vectors that are contained in both U and V. It is easy to verify that $U \cap V$ is a subspace. Let $U \oplus V$ denote the subspace consisting of all linear combinations $a\mathbf{u} + b\mathbf{v}$, where $\mathbf{u} \in U$, $\mathbf{v} \in V$, and a and b are scalars.

THEOREM 2.17. *The sum of the dimensions of $U \cap V$ and $U \oplus V$ equals the sum of the dimensions of U and V.*

Proof. Let k_1 denote the dimension of U, k_2 the dimension of V, and k_0 the dimension of $U \cap V$. Then there exists a basis of k_0 vectors for $U \cap V$. It will be possible to find a basis for U consisting of these k_0 vectors and $k_1 - k_0$ others not in $U \cap V$, and a basis for V consisting of the basis of $U \cap V$ and $k_2 - k_0$ others. Then together, the k_0 vectors in the basis of $U \cap V$, the $k_1 - k_0$ additional vectors in the basis of U and the $k_2 - k_0$ vectors in the basis of V form a basis of $U \oplus V$. Therefore, the dimension of $U \oplus V$ is $k_0 + (k_1 - k_0) + (k_2 - k_0)$. Q.E.D

THEOREM 2.18. *Let U_2 be the null space of U_1 and V_2 the null space of V_1. Then $U_2 \cap V_2$ is the null space of $U_1 \oplus V_1$.*

Proof. Since U_1 is contained in $U_1 \oplus V_1$, every vector in the null space of $U_1 \oplus V_1$ must be in U_2, the null space of U_1. Similarly, every vector in the null space of $U_1 \oplus V_1$ must be in V_2, the null space of V_1. Therefore, the null space of $U_1 \oplus V_1$ is contained in $U_2 \cap V_2$. Every vector in $U_1 \oplus V_1$ can be written in the form $a\mathbf{u}_1 + b\mathbf{v}_1$. If $\mathbf{w}$ is any element of $U_2 \cap V_2$, then $\mathbf{u}_1 \cdot \mathbf{w} = \mathbf{v}_1 \cdot \mathbf{w} = 0$ and hence $(a\mathbf{u}_1 + b\mathbf{v}_1) \cdot \mathbf{w} = 0$. Therefore, $U_2 \cap V_2$ is contained in the null space of $U_1 \oplus V_1$. It follows that the null space of $U_1 \oplus V_1$ equals $U_2 \cap V_2$. Q.E.D

There are many important concepts and theorems of matrix theory that have not been mentioned. It should be emphasized that, while the material presented here may be adequate for understanding what follows, it is certainly no substitute for books or courses on modern algebra, which can provide a well-rounded understanding of the subject.

Notes

There are many good textbooks on algebra and on matrices. Birkhoff and Mac Lane (1941) covers all the material of this chapter and much more. It is clearly written and is probably the most easily understood text on modern algebra. It also contains an extensive bibliography. Van der Waerden (1949) is also well written and highly regarded, and goes generally deeper into the subject.

Problems

2.1. Show that there is only one group of three elements. Show that there are only two distinct groups with four elements, and that both are Abelian.

2.2. Show that if the operation is taken as addition in the groups of Problem 2.1, multiplication can be defined to make them rings.

2.3. The set of all nonnegative integers is not a group with the operation addition. Why? It is also not a group with the operation multiplication. Why?

2.4. The set of all $n \times n$ matrices is not a skew field. Why? The set of all nonsingular $n \times n$ matrices and the all-zero matrix is also not a skew field. Why?

2.5. Show that the set of all integers with the operation subtraction does not satisfy the associative law.

2.6. Solve these simultaneous equations for x and y, assuming the coefficients to be in the field of 4 elements as given in Table 2.3:

$$ax + y = b,$$
$$x + ay = b.$$

(Answer: $x = y = 1$.)

2.7. Calculate the determinant of the following matrix. Put the matrix in echelon canonical form and show that the rank is 3. Express the inverse as a product of elementary matrices. Assume the field of three elements.

$$\begin{bmatrix} 1 & 2 & 0 \\ 2 & 2 & 1 \\ 1 & 1 & 1 \end{bmatrix}$$

2.8. By row operations, find the echelon canonical form for the following matrix. Also calculate the determinant. Assume the field with two elements.

$$\begin{bmatrix} 1 & 1 & 0 & 1 \\ 1 & 1 & 1 & 0 \\ 0 & 1 & 1 & 0 \\ 0 & 1 & 0 & 1 \end{bmatrix}$$

2.9. Show that in the vector space of n-tuples over the field of two elements, every subgroup (under addition) is a subspace. (Compare Problem 6.8.)

2.10. Define the Hamming weight $w(\mathbf{v})$ of an n-tuple $\mathbf{v}$ as its Hamming distance from the zero n-tuple. Show that

$$d(\mathbf{u}, \mathbf{v}) = w(\mathbf{u} - \mathbf{v}).$$

2.11. Let H be a subspace of n-tuples, and define the Hamming weight of a coset of H as the minimum Hamming weight of elements of the coset. Define the distance between two cosets as the weight of the difference of the two cosets, which is also a coset. Show that this distance function is a metric. (Compare Problem 1.2.)

2.12. If an $n \times n$ matrix has the form

$$\begin{bmatrix} \mathbf{I}_k & \mathbf{P} \\ \mathbf{0} & \mathbf{I}_{n-k} \end{bmatrix} = \mathbf{M}$$

where $\mathbf{I}_k$ is a $k \times k$ identity matrix, $\mathbf{I}_{n-k}$ is an $(n-k) \times (n-k)$ identity matrix, $\mathbf{0}$ is an $(n-k) \times k$ matrix of all 0's, and $\mathbf{P}$ is an arbitrary $(k \times n-k)$ matrix, show that the inverse of $\mathbf{M}$ has the same form with $\mathbf{P}$ replaced by $-\mathbf{P}$.

2.13. Prove that the set of all $n \times n$ square matrices that have 1's on the main diagonal and 0's below the main diagonal forms a group under multiplication.

2.14. Show that the integers modulo 4 form a commutative ring but not a field. Compare Table 2.2. and Problem 2.1.

3 Linear Codes

In this chapter attention is focused on a subclass of the class of all codes, the linear codes. Almost all known block and tree codes are of this type, and so with one exception, only these codes are considered in the remainder of this book. Linear codes can be defined with symbols chosen from a set of arbitrary size (Problems 3.1 and 3.2). However, nearly all the major results of coding theory have been derived assuming that the code symbols are elements of a finite field. Thus in the sequel the number of symbols q will be taken to be a power of a prime. Of course, binary codes with symbols 0 and 1 result when $q = 2$.

3.1 The Hamming and Lee Metrics

The set of all n-tuples with entries chosen from the field of q elements is a vector space. A set of these vectors of length n is called a *linear block code* if and only if it is a subspace of the vector space of n-tuples. Similarly, a linear tree code (defined in Section 3.3) is a set of semi-infinite sequences which forms a subspace of the vector space of all such sequences. In the binary case, and in fact over a field of p elements where p is prime, every group of vectors is also a subspace (Problems 2.9 and 6.8). The term *group code* is common terminology for binary linear codes. The term *group alphabet* is also used with reference to linear block codes.

The *Hamming weight* of a vector $\mathbf{v}$, denoted $w(\mathbf{v})$, is defined to be the number of nonzero components. Since the Hamming distance between two vectors $\mathbf{v}_1$ and $\mathbf{v}_2$ is the number of positions in which they differ, the distance between $\mathbf{v}_1$ and $\mathbf{v}_2$ is equal to $w(\mathbf{v}_1 - \mathbf{v}_2)$. If $\mathbf{v}_1$ and $\mathbf{v}_2$ are both code words of a linear block code, then $\mathbf{v}_1 - \mathbf{v}_2$ must also be a code word, since the set of all code words is a vector space. Therefore, the distance between any two code vectors equals the weight of some other code vector, and *the minimum distance for a linear code equals the minimum weight* of its nonzero vectors. This property is extremely helpful in analyzing the error-correction capabilities of linear codes.

> *Example.* For a block code with $q = 2$ and $n = 5$, the set of vectors (00000), (10011), (01010), (11001), (00101), (10110), (01111), and (11100) form a vector space V_1 and hence a linear, or group, binary code. The minimum weight is 2, and hence the minimum distance is 2. This code will be used as an example throughout this chapter.

Nearly all known block and convolutional codes are based on the concept of Hamming distance. With one exception all of the codes discussed in this book employ this metric. The concept of Lee distance, though not as widely used as Hamming distance, is useful and for certain types of channels is more a natural metric than Hamming distance.

The *Lee weight* of an n-tuple $(a_{n-1}, \ldots, a_1, a_0)$, a_i chosen from the set $(0, 1, \ldots, q-1)$, where q is an arbitrary positive integer, is defined as

$$w_L = \sum_{i=0}^{n-1} |a_i|$$

where

$$|a_i| = a_i, \qquad 0 \leqq a_i \leqq \frac{q}{2};$$

$$= q - a_i, \quad \frac{q}{2} < a_i \leqq q - 1.$$

The *Lee distance* between two n-tuples is defined as the Lee weight of their difference. For $q = 2$ and 3, Lee and Hamming distance coincide; for $q > 3$, the Lee distance between two n-tuples is greater than or equal to the Hamming distance between them.

> *Example.* Let $q = 5$ and $n = 6$. Then the Lee distance between the two 6-tuples

$a = (200234)$

and

$b = (204000)$

is the weight of their term by term difference modulo 5,

$a - b = (001234)$.

Thus,

$w_L(a - b) = 0 + 0 + 1 + 2 + 2 + 1 = 6.$

3.2 Description of Linear Block Codes by Matrices

Any set of basis vectors for a linear block code V can be considered as rows of a matrix **G**, called a *generator matrix* of V. The row space of **G** is the linear code V, and the vector is a code vector if and only if it is a linear combination of the rows of **G**. If the dimension of the vector space V is k, the number of rows of **G** (which equals the rank of **G**, since the rows must be linearly independent) is k. If any two linear combinations were equal, there would be a dependence relation among rows of **G**. Thus, each distinct linear combination gives a distinct code vector, and since there are k coefficients with q possible values for each, there are q^k code vectors in V. Such a code is called an (n, k) code.

Unless both q and k are small, the matrix description is much more compact than a list of code vectors. A (50, 30) binary group code is described by a 30×50 matrix but has more than 10^9 code vectors.

Example. The code V_1 in the preceding example is the row space of either of the following matrices:

$$\begin{bmatrix} 1&0&0&1&1 \\ 0&1&0&1&0 \\ 0&0&1&0&1 \end{bmatrix} \qquad \begin{bmatrix} 1&0&0&1&1 \\ 1&1&0&0&1 \\ 1&1&1&0&0 \end{bmatrix}$$

There is an alternative description by matrices. Again, if V is a subspace of dimension k, its null space is a vector space V' of dimension $n - k$. A matrix **H** of rank $n - k$ whose row space is V' can be made with a basis for V' as rows. Then V is the null space of V', and a vector **v** is in V if and only if it is orthogonal to every row of **H**, that is, if and only if

$$\mathbf{v}\mathbf{H}^T = \mathbf{0}. \tag{3.1}$$

If $\mathbf{v} = (a_1, a_2, a_3, \ldots, a_n)$ and the element in the ith row and jth column of $\mathbf{H}$ is denoted h_{ij}, then Equation 3.1 implies that for each i (that is, each row of $\mathbf{H}$),

$$\sum_j a_j h_{ij} = 0. \tag{3.2}$$

Thus, the meaning of Equation 3.1 is that the components of $\mathbf{v}$ must satisfy a set of $n - k$ independent equations. Of course, any linear combination of the Equations 3.2 also gives an equation that the components of $\mathbf{v}$ must satisfy, and this corresponds to the fact that $\mathbf{v}$ is orthogonal to every vector of V'. These equations are called generalized parity checks, since in the binary case they are simply checks for even parity on certain sets of symbols in the code word. That is, for each row of $\mathbf{H}$, the number of 1's in $\mathbf{v}$ that corresponds to 1's in that row of $\mathbf{H}$ is even (for the binary case) if and only if $\mathbf{v}$ satisfies Equations 3.2. The matrix $\mathbf{H}$ is called a *parity-check matrix of V.*

Equation 3.1 holds for every vector $\mathbf{v}$ in V. In particular it holds for the k basis vectors of the matrix $\mathbf{G}$. These k equations can be expressed as follows, with $\mathbf{0}$ denoting the $k \times (n\text{-}k)$ all-zero matrix:

$$\mathbf{G}\mathbf{H}^T = \mathbf{0}. \tag{3.3}$$

Example. The null space V_2 of the vector space V_1 of previous examples consists of the four vectors (0 0 0 0 0), (1 1 0 1 0), (1 0 1 0 1), and (0 1 1 1 1). These four vectors form a vector space. The first two nonzero vectors are linearly independent and are a basis. Thus, V_1 is the row space of the matrix

$$\mathbf{H} = \begin{bmatrix} 1\,1\,0\,1\,0 \\ 1\,0\,1\,0\,1 \end{bmatrix}$$

The code V_1 is the null space of this matrix. For each vector in V_2 there is an equation that the components of every code vector must satisfy. For example, corresponding to (0 1 1 1 1) is the equation

$$0a_1 + 1a_2 + 1a_3 + 1a_4 + 1a_5 = 0$$

that must be satisfied by every code vector $(a_1, a_2, a_3, a_4, a_5)$. For binary codes, this is equivalent to having an even number of 1's among the last four components or an even parity check on the last four components. Note that, unlike vectors over the field of real numbers, a nonzero vector over a finite field can be orthogonal to itself. For example, (0 1 1 1 1) is in both V_1 and V_2.

It is easily verified that the Equation 3.3 is satisfied for the matrix **H** (above) and either of the two generator matrices of the previous example.

Both a vector space V and its null space V' are subspaces of the space of all n-tuples, and therefore both are linear codes. They are called *dual codes*. If V is an (n, k) code, V' is an $(n, n-k)$ code. If a code is the row space of a matrix, its dual is the null space, and vice versa.

THEOREM 3.1. *Let V be a linear code which is the null space of a matrix* **H**. *Then for each code word of Hamming weight w, there is a linear dependence relation among w columns of* **H**, *and conversely, for each linear dependence relation involving w columns of* **H**, *there is a code word of weight w.*

Proof. A vector $\mathbf{v} = (a_1, a_2, \ldots, a_n)$ is a code word if and only if

$$\mathbf{v}\mathbf{H}^T = \mathbf{0}$$

or, if the ith column vector in the matrix **H** is denoted $\mathbf{h}_i$,

$$\sum_{i=1}^{n} a_i \mathbf{h}_i = \mathbf{0}$$

This is exactly a linear dependence relation among columns of H, and the number of columns of H that appear with nonzero coefficients is the number of nonzero components a_i of $\mathbf{v}$, which is exactly the weight of $\mathbf{v}$. Similarly, the coefficients of any dependence relation among columns of **H** are components of a vector that must be in the null space of **H**. Q.E.D.

COROLLARY 3.1. *A block code that is the null space of a matrix* **H** *has minimum weight (and hence minimum distance) at least w if and only if every combination of $w - 1$ or fewer columns of H is linearly independent.*

Note the distinction between this condition and the definition of rank of a matrix. For a matrix to have column rank r or greater, there must be at least one set of r columns that is linearly independent.

For the purpose of studying the error-correcting properties of codes for any channel with independent errors, two codes that differ only in the arrangement of symbols have the same probability of error. In general, two such codes are very closely related and are therefore called *equivalent*. More precisely, if V is the row space of a matrix $\mathbf{G}$, then V' is a code equivalent to V if and only if V' is the row space of a matrix $\mathbf{G}'$ that is obtained from $\mathbf{G}$ by rearranging columns. Thus, permuting the columns of a generator matrix leads to a generator matrix for an equivalent code. Any elementary row operation on a matrix results in a matrix with the same row space, and therefore the altered matrix is a generator matrix for the same code. If one matrix can be obtained from another by a combination of row operations and column permutations, the two matrices are called *combinatorially equivalent*.

Every generator matrix $\mathbf{G}$ is combinatorially equivalent to one $\mathbf{G}'$ in echelon canonical form. The matrix $\mathbf{G}'$ can be obtained from $\mathbf{G}$ as follows: Starting with the first row, for each of the k rows do the following steps:

1. There must be at least one nonzero element in the ith row, because the rows are linearly independent. Say the jth column is the first with a nonzero element. Divide every element in the row by this element a_{ij}. As a result, the new a'_{ij} becomes 1.
2. Add to each other row, row l, $-a_{lj}$ times the ith row. The result will be that in the jth column, row i contains a 1 and all other rows contain 0.

Note that once a column takes the form in which it has one 1 and all the rest 0's, doing Steps 1 and 2 on another row will not change that column. Thus, after this is done on each row of the matrix, the resulting matrix $\mathbf{G}'$ has k columns each containing one 1 and $k-1$ 0's, and each row contains one of these 1's.

In fact, since $\mathbf{G}'$ can be obtained from $\mathbf{G}$ by row operations, they generate the same code. Then by column permutations, the k columns that contain the leading 1's of each row can be arranged at the left in the form of a $k \times k$ identity matrix, resulting in a combinatorially equivalent matrix $\mathbf{G}''$ of the following form:

$$\mathbf{G}'' = \begin{bmatrix} 1 & 0 & \cdots & 0 & p_{11} & \cdots & p_{1,n-k} \\ 0 & 1 & \cdots & 0 & p_{21} & \cdots & p_{2,n-k} \\ \vdots & \vdots & \vdots & \vdots & & & \\ 0 & 0 & \cdots & 1 & p_{k1} & \cdots & p_{k,n-k} \end{bmatrix} = [\mathbf{I}_k \mathbf{P}] \qquad (3.4)$$

This is called *reduced-echelon form.* (The terminology is not uniform on this subject.) Thus, there is a reduced-echelon matrix $\mathbf{G}''$ that is combinatorially equivalent to every generator matrix $\mathbf{G}$, and every code is equivalent to the row space of some matrix in reduced-echelon form.

Now let $\mathbf{v} = (a_1, a_2, \ldots, a_k)$ be an arbitrary k-tuple, and consider the vector $\mathbf{u}$ that is the linear combination of rows of $\mathbf{G}''$ with a_i as the ith coefficient:

$$\mathbf{u} = \mathbf{v}\mathbf{G}'' = (a_1, a_2, \ldots, a_k, c_1, c_2, \ldots, c_{n-k}), \tag{3.5}$$

where

$$c_j = \sum_{i=1}^{k} a_i p_{ij}. \tag{3.6}$$

Thus, the first k components of the code vector can be arbitrarily chosen information symbols, and each of the last $n-k$ components is a linear combination of the first k components. Encoding is thereby greatly simplified. A code of this type is called a *systematic code*; the first k components are called *information symbols*, and the last $n-k$ components are called *redundant* or *check symbols*. Thus, the following theorem holds.

THEOREM 3.2. *Every linear code is equivalent to a systematic code.*

There is a simple way to find a parity-check matrix for a code if a generator matrix in reduced-echelon form is given.

THEOREM 3.3. *If V is the row space of the matrix $\mathbf{G} = [\mathbf{I}_k \mathbf{P}]$, where $\mathbf{I}_k$ is a $k \times k$ identity matrix and $\mathbf{P}$ is a $k \times (n-k)$ matrix, then V is the null space of $\mathbf{H} = [-\mathbf{P}^T \mathbf{I}_{n-k}]$, where $\mathbf{I}_{n-k}$ is an $(n-k) \times (n-k)$ identity matrix.*

Proof. It can be easily verified that $\mathbf{G}\mathbf{H}^T = \mathbf{0}$, and, since the sum of their ranks is n, the row space of $\mathbf{G}$ is the null space of $\mathbf{H}$. Q.E.D.

If $\mathbf{u} = (a_1, a_2, \ldots, a_k, c_1, c_2, \ldots, c_{n-k})$ is a code vector, then

$$\mathbf{u}\mathbf{H}^T = \mathbf{0} = (-\sum_i a_i p_{i1} + c_1, \cdots, -\sum_i a_i p_{i,n-k} + c_{n-k}), \tag{3.7}$$

which is exactly the same as Equation 3.6. The connection between $\mathbf{G}$ and $\mathbf{H}$ in this form can be seen by noting that in either case p_{ij}, the element in the ith row and jth column of $\mathbf{P}$, is just exactly the coefficient of the ith information symbol a_i in the sum that gives the jth parity-check symbol c_j.

Example. The generator matrix

$$\mathbf{G} = \begin{bmatrix} 10011 \\ 01010 \\ 00101 \end{bmatrix} = [\mathbf{I}_3 \mathbf{P}]$$

for the code used in previous examples is in reduced-echelon form. If

$$\mathbf{H} = \begin{bmatrix} 11010 \\ 10101 \end{bmatrix} = [-\mathbf{P}^T \mathbf{I}_2]$$

then $\mathbf{GH}^T = \mathbf{HG}^T = 0$, and the row space of each is the null space of the other. In this form, the first three components of each code word $(a_1, a_2, a_3, a_4, a_5)$ can be chosen arbitrarily. The other two are parity-check symbols; that is,

$$a_4 = a_1 + a_2,$$
$$a_5 = a_1 + a_3,$$

as can be seen from either matrix. In **G**, the fourth column has 1's in the first and second rows, and therefore the first and second information symbols are involved in the calculation of the parity check symbol a_4. In **H**, because each row is in the null space of the code, every code word is orthogonal to each row of **H**. In particular, for the first row of **H**,

$$1a_1 + 1a_2 + 0a_3 + 1a_4 + 0a_5 = 0,$$

and this equation can be solved for a_4.

3.3 Description of Linear Tree Codes by Matrices

Let $\mathbf{F}_i$ denote a matrix whose k_0 rows are linearly independent semi-infinite vectors over $GF(q)$ where $GF(q)$ is the finite field of q elements (see Chapter 6). Further assume that the first $(i-1)n_0$ columns of $\mathbf{F}_i$ are zero and that some entry in columns $(i-1)n_0 + 1$ through in_0 is nonzero. Then a *linear tree code* is defined as the set of semi-infinite row vectors which is the row space of

$$\mathbf{G} = \begin{bmatrix} \mathbf{F}_1 \\ \mathbf{F}_2 \\ \mathbf{F}_3 \\ \vdots \end{bmatrix} \tag{3.8}$$

The matrix of **G** is a *generator matrix* of the code and has the form

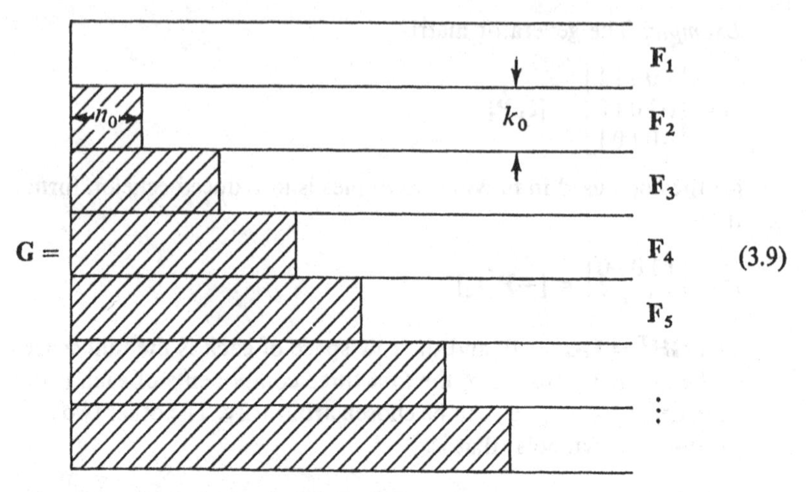

(3.9)

where the shaded area is filled with zeros.

A semi-infinite code sequence **c** in the linear tree code generated by **G** is obtained from a semi-infinite information sequence *i* according to the equation

$$\mathbf{c} = \mathbf{i}\mathbf{G} \tag{3.10}$$

Certain elements of **G** are required to be zero, because in a tree code the *i*th information block cannot affect the code blocks corresponding to information blocks 1, 2, ..., $i - 1$.

The most interesting class of linear tree codes, called *convolutional* or *recurrent codes*, is obtained by restricting the matrices $\mathbf{F}_i$ to shifted versions of $\mathbf{F}_1$. That is, $\mathbf{F}_i$ is obtained by shifting $\mathbf{F}_1$ exactly in_0 positions to the right and filling the in_0 leftmost positions with zeros. Most of the tree codes that have been studied in detail are of this type, and so only these convolutional tree codes will be considered throughout the remainder of this book.

Example. The binary tree code used in the examples of Chapter 1 is, in fact, a convolutional code. Its generator matrix is

$$\mathbf{G} = \begin{bmatrix} 1101 & & & \\ & 1101 & & \\ & & 1101 & \\ & & & \ddots \end{bmatrix} \tag{3.11}$$

(Throughout this book blank spaces in matrices of this type are filled with zeros.) The code sequence associated with the information sequence $\mathbf{i} = 1\,0\,1\,1\,0 \cdots$ begins

$$\mathbf{iG} = 1\,1\,0\,1\,1\,1\,1\,0\,0\,1 \ldots$$

(Compare Section 1.5.)

Any real encoder or decoder can store only a finite number of code digits; let n denote the number of digits which the decoder stores. The set of n-digit code words employed in decoding the first n_0 = symbol code block forms a group under addition and hence a linear subspace of the space of n-tuples. The generator matrix of this space is the k by n upper left corner of the matrix $\mathbf{G}$. It has the form

$$\mathbf{G} = \begin{bmatrix} \mathbf{G}_0 & \mathbf{G}_1 & \mathbf{G}_2 & \cdots\cdots & & \mathbf{G}_{m-1} \\ & \mathbf{G}_0 & \mathbf{G}_1 & \cdots\cdots & & \mathbf{G}_{m-2} \\ & & \mathbf{G}_0 & \ddots & & \\ & & & & & \\ & & & & \mathbf{G}_0 & \mathbf{G}_1 \\ & & & & & \mathbf{G}_0 \end{bmatrix} \tag{3.12}$$

where the submatrices $\mathbf{G}_i$ have k_0 rows and n_0 columns. The matrix $\mathbf{G}_0$ is always chosen to have rank k_0; hence the rank of $\mathbf{G}$ is $k = mk_0$. The row space of the matrix 3.12 is referred to as an (n, k) *convolutional code*. The upper k_0 rows of $\mathbf{G}$ form the *basic generator matrix* of the code.

Example. Let $n = 4$ in the preceding example. The generator matrix for the set of first code words in this (4, 2) code is

$$\mathbf{G} = \begin{bmatrix} 1\,1\,0\,1 \\ 0\,0\,1\,1 \end{bmatrix}$$

If the first block is decoded correctly, it is possible to remove its effect from subsequent decodings. Thus, it is possible to treat each block as the first one, provided all previous decodings are correct; the effect of previous blocks on the code words at a particular node is simply to add a fixed pattern to each of them. This pattern does not affect the error-correcting capability of the code and can be removed. For this *feedback decoding,* as it is called, the set of n-digit code words emanating from each node of the tree is the row space of the matrix $\mathbf{G}$ of Equation 3.12.

The question of what happens when a decoding error occurs is an important one. Because the information fed back to modify the set of code words is incorrect in this case, additional decoding errors are likely to be made. This *error propagation* effect, which is discussed in Chapter 13 can be eliminated by *definite decoding* (without feedback). However, most analyses of convolutional codes have assumed feedback decoding and so, with a few important exceptions in Chapter 13, feedback decoding is emphasized in this book.

Most of the results derived in the preceding section for linear block codes apply to the row space of the matrix **G** of Equation 3.12. In particular, the minimum weight of a code word *whose first* n_0 *digits are not all zero* equals the minimum distance d of the code. Also, the code can be described as the null space of a matrix **H** of rank $n - k$. Each of the $n - k$ (linearly independent) rows of **H** describes a generalized parity check on some set of symbols in each code word.

Example. For the code of the previous example,

$$\mathbf{H} = \begin{bmatrix} 1100 \\ 1011 \end{bmatrix}$$

In words, **H** states that the sum of the first two digits and the sum of digits one, three, and four of every code word must be zero.

In addition, Theorem 3.1 holds for the matrix **H**. However, its corollary must be modified to read as follows:

COROLLARY 3.2. *A code that is the null space of a matrix* **H** *has minimum weight at least* w *if and only if every combination of* $w - 1$ *or fewer columns of* **H** *is linearly independent, where at least one column is chosen from among the first* n_0.

Again as for linear block codes, every convolutional code generator matrix is combinatorially equivalent to one in echelon canonical form:

$$\mathbf{G} = \begin{bmatrix} \mathbf{IP}_0 & \mathbf{OP}_1 & \cdots & \mathbf{OP}_{m-1} \\ & \mathbf{IP}_0 & \cdots & \mathbf{OP}_{m-2} \\ & & \ddots & \\ & & & \mathbf{IP}_0 \end{bmatrix} \tag{3.13}$$

Here $\mathbf{P}_i$ represents an arbitrary $k_0 \times (n_0 - k_0)$ matrix and **I** and **O** represent the identity and all-zero matrices of order k_0, respectively. The first k_0 symbols in each n_0-symbol block of a code word in the code generated by **G** in Equation 3.13 are information symbols; the last

$n_0 - k_0$ are parity-check symbols. A code of this type is called *systematic*. Because the matrix $\mathbf{G}_0$ has rank k_0, Theorem 3.2 holds for convolutional codes as well as block codes. That is, every convolutional code is equivalent to a systematic convolutional code. (*Equivalent* convolutional codes are obtained by permutating only columns within the n_0-symbol blocks with the same permutation applied to all blocks).

Example. The code considered in the previous examples is in systematic form. Since $k_0 = n_0 - k_0 = 1$, the matrices $\mathbf{P}_i$ are simply binary digits, namely $\mathbf{P}_0 = \mathbf{P}_1 = [1]$.

Example. A systematic (12, 6) convolutional code with generator matrix $\mathbf{G}$ is also generated (in nonsystematic form) by the matrix $\mathbf{G}'$ and is equivalent to the code generated by the matrix $\mathbf{G}''$, where

$$\mathbf{G} = \begin{bmatrix} 11 & 01 & 01 & 00 & 01 & 01 \\ & 11 & 01 & 01 & 00 & 01 \\ & & 11 & 01 & 01 & 00 \\ & & & 11 & 01 & 01 \\ & & & & 11 & 01 \\ & & & & & 11 \end{bmatrix}$$

$$\mathbf{G}' = \begin{bmatrix} 11 & 10 & 11 & 00 & 00 & 00 \\ & 11 & 10 & 11 & 00 & 00 \\ & & 11 & 10 & 11 & 00 \\ & & & 11 & 10 & 11 \\ & & & & 11 & 10 \\ & & & & & 11 \end{bmatrix}$$

$$\mathbf{G}'' = \begin{bmatrix} 11 & 01 & 11 & 00 & 00 & 00 \\ & 11 & 01 & 11 & 00 & 00 \\ & & 11 & 01 & 11 & 00 \\ & & & 11 & 01 & 11 \\ & & & & 11 & 01 \\ & & & & & 11 \end{bmatrix}$$

The last code is said to have an *encoding constraint length* of 6 bits; this point is discussed in Chapter 13.

Analogous to Theorem 3.3 for block codes is the following result for convolutional codes.

THEOREM 3.4. *The row space of the matrix* $\mathbf{G}$ *of Equation* 3.13 *is the null space of the matrix*

$$\mathbf{H} = \begin{bmatrix} \mathbf{P}_0^T\mathbf{I} & & & \\ \mathbf{P}_1^T\mathbf{O} & \mathbf{P}_0^T\mathbf{I} & & \\ \vdots & \vdots & \ddots & \\ \mathbf{P}_{m-1}^T\mathbf{O} & \mathbf{P}_{m-2}^T\mathbf{O} & \cdots & \mathbf{P}_0^T\mathbf{I} \end{bmatrix} \quad (3.14)$$

Proof. The sum of the ranks of $\mathbf{G}$ and $\mathbf{H}$ is n. The theorem follows from the fact that $\mathbf{G}\mathbf{H}^T = \mathbf{0}$. Q.E.D.

Equation (3.14) illustrates the basic structure of convolutional codes rather well. Consider a binary code with $n_0 - k_0 = 1$; then each of the matrices $\mathbf{P}_i^T$ is an $(n_0 - 1)$-place binary row vector. The bottom $n_0 - k_0$ rows of the matrix $\mathbf{H}$, which form the *basic parity-check matrix* of the code, state that the parity bit in a block is the sum of the information bits in that block which correspond to the 1's of $\mathbf{P}_0^T$, the information bits in the first preceding block which correspond to the 1's of $\mathbf{P}_1^T, \ldots,$ and the information bits in the $(m - 1)$st preceding block which correspond to the 1's of P_{m-1}^T. Because of the restriction to convolutional codes, the parity digit in every block is the sum of information digits in the same relative positions. The top row of $\mathbf{H}$ illustrates the fact that although the parity bit in the leftmost block originally checked information bits in blocks other than its own, the effect of these bits has been removed since they have already been decoded and so are presumably known to the decoder. These ideas generalize in an obvious manner to the case of $n_0 - k_0 \neq 1$.

3.4 The Standard Array

Let V be an (n, k) linear code, let $\mathbf{h}_1$ be the all-zero (identity) vector, and let $\mathbf{h}_2, \mathbf{h}_3, \ldots, \mathbf{h}_{q^k}$ be the other code vectors. Then a decoding table can be formed as follows. The code vectors are placed in a row with the identity element at the left. Next, of all the remaining n-tuples, one, say $\mathbf{g}_1$, is placed under the identity element. (This would ordinarily be one of the most likely to be received if the identity vector is transmitted.) Then the row is completed by placing under each code vector $\mathbf{h}_i$ the vector $\mathbf{g}_1 + \mathbf{h}_i$. Similarly, a second vector $\mathbf{g}_2$ is placed in the first column and the row similarly completed. The process is continued until each possible n-tuple appears somewhere in the array. This standard array is, of course, exactly the array of cosets described in Chapter 2. The rows are cosets, and the vectors in the first column are coset leaders.

The standard array is useful in analyzing both block and convolutional codes. On the following pages several results pertaining to the standard array are proved for block codes. Following this discussion, the results are modified, where necessary, to cover convolutional codes.

If a vector $\mathbf{u}$ is transmitted and a vector $\mathbf{v}$ is received, then $\mathbf{v} - \mathbf{u}$ is called the error pattern.

THEOREM 3.5. *If the standard array is used as a decoding table for a block code, then a received vector* $\mathbf{v}$ *will be decoded correctly into the transmitted vector* $\mathbf{u}$ *if and only if the error pattern* $\mathbf{v} - \mathbf{u}$ *is a coset leader.*

Proof. If $\mathbf{v} - \mathbf{u} = \mathbf{g}_i$, the coset leader of the ith coset, then $\mathbf{v} = \mathbf{g}_i + \mathbf{u}$ must appear in the standard array in the ith coset under the code word $\mathbf{u}$ and will be decoded correctly. If, on the other hand, $\mathbf{v} - \mathbf{u}$ is not a coset leader, $\mathbf{v}$ must still be in some coset, say the jth, with coset leader $\mathbf{g}_j$. Then $\mathbf{v}$ is in the jth row but not under $\mathbf{u}$, for $\mathbf{v} \neq \mathbf{g}_j + \mathbf{u}$.

Q.E.D.

Suppose that a linear code is the null space of an $(n - k) \times n$ matrix $\mathbf{H}$. For any received vector $\mathbf{v}$, the $(n - k)$-component vector $\mathbf{S} = \mathbf{v}\mathbf{H}^T$ is called the *syndrome.* Since the code is the null space of $\mathbf{H}$, a vector is a code word if and only if its syndrome is zero. In general, each row of $\mathbf{H}$ corresponds to a parity-check equation that code words must satisfy. The components of $\mathbf{S}$ are zero for all equations that are satisfied and otherwise are nonzero.

THEOREM 3.6. *Two vectors* $\mathbf{v}_1$ *and* $\mathbf{v}_2$ *are in the same coset if and only if their syndromes are equal.*

Proof. It was shown in Chapter 2 that two group elements $\mathbf{v}_1$ and $\mathbf{v}_2$ are in the same coset if and only if $(-\mathbf{v}_2) + \mathbf{v}_1 = \mathbf{v}_1 - \mathbf{v}_2$ is an element of the subgroup, which in this case is the code vector space. If the code space is the null space of $\mathbf{H}$, then $\mathbf{v}_1 - \mathbf{v}_2$ is in the code space if and only if

$$(\mathbf{v}_1 - \mathbf{v}_2)\mathbf{H}^T = \mathbf{0}.$$

Since the distributive law holds for multiplication of matrices,

$$(\mathbf{v}_1 - \mathbf{v}_2)\mathbf{H}^T = \mathbf{v}_1\mathbf{H}^T - \mathbf{v}_2\mathbf{H}^T = \mathbf{0},$$

so that $\mathbf{v}_1 - \mathbf{v}_2$ is a code vector if and only if the syndromes of $\mathbf{v}_1$ and $\mathbf{v}_2$ are equal.

Q.E.D.

The decoding process can now be greatly simplified by the use of a decoding table. A table is formed that shows the coset leader and the syndrome for each of the 2^{n-k} cosets. When a vector is received, the syndrome is calculated. Then the coset leader is looked up in the table. This is the presumed error pattern, and subtracting it from the received vector gives a code vector that is assumed to have been sent. While in many cases such a procedure reduces memory requirements for the table by a large factor, the table may still be very large. For example, for a binary (100, 80) code the decoding table would require 2^{100} entries, which is a number beyond consideration. The number of cosets is 2^{20}, a much smaller value but still impractically large.

THEOREM 3.7. *Let V be an (n, k) binary block code (that is, a group code) to be used with the binary symmetric channel, and assume that the code vectors are equally likely to be transmitted. Then the average probability of correct decoding is as large as possible for this code if the standard array, with each coset leader chosen to have minimum weight in its coset, is used as the decoding table.*

Proof. Denote by $\mathbf{v}_{ij}$ the vector in the ith row and jth column of the decoding table. The code words placed at the top of the column are denoted $\mathbf{v}_{0j}$. Denote by d_{ij} the Hamming distance between a received $\mathbf{v}_{ij}$ and the code word into which it is decoded, $\mathbf{v}_{0j}$. Then the probability of correct decoding if the code word $\mathbf{v}_{0j}$ is transmitted is

$$\sum_{i=0}^{2^{n-k}-1} P^{d_{ij}} Q^{n-d_{ij}},$$

where P is the channel probability of error and $Q = 1 - P$. (See Figure 1.4.) Since the 2^k code words are assumed to be equally probable, in averaging the probability of correct decoding, the weighting factor 2^{-k} is used:

$$P_c = 2^{-k} \sum_{i,j} P^{d_{ij}} Q^{n-d_{ij}}.$$

There is one term in the sum for each possible received vector of binary symbols, and that term is maximized in each case if that particular vector is decoded into the closest code vector in the Hamming sense, since $P^{d_{ij}} Q^{n-d_{ij}}$ is a monotone decreasing function of d_{ij}. Therefore, the probability of correct decoding will be maximized if each received vector is decoded into the closest code vector.

Now suppose that a particular vector $\mathbf{v}$ appears in the decoding table under the code vector $\mathbf{u}$, which is at Hamming distance w. Suppose that the closest code vector $\mathbf{u}_1$ is at distance w_1. Let $\mathbf{g}$ denote the coset leader of the coset that contains $\mathbf{v}$. Then $\mathbf{g} = \mathbf{v} - \mathbf{u}$ has weight w. The element $\mathbf{v} - \mathbf{u}_1 = \mathbf{g} + (\mathbf{u} - \mathbf{u}_1)$ has weight w_1 and is in the same coset.

Because it was assumed that **g** has minimum weight in its coset, then $w_1 \geqq w$, and therefore **v** is at least as close to **u** as to $\mathbf{u}_1$. Q.E.D.

The number of coset leaders of weight i is denoted α_i. The probability of correct decoding can be written

$$P(\text{correct decoding}) = \alpha_0 Q^n + \alpha_1 P Q^{n-1} + \alpha_2 P^2 Q^{n-2} \cdots. \quad (3.15)$$

Example. A standard array for the code used in previous examples is

00000 10011 01010 11001 00101 10110 01111 11100
00001 10010 01011 11000 00100 10111 01110 11101
00010 10001 01000 11011 00111 10100 01101 11110
10000 00011 11010 01001 10101 00110 11111 01100

In each case, the coset leader was chosen to be a remaining vector of smallest weight. Such a procedure leads to optimum decoding. (Note that this does not mean an optimum code. Though it is not true in the present case, it might be that a different choice of code words would give smaller probability of error.) This code corrects three of the five possible single-error patterns. Note that 00001 and 00100 are in the same coset, since 00101, their difference, is a code vector. Therefore, these two error patterns cannot both be corrected. A similar result occurs whenever there is a code word of weight 2; minimum weight 3 is necessary and sufficient for correcting all single errors.

For the code itself, both parity checks are satisfied. For the next coset in the array, the syndrome is 01; for the next, 10; and for the last, 11. Note that in each coset there is a vector with 0's as the information symbols and the syndrome as check symbols.

On a binary symmetric channel the probability of receiving the transmitted code word is Q^n. If $P < \frac{1}{2}$, then this is the most probable received word. It can also be shown (Sullivan 1969) that if a code word is transmitted, the total probability that the received word is a code word, either the transmitted one or a different one, is greater than the probability that the received word is in any other given coset.

The standard array for a convolutional code has the same form as that of a block code. Now, however, correct decoding results whenever the received n-tuple falls in a column whose code vector is identical to the transmitted vector in the first n_0 positions. This is because only n_0 symbols are decoded at a time. That is, correct decoding results when the received n-tuple is in the same subset (see Chapter 1) as the transmitted code word.

A slightly modified version of Theorem 3.5 holds for convolutional codes.

THEOREM 3.8. *If the standard array is used as a decoding table for a convolutional code, then the first n_0-symbol block in a received vector* **v** *will be decoded correctly into the corresponding block of the transmitted vector* **u** *if and only if the error pattern* **v** – **u** *is in the correct (first) subset.*

Proof. The proof is identical to that of Theorem 3.5 with the correct subset playing the role of coset leader. If the error pattern **v** – **u** is in the correct subset, the first n_0 digits of the code word **u**′ – **u** at the head of its column must be zero. Thus, the code word

$$\mathbf{u}' = \mathbf{u} + (\mathbf{u}' - \mathbf{u})$$

must be identical to **u** in the first n_0 positions, and correct decoding results. On the other hand, if the error pattern is not in the correct subset, the first n_0 digits of the code word **u**′ – **u** are necessarily not all zero and the code word produced by the decoder differs from the transmitted word in the first n_0 positions. Q.E.D.

One fundamental difference between block and convolutional codes is that in the latter the "correction pattern" subtracted from the received vector by the decoder and the error pattern added by the channel can be different even when the decoding is correct. For block codes the two must be identical, of course.

Theorem 3.6 holds for convolutional codes without modification.

Theorem 3.7 does not hold for convolutional codes. In constructing the decoding table for a convolutional code it is desirable to have the received n-tuples of low weight in the correct subset. However, since the n-tuples in a particular coset are determined by the choice of code words and coset leader, not every low-weight element of each coset can be listed in the correct subset. In general, the coset leader should be chosen so that the total probability of the n-tuples in the correct subset is as large as possible. This does not seem to be a particularly meaningful result, however, and is not used in decoding practical codes.

3.5 Step-by-Step Decoding of Block Codes

Assume that for each received vector in a linear block code it is possible to determine the weight of the minimum weight element in its coset. This would be possible if a table showing the correspondence between syndrome and coset leader were available and conceivably could be accomplished with much less memory than such a table would require. Then decoding can be done in the following step-by-step manner:

Number the field elements from 1 to q, making the zero element last, but in any manner otherwise. Now order the vectors lexicographically, that is, $(b_1, \ldots, b_n)$ follows $(a_1, \ldots, a_n)$ if b_j follows a_j in the order of the field elements, and the jth position is the first in which the two vectors differ. Define the *weight of a coset* to be the weight of the minimum weight element in the coset.

Given a received vector $(a_1, a_2, \ldots, a_n)$, first the weight of the coset is determined. Then a_1 is replaced successively by $a_1 - f_1$, $a_1 - f_2$, and so on, where f_i is the ith field element in the defined order. The weight of the coset containing the received vector with the altered first component is determined.

If the weight is smaller in any other case, a_1 is replaced by $a_1 - f_i$, where f_i is the first field element resulting in smaller weight. If smaller weight does not occur, a_1 is retained as the first component. Then the same procedure is applied to the second, third, and all components in succession until a vector results that is in a coset of weight 0, that is, in the code. This is the code vector assumed to have been transmitted. This procedure is called *step-by-step decoding*. It will be shown that step-by-step decoding decodes every received vector into the nearest code vector, and that the coset leaders in the decoding table have an interesting property.

A vector $\mathbf{v}$ is called an *immediate descendant* of $\mathbf{u}$ if $\mathbf{v}$ can be obtained from $\mathbf{u}$ by changing one nonzero component to zero. A vector $\mathbf{v}$ is called a *descendant* of $\mathbf{u}$ if there is a chain $\mathbf{u}_0 = \mathbf{u}, \mathbf{u}_1, \mathbf{u}_2, \ldots, \mathbf{u}_n = \mathbf{v}$ such that, for each i, $\mathbf{u}_i$ is an immediate descendant of $\mathbf{u}_{i-1}$.

THEOREM 3.9. *If* $\mathbf{v}$ *is a vector of minimum weight in its coset and* $\mathbf{u}$ *is a descendant of* $\mathbf{v}$, *then* $\mathbf{u}$ *has minimum weight in its coset.*

Proof. It is sufficient to prove the theorem for immediate descendants, since the property is hereditary. Then $\mathbf{v} - \mathbf{e} = \mathbf{u}$, where $\mathbf{e}$ has weight one. Each element of $\{\mathbf{u}\}$, the coset that contains $\mathbf{u}$, is of the form $\mathbf{s} + \mathbf{u} = \mathbf{s} + \mathbf{v} - \mathbf{e}$, where $\mathbf{s}$ is a code vector. Since $\mathbf{s} + \mathbf{v}$ is in $\{\mathbf{v}\}$, and since $\mathbf{e}$ has weight one, each vector in the $\{\mathbf{u}\}$ differs in only one component from some vector in $\{\mathbf{v}\}$. Therefore the weight of $\{\mathbf{u}\}$ could differ by no more than one from the weight of $\{\mathbf{v}\}$. Since the weight of $\mathbf{u}$ is one less than that of $\mathbf{v}$, $\mathbf{u}$ must have minimum weight in its coset.

Q.E.D.

THEOREM 3.10. *If* $\mathbf{u}$ *is the minimum weight vector in its coset which precedes all other minimum weight vectors in its coset, and if* $\mathbf{v}$ *is a descendant of* $\mathbf{u}$, *then* $\mathbf{v}$ *is the minimum weight element in its coset which precedes all other minimum weight vectors in its coset.*

Proof. Again it is sufficient to prove the theorem for immediate descendants. Assume that $\mathbf{v} - \mathbf{u} = \mathbf{e}$, which is 0 except in the kth position. Then each element of $\{\mathbf{v}\}$ differs from some element of $\{\mathbf{u}\}$ only by $\mathbf{e}$. Consequently every element of minimum weight in $\{\mathbf{v}\}$ must be 0 in the kth position, since every element of minimum weight in $\{\mathbf{v}\}$ has more 0's than any element in $\{\mathbf{u}\}$. Therefore every element of minimum weight in $\{\mathbf{v}\}$ must be the result of subtracting $\mathbf{e}$ from some minimum weight element of $\{\mathbf{u}\}$. Consider the comparison of $\mathbf{v}$ with any other minimum weight element $\mathbf{v}_1$ in $\{\mathbf{v}\}$. The element $\mathbf{v}$ is obtained by subtracting $\mathbf{e}$ from $\mathbf{u}$, and $\mathbf{v}_1$ is obtained by subtracting $\mathbf{e}$ from some other minimum weight element $\mathbf{u}_1$ of $\{\mathbf{u}\}$. The vectors $\mathbf{u}$ and $\mathbf{u}_1$ must both have their kth components equal to the kth component of $\mathbf{e}$. Therefore, since $\mathbf{u}$ precedes $\mathbf{u}_1$, $\mathbf{v}$ precedes $\mathbf{v}_1$. Q.E.D.

THEOREM 3.11 (*Slepian–Moore*). *If in each coset the minimum weight element that precedes all other minimum weight elements is taken as coset leader, then every descendant of a coset leader is a coset leader.*

This theorem follows directly from Theorem 3.10.

THEOREM 3.12 (*Prange*). *Step-by-step decoding always results in a code vector. The corresponding coset leader, that is, the difference between the received vector and the resulting code word, has minimum weight in its coset and precedes all other minimum weight elements in this coset.*

Proof. Let $\mathbf{v}$ be the received vector and $\mathbf{g}$ the minimum weight vector in the coset $\{\mathbf{v}\}$ that precedes all other minimum weight vectors in $\{\mathbf{v}\}$. Let $\mathbf{e}_i$ denote a vector that has a 1 in the ith component and 0's in all other components, and let

$$\mathbf{g} = f_1 \mathbf{e}_{i_1} + \cdots + f_w \mathbf{e}_{i_w},$$

where w is the weight of $\mathbf{g}$, where

$$i_1 < \cdots < i_w,$$

and where $f_1, \ldots, f_w$ are field elements.

The first step in the proof is to note that the first component of $\mathbf{v}$ altered by the step-by-step decoding process would be the i_1 component, and it would have f_1 subtracted from it. Certainly if no earlier component is changed, and if no preceding field element is subtracted from the i_1 component, then f_1 would be subtracted from the i_1 component, for then $\mathbf{g}' = \mathbf{g} - f_1\mathbf{e}_{i_1}$, which has weight $w - 1$, would be in the coset containing the altered vector, and hence the coset would have weight less than w. Suppose that either an earlier component is changed or that the i_1 component has a field element preceding f_1 subtracted from it. Suppose that the first change is $f'\mathbf{e}_i'$. Then the resulting coset must have weight at most $w - 1$, and hence a coset leader $\mathbf{g}'$ of weight at most $w - 1$. Then $\mathbf{g}' + f'\mathbf{e}_i$ is a minimum weight element in $\{\mathbf{v}\}$ which precedes $\mathbf{g}$, contrary to hypothesis. Therefore the first component of $\mathbf{v}$ altered in step-by-step decoding is the i_1 component, and it has f_1 subtracted from it.

Let $\mathbf{v}_j$ denote the vector that results after j changes in $\mathbf{v}$ by the step-by-step decoding process. Next it will be shown by induction on j that the jth change in $\mathbf{v}$, which is $\mathbf{v}_j - \mathbf{v}_{j-1}$, is $f_j\mathbf{e}_{ij}$. The proof for $j = 1$ is given in the preceding paragraph. Assume that it is true for $j < l$. Then the vector $g_l = f_l\mathbf{e}_{i_l} + f_{l+1}\mathbf{e}_{i_{l+1}} + \cdots + f_w\mathbf{e}_{i_w}$ is in the same coset as $\mathbf{v}_l$, for $\mathbf{g}_l - \mathbf{v}_l = \mathbf{g} - \mathbf{v}$, which is a code vector. Since $\mathbf{g}_l$ is a descendant of $\mathbf{g}$, it is a minimum weight element in its coset which precedes all other minimum weight elements in its coset, by Theorem 3.10. The argument in the preceding paragraph then shows that the next change which will result in the step-by-step decoding process is subtraction of $f_l\mathbf{e}_{i_l}$ from $\mathbf{v}_l$ to form $\mathbf{v}_{l+1}$. This is true whether the step-by-step decoding is started again from the first component or simply continued from the last change.

Thus the step-by-step decoding process will make the w changes $f_1\mathbf{e}_{i_1}, \ldots, f_w\mathbf{e}_{i_w}$ successively in the received vector, and the resulting vector will be $\mathbf{v} - \mathbf{g}$, which is the desired code vector. Q.E.D.

3.6 Modular Representation of Linear Block Codes

Let $\mathbf{G}$ be a generator matrix for an (n, k) linear code. Since the generator has k rows, and since a column of all 0's would be ruled out as useless, there are $q^k - 1$ different types of columns possible. If rearrangement of columns is unimportant, a code can be described by a list of the number of columns of each type. This is called the modular representation.

Let $\mathbf{M}$ be a special $k \times (q^k - 1)$ matrix that has as columns all possible vectors of k field elements except the vector of all 0's. Then the jth column of $\mathbf{M}$ can be considered a column of type j, and a code can be described by a vector of $q^k - 1$ positive integers,

$$\mathbf{N} = (n_1, n_2, \ldots, n_{q^k-1}),$$

in which n_i is the number of columns of type i.

Note that the $(q^k - 1) \times n$ matrix

$$\mathbf{K} = \mathbf{M}^T\mathbf{G} \tag{3.16}$$

has as rows all possible nonzero linear combinations of rows of $\mathbf{G}$ and thus has all nonzero code vectors as rows. An important case is the matrix that is the entire code generated by $\mathbf{M}$ considered as a generator matrix:

$$\mathbf{C} = \mathbf{M}^T\mathbf{M}. \tag{3.17}$$

It is clearly symmetric, and contains one column of each possible type.

Now assume the binary case.

THEOREM 3.13. (*MacDonald*). *A list of the weights of the* $2^k - 1$ *nonzero code words of a binary group code can be found as the components of the vector resulting from multiplying as matrices of real numbers the modular representation vector* $\mathbf{N}$ *by the matrix* $\mathbf{C}$:

$$\mathbf{W} = \mathbf{NC}, \quad \textit{or} \quad \mathbf{W}^T = \mathbf{CN}^T. \tag{3.18}$$

Proof. (The weights of the code words appear in the same order as the code words appear in the matrix in Equation 3.16.) Equation 3.18 can be seen by noting that the ith component of $\mathbf{W}^T$ is obtained by multiplying the ith row of $\mathbf{C}$ by $\mathbf{N}$. Since all the elements of $\mathbf{C}$ are 1's and 0's, this is just the sum of a certain subset of the components of $\mathbf{N}$, those particular components referring to columns that have 1's in the ith code word. Q.E.D.

The matrix $\mathbf{C}$ considered as a matrix of real numbers is nonsingular. The inverse can be found by changing each 0 in $\mathbf{C}$ to -1, and dividing each element by 2^{k-1}. The first step in proving this is to show that two different columns of $\mathbf{C}$ have 1's in common in 2^{k-2} rows.

The rows of $\mathbf{C}$ together with a vector of all 0's form a group, since they are the row space of $\mathbf{M}$. Consider the set of rows that have 0's in the ith and jth columns. It is easily verified that they form a subgroup. There are four cosets, each with an equal number of elements — namely, the subgroup, the set containing every row with 0 in column i

and 1 in column j, the set containing every row with 1 in column i and 0 in column j, and the set of rows with 1's in both columns. Thus one-fourth of the rows, or 2^{k-2} rows altogether, have 1's in both column i and column j. It can similarly be shown that each column has 2^{k-1} ones. (See Problem 3.5.)

Since $\mathbf{C}$ is symmetric, if $\mathbf{C}$ is multiplied by itself, the diagonal elements are 2^{k-1}, while all off-diagonal terms are 2^{k-2}. Thus

$$\mathbf{C}^2 = 2^{k-2}(\mathbf{I} + \mathbf{J}),$$

where $\mathbf{I}$ denotes the identity matrix and $\mathbf{J}$ denotes a matrix of all 1's. It is easily verified that $\mathbf{CJ} = 2^{k-1}\mathbf{J}$. Therefore,

$$\mathbf{I} = \frac{2\mathbf{C}^2 - 2^{k-1}\mathbf{J}}{2^{k-1}} = \frac{2\mathbf{C}^2 - \mathbf{CJ}}{2^{k-1}} = \mathbf{C}\frac{2\mathbf{C} - \mathbf{J}}{2^{k-1}} = \mathbf{CC}^{-1}$$

and so

$$\mathbf{C}^{-1} = \frac{2\mathbf{C} - \mathbf{J}}{2^{k-1}}. \tag{3.19}$$

Thus if a list of weights, in the order in which the code words appear in Equation 3.18, is given, the modular representation vector can be found and thus the code determined except for the arrangement of columns. A given set of weights is possible if it can be arranged in a vector $\mathbf{W}$ in such a way that $\mathbf{N} = \mathbf{WC}^{-1}$ has components that are non-negative integers.

As a simple application of this principle, let us consider under what circumstances a code can have all its code words of equal weight w_0. Only one arrangement of the elements of $\mathbf{W}$ is possible. The product $\mathbf{WC}^{-1}$ then has every component equal to $w_0 2^{-(k-1)}$, since each row of $\mathbf{C}^{-1}$ has one more positive than negative term. Since $\mathbf{N} = \mathbf{WC}^{-1}$ must have integral components, w_0 must be a multiple of 2^{k-1}, say $t2^{k-1}$. Then every component of vector $\mathbf{N}$ is t, and the code consists of t columns of each type.

Example. For $k = 3$, $\mathbf{M}$ might be chosen as follows:

$$\mathbf{M} = \begin{bmatrix} 0001111 \\ 0110011 \\ 1010101 \end{bmatrix}$$

(The columns are in order as binary numbers.) Then

$$\mathbf{C} = \mathbf{M}^T\mathbf{M} = \begin{bmatrix} 1010101 \\ 0110011 \\ 1100110 \\ 0001111 \\ 1011010 \\ 0111100 \\ 1101001 \end{bmatrix}$$

$$\mathbf{C}^{-1} = \tfrac{1}{4}\begin{bmatrix} 1 & -1 & 1 & -1 & 1 & -1 & 1 \\ -1 & 1 & 1 & -1 & -1 & 1 & 1 \\ 1 & 1 & -1 & -1 & 1 & 1 & -1 \\ -1 & -1 & -1 & 1 & 1 & 1 & 1 \\ 1 & -1 & 1 & 1 & -1 & 1 & -1 \\ -1 & 1 & 1 & 1 & 1 & -1 & -1 \\ 1 & 1 & -1 & 1 & -1 & -1 & 1 \end{bmatrix}$$

For the code used in previous examples,

$$\mathbf{G} = \begin{bmatrix} 10011 \\ 01010 \\ 00101 \end{bmatrix} \qquad \mathbf{M}^T\mathbf{G} = \begin{bmatrix} 00101 \\ 01010 \\ 01111 \\ 10011 \\ 10110 \\ 11001 \\ 11100 \end{bmatrix}$$

$$\mathbf{N} = (1, 1, 0, 1, 1, 1, 0) \qquad \mathbf{W} = (2, 2, 4, 3, 3, 3, 3).$$

3.7 Linear Block Code Equivalence

In studying properties of block codes in which the arrangement of columns is immaterial, that is, properties common to equivalent codes, the modular representation is especially convenient. However, there are many possible choices as basis for the same code and, hence, many different generator matrices. In general they will result in different modular representation vectors, and it would be desirable to know when modular representations describe equivalent codes.

There are two obvious necessary conditions. If two columns are identical in a code, they will be identical in any basis, and therefore if a column of type i occurs n_i times in one representation, some other type of column occurs n_i times in any other representation of the same or an equivalent code. Thus the components of the vector $\mathbf{N}$ are permuted but not otherwise changed. Similarly, the components of the weight vector $\mathbf{W}$ are permuted but not otherwise changed. Now the problem is to characterize the permutations.

Let $\mathbf{S}$ be any $k \times k$ nonsingular matrix. If $\mathbf{v}_1$ and $\mathbf{v}_2$ are k-component vectors, $\mathbf{v}_1\mathbf{S} - \mathbf{v}_2\mathbf{S} = (\mathbf{v}_1 - \mathbf{v}_2)\mathbf{S}$ is a linear combination of rows of $\mathbf{S}$, and, since the rows of $\mathbf{S}$ are linearly independent, $\mathbf{v}_1\mathbf{S} - \mathbf{v}_2\mathbf{S}$ is $\mathbf{0}$ only if $\mathbf{v}_1 - \mathbf{v}_2$ is $\mathbf{0}$. Therefore if $\mathbf{v}_1$ and $\mathbf{v}_2$ are unequal, so are $\mathbf{v}_1\mathbf{S}$ and $\mathbf{v}_2\mathbf{S}$. Then the $q^k - 1$ rows of $\mathbf{M}^T\mathbf{S}$ will all be different, where $\mathbf{M}$ is the matrix defined in Section 3.6. Since there are exactly $q^k - 1$ different nonzero vectors, $\mathbf{M}^T\mathbf{S}$ must differ from $\mathbf{M}^T$ only in having its rows permuted:

$$\mathbf{M}^T\mathbf{S} = \mathbf{P}_S\mathbf{M}^T, \tag{3.20}$$

where $\mathbf{P}_S$ is a permutation matrix. This matrix is called the *A-permutation* corresponding to $\mathbf{S}$. (Note that $\mathbf{P}_S$ depends also on the choice of $\mathbf{M}$.)

There is for each i somewhere among the rows of $\mathbf{M}^T$, say in the kth row, a vector that has 0's in every position except the ith, and a 1 in that position. Then the ith row of $\mathbf{S}$ appears as the kth row of $\mathbf{P}_S\mathbf{M}^T$, and therefore different matrices $\mathbf{S}$ result in different permutations $\mathbf{P}_S$. Furthermore, if $\mathbf{S}$ and $\mathbf{U}$ are nonsingular $k \times k$ matrices,

$$\mathbf{M}^T\mathbf{S}\mathbf{U} = \mathbf{P}_S\mathbf{M}^T\mathbf{U} = \mathbf{P}_S\mathbf{P}_U\mathbf{M}^T; \tag{3.21}$$

that is, the product $\mathbf{SU}$ corresponds to the permutation $\mathbf{P}_S\mathbf{P}_U$. It follows that the A-permutations form a group isomorphic to (that is, the same in structure as) the group of nonsingular $k \times k$ matrices.

Now consider the effect of an A-permutation on the rows of the matrix $\mathbf{C} = \mathbf{M}^T\mathbf{M}$. Let $\mathbf{U} = (\mathbf{S}^{-1})^T$. Then

$$\begin{aligned}\mathbf{P}_S\mathbf{C}\mathbf{P}_U^T &= \mathbf{P}_S\mathbf{M}^T\mathbf{M}\mathbf{P}_U^T = \mathbf{P}_S\mathbf{M}^T(\mathbf{P}_U\mathbf{M}^T)^T \\ &= (\mathbf{M}^T\mathbf{S})(\mathbf{M}^T\mathbf{U})^T = \mathbf{M}^T\mathbf{S}\mathbf{U}^T\mathbf{M} = \mathbf{M}^T\mathbf{M} = \mathbf{C}.\end{aligned}$$

Since a permutation matrix is an orthogonal matrix, $\mathbf{P}^T = \mathbf{P}^{-1}$, and

$$\mathbf{P}_S\mathbf{C} = \mathbf{C}\mathbf{P}_U. \tag{3.22}$$

Therefore applying an A-permutation on the rows is equivalent to applying a different but related A-permutation to the columns of $\mathbf{C}$.

Choosing a new basis and generator matrix for a group code corresponds to multiplying the generator matrix on the left by some nonsingular matrix $\mathbf{S}$. The nonzero code vectors for the generator $\mathbf{SG}$ are the rows of

$$\mathbf{M}^T(\mathbf{SG}) = (\mathbf{M}^T\mathbf{S})\mathbf{G} = (\mathbf{P}_S\mathbf{M}^T)\mathbf{G} = \mathbf{P}_S(\mathbf{M}^T\mathbf{G}), \tag{3.23}$$

and these are the rows of $\mathbf{M}^T\mathbf{G}$ permuted by $\mathbf{P}_S$. Thus choosing a new basis is equivalent to applying an A-permutation to the code words. The argument is clearly reversible.

Also a column of type i in the matrix $\mathbf{M}^T\mathbf{G}$, which lists all the code words, is identical to the ith column of the matrix $\mathbf{C}$. Then in $\mathbf{M}^T(\mathbf{SG}) = \mathbf{P}_S(\mathbf{M}^T\mathbf{G})$, this column is still like the ith column of $\mathbf{P}_S\mathbf{C}$. But $\mathbf{P}_S\mathbf{C} = \mathbf{C}\mathbf{P}_U$, where $\mathbf{U} = (\mathbf{S}^{-1})^T$, and therefore the column of $\mathbf{C}$ which corresponds to the ith column of $\mathbf{P}_S\mathbf{C}$ is the column which $\mathbf{P}_U$ permutes into the ith column. Therefore

$$\mathbf{N}_{SG}^T = \mathbf{P}_S\mathbf{N}_G^T \tag{3.24}$$

where $\mathbf{N}_{SG}$ and $\mathbf{N}_G$ are modular representations of the codes whose generator matrices are $\mathbf{SG}$ and $\mathbf{G}$, respectively. Therefore two different generator matrices result in modular representations that differ by an A-permutation. The converse can similarly be shown.

3.8 Weight Distributions and the MacWilliams Identities

Let A_i denote the number of code words of weight i in an (n, k) block code. The numbers A_i, $i = 0, 1, \ldots, n$, form the *weight distribution* or *weight spectrum* of the code. The weight distribution has a number of applications in the study of codes. For example, from the A_i, the probability of an undetectable error for a group code used strictly for error detection on the binary symmetric channel can be calculated. An undetectable error occurs only when the error pattern is a nonzero code word, therefore

$$P_e = \sum_{i=1}^{n} A_i P^i Q^{n-i}. \tag{3.25}$$

Similar but more complex results can be obtained when some correction is performed (see Berlekamp 1968*b*, Chap. 16).

It is possible to determine the weight distribution of a code with today's digital computers by simply examining all 2^k code words, provided k does not exceed 25 or so. The weight distribution of codes with no more than about 25 check symbols can be found with the help of MacWilliams's identities, which state that the weight distribution of a code can be calculated from that of its null space, that is, its dual code. These are given in the following theorem.

THEOREM 3.14. (*MacWilliams* 1963*a*). *Let V_1 be an (n, k) block code, and V_2 the $(n, n-k)$ code which is the null space of V_1. Let A_i and*

B_i denote the number of vectors of weight i in V_1 and V_2, respectively. Then

$$q^k \sum_{i=0}^{n} B_i X^i = \sum_{j=0}^{n} A_j (1 - X)^j [1 + (q-1)X]^{n-j}. \tag{3.26}$$

Proof. These formulas can be written more compactly in terms of generating functions,

$$A(X) = \sum_{i=0}^{n} A_i X^i, \qquad B(X) = \sum_{i=0}^{n} B_i X^i.$$

Then Equation 3.25 becomes

$$P_e = Q^n A\left(\frac{P}{Q}\right)$$

and Equation 3.26 becomes

$$q^k B(X) = [1 + (q-1)X]^n A\left[\frac{1 - X}{1 + (q-1)X}\right]$$

There are a number of sets of identities that are equivalent to Equation 3.26, and it is more convenient to prove one of these rather than Equation 3.26 itself. Therefore, these will be given first and the proof afterward.

First, equating the coefficients of X^i on both sides of Equation 3.26 gives an explicit formula for each B_i as a function of all the A_j:

$$\sum_{i=0}^{n} B_i X^i = q^{-k} \sum_{j=0}^{n} A_j (1 - X)^j [1 + (q-1)X]^{n-j}$$

$$= q^{-k} \sum_{j=0}^{n} \sum_{s=0}^{j} \sum_{t=0}^{n-j} A_j \binom{j}{s} (-1)^s X^s \binom{n-j}{t} (q-1)^t X^t$$

Now let $s + t = i$, and eliminate t from the expression:

$$\sum_{i=0}^{n} B_i X^i = q^{-k} \sum_{j=0}^{n} \sum_{s=0}^{j} \sum_{i=s}^{n-j+s} A_j \binom{j}{s} \binom{n-j}{i-s} (-1)^s (q-1)^{i-s} X^i$$

$$= q^{-k} \sum_{j=0}^{n} \sum_{s=0}^{n} \sum_{i=0}^{n} A_j \binom{j}{s} \binom{n-j}{i-s} (-1)^s (q-1)^{i-s} X^i$$

$$= q^{-k} \sum_{i=0}^{n} X^i \sum_{j=0}^{n} A_j \sum_{s=0}^{n} \binom{j}{s} \binom{n-j}{i-s} (-1)^s (q-1)^{i-s}.$$

Summing from $i = 0$ to n as in the second expression rather than from $i = s$ to $n - j + s$ introduces additional terms, all of which are zero. In this form, however, the order of summation can be changed. Now the coefficients of X^i on the left and the right must be equal:

$$B_i = q^{-k} \sum_{j=0}^{n} A_j \sum_{s=0}^{n} \binom{j}{s} \binom{n-j}{i-s} (-1)^s (q-1)^{i-s}. \tag{3.27}$$

Letting $X = 1 + Y$ in Equation 3.26, one has

$$q^k \sum_{i=0}^{n} B_i (1+Y)^i = \sum_{j=0}^{n} A_j (-Y)^j [q + (q-1)Y]^{n-j}, \tag{3.28}$$

and expanding and equating coefficients of Y^m on both sides, as was done in deriving Equation 3.27, gives

$$\sum_{i=m}^{n} B_i \binom{i}{m} = q^{n-k-m} \sum_{j=0}^{m} A_j \binom{n-j}{n-m} (-1)^j (q-1)^{m-j}. \tag{3.29}$$

Similarly letting $X = 1/(1+Y)$ in Equation 3.26, one has

$$q^k \sum_{i=0}^{n} B_i (1+Y)^{n-i} = \sum_{j=0}^{n} A_j Y^j (Y+q)^{n-j}, \tag{3.30}$$

and expanding and equating coefficients of Y^m on both sides, yields

$$\sum_{i=0}^{n-m} B_i \binom{n-i}{m} = q^{n-k-m} \sum_{j=0}^{n} A_j \binom{n-j}{n-m}. \tag{3.31}$$

Now a proof will be given for Equation 3.31. Let $s = (s_1, s_2, \ldots, s_m)$ be a set of m different integers, $1 \leq s_i \leq n$, and let $t = (t_1, t_2, \ldots, t_{n-m})$ denote the complementary set, that is, all integers between 1 and n which are not in s. Let F_s be the subspace of all vectors whose components in positions $s_1, s_2, \ldots, s_m$ may be nonzero but whose components in positions $t_1, t_2, \ldots, t_{n-m}$ are zero, and similarly define F_t. Then F_t is the null space of F_s.

Next consider the subspace of all vectors in V_1 which are zero in positions $t_1, t_2, \ldots, t_{n-m}$. This subspace is the intersection of V_1 and F_s, $V_1 \cap F_s$. Similarly, the subspace of all vectors of V_2 which are zero in positions $s_1, s_2, \ldots, s_m$ is $F_t \cap V_2$. By Theorem 2.18, the null space of $V_1 \cap F_s$ is $V_2 \oplus F_t$, If we denote by d_s the dimension of $V_1 \cap F_s$ and by d_t the dimension of $V_2 \cap F_t$, then the dimension of $V_2 \oplus F_t$ is $n - d_s$ because it is the null space of $V_1 \cap F_s$. On the other hand, by Theorem 2.17, the dimension of $V_2 \oplus F_t$ is $(n-k) + (n-m) - d_t$. Therefore

$$n - d_s = (n-k) + (n-m) - d_t$$

or

$$d_t = d_s + n - k - m.$$

Now consider pairs consisting of a set s of m integers and a vector $\mathbf{v}_1$ in $V_1 \cap F_s$. For each choice of s, the number of such pairs is q^{d_s}, the number of elements in $V_1 \cap F_s$. Considering all possible choices of s, the total number of such pairs is

$$\sum_{\text{all } s} q^{d_s}.$$

On the other hand, for each vector of weight j in V_1, there are $n - j$ zero components, and any set t which is a subset of $n - m$ of the indices of these positions will define a set s which can be paired with this vector. There are $\binom{n-j}{n-m}$ choices with m integers in the set s. There are A_j vectors of weight j in V_1, and so the number of pairs is given by a second expression:

$$\sum_{\text{all } s} q^{d_s} = \sum_{j=0}^{n} A_j \binom{n-j}{n-m}.$$

Similarly, considering V_2 and sets t of $n - m$ integers, one has the following result:

$$\sum_{\text{all } t} q^{d_t} = \sum_{i=0}^{n} B_i \binom{n-i}{m}.$$

But since $d_t = d_s + n - k - m$, and since each set t determines a unique set s,

$$\sum_{\text{all } t} q^{d_t} = \sum_{\text{all } t} q^{d_s+n-k-m} = \sum_{\text{all } s} q^{d_s+n-k-m}$$
$$= q^{n-k-m} \sum_{\text{all } s} q^{d_s}$$

and hence

$$\sum_{i=0}^{n} B_i \binom{n-i}{m} = q^{n-k-m} \sum_{j=0}^{n} A_j \binom{n-j}{n-m}.$$

This is the Identity 3.31. From it, Equation 3.30 follows, and using the substitution $X = 1/(1 + Y)$ to eliminate Y from 3.30 results in Equation 3.26. Q.E.D.

Mrs. MacWilliams (1963*a*) gave two proofs of the theorem in her paper. The one presented here is the simpler. The other depends strongly on the theory of group characters and gives a more general result which will be stated here without proof.

Let $X(\alpha, \beta)$, where α and β are elements of a field of q elements, denote the complex-valued function of α which is the character of the additive group of $GF(q)$ corresponding to β (see Chapter 6). Since the definition and theory of group characters is not needed elsewhere in this book, it will not be included here. If q is a prime, then the characters can be taken to be the functions

$$X(\alpha, \beta) = e^{\alpha\beta[(2i\pi)/q]} \tag{3.32}$$

where e is the base of the natural logarithm and $i = \sqrt{-1}$. If $q = p^m$ and $m > 1$, then it is shown in Chapter 6 that α and β can be expressed as m-tuples whose components are elements of the field of p elements, and the character can be taken to be

$$X(\alpha, \beta) = e^{(\alpha \cdot \beta)(2i\pi/q)}$$

where $\alpha \cdot \beta$ is the inner product of α and β as n-tuples. Then the following theorem appears as Lemma 2.7 in Mrs. MacWilliams's paper (1963*a*).

THEOREM 3.15. *Let $\alpha_0 = 0, \alpha_1, \ldots, \alpha_{q-1}$ denote all the elements of the field, and $X_0, X_1, \ldots, X_{q-1}$ be q indeterminants. Let V_1 be a k-dimensional vector space and V_2 its null space. Let $A_{i_1, i_2, \ldots, i_{q-1}}$ denote the number of vectors in V_1 in which the field element α_1 occurs i_1 times, α_2 occurs i_2 times, and so on. The element 0 must occur $i_0 = n - i_1 - i_2 - \cdots - i_{q-1}$ times. Define $B_{i_1, i_2, \ldots, i_{q-1}}$ similarly. Then*

$$\sum_{i_1, i_2, \ldots, i_{q-1}=1}^{n} A_{i_1, i_2, \ldots, i_{q-1}} \prod_{j=0}^{q-1} \left(\sum_{s=1}^{q} X(\alpha_j, \alpha_s) X_s \right)^{i_j}$$
$$= q^k \sum_{i_1, i_2, \ldots, i_{q-1}=1}^{n} B_{i_1, i_2, \ldots, i_{q-1}} X_1^{i_1} \cdots X_{q-1}^{i_{q-1}} X_q^{i_q}. \tag{3.33}$$

Theorem 3.14 states that if we know only how many vectors in V_1 have each possible composition, then the number of vectors in V_2 with each possible composition can be calculated.

At first sight, this looks too complicated to have any application. Let us look at two special cases, in order to see more clearly its structure. First consider the case $q = 2$. Then by Equation 3.32, $X(0, 0) = X(0, 1) = X(1, 0) = 1$, $X(1, 1) = -1$. Let $\alpha_1 = 1$, $\alpha_2 = 0$. Then A_{i_1} is simply the number of vectors of weight i; Equation 3.33 becomes

$$\sum_{i_1=0}^{n} A_{i_1}(X_0 + X_1)^{i_0}(X_0 - X_1)^{i_1} = 2^k \sum_{i_1=0}^{n} B_{i_1} X_0^{i_0} X_1^{i_1}. \tag{3.34}$$

If we let $X_0 = 1$ and $i_0 = n - i_1$ in this expression, it makes it the same as Equation 3.26 for the binary case.

Now let us consider the case $q = 3$, and let ξ denote the cube root of unity; that is, $\xi = (1 + i\sqrt{3})/2$. Then $X(\alpha, \beta) = \xi^{\alpha\beta}$. The three field elements are $\alpha_1 = 1$, $\alpha_2 = 2$, and $\alpha_3 = 0$. Then $A_{i_1 i_2}$ is the number of vectors with i_1 ones and i_2 twos as components, and Equation 3.33 becomes

$$\sum_{i_1=1}^{n} \sum_{i_2=1}^{n} A_{i_1 i_2}(X_1 + X_2 + X_3)^{i_0}(\zeta X_1 + \zeta^2 X_2 + X_3)^{i_1} \times (\zeta^2 X_1 + \zeta X_2 + X_3)^{i_2} = q^k \sum_{i_1=1}^{n} \sum_{i_2=1}^{n} B_{i_1 i_2} X_0^{i_0} X_1^{i_1} X_2^{i_2}. \quad (3.35)$$

Theorem 3.14 can be derived from Theorem 3.15 by setting $X_0 = 1$ and all other $X_i = X$ and using some simple properties of characters. The following theorem is derived similarly from Theorem 3.15 by letting $X_j = X$ and $X_i = 1$ if $i \neq j$, and doing some simplification:

THEOREM 3.16. *Let B_s' denote the number of vectors in V_2 in which i components have the value $\alpha_j \neq 0$, let A_{0s} be the number of vectors of weight s in V_1 whose components sum to zero, and A_{1s} the number of vectors of weight s in V_1 whose components do not sum to zero. Then*

$$\sum_{s=0}^{n} B_s' X^s = \sum_{s=0}^{n} \left(A_{0s} - \frac{A_{1s}}{q-1}\right)(X-1)^s(X+q-1)^{n-s}. \quad (3.36)$$

Pless (1963) observed that it is possible to derive from MacWilliams' identities expressions for the sum of the jth powers of the weight of the vectors in a space:

$$\left(X\frac{d}{dx}\right)^j \sum_{i=0}^{n} B_i X^i = \sum_{i=0}^{n} i^j B_i X^i. \quad (3.37)$$

Substituting $X = 1$ in this expression one has the desired result. To carry out the differentiation in general is complicated, but Mrs. Pless has found a closed-form formula for the result in Equation 3.37. Note that after $\left(X\frac{d}{dx}\right)^j$ acts on the right side of Equation 3.26, A_i will be multiplied by $X-1$ in the result if $i > j$, and thus all terms involving A_i for $i > j$ will disappear.

The resulting expressions for the special cases $j = 0$, 1, and 2 are useful; they are

$$\begin{aligned}\sum B_i &= q^{n-k},\\ \sum iB_i &= q^{(n-k-1)}[n(q-1) - A_1], \qquad (3.38)\\ \sum i^2 B_i &= q^{(n-k-2)}\{n(q-1)(nq-n+1)\\ &\qquad - A_1[q + 2(n-1)(q-1)] + 2A_2\}.\end{aligned}$$

The first is simply the number of vectors. The second is the sum of the weights of the code words, and the third the sum of the squares of the weights. The coefficient A_1 will be zero if and only if there is no column in the generator matrix for V_2 which is all zeros, and A_2 will be zero if and only if no two columns of the generator matrix of V_2 are scalar multiples of each other. For almost every interesting code both A_1 and A_2 will be zero. An alternate proof of the second equation is suggested in Problem 3.6.

Considerable effort has been expended in determining the weight distributions of various types of codes; several of these results are included in Chapters 9 and 10. Berlekamp (1968*b*) provides a comprehensive treatment of this problem.

3.9 Maximum-Distance-Separable Codes

The minimum distance for an (n, k) code over $GF(q)$ is not greater than $n - k + 1$, since code words exist with only one nonzero information symbol. Codes with the property that $d = n - k + 1$ have been referred to as *maximum-distance-separable* codes. See Kasami, Lin, Peterson (1966), Forney (1966), and Assmus, Mattson, and Turyn (1965). There are no nontrivial binary maximum-distance-separable block codes, but nonbinary codes do exist. The Reed-Solomon codes of Chapter 9 are of this type. In the following paragraph an expression for the number of code words of a given weight in a maximum-distance-separable block code is derived.

If $d = n - k + 1$, then by Corollary 3.1 every set of $n - k$ columns of the parity-check matrix of the code is linearly independent. Now let $N(i_1, i_2, \ldots, i_h)$ be the set of code vectors whose i_1th, i_2th, ..., i_hth components are zero and let $|N(i_1, i_2, \ldots, i_h)|$ be the number of code vectors in $N(i_1, i_2, \ldots, i_h)$. For $h \geq k$, $N(i_1, i_2, \ldots, i_h)$ consists of only the zero vector; that is,

$$|N(i_1, i_2, \ldots, i_h)| = 1; \qquad h \geq k.$$

For $h \leqq k-1$, it follows from Corollary 3.1 that the rank of the matrix $\mathbf{H}(i_1, i_2, \ldots, i_h)$ which is obtained by deleting the i_1th, i_2th, ..., i_hth columns of $\mathbf{H}$ is equal to $n-k$. Therefore, the dimension of the null space of $\mathbf{H}(i_1, i_2, \ldots, i_h)$ is $k-h$. Hence,

$$|N(i_1, i_2, \ldots, i_h)| = q^{k-h}; \qquad h \leqq k-1.$$

If A_j is the number of code vectors with weight j, then by definition, A_j is the number of code vectors which have exactly $n-j$ zero components. Let U_s be the sum of the numbers of vectors in all the sets $N(i_1, i_2, \ldots, i_s)$ which have zeros in s or more positions. Then

$$\begin{aligned} U_s &= \sum_{1 \leqq i_1 < \cdots < i_s \leqq n} |N(i_1, i_2, \ldots, i_s)| \\ &= \binom{n}{s} q^{k-s}. \end{aligned} \tag{3.39}$$

for $k \geqq s$, while for $k < s$,

$$U_s = \binom{n}{s}. \tag{3.40}$$

In the sum U_s, vectors of weight less than $n-s$ are counted more than once. In fact,

$$U_s = A_{n-s} + \binom{s+1}{1} A_{n-s-1} + \binom{s+2}{2} A_{n-s-2} + \cdots + \binom{n}{n-s} A_0. \tag{3.41}$$

Equations 3.39 and 3.41 can be used to solve for the A_i iteratively. However, a closed-form expression can be derived using the principle of inclusion and exclusion (see Riordan 1958). This yields

$$A_j = \sum_{h=0}^{j} (-1)^h \binom{n-j+h}{h} U_{n-j+h}. \tag{3.42}$$

Substituting Equations 3.39 and 3.40 into Equation 3.42, one has

$$\begin{aligned} A_j &= \sum_{h=0}^{j-(n-k)-1} (-1)^h \binom{n-j+h}{h} \binom{n}{n-j+h} q^{j-h-(n-k)} \\ &\quad + \sum_{h=j-(n-k)}^{j} (-1)^h \binom{n-j+h}{h} \binom{n}{n-j+h} \\ &= \binom{n}{j} \left[\sum_{h=0}^{j-(n-k)-1} (-1)^h \binom{j}{h} q^{j-h-(n-k)} + \sum_{h=j-(n-k)}^{j} (-1)^h \binom{j}{h} \right]. \end{aligned} \tag{3.43}$$

The identity

$$-\sum_{h=0}^{j-(n-k)-1}(-1)^h\binom{j}{h}=\sum_{h=j-(n-k)}^{j}(-1)^h\binom{j}{h}$$

can be used in Equation 3.42 to give

$$A_j=\binom{n}{j}\sum_{h=0}^{j-1-(n-k)}(-1)^h\binom{j}{h}(q^{j-h-(n-k)}-1) \tag{3.44}$$

for $n-k+1 \leqq j \leqq n$. For $1 \leqq j \leqq n-k$, of course $A_j=0$ and $A_0=1$. Thus, the complete weight distribution of any maximum-distance-separable code can be calculated quite simply.

Example. There exists an (8, 4) maximum-distance-separable code with symbols chosen from the field of 8 elements. That is, $q=8$ and $d=5$. For this code, from Equation 3.44,

$A_0=1$ $\qquad$ $A_6=588$
$A_1=A_2=A_3=A_4=0$ $\qquad$ $A_7=1736$
$A_5=392$ $\qquad$ $A_8=1379$

Note that

$$\sum_{j=0}^{8}A_j=q^k,$$

Notes

The relationship between parity-check codes and groups or vector spaces was first noted by Kiyasu (1953). Most of the material in Sections 3.1 to 3.3, as well as several of the problems, was adapted from Slepian's fundamental work (1956*a*, 1960). Hamming (1950) and Golay (1949) had previously considered systematic codes. The description of a code as a null space of a matrix was used by a number of people, and Theorem 3.1 and the corollary were apparently found independently by Sacks (1958) and Dwork and Heller (1959) and earlier by Bose in connection with the design of statistical experiments.

Theorem 3.11 was first suggested by Slepian (1960) and proved by Moore in a slightly weaker form. The rest of Section 3.5, including the present form of Theorem 3.11, consists of ideas and proofs of Prange, modified since Prange used Lee (1958) distance rather than Hamming distance in his original presentation.

Section 3.6 is adapted from MacDonald's work (1958, 1960), though equivalent relations between weights of code words and modular representations have been derived by Slepian (1956*a*), using the theory of group characters, and Bose and Kuebler (1958), using a geometric argument. [See also Fontaine and Peterson (1958) and McCluskey (1959).] Section 3.7 is taken from Fontaine and Peterson (1959). [See also Slepian (1960).] Singleton (1964) was the first to study maximum-distance-separable codes. The results in Section 3.9 were derived independently at about the same time by Kasami,

Lin, and Peterson (1966); Forney (1966) and Assmus, Mattson, and Turyn (1965).

Although the description of linear tree codes given in Section 3.3 is restricted to convolutional codes, the results carry over to more general linear tree codes, virtually without exception. This material is based largely on the work of Elias (1954); Wozencraft (1957); and Wyner and Ash (1963), although the presentation here differs in that the close structural relationships between convolutional and linear block codes are emphasized.

Problems

3.1. Show that linear codes can be defined with symbols chosen from a ring and thus that the number of symbols is arbitrary.

3.2. Show that it is not always possible to put the generator (or parity check) matrix of a linear code into echelon canonical form unless the code symbols are chosen from a field.

3.3. For the binary group code whose generator matrix is

$$\begin{bmatrix} 1\,0\,1\,0\,1\,1 \\ 0\,1\,1\,1\,1\,0 \\ 0\,0\,0\,1\,1\,1 \end{bmatrix},$$

a. Find the generator matrix **G** in reduced-echelon form for an equivalent code.
b. Find the parity-check matrix **H** for the code in (a).
c. Find the code word that has 110 as information symbols. Show that it is in the row space of **G** and in the null space of **H**.
d. Form the standard array for this code. Choose a minimum-weight leader for each coset and find a_i, the number of coset leaders of weight i for $i = 0, 1, 2, \ldots, 6$.
(Answer: $a_0 = 1$, $a_1 = 6$, $a_2 = 1$.)
e. Find the modular representation vector.
(Answer: It consists of six 1's and one 0.)
f. Find the weight vector.
(Answer: One of weight 0, three of weight 4, four of weight 3.)

3.4. Let **H** be the parity-check matrix for a linear code. Show that the coset whose syndrome is **v** contains a vector of weight w if and only if some linear combination of w columns of **H** equals **v**. (Compare with Theorem 3.1.)

3.5. Show that if all the code vectors in an (n, k) linear block code are arranged as rows of a matrix, each field element appears q^{k-1} times in each column. Assume that no column consists of all 0's. (Hint: Show that the set of all code words with 0's in a particular component forms a subspace, and consider cosets.)

3.6. Using the result of Problem 3.5, show that the sum of the weights of all code words in an (n, k) block code is $n(q-1)q^{k-1}$. Assume that no column consists of all 0's.

3.7. Show that in a binary group block code either all the code words have even weight or half have even weight, half odd. (Hint: Show that the code words of even weight form a subgroup.)

3.8. Show that if a binary group block code has odd minimum weight, adding a parity-check digit that is a check on every digit in the code increases the minimum weight by 1.

3.9. Show that if an (n, k) linear code with minimum weight w is used with an erasure channel and if $w-1$ or fewer erasure. occur, it is possible to find a set of linearly independent equations that can be solved for the unknown symbols. Show that there is at least one case with w erasures that cannot be corrected.

3.10. For the binary block code used as an example in this chapter, decode the received vector $\mathbf{v} = (1\,0\,1\,1\,1)$ by the step-by-step decoding process. Verify that the resulting vector $\mathbf{u}$ is a code vector, and that $\mathbf{v}-\mathbf{u}$ is the minimum weight vector in its coset which precedes all other minimum weight vectors.

3.11. Assume that it is known that a (13, 5) block code has $a_0 = 1$, $a_1 = 13$, $a_2 = 78$, and $a_3 = 152$. Show that $a_5 \leqq 2$ and all other $a_i = 0$ for $i > 5$. (Hint: Use Theorem 3.11.)

3.12. Find the modular representation for a binary block code with $\mathbf{W} = (3, 4, 3, 4, 3, 4, 3)$. Construct a generator matrix for the code. Assume the matrix $\mathbf{M}$ given in the example of Section 3.6.

3.13. Find the A-permutations corresponding to the elementary 3×3 matrices over the field of two elements.

3.14. Construct the $\mathbf{G}$ and $\mathbf{H}$ matrices for the (8, 4) convolutional code for which $\mathbf{P}_0 = \mathbf{P}_1 = \mathbf{P}_3 = 1$, $\mathbf{P}_2 = 0$. Show that for this code $d = 4$. Can you construct a (6, 3) code with $d = 4$?

Problems 3.15–3.19 refer to systematic binary convolutional codes.

3.15. Construct the $\mathbf{G}$ and $\mathbf{H}$ matrices for the (12, 9) convolutional code for which $\mathbf{P}_2^T = 110$, $\mathbf{P}_1^T = 101$, and $\mathbf{P}_0^T = 111$. Show that $d = 3$.

3.16. Show that there does not exist a convolutional code with $n - k = 3$ and $d = 3$ which has a higher rate than the (12, 9) code of the previous problem.

3.17. The (4, 2) code used in the examples of this chapter and the (12, 9) code above are optimum, single-error-correcting convolutional codes with $n - k = 2$ and 3, respectively. Construct the next code in this family, the (32, 28), $d = 3$ code. (Hint: Examine the form of the $\mathbf{H}$ matrices of these codes and employ Theorem 3.1 and its Corollary 3.2.)

3.18. (Wyner-Ash) For any integer m there exists a binary convolutional $[m2^{m-1}, m(2^{m-1}-1)]$ code with $d = 3$. Prove this constructively, that is, by specifying the form of the $\mathbf{H}$ (or $\mathbf{G}$) matrix of the code. Do Problem 3.17 first.

3.19. The *dual* of a convolutional code has been defined as the code whose generator matrix is obtained by interchanging the ith and $n - i$th, $1 \leqq i \leqq n$, columns of the parity check matrix of the original code (reflection) and then suitably rearranging rows. Show that the dual of the (12, 9) code of Problem 3.15 is a (12, 3) code with $\mathbf{P}_0 = 111$, $\mathbf{P}_1 = 101$, and $\mathbf{P}_2 = 011$. Show that this code has $d = 8$.

3.20. The set of code words at a particular node of a convolutional tree code forms a group provided the results of previous decodings are taken into account. Show that if this feedback information is ignored, the set of code words forms a coset of this group.

3.21. Assume that for a (24, 12) code, and also for its null space, there is a code word of weight zero, one of weight 24, and the only other weights that occur are 8, 12, 16. Find the weight distribution of both codes. (These are the Golay codes described in Section 5.2.) (Hint: Use Equation 3.28.)

3.22. The Hamming codes, which are described in Section 5.1, have $n = (q^m - 1)/(q - 1)$, $k = n - m$, and in the null space all vectors have the same weight. (See Problem 3.5.) Show that for the Hamming codes,

$$A(X) = \sum_{i=0}^{u} A_i X^i$$

$$= \frac{1}{q^m} \{(1 + (q-1)X)^n + (q^m - 1)[1 + (q-1)X]^{(n-1)/q} (1 - X)^{q^{m-1}}\}.$$

Find the A_i for the (7, 4) binary code.

3.23. Show that if the columns of the generator matrix $\mathbf{G}$ for a binary code consist of all $2^k - 1$ nonzero k-tuples, than all nonzero code words have weight 2^{k-1}.

3.24. More generally, show that if the columns of the generator matrix $\mathbf{G}$ for a q-ary code consist of all $q^K -$ nonzero k-tuples, then all nonzero code words have weight $(q - 1)q^{K-1}$.

3.25. Show that if the columns of the generator matrix $\mathbf{G}$ of a code consist of $(q^k - 1)/(q - 1)$ vectors, none of which is a scalar multiple of another, then all nonzero code vectors have weight q^{k-1}. (Hint: Use the results of the previous two problems.)

4 Error-Correction Capabilities of Linear Codes

It is important to know the ultimate capabilities and limitations of error-correcting codes. This information, coupled with a knowledge of what is practically achievable, indicates which problems are virtually solved and which need further work. In addition, performance bounds are useful in the early stages of communication system design; they permit the designer to estimate in a simple manner the relative efficacy of various codes.

In the first section of this chapter, upper and lower bounds are given on the minimum distance attainable with linear block codes of a given length and rate. In Section 4.2, bounds on the probability of erroneous decoding with the best linear block codes used on the binary symmetric channel are derived. The significance of these bounds is discussed in the third section. In Sections 4.4 and 4.5, the corresponding bounds for convolutional codes are given. The last section presents bounds on the burst-correcting ability of both block and convolutional codes.

4.1 Bounds on Minimum Distance for Block Codes

For given values of n and k it is possible to derive both upper and lower bounds on the largest minimum distance attainable with a linear code. The lower bounds apply to larger classes of codes, of course, since they merely state what is possible; the upper bounds can also be proved for nonlinear codes but this is not done here.

The *Plotkin upper bound* employs the following rather crude bound on d:

LEMMA 4.1. *The minimum weight of a code word in an (n, k) linear code is at most as large as the average weight $nq^{k-1}(q-1)/(q^k-1)$.*

Proof. The sum of the weights of the code words of an (n, k) linear code with symbols taken from the field of q elements is $nq^{k-1}(q-1)$. (See Problem 3.6.) From the fact that there are $q^k - 1$ elements with nonzero weight, and the minimum weight element has at most average weight, the lemma follows directly. Q.E.D.

Now let $B(n, d)$ be the maximum number of code words possible in a linear code of length n with minimum weight at least d.

LEMMA 4.2. *If $n > d$, $B(n,d) \leqq qB(n-1, d)$.*

Proof. Let G be a code with n symbols and minimum weight at least d that has $B(n, d)$ code words. The set F of all code words in G whose last symbol is 0 forms a subspace of G, since the sum of any two elements of F is in F, and any scalar multiple of an element of F is in F. There will be q cosets of F in G, one for each symbol that may appear in the last position, and thus a fraction $1/q$ of the elements of G is in F. Then the subgroup F is a linear code of $(1/q)B(n, d)$ symbols and minimum weight at least d, each of whose vectors has the last component 0. The last component can be dropped to give a linear code of $n - 1$ symbols without affecting the number of code words in the subgroup or the minimum weight. There may be other columns of all zeros in the resulting code F, but these could be replaced by any other type of column without reducing the minimum weight. (Note that $B(n-1, n-1) = q$, the code consisting of $n - 1$ repetitions of a single information symbol. Thus, with the assumption that $n > d$, nonzero columns are possible in the $n - 1$-symbol code.) Therefore, $B(n-1, d) \geqq (1/q)B(n, d)$. Q.E.D.

Lemma 4.1 applied to a code of length i can be rearranged to give

$$d(q^k - 1) \leqq iq^{k-1}(q-1),$$

$$q^{k-1}(qd + i - iq) \leqq d,$$

and if

$$qd + i - iq > 0,$$

then

$$q^k = B(i, d) \leqq \frac{qd}{qd + i - iq}. \tag{4.1}$$

Now choose i so that $(qd - 1)/(q - 1) = i + f$, where i is an integer and $0 \leqq f < 1$; then

$$B(i, d) \leqq \frac{qd}{qd - (q - 1)i} = \frac{qd}{1 + (q - 1)f}. \tag{4.2}$$

If $n \geqq i$, repeated application of Lemma 4.2 gives

$$B(n, d) \leqq q^{n-i} B(i, d) \leqq \frac{q^{n-[(qd-1)/(q-1)]+f} qd}{1 + (q - 1)f}. \tag{4.3}$$

It can be shown that $q^f \leqq 1 + (q - 1)f$, and therefore

$$B(n, d) \leqq q^{n-(qd-1)/(q-1)} qd. \tag{4.4}$$

Since $B(n, d) = q^k$ for the code with maximum minimum distance, where k is the number of information symbols for that code,

$$k \leqq n - \frac{qd - 1}{q - 1} + 1 + \log_q d. \tag{4.5}$$

This can be stated as follows:

THEOREM 4.1. *If* $n \geqq (qd - 1)/(q - 1)$, *the number of check symbols required to achieve minimum weight* d *in an* n*-symbol linear block code is at least* $[(qd - 1)/(q - 1)] - 1 - \log_q d$.

If d is very large, the last two terms in this expression are negligible. This asymptotic bound is plotted for the binary case in Figure 4.1.

The Plotkin bound can be proved for nonlinear codes also. Theorems 4.2, 4.3, and 4.4 provide a refinement of this bound.

THEOREM 4.2. *If there exists an* (n, k) *code over* $GF(q)$ *with minimum distance* d, *then there exists an* $(n - d, k - 1)$ *code with minimum distance at least* d/q.

Proof. Arrange all the code vectors in a column with the all-zero vector first and a vector $\mathbf{v}_0$ of weight d second, followed by all scalar multiples of $\mathbf{v}_0$. Now rearrange the columns so that the first $n - d$ columns contain the zeros of $\mathbf{v}_0$ and its scalar multiples and the last d columns contain the nonzero components. These first q vectors form a subspace, and the whole code consists of q^{k-1} cosets of this subspace. In each coset the first $n - d$ components are equal. Thus, if the last d columns are dropped from every vector, the $n - d$-component vectors that remain make q copies of a $k - 1$-dimensional subspace of $(n - d)$-tuples. It will now be shown that this subspace has minimum distance at least d/q.

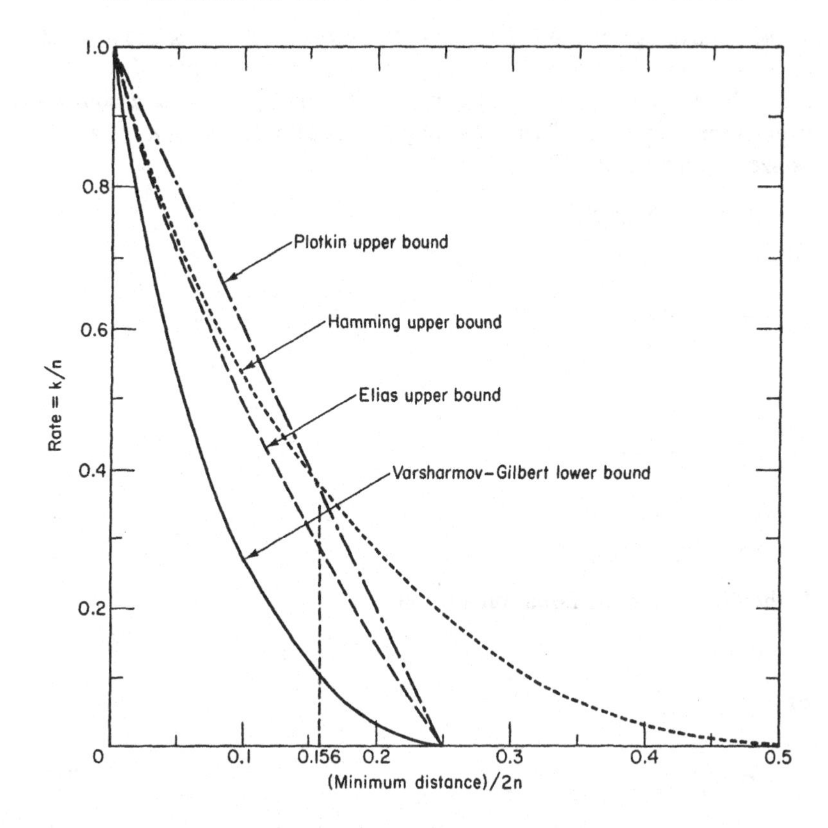

Figure 4.1. Bounds on minimum distance for the best binary block code. (The code length n is assumed to be very large.)

Let $\mathbf{v}_1$ be any vector in the original code which is not a scalar multiple of $\mathbf{v}_0$, and let $\mathbf{v}_1$ have a_1 nonzero components among the first $n - d$ components and a_2 nonzero components among the last d components. Then since the minimum weight in the original code is d,

$$a_1 + a_2 \geqq d. \tag{4.6}$$

Let b_i, $i = 2, 3, \ldots, q$, be the number of nonzero components of $\mathbf{v}_1$ that match with the ith code word among the $q - 1$ nonzero scalar multiples of $\mathbf{v}_0$. Then, since each of the a_2 nonzero components of $\mathbf{v}_1$ will match with exactly one scalar multiple of $\mathbf{v}_0$,

$$\sum_{i=2}^{q} b_i = a_2. \tag{4.7}$$

Thus, the average of the b_i is $a_2/(q-1)$, and at least one of the b_i must be this large. Therefore there must be a scalar multiple of $\mathbf{v}_0$, say $\beta\mathbf{v}_0$, which has $b_i \geqq a_2/(q-1)$ components among the last d components that match $\mathbf{v}_1$. Then $\mathbf{v}_1 - \beta\mathbf{v}_0$ is a code word with $a_1 + d - b_i$ nonzero components. Thus,

$$a_1 + d - b_i \geqq d,$$

or

$$a_1 - b_i \geqq 0,$$

or

$$a_1 \geqq \frac{a_2}{q-1},$$

or

$$qa_1 \geqq a_1 + a_2.$$

It then follows from Equation 4.6 that

$$qa_1 \geqq d,$$

or

$$a_1 \geqq \frac{d}{q}. \tag{4.8}$$

But a_1 is the weight of an arbitrary vector in the $(n-d, k-1)$ code formed by dropping the last d columns of every code vector. Q.E.D.

THEOREM 4.3. *The smallest value of n for which an (n, k) code with minimum distance d exists satisfies the inequality*

$$n \geqq \frac{sq^k - 1}{q-1} - \sum_{i=0}^{k-2} \delta_i \frac{q^{i+1}-1}{q-1}, \tag{4.9}$$

where sq^{k-1} is the smallest multiple of q^{k-1} that is equal to or greater than d, and

$$sq^{k-1} - d = \sum_{i=0}^{k-2} \delta_i q^i, \qquad 0 \leqq \delta_i < q; \tag{4.10}$$

that is, the δ_i are the digits in the expression for $sq^{k-1} - d$ in a radix-q system.

Proof. The proof is by induction on d. If $d = 1$, then $s = 1$ and the δ_i all have the value $q - 1$. This gives for the bound on n,

$$n \geqq \frac{q^k - 1}{q - 1} - \sum_{i=0}^{k-2} (q^{i+1} - 1)$$

$$= \frac{q^k - 1}{q - 1} - q^{k-1} - q^{k-2} - \cdots - q + k - 1 = k. \tag{4.11}$$

This is the correct value — the (k, k) code consisting of all k-tuples has minimum distance exactly 1.

Now assume that the theorem holds for every value of d less than d_0. By Theorem 4.2, if there exists an (n, k) code with minimum distance d_0, there exists an $(n - d_0, k - 1)$ code of distance at least d_1, which is the smallest integer equal to or greater than d_0/q. By the induction hypothesis, Formula 4.9 holds and gives a bound on $n - d_0$. If

$$d_0 = sq^{k-1} - \sum_{i=0}^{k-2} \delta_i q^i,$$

then

$$d_1 = sq^{k-2} - \sum_{i=1}^{k-2} \delta_i q^{i-1}$$

and

$$n - d_0 \geqq \frac{sq^{k-1} - 1}{q - 1} - \sum_{i=1}^{k-2} \delta_i \frac{q^i - 1}{q - 1}$$

so that

$$n \geqq (n - d_0) + d_0 = \frac{sq^{k-1} - 1}{q - 1} + sq^{k-1} - \sum_{i=1}^{k-2} \delta_i \frac{q^i - 1}{q - 1} - \sum_{i=0}^{k-2} \delta_i q^i,$$

$$n \geqq \frac{sq^k - 1}{q - 1} - \sum_{i=0}^{k-2} \delta_i \frac{q^{i+1} - 1}{q - 1}.$$

Q.E.D.

For a generator matrix, $\mathbf{G}_1$ whose $(q^k - 1)/(q - 1)$ columns are k-tuples, none of which is a scalar multiple of another, all nonzero code words have weight exactly q^{k-1}. An $(s(q^k - 1)/(q - 1), k)$ code all of whose nonzero code words have weight sq^{k-1} can be generated, for example, by a matrix $\mathbf{G}_s$ that consists of s copies of $\mathbf{G}_1$ side by side. These codes meet the bound in Theorem 4.3. Next, additional codes formed by dropping columns from $\mathbf{G}_s$ will be derived.

For any $i < k$, consider a matrix formed by taking from $\mathbf{G}_1$ exactly i linearly independent columns and all the columns of $\mathbf{G}_1$ that are linear combinations of these chosen i columns, and call this matrix $\mathbf{K}_i$. Altogether there are q^i linear combinations of i independent columns. However, because $\mathbf{G}_1$ does not include the column of all zeros and includes only one column from each set of $q - 1$ columns that are multiples, $\mathbf{K}_i$ has $(q^i - 1)/(q - 1)$ columns. The column rank of $\mathbf{K}_i$ is i by definition, and because column rank equals row rank, the row rank of $\mathbf{K}_i$ is also i. This means that among the rows of $\mathbf{K}_i$ there exist i linearly independent rows, and all other rows are linear combinations of these. Let $\mathbf{K}_i'$ be an $i \times (q^i - 1)/(i - 1)$ matrix consisting of i independent rows of $\mathbf{K}_i$. Then no two columns of $\mathbf{K}_i'$ are scalar multiples of each other, and every nonzero linear combination of rows of $\mathbf{K}_i'$, and hence of $\mathbf{K}_i$, has weight exactly q^{i-1}. Therefore, if the columns of $\mathbf{K}_i$ are dropped from $\mathbf{G}_1$ to form a new matrix $\mathbf{G}_1'$ having k rows and $(q^k - 1)/(q - 1) - (q^i - 1)/(q - 1)$ columns, the minimum weight for the code is $q^{k-1} - q^{i-1}$. (There will be some code words of weight q^{k-1} yet, corresponding to linear combinations of rows of $\mathbf{K}_i$ that result in zero vectors.) The code generated by $\mathbf{G}_1'$ still meets the bound of Theorem 4.3.

More generally, codes that meet the bound of Theorem 4.3 can be formed from the matrix $\mathbf{G}_s$ by dropping sets of $(q_i - 1)/(q - 1)$ columns, chosen in the manner just described from one or another of the matrices $\mathbf{G}_1$ which make up $\mathbf{G}_s$, as long as no more than $q - 1$ sets are dropped for any given i, and as long as there remain sets of $(q_i - 1)/(q - 1)$ columns of this type. In particular, this will always be assured if the conditions of the following theorem are met and can sometimes be done even when these conditions are not met:

THEOREM 4.4. *There exists a code which meets the bound of Theorem 4.3 if:*

1. $s \geqq \delta_i$ *for all* i, *and*
2. *The sum of the* i*'s for which* $\delta_i \neq 0$ *does not exceed* k.

The bound in Theorem 4.4 depends on the digits in the expression for $sq^{k-1} - d$. In general they may or may not be zero. A simpler bound results if we assume that the δ_i are zero. Since s is roughly d/q^{k-1}, this gives

$$n \geqq \frac{d}{qk - 1} \cdot \frac{q^k - 1}{q - 1},$$

which is exactly the Plotkin bound. This bound is met by a much smaller class of codes than the bound of Theorem 4.4.

The *Hamming upper bound* on d can be proved as follows. An (n, k) linear code has q^k code vectors and q^{n-k} cosets. If a code is to correct all combinations of t or fewer errors, all vectors of weight t or less must be coset leaders. Thus the number of vectors of weight t or less must be no greater than the number of cosets:

$$1 + \binom{n}{1}(q-1) + \binom{n}{2}(q-1)^2 + \cdots + \binom{n}{t}(q-1)^t \leqq q^{n-k}.$$

THEOREM 4.5. *For any (n, k) block code with minimum weight $2t + 1$ or greater, the number of check symbols satisfies*

$$n - k \geqq \log_q\left[1 + \binom{n}{1}(q-1) + \binom{n}{2}(q-1)^2 + \cdots + \binom{n}{t}(q-1)^t\right]. \tag{4.12}$$

This bound can be proved for nonlinear codes.

Asymptotic formulas can be obtained again. As a simple example, let $q = 2$, and let t_h be the largest integer t for which Equation 4.12 holds. Then

$$1 - \frac{k}{n} \geqq \frac{1}{n}\log\left[1 + \binom{n}{1} + \cdots + \binom{n}{t_h}\right].$$

With use of the results of Appendix A, it is easily shown that in the limit as n approaches infinity, the ratio t/n for any (n, k) block code cannot exceed t_h/n, where

$$1 - \frac{k}{n} = H\left(\frac{t_h}{n}\right). \tag{4.13}$$

This limiting form of the Hamming bound is plotted in Figure 4.1.

Another upper bound on the minimum distance achievable with a block code, either linear or nonlinear, can be proved. This *Elias upper bound* employs the concepts used in both the Plotkin and Hamming bounds and for large n is tighter than either. The bound can be proved for codes with q-ary symbols (Berlekamp 1968); however, the proof presented here is for binary codes.

Consider an (n, k) block code. A sphere of radius t centered on the ith n-tuple in this n-space will contain K_i code vectors, $i = 1, 2, \ldots, 2^n$.

The number of points in each sphere is $\sum_{j=0}^{t} \binom{n}{j}$, and each of the 2^k code words appears in exactly this many spheres. Thus,

$$\sum_{i=1}^{2^n} K_i = 2^k \sum_{j=0}^{t} \binom{n}{j}. \tag{4.14}$$

Let K denote the largest of the K_i; since K is at least as large as the average K_i,

$$K \geqq \frac{\sum_{j=0}^{t} \binom{n}{j}}{2^{n-k}}. \tag{4.15}$$

Thus, there exists a sphere of radius t containing K code words. Note that this sphere is not necessarily centered on a code word.

The next step in deriving the Elias bound is to compute the average distance between these K code words. It will be shown that for an appropriate choice of t, the code words must be closer together than is guaranteed by either the Hamming or Plotkin bounds.

Consider the K n-tuples which are produced by subtracting the center n-tuple from the K code words. Denote these by

$$\begin{matrix} a_{11} & a_{12} & \cdots & a_{1n} \\ a_{21} & a_{22} & \cdots & a_{2n} \\ \vdots & & & \\ a_{K1} & a_{K2} & \cdots & a_{Kn} \end{matrix} \tag{4.16}$$

Let w_i denote the weight of the ith of these n-tuples. Since the sphere has radius t, the total weight of these n-tuples is not greater than Kt; that is,

$$\sum_{i=1}^{K} w_i \leqq Kt.$$

Let $v_j, j = 1, 2, \ldots, n$, denote the weight of the jth column of the Array 4.16; thus, this column has $K - v_j$ zeros and v_j ones. Clearly,

$$\sum_{j=1}^{n} v_j \leqq Kt.$$

The total distance d_{TOTAL} of Array 4.16 is the sum of the $\binom{K}{2}$ distances between n-tuples in the array. The jth column of the array contributes

$$i_1 > i_2 \sum (a_{i_1 j} + a_{i_2 j}) = \binom{K}{2} - \binom{v_j}{2} - \binom{K - v_j}{2} = v_j(K - v_j)$$

to d_{TOTAL}. Summing on j, one has

$$d_{\text{TOTAL}} = K \sum_{j=1}^{n} v_j - \sum_{j=1}^{n} v_j^2. \tag{4.17}$$

Now consider the sum $v_{j_1}^2 + v_{j_2}^2$. If $v_{j_1} > v_{j_2} + 1$, then increasing v_{j_2} by 1 and decreasing v_{j_1} by the same amount decreases the sum $v_{j_1}^2 + v_{j_2}^2$. For

$$(v_{j_1} - 1)^2 + (v_{j_2} + 1)^2 - (v_{j_1}^2 + v_{j_2}^2) = 2(v_{j_2} - v_{j_1} + 1) < 0.$$

It follows for any choice of the v_j such that $\sum_{j=1}^{n} v_j = Kt - \Delta$, $\Delta \geqq 0$,

$$\sum_{j=1}^{n} v_j^2 \geqq n\left(\frac{Kt - \Delta}{n}\right)^2.$$

Equation 4.17 then gives

$$d_{\text{TOTAL}} \leqq K(Kt - \Delta) - n\left(\frac{Kt - \Delta}{n}\right)^2$$

$$\leqq tK^2\left(1 - \frac{t}{n}\right) - \Delta K\left(1 - \frac{2t}{n}\right).$$

For any code $t < n/2$; thus

$$d_{\text{TOTAL}} \leqq tK^2\left(1 - \frac{t}{n}\right).$$

However of the $\binom{K}{2}$ distances, at least one is not greater than average; denote this by d. Then,

$$\frac{d}{n} \leqq 2\frac{t}{n}\left(1 - \frac{t}{n}\right)\left(\frac{K}{K - 1}\right). \tag{4.18}$$

This result holds for any choice of t/n for which the right side of Equation 4.15 exceeds unity. (If $K = 1$, the argument disintegrates because there are no distances to consider within the sphere.) The tightest bound results when t/n is chosen to be just slightly greater than its minimum value. This result can be stated as follows:

THEOREM 4.6. *For any (n, k) block code, the minimum distance is bounded by*

$$d \leqq 2t\left(1 - \frac{t}{n}\right)\left(\frac{K}{K - 1}\right)$$

where t is any integer such that

$$\sum_{j=0}^{t} \binom{n}{j} > 2^{n-k}$$

and K is the smallest integer such that

$$K \geqq \frac{\sum_{j=0}^{t} \binom{n}{j}}{2^{n-k}}.$$

The limiting form of the Elias bound for large n is

$$\frac{d}{n} \leqq 2\frac{t_h}{n}\left(1 - \frac{t_h}{n}\right)$$

where t_h is given by Equation 4.13. This is plotted in Figure 4.1.

Other upper bounds on d have been derived which improve on the foregoing bounds in certain cases. See, for example, Wax (1959), and Johnson (1962, 1963). None of these bounds improve on the Elias asymptotic bound, however, and for small n they are generally more difficult than either the Hamming or Plotkin bounds.

The preceding bounds prove that codes with certain parameters do not exist. This raises the question of what ranges of parameters are possible. Numerous specific answers are given by the codes of later chapters; a general answer is given by the *Varsharmov-Gilbert lower bound* on minimum distance, which follows.

By Theorem 3.1, if a matrix can be found for which no set of $d - 1$ or fewer columns is linearly dependent, the null space of the matrix is a linear code with minimum distance at least d. This suggests the following method for constructing a code with r parity-check symbols and minimum weight d. Select any nonzero r-tuple as the first column of a parity-check matrix. Then select any nonzero r-tuple except multiples of the first as a second column in the parity-check matrix. The third column may be any r-tuple that is not a linear combination of the first two. In general, the ith column is chosen as any r-tuple that is not a linear combination of any $d - 2$ or fewer previous columns. This construction assures that no linear combination of $d - 1$ or fewer columns will be zero.

As long as the set of all linear combinations of $d - 2$ or fewer columns does not include all r-tuples, another column can be added. In the worst possible case, all these linear combinations might be distinct. There are $q - 1$ possible nonzero coefficients, and thus there are

$$\binom{j-1}{1}(q-1)+\binom{j-1}{2}(q-1)^2+\cdots+\binom{j-1}{d-2}(q-1)^{d-2} \tag{4.19}$$

linear combinations of $d-2$ or fewer columns out of a total of $j-1$ columns. If this is less than the total number of nonzero r-tuples, then there is certainly one more column that can be added to the matrix. That is, if

$$\binom{j-1}{1}(q-1)+\binom{j-1}{2}(q-1)^2+\cdots+\binom{j-1}{d-2}(q-1)^{d-2}<q^r-1 \tag{4.20}$$

there exists a code with j digits and at most r parity-check symbols (and therefore at least $k=j-r$ information symbols) with minimum distance d. The code is the null space of the $r \times j$ matrix that is formed from the chosen columns.

Now let n be the largest value of j for which Inequality 4.20 holds. Then an (n, k) code with minimum distance d exists which satisfies the inequality

$$\binom{n}{1}(q-1)+\binom{n}{2}(q-1)^2+\cdots+\binom{n}{d-2}(q-1)^{d-2}\geqq q^r-1 \tag{4.21}$$

This provides a lower bound on the minimum distance attainable with an (n, k) code.

THEOREM 4.7. *It is possible to construct an (n, k) code with minimum distance at least d for which the following inequality holds:*

$$\sum_{i=0}^{d-2}\binom{n}{i}(q-1)^i \geqq q^{n-k}.$$

For large n, asymptotic results can be obtained using the formulas of Appendix A. For example for the case of $q=2$, using the Chernoff bound (Equation A.8) with Equation A.10 yields

$$2^{n-k} \leqq \sum_{i=0}^{d-2}\binom{n}{i} = \sum_{i=n-d+2}^{n}\binom{n}{i}$$
$$\leqq \left(\frac{n-d+2}{n}\right)^{-(n-d+2)}\left(\frac{d-2}{n}\right)^{-(d-2)} = 2^{nH[(d-2)/n]}$$

or taking the logarithm of both sides,

$$n - k \leqq nH\left(\frac{d-2}{n}\right). \tag{4.22}$$

This bound is plotted in Figure 4.1, assuming that d and n are large enough so that the 2 in Inequality 4.22 can be neglected.

4.2 Bounds on the Probability of Error for Block Codes Used on the Binary Symmetric Channel

The bounds of the preceding section can be used to obtain bounds on P_e, the probability of erroneous decoding for the best binary code of a given rate and length on the binary symmetric channel. If it is known that a binary code has minimum distance d or less, then P_e is certainly not less than the probability of confusing the transmitted code word with another word a distance d away. Thus on a binary symmetric channel,

$$P_e \geqq \sum_{i=[d/2]+1}^{d} \binom{d}{i} P^i Q^{d-i} \tag{4.23}$$

since the $n - d$ positions in which the two words match cannot affect the probability of confusing them.* This result can be used in conjunction with the Elias upper bound on minimum distance to obtain a lower bound on P_e which is reasonably tight for low rates.

If a binary (n, k) code has distance less than or equal to d, then P_e for any code is not greater than the number of code words times the probability of interpreting the transmitted word as its nearest neighbor. This *union bound* can then be written as

$$P_e \leqq 2^k \sum_{i=[d/2]}^{d} \binom{d}{i} P^i Q^{d-i}. \tag{4.24}$$

Similarly if a binary (n, k) code has minimum distance d, then all patterns of $t = [(d-1)/2]$ or fewer errors can be corrected. Therefore, the probability of correct decoding for the best (n, k) code can be lower bounded by

$$P_e \leqq \sum_{i=t+1}^{n} \binom{n}{i} P^i Q^{n-i}. \tag{4.25}$$

* The symbol $[x]$ denotes the greatest integer contained in x; thus $[7/2] = 3$.

This result and the Varsharmov-Gilbert bound provide an upper bound to P_e which is reasonably good for low rates. (See Problem 4.2.)

It is possible to obtain much better bounds than Equations 4.23, 4.24, and 4.25, however. The two most important of these, the sphere-packing and random-coding bounds, will now be derived. First, however, some definitions are required. A linear code that for some t has all patterns of weight t or less and no others as coset leaders is called a *perfect* code. A code which, for some t, has all patterns of weight t or less, some of weight $t + 1$, and none of greater weight as coset leaders is called *quasi-perfect.* A binary group code is called *optimum* for the binary symmetric channel if its probability of error is as small as for any group code with the same total number of symbols and the same number of information symbols.

The *sphere-packing lower bound* on P_e employs the Hamming bound on minimum distance. Assume for the moment that there exists a quasi-perfect (n, k) code, that is, a code for which, for some t, all vectors of weight t or less and no vectors of greater weight than $t + 1$ are coset leaders. The following argument shows that this code must be optimum. The probability of correct decoding can be written

$$P_c = \alpha_0 Q^n + \alpha_1 P Q^{n-1} + \alpha_2 P^2 Q^{n-2} + \cdots$$

where α_i is the number of coset leaders of weight i. Since the quantities $P^i Q^{n-i}$ decrease as i increases (if $P < Q$), the probability of correct decoding is increased whenever one α_i is increased and another later in the sequence decreased. (Note that $\alpha_0 + \alpha_1 + \alpha_2 + \cdots = 2^{n-k}$, the number of cosets.) For a quasi-perfect code, each of the first m coefficients α_i is equal to the number of vectors of weight i and so is as large as possible. The terms beyond the $(t + 1)$st are 0, and α_{t+1} accounts for the rest of the cosets. Since no α_i could be increased at the expense of one later in the sequence, the probability of correct decoding is as great as possible. Then the expression for the probability of correct decoding is

$$P_c = Q^n + \binom{n}{1} P Q^{n-1} + \binom{n}{2} P^2 Q^{n-2} + \cdots + \binom{n}{t} P^t Q^{n-t} + \alpha_{t+1} P^{t+1} Q^{n-t-1}, \tag{4.26}$$

where t is the greatest integer such that

$$\alpha_{t+1} = 2^{n-k} - 1 - \binom{n}{1} - \binom{n}{2} - \cdots - \binom{n}{t} \geqq 0. \tag{4.27}$$

Quasi-perfect (n, k) codes do not exist for all choices of n and k. In the cases where they do not exist, the best code has probability of correct decoding which is less than P_c in Equations 4.26 and 4.27.

THEOREM 4.8. *For any (n, k) code,*

$$P_e \geqq \left[\binom{n}{t+1} - \alpha_{t+1}\right] P^{t+1} Q^{n-t-1} + \sum_{i=t+2}^{n} \binom{n}{i} P^i Q^{n-i}, \tag{4.28}$$

where t and α_{t+1} are defined by Equation 4.27.

A simple asymptotic result can be obtained as follows. It is convenient to work with a quantity E, called *reliability* or *error exponent,*

$$E = -\lim_{n \to \infty} \frac{1}{n} [\log_2 (P_e \text{ for the best binary group code})],$$

and to define E_s to be the sphere-packing bound on reliability:

$$E \leqq E_s = -\lim_{n\to\infty} \frac{1}{n} \log_2 \left[\binom{n}{t+2} P^{t+2} Q^{n-t-2} + \binom{n}{t+3} P^{t+3} Q^{n-t-3} + \cdots + \binom{n}{n} P^n\right] = E\left(\frac{t}{n}, P\right), \tag{4.29}$$

where $E(\lambda, P)$ is the function defined in Appendix A. Also, from Equation 4.27,

$$\frac{1}{n} \log_2 \left[1 + \binom{n}{1} + \cdots + \binom{n}{t}\right] \leqq 1 - \frac{k}{n} \leqq \frac{1}{n} \log_2 \left[1 + \binom{n}{1} + \cdots + \binom{n}{t+1}\right]. \tag{4.30}$$

The limit for very large n, using the results of Appendix A, is the same for both the upper and lower bounds of Equation 4.30, so that

$$\lim_{n\to\infty} \left(1 - \frac{k}{n}\right) = H\left(\frac{t}{n}\right). \tag{4.31}$$

Thus, for very large n, the value of t to be used in Equation 4.29 is approximately equal to half the distance given by the Hamming bound, or in other words, the distance given by the Gilbert bound. Bounds that are somewhat tighter than the foregoing result can be found, but they are lengthy; Elias (1955, 1956), Fano (1961), and Shannon (1957) give further details. The bound on E given by Equations 4.29 and 4.31 is plotted in Figure 4.2 for $P = 10^{-2}$.

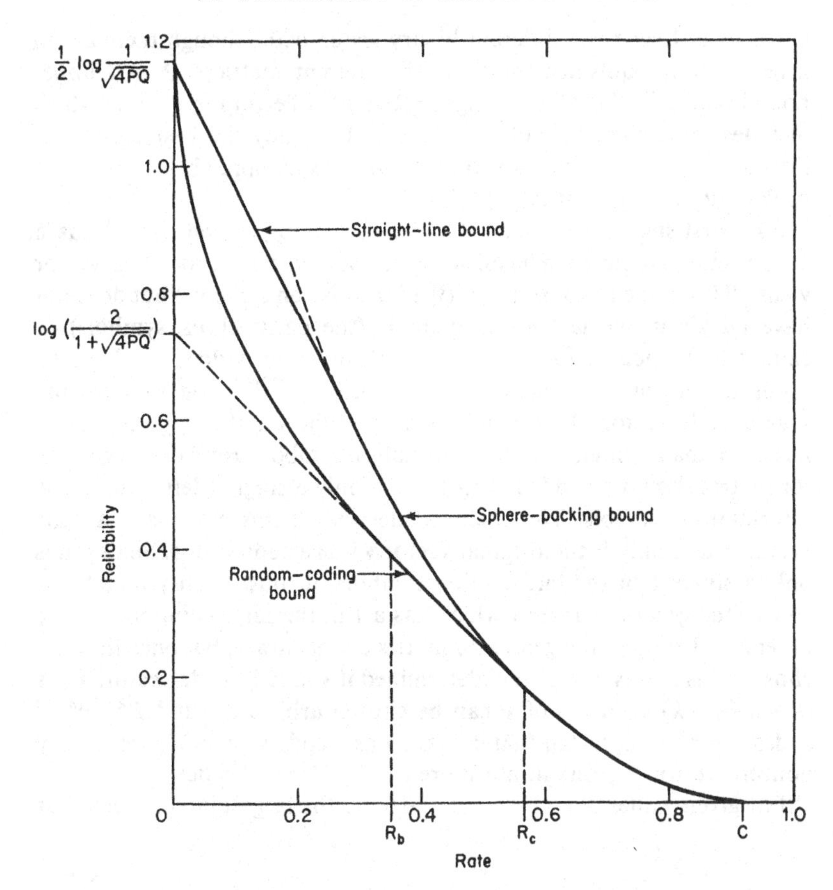

Figure 4.2. Plot of bounds on reliability as a function of rate for block codes on the binary symmetric channel with $P = 0.01$.

Asymptotic forms for the bounds of Equations 4.23 and 4.24 can also be derived. (See Problem 4.1.)

The *random-coding upper bound* on P_e derived in this section applies specifically to group codes for the binary symmetric channel, though Shannon and others have derived more general results. It is based on the fact that the average probability of error for a class of codes can often be calculated more easily than the probability of error for an individual code and that some code in the class must be as good as average.

The class of codes considered is a subset of the row spaces of all matrices of the form $[\mathbf{I}_k \ \mathbf{P}]$, where $\mathbf{I}_k$ is a $k \times k$ identity matrix and $\mathbf{P}$ is a $k \times (n-k)$ matrix of 0's and 1's. Each of the $2^{k(n-k)}$ possible matrices **P** describes a different binary group code, though there are in general many equivalent codes with different matrices **P**. An upper bound is described for the average probability of error for a subset which includes more than half of these codes. Certainly the best code is at least as good as average, and so this also gives an upper bound on error probability for the best code.

As a first step, the number of codes containing a given n-tuple as a code vector is required. The all-zeros vector is in every code. If a vector $\mathbf{v}$ has all 0's in the first k symbols (the information symbols) but does not have all 0's in the last $n - k$ symbols (the parity-check symbols), it cannot be a code vector in any code. If, however, $\mathbf{v}$ does not have all 0's in the information places, then there are $2^{(k-1)(n-k)}$ codes containing $\mathbf{v}$ as a code vector. This can be seen as follows: If the given vector has more than a single 1 in the information symbols, rows of the generator matrix should be added until there is only a single 1 left among the information symbols. The vector $\mathbf{v}'$ derived in this manner is a code vector if and only if the original vector $\mathbf{v}$ was a code vector. Since it has only a single 1 in the information symbols, it must exactly match the row of the generator matrix which has a 1 in the same component. The other $k - 1$ rows of the generator matrix are arbitrary, but once they are chosen, this row is completely determined if $\mathbf{v}$ is to be code vector. Thus $(k - 1)(n - k)$ elements of **P** can be chosen arbitrarily, and $2^{(k-1)(n-k)}$ codes can be constructed that contain $\mathbf{v}$ as a code vector. Therefore any nonzero vector appears in not more than $2^{(k-1)(n-k)}$ codes.

For given values of n and k, let d_g denote the largest integer such that

$$2^{n-k} \geqq 2\sum_{i=0}^{d_g-1}\binom{n}{i}. \tag{4.32}$$

Thus the number of nonzero code words of weight less than d_g in all codes is less than

$$2^{(k-1)(n-k)}\sum_{i=0}^{d_g-1}\binom{n}{i} < \frac{2^{k(n-k)}}{2}.$$

Because there are fewer than half as many vectors of weight less than d_g as there are codes, the following theorem holds:

THEOREM 4.9. *Most (more than half) binary linear codes have minimum distance at least d_g, where d_g is defined by Equation* 4.32.

It can be shown that as n increases with the ratio k/n fixed, d_g/n approaches the ratio of Gilbert distance to code length. (See Theorem

4.7.) Thus it can be said that the minimum distance of most binary linear block codes is at least very near the Gilbert distance. It can also be shown that very few codes have minimum distance which exceeds this value by any appreciable amount (Pierce, 1967).

Now let us calculate an upper bound on the average error probability for the class of all codes with minimum distance at least d_g.* To do this, it is necessary to determine, or at least to overbound $N(j)$, the number of codes in which the occurrence of an error pattern of weight j results in a decoding error. Without loss of generality, it can be assumed that the zero word was transmitted and that j errors occurred in transmission. A decoding error occurs in any code in which a nonzero code word lies within distance j or less of the received n-tuple. There are then three cases to consider.

For $j < [d_g/2]$ no codes will commit errors; that is,

$$N(j) = 0. \tag{4.33a}$$

For $[d_g/2] \leqq j < d_g$ the number of n-tuples which results in a decoding error must be determined. Since each n-tuple can be a code vector in at most $2^{(k-1)(n-k)}$ codes, $2^{(k-1)(n-k)}$ times this number gives an upper bound on the number of n-tuples in all codes which result in a decoding error. The number of n-tuples at distance i from the received sequence is

$$\sum_{x=0}^{\min(i,j)} \binom{j}{x}\binom{n-j}{i-x}.$$

Only those n-tuples that have weight d_g or greater can be code words in any code. Setting h equal to $i + j - 2x$, the weight of the n-tuples, in the preceding sum gives

$$\sum_{h=d_g}^{j+i} \binom{n-j}{\frac{h+i-j}{2}}\binom{j}{\frac{i+j-h}{2}} = \sum_{h=d_g}^{j+i} \binom{n-j}{\frac{h+i-j}{2}}\binom{j}{\frac{h+j-i}{2}}$$

where the sum is over those values of h for which $h + i - j$ is even. Then summing on i gives the number of n-tuples within distance j of the received sequence which can be code words; that is,

$$\sum_{i=d_g-j}^{j} \sum_{h=d_g}^{j+i} \binom{n-j}{\frac{h+i-j}{2}}\binom{j}{\frac{h+j-i}{2}}.$$

* It is possible to consider the class of all codes rather than this subset. If all codes are included in the average the results are weaker. The first random-coding bounds were of this type. (See the first edition of this book, for example.) The present bound is usually referred to as the "expurgated" random-coding bound.

It is assumed that in the case where two code words are equidistant from the received sequence an error occurs. Thus the upper limit on the i-sum is j. Therefore,

$$N(j) \leq 2^{(k-1)(n-k)} \sum_{i=d_g-j}^{j} \sum_{h=d_g}^{j+i} \binom{n-j}{\frac{h+i-j}{2}} \binom{j}{\frac{h+j-i}{2}}; \qquad (4.33b)$$

$$\left[\frac{d_g}{2}\right] \leq j < d_g.$$

For $j \geq d_g$ it is certainly true that

$$N(j) \leq \text{total number of codes in class.} \qquad (4.33c)$$

Each pattern of j errors has probability $P^j Q^{n-j}$ and there are $\binom{n}{j}$ such patterns. Now summing on j and dividing by the number of codes in the class being considered, one has an upper bound on the average probability of error for the class of good codes. Since the number of good codes is lower bounded by $2^{k(n-k)-1}$, this number can be used in place of the actual number of codes. Then since there is at least one code in the class which is as good as average, the bound obtained applies to the best code as well.

THEOREM 4.10. *The probability of erroneous decoding for the best (n, k) code is overbounded by*

$$P_e = \sum_{j=[d_g/2]}^{d_g-1} \sum_{i=d_g-j}^{j} \sum_{h=d_g}^{j+i} \binom{n-j}{\frac{h+i-j}{2}} \binom{j}{\frac{h+j-i}{2}} \frac{\binom{n}{j} P^j Q^{n-j}}{2^{n-k-1}}$$

$$+ \sum_{j=d_g}^{n} \binom{n}{j} P^j Q^{n-j}. \qquad (4.34)$$

It is interesting to examine the behavior of Equation 4.34 when n is considered to be large. If

$$j \leq j_b = \left[\frac{n}{2} - \frac{n}{2}\sqrt{1 - \frac{2d_g - \delta}{n}}\right],$$

it can be shown by a simple ratio test that the largest term in the h-sum is the first. (The quantity δ is always less than 3 and approaches zero as n approaches infinity.) Thus for this range of j, the h-sum can be overbounded by the product of the first term and the number of terms in the sum. In general the entire i-sum is less than $\binom{n}{j}$. This provides a useful upper bound for $j > j_b$. Thus, Equation 4.34 reduces to

$$P_e \leqq \sum_{j=[d_g/2]}^{j_b} \sum_{i=d_g-j}^{j} (j+i-d_g)\binom{n-j}{\frac{d_g+i-j}{2}}\binom{j}{\frac{d_g+j-i}{2}} \frac{\binom{n}{j}P^jQ^{n-j}}{2^{n-k-1}}$$
$$+ 2^{k-n+1}\sum_{j=j_b+1}^{d_g-1}\binom{n}{j}^2 P^jQ^{n-j} + \sum_{j=d_g}^{n}\binom{n}{j}P^jQ^{n-j}. \quad (4.35)$$

The remaining i-sum can also be overbounded by the product of the number of terms and its largest term, which is the last. That is,

$$i\text{-sum} \leqq (2j-d_g)^2\binom{n-j}{[d_g/2]}\binom{j}{[d_g/2]}.$$

Then, since

$$\binom{n-j}{[d_g/2]}\binom{j}{[d_g/2]}\binom{n}{j} \leqq \binom{n-d_g}{j-[d_g/2]}\binom{n}{d_g}2^{d_g}$$

for large n, Equation 4.35 reduces to

$$P_e \leqq \frac{2^{d_g+1}\binom{n}{d_g}}{2^{n-k}} \sum_{j=[d_g/2]}^{j_b} (2j-d_g)^2\binom{n-d_g}{j-[d_g/2]}P^jQ^{n-j}$$
$$+ 2^{k-n+1}\sum_{j=j_b+1}^{d_g-1}\binom{n}{j}^2 P^jQ^{n-j} + \sum_{j=d_g}^{n}\binom{n}{j}P^jQ^{n-j}. \quad (4.36)$$

This result can be overbounded by n times the largest term. Now, however, it is not so simple to find this term; for, depending on the ratio d_g/n, it may be in any one of the three sums of Equation 4.36. One way to locate this largest term is by a sequence of ratio tests. Before attempting this it is useful to determine the largest term in each of the three partial sums.

If n is large enough so that the factor $(2j - d_g)^2$ is unimportant, then the first sum is simply a part of a binomial distribution whose largest term occurs when $j - [d_g/2] = P(n - d_g)$. Thus for $0 \leqq (n - d_g)P \leqq j_b - [d_g/2]$, the largest term has $j = P(n - d_g) + [d_g/2]$; for $j_b - [d_g/2] < (n - d_g)P$, the largest term is the last.

The second sum has similar properties. The ratio of the $(j + i)$st to the jth term is

$$\frac{P(n-j)^2}{Q(j+1)^2}$$

and the largest term occurs when this ratio is as close as possible to unity. Again if the n and j are large, so that the 1 in the denominator can be neglected, this ratio is unity for

$$\frac{j}{n} = P_c = \frac{\sqrt{P}}{\sqrt{P} + \sqrt{Q}}. \tag{4.37}$$

Thus, for

$nP_c \leqq j_b + 1$, the largest term is the first;

$j_b + 1 < nP_c < d_g - 1$, the largest term has $j = nP_c$;

$d_g - 1 \leqq nP_c$, the largest term is the last.

The third sum is again a binomial distribution. Therefore, for

$nP \leqq d_g$, the largest term is the first;

$d_g < nP \leqq n$, the largest term has $j = nP$.

With this information it is a simple matter to determine, by means of ratio tests, which of the three candidates is the largest. The results are

Case 1. $0 < d_g \leqq nP$. The largest term is the term in the third sum for which $j = nP$. A good upper bound on P_e in this range of d_g is unity. Applying the results of Appendix A to Equation 4.32 gives

$$1 - R = H\left(\frac{d_g}{n}\right). \tag{4.38}$$

The value of R corresponding to the largest value of d_g/n for which the third sum dominates is Shannon's channel capacity, C. Thus,

$$C = 1 - H(P). \tag{4.39}$$

Case 2. $nP < d_g \leqq nP_c$. The largest term is the first term of the third sum. The resulting bound on reliability for the best code is

$$E \geqq -\lim_{n\to\infty} \frac{1}{n} \log\left[n\binom{n}{d_g} P^{d_g} Q^{n-d_g}\right] \geqq E\left(\frac{d_g}{n}, P\right), \tag{4.40}$$

which is the function defined in Appendix A and the same function that was found as a lower bound for E by the sphere-packing bound. Thus, for this range of d_g, $E = E(d_g/n, P)$.

From the definition of this function in Appendix A it can be seen that a necessary and sufficient condition for E to be greater than 0 is that $d_g/n > P$. But then,

$$H\left(\frac{d_g}{n}\right) > H(P)$$

and from Equations 4.38 and 4.39, $R < C$.

Thus the probability of error will approach 0 as n approaches infinity for the best code of length n, provided $R < C$. This is a special case of Shannon's fundamental theorem for noisy channels, which states that it is possible to make the probability of error as small as desired by choosing long enough codes, provided the rate is less than the channel capacity.

A converse of this theorem can also be proved. It states that for $R > C$ it is not possible to obtain vanishingly small P_e on a noisy channel.

Case 3. $nP_c < d_g \leqq nP_b$, where

$$P_b = \frac{\sqrt{4PQ}}{1 + \sqrt{4PQ}}. \tag{4.41}$$

The quantity P_b is the value assumed by dg/n when $j_b = nP_c$, that is, when the largest term in the second sum is the first. From Appendix A and Equation 4.38,

$$E \geqq -\lim_{n\to\infty} \frac{1}{n} \log P_e \geqq H\left(\frac{d_g}{n}\right) - H(P_c) + E(P_c, P). \tag{4.42}$$

This lower bound on reliability is definitely lower than the sphere-packing upper bound.

Case 4. $nP_b < d_g \leqq n$. The largest term is the term in the first sum for which $j - [d_g/2] = (n - d_g)P$. Because

$$-\lim_{n\to\infty} \frac{1}{n} \log\binom{n}{d_g} 2^{-(n-k)} = 0$$

for this range of d_g, the reliability is bounded by

$$E \geqq \frac{d_g}{n} \log \frac{1}{\sqrt{4PQ}}. \tag{4.43}$$

Equations 4.40, 4.41, and 4.42 and the relationship between d_g/n and code rate can be used to construct a lower bound for the reliability-versus-rate curve for the best binary codes. This is plotted in Figure 4.2 for $P = 10^{-2}$. The bound consists of three nonzero sections. For $C > R \geqq R_c$, Equation 4.40 applies. The quantity R_c is the rate corresponding to the condition $d_g = nP_c$, where P_c is given by Equation 4.37.

Thus,

$$R_c = 1 - H\left(\frac{\sqrt{P}}{\sqrt{P} + \sqrt{Q}}\right).$$

For $R_c > R \geqq R_b$, Equation 4.42 applies.

The quantity R_b is the rate corresponding to the condition $d_g = nP_b$ where P_b is given by Equation 4.41. Thus,

$$R_b = 1 - H\left(\frac{\sqrt{4PQ}}{1 + \sqrt{4PQ}}\right).$$

In this range of rates the bound takes the form of a straight line:

$$E \geqq \log\left(\frac{2}{1 + \sqrt{4PQ}}\right) - R. \tag{4.44}$$

For rates between 0 and R_b, Equation 4.43 provides the best bound. With the aid of Equation 4.38, this states that

$$H\left(\frac{E}{\log\dfrac{1}{\sqrt{4PQ}}}\right) \geqq 1 - R. \tag{4.45}$$

These results show that the random-coding bound consists of two curved and one straight-line section. It is easily verified that the curve is continuous and in fact that the curved sections are tangent to the straight line, so that even the derivative is continuous.

Had not the bad codes been excluded from the averaging, the upper bound on P_e would have been slightly higher. In particular, the domain of Equation 4.44 would then be extended from $R = R_c$ to $R = 0$, and Equation 4.45 would not apply. This is shown as a dashed line in Figure 4.2.

It is interesting to note also that fairly good codes can be found by choosing a modest number of codes at random and keeping the best. Encoding is fairly easy for these codes since they are linear, and they might well be used except for the difficulties involved in decoding.

At $R = 0$, Equation 4.45 shows that the reliability is lower-bounded by the quantity $\frac{1}{2}\log(1/\sqrt{4PQ})$, which is exactly half of the value assumed by the sphere-packing bound at $R = 0$. Equation 4.23, when expressed in asymptotic form (see Problem 4.1), states that for $R = 0$ the reliability is also upper-bounded by $\frac{1}{2}\log(1/\sqrt{4PQ})$. Thus, at $R = 0$ the reliability of the best code is known exactly.

This fact has been used by Shannon, Gallager, and Berlekamp (1967) to derive another bound which is uniformly better than the bound of Equation 4.23. The derivation of this *straight-line upper bound* on reliability involves notions otherwise unnecessary in this book and hence is omitted. The bound itself states that the reliability-versus-rate curve for the sequence of best codes cannot lie above a straight line that is tangent to the sphere-packing bound and passes through the known zero-rate point. This bound is also plotted in Figure 4.2.

4.3 Discussion of Bounds for Block Codes

Upper and lower bounds have been given that can be interpreted as bounds on the minimum distance d possible for an (n, k) code. As n becomes very large, if the rate k/n is kept constant, the bounds on the ratio d/n become fixed constants independent of n, and these bounds are plotted in Figure 4.1.

The Hamming codes, and the equivalent highest rate Reed-Muller and Bose-Chaudhuri-Hocquenghem (BCH) codes described in later chapters, meet the Hamming bound and are optimum. The codes of Theorem 4.6 and the lowest rate Reed-Muller and BCH codes meet the Plotkin bound. Hence, these codes all have maximum minimum distance. For large n, their rates all approach 0 or 1, however. In the middle rate range, for both the BCH and majority-logic decodable codes of Chapters 10 and 11, with any fixed nonzero rate the ratio d/n approaches zero as n approaches infinity. The BCH codes, however, still lie approximately on the Varsharmov-Gilbert bound for $n = 1023$. There is no known coding system for which it has been proved that d/n remains nonzero as n approaches infinity with the rate k/n held fixed, though the Varsharmov-Gilbert bound shows that such codes exist. In fact, Theorem 4.9 states that most codes have this property.

Now consider codes for the binary symmetric channel. By Shannon's fundamental theorem for the noisy channel, it is known that for any rate k/n less than channel capacity there exist codes for which the probability of error is arbitrarily small. Yet only two nonrandom coding systems, Elias's error-free coding in (Section 5.8) and Forney's concatenated BCH codes (Section 5.10), are known to be capable of achieving error probability approaching zero and maintaining a rate that does not approach zero as the code length n is increased.

There is one more noteworthy fact. The number of errors occurring in a block of n symbols in a binary symmetric channel has a binomial distribution with mean nP and standard deviation $\sqrt{nPQ}$. The fraction of positions in error then has mean P and standard deviation $\sqrt{PQ/n}$. As n approaches infinity, this standard deviation approaches zero, and for a fixed value of $P_0 > P$, the probability that $P_0 n$ or more errors will occur approaches zero. On the other hand if $P_0 \leqq P$, the probability that $P_0 n$ or more errors will occur certainly does not approach zero. A code that has minimum distance d and is decoded with *bounded distance decoding* corrects all error patterns of weight $t = [(d-1)/2]$ or less and no others. If $t = nP_0$, the probability of error approaches zero with increasing n if and only if $P_0 > P$. The rate for such a code is bounded by the Elias bound to a value below channel capacity, although for $P < 10^{-3}$ or so the difference is quite small. (See Problem 4.4.) In other words, a coding system which achieves channel capacity must do so by correcting *most error patterns of weight somewhat greater than* $[(d-1)/2]$ even though it is possible to correct *all* patterns only up to weight $[(d-1)/2]$.

Thus the best codes known now, while they are useful for practical applications, fall significantly short of theoretical limits. It would be of great theoretical interest to find explicit constructions for codes that achieve what the bounds indicate is possible, or to show that explicit constructions are impossible. Whether such codes would be of practical interest would depend on whether they could be implemented simply. Little is known about theoretical limits on the complexity of decoders or on the amount of computation necessarily involved in decoding block codes (Savage 1969).

4.4 Bounds on Minimum Distance for Convolutional Codes

The results of this section show what values of minimum distance are and are not attainable with an (n, k) convolutional code. Bounds similar to the Varsharmov-Gilbert and Plotkin bounds for block codes are derived, and large n are shown to be identical to the corresponding results for block codes.

The following upper bound on the largest minimum distance attainable with a systematic convolutional code is analogous to the *Plotkin bound* for block codes (Robinson 1965). The parity-check matrix $\mathbf{H}$ of an (mn_0, mk_0) convolutional code with minimum distance d can be regarded as the parity-check matrix of a linear block code of the same length and having the same number of information symbols. Of course, the block code so obtained is not systematic but is equivalent to one that is.

Now "shorten" this code by setting equal to zero the $k - k_b$ information digits (corresponding to the rightmost $k - k_b$ columns of $\mathbf{H}$). The new code obtained in this manner has the same number of parity checks as the original but has only k_b information symbols. Its code words form a subset of the original set of code words and so it follows that the minimum distance of the new block code d_b is not less than that of the original block code. By similar reasoning, the weight of a code word which is not all zeros in the first n_0 positions, denoted d_c, is at least d. That is,

$$d \leqq d_c. \tag{4.46}$$

On the other hand, it can be seen that

$$d_c \leqq d_b + \left[\frac{k_b - 1}{k_0}\right](n_0 - k_0). \tag{4.47}$$

For assume that a code word of minimum weight d_b has its first nonzero digit in the ith n_0-symbol block. If $i = 1$, then $d_c = d_b$ and Equation 4.47 holds. If $i = 2$, then because of the form of $\mathbf{H}$ there must be a code word whose first nonzero digit is in the first block and whose weight is $d_b + (n_0 - k_0)$ or less. This word matches the original word shifted left one block except in the last $n_0 - k_0$ parity digits where it can have at most $n_0 - k_0$ nonzero symbols. More generally, there must be a code word of weight $d_b + (i - 1)(n_0 - k_0)$ or less whose first block is nonzero. But with only k_b information digits, i must be less than or equal to the least integer that is greater than or equal to k_b/k_0;

$$i \leqq \left[\frac{k_b - 1}{k_0}\right] + 1. \tag{4.48}$$

Equation 4.47 follows directly.

Now the quantity d_b can be overbounded by the Plotkin bound for block codes, Theorem 4.1. The tightest bound is obtained by choosing k_b to be as small as possible. Because $k_b + m(n_0 - k_0)$ must be at least $(qd_b - 1)/(q - 1)$ for Theorem 4.1 to apply, choose

$$k_b = \left[\frac{(qd_b - 2)}{q - 1}\right] - (n_0 - k_0)m + 1. \tag{4.49}$$

Then combining Equations 4.46, 4.47, and 4.49 with Theorem 4.1 and noting that every convolutional code is equivalent to a systematic code gives

THEOREM 4.11. *The minimum distance of an* (mn_0, mk_0) *convolutional code with decoding constraint length* $n = mn_0$ *is bounded by*

$$d \leqq d_b + (n_0 - k_0)\left\lceil \frac{\left\lceil \frac{qd_b - 2}{q - 1} \right\rceil - m(n_0 - k_0)}{k_0} \right\rceil, \tag{4.50}$$

where d_b *is the largest integer i such that*

$$\frac{qi - 1}{q - 1} - 1 - \log_q i \leqq m(n_0 - k_0).$$

For n large and $q = 2$, Equation 4.50 reduces to

$$d \leqq \frac{n - k}{2}, \tag{4.51}$$

which is identical to the corresponding result for block codes.

In Robinson (1965) a tighter, although more complex version of this result is derived. Also, another upper bound on d is obtained by Wyner and Ash (1963). No simple expression for this latter bound has been obtained, however, and its limiting form as n approaches infinity is not known.

A version of the Hamming bound for convolutional codes can be derived using the results of the next section (Equation 4.61). The argument used is somewhat artificial, however, and the problem of deriving a true Hamming bound for convolutional codes remains open. (See Problem 4.10.)

A lower bound on the minimum distance attainable with an (n, k) convolutional code can be derived. This result, which also applies to the more general class of linear tree codes, is analogous to the *Varsharmov-Gilbert bound* for block codes (Bussgang 1965, Lin and Lyne 1967, Massey 1963, Robinson 1967, Wozencraft and Reiffen 1961, and Wyner and Ash 1963).

A convolutional code in systematic form is completely specified by the choice of the k_0 by $(n_0 - k_0)$ matrices $\mathbf{P}_i$, $0 \leqq i \leqq m - 1$, in Equation 3.13. Thus, with symbols chosen from an alphabet of size q, there are $q^{mk_0(n_0 - k_0)}$ possible convolutional codes. Any n-tuple that does not have all zeros in the first block appears in exactly $q^{m(k_0 - 1)(n_0 - k_0)}$ of these codes. This can be seen as follows: Consider an n-tuple which has only a single 1 in the information section of the first block (any other n-tuple which does not have all zeros in the first block can be put in this form by elementary row operations) and use this n-tuple as one of the first k_0

rows of G. The other $k_0 - 1$ of these first k_0 rows can be specified arbitrarily, but once this is done the entire matrix G is determined. In systematic form, each of these rows has $m(n_0 - k_0)$ arbitrary symbols. Thus, $m(k_0 - 1)(n_0 - k_0)$ symbols can be chosen arbitrarily, and there are exactly $q^{m(k_0-1)(n_0-k_0)}$ codes in which an n-tuple which does not have all zeros in the first block appears.

For an n-tuple that does not have all zeros in the first block to be a code word, at least one of the k_0 information symbols in the first block must be nonzero. Let i be the number of nonzero information symbols in the first block; let j denote the weight of the n-tuple. For a particular pattern of i digits in the first k_0 positions, there are

$$\sum_{j=0}^{d-i-1} \binom{n-k_0}{j}(q-1)^j$$

patterns which can occur in the last $n - k_0$ positions such that the total weight is less than d. Summing on i gives $N(d)$, the total number of n-tuples of weight less than d which have at least one nonzero digit in the first k_0 positions; that is,

$$N(d) = \sum_{i=1}^{k_0} \binom{k_0}{i}(q-1)^i \sum_{j=0}^{d-i-1} \binom{n-k_0}{j}(q-1)^j.$$

Now define d_g, the Gilbert distance, to be the largest value of d such that $N(d) < q^{n-k}$. Then the product of the number of n-tuples of weight less than d_g which do not have all zeros in the first k_0 positions times the number of codes in which each appears is strictly less than the number of codes. Consequently, there is at least one code with minimum distance at least d if

$$\sum_{i=1}^{k_0} \binom{k_0}{i}(q-1)^i \sum_{j=0}^{d-i-1} \binom{n-k_0}{j}(q-1)^j < q^{m(n_0-k_0)}. \tag{4.52}$$

In particular, a code exists with minimum distance d_g where d_g is the largest value of d satisfying Inequality 4.52. If d_g is the largest value of d satisfying Inequality 4.52, then the opposite inequality is satisfied if $d_g + 1$ is substituted for d. Thus the following theorem holds:

THEOREM 4.12. *There exists an (mn_0, mk_0) convolutional code whose minimum distance is at least d_g, where*

$$\sum_{i=1}^{k_0} \binom{k_0}{i}(q-1)^i \sum_{j=0}^{d_g-i} \binom{n-k_0}{j}(q-1)^j \geq q^{m(n_0-k_0)} \tag{4.53}$$

It is easily shown that, as for block codes, most codes have minimum distance which is at least only slightly less than d_g. For $q = 2$, the same asymptotic form is obtained as for block codes when n approaches infinity; that is,

$$1 - R = H\left(\frac{d_g}{2}\right). \tag{4.54}$$

The bounds on minimum distance presented in this section have assumed a systematic convolutional code. Every nonsystematic code with decoding constraint length n is equivalent to a systematic code with the same decoding constraint length, and so these bounds apply to all convolutional codes.

Equations 4.22 and 4.54 suggest that for n large there is relatively little difference between the minimum distances of the best block and convolutional codes. For small values of n, the best bounds on d for convolutional codes tend to be slightly higher than the corresponding results for block codes. This seems to indicate that for given values of n and k, slightly larger minimum distance is attainable with convolutional codes. The best known codes discussed in Chapters 5, 10, and 13 bear this out.

4.5 Bounds on the Probability of Error for Convolutional Codes Used on the Binary Symmetric Channel

For block codes used on a memoryless channel, successive decodings are independent. Thus, it is a conceptually simple matter to determine the probability of erroneous decoding P_e. The situation is fundamentally different for convolutional codes, however, since the probability of decoding a particular block erroneously is strongly influenced by the results of preceding decodings. That is, P_e for a particular block may be affected by channel errors which occurred at any time in the past. Let $P_e(-i)$ denote the probability that the last error occurred on the $(-i)$th block and let $P_e(0 \mid -i)$ denote the conditional probability of decoding the 0th block incorrectly given that the $(-i)$th block was so decoded. Then the probability of erroneously decoding the 0th block is

$$P_e = \sum_{i=1}^{\infty} P_e(0 \mid -i) P_e(-i).$$

Assuming that unlimited or catastrophic error propagation never occurs, for i large, one would expect that $P_e(0 \mid -i)$ would be closely approximated by P_{1e}, the probability of error for the first block transmitted. Then if it can be assumed that this approximation holds for all values of i,

$$P_e \cong P_{1e} \sum_{i=1}^{\infty} P_e(-i) = P_{1e}. \tag{4.55}$$

The quantity P_{1e} can be calculated readily and, subject to the above restrictions, can be used to approximate the probability of error. Note that if the channel error probability is small each factor $P_e(-i)$ in Eq. 4.55 will be small and so the difference between P_{1e} and P_e will be slight. In any case P_{1e} does provide an indication of the reliability achievable with convolutional codes, and in some situations nothing better is available. In what follows both P_e and P_{1e} are employed.

The probability of first error can be computed for a particular convolutional code in a conceptually straightforward way. In terms of the standard array, P_{1e} is simply the sum of the probabilities of the n-tuples in subsets 2 through 2^{k_0}, that is, the incorrect subsets. Again, as for block codes, the sheer size of the standard array usually makes any enumerative procedure impractical.

The most important of the bounds, the *random coding bound*, can be proved for convolutional codes. The proof is quite similar to that for block codes. Now, however, the codes considered are the row spaces of matrices of the form of Equation 3.13:

$$\mathbf{G} = \begin{bmatrix} \mathbf{IP}_0 & \mathbf{0P}_1 & \cdots & \mathbf{0P}_{m-1} \\ & \mathbf{IP}_0 & \cdots & \mathbf{0P}_{m-2} \\ & & \ddots & \vdots \\ & & & \mathbf{IP}_0 \end{bmatrix}$$

It was shown in the derivation of the Gilbert bound that there are $2^{mk_0(n_0-k_0)}$ ways of choosing the matrices $\mathbf{P}_i$, $0 \leqq i \leqq m-1$, and so there are as many codes as this in the class. Also, it was shown that any n-tuple whose first block is nonzero can be a code word in not more than $2^{m(k_0-1)(n_0-k_0)}$ codes.

Let d_g be defined as in Equation 4.32. That is, d_g is the largest integer such that

$$2^{n-k} \geqq 2 \sum_{i=0}^{d_g-1} \binom{n}{i} > \left\{ \begin{matrix} \text{number of } n \text{ tuples of weight less} \\ \text{than } d_g \text{ whose first block is nonzero} \end{matrix} \right\}. \tag{4.56}$$

Thus, the number of code words of weight less than d_g whose first block is nonzero in all codes is overbounded by

$$2^{m(k_0-1)(n_0-k_0)} \sum_{i=0}^{d_g-1} \binom{n}{i} < \frac{2^{mk_0(n_0-k_0)}}{2}.$$

Thus, fewer than half of the convolutional codes can contain an n-tuple of weight less than d_g whose first block is nonzero. In other words, Theorem 4.9 holds for convolutional as well as for block codes.

For large n, the difference between d_g in Equation 4.56 and the Gilbert distance of Theorem 4.12 is negligibly small. Thus, it can be said that the minimum distance of most convolutional codes is at least quite close to the Gilbert distance.

Now, as earlier, the number of codes with minimum distance $d \geqq d_g$ in which the occurrence of an error pattern of weight j causes an error must be overbounded. A decoding error occurs in any code in which a code word whose first block is nonzero lies within distance j or less of the received n-tuple. Now the number of n-tuples whose first block is nonzero, and which have weight d_g or greater, and which are within distance j of the received n-tuple is strictly less than the number of n-tuples which have weight d_g or greater and which are within distance j of the received n-tuple. This latter number is determined in the derivation of Equation 4.33. Multiplying this overbound to the number of possible code words within distance j of the received sequence by $2^{m(k_0-1)(n_0-k_0)}$, the number of codes in which a code word can appear, gives an upper bound on $N(j)$, the number of codes in which an error pattern of weight j causes a first decoding error. Thus, from the derivation of Equation 4.33,

$$N(j) = 0; \qquad 0 \leqq j < \left[\frac{d_g}{2}\right],$$

$$N(j) \leqq 2^{m(k_0-1)(n_0-k_0)} \sum_{i=d_g-j}^{j} \sum_{n=d_g}^{j+i} \binom{n-j}{\frac{n+i-j}{2}} \binom{j}{\frac{n+j-i}{2}}; \qquad \left[\frac{d_g}{2}\right] \leqq j < d_g,$$

$$N(j) \leqq \text{total number of codes with } d > d_g; \qquad d_g \leqq j. \tag{4.57}$$

Now each pattern of j errors has probability $P^j Q^{n-j}$ and there are $\binom{n}{j}$ such patterns. Summing on j gives an upper bound on the average P_{1e} for codes with $d \geqq d_g$. By Theorem 4.9 the number of such codes is at least $2^{mk_0(n_0-k_0)-1}$; thus, in the averaging this number can be used in place of the actual number of codes. Finally, as there is at least one code in the class which is as good as average, the upper bound on P_{1e} applies to it as well. The statement of this bound is identical to that for block codes, given as Theorem 4.10, with P_{1e} replacing P_e.

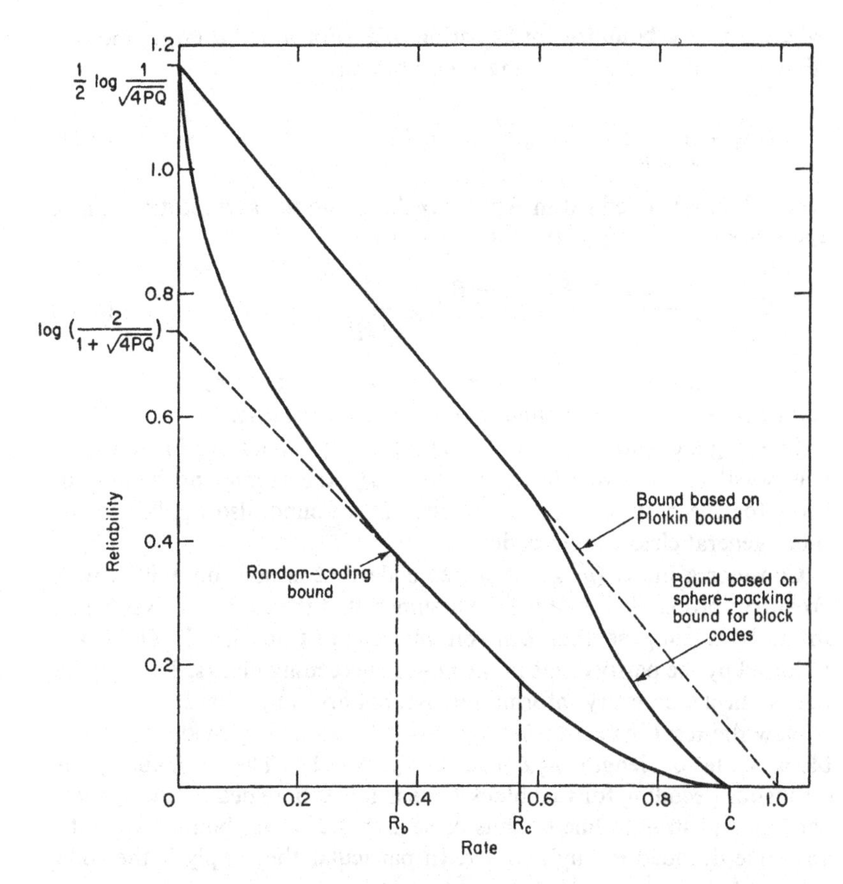

Figure 4.3. Plot of bounds on reliability as a function of rate for systematic convolutional codes on a binary symmetric channel with $P = 10^{-2}$.

Of course the behavior of the bound as n approaches infinity is also identical to that for block codes. This asymptotic bound is stated in Equations 4.40, 4.42, and 4.43 and is plotted in Figure 4.3 for $P = 10^{-2}$.

The Plotkin upper bound on minimum distance derived in the preceding section can be used to derive a lower bound on P_{1e}, the probability of first error. The argument employed is identical to that for block codes. Let d denote the maximum minimum distance allowed by the Plotkin bound. The probability P_{1e} is not less than the probability of confusing the transmitted word with another word distance d away. Thus for the binary symmetric channel (BSC),

$$P_{1e} \geqq \sum_{i=[(d+1)/2]}^{d} \binom{d}{i} P^i Q^{d-i} \tag{4.58}$$

where d is overbounded by Equation 4.50. For n and d large, the reliability E satisfies the following upper bound:

$$E \leqq -\lim_{n\to\infty} \frac{1}{n} \log_2 P_{1e} \leqq \frac{d}{n} E(0.5, P) \tag{4.59}$$

where $E(\lambda, P)$ is defined in Appendix A. Using the asymptotic form of the Plotkin bound, Equation 4.51, gives

$$E \leqq \frac{(1-R)E(0.5, P)}{2} = \frac{1-R}{2} \log \frac{1}{\sqrt{4PQ}}. \tag{4.60}$$

This result is plotted in Figure 4.3 for $P = 10^{-2}$. As can be seen, for rates near capacity the bound is obviously quite loose.

By using the straight-line and sphere-packing bounds for block codes, it is possible to derive a lower bound on P_e, the average probability of error for the best convolutional code. This bound also applies to the more general class of tree codes.

Consider a linear (mn_0, mk_0) tree code that is used on a BSC with crossover probability P. It will be assumed that the code is in systematic form. Now suppose that B n_0-bit blocks are transmitted. These are followed by the parity digits in the $m - 1$ succeeding blocks. Thus all the parity checks on every information symbol are transmitted.

Now the resulting set of 2^{Bk_0} code words can be regarded as a linear block code of length $n_0 B + (n_0 - k_0)(m - 1)$. The probability of erroneous decoding for this block code is lower bounded by the sphere-packing and straight-line bounds of Section 4.2. These bounds apply to any code decoded in any manner. In particular they apply if the code constructed above is decoded as a tree code.

Let P_e denote the average probability that an n_0-bit block is decoded incorrectly when the code is decoded as a tree code. Clearly, P_e is not less than the average probability that a block is wrong when the code is viewed as a block code and maximum-likelihood decoding is employed. This latter probability in turn is lower bounded by $1/B$ times the value of the lower bound on the probability of error for block codes. For when a word error occurs, at least one block must be in error. Thus, for an (mn_0, mk_0) tree code,

$$P_e \geqq \frac{1}{B} \begin{bmatrix} \text{value of lower bound on probability of error} \\ \text{for best } (Bn_0 + (m-1)(n_0 - k_0), Bk_0) \text{ block} \\ \text{code} \end{bmatrix}. \tag{4.61}$$

Now consider the length of the code to be large and denote the ratio

B/m by μ. With μ regarded as a constant, the reliability of the tree code E_t is then overbounded as follows:

$$E_t = -\lim_{n\to\infty} \frac{1}{mn_0} \log P_e$$

$$= (\mu + 1 - R_t)\bar{E}_b \tag{4.62}$$

where $R_t = k_0/n_0$ and $\bar{E}_b$ denotes the block code upper bound on reliability. The rate for the block code is

$$R_b = \frac{R_t}{\mu + 1 - R_t}. \tag{4.63}$$

Since Equation 4.62 holds for all values of the parameter μ, the best upper bound on E_t is obtained by taking the lower envelope of the family of bounds. This result is plotted in Figure 4.3 for $P = 10^{-2}$. It is worth noting that since the straight-line and sphere-packing bounds hold for the more general discrete memoryless channel, so does the bound derived here.

4.6 Bounds for Burst-Error Correcting and Detecting Codes

A burst of length l is defined as a vector whose only nonzero components are among l successive components, the first and last of which are nonzero.

THEOREM 4.13. *A linear block code that has no burst of length l or less as a code word must have at least l parity-check symbols.*

Proof. If no burst of length l is a code vector, no two vectors that are 0 except in their first l symbols could be in the same coset, because if they were, their difference, which must be a burst of length l or less, would have to be a code vector. The number of vectors that are 0 except in the first l symbols is q^l, and therefore there must be at least q^l cosets and at least l check symbols. Q.E.D.

THEOREM 4.14. *For detecting all burst errors of length l or less with a linear block code of length n, l parity-check symbols are necessary and sufficient.*

Proof. The necessity follows from Theorem 4.13. The sufficiency follows from the fact that all bursts of length l or less are detected by a code in which the first $n - l$ symbols are information symbols and

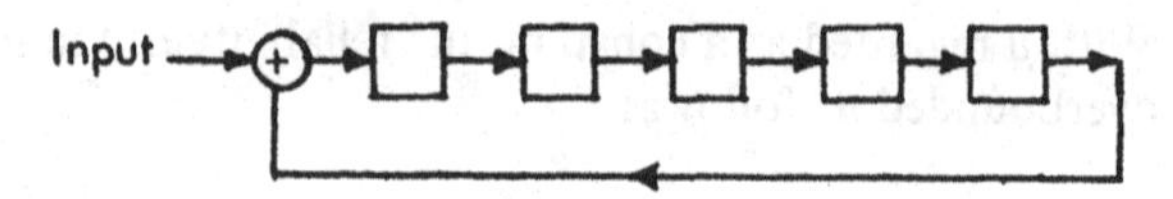

Figure 4.4. Shift register for calculating parity checks for (23, 18) code with $l = 5$.

the last l symbols are parity-check symbols, chosen to make 0 the sum of each of the l sets of symbols consisting of one of the first l symbols and every lth symbol following it. Then at most one of the nonzero symbols of a burst of length l or less can affect any particular parity check, and so every such burst will be detected, along with many other error patterns. Q.E.D.

The parity-check matrix for such a code for $n = 23$ and $l = 5$ is

$$\mathbf{H} = \begin{bmatrix} 10000100001000010000100 \\ 01000010000100001000010 \\ 00100001000010000100001 \\ 00010000100001000010000 \\ 00001000010000100001000 \end{bmatrix}$$

and a method of mechanizing it which uses a shift register is shown in Figure 4.4. This is an elementary example of a cyclic code, the subject of Chapter 8.

THEOREM 4.15. (Rieger 1960.) *In order to correct all burst errors of length b or less, a linear block code must have at least* $2b$ *parity-check symbols. In order to correct all bursts of length b or less and simultaneously detect all bursts of length* $l \geqq b$ *or less, the code must have at least* $b + l$ *parity-check symbols.*

Proof. Any vector that has the form of a burst of length $2b$ or less can be written as the difference of two bursts of length b or less (except in the degenerate case of a burst consisting of a single nonzero element). Since in order to correct all bursts of length b or less these must be in different cosets, their difference cannot be a code word. Therefore, a burst of length $2b$ or less cannot be a code word. The first part of the theorem (including the exceptional case) then follows from Theorem 4.13.

Similarly, every burst of length $b + l$ or less can be written as the difference of a burst of length l or less and a burst of length b or less. If the code is simultaneously to correct bursts of length b or less and to detect all bursts of length l, the burst of length b and the burst of length l must be in different cosets, and their sum must not be a code word. This theorem then follows from Theorem 4.13. Q.E.D.

Another lower bound on the number of parity checks required for a linear code that corrects all bursts of length b or less can be found by noting that, because every burst of length b or less must be in a different coset, the number of cosets is at least as great as the number of burst-error patterns of length b or less.

There are $(q-1)n$ different bursts of length 1, since the nonzero component may appear in any one of n symbols and any of the $q-1$ nonzero field elements. There are $(q-1)^2(n-1)$ possible burst errors of length 2, since each of the two nonzero components may be any of the $q-1$ nonzero field elements, and the burst may start in any position except the last. For bursts of length $i > 2$, there are $(q-1)^2q^{i-2}(n-i+1)$ patterns, since there are $q-1$ choices for each end symbol, q choices for the symbols in between, and $(n-i+1)$ possible starting positions. The total number of error patterns, including the pattern of all zeros, is therefore

$$1 + n(q-1) + \sum_{i=2}^{b} (q-1)^2 q^{i-2}(n-i+1).$$

By use of the two identities

$$\sum_{i=0}^{n} x^i = \frac{1-x^{n+1}}{1-x}$$

and (4.64)

$$\sum_{i=0}^{n} ix^{i-1} = \frac{d}{dx}\left(\frac{1-x^{n+1}}{1-x}\right),$$

the expression for the total number of error patterns can be simplified to

$$q^{b-1}[(q-1)(n-b+1)+1]$$

and, because there must be at least this number of cosets, the following theorem holds:

THEOREM 4.16. *The number of parity-check symbols in any linear block code that corrects all bursts of length b or less is at least*

$$b - 1 + \log_q[(q-1)(n-b+1)+1].$$

Some of the codes described in Chapter 11 require the minimum or very few more than the minimum number of parity checks indicated by the preceding theorems.

A bound analogous to the Varsharmov-Gilbert bound can be found for burst-error-correcting codes. Suppose that the matrix $\mathbf{H}$ of parity-check rules is being constructed for a code to correct any single burst of length b or less. It is necessary and sufficient that no code vector consist of the sum of two bursts of length b or less. Thus, by Theorem 3.1, it is necessary and sufficient that no linear combination involving two sets of b or fewer consecutive columns of $\mathbf{H}$ be $\mathbf{0}$. Suppose that $n-1$ columns $\mathbf{h}_1, \mathbf{h}_2, \ldots, \mathbf{h}_{n-1}$ have been chosen. Then any column $\mathbf{h}_n$ may be added, provided that it is not a linear combination of the last $b-1$ columns $\mathbf{h}_{n-b+1}, \ldots, \mathbf{h}_{n-1}$ and any set of b consecutive columns among $\mathbf{h}_1, \ldots, \mathbf{h}_{n-b}$;

$$\begin{aligned}\mathbf{h}_n \neq (a_{n-1}\mathbf{h}_{n-1} + \cdots + a_{n-b+1}\mathbf{h}_{n-b+1}) \\ + (b_{n-b-i}\mathbf{h}_{n-b-i} + \cdots + b_{n-b-i-b+1}\mathbf{h}_{n-b-i-b+1}).\end{aligned} \tag{4.65}$$

The worst conceivable case would be for each choice of coefficients a_j and b_j to yield a distinct sum in Equation 4.65. There are q^{b-1} choices for the a_j. The coefficients b_j form a burst of length b or less in a vector of length $n-b$, and by the argument preceding Theorem 4.16 it can be seen that there are $q^{b-1}[(q-1)(n-2b+1)+1]$ choices for these coefficients, including the case in which they are all zeros. Thus the total number of choices of coefficients is

$$q^{b-1}q^{b-1}[(q-1)(n-2b+1)+1].$$

If the number of possible vectors of length $n-k$ is greater than this, there certainly must exist a vector $\mathbf{h}_n$ satisfying Inequality 4.65 for all choices of coefficients, and thus it is possible to construct a code of length n which corrects all bursts of length b or less. Since there are q^{n-k} vectors of length $n-k$, this is possible if

$$q^{n-k} > q^{2(b-1)}[(q-1)(n-2b+1)+1].$$

Now let b_g be the largest value of b satisfying this inequality. Then for $b = b_g + 1$, the opposite inequality is satisfied, and the following theorem holds:

THEOREM 4.17. *There exists an (n, k) linear code that corrects any single burst of length $b_g < n/2$ or less for which the following inequality is satisfied:*

$$n-k \leqq 2b_g + \log_q[(q-1)(n-2b_g-1)+1].$$

For large n, Theorems 4.15 and 4.17 state that $(n - k)/2$ is a practically attainable maximum for the burst-correcting ability of a linear block code.

The following theorem for convolutional codes is analogous to Theorem 4.13 for block codes:

THEOREM 4.13′. *A convolutional code that has no burst of length sn_0 or less in the first s blocks as a code word must have at least sn_0 parity checks.*

The proof is identical to that of Theorem 4.13.

An upper bound on the burst-error-correcting ability of a convolutional code can be derived with the aid of the following result.

THEOREM 4.18. (*Wyner-Ash*) *In order to correct all bursts of length b_2 which are confined to r (adjacent) blocks,* an (mn_0, mk_0) convolutional code must have at least $2b_2 - (r - 1)(n_0 - k_0)$ parity checks.*

Proof. If a code can correct all patterns of errors that are confined to r blocks, then no code word in the incorrect subsets can consist of two bursts of length rn_0 or less, where each burst is confined to r blocks. For otherwise there would be a coset containing two error patterns that are bursts of length rn_0 and that differ in the first block. It remains to show that if no code word consists of two such bursts, then the code must have at least $2rn_0 - (r - 1)(n_0 - k_0)$ parity checks. This is done by showing that if the code has fewer check digits then there is at least one code word in the incorrect subsets which consists of two bursts each confined to r blocks.

Consider the parity check matrix $\mathbf{H}$ of a convolutional code with parameters n_0, k_0, m' and fewer than $2rn_0$ parity checks. By Theorem 4.13′ there is a code word in this code which consists of a burst of length $2rn_0$ or less in the first $2r$ blocks. There are $2r$ situations to consider corresponding to the possible locations of the first nonzero block in the burst. If the first nonzero block of this code word is block 1, then there is a code word in the incorrect subsets that consists of two bursts each of length less than or equal to rn_0. If the first nonzero block is block 2, then shift this word to the left one block. A code word $\mathbf{c}$ is obtained in this manner which consists of a burst in the first $2r - 1$ blocks and possibly another burst in the last block. Construct the

* These error patterns are called Type B2 bursts.

parity-check matrix of a new code of length $n_0(m' - 1)$ from the upper $(m' - 1)(n_0 - k_0)$ rows of the **H** matrix of the original code. In this new code there is a code word **c**′ that is identical to the first $(m' - 1)n_0$ symbols of **c**. Thus, there is a code word in the incorrect subsets of the new code which consists of two bursts each of length less than or equal to rn_0.

Now, if the first nonzero block is block i, where $1 \leqq i \leqq r$, then shortening the code by $r - 1$ blocks guarantees that there is a code word in the incorrect subsets of the shortened code which consists of a single burst of length less than or equal to $2rn_0$ which is confined to the first $2rn_0$ blocks. Hence, there is a code word that consists of two bursts each of length less than or equal to rn_0.

If the first nonzero block is block $r + 1$, no shortening is necessary. There is a code word in the incorrect subsets which consists of two bursts in the first and last r blocks. If the first nonzero digit is in block i, where $r + 2 \leqq i \leqq 2r$, then shortening the code by $r - 1$ blocks guarantees that there is a code word in the incorrect subsets of the new code which consists of two bursts of length not greater than rn_0. One burst occurs in the first r blocks, the other in the last r blocks.

Shortening the original code by $r - 1$ blocks always produces a code with at least $2rn_0 - (r - 1)(n_0 - k_0)$ parity checks and whose burst-correcting ability is less than rn_0. Q.E.D.

This result can be used to overbound b, the burst-correcting ability of a convolutional code. Theorem 4.18 provides an upper bound on b_2, the burst-correcting ability for bursts confined to $[b_2/n_0]$ blocks; denote this by $\bar{b}_2$. Then

$$b \leqq \bar{b}_2 + n_0 - 1. \tag{4.66}$$

For if b were larger, it would imply that $b_2 > \bar{b}_2$, a condition which is impossible by Theorem 4.18. Equation 4.66 can be combined with Theorem 4.18 to give the following theorem:

THEOREM 4.19. *The burst-correcting ability b of an (mn_0, mk_0) convolutional code is overbounded by*

$$n - k \geqq \left[\frac{n_0 + k_0}{n_0}\right](b + 1 - n_0) + n_0 - k_0. \tag{4.67}$$

In addition, it is clearly always true that

$$b \leqq \left[\frac{n - 1}{2}\right]. \tag{4.68}$$

There is no need to prove a result for convolutional codes analogous to Theorem 4.17. Good burst-error-correcting convolutional codes can be constructed using the methods of Chapter 14. For large n, these codes and Theorem 4.16 show that $(n - k)/(1 + R)$ is a practically attainable maximum for convolutional codes. Because the code rate R is always less than unity, for a given (large) n and k, convolutional codes have greater burst-error-correcting ability than block codes. The opposite seems to be true when n is small, however.

Notes

The Plotkin bound is taken from Plotkin (1951), and the refinement in Theorem 4.1 is due to Elias. The Varsharmov-Gilbert bound was found by Varsharmov (1957). It is a refinement of a bound of Gilbert's (1952) and was also found by Sacks (1958). Sacks's proof is used here because of its simplicity. The refinement in Theorem 4.3 is due to Greismer (1960) and codes that meet this bound were found by MacDonald (1960) and Solomon and Stiffler (1965). The Hamming bound appears in Hamming (1950) and a refinement of it in Wax (1959).

Bounds for the binary symmetric channel were first published by Elias (1955, 1956), and were based on Shannon's original work (1949). Error probability bounds for more general channels are an important part of Gallager's book (1968), and the results and proofs presented in this book include some refinements due to Gallager. Theorem 4.9 and its converse are due to Pierce (1967).

The Gilbert bound for convolutional codes was first derived by Wozencraft and Reiffen (1961). Several refinements of their work have been devised but none of these have improved on its asymptotic form. The Plotkin-like bound for these codes is due to Robinson (1965). The upper bound on minimum distance derived by Wyner and Ash (1963) is the tightest known bound in some cases but an asymptotic form for this bound has not yet been derived. The use of block code bounds to derive similar bounds for convolutional codes is due to Viterbi (1967).

Bounds for burst-error detection and correction, results equivalent to Theorem 4.15, appear in Reiger (1960) and are similar to some results of Fire (1959). Theorem 4.16 appears in Fire's paper. Theorem 4.17 was found by C. N. Campopiano.

Theorems 4.18 and 4.19 were first proved by Wyner and Ash (1963).

Problems

4.1. Using the results of Appendix A, determine the asymptotic forms of the bounds of Equations 4.23 and 4.24 as $n \to \infty$. Compare the results to the other asymptotic bounds on P_e plotted in Figure 4.2.

4.2. Derive and plot the lower bound on reliability implied by Equation 4.25 for $P = 10^{-2}$. This forms a lower bound on the reliability of the best code decoded with this *bounded distance decoding* (that is, when only $[d/2]$ errors or fewer can be corrected in any word).

4.3. Using the Elias upper bound on the ratio d/n, show that for the best code decoded with bounded distance decoding (Problem 4.1),

$$\text{Reliability} < E[\lambda(1-\lambda), P]$$

where

$$H(\lambda) = 1 - R.$$

4.4. Derive upper and lower bounds on the capacity of the binary symmetric channel when bounded distance decoding is used. Plot and compare with the true channel capacity (Equation 4.39). (Hint: Determine the values of R for which the bounds of Problems 4.1, 4.2, and 4.3 equal zero.)

4.5. Show that for a linear block code of length n, b parity-check symbols are necessary and sufficient for all correcting all bursts of erasures of length b or less.

4.6. Determine N, the number of systematic (n, k) codes. Determine an upper bound on the number of these codes in which a particular n-tuple can be a code word; call this M. Let J denote the number of nonzero n-tuples of weight less than d_g and choose d_g as large as possible such that $JM < N$. Clearly, there must be at least one code with no nonzero words of weight less than d_g.

Derive an asymptotic lower bound on d_g/n using this result and considering n to be large and show that this is identical to the Gilbert bound.

4.7. Let $n = 100$ and $\lambda = 0.6$. Calculate upper and lower bounds on $\binom{n}{\lambda n}$ and $\sum_{i=\lambda n}^{n} \binom{n}{i}$, using the results in Appendix A.

4.8. A one-way data communication system requires a binary block code with $R = 0.5$. Is it possible to build either a decoder capable of correcting only single errors or all single and double errors? Construct codes for this system. Why should you strive to make each code as short as possible?

4.9. Compare the probability of decoding incorrectly on the binary symmetric channel for the following codes for $10^{-4} \leqq P \leqq 1$. Bounded distance decoding is used.

a. (23, 12) $t = 3$ (Golay code)
b. (57, 30) $t = 5$ (shortened (63, 36) BCH code)

Discuss the region around $P = 10^{-1}$.

4.10. Using the lower bound on the probability of decoding a block erroneously for convolutional codes stated in Equations 4.62 and 4. 63, derive an upper bound on minimum distance.

5 Important Linear Block Codes

The title notwithstanding, the most important linear block codes are not discussed in this chapter. These are the cyclic codes, and Chapters 6 through 11 are devoted to them. In this chapter various classes of non-cyclic block codes are presented. Several of these, including the Hamming codes, the Golay code, the Reed-Muller codes, and some product codes, are equivalent to cyclic codes and so are discussed in later chapters also.

5.1 The Hamming Codes

The binary Hamming code is most easily described in terms of its parity-check matrix. Consider a matrix **H** of 1's and 0's, which has m rows and $2^m - 1$ columns, the column vectors being all possible m-tuples except the zero m-tuple. Over the field of two elements, if two vectors add to zero, they must be equal. Therefore, no two columns of this matrix add to zero, and, since the only nonzero scalar is 1, no linear combination of two columns is zero. Therefore, the null space of this matrix has minimum weight 3 and is capable of correcting all single errors. The code vectors have length $2^m - 1$, with m parity-check symbols and therefore $2^m - 1 - m$ information symbols.

Since each of the $2^m - 1$ single-error patterns is in a different coset, these together with the code space account for all the 2^m cosets. Therefore this code has as coset leaders the zero vector and all single-error patterns, and no others, and is an example of a perfect code. The

Hamming code can be modified to any length n by setting up the matrix **H** for the smallest m in such a way that $2^m - 1 \geqq n$ and by simply omitting all but n columns. No matter which columns are omitted, the code will still have minimum weight 3. It is possible to choose the columns so that the resulting code is quasi-perfect. (See Problems 5.1 and 5.3.) Thus for every n there is a Hamming single-error-correcting code that is optimum for the binary symmetric channel.

If a code vector **u** is transmitted and a single error occurs, the received vector is $\mathbf{u} + \mathbf{e}$, where **e** is a vector that has a 1 in the error position and 0's in all other components. Then the syndrome is

$$(\mathbf{u} + \mathbf{e})\mathbf{H}^T = \mathbf{u}\mathbf{H}^T + \mathbf{e}\mathbf{H}^T = \mathbf{e}\mathbf{H}^T$$

since **u** is a code vector and therefore in the null space of **H**. But since **e** is a vector that has a single 1 in the position corresponding to the error, the syndrome $\mathbf{e}\mathbf{H}^T$ is just the row of $\mathbf{H}^T$ corresponding to the error. Thus by comparing the syndrome with the matrix $\mathbf{H}^T$, the position of the error can be found, and simply changing that symbol corrects the error. A clever way of doing this is to use as the ith column of **H** the binary representation of the number i. Then the syndrome gives, for each single error, the binary representation of the position in error. This is the arrangement originally used by Hamming (1950).

Example. For $m = 3$, $n = 2^3 - 1 = 7$, the parity-check matrix may be chosen as follows:

$$\mathbf{H} = \begin{bmatrix} 0\,0\,0\,1\,1\,1\,1 \\ 0\,1\,1\,0\,0\,1\,1 \\ 1\,0\,1\,0\,1\,0\,1 \end{bmatrix}$$

It is easy to encode if the first, second, and fourth symbols are taken to be the parity-check symbols, because each is involved in only one of the parity-check relations described by **H**. To encode information symbols 1 1 0 0, three parity-check symbols $p_1 p_2\, 1 p_3\, 1 0 0$ are inserted. Then p_1 is chosen to satisfy the parity relation given by the last row of **H**; that is,

$$p_1 + 1 + 1 + 0 = 0$$

Therefore, $p_1 = 0$. Similarly, $p_2 = 1$ and $p_3 = 1$, and the code vector is 0 1 1 1 1 0 0. If the fifth symbol is received in error, the received vector is 0 1 1 1 0 0 0. The syndrome is easily found to be 1 0 1, a value that matches the fifth column of **H**, indicating an error in the fifth symbol of the received vector. The syndrome is the binary code for 5, since each column of **H** was chosen as the binary representation of the column number.

A binary code with minimum weight 4 can be formed by adding to a binary Hamming code one parity check that is a check on all the symbols in the code. In fact, adding one check symbol that includes all symbols to any binary code will always add a 0 to all words of even weight, a 1 to all words of odd weight, and therefore, if the minimum weight in a code is odd, the over-all parity check increases the minimum weight by 1. There are $m + 1$ parity-check symbols, $2^m - m - 1$ information symbols (the same as for the single-error-correcting code), and therefore a total of $n = 2^m$ symbols.

Example. The parity-check matrix for the Hamming (8, 4) single-error-correcting, double-error-detecting code is

$$\mathbf{H} = \begin{bmatrix} 00001111 \\ 00110011 \\ 01010101 \\ 11111111 \end{bmatrix}$$

Decoding for this code is accomplished in the following way:

1. If the syndrome is **0**, assume that no error occurred.
2. If the overall check (corresponding to the last row in **H** in the example above) is 1, assume that a single error occurred. The syndrome will match the column vector in **H** corresponding to the error.
3. If the overall check symbol is 0, but other parity checks fail, an uncorrectable error has been detected.

The distance-4 Hamming codes can be shown to be quasi-perfect. (See Problem 5.2.) Again it is possible to omit columns from the parity-check matrix so as to form a distance-4 code of any length $n < 2^m$.

At first sight it might appear that to generalize the Hamming codes to codes with symbols taken from the field of $q > 2$ elements it would be necessary only to take as the parity-check matrix **H** an $m \times (q^m - 1)$ matrix in which the columns are all possible distinct m-tuples. This does not work, since now some nontrivial linear combinations of two columns are zero. For example, over the field of three elements, (2, 1) and (1, 2) add to (0, 0). The difficulty is that (1, 2) is a scalar multiple of (2, 1). In the binary case the only scalars are trivial.

The difficulty is overcome if, out of each class of vectors that are scalar multiples of each other, only one is chosen, say the one having a

1 as its first nonzero component. Then no two columns of **H** are linearly dependent, and the null space of **H** is a distance-3 code, capable of correcting any error involving a single component. There are altogether $q^m - 1$ nonzero m-tuples, of which a fraction $1/(q-1)$ have their leading nonzero element equal to 1. The maximum number of columns in **H** is therefore $(q^m - 1)/(q-1)$.

Example. A code with symbols from the field of three elements, with three parity-check symbols, is the null space of the matrix

$$\mathbf{H} = \begin{bmatrix} 0000111111111 \\ 0111000111222 \\ 1012012012012 \end{bmatrix}$$

This code of $(3^3 - 1)/(3-1) = 13$ symbols, of which 10 are information symbols, can correct any error in any single symbol. It is simple to encode if the check symbols are taken to be the first, second, and fifth, corresponding to the columns with only one nonzero element.

If a code word **u** is transmitted and an error amounting to adding b to the jth symbol in **u** occurs, the received vector is $\mathbf{u} + \mathbf{e}$, where **e** is a vector with b in the jth symbol and 0's elsewhere. Then the syndrome is

$$(\mathbf{u} + \mathbf{e})\mathbf{H}^T = \mathbf{u}\mathbf{H}^T + \mathbf{e}\mathbf{H}^T = \mathbf{e}\mathbf{H}^T, \tag{5.1}$$

which is merely the transpose of the jth column of **H**, multiplied by b. The syndrome will therefore have b as its leading nonzero symbol. Then decoding can be effected by dividing the syndrome by its leading symbol b. The resulting vector will match the column of **H** corresponding to the position of the error, and correction is accomplished by subtracting b from this symbol in the received vector.

A generalized Hamming code with the maximum number $n = (q^m - 1)/(q-1)$ of symbols is perfect, since the $n(q-1) = q^m - 1$ single-error patterns and the zero vector must all be coset leaders, thus accounting for the total of q^m cosets. (See Problem 5.3.)

The weight distribution is easily found for the null space of the Hamming codes (see Section 8.4), and therefore the weight distribution for the Hamming codes can be found from MacWilliams's formula. (See Problems 5.7, 5.8, and 5.9.)

5.2 The Golay (23, 12) Code

Golay, in a search for perfect codes, noticed that

$$\binom{23}{0} + \binom{23}{1} + \binom{23}{2} + \binom{23}{3} = 2^{11}$$

and that this indicated the possibility of a (23, 12) perfect binary code that corrects all patterns of three or fewer errors. He found that such a code did exist. It will not be described here, since it reappears later as a cyclic code and will be discussed as such.

The number of code vectors for the (23, 12) code and for the code formed by adding to it an over-all parity check to form a (24, 12) code are listed in Table 5.1.

Table 5.1. Weight of Code Vectors in the Golay Codes

Weight	Number of Code Words of This Weight	
	(23, 12) Code	(24, 12) Code
0	1	1
7	253	0
8	506	759
11	1288	0
12	1288	2576
15	506	0
16	253	759
23	1	0
24	0	1
Total	4096	4096

The codes that have one information symbol repeated $2m + 1$ times correct all combinations of m or fewer errors and no patterns of more than m errors. These trivial codes, the Hamming codes, and the Golay (23, 12) code are the only known perfect binary codes. The only known nontrivial perfect nonbinary code is an (11, 6) ternary code with $t = 3$ (see Problem 5.19). There are a number of results indicating that perfect codes are scarce, and it even seems quite likely that there are no others (Lloyd 1957; Shapiro and Slotnick 1959; Cohen 1964; Alter 1968).

5.3 Optimum Codes for the Binary Symmetric Channel

The search for optimum codes for the binary symmetric channel has so far met with very limited success. The codes with one information symbol repeated an odd number of times are optimum in a trivial way, and the Hamming codes provide another infinite class. Certain codes found by omitting columns from Hamming codes can be shown to be quasi-perfect and therefore optimum. (See Problem 5.3.) Double-error-correcting Bose-Chaudhuri-Hocquenghem (BCH) codes are quasi-perfect and therefore optimum (Gorenstein 1960). The values of n and k for other known optimum codes are listed in Table 5.2.

Table 5.2. Values of (n, k) for Known Nontrivial Optimum Group Codes for the Binary Symmetric Channel for $n \leq 31$. Some longer codes are listed in Wagner (1966*b*, 1967) (t = the largest number such that all patterns of t or fewer errors are coset leaders)

Quasi-Perfect Codes					
(n, k)	t	Reference	(n, k)	t	Reference
(5, 2)	1	Slepian (1956*a*)	(22, 12)	2	Fontaine & Peterson (1959)
(6, 2)	1	”	(22, 13)	2	Wagner (1966*b*)
(8, 2)	2	”	(22, 15)	1	Fontaine & Peterson (1959)
(9, 5)	1	”	(23, 12)	3	Golay (1954)
(10, 5)	1	”	(23, 14)	2	Wagner (1966*b*)
(11, 4)	2	”	(23, 16)	1	Fontaine & Peterson (1959)
(11, 6)	1	”	(24, 12)	3	Golay (1954)
(14, 6)	2	Fontaine & Peterson (1959)	(25, 12)	3	Fontaine & Peterson (1959)
(14, 8)	1	”	(25, 15)	1	Wagner (1966*b*)
(15, 9)	1	”	(26, 16)	1	”
(17, 9)	2	Prange (private communication)	(27, 17)	1	”
(19, 10)	2	Wagner (1967)	(28, 18)	1	”
(20, 11)	2	Wagner (1966*b*)	(29, 19)	1	”
(21, 12)	2	Prange (1958)	(30, 20)	1	”
(21, 14)	1	Fontaine & Peterson (1959)	(31, 20)	2	Wagner (1967)

Other Codes					
(n, k)	t	Reference	(n, k)	t	Reference
(7, 2)	1	Slepian (1965*a*)	(14, 3)	3	Fontaine & Peterson (1959)
(8, 3)	1	”	(14, 4)	3	”
(9, 2)	2	”	(14, 5)	2	”
(9, 3)	1	”	(15, 2)	4	”
(10, 2)	2	”	(15, 3)	3	”
(10, 3)	2	”	(15, 4)	3	”
(10, 4)	1	”	(15, 5)	3	”
(11, 2)	3	”	(16, 2)	4	”
(11, 3)	2	”	(16, 3)	3	”
(11, 5)	1	Fontaine & Peterson (1959)	(16, 4)	3	”
(12, 2)	3	Slepian (1956*a*)	(16, 5)	3	Tokura, Taniguchi, Kasami (1967)
(12, 3)	2	”	(16, 8)	2	”
(12, 4)	2	Fontaine & Peterson (1959)	(17, 2)	5	Fontaine & Peterson (1959)
(12, 5)	1	”	(17, 3)	4	”
(12, 6)	1	”	(17, 6)	3	Tokura, Taniguchi, Kasami (1967)
(13, 2)	3	”	(18, 2)	5	Fontaine & Peterson (1959)
(13, 3)	3	”	(18, 3)	4	”
(13, 4)	2	”	(18, 7)	3	Tokura, Taniguchi, Kasami (1967)
(13, 5)	2	”	(19, 8)	3	”
(13, 6)	1	”	(20, 9)	3	”
(13, 7)	1	”	(21, 10)	3	”
(14, 2)	4	”	(22, 11)	3	”

Known optimum codes fall in one of two classes: (1) codes that have been found to be quasi-perfect and therefore must be optimum, and (2) codes that have been proved to be as good as any other code with the same total number of symbols and the same number of information symbols. In the latter case, the procedure used was typically to obtain as good a code as possible with reasonable effort, and then to compare all others with it. With the best use of present knowledge of coding theory, the task is long and tedious even for short codes (Slepian 1956*a*; Fontaine and Peterson 1959).

Since the sets of weights, numbers in the modular representation, and the α_i (the number of coset leaders of weight i) are very closely related, one is tempted to make several conjectures about them. A number of counterexamples have been found. For example, two codes have been found that have the same set of weights of code words but different sets of numbers in their modular representation and different sets of α_i. The combinations for which counterexamples have been found are listed in Table 5.3. The details are in Fontaine and Peterson (1959). It is also

Table 5.3. Counterexamples to Typical Conjectures

(n, k)	Sets of Numbers in Modular Representation	Sets of Weights of Code Words	Set of α's	Remarks
(16, 3)	Same	Different	Different	Nonoptimum
(14, 3)	Different	Same	Different	Nonoptimum
(14, 3)	Different	Different	Same	Optimum
(14, 6)	Same	Same	Different	Nonoptimum
(14, 6)	Same	Different	Same	Optimum

interesting to note that for all known cases *except the (15, 3) code* the same code is optimum for all values of channel error probability P less than one-half.

With a less stringent definition of optimum, Bose and Kuebler (1958) were able to make limited progress in finding optimum codes. They considered a code optimum if it would correct all errors of weight m or less, with m as great as possible, and would correct as many errors as possible of weight $m + 1$.

5.4 Binary Codes with Large Minimum Distance

The difficulties encountered in extending the search for optimum codes suggest that it may be more fruitful to search instead for good codes. This has been done by several authors, and some of the results are tabulated in this section.

Table 5.4. List of Largest Known Values of k for Given Values of n and d

n/d	3	4	5	6	7	8	9	10	11	12	13	14
3	1_H											
4	1	1_E										
5	2	1	1									
6	3	2	1	1								
7	4_H	3_A	1	1	1							
8	4	4_E	2_S	1	1	1						
9	5	4	2	2_B	1	1	1					
10	6	5	3	2_D	1	1	1	1				
11	7	6	4_S	3	2_S	1	1	1	1			
12	8	7	4	4_E	2	2_S	1	1	1	1		
13	9	8	5	4	3_F	2_D	1	1	1	1	1	
14	10	9	6	5	4	3_E	2_F	1	1	1	1	1
15	11_H	10_A	7_B	6_A	5_B	4_A	2_D	2_F	1	1	1	1
16	11	11_E	8	7	5	5_E	2	2_D	1	1	1	1
17	12	11	9_P	8_A	6	5	3_F	2	2_D	1	1	1
18	13	12	9	9_E	7	6	3	3_E	2_D	2_F	1	1
19	14	13	10	9	8	7	4	3	2	2_D	1	1
20	15	14	11	10	9	8	5_D	4	3_D	2	2_D	1
21	16	15	12_B	11_A	10	9	5	5_B	3	3_B	2_I	2_F
22	17	16	13_W	12_E	11	10	6_W	5	4	3	2_I	2_I
23	18	17	14_W	13_E	12_G	11_A	6_I	6_E	5_D	4	2_I	2_I
24	19	18	14	14_E	12_I	12_E	7_{PA}	6_W	5	5_M	3_C	2_I
25	20	19	15	14	12	12_I^*	7	7_E	6	5_I^*	3	3_E^*
26	21	20	16	15	13_Q	12	8	7	6	6_Z	4*	3
27	22	21	17	16	14_D	13	9	8	7	6	5_D^*	4*
28	23	22	18	17	14_D	14_Q^*	10	9	8	7	5	5_M^*
29	24	23	19	18	15_D	14	11_D	10	9	8	6_D^*	5
30	25	24	20	19	16_D	15_Q^*	11_I	11_D	10	9	6_I	6_D^*
31	26_H	25_A	21_B	20_A	16_B	16_K	11_I	11_I	11_B	10_A	6_I	6_I

* Known to be best.
No subscript Shortened version of code below.
A Code obtained by discarding all odd-weight code words in the code to the left.
B BCH code.
C Calabi and Myrvaagnes (1964).
D Code obtained by dropping a parity digit of code to right and below.
E Code obtained by adding over-all parity check to code to left and above.
F Fontaine and Peterson (1959).
G Golay code.
H Hamming code.
I Code obtained by inserting a dummy parity digit in code above.
K Karlin (1969).
M MacDonald code (1958,1960).
P Prange (private communication).
Q Quasi-cyclic code (Chen 1969).
S Slepian (1956*b*).
W Wagner (1965) and Calabi and Myrvaagnes (1964).
Z Goethals (1969) (see Problem 5.15) and Calabi and Myrvaagnes (1964).

A good code will be taken here to be one that has the largest number of information symbols for given values of code length and minimum distance. Binary linear codes of this type are listed in Table 5.4 for $n \leqq 31$ and $d \leqq 14$. The table can also be used to determine the largest known value of d for given values of n and k, of course.

For $n \leqq 24$ or $d \leqq 6$, the various bounds on minimum distance show that all listed codes are best in the sense that it is not possible to find a code with the same n and d for which k is larger. For $n \geqq 25$ and $d \geqq 7$, the codes marked with an asterisk are also known to be best. (See Calabi and Myrvaagnes 1964; Wagner 1965, 1966b, 1967; and Tokura, Taniguchi and Kasami 1967.)

Every code in the table is subscripted (some with a blank). This subscript and the legend enable one to construct any code listed.

It is interesting to note that in several cases it is possible to construct a nonlinear code with more code words than the best linear code with the same n and d. Sloane (1970) has developed a class of nonlinear binary single-error-correcting codes having more code words than the best comparable linear codes. Preparata (1968), generalizing the work of Green (1966) and Nordstrom and Robinson (1967), has constructed a class of systematic, double-error-correcting, nonlinear codes with the largest possible number of code words. These latter codes are closely related to cyclic codes and can be encoded with a nonlinear feedback shift register. A decoding procedure has also been devised for these codes.

5.5 Reed-Muller Codes

The Reed-Muller codes are a class of binary group codes covering a wide range of rate and minimum distance. They are, in fact, equivalent to cyclic codes with an over-all parity check added and are the basis for the majority-logic decodable codes discussed in Chapter 10.

For any m and $r < m$, there is a Reed-Muller code for which

$$\begin{aligned} n &= 2^m, \\ k &= 1 + \binom{m}{1} + \cdots + \binom{m}{r}, \\ n - k &= 1 + \binom{m}{1} + \cdots + \binom{m}{m-r-1}, \\ d &= 2^{m-r} = \text{minimum weight}. \end{aligned} \tag{5.2}$$

The construction of these codes requires a little mathematical development. Consider the following set of vectors over the field of two elements. Let $\mathbf{v}_0$ be a vector whose 2^m components are all 1's, and let $\mathbf{v}_1, \mathbf{v}_2, \ldots, \mathbf{v}_m$ be the rows of a matrix that has all possible m-tuples as columns, as illustrated for $m = 4$ in Figure 5.1. Now define the vector product of two vectors as follows:

$$\begin{aligned} \mathbf{u} &= (a_1, a_2, \ldots, a_n), \\ \mathbf{v} &= (b_1, b_2, \ldots, b_n), \\ \mathbf{uv} &= (a_1 b_1, a_2 b_2, \ldots, a_n b_n). \end{aligned} \tag{5.3}$$

With this definition, the vectors form a commutative linear associative algebra. Finally consider the collection of vectors formed by multiplying the vectors $\mathbf{v}_i$ two at a time, three at a time, and so forth, up to m at a time, as illustrated in Figure 5.1. It can be shown that these vectors are linearly independent. (Note that in Figure 5.1 the rows could be rearranged to form a matrix with 1's on the main diagonal and 0's below.)

The rth-order Reed-Muller code is formed by using as a basis the vectors $\mathbf{v}_0, \mathbf{v}_1, \ldots, \mathbf{v}_m$, and all vector products of these vectors r or fewer at a time. Clearly the inner product of two vectors is zero if the number of 1's in the vector product is even, one if it is odd. Also, for any vector

$$\begin{aligned}
\mathbf{v}_0 &= (1111111111111111) \\
\mathbf{v}_4 &= (0000000011111111) \\
\mathbf{v}_3 &= (0000111100001111) \\
\mathbf{v}_2 &= (0011001100110011) \\
\mathbf{v}_1 &= (0101010101010101) \\
\mathbf{v}_4\mathbf{v}_3 &= (0000000000001111) \\
\mathbf{v}_4\mathbf{v}_2 &= (0000000000110011) \\
\mathbf{v}_4\mathbf{v}_1 &= (0000000001010101) \\
\mathbf{v}_3\mathbf{v}_2 &= (0000001100000011) \\
\mathbf{v}_3\mathbf{v}_1 &= (0000010100000101) \\
\mathbf{v}_2\mathbf{v}_1 &= (0001000100010001) \\
\mathbf{v}_4\mathbf{v}_3\mathbf{v}_2 &= (0000000000000011) \\
\mathbf{v}_4\mathbf{v}_3\mathbf{v}_1 &= (0000000000000101) \\
\mathbf{v}_4\mathbf{v}_2\mathbf{v}_1 &= (0000000000010001) \\
\mathbf{v}_3\mathbf{v}_2\mathbf{v}_1 &= (0000000100000001) \\
\mathbf{v}_4\mathbf{v}_3\mathbf{v}_2\mathbf{v}_1 &= (0000000000000001)
\end{aligned}$$

Figure 5.1. Vectors used as a basis for the Reed-Muller codes of length 16.

$\mathbf{v}$, $\mathbf{v}^2 = \mathbf{v}$. Finally, the only product that has an odd number of 1's is the product of all the vectors $\mathbf{v}_1, \ldots, \mathbf{v}_m$. Thus the vector product of any vector in the basis of an rth-order code with any vector in the basis for an $(m-r-1)$-order code is a vector in the basis for an $(m-1)$-order code and therefore has an even number of 1's in it. Therefore any vector in the rth-order code is orthogonal to any vector in the basis for the $(m-r-1)$-order code, that is, any vector which is the product of $m-r-1$ or fewer of the vectors $\mathbf{v}_1, \ldots, \mathbf{v}_m$. The sum of the dimensions of these codes is n, and hence each is the dual code of the other. It follows also that the rth-order Reed-Muller code is the null space of the matrix whose row vectors are $\mathbf{v}_0, \mathbf{v}_1, \ldots, \mathbf{v}_m$, and all vector products of these vectors taken no more than $m-r-1$ at a time. Because the matrix formed by the rows $\mathbf{v}_0, \mathbf{v}_1, \mathbf{v}_2, \ldots, \mathbf{v}_m$ is the parity-check matrix for the Hamming single-error-correcting double-error-detecting code, this code is the same as the Reed-Muller code of order $m-2$.

An important feature of the Reed-Muller codes is that they can be decoded in a simple manner. This can best be seen by an example. Consider the second-order code for $m = 4$. Then this is a (16, 11) code, and the 11 information symbols $a_0, a_4, a_3, a_2, a_1, a_{43}, a_{42}, a_{41}, a_{32}, a_{31}, a_{21}$ are coded into the vector:

$$a_0\mathbf{v}_0 + a_4\mathbf{v}_4 + a_3\mathbf{v}_3 + a_2\mathbf{v}_2 + a_1\mathbf{v}_1 + a_{43}\mathbf{v}_4\mathbf{v}_3 + a_{42}\mathbf{v}_4\mathbf{v}_2$$

$$+ a_{41}\mathbf{v}_4\mathbf{v}_1 + a_{32}\mathbf{v}_3\mathbf{v}_2 + a_{31}\mathbf{v}_3\mathbf{v}_1 + a_{21}\mathbf{v}_2\mathbf{v}_1 = (b_1, b_2, \ldots, b_n).$$

The problem is to determine the a's from a received vector even though errors may have occurred. Note that the sum of the first four components, as elements of the field of two elements, is zero for every basis vector except $\mathbf{v}_2\mathbf{v}_1$. Thus, in the absence of errors,

$$b_1 + b_2 + b_3 + b_4 = a_{21}.$$

The same is true of the next four components, and

$$b_5 + b_6 + b_7 + b_8 = a_{21}.$$

and also

$$b_9 + b_{10} + b_{11} + b_{12} = a_{21},$$

$$b_{13} + b_{14} + b_{15} + b_{16} = a_{21}.$$

Thus there are four independent determinations of a_{21}. In general there would be 2^{m-r} independent determinations. Errors may cause some of these to be incorrect, but each error can affect only one determination, and therefore, if a_{21} is taken to be equal to the value occurring most frequently, with any combination of $2^{m-r-1} - 1$ or fewer errors, a_{21} will still be decoded correctly. Similar determinations of a_{31}, a_{32}, a_{41}, a_{42}, and a_{43} can be made.

After these have been determined,

$$a_{43}\mathbf{v}_4\mathbf{v}_3 + a_{42}\mathbf{v}_4\mathbf{v}_2 + a_{41}\mathbf{v}_4\mathbf{v}_1 + a_{32}\mathbf{v}_3\mathbf{v}_2 + a_{31}\mathbf{v}_3\mathbf{v}_1 + a_{21}\mathbf{v}_2\mathbf{v}_1$$

can be subtracted from the received vector. This, in the absence of errors, would leave

$$\mathbf{r}' = a_0\mathbf{v}_0 + a_4\mathbf{v}_4 + a_3\mathbf{v}_3 + a_2\mathbf{v}_2 + a_1\mathbf{v}_1 = (b'_1, b'_2, \ldots, b'_n).$$

and the next set of coefficients can be determined in a similar way. There are eight equations that a_1 should satisfy:

$$a_1 = b'_1 + b'_2 = b'_3 + b'_4 = b'_5 + b'_6 = b'_7 + b'_8 = b'_9 + b'_{10}$$
$$= b'_{11} + b'_{12} = b'_{13} + b'_{14} = b'_{15} + b'_{16}.$$

Similar equations hold for a_2, a_3, and a_4. Finally, in the absence of errors,

$$\mathbf{r}' - a_4\mathbf{v}_4 - a_3\mathbf{v}_3 - a_2\mathbf{v}_2 - a_1\mathbf{v}_1 = a_0\mathbf{v}_0.$$

This should be all 0's if $a_0 = 0$, all 1's if $a_0 = 1$, and a_0 can be taken to be whichever occurs more frequently.

Since this decoding system can correct all combinations of $2^{m-r-1} - 1$ or fewer errors, the minimum distance must be at least $2(2^{m-r-1} - 1) + 1 = 2^{m-r} - 1$, and, since the code vectors all have even weight, it must be at least 2^{m-r}. But the last basis vectors have weight 2^{m-r}, so this is exactly the minimum weight.

The scheme for determining which sums of symbols in the received vector should equal a given information symbol can be described as follows. Arrange the symbols in each of the original vectors $\mathbf{v}_1, \ldots, \mathbf{v}_m$ as in Figure 5.1, and call the component corresponding to the jth 0 in $\mathbf{v}_i$ and the component corresponding to the jth 1 in $\mathbf{v}_i$ matching components for $\mathbf{v}_i$. Then the 2^{m-1} sums of matching components of $\mathbf{v}_i$ are used in determining a_i. The 2^{m-2} sums of four components used to determine a_{ij} are found by taking a matching pair of components for $\mathbf{v}_i$, and with each of them the component that matches for $\mathbf{v}_j$. Similarly, each determination of a_{ijk} is a sum of a pair of matching components $\mathbf{v}_i$, together with their matching components for $\mathbf{v}_j$, and the matching component for $\mathbf{v}_k$ for each of these, to make a total of eight components. The process can be continued in a similar manner.

These codes have an interesting geometric interpretation. Consider a space of m dimensions in which the coordinates are elements of the field of two elements. There are 2^m points, and each column in Figure 5.1 corresponds to one of these points. The vector $\mathbf{v}_i$ has a 1 for all points that have their ith coordinate X_i equal to 0, that is, for every point in the $(m-1)$-dimensional X_i-hyperplane. (This is an incidence vector.) The vector $\mathbf{v}_i\mathbf{v}_j$ has a 1 for every point that is in both the X_i and X_j hyperplanes and hence is the incidence matrix for an $(m-2)$-dimensional *flat* through the origin, and so on.

Since the rth-order code is the null space of the $(m-r-1)$-order code, each product of $m-r-1$ or fewer vectors $\mathbf{v}_i$ defines a parity-check rule. Geometrically, if the symbols of the code are placed at the corresponding points in the m-dimensional space, each parity-check rule is a parity check on the symbols associated with the points of a flat of $r+1$ or more dimensions through the origin, and every such flat gives an independent parity-check rule.

The decoding method has the following geometric interpretation: Each basis vector in the code is a product of r or fewer vectors $\mathbf{v}_i, \ldots, \mathbf{v}_m$. An r-dimensional flat has 2^r points, and hence a product of r vectors $\mathbf{v}_i$ has 2^{m-r} ones. Now through each of these points there is a perpendicular flat of r dimensions, or 2^r points. These are the sets of points that correspond to the sums used to determine the information symbols during decoding. Such a set of points will serve that purpose if its incidence vector has an odd number of 1's in common with the vector whose coefficient is to be determined but an even number in common with all other vectors that are products of r or fewer of the vectors $\mathbf{v}_i$, because then in the sum the desired coefficient will not drop out, but all others will cancel. These sets of points have this property because, being perpendicular to the given flat, each intersects it in one point, but each intersects every other flat of dimension r or more either not at all or in a line or higher-dimensional flat and so has in common with it an even number of points 2^j, where j is the dimension of the intersection.

In Chapter 10 the Reed-Muller code will be shown to be equivalent to binary Euclidean geometry codes, which are cyclic with an over-all parity check.

5.6 Codes Derived from Hadamard Matrices

A *Hadamard matrix* is an orthogonal $n \times n$ matrix whose elements are the real numbers $+1$ and -1. An *orthogonal matrix* is a matrix whose rows are orthogonal n-tuples (over the field of real numbers in this case).

THEOREM 5.1. *If there exists an $n \times n$ Hadamard matrix, there exists a binary code with n symbols, $2n$ code vectors, and minimum distance $n/2$. (This is not necessarily a linear code.)*

Proof. Let **H** be a Hadamard matrix. The code is constructed as follows: Form a set of $2n$ vectors $\mathbf{v}_1, \mathbf{v}_2, \ldots, \mathbf{v}_n, -\mathbf{v}_1, -\mathbf{v}_2, \ldots, -\mathbf{v}_n$, where $\mathbf{v}_1, \mathbf{v}_2, \ldots, \mathbf{v}_n$ are the rows of **H**. Then in each of these change the 1's to 0's, and the -1's to 1's. This gives a set of $2n$ vectors of n binary symbols each. Since corresponding components of $\mathbf{v}_i$ and $-\mathbf{v}_i$ are different, the distance between $\mathbf{v}_i$ and $-\mathbf{v}_i$ is n. Since $\pm\mathbf{v}_i$ and $\pm\mathbf{v}_j$ are orthogonal if $i \neq j$, they must match in half the positions and differ in the other half, and thus the corresponding binary vectors are at distance $n/2$.

Q.E.D.

THEOREM 5.2. *If* **H** *is an $n \times n$ Hadamard matrix, then the matrix*

$$\mathbf{H}' = \begin{bmatrix} \mathbf{H} & \mathbf{H} \\ \mathbf{H} & -\mathbf{H} \end{bmatrix}$$

is a $2n \times 2n$ Hadamard matrix.

Proof. The matrix $\mathbf{H}'$ is clearly a square matrix with $+1$ and -1 as elements. The dot product of the jth and $(n+j)$th rows $(j \leqq n)$ is

$$(\mathbf{v}_j, \mathbf{v}_j) \cdot (\mathbf{v}_j, -\mathbf{v}_j) = \mathbf{v}_j \cdot \mathbf{v}_j + \mathbf{v}_j \cdot (-\mathbf{v}_j) = n - n = 0$$

For any other combination of rows,

$$(\mathbf{v}_i, \pm\mathbf{v}_i) \cdot (\mathbf{v}_j, \pm\mathbf{v}_j) = \mathbf{v}_i \cdot \mathbf{v}_j \pm \mathbf{v}_i \cdot \mathbf{v}_j = 0 \pm 0 = 0$$

and thus $\mathbf{H}'$ is an orthogonal matrix. Q.E.D.

It is easily verified that

$$\mathbf{H}_2 = \begin{bmatrix} 1 & 1 \\ 1 & -1 \end{bmatrix}$$

is a Hadamard matrix, and therefore

$$\mathbf{H}_4 = \begin{bmatrix} 1 & 1 & 1 & 1 \\ 1 & -1 & 1 & -1 \\ 1 & 1 & -1 & -1 \\ 1 & -1 & -1 & 1 \end{bmatrix}$$

is also, by Theorem 5.2. By repeated application of Theorem 5.2, a $2^m \times 2^m$ Hadamard matrix $\mathbf{H}_{2^m}$ can be constructed for any positive integer m. The resulting code is the same as a first-order Reed-Muller code. In fact, the seven nonzero code words in the code derived from $\mathbf{H}_4$ match exactly the last four columns of the matrix **C** on page 62, and therefore the code has a modular representation $(0, 0, 0, 1, 1, 1, 1)$. It is true in general that the codes derived from $\mathbf{H}_{2^m}$ have a modular representation vector consisting of $2^{m-1} - 1$ zeros followed by 2^{m-1} ones if the matrix $\mathbf{M}$ in Equation 3.17 has its columns arranged in order as binary numbers.

For other values of n, the binary code derived from a Hadamard matrix cannot be a group code, since the number of code vectors is not a power of 2. It can be shown easily that, if n is greater than 2, it must be a multiple of 4. Many methods found for constructing Hadamard matrices are presented in Hall (1967), and recent papers by Spence (1967), Goethals and Seidl (1967), and Wallis (1969). These include a number of infinite classes, and all possible multiples of 4 up to 200 with the single exception of 188. Also, the existence of a Hadamard matrix has not been disproved for any m that is a multiple of 4.

5.7 Product Codes

It is possible to combine the use of two or more codes so as to obtain a more powerful code. For example, a single parity check on a vector is capable of detecting all single errors. Now consider information symbols arranged in a rectangular array, as shown in Figure 5.2, with a single over-all parity check on each row and each column. This iteration of a simple parity-check code is capable of correcting all single errors, for if a single error occurs, the row and column in which it occurs are indicated by parity-check failures. In fact, this code, which is a linear code, has minimum weight 4, the minimum weight code word having nonzero components at the intersections of two rows and two columns. This code is actually used for error detection on magnetic-tape units used with computers.

Information Symbols	Checks on Rows
Checks on Columns	Checks on Checks

(a) General arrangement

11010	1
10001	0
10110	1
10000	1
11111	1
01001	0
11011	0

(b) A binary product code

Figure 5.2. Structure of product codes.

An important generalization results if each row of the array is a vector taken from one code and each column a vector from a different code. Product codes can also be generalized to three or higher dimensional arrays. These are all linear codes, and the generator matrix for the product of two codes is combinatorially equivalent to the tensor product of the generator matrices of the two original codes.

It should be noted that certain symbols, such as those in the lower right-hand corners in Figure 5.2, are checks on check symbols. These can be filled in as checks on rows and will be consistent as checks on columns, or vice versa. If they are filled in as checks on rows according to the parity-check rules for the row code, then each parity-check column is actually a linear combination of the columns that contain information symbols. Each of these has parity symbols added to it to make it a code vector, and therefore the parity-check columns, being linear combinations of code vectors for the column code, are also code vectors for the column code.

Several observations can be made about the error-correcting ability of these codes:

THEOREM 5.3 (*Elias*). *The minimum weight for the product of two codes is the product of the minimum weights for the codes.*

Proof. If one code has a minimum weight w_1 and the other w_2, a vector in the product code must have at least w_1 nonzero elements in each row that contains a nonzero element and at least w_2 nonzero elements in each column that contains a nonzero element and therefore has $w_1 w_2$ nonzero elements if it has any at all. Also, at least one such pattern is possible if the first code has a vector of weight w_1 and the second a vector of weight w_2. Q.E.D.

In what follows, the subscripts 1 and 2 refer to the row and column codes, respectively. If a product code array is filled with received digits on a row-by-row basis, then at most b_2 digits of a burst of length not greater than $n_1 b_2$ can be in any column. Thus if the column code has burst-correcting ability b_2, the burst-correcting ability of the product code, b, is at least $b_2 n_1$. A similar argument applies if the array is filled column-by-column,

$$b \geq \max(b_2 n_1, b_1 n_2). \tag{5.4}$$

In fact, it is possible to improve on this result slightly (Problem 5.11).

Because product codes have some random and burst-correcting capabilities, it is natural to ask what is the burst-correcting ability when the code is used to correct all patterns of weight $t = [(d_1 d_2 - 1)/2]$ or less. The following theorem provides a partial answer:

THEOREM 5.4 (*Burton and Weldon*). *The product of an* (n_1, k_1) *code with error-correcting ability* $t_1 = [(d_1 - 1)/2]$ *and an* (n_2, k_2) *code with* $t_2 = [(d_2 - 1)/2]$ *can correct all patterns of weight* $t = [(d_1 d_2 - 1)/2]$ *or less and all bursts of length up to* $b = \max(n_1 t_2, n_2 t_1)$.

Proof. The random-error-correcting ability of the code is given by Theorem 5.3; it remains to show only that no coset contains a pattern of weight t or less and a burst of length b or less.

As before, suppose the code array is filled on a row-by-row basis. Then each column can contain at most t_2 errors in a burst of length $n_1 t_2$ or less. If this burst and a random-error pattern of weight not greater than t are in the same coset, then their sum is a code word. Each column of such a code word has either weight zero or weight at least d_2. Each nonzero column must be composed of at least $d_2 - t_2$ random errors and at most t_2 errors from the burst. Thus the random errors must be distributed among at most

$$\left[\frac{t}{d_2 - t_2}\right]$$

columns. Hence the sum array contains at most

$$\left[\frac{t}{d_2 - t_2}\right] \cdot t_2 + t < 2t < d$$

nonzero elements. But since the code has minimum weight d, the array cannot be a code word and $b \geqq n_1 t_2$. By interchanging the function of row and column, it can also be shown that $b \geqq n_2 t_1$. Q.E.D.

THEOREM 5.5. *For a binary symmetric channel, if one code has probability of error* $f_1(P)$ *and another* $f_2(P)$, *their product is capable of decoding with probability of error no greater than* $f_2[f_1(P)]$.

Proof. Suppose that the first code applies to rows, and that after all the information is received, the decoding is done on rows alone. Then the probability of an error in any row is $f_1(P)$, and therefore, the probability that any particular symbol is in error is no greater than this. Also, the rows are independent, and, since each column contains only one symbol from each row, the symbols in each column are independent. Then the columns are decoded using the column code, and the resulting probability of error is no greater than $f_2[f_1(P)]$. There might, of course, be a better way to decode. Q.E.D.

Elias used these ideas in an interesting way to find for the binary symmetric channel a sequence of codes whose probabilities of error approach zero and whose rates approach a limit greater than zero as the length of the codes approaches infinity. This is one of the few known examples of a coding system with both of these properties.

The system uses the Hamming single-error-correcting, double-error-detecting code. This code has $n = 2^m$ symbols, of which $m + 1$ are parity-check symbols and $2^m - m - 1$ are information symbols. (See Section 5.1.) It is capable of correcting single errors. All combinations of an even number of errors are either detected or form a code word; in either case no change is made in the received vector. However, if the number of errors is odd and at least three, the correction procedure will be applied, and one symbol that probably was correct will be changed, thus introducing an extra error. The probability for a particular pattern of i errors is P^iQ^{n-i}; there are $\binom{n}{i}$ such patterns, and therefore the probability that i errors will occur is $P(i) = \binom{n}{i}P^iQ^{n-i}$. The average number of errors expected per block, then, is

$$\begin{aligned}
nP_1 &\leqq \sum_{\text{even } i \geqq 2}^{n} iP(i) + \sum_{\text{odd } i \geqq 3}^{n-1} (i+1)P(i) \\
&\leqq 2\binom{n}{2}P^2Q^{n-2} + \sum_{i=3}^{n}(i+1)\binom{n}{i}P^iQ^{n-i} \\
&= 2\binom{n}{2}P^2\left[Q^{n-2} + \sum_{i=3}^{n} \frac{(i+1)\binom{n}{i}}{2P^2\binom{n}{2}} P^iQ^{n-i}\right] \\
&= 2\binom{n}{2}P^2\left[Q^{n-2} + \sum_{i=3}^{n} \frac{i+1}{i(i-1)} \binom{n-2}{i-2}P^{i-2}Q^{n-i}\right] \\
&\leqq 2\binom{n}{2}P^2\left[Q^{n-2} + \sum_{i=3}^{n} \binom{n-2}{i-2}P^{i-2}Q^{n-i}\right] \\
&= 2\binom{n}{2}P^2\left[Q^{n-2} + \sum_{i=1}^{n-2} \binom{n-2}{i}P^{i}Q^{n-2-i}\right] \\
&= 2\binom{n}{2}P^2 = n(n-1)P^2
\end{aligned}$$

and therefore, the probability that an error will remain in any symbol after correction is

$$P_1 \leqq (n-1)P^2 < nP^2. \tag{5.5}$$

Now consider the product of r of these codes starting with $n = 2^m$ and doubling the length of the code introduced at each stage, so that the code used at the ith stage has length 2^{m+i-1}. Let $P_0 = P$ denote the channel probability of error and P_i the probability of error after i iterations. Then by Equation 5.5,

$$P_i \leqq 2^{m+i-1} P_{i-1}^2 \tag{5.6}$$

and repeated use of Equation 5.6 together with Equation 4.64 yields

$$\begin{aligned} P_r &\leqq (2^m)^{2^{r-1}} (2^{m+1})^{2^{r-2}} (2^{m+2})^{2^{r-3}} \cdots (2^{m+r-1}) P_0^{2^r} \\ &\leqq 2^{m2^r + 2^r} P^{2^r} = (2^{m+1} P_0)^{2^r} \end{aligned} \tag{5.7}$$

and this approaches zero as r approaches infinity as long as $2^m P_0 < 1/2$, that is, if the expected number of errors per row in the first iteration is less than 1/2.

Finally the fraction of the symbols that will be information symbols after r iterations can be estimated as follows: The number of parity-check symbols in the code used at the ith iteration is $\log_2 n + 1 = m + i$, so the fraction of information symbols is

$$1 - \frac{m+i}{2^{m+i-1}}$$

and at each stage check symbols are added, cutting down the overall fraction of information symbols by this ratio. Therefore, the overall rate is

$$R = \left(1 - \frac{m+1}{2^m}\right)\left(1 - \frac{m+2}{2^{m+1}}\right) \cdots \left(1 - \frac{m+r}{2^{m+r-1}}\right).$$

This can be bounded by use of the relation

$$(1-a)(1-b) > 1 - (a+b) \qquad \text{if } a > 0, b > 0,$$

and this together with Equation 4.53 yields

$$R > 1 - \left(\frac{m+1}{2^m} + \frac{m+2}{2^{m+1}} + \cdots + \frac{m+r}{2^{m+r-1}}\right) > 1 - \frac{m+2}{2^{m-1}}. \tag{5.8}$$

In summary, then, if the channel probability of error is sufficiently small that the expected number of errors in each row of the first iteration is less than one-half, the probability of error can be made arbitrarily small by taking enough iterations, and still the rate, or fraction of symbols that carry information, is greater than a fixed constant for any number of iterations.

The rate for this code falls short of the rate known to be possible by Shannon's fundamental theorem for the noisy channel. In fact, the efficiency in this respect is limited in a sense by the efficiency of the first iteration. The probability of error (and efficiency) of the first iteration is limited for short codes by the sphere-packing bound, so that, in order to increase efficiency beyond a certain point, the length of the first iteration would have to be increased. (This notion of efficiency can be made precise. (See Peterson 1958*b*.)) This may, however, be the fault only of the decoding method, and not of the code itself.

Another important point is that the minimum weight of the product of r codes is 4^r, since a code of minimum weight 4 is used at each step. The ratio of minimum weight to code length,

$$\frac{d}{b} = \frac{2^{2r}}{2^m \times 2^{m+1} \ldots 2^{m+r-1}} = 2^{2r-mr-(r(r-1)/2)}, \tag{5.9}$$

approaches zero as r approaches infinity and therefore falls short of what the Varsharmov-Gilbert bound shows is possible. In addition, the decoding system described is not optimum, and so not even all the errors that Equation 5.9 indicates could be corrected. The code succeeds by correcting the overwhelming majority of the likely error patterns, many of which consist of many more than $d/2$ errors.

Under certain conditions product codes are equivalent to cyclic codes. These codes are discussed in Section 8.12.

5.8 Graph-Theoretic Codes

A *linear undirected graph* is a collection of m nodes and n branches. Figure 5.3 shows a graph with $m = 10$ and $n = 15$. Now number the branches from 1 to n in an arbitrary manner. Then corresponding to any subset of branches there is a binary n-tuple whose ith component is 1 if the ith branch is in the subset, 0 if it is not. For example, the set of three branches (2, 3, and 8) labeled "cut-set" corresponds to the n-tuple (0 1 1 0 0 0 0 1 0 0 0 0 0 0 0).

There are two types of linear codes associated with any linear graph:

1. The *circuit code* of a graph consists of the set of n-tuples which correspond to circuits (closed paths) and disjoint unions of circuits. This set forms a group under modulo-2 addition since the modulo-2 sum of two circuits is either another circuit or a disjoint union of circuits.

2. A *cut-set* is a collection of branches crossed by a line dividing the set of nodes into two disjoint subsets. The *cut-set code* of a graph consists of the set of n-tuples which correspond to cut-sets and disjoint unions of cut-sets. Again the set of n-tuples forms a group under

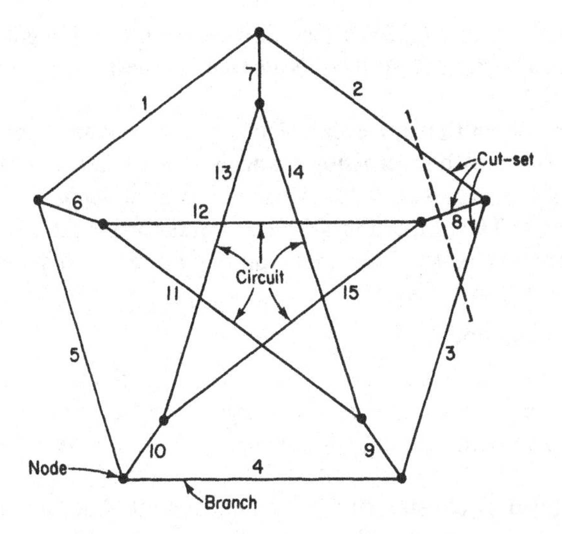

Figure 5.3. The Peterson graph; $n = 15$, $m = 10$.

modulo-2 addition since the modulo-2 sum of two cut-sets is either another cut-set or a disjoint union of cut-sets. An example of a cut-set and a circuit are shown in Figure 5.3.

It can be proved (by induction on n for example) that the dimension of the linear subspace of circuits is $n - m + 1$ and that of the subspace of cut-sets is $m - 1$. Since a cut-set always intersects a circuit in an even number of places, the inner product of a circuit n-tuple and a cut-set n-tuple is zero. Thus the circuit code is the null space of the cut-set code, and vice versa.

The minimum distance of a circuit (cut-set) code is just the number of branches in the circuit (cut-set) having the fewest branches. In the (15, 6) circuit code of Figure 5.3, $d = 5$; in the (15, 9) cut-set code, $d = 3$. For circuit codes, $d \leqq m$ because a circuit cannot have more branches than nodes.

In order to have distance d, every node in a cut-set code must have degree $\geqq d$, that is, at least d branches incident on it. Since a branch is incident on two nodes, it follows that

$$n \geqq \frac{md}{2}.$$

However, in this case, $k = m - 1$; therefore

$$d \leqq 2\left[\frac{n}{k+1}\right] < \left[\frac{2}{R}\right]. \tag{5.10}$$

In Hakimi and Frank (1965) a technique for constructing cut-set codes that meet this bound is described. Note that for these codes either d or R must be small.

It can be shown that for every planar graph (a graph which can be drawn in a plane with no crossing branches) there is a dual graph which is also planar. The cut-set code for one is the circuit code for the other, and vice versa. Thus Equation 5.10 also holds for planar circuit codes. Furthermore, if a code of planar graph has no repeated symbols, then by employing Euler's formula

$$n - m = \text{number of faces} - 2,$$

it is a relatively simple matter to show that $d \leqq 5$. (A face is an area bounded by branches and containing neither branches nor nodes in its interior.) Thus both cut-set codes and planar codes have poor distance properties.

The problem of constructing nonplanar circuit codes has been considered by several authors, thus far with rather limited success. Of the best-known codes tabulated in Table 5.4, only the (9, 4) and (6, 3) codes are known to be circuit codes; for even moderately large n, it has proved difficult to construct good codes. This has led several investigators to consider augmented circuit codes, that is, codes generated by the set of linearly independent circuits of a graph plus some other linearly independent n-tuples. Several computer-aided methods of choosing these additional n-tuples have been proposed, and in many cases the codes obtained are only slightly inferior to the best-known codes (Hakimi and Bredeson 1968).

Perhaps the most appealing feature of these augmented circuit codes is that they can be decoded with majority-logic techniques (Bredeson and Hakimi 1967; Hakimi and Bredeson 1968). (See Chapter 10.) As things stand now, however, the implementation of these codes appears to be somewhat more difficult than that of the random-error-correcting cyclic codes of Chapters 8, 9, and 10.

5.9 Low-Density Codes

As they were originally defined by Gallager (1963), a binary, low-density, parity-check code is the null space of an $(n - k) \times n$ matrix $\mathbf{H}$ with the property that every row of $\mathbf{H}$ contains K ones and every column contains J ones. Since $K(n - k) = Jn$, the code rate R is given by

$$R = 1 - \frac{J}{K}.$$

The codes are termed *low-density* because the integers J and K are usually taken to be relatively small, typically less than $0.02n$.

Every digit of a code word in a low-density code is involved in exactly J of the parity-check relationships represented by the rows of $\mathbf{H}$. Consider the set of J parity-check sums which check a particular digit. Because of the rather low density of 1's in $\mathbf{H}$, very few (usually none) of the other $n - 1$ digits will be involved in more than one of these J sums. Thus an incorrectly received bit is more likely to be involved in a large number of parity-check equations that fail than is a correct bit. Then a reasonable decoding procedure is to decide that a bit is incorrect if more than λ of the check digits in which it is involved are incorrect, where λ is a design parameter which depends on the channel error probability and the code.

Somewhat better performance can be obtained by making λ a variable (Townsend and Weldon 1967). This procedure works as follows: Examine the set of J parity-check sums associated with the first digit of the received word. If all of these sums are 1, change the first digit and recompute all check sums; otherwise do not. Examine the received digits successively, and after testing the nth digit return to the first digit and continue. When no changes have been made in the last n tests, change the decision rule to permit changes when $J - 1$ or more of the check sums are 1. Proceed until no changes have been made in the last n tests and lower the threshold by one again.

Gallager (1963) has also proposed a more complex decoding procedure that utilizes the demodulator's *a posteriori* probabilities. By means of a form of the random-coding argument of Chapter 4 he has shown that the average probability of erroneous decoding with this algorithm approaches zero exponentially with increasing code length, although not as fast as for the general class of codes. (This assumes a memoryless, binary-input, continuous-output channel.)

Low-density codes as just described do not appear to be as attractive for use in practical systems as do some of the other codes presented in this book. However, the decoding algorithms proposed for these codes have provided the basis for much of the work on majority-logic decoding described in Chapter 10.

5.10 Concatenated Codes

Forney (1966) has devised a method of combining two codes to form a larger code in a manner that resembles product codes somewhat. Figure 5.4 shows a general concatenated coding system. One code, called the

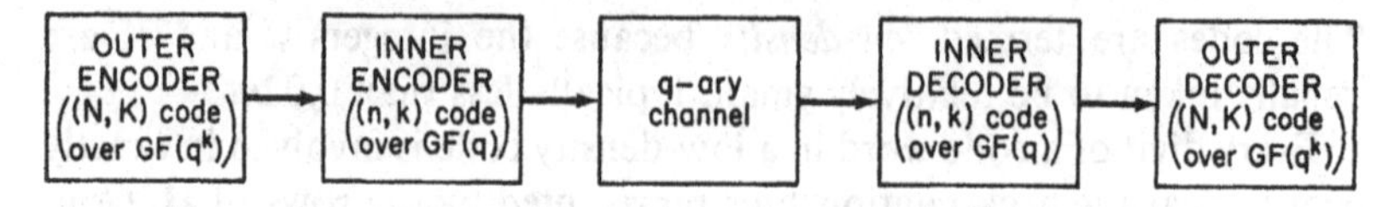

Figure 5.4. Communication channel using a concatenated code.

inner code, is an (n, k) code with symbols from $GF(q)$. The other, called the outer code, is an (N, K) code with symbols from $GF(q^k)$. Encoding is done as follows:

1. A block of kK information symbols is divided into K "bytes" of k symbols.
2. Each byte of k symbols is considered to be a symbol in $GF(q^k)$. The K bytes are then encoded into an N-byte code word in the outer code.
3. Each of the N bytes of k symbols is encoded as information symbols into an n-symbol code word in the inner code.

The set of N code words of the (n, k) inner code then is a code word in the concatenated (Nn, Kk) code.

Decoding is accomplished in the obvious way. First decoding is done on the inner code, resulting in reducing the N inner-code words to N bytes of k symbols. Then these N bytes are decoded into K bytes by the decoding for the outer code. The error-correcting ability of a concatenated code is easily characterized: There will be an uncorrectable error if the pattern of inner-code words that are uncorrectable is an uncorrectable pattern in the outer code.

Usually the inner code is chosen to be a binary (n, k) code, and the outer code is chosen to be a Reed-Solomon code or shortened Reed-Solomon code, using symbols from $GF(2^k)$. (See Chapter 9.) Forney (1966) has done extensive studies of concatenated words, how to choose the inner and outer codes, and what error probabilities can be achieved. In particular, he has shown that for the binary symmetric channel, for any rate R less than channel capacity, and for any specified ε, there exists a concatenated code with rate at least as great as R and with error probabilities not exceeding ε.

Example. The (7, 4) binary single-error-correcting Hamming code could be used as an inner code. There exists a (15, 7) Reed-Solomon code with symbols from $GF(2^4)$, which corrects any combination of four or fewer errors. A symbol from $GF(2^4)$ can be represented as four binary symbols as in Table 6.1. For this code, the 28 information bits are treated as seven 4-symbol bytes. Then each of these is coded as a (7, 4) Hamming code word. Thus the resulting code has 105 binary symbols in each code word, of which 28 are information symbols. A code word will be decoded correctly if and only if no more than four of the (7, 4) inner code words have more than a single error.

Notes

The Hamming codes were first described in Hamming (1950). Generalizations to the nonbinary case were made first by Golay (1954, 1958), and finally to the case where the symbols are taken from an arbitrary finite field by Cocke (1959). See also Slepian (1956*b*) and Zaremba (1952) and the material on Hamming codes in Chapter 8. The Golay (23, 12) code is described in Golay (1949) and as a cyclic code by Prange (1957, 1959).

Mitani (1951) discovered the Reed (1954)-Muller (1954) codes; the decoding procedure of Section 5.5 is due to Reed. These codes were also discovered by Honda (1956) in a different way, and still another description is given by Slepian (1956*a*, 1956*b*). The geometric treatment of Reed-Muller codes and others appears in a well-written and interesting report by Kautz (1959). Dwork and Heller (1959) have found a generalization beyond simply using a different field; a more natural generalization is given in Chapter 10.

Codes derived from Hadamard matrices were first found by Plotkin (1951). The connection with Hadamard matrices and symmetrical block designs was pointed out by Bose and Shrikhande (1959). (Also see Harmuth (1960).) The material on product codes is based primarily on Elias's work (1954). Some additional material appears in Burton and Weldon (1965), Calabi and Haefeli (1959), Peterson (1958*b*), and Abramson (1968). Recently, Weldon (1970) and Reddy and Robinson (1970) have devised a procedure for decoding product codes that uses the decoders for the component codes in a simple way. Berlekamp (1968*b*) has improved slightly on the rate at which Elias' error-free coding can operate. Problem 5.3 is an extension of Slepian's Proposition 5 (1956*a*, 1956*b*). Graph codes were first studied by Kasami (1961), and later by Huffman (1964) and Frazer (1964). Gallager's study of low-density codes is available as a monograph (1960).

Problems

5.1. Let **H** be an $m \times n$ matrix, $2^{m-1} \leqq n < 2^m$, whose columns are the binary representation of the column number. Show that for the code which is the null space of **H**, every coset contains a vector of weight 2 or less. Show that the code corrects all single errors and is therefore quasi-perfect. (Hint: Use Problem 3.2.)

5.2. Show that the Hamming single-error-correcting double-error-detecting binary code is quasi-perfect if it is of length $n = 2^m$ and has $m + 1$ parity checks, but that if any column is dropped from the parity-check matrix there is a coset with minimum weight 3.

5.3. Show that there is a quasi-perfect single-error-correcting binary code with m parity-check symbols for any length n satisfying $2^{m/2+1} - 2 \leq n < 2^m$ if m is even, $2^{(m+1)/2} + 2^{(m-1)/2} - 2 \leq n < 2^m$ if m is odd. (Hint: Include in the parity-check matrix all columns that have 0's in the upper half of the rows and all columns that have 0's in the lower half of the rows.)

This result can be generalized directly to linear codes with q symbols.

5.4. Devise a procedure for correcting double erasures for the Hamming distance-3 code.

5.5. Devise a way of decoding in spite of $2^{m-r} - 1$ erasures with the Reed-Muller codes.

5.6. Show that with the simple iterated code consisting of a parity check on rows and a parity check on columns it is possible to correct all combinations of three erasures, but there are combinations of four erasures which are uncorrectable.

5.7. Show that all code words in the null space of the binary single-error-correcting Hamming code have the same weight, and then using the MacWilliams formula, show that the generating function for the weight distribution for the Hamming code is

$$f_0(x) = \frac{1}{n+1}[(1+x)^n + n(1+x)^{(n-1)/2}(1-x)^{(n+1)/2}].$$

5.8. Show that the weight distribution for the distance-4 binary Hamming code of length $n = 2^m$ is

$$f_1(x) = \frac{1}{2n}[(1+x)^n + (1-x)^n + 2(n-1)(1-x^2)^{n/2}]$$

(This can be derived either by finding the weight distribution of the dual code and using the MacWilliams formula, or it can be derived directly from the $f_0(x)$ given in Problem 5.7.)

5.9. The results of Problems 5.7 and 5.8 can be used to derive an expression for the probability of undetected error when a Hamming code is used only for error detection on the BSC. Show that

$$P(\text{undetected error}) = Q^n\left[f\left(\frac{P}{Q}\right) - 1\right],$$

where P is the BSC crossover probability, $Q = 1 - P$, and $f(X)$ is given in the preceding problems.

5.10. Show that for the dual of the generalized Hamming code, all code words have the same weight, and thus from the MacWilliams formula, the generating function for the weight distribution of the generalized Hamming code is

$$f(X) = \frac{1}{n(q-1)+1}\{[(1+(q-1)x]^n$$
$$+ n(q-1)[1+(q-1)x]^{(n-1)/q}(1-x)^{(n(q-1)+1)/q}\}$$

5.11. Show that the digits in any product code can be reordered to create a code with burst-correcting ability

$$b \geq \max(b_1 n_2 + t_2, b_2 n_1 + t_1)$$

where b_1, n_1, and t_1 are defined in Section 5.7.

5.12. Some authors have considered the duals of product codes. If d_1 and d_2 denote, respectively, the minimum distance of the duals of the row and column codes, show that the minimum distance of the dual of a product code is

$$d = \min(d_1, d_2).$$

5.13. The bottom row of the generator matrix of a binary linear (15, 7) code is

[000000110110001].

This code has the peculiar property that a cyclic shift of a code word (in either direction) is another code word. That is, if

$$a_{14}\, a_{13} \ldots a_0$$

is a code word, so is

$$a_{13}\, a_{12} \ldots a_0\, a_{14}.$$

Construct the generator matrix of this code in reduced-echelon form.

This code is an example of a cyclic code. Chapters 6 through 12 are devoted to their study.

5.14. Given an (n_1, k) code with minimum distance d_1 and an (n_2, k) code with minimum distance d_2, construct an $(n_1 + n_2, k)$ code with minimum distance at least $d_1 + d_2$.

5.15. (Goethals 1967) Assume that there exists an (n, k) code with minimum distance d whose dual code has minimum distance $\bar{d}$. Prove that this code contains, as a proper subcode, an $(n - d, k - \bar{d} + 1)$ code with minimum distance d.

5.16. Use the result of the previous problem and the data on binary cyclic codes of length 31 given in Appendix D to construct a (26, 6) code with $d = 12$. Compare Table 5.4.

5.17. A general purpose digital computer with 4,096 twelve-bit words of memory is to be used to decode a Golay code. An instruction for performing a full word exclusive — OR is available and execution time for all instructions is 1 μsecond. Devise a table look-up procedure for decoding this code. Determine the maximum data rate that this decoder can handle.

5.18. Consider the class of codes formed by taking the product of a code with itself. Show that for n large the radio d/n must lie below the Gilbert bound. Generalize to two different component codes. (This result implies that long product codes have relatively low minimum distance.)

5.19. Confirm the possibility of the existence of a perfect double-error-correcting (11, 6) code over $GF(3)$. (In fact, such a code exists and was discovered by Golay (1949).) Determine A_5, the number of minimum weight code words.

6 Polynomial Rings and Galois Fields

Much of the remainder of this book requires some knowledge of rings, ideals, residue classes, and the basic structure of finite fields. The purpose of this chapter is to present the minimum background necessary for understanding subsequent chapters.

6.1 Ideals, Residue Classes, and the Residue Class Ring

In the theory of groups, subgroups, particularly normal subgroups, are very important. In the theory of rings, ideals play the corresponding role. An *ideal* I is a subset of elements of a ring R with the following two properties: (1) I is a subgroup of the additive group of R, and (2) for any element a of I and any element r of R, ar and ra are in I. (This is sometimes called a two-sided ideal.)

> *Example.* In the ring of all positive and negative integers and 0, the set of all multiples of any particular integer is an ideal.

Since an ideal is a subgroup, cosets can be formed. In this case the cosets are called *residue classes.* The ideal forms the first row of an array, with the 0 element at the left. Then any ring element not in the ideal can be chosen as leader of the first residue class, and the rest of the class is formed by adding the leader to each of the elements of the ideal:

$$\begin{array}{llllll}
0 = a_1, & a_2, & a_3, & a_4, & a_5, & \ldots \\
r_1 = r_1 + a_1, & r_1 + a_2, & r_1 + a_3, & r_1 + a_4, & r_1 + a_5, & \ldots \\
r_2 = r_2 + a_1, & r_2 + a_2, & r_2 + a_3, & r_2 + a_4, & r_2 + a_5, & \ldots \\
\vdots & \vdots & & & &
\end{array}$$

The first element in each row is, as before, a previously unused element.

Of course, all properties of cosets apply to residue classes also. In particular since addition, the group operation, is commutative, an ideal is a normal subgroup and addition of cosets is defined:

$$\{r\} + \{s\} = \{r + s\}$$

where $\{r\}$ denotes the residue class containing r. With this definition the residue classes form a group under addition, the factor group discussed in Section 2.4. It is possible also to define multiplication of residue classes:

$$\{r\}\{s\} = \{rs\}. \tag{6.1}$$

This is a valid definition only if, no matter which elements are chosen in the residue classes that are being multiplied, Equation 6.1 defines the same residue class as the product. That is, if r and r' are in the same residue class and if s and s' are in the same residue class, then rs and $r's'$ must be in the same residue class, and this will be the case if and only if $r's' - rs$ is in the ideal:

$$r's' - rs = r's' - r's + r's - rs = r'(s' - s) + (r' - r)s.$$

Since $s' - s$ and $r' - r$ are in the ideal, so is each term on the right side of this equation, and hence so is $r's' - rs$. Therefore, this definition of multiplication of residue classes is consistent.

It is easily verified that the associative and distributive laws hold:

$$\begin{aligned}
\{a\}(\{b\}\{c\}) &= \{a\}\{bc\} = \{abc\} = \{ab\}\{c\} = (\{a\}\{b\})\{c\}, \\
\{a\}(\{b\} + \{c\}) &= \{a\}\{b + c\} = \{a(b + c)\} = \{ab\} + \{ac\} \\
&= \{a\}\{b\} + \{a\}\{c\},
\end{aligned}$$

and similarly for the other distributive law. Clearly, multiplication is defined for any pair of residue classes. Therefore:

THEOREM 6.1. *The residue classes of a ring with respect to an ideal form a ring.*

This ring is called the *residue class ring*.

Example. In the ring of all integers, consider the ideal that consists of all even integers. Then there will be 2 residue classes, $\{0\}$ and $\{1\}$. It is easily seen that the arithmetic in the residue class ring is exactly arithmetic modulo 2.

6.2 Ideals and Residue Classes of Integers

If r, s, and t are integers and $rs = t$, then it is said that t is divisible by r or that r divides t. An integer $p \geqq 1$ that is divisible only by $\pm p$ or ± 1 is called *prime*. The *greatest common divisor* of two integers is the greatest positive integer that divides both of them. Two integers are said to be *relatively prime* if their greatest common divisor is 1.

If r divides s and s divides r, then either $r = s$ or $r = -s$, for if r divides s and s divides r, then for some a and b, $r = sa$ and $s = rb$, and therefore $r = rab$, and ab must equal 1. Therefore $a = b^{-1}$, and a and b must both be either $+1$ or -1.

For every pair of integers s and d there is a unique pair of integers q, the quotient, and r, the remainder, such that

$$s = dq + r \qquad \text{where} \qquad 0 \leqq r < |d|. \tag{6.2}$$

This is known as the *Euclidean division algorithm*, and from it some very important algebraic properties of the integers can be proved, including the fact that every integer can be expressed uniquely as a product of powers of primes, and the fact that the greatest common divisor d of two integers r and s can always be expressed in the form

$$d = ar + bs \tag{6.3}$$

where a and b are integers. An illustration of how the greatest common divisor is found using the division algorithm will indicate the method of proof. The greatest common divisor d of 973 and 301 is found as follows:

$$\begin{aligned} 973 &= 3 + 301 + 70 \\ 301 &= 4 \times 70 + 21 \\ 70 &= 3 \times 21 + 7 \\ 21 &= 3 \times 7 + 0 \end{aligned}$$

Since d divides 973 and 301, it must divide the remainder 70. Since it divides 301 and 70, it divides 21. Since it divides 70 and 21, it divides 7. On the other hand, 7 divides 21, therefore 70, therefore 301, and finally also 973, and therefore d must be 7.

Now the foregoing equations can be used to express 7 in the form of Equation 6.3, for

$$\begin{aligned} 7 &= 70 - 3 \times 21 \\ &= 70 - 3 \times (301 - 4 \times 70) \\ &= -3 \times 301 + 13 \times 70 \\ &= -3 \times 301 + 13 \times (973 - 3 \times 301) \\ &= 13 \times 973 - 42 \times 301. \end{aligned}$$

THEOREM 6.2. *A set of integers is an ideal if and only if it consists of all multiples of some integer.*

Proof. Let r be the smallest positive integer in an ideal and s be any other integer in the ideal. Then their greatest common divisor d is in the ideal, for by the definition of an ideal both terms on the right side of Equation 6.3 are in the ideal, and hence their sum is also. Since r is the smallest positive integer in the ideal, $r \leqq d$. Since d divides r, $d \leqq r$. Therefore $r = d$, and r divides s and hence divides every integer in the ideal. Finally, every multiple of r is in the ideal, by the definition of an ideal. Q.E.D.

An ideal that consists of all multiples of one ring element is called a *principal ideal*, and a ring in which every ideal is a principal ideal is called a *principal ideal ring*. Theorem 6.2 states that the ring of integers is a principal ideal ring.

The ideal that consists of all multiples of a positive integer m is denoted (m). The residue class ring formed of residue classes of (m) is called the *ring of integers modulo m*.

THEOREM 6.3. *Every residue class modulo m contains either* 0 *or a positive integer less than m. Zero is an element of the ideal, and each positive integer less than m is in a distinct residue class.*

Proof. If s is any element of a residue class, then since

$$s = mq + r,$$

r is in the same residue class, and $0 \leqq r < m$. If r and s are in the same residue class, $r - s$ is an element of the ideal and hence a multiple of m. If $r \neq s$, clearly they could not both be less than m and nonnegative. Q.E.D.

It follows from Theorem 6.3 that the list $\{0\}, \{1\}, \{2\}, \ldots, \{m-1\}$ includes each residue class once and only once. Commonly the residue classes are named $0, 1, 2, \ldots, m-1$. This notation will be used in this book, since it should be clear from the context whether integers or residue classes are meant.

THEOREM 6.4. *The residue class ring modulo m is a field if and only if m is a prime number.*

Proof. If m is not prime, then $m = rs$ for some integers r and s that are not multiples of m. Then $\{r\}\{s\} = \{m\} = 0$, and if $\{r\}$ had an inverse $\{r\}^{-1}$, then $\{r\}^{-1}\{r\}\{s\} = \{s\} = \{r\}^{-1}0 = 0$, which is a contradiction. Therefore $\{r\}$ can have no inverse, and the residue class ring is not a field.

It remains only to show that if m is prime, every residue class except 0 (the ideal) has an inverse. Every such residue class contains an integer s that is less than m and is not 0. Since 1 is its own inverse, it may be assumed that $s > 1$. Then since m is assumed prime, the greatest common divisor of s and m must be either m or 1. Since $m > s$ and therefore cannot divide s, the greatest common divisor is 1. By Equation 6.3,

$$1 = am + bs$$

and therefore $\{b\}\{s\} = \{1\}$, and the residue class $\{s\}$ has $\{b\}$ as its inverse.

Q.E.D.

These fields are called *prime fields,* or *Galois fields of p elements, GF(p).*

6.3 Polynomial Ideals and Residue Classes

Now consider polynomials $f(X)$, with one indeterminant (or variable) X and with coefficients from any field F:

$$f(X) = f_0 + f_1X + f_2X^2 + \cdots + f_nX^n.$$

The *degree* of a polynomial is the largest power of X in a term with a nonzero coefficient. The degree of the 0 polynomial is 0. A polynomial is called *monic* if the coefficient of the highest power of X is 1. Polynomials can be added and multiplied in the usual way, and they form a ring.

If $r(X)$, $s(X)$, and $t(X)$ are polynomials and $r(X)\,s(X) = t(X)$, then it is said that $t(X)$ is divisible by $r(X)$ or that $r(X)$ divides $t(X)$, and that $r(X)$ is a factor of $t(X)$. A polynomial $p(X)$ of degree n which is not divisible by any polynomial of degree less than n but is greater than 0 is called *irreducible.* The *greatest common divisor* of two polynomials is the monic polynomial of greatest degree which divides both of them. Two polynomials are said to be *relatively prime* if their greatest common divisor is 1.

The degree of the product of two polynomials is the sum of their degrees. A polynomial of degree 0 is a field element and therefore has an inverse, but no nonzero polynomial of higher degree has an inverse. If $r(X)$ divides $s(X)$ and $s(X)$ divides $r(X)$, they differ at most by a factor that is a field element. This can be shown in the following way. For some $a(X)$ and $b(X)$, $r(X) = s(X)\,a(X)$ and $s(X) = r(X)\,b(X)$. Then, since the degree of $r(X)$ equals the sum of degrees of $s(X)$ and $a(X)$, the degree of $r(X)$ is equal to or greater than the degree of $s(X)$. Similarly, the degree of $s(X)$ is equal to or greater than the degree of $r(X)$, and thus their degrees must be equal. Therefore $a(X)$ and $b(X)$ have degree 0 and must be field elements.

For every pair of polynomials $s(X)$ and $d(X)$, there is a unique pair of polynomials $q(X)$, the quotient, and $r(X)$, the remainder, such that

$$s(X) = d(X)\,q(X) + r(X) \tag{6.4}$$

and the degree of $r(X)$ is less than the degree of $d(X)$. This is the Euclidean division algorithm, and $q(X)$ and $r(X)$ can be obtained by ordinary long division of polynomials.

Several important results are obtained by assuming a first-degree divisor $X - a$ in the division algorithm:

$$f(X) = (X - a)\,q(X) + r. \tag{6.5}$$

Since r must have degree less than the degree of the divisor, it must have degree 0; that is, it must be a field element. Substitution of a for X then shows that $r = f(a)$. This is the *remainder theorem.* Then if $f(a) = 0$, that is, a is a root of $f(X)$, then $r = 0$, and $x - a$ is a factor $f(X)$. This result is known as the *factor theorem.* Thus, for each distinct root of $f(X)$ there is a distinct first-degree factor. Since the degree of a product of polynomials is the sum of the degrees of the factors, *the degree of $f(X)$ is at least as great as the number of roots of $f(X)$.*

The parallel between the ring of integers and rings of polynomials over a field must be apparent. Both are special cases of an algebraic structure called a *Euclidean ring.* The remainder of this section and the next two sections consist largely of the analogs of theorems in Section 6.2. Proofs will not be given, but the reader can construct them from proofs in Section 6.2 by changing the word "integer" to "polynomial" and the phrase "a is less than b" to "the degree of $a(X)$ is less than the degree of $b(X)$" and a few very minor additional changes.

The greatest common divisor $d(X)$ of two polynomials $r(X)$ and $s(X)$ can always be expressed in the form

$$d(X) = a(X)\, r(X) + b(X)\, s(X), \tag{6.6}$$

where $a(X)$ and $b(X)$ are polynomials. This can be accomplished by use of the division algorithm in a manner exactly analogous to the method used for integers.

THEOREM 6.5. *A set of polynomials is an ideal if and only if it consists of all multiples of some polynomial.*

That is, the ring of polynomials is a principal ideal ring. The ideal which consists of all multiples of $f(X)$ is denoted $(f(X))$. The residue class ring formed from this ideal is called the ring of polynomials modulo $f(X)$.

THEOREM 6.6. *Every residue class modulo a polynomial $f(X)$ of degree n contains either 0 or a polynomial of degree less than n. Zero is an element of the ideal, and every polynomial of degree less than n is in a distinct residue class.*

6.4 The Algebra of Polynomial Residue Classes

THEOREM 6.7. *The residue classes of polynomials modulo a polynomial $f(X)$ of degree n form a commutative linear algebra of dimension n over the coefficient field.*

Proof. Scalar multiplication is defined by the equation $a\{r(X)\} = \{ar(X)\}$, and it is easily verified that all the axioms are satisfied for a vector space and algebra. For example, the distributive law is verified as follows:

$$\begin{aligned}\{r(X)\}(\{s(X)\} + \{t(X)\}) &= \{r(X)(s(X) + t(X))\} \\ &= \{r(X)s(X) + r(X)t(X)\} \\ &= \{r(X)\}\{s(X)\} + \{r(X)\}\{t(X)\}.\end{aligned}$$

That it has dimension n can be seen from the fact that the n residue classes $\{1\}, \{X\}, \{X^2\}, \ldots, \{X^{n-1}\}$ span the space, since every residue class contains a polynomial of degree less than n, and

$$\{a_0 + a_1X + \cdots + a_{n-1}X^{n-1}\} = a_0\{1\} + a_1\{X\} + \cdots + a_{n-1}\{X^{n-1}\}. \tag{6.7}$$

Also, these n residue classes are linearly independent, for the right-hand side of Equation 6.7 is an arbitrary linear combination of $\{1\}, \{X\}, \ldots, \{X^{n-1}\}$ and the left side is 0 only if $a_0 + a_1X + \cdots + a_{n-1}X^{n-1}$ is divisible by $f(X)$, which is impossible, or if all the a_i are 0. Q.E.D.

It is quite common to use the polynomial of minimum degree in a residue class to represent that residue class, but here using the same notation for both may lead to some confusion. In this book, whenever the brace notation for residue classes is not used, the following system will be used. Some symbol, typically S or α, will be used to represent the residue class containing X. The residue class containing a field element will be given the same name as the field element — this should not cause confusion. Then the coset that contains $a_0 + a_1X + \cdots + a_{n-1}X^{n-1}$ is

$$\begin{aligned}\{a_0 + a_1X + \cdots + a_{n-1}X^{n-1}\} &= \{a_0\} + \{a_1\}\{X\} + \cdots + \{a_{n-1}\}\{X\}^{n-1} \\ &= a_0 + a_1S + \cdots + a_{n-1}S^{n-1}.\end{aligned}$$

Thus, every residue class equals a polynomial of degree less than n in S.

THEOREM 6.8. *In the algebra of polynomials modulo a polynomial $f(X)$ of degree n, $f(S) = 0$, but no polynomial in S of degree less than n is 0.*

Proof.

$$\begin{aligned}f(S) &= f_0 + f_1S + \cdots + f_nS^n \\ &= f_0 + f_1\{X\} + \cdots + f_n\{X^n\} \\ &= \{f_0 + f_1X + \cdots + f_nX^n\} = \{f(X)\} = 0.\end{aligned}$$

Similarly, if $g(X)$ is any polynomial of degree less than n, $g(S) = \{g(X)\}$, and by Theorem 6.6 this is not the ideal. Q.E.D.

It follows from this theorem that every polynomial in S of degree less than n is a distinct residue class, for otherwise their difference would be a polynomial of degree less than n in S equal to 0.

THEOREM 6.9. *Let J be an ideal in the algebra of polynomials modulo $f(X)$ and let $g(X)$ be a nonzero polynomial of smallest degree such that the residue class $\{g(X)\}$ is in J. Then $\{s(X)\}$ is in J if and only if $s(X)$ is divisible by $g(X)$. Furthermore, $g(X)$ divides $f(X)$.*

Proof. By the division algorithm,

$$s(X) = g(X)\ q(X) + r(X),$$

where $r(X)$ has degree less than the degree of $g(X)$. Therefore,

$$\{s(X)\} = \{g(X)\}\{q(X)\} + \{r(X)\}$$

and if $\{s(X)\}$ and $\{g(X)\}$ are in J, so is $\{s(X)\} - \{g(X)\}\{q(X)\} = \{r(X)\}$. Since $r(X)$ has degree less than the degree of $g(X)$, and $g(X)$ was assumed to be a nonzero polynomial of smallest degree such that $\{g(X)\}$ is in J, $r(X)$ must equal 0. Therefore, $s(X)$ is a multiple of $g(X)$. Conversely, if $s(X)$ is a multiple of $g(X)$, then $s(X) = g(X)\,q(X)$ and $\{s(X)\} = \{g(X)\} \cdot\{q(X)\}$, and since $\{g(X)\}$ is in J, $\{s(X)\}$ must be in J also.

By the division algorithm,

$$f(X) = g(X)\,q(X) + r(X)$$

where $r(X)$ has degree less than the degree of $g(X)$. Then

$$\{0\} = \{f(X)\} = \{g(X)\}\{q(X)\} + \{r(X)\}$$

and so $\{r(X)\}$ is in J. Since $r(X)$ has degree less than the degree of $g(X)$, $r(X)$ must be 0, and $f(X)$ is a multiple of $g(X)$. Q.E.D.

THEOREM 6.10. *For every ideal J in the algebra of polynomials modulo $f(X)$ there is a unique monic polynomial $g(X)$ of minimum degree such that $\{g(X)\}$ is in J. Conversely, every monic polynomial $g(X)$ that divides $f(X)$ generates an ideal J in which $g(X)$ is the monic polynomial of minimum degree in J.*

Proof. There must be a polynomial $h(X) = h_0 + h_1 X + \cdots + h_k X^k$ of minimum degree such that $\{h(X)\}$ is in J. Then $h_k^{-1} h(X)$ is a monic polynomial of minimum degree whose residue class is also in J, and therefore there exists at least one monic polynomial of minimum degree in J. If there are two, $g(X)$ and $g'(X)$, then, by Theorem 6.9, $g(X)$ divides $g'(X)$ and $g'(X)$ divides $g(X)$, and so they differ at most by a factor that is a field element. Since both are assumed monic, the field element must be 1, and $g(X) = g'(X)$. Thus there is a unique minimum degree monic polynomial $g(X)$ such that $\{g(X)\}$ is in J.

Now assume that $g(X)$ is a monic polynomial that divides $f(X)$ and consider the ideal J generated by $\{g(X)\}$, that is, the ideal consisting of all multiples of $\{g(X)\}$. Suppose that $\{r(X)\}$ is in J. Then

$$\{r(X)\} = \{g(X)\}\{a(X)\} = \{g(X)\,a(X)\}$$

for some $a(X)$, and therefore

$$r(X) = g(X)\,a(X) + f(X)\,b(X)$$

for some $b(X)$. Since $f(X)$ is a multiple of $g(X)$, $r(X)$ is also, and therefore if it is not 0 it has degree at least as great as the degree of $g(X)$. Thus $g(X)$ is a monic polynomial of minimum degree such that $\{g(X)\}$ is in J. Q.E.D.

THEOREM 6.11. *Let $f(X) = g(X)\,h(X)$ where $f(X)$ has degree n and $h(X)$ has degree k. Then the ideal generated by $\{g(X)\}$ in the algebra of polynomials modulo $f(X)$ has dimension k.*

Proof. In the ideal, which is a subspace, the vectors $\{g(X)\}, \{Xg(X)\}, \ldots, \{X^{k-1}g(X)\}$ are linearly independent, for any linear combination of them is of the form $\{(a_0 + \cdots + a_{k-1}X^{k-1})g(X)\}$ and thus cannot be 0 by Theorem 6.6, since the residue class contains a polynomial of degree less than n. Furthermore, if $\{s(X)\}$ is in the ideal, then $s(X)$ is divisible by $g(X)$ by Theorem 6.9, and if $s(X)$ is the polynomial of minimum degree in the residue class, it has degree less than n. Thus

$$s(X) = g(X)\,q(X) = g(X)(q_0 + q_1X + \cdots + q_{k-1}X^{k-1}),$$

and

$$\{s(X)\} = q_0\{g(X)\} + q_1\{Xg(X)\} + \cdots + q_{k-1}\{X^{k-1}g(X)\},$$

and the k vectors $\{g(X)\}$, $\{Xg(X)\}$, $\ldots$, $\{X^{k-1}g(X)\}$ span the ideal. Therefore, the dimension of the ideal is k. Q.E.D.

The monic polynomial $g(X)$ of minimum degree such that $\{g(X)\}$ is in an ideal J is called the *generator* of the ideal.

Theorems 6.9 to 6.11 can be summarized as follows: Every ideal in the algebra of polynomials modulo $f(X)$ has a generator polynomial $g(X)$ that divides $f(X)$, and every monic polynomial that divides $f(X)$ generates a different ideal. Every residue class in the ideal generated by $g(X)$ contains a unique polynomial that is divisible by $g(X)$ and has degree less than the degree of $f(X)$, and every such polynomial is in a residue class that is in the ideal.

There is a natural correspondence between n-tuples and polynomials in the algebra of polynomials modulo $f(X)$ of degree n. The n-tuple $(a_0, a_1, \ldots, a_{n-1})$ corresponds to the polynomial $a_0 + a_1S + \cdots + a_{n-1}S^{n-1}$. The sum of two n-tuples corresponds to the sum of the corresponding polynomials, and multiplication by scalars carries over similarly. In subsequent chapters the n-tuple $(a_0, a_1, \ldots, a_{n-1})$ and the polynomial $a_0 + a_1S + \cdots + a_{n-1}S^{n-1}$ will be considered to be only different ways of representing the same element of the algebra, and whichever notation is more convenient will be used. Similarly, an element of the algebra will sometimes be called a vector, sometimes a polynomial.

A polynomial $r(S)$ will be said to be in the null space of an ideal J if $r(S)s(S) = 0$ for every polynomial $s(S)$ in J. This definition differs from the definition given in Chapter 2 for a null space because the requirements that the inner product of vectors be 0 and that the product of polynomials be 0 are not the same. There is, however, a very close connection if $f(X) = X^n - 1$. Let

$$a(S) = a_0 + a_1 S + \cdots + a_{n-1} S^{n-1};$$
$$b(S) = b_0 + b_1 S + \cdots + b_{n-1} S^{n-1}.$$

Then the coefficient of S^j in $c(S) = a(S)\, b(S)$ is

$$c_j = a_0 b_j + a_1 b_{j-1} + \cdots + a_j b_0 + a_{j+1} b_{n-1} + a_{j+2} b_{n-2} + \cdots + a_{n-1} b_{j+1}. \quad (6.8)$$

The terms involving $a_{j+1}, \ldots, a_{n-1}$ come from terms in the product $a(S)\, b(S)$ which involve S^{n+j}, but since $S^n - 1 = 0$, $S^{n+j} = S^j$. This can be rewritten as a dot, or inner, product:

$$c_j = (a_0, a_1, \ldots, a_{n-1})(b_j, b_{j-1}, \ldots, b_0, b_{n-1}, b_{n-2}, \ldots, b_{j+1}).$$

The first vector is the vector corresponding to $a(S)$. The second is a vector consisting of the coefficients of $b(S)$ *in reverse order and shifted cyclically* $j + 1$ *units to the right*. Thus if $a(S)\, b(S)$ is 0, then the vector corresponding to $a(S)$ is orthogonal to the vector corresponding to $b(S)$ with the order of its components reversed, and to every cyclic shift of this vector. The converse is also true: if $(a_0, \ldots, a_{n-1})$ is orthogonal to $(b_{n-1}, \ldots, b_0)$ and to every cyclic shift of this vector, then $a(S)\, b(S) = 0$.

THEOREM 6.12. *Let $f(X)$, $g(X)$, and $h(X)$ be monic polynomials, and let $f(X) = g(X)\, h(X)$. Then $\{a(X)\}$ is in the null space of the ideal generated by $h(X)$ if and only if it is in the ideal generated by $g(X)$.*

Proof. If $\{a(X)\}$ is in the ideal generated by $g(X)$ and $\{b(X)\}$ is any residue class in the ideal generated by $h(X)$, then $a(X)$ is a multiple of $g(X)$ and $b(X)$ is a multiple of $h(X)$, and $a(X)\, b(X)$ is a multiple of $f(X)$. Therefore, $\{a(X)\}\{b(X)\} = \{a(X)\, b(X)\} = 0$, and thus $\{a(X)\}$ is in the null space of the ideal generated by $h(X)$. Conversely, if $\{a(X)\}\{h(X)\} = 0$, then $a(X)\, h(X)$ must be a multiple of $f(X)$. It follows that $a(X)$ must be divisible by $g(X)$, and therefore $\{a(X)\}$ is in the ideal generated by $g(X)$. Q.E.D.

Examples of the use of these ideas appear in Sections 8.1 and 8.2.

6.5 Galois Fields

THEOREM 6.13. *Let $p(X)$ be a polynomial with coefficients in a field F. Iff $p(X)$ is irreducible in F, that is, iff $p(X)$ has no factors with coefficients in F, then the algebra of polynomials over F modulo $p(X)$ is a field.*

The proof is exactly analogous to the proof of Theorem 6.4.

Example. Consider the ring of polynomials with real-number coefficients modulo the irreducible polynomial $X^2 + 1 = p(X)$. Denote the residue class that contains $X, \{X\} = i$. Then every element of the resulting field can be expressed as a polynomial of degree less than 2 in i, that is, in the form $a + bi$. Since i satisfies the equation $p(X) = 0$, by Theorem 6.8, $i^2 + 1 = 0$, or $i^2 = -1$. This is merely one way of describing the field of complex numbers.

The field formed by taking polynomials over a field F modulo an irreducible polynomial $p(X)$ of degree k is called an *extension field of degree k over F.* If the residue class containing X is called α, the extension field is denoted $F[\alpha]$. The original field F is called the *ground field.* The new field contains an element (a residue class) corresponding to each element in the ground field, and it is said that it contains the ground field. Since $p(\alpha) = 0$, α is a root of $p(X)$, and it is said that the extension field is obtained by adjoining a root of $p(X)$ to the ground field. This language is suggestive and convenient, but it should only be thought of as a heuristic description of the process of forming a field in which the elements are residue classes.

In Section 6.2 it was shown that residue classes of integers modulo any prime number p form a field of p elements called the Galois field $GF(p)$. It can be shown that the ring of polynomials over any finite field has at least one irreducible polynomial of every degree. The field of polynomials over $GF(p)$ modulo an irreducible polynomial of degree m is called the Galois field of p^m elements, or $GF(p^m)$. It is, by Theorem 6.7, a vector space of dimension m over $GF(p)$ and hence has p^m elements. For any number $q = p^m$ that is a power of a prime number, therefore, there is a field, $GF(q)$, which has q elements. It can be shown also that every finite field is isomorphic to some Galois field; that is, every finite field has the same structure as some Galois field and differs only in the way the elements are named. It can also be shown that any two finite fields with the same number of elements are isomorphic; that is, they differ only in the way the elements are named.

The Galois fields that can be realized by taking residue classes of polynomials modulo an irreducible polynomial over $GF(p)$ are said to be fields of *characteristic p*. Thus $GF(p^m)$ is a field of characteristic p for any choice of m. In the field $GF(p)$, $p = 0$. Since this is the coefficient field for $GF(p^m)$, it is true for all fields of characteristic p that $p = 0$. Then

$$(a + b)^p = a^p + \binom{p}{1} a^{p-1}b + \binom{p}{2} a^{p-2}b^2 + \ldots + b^p$$

and all the binomial coefficients $\binom{p}{i}$ for $0 < i < p$ have p as a factor and therefore are 0, so that the following theorem is valid:

THEOREM 6.14. *In a field of characteristic p,* $(a + b)^p = a^p + b^p$.

Now consider a ground field F and an extension field, and let β be any element of the extension field. The monic polynomial $m(X)$ of smallest degree with coefficients in the ground field F such that $m(\beta) = 0$ is called the *minimum polynomial* or *minimum function* of β.

THEOREM 6.15. *The minimum function $m(X)$ of any element β is irreducible.*

Proof. Suppose that on the contrary $m(X) = m_1(X)\, m_2(X)$. Then $m(\beta) = m_1(\beta)m_2(\beta)$, and at least one of the factors $m_1(\beta)$ or $m_2(\beta)$ must be 0. If these are nontrivial factors, the hypothesis that $m(X)$ is the minimum degree polynomial is contradicted. Q.E.D.

THEOREM 6.16. *If $f(X)$ is a polynomial with coefficients in the ground field F and if $f(\beta) = 0$, then $f(X)$ is divisible by $m(X)$, the minimum function of β.*

Proof. By the Euclidean algorithm,

$$f(X) = m(X)\, q(X) + r(X),$$

where $r(X)$ has degree less than the degree of $m(X)$. Since $f(\beta) = 0$ and $m(\beta) = 0$, $r(\beta) = 0$. Since $m(X)$ is the minimum function of β and $r(X)$ has degree less than that of $m(X)$, $r(\beta) = 0$ only if $r(X) = 0$. Q.E.D.

It follows from Theorem 6.16 that the minimum function of β is unique. It follows also that if $p(X)$ is a monic irreducible polynomial and $p(\beta) = 0$, then $p(X)$ is the minimum function of β.

THEOREM 6.17. *Every element of an extension field of degree k over F has a minimum function of degree k or less.*

Proof. By Theorem 6.7, the extension field is a vector space of dimension k. Therefore for any element β, the $k+1$ elements $1, \beta, \beta^2, \ldots, \beta^k$ cannot be linearly independent. Consequently, there must be some polynomial of degree k or less in β which is equal to 0, and this polynomial can be made monic by dividing it by its leading coefficient.

Q.E.D.

6.6 The Multiplicative Group of a Galois Field

Consider in any finite group the set of elements formed by any element g and all its powers $gg = g^2$, $gg^2 = g^3$, and so on. There can be at most a finite set of such elements, and therefore at some point there must be repetition; that is, $g^i = g^j$ for some i and j. Then, multiplying by $(g^i)^{-1} = (g^{-1})^i$ gives $1 = g^{j-i}$. Therefore, some power of g equals 1. Let e be the smallest positive integer such that $g^e = 1$. Then e is called the *order* of the element g. The set of elements $1, g, g^2, \ldots, g^{e-1}$ forms a subgroup, for the product of two such elements is another of the same form, and the inverse of g^j is g^{e-j} and hence is one of the elements of this set. A group that consists of all the powers of one of its elements is called a *cyclic group.*

The order e of any element g of a group divides the order of the group, for the group consists of the cyclic subgroup of e elements generated by g, and a number of cosets of this subgroup, each of which has e elements also.

THEOREM 6.18. *The polynomial $X^{q-1} - 1$ has as roots all the $q - 1$ nonzero elements of $GF(q)$.*

Proof. The set of $q - 1$ nonzero elements of $GF(q)$ forms a group. The order of each element of $GF(q)$ must divide $q - 1$, and therefore each of the $q - 1$ elements is a root of the polynomial $X^{q-1} - 1$. But this polynomial has at most $q - 1$ roots, since it is of degree $q - 1$, and therefore these must be all of the roots. Q.E.D.

THEOREM 6.19. *The polynomial $X^m - 1$ divides $X^n - 1$ if and only if m divides n.*

Proof. Suppose that $n = md$. Then $Y - 1$ divides $Y^d - 1$, since $Y = 1$ is a root of $Y^d - 1$. Substituting $X^m = Y$ then shows that $X^m - 1$ divides $X^{md} - 1$.

Now suppose that $n = md + r$, where $r < m$. Then

$$X^n - 1 = X^r(X^{md} - 1) + X^r - 1$$

and, by the division algorithm,

$$X^n - 1 = q(X)(X^m - 1) + r(X).$$

Comparison of these equations shows that

$$q(X) = \frac{X^r(X^{md} - 1)}{X^m - 1} \quad \text{and } r(X) = X^r - 1,$$

since the former is a polynomial and the latter has degree less than m. Then the remainder is 0 only if $r = 0$, that is, if m divides n. Q.E.D.

THEOREM 6.20. *In $GF(q)$ there is a primitive element α, that is, an element of order $q - 1$. Every nonzero element of $GF(q)$ can be expressed as a power of α; that is, the multiplicative group of $GF(q)$ is cyclic.*

Proof Let $q - 1 = p_1^{e_1} p_2^{e_2} \cdots p_r^{e_r}$ and let β_i be a field element of order $p_i^{e_i}$, $i = 1, 2, \ldots, r$. (There are $p_i^{e_i} - p_i^{e_i - 1}$ such elements; these are the roots of $X^{p_i^{e_i}} - 1$ but not of $X^{p_i^{e_i - 1}} - 1$.) Since $p_1^{e_1}$ and $p_2^{e_2}$ are relatively prime, there exists s and t such that $sp_1^{e_1} + tp_2^{e_2} = 1$. Then $(\beta_1\beta_2)^{sp_1^{e_1}} = (\beta_2)^{sp_1^{e_1}} = (\beta_2)^{1 - tp_2^{e_2}} = \beta_2$; similarly $(\beta_1\beta_2)^{tp_2^{e_2}} = \beta_1$. Thus β_1 and β_2 are powers of $\beta_1\beta_2$ and so the order of the field element $\beta_1\beta_2$ divides $p_1^{e_1} p_2^{e_2}$. But if $(\beta_1\beta_2)^{p_1 p_2^{e_2}/a} = 1$ for some $a > 1$, then either β_1 has order less than $p_1^{e_1}$ or β_2 has order less than $p_2^{e_2}$, which is a contradiction. Thus $\beta_1\beta_2 \ldots \beta_r$ has order $p_1^{e_1} p_2^{e_2}$. By induction on i it follows that the element $\alpha = \beta_1\beta_2 \cdots \beta_r$ has order $p_1^{e_1} p_2^{e_2} \cdots p_r^{e_r} = q - 1$. Consequently the elements $\alpha, \alpha^2, \ldots, \alpha^{q-2} = 1$ are distinct field elements and so $GF(q)$ is cyclic. Q.E.D.

Example. The Galois field of 2^4 elements $GF(2^4)$ may be formed as the field of polynomials over $GF(2)$ modulo $X^4 + X + 1$. Let α denote the residue class that contains X. Then α is a root of $X^4 + X + 1$, and this happens to be a primitive element of the field. Then the 15 nonzero field elements are as given in Table 6.1.

The following seven theorems give further details on the relationships between the multiplicative properties of field elements, the minimum polynomials of field elements, and the polynomial $X^q - X$. Following these theorems is an illustration of their application to the factorization of polynomials of the form $X^n - 1$, which should enable the reader to gain further insight into the structure of the field.

Table 6.1. Representation of $GF(2^4)$

α^0	$= 1$	$= 0001$
α^1	$= \alpha$	$= 0010$
α^2	$= \alpha^2$	$= 0100$
α^3	$= \alpha^3$	$= 1000$
α^4	$= \alpha + 1$	$= 0011$
α^5	$= \alpha^2 + \alpha$	$= 0110$
α^6	$= \alpha^3 + \alpha^2$	$= 1100$
α^7	$= \alpha^3 + \alpha + 1$	$= 1011$
α^8	$= \alpha^2 + 1$	$= 0101$
α^9	$= \alpha^3 + \alpha$	$= 1010$
α^{10}	$= \alpha^2 + \alpha + 1$	$= 0111$
α^{11}	$= \alpha^3 + \alpha^2 + \alpha$	$= 1110$
α^{12}	$= \alpha^3 + \alpha^2 + \alpha + 1$	$= 1111$
α^{13}	$= \alpha^3 + \alpha^2 + 1$	$= 1101$
α^{14}	$= \alpha^3 + 1$	$= 1001$
α^{15}	$= 1$	$= \alpha^0$

THEOREM 6.21. *If $f(X)$ is a polynomial with coefficients in $GF(q)$ and β is a root of $f(X)$ in an extension field of $GF(q)$, then β^q is also a root of $f(X)$.*

Proof. Let $f(X) = a_0 + a_1 X + \cdots + a_n X^n$. Then

$$[f(X)]^q = (a_0)^q + (a_1 X)^q + \cdots + (a_n X^n)^q$$
$$= a_0^q + a_1^q X^q + \cdots + a_n^q (X^q)^n$$

by Theorem 6.14. Then by Theorem 6.18, $a^{q-1} = 1$, and therefore $a^q = a$ for any element a of $GF(q)$. Therefore $[f(X)]^q = a_0 + a_1 X^q + \cdots + a_n (X^q)^n = f(X^q)$, and, if $f(\beta) = 0$, then $[f(\beta)]^q = f(\beta^q) = 0$. Q.E.D.

THEOREM 6.22. *Consider an extension field of $GF(q)$ which contains all the roots of $X^{q^m} - X$. Then all these roots form a subfield.*

Proof. By Theorem 6.14, if a and b are two roots, $(a + b)^{q^m} = a^{q^m} + b^{q^m} = a + b$, and so $a + b$ is a root of $X^{q^m} - X$. Also $(-a)^{q^m} = -(a^{q^m}) = -a$, and so $-a$ is a root if a is. (Note that $-a = a$ if the characteristic of the field is 2.) Therefore the roots form a group under addition. If a and b are roots, ab is a root, and a^{-1} is also (if $a \neq 0$). The other axioms are satisfied by virtue of the fact that the roots belong to a field. Q.E.D.

THEOREM 6.23. *Every polynomial $p(X)$ of degree m irreducible over $GF(q)$ is a factor of $X^{q^m} - X$.*

Proof. If $p(X) = X$, the theorem is obviously true. If $p(X) \neq X$, let α (which is not 0) be a root of $p(X)$ in the extension field of polynomials modulo $p(X)$ over $GF(q)$. This is a field of q^m elements, and the set of all nonzero elements forms a group of order $q^m - 1$. Therefore the order of α must divide $q^m - 1$, and α must be a root of $X^{q^m-1} - 1$. Then by Theorem 6.16, $p(X)$ divides $X^{q^m-1} - 1$. Q.E.D.

THEOREM 6.24. *Every factor of $X^{q^m} - X$ irreducible over $GF(q)$ has degree m or less.*

Proof. Assume that $p(X)$ of degree k is an irreducible factor of $X^{q^m} - X$ over $GF(q)$, and consider the extension field of polynomials over $GF(q)$ modulo $p(X)$. It has q^k elements, each of which can be expressed in the form $a_0 + a_1\alpha + \cdots + a_{k-1}\alpha^{k-1} = \beta$, where α is a root of $p(X)$ and $a_0, a_1, \ldots, a_{k-1}$ are elements of $GF(q)$. Then by Theorem 6.14,

$$\beta^{q^m} = a_0^{q^m} + a_1^{q^m}\alpha^{q^m} + \cdots + a_{k-1}^{q^m}\alpha^{q^m(k-1)}.$$

By Theorem 6.18, $a^{q^m-1} = 1$, and hence $a^{q^m} = a$ for any a in $GF(q^m)$, and since $a_0, a_1, \ldots, a_{k-1}$ are in $GF(q)$ and therefore also in the extension field $GF(q^m)$,

$$\beta^{q^m} = a_0 + a_1\alpha^{q^m} + \cdots + a_{k-1}\alpha^{q^m(k-1)}.$$

But α is a root of $X^{q^m} - X$, and so $\alpha^{q^m} = \alpha$, and $\alpha^{jq^m} = a^j$ for all j. Therefore,

$$\beta^{q^m} = a_0 + a_1\alpha + \cdots + a_{k-1}\alpha^{k-1} = \beta,$$

and β is a root of $X^{q^m} - X$ also. Since there are q^k such elements, while $X^{q^m} - X$ has no more than q^m roots, $q^m \geqq q^k$, and hence $m \geqq k$. Q.E.D.

THEOREM 6.25. *If β is an element of an extension field of $GF(q)$, then the order e of β divides $q^k - 1$ but no smaller number of the form $q^n - 1$, where k is the degree of its minimum function.*

Proof. Let $m(X)$ be the minimum function of β, and assume its degree is k. Then $m(X)$ divides $X^{q^k-1} - 1$, by Theorem 6.23, and β is a root of $X^{q^k-1} - 1$. Therefore, the order of β divides $q^k - 1$. Suppose that the order of β divides $q^n - 1$ for $n \leqq k$. Then β is a root of $X^{q^n} - X$, and $m(X)$ is a factor of $X^{q^n} - X$, by Theorem 6.16. Then the degree of $m(X)$ is equal to or less than n, by 6.24. Q.E.D.

THEOREM 6.26. *Let $p(X)$ be a polynomial of degree m with coefficients in $GF(q)$, which is irreducible in this field, and let β be a root of $p(X)$ in an extension field. Then $\beta, \beta^q, \ldots, \beta^{q^{m-1}}$ are all the roots of $p(X)$.*

Proof. By Theorem 6.21, $\beta, \beta^q, \ldots, \beta^{q^{m-1}}$ are roots of $p(X)$. The following argument shows that these m field elements are distinct. Suppose that they are not, and $\beta^{q^i} = \beta^{q^j}$, and suppose that $j < i$. Then

$$\beta = \beta^{q^m} = (\beta^{q^i})^{q^{m-i}} = (\beta^{q^j})^{q^{m-i}} = \beta^{q^{m+j-i}};$$
$$1 = \beta^{(q^{m+j-i}-1)}.$$

Thus the order of β divides $q^{m+j-i} - 1$. But $p(X)$ differs from the minimum polynomial of β by at most a constant factor, and $m + j - i < m$, the degree of $p(X)$. This contradicts Theorem 6.25, and therefore $\beta, \beta^q, \ldots, \beta^{q^{m-1}}$ are distinct. Since $p(X)$ can have at most m roots, these must be all the roots. Q.E.D.

THEOREM 6.27. *All the roots of an irreducible polynomial have the same order.*

Proof. By Theorem 6.26, if β is one root, every other root can be expressed in the form β^{q^j} for some j. Let e denote the order of β and e' the order of β^{q^j}. Then

$$(\beta^{q^j})^e = \beta^{eq^j} = (\beta^e)^{q^j} = 1^{q^j} = 1,$$

and therefore e' divides e. Similarly,

$$\beta^{e'} = (\beta^{q^m})^{e'} = \beta^{q^j q^{m-j} e'} = [(\beta^{q^j})^{e'}]^{q^{m-j}} = 1^{q^{m-j}} = 1,$$

and therefore e divides e'. Since they are both positive integers, $e' = e$. Q.E.D.

The order of the roots of an irreducible polynomial is called the *exponent* to which that polynomial belongs. If an irreducible polynomial belongs to e, then it divides $X^e - 1$ but no polynomial of the form $X^n - 1$ for $n < e$. An irreducible polynomial of degree m over $GF(q)$ is called *primitive* if it has a primitive element of $GF(q^m)$ as a root. Then this root and hence all roots have order $q^m - 1$, and they are all primitive, by Theorem 6.27. An irreducible polynomial of degree m is primitive if and only if it belongs to $q^m - 1$. Finally, an irreducible polynomial of degree m is primitive if and only if it divides $X^n - 1$ for no n less than $q^m - 1$.

6.7 Structure of Finite Fields—Summary

The contents of the theorems of the preceding section are summarized in this section in the form of a discussion of the factorization of $X^{63} - 1$ over $GF(2)$. The ideas carry over to the general case of factorization of $X^n - 1$ over $GF(q)$, where the roots of $X^n - 1$ lie in $GF(q^m)$. Careful study and thorough understanding of the ideas presented in this section will prove invaluable in understanding the theory of cyclic codes.

The nonzero elements of the field $GF(64)$ can all be expressed as powers of any primitive element α. Thus, all the elements are 0, 1, α, $\alpha^2, \alpha^3, \ldots, \alpha^{62}$, and

$$X^{63} - 1 = (X - 1)(X - \alpha)(X - \alpha^2) \cdots (X - \alpha^{62}). \tag{6.9}$$

Now since $(\alpha^{21})^3 = \alpha^{63} = 1$, α^{21} has order 3. So has α^{42}. Similarly $\alpha(^9)^7 = \alpha^{63}$, and so α^9 has order 7, and so do $\alpha^{18}, \alpha^{27}, \alpha^{36}, \alpha^{45}$, and α^{54}. The elements $\alpha^7, \alpha^{14}, \alpha^{28}, \alpha^{35}, \alpha^{49}$, and α^{56} have order 9. Note that $(\alpha^{21})^9 = 1$, but the order of α^{21} is three, not nine, because the order of an element β is the smallest e such that $\alpha^e = 1$. Similarly, every power of α for which the exponent is a multiple of 3 but not a multiple of 7 or 9 is an element of order 21; there are twelve of them. The remaining 36 elements must have order 63. Now define the *cyclotomic polynomial* $\psi_i(X) = (X - \beta_1)(X - \beta_2) \cdots (X - \beta_r)$, where $\beta_1, \beta_2, \ldots, \beta_r$ are all the elements of order i. Then $\psi_1 = X - 1$, $\psi_3 = (X - \alpha^{21})(X - \alpha^{42})$, $\psi_7 = (X - \alpha^9)(X - \alpha^{18})(X - \alpha^{27})(X - \alpha^{36}) \cdot (X - \alpha^{45})(X - \alpha^{54})$, and so on. Also, Equation (6.9) can be written

$$X^{63} - 1 = \psi_1(X)\psi_3(X)\psi_7(X)\psi_9(X)\psi_{21}(X)\psi_{63}(X). \tag{6.10}$$

The polynomial $X^{21} - 1$ has as roots all elements β for which $\beta^{21} = 1$, and this includes $\psi_i(X)$ for all i which divide 21 evenly. Thus,

$$X^{21} - 1 = \psi_{21}(X)\psi_7(X)\psi_3(X)\psi_1(X),$$

and similarly,

$$\begin{aligned} X^9 - 1 &= \psi_9(X)\psi_3(X)\psi_1(X), \\ X^7 - 1 &= \psi_7(X)\psi_1(X), \\ X^3 - 1 &= \psi_3(X)\psi_1(X), \\ X - 1 &= \psi_1(X). \end{aligned} \tag{6.11}$$

These equations can be rewritten

$$\begin{aligned} \psi_1(X) &= X - 1 && \text{(degree 1)}, \\ \psi_3(X) &= \frac{X^3 - 1}{\psi_1(X)} && \text{(degree 2)}, \\ \psi_7(X) &= \frac{X^7 - 1}{\psi_1(X)} && \text{(degree 6)}, \\ \psi_9(X) &= \frac{X^9 - 1}{\psi_1(X)\psi_3(X)} && \text{(degree 6)}, \\ \psi_{21}(X) &= \frac{X^{21} - 1}{\psi_1(X)\psi_3(X)\psi_7(X)} && \text{(degree 12)}, \\ \psi_{63}(X) &= \frac{X^{63} - 1}{\psi_1(X)\psi_3(X)\psi_7(X)\psi_9(X)\psi_{21}(X)} && \text{(degree 36)}. \end{aligned} \tag{6.12}$$

The degree of $\psi_i(X)$ is the same as the number of elements of order i, which has already been determined by counting. Alternatively, ψ_1 obviously has degree 1. The degree of ψ_3 is the difference between the degree of $X^3 - 1$ and the degree of the denominator $\psi_1(X)$, and so forth.

By Theorem 6.25 the elements of order 3 should have minimum polynomials over $GF(2)$ with degree 2, because they are elements of $GF(2^2)$, and thus $\psi_3(X)$ is irreducible over $GF(2)$. In fact the nonzero elements of $GF(2^2)$ are the roots of $X^3 - 1$, so they are $1, \alpha^{21}$, and α^{42}. Similarly, the elements of order 7 belong to $GF(2^3)$ and have minimum polynomials of degree 3, and thus $\psi_7(X)$ must factor into two irreducible polynomials of degree 3. All the other elements of $GF(2^6)$ are elements of no subfield, and therefore all their minimum polynomials have degree 6. Note also that because all the roots of an irreducible polynomial have the same order (Theorem 6.27), if one root of an irreducible polynomial $p(X)$ has order i, all the roots have order i and are therefore roots of $\psi_i(X)$, and thus $p(X)$ divides $\psi_i(X)$. Therefore, $\psi_9(X)$ must be irreducible, $\psi_{21}(X)$ has two factors of degree 6, and $\psi_{63}(X)$ has six factors of degree 6.

We can go one step further. If β is a root of an irreducible polynomial $p(X)$, then all the other roots are $\beta^2, \beta^4, \beta^8, \beta^{16}$, and β^{32}. Let us denote by $m_i(X)$ the minimum polynomial of α^i. Then,

$$m_1(X) = (X - \alpha)(X - \alpha^2)(X - \alpha^4)(X - \alpha^8)(X - \alpha^{16})(X - \alpha^{32})$$

and

$$m_3(X) = (X - \alpha^3)(X - \alpha^6)(X - \alpha^{12})(X - \alpha^{24})(X - \alpha^{48})(X - \alpha^{33}),$$

and so on.

Note that $(\alpha^{48})^2 = \alpha^{96} = \alpha^{33}$ because $\alpha^{63} = 1$. Also, note that $(\alpha^{32})^2 = \alpha^{64} = \alpha$ because $\alpha^{63} = 1$, and thus only the six distinct roots of $m_1(X)$ are generated by this process of successive squaring. Similarly $(\alpha^{33})^2 = \alpha^{66} = \alpha^3$. Note also that $(\alpha^9)^2 = \alpha^{18}$, $(\alpha^{18})^2 = \alpha^{36}$, and $(\alpha^{36})^2 = \alpha^{72} = \alpha^9$, and thus successive squaring produces only three distinct roots for $m_9(X)$, which agrees with the fact that $m_9(X)$ must have degree 3, since the elements of order 9 belong to $GF(2^3)$.

All this is summarized in Table 6.2.

Define the reciprocal polynomial $f^*(X)$ of $f(X)$ to be $X^m f(1/X)$, where m is the degree of $f(X)$. (The coefficients of $f^*(X)$ are the same as those of $f(X)$ but in reverse order.) Several facts about reciprocal polynomials are suggested in Problem 6.7. For the case at hand, because the order of β and β^{-1} are the same, if β is a root of $\psi_i(X)$, then β^{-1} is also, and it follows that $\psi_i(X)$ is self-reciprocal. Hence, $m_7(X)$ is

Table 6.2. Factorization of $X^{63}-1$

$$
\begin{aligned}
&X^{63}-1=\psi_1(X)\psi_3(X)\psi_7(X)\psi_9(X)\psi_{21}(X)\psi_{63}(X)\\
&\quad\psi_1(X)=X-1\\
&\quad\psi_3(X)=m_{21}(X)\\
&\qquad m_{21}(X)=(X-\alpha^{21})(X-\alpha^{42})\\
&\quad\psi_7(X)=m_9(X)m_{27}(X)\\
&\qquad m_9(X)=(X-\alpha^{9})(X-\alpha^{18})(X-\alpha^{36})\\
&\qquad m_{27}(X)=(X-\alpha^{27})(X-\alpha^{54})(X-\alpha^{45})\\
&\quad\psi_9(X)=m_7(X)\\
&\qquad m_7(X)=(X-\alpha^{7})(X-\alpha^{14})(X-\alpha^{28})(X-\alpha^{56})(X-\alpha^{49})(X-\alpha^{35})\\
&\quad\psi_{21}(X)=m_3(X)m_{15}(X)\\
&\qquad m_3(X)=(X-\alpha^{3})(X-\alpha^{6})(X-\alpha^{12})(X-\alpha^{24})(X-\alpha^{48})(X-\alpha^{33})\\
&\qquad m_{15}(X)=(X-\alpha^{15})(X-\alpha^{30})(X-\alpha^{60})(X-\alpha^{57})(X-\alpha^{51})(X-\alpha^{39})\\
&\quad\psi_{63}(X)=m_1(X)m_5(X)m_{11}(X)m_{13}(X)m_{23}(X)m_{31}(X)\\
&\qquad m_1(X)=(X-\alpha)(X-\alpha^{2})(X-\alpha^{4})(X-\alpha^{8})(X-\alpha^{16})(X-\alpha^{32})\\
&\qquad m_5(X)=(X-\alpha^{5})(X-\alpha^{10})(X-\alpha^{20})(X-\alpha^{40})(X-\alpha^{17})(X-\alpha^{34})\\
&\qquad m_{11}(X)=(X-\alpha^{11})(X-\alpha^{22})(X-\alpha^{44})(X-\alpha^{25})(X-\alpha^{50})(X-\alpha^{37})\\
&\qquad m_{13}(X)=(X-\alpha^{13})(X-\alpha^{26})(X-\alpha^{52})(X-\alpha^{41})(X-\alpha^{19})(X-\alpha^{38})\\
&\qquad m_{23}(X)=(X-\alpha^{23})(X-\alpha^{46})(X-\alpha^{29})(X-\alpha^{58})(X-\alpha^{53})(X-\alpha^{43})\\
&\qquad m_{31}(X)=(X-\alpha^{31})(X-\alpha^{62})(X-\alpha^{61})(X-\alpha^{59})(X-\alpha^{55})(X-\alpha^{47})
\end{aligned}
$$

self-reciprocal. Both $\psi_7(X)$ and $\psi_{21}(X)$ are products of two irreducible polynomials, so either both factors must be self-reciprocal or else one factor must be the reciprocal of the other; for $\psi_7(X)$ and $\psi_{21}(X)$, the latter is the case. (However, $\psi_{17}(X)$ is the product of two irreducible polynomials of degree eight, and both are self-reciprocal.) No primitive polynomial can be self-reciprocal (Problem 6.7), and therefore the six factors of $\psi_{63}(X)$ must consist of three reciprocal pairs:

As $\alpha^{-1}=\alpha^{62}$ is a root of $m_{31}(X)$, $m_{31}(X)=m_1^*(X)$.
As $\alpha^{-5}=\alpha^{58}$ is a root of $m_{23}(X)$, $m_{23}(X)=m_5^*(X)$.
As $\alpha^{-11}=\alpha^{52}$ is a root of $m_{13}(X)$, $m_{13}(X)=m_{11}^*(X)$.

All this can be said without looking at a polynomial explicitly. The factoring can be completed by direct computation of the type that was done in producing Appendix C, or alternatively, for small polynomials over $GF(2)$, the factoring can be completed using Appendix C or Marsh's tables.

6.8 Vector Subspaces and Linear Transformations of Finite Fields

Let $\bar{f}(X)$ be a polynomial with coefficients in $GF(q^m)$ of the following kind:

$$\bar{f}(X)=\sum_{i=0}^{r} a_i X^{q^i}. \tag{6.13}$$

By Theorem 6.14, this is a linear transformation of $GF(q^m)$ into itself, considered as a vector space over $GF(q)$. Because it is a linear transformation, the set of roots and the set of possible values are both subspaces of $GF(q^m)$. In this section, the following two questions are answered affirmatively:

1. Can every subspace of $GF(q^m)$ be described as the set of roots of such a polynomial $\bar{f}(X)$ which factors completely in $GF(q^m)$?
2. Can every subspace of $GF(q^m)$ be described as the range of values occurring when all elements of $GF(q^m)$ are substituted into a polynomial $\bar{f}(X)$ which factors completely in $GF(q^m)$?

In this section, L is used to denote the map of $GF(q^m)$ onto itself which sends each field element β into β^q:

$$L\beta = \beta^q.$$

THEOREM 6.28. *Every linear transformation of $GF(q^m)$ into itself can be represented uniquely as $f(L)$, where $f(X)$ is a polynomial of degree $\leq m - 1$.*

Proof. Because the number of linear transformations of $GF(q^m)$ into itself is q^{m^2} and the number of polynomials $f(X)$ of degree $\leq m - 1$ with coefficients in $GF(q^m)$ is also q^{m^2}, it suffices to show that $f(L) \neq g(L)$ for $f(X) \neq g(X)$. This in turn is the same as showing that $f(L) \neq 0$ for $f(X) \neq 0$ and $\deg f(X) \leq m - 1$.

Thus let $f(X) = a_0 + a_1X + \cdots + a_sX^s$ with $s \leq m - 1$, $a_i \in GF(q^m)$, and not all $a_i = 0$. For $\beta \in GF(q^m)$,

$$f(L)(\beta) = a_0\beta + a_1\beta^q + \cdots + a_s\beta^{q^s}.$$

Because $q^s < q^m$ and not all the a_i are zero, there must exist a $\beta \in GF(q^m)$ that is not a zero of the polynomial

$$a_0X + a_1X^q + \cdots + a_sX^{q^s}.$$

For such a β, $f(L)(\beta) \neq 0$, and therefore $f(L) \neq 0$. Q.E.D.

The following notation will be convenient: For

$$f(X) = \sum_{i=0}^{s} a_iX^i$$

denote by $\bar{f}(X)$ the polynomial

$$\bar{f}(X) = \sum_{i=0}^{s} a_iX^{q^i}.$$

Because each subspace occurs both as range and null space of linear maps of $GF(q^m)$, we have the following corollary to Theorem 6.28.

COROLLARY 6.1. *Every subspace of $GF(q^m)$ occurs both as the set of zeros and as the range of values of a polynomial of the form $\bar{f}(X)$.*

The corollary of course is only a partial answer to previous questions (1) and (2). In addition it must be shown that the polynomials can be chosen such that they factor completely in $GF(q^m)$. To answer these questions, the following ideas will be useful.

Consider the set of polynomials with coefficients in $GF(q^m)$ with addition defined as usual, but with multiplication $*$ defined by

$$X^i * Y^j = X^{i+j}, \qquad X * a = a^q * X, \text{ for } a \text{ in } GF(q^m). \tag{6.14}$$

It can be verified that relative to these operations the polynomials form a noncommutative ring. There are no zero divisors; that is, if $f(X) * g(X) \neq 0$, then neither $f(X)$ nor $g(X)$ is zero. Note that with this definition of multiplication, the linear transformations $[f(X) * g(X)]_{X=L}$ and $f(L) \cdot g(L)$ are identical.

The following theorem is not difficult to verify:

THEOREM 6.29: *Let $f(X)$ and $g(X)$ be polynomials with coefficients in $GF(q^m)$ and suppose $g(X) \neq 0$. Then there exist unique polynomials $q(X)$ and $r(X)$ such that*

$$f(X) = q(X) * g(X) + r(X)$$

and either $r(X) = 0$ or the degree of $r(X)$ is less than the degree of $g(X)$.

In a noncommutative ring, a *left ideal* is defined as a subring I with the property that if $f(X)$ is in I and $a(X)$ is any other polynomial, then $a(X) * f(X)$ is in I. (Note that $f(X) * a(X)$ may not be in I.) It can be shown then, in a manner exactly analogous to the proof of Theorem 6.5, that every left ideal is a principal left ideal; that is, in every ideal I there is a unique monic polynomial $g(X)$ of minimum degree, and every polynomial in I is in the form $f(X) * g(X)$ for some $f(X)$.

Now let V be any k-dimensional subspace of $GF(q^m)$ considered as a vector space over $GF(q)$. Consider the set I of all polynomials $f(X)$ such that $f(L)V = 0$. Then this is a left ideal, because

$$[a(X) * f(X)]_{X=L} V = a(L) f(L) V = 0,$$

and hence for any $a(X)$, $a(X) * f(X)$ is in I. Also clearly if $f_1(X)$ and $f_2(X)$ are in I, $f_1(X) + f_2(X)$ is in I. Thus, in I there is a unique monic polynomial $g(X)$ of minimum degree k, and every other polynomial in I is a left multiple of $g(X)$.

By Theorem 6.28 there exists a polynomial $f(L)$ such that the elements of V are the set of zeros of $f(L)$; that is, $f(L)\beta = 0$ if and only if $\beta \in V$. Then $f(X)$ is in I, and it follows that $f(X) = f_1(X) * g(X)$. Therefore, $f_1(L)g(L)\beta = 0$ if and only if $\beta \in V$, and this implies that $g(L)\beta = 0$ if and only if $\beta \in V$.

The polynomial $X^m - 1$ is an element of I also, because for any field element β,

$$(L^m - 1)\beta = \beta^{q^m} - \beta = 0.$$

Therefore there exists an $h(X)$ such that

$$X^m - 1 = h(X) * g(X),$$

and

$$g(X) * (X^m - 1) = g(X) * h(X) * g(X).$$

Furthermore, for any field element β, $\beta^{q^m} = \beta$, and therefore $X^m\beta = \beta X^m$. It follows that for any polynomial $f(X)$, $X^m * f(X) = f(X) * X^m$. Therefore,

$$g(X) * (X^m - 1) = (X^m - 1) * g(X) = g(X) * h(X) * g(X);$$

and as there are no zero divisors, it follows that the $g(X)$ can be canceled, and

$$X^m - 1 = h(X) * g(X) = g(X) * h(X).$$

Now let U denote the subspace of $GF(q^m)$ consisting of all elements that occur when $g(L)$ is applied to a field element. That is,

$$U = g(L)\, GF(q^m).$$

If one considers $g(L)$ to be a matrix, V is the null space, and because V has dimension k, then $g(L)$ has row rank $m - k$ by Theorem 2.15. Then U is the column space of $g(L)$, but because the row rank and column rank of a matrix are equal, U has dimension $m - k$ also. Now,

$$h(L)\, g(L)\, GF(q^m) = h(L)U = 0.$$

As all the elements of V are roots of $\bar{g}(X)$, $\bar{g}(X)$ has degree at least q^k, and therefore $g(X)$ has degree at least k. Similarly $\bar{h}(X)$ has all the elements of U as roots; therefore $\bar{h}(X)$ has degree at least q^{m-k}, and

$h(X)$ has degree at least $m-k$. However, $g(X) * h(X) = X^m - 1$ has degree m, and therefore the degree of $g(X)$ must be exactly k, and the degree of $h(X)$ must be exactly $m-k$. It follows from this that $\bar{g}(X)$ has degree q^k, and therefore, it has as roots exactly all elements of V and it factors into q^k linear factors in $GF(q^m)$. Similarly $h(X)$ has as roots exactly all elements of U and thus factors completely, and U has dimension exactly $m-k$.

Finally,

$$g(L)\, h(L)\, GF(q^m) = 0,$$

and therefore $h(L)\, GF(q^m)$ is contained in V; because U, the null space of $h(L)$, has dimension $m-k$, the range must have dimension k and therefore must equal V. Thus the following theorem holds:

THEOREM 6.30. *Let V be a k-dimensional subspace of $GF(q^m)$ considered as a vector space over $GF(q)$. Then there exist a unique $m-k$-dimensional subspace U and unique monic polynomials $g(X)$ of degree k and $h(X)$ of degree $m-k$ such that V is the null space of $g(L)$ and the range of $h(L)$, and U is the null space of $h(L)$ and the range of $g(L)$. Furthermore, $g(X) * h(X) = h(X) * g(X) = X^m - 1$.*

COROLLARY 6.2. *The polynomial $\bar{g}(X)$ of degree q^k factors completely into linear factors and has the elements of V as roots and all the elements of U as possible values when all elements of $GF(q^m)$ are substituted for X. Similarly, $\bar{h}(X)$ has the elements of U as roots and the elements of V as values. Finally, $\bar{g}[\bar{h}(X)] = \bar{h}[\bar{g}(X)] = X^{q^m} - X$.*

Notes

Material in the first part of this chapter can be found in any of the books on algebra listed here, and many others. On Galois fields, the exposition in Carmichael (1937) is particularly straightforward. Van der Waerden (1949) is also a very good source. Albert (1956) is harder to read but is deeper and is oriented to the reader interested in finite fields.

The results of Section 6.8 were proved independently by Pele (1969) and Berlekamp (1968*b*).

Problems

6.1. Construct an addition and multiplication table for GF(7). Find the order of each element. Which elements are primitive?

6.2. Find all irreducible polynomials of degree 5 or less over $GF(2)$. (Note that if a polynomial of degree m is not irreducible it has a factor of degree less than or equal to $m/2$.) Find an irreducible polynomial of degree 5 over $GF(3)$. (The first part can be checked against Appendix C.)

6.3. How many ideals are there in the algebra of polynomials modulo $X^6 - 1$ over $GF(2)$? List their generators. (Answer: There are 7 nontrivial ideals.)

6.4. The polynomial $X^4 + X^3 + X^2 + X + 1 = p(X)$ is irreducible over $GF(2)$, and therefore the algebra of polynomials modulo $p(X)$ is $GF(2^4)$. Let α designate the residue class $\{X\}$, and show that α is not a primitive element, and therefore $p(X)$ is not a primitive polynomial. Show that $\alpha + 1$ is primitive and find its minimum polynomial, which is a primitive polynomial. (Answer: The minimum polynomial of $\alpha + 1$ is $X^4 + X^3 + 1$.)

6.5. Form tables similar to Table 6.1 for $GF(2^3)$ and $GF(3^2)$.

6.6. Determine which cyclotomic polynomials are factors of each of the following polynomials: $X^{15} - 1$, $X^{31} - 1$, $X^{127} - 1$, and $X^{255} - 1$. Determine for each of the cyclotomic polynomials the number and degree of the irreducible factors over $GF(2)$. Check by finding the factors in Appendix C.

6.7. Define the reciprocal polynomial $f^*(X)$ of any polynomial $f(X)$ to be $f^*(X) = X^m f(1/X)$, where m is the degree of $f(X)$. Prove the following:

a. The polynomial $f^*(X)$ is irreducible if and only if $f(X)$ is.
b. If $f(X)$ is irreducible, $f(X)$ and $f^*(X)$ belong to the same exponent. Therefore, $f^*(X)$ is primitive if and only if $f(X)$ is also.
c. If $f^*(X) = f(X)$ and $f(X)$ has degree greater than 2, $f(X)$ is not primitive. (The only self-reciprocal primitive polynomials are $X^2 + X + 1$ and $X + 1$ over $GF(2)$ and $X + 1$ over $GF(3)$.)
d. If $f(X) = g(X)h(X)$, $g(X)$ and $h(X)$ are irreducible, and $f(X) = f^*(X)$, then either $h(X) = g^*(X)$ or $g(X) = g^*(X)$ and $h(X) = h^*(X)$.

6.8. Show that in the vector space of n-tuples over a field $GF(p)$, where p is a prime, every subgroup (under addition) is a subspace.

6.9. Choose a 2-dimensional subspace V of $GF(2^4)$ and check Theorem 6.30 and Corollary 6.31 by calculating $\bar{g}(X)$, $\bar{h}(X)$, $g(X)$, $h(X)$, and U, and check that $g(X) * h(X) = h(X) * g(X)$. (Do not choose V to be subfield of $GF(2^4)$.)

7 Linear Switching Circuits

The heart of equipment for encoding and error correction or detection with linear codes consists of linear finite-state switching circuits. Some circuits useful for implementing linear codes are described in Sections 7.2, 7.3, and 7.4. Further properties of these circuits are presented in Section 7.5. The theory of the general linear finite-state switching circuit is introduced in Section 7.6, and it is shown that every such circuit is equivalent to a circuit of the type described in Section 7.2.

7.1 Definitions

In linear switching circuits, information is assumed to be some representation of elements of $GF(q)$. Three types of devices are used. The first is an adder, which has two inputs and one output, the output being the sum $GF(q)$ of the two inputs. The second is a storage device, which has one input and one output. It can be a delay device, for which the output always is the same as the input was one unit of time earlier. It can also be considered to be a single stage of shift register. In a shift register, there is a shift signal, not shown in the diagrams, which would usually be supplied by timing circuits. When this signal appears, the output of each stage takes the value that the input took immediately before the shift signal appeared. The third type of device is a constant multiplier, which has one input and one output, the output being simply the input multiplied by a constant, which may be any field element. The rule for interconnection of these devices is that any number of

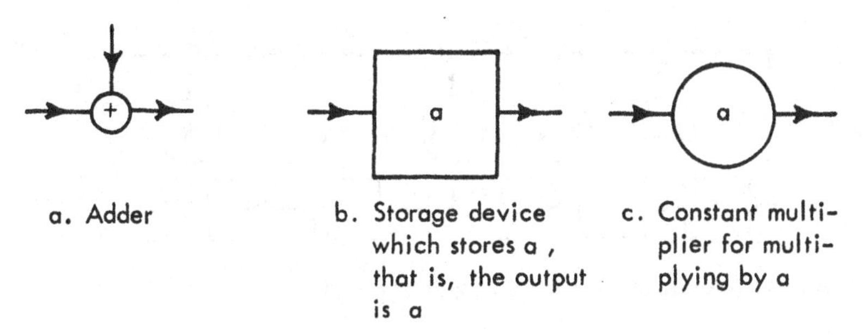

Figure 7.1. The building blocks for linear switching circuits.

inputs may be connected to any output, but that two outputs are never connected together. The representation of these devices in circuit diagrams is shown in Figure 7.1.

A linear finite-state switching circuit is any circuit consisting of a finite number of adders, memory devices, and constant multipliers connected in any permissible way. Any linear finite-state switching circuit can be constructed out of vacuum tubes, transistors, magnetic cores, or other computer logical circuitry using the techniques of digital computer design. In the binary case, the adder is an "exclusive-or" logical block, and the memory device is either a delay device or a single stage of ordinary binary shift register. The constant multiplier for the constant 1 is simply a connection, and for the constant 0, simply no connection.

Input and output is assumed to be serial; that is, it consists of field elements entering an input line one at a time, one for each unit of time. When an input or output is a polynomial, as is often the case, only the coefficients appear on the input or output line, and they are transmitted *high-order coefficients first*. The reason is that in division, the high-order coefficients of the dividend must be processed first. Thus the polynomial

$$f(X) = f_n X^n + f_{n-1} X^{n-1} + \cdots + f_0$$

would be entered on an input line or appear on an output line as a succession of n field elements, with f_n coming first, then f_{n-1} one unit of time later, f_{n-2} after another unit of time, and so forth.

7.2 Multiplication and Division of Polynomials

Circuits are given in this section for multiplication or division of any polynomial by a fixed polynomial.

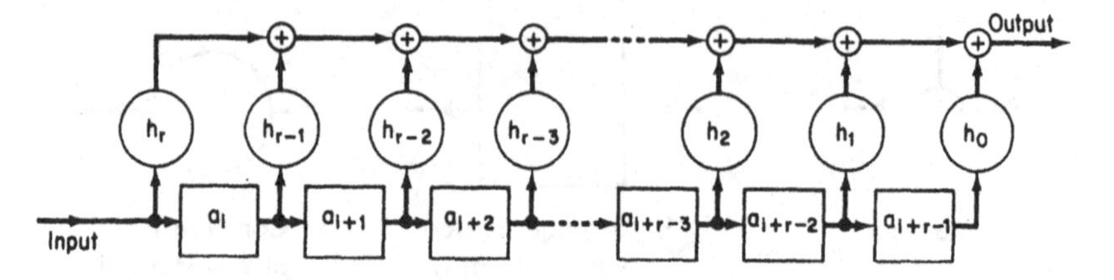

Figure 7.2. A circuit for multiplying polynomials.

The circuit shown in Figure 7.2 multiplies any input polynomial

$$a(X) = a_k X^k + a_{k-1}X^{k-1} + \cdots + a_1 X + a_0$$

by the fixed polynomial

$$h(X) = h_r X^r + h_{r-1}X^{r-1} + \cdots + h_1 X + h_0.$$

The storage devices are assumed to contain 0's initially, and the coefficients of $a(X)$ are assumed to enter high-order first and to be followed by r zeros.

The product is

$$\begin{aligned} a(X)\,h(X) = {} & a_k h_r X^{k+r} \\ & + (a_{k-1}h_r + a_k h_{r-1})X^{k+r-1} \\ & + (a_{k-2} h_r + a_{k-1}h_{r-1} + a_k h_{r-2})X^{k+r-2} + \cdots \\ & + (a_0 h_2 + a_1 h_1 + a_2 h_0)X^2 \\ & + (a_0 h_1 + a_1 h_0)X + a_0 h_0 . \end{aligned}$$

When the first coefficient in a_k in $a(X)$ appears at the input, the first coefficient $a_k h_r$ of $a(X)h(X)$ appears at the output. At that point all the storage devices contain 0's. After one unit of time, a_{k-1} appears at the input, a_k is in the first storage device, and the rest of the storage devices contain 0's. The output can be seen from Figure 7.2 to be $a_{k-1}h_r + a_k h_{r-1}$, which is the correct second coefficient in the product $a(X)\,h(X)$. Similarly, after two units of time a_{k-2} is at the input, and the shift register stages contain $a_{k-1}, a_k, 0, \ldots, 0, 0, 0$. The output is $a_{k-2} h_r + a_{k-1}h_{k-1} + a_k h_{r-2}$, which is the correct third coefficient of $a(X)\,h(X)$. The operation continues in a similar manner. After $r + k - 1$ shifts, the shift register contains $0, 0, 0, \ldots, 0, a_0, a_1$, and the output is $a_0 h_1 + a_1 h_0$, which is the next-to-last coefficient in $a(X)\,h(X)$. After $r + k$ shifts, the shift register contains $0, 0, 0, \ldots, a_0$, and the output is $a_0 h_0$, the last coefficient of $a(X)\,h(X)$, and the product is complete.

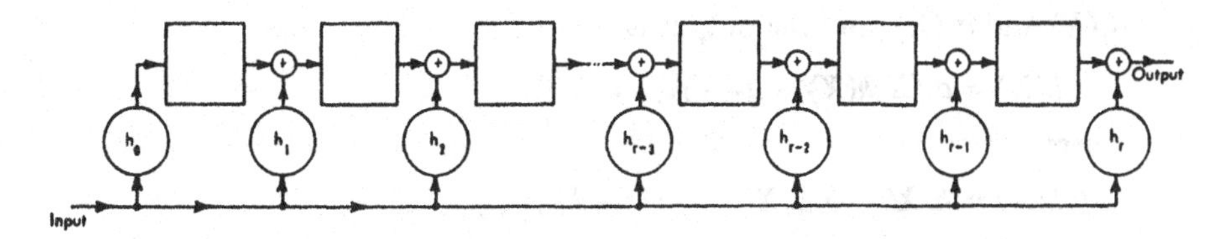

Figure 7.3. Another circuit for multiplying polynomials.

Another circuit for multiplication is shown in Figure 7.3. The product coefficients are developed in the shift register. As the first symbol enters the input, the output is $a_k h_r$, and the storage devices contain all 0's. After one shift the storage devices contain $a_k h_0, a_k h_1, \ldots, a_k h_{r-1}$, and the input is a_{k-1}. The output is therefore $a_k h_{r-1} + a_{k-1} h_r$, which is the correct second coefficient. After the next shift the storage devices contain $a_{k-1}h_0, a_k h_0 + a_{k-1}h_1, a_k h_1 + a_{k-1}h_2, \ldots, a_k h_{r-2} + a_{k-1}h_{r-1}$, and the input is a_{k-2}. The output is therefore $a_k h_{r-2} + a_{k-1}h_{r-1} + a_{k-2} h_r$, which is the correct third coefficient. The operation continues in a similar manner.

This circuit can be understood in another manner. The set of r storage devices forms a register that stores a polynomial. Initially, it is 0. The presence of a_k at the input adds $a_k h(X)$ into the register. Shifting multiplies by X and delivers the first coefficient, whose calculation is complete to the output. The appearance of a_{k-1} at the input adds $a_{k-1}h(X)$ into the register, and shifting again multiplies by X and delivers the second coefficient to the output, and so forth.

Circuits of the type shown in Figure 7.3 can have more than one input. For example, the circuit shown in Figure 7.4 has two inputs,

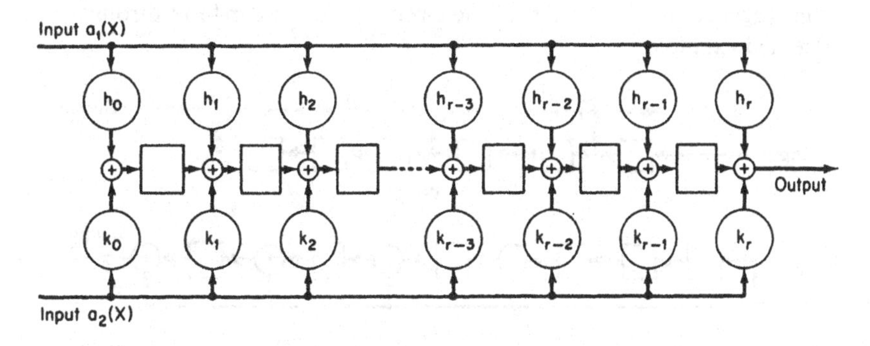

Figure 7.4. A two-input multiplier.

$a_1(X)$ and $a_2(X)$, and the output is

$$b(X) = a_1(X)h(X) + a_2(X)k(X),$$

where

$$h(X) = h_r X^r + h_{r-1}X^{r-1} + \cdots + h_0,$$

$$k(X) = k_r X^r + k_{r-1}X^{r-1} + \cdots + k_0.$$

The circuit is shown as if $h(X)$ and $k(X)$ have the same degree, but in case the degrees are not equal, r can be taken as the larger degree, and the high-order coefficients of one polynomial can be 0.

Note that in all these circuits, the coefficient of X^{r+i} comes out at the same time that the coefficient of X^i goes in. The coefficient of X^r in the product comes out r units of time after the coefficient of X^0 enters the input. Thus, in a sense, the output is delayed r units of time.

Example. The circuits shown in Figure 7.5 multiply the input polynomial by $h(X) = X^6 + X^5 + X^4 + X^3 + 1$ over the field of two elements. It is instructive to write out the contents of the storage devices at each step in the process and to compare with the ordinary hand calculation of the product.

A circuit for dividing $d(X) = d_n X^n + d_{n-1}X^{n-1} + \cdots + d_0$ by $g(X) = g_r X^r + g_{r-1}X^{r-1} + \cdots + g_0$ is shown in Figure 7.6. The storage devices must be set to 0 initially. The output is 0 for the first r shifts, that is, until the first input symbol reaches the end of the shift register. Then the first nonzero output appears, and its value is $d_n g_r^{-1}$, the first coefficient of the quotient. For each quotient coefficient q_j, the polynomial $q_j g(X)$ must be subtracted from the dividend. The feedback connections accomplish this subtraction. After a total of n shifts, the entire quotient has appeared at the output, and the remainder is in the shift register. The operation of the circuit is best understood through a detailed example.

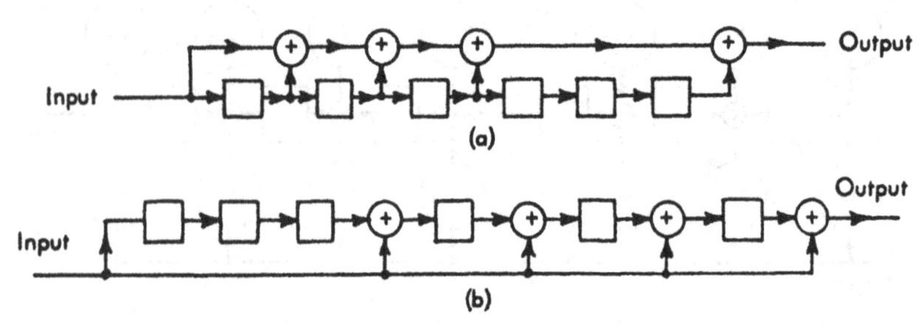

Figure 7.5. Circuits for multiplying by $X^6 + X^5 + X^4 + X^3 + 1$.

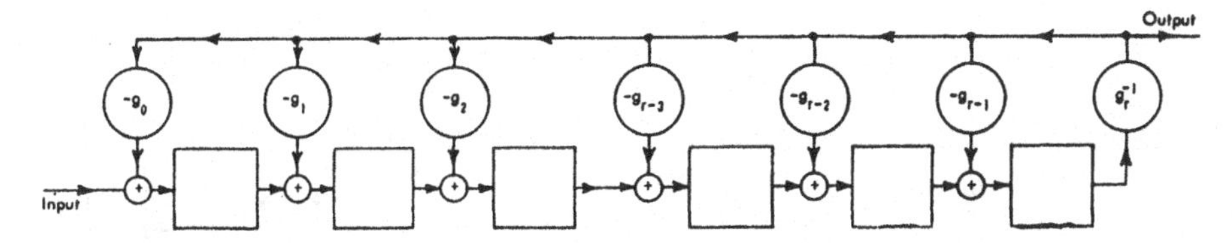

Figure 7.6. A circuit for dividing polynomials.

Example. The circuit shown in Figure 7.7 divides the input polynomial by $g(X) = X^6 + X^5 + X^4 + X^3 + 1$, over the field of two elements. The step-by-step division of $X^{13} + X^{11} + X^{10} + X^7 + X^4 + X^3 + X + 1$ by $X^6 + X^5 + X^4 + X^3 + 1$ is compared with the step-by-step operation of this circuit in Table 7.1. Note that in ordinary long division the high-order terms are at the left, while in the shift register the high-order terms are at the right.

The first six shifts have no counterpart in long division. After six shifts the contents of the shift register match the polynomial marked A in Table 7.1a. The leading coefficient is the first quotient symbol and is also the output after the seventh shift. The feedback matches the polynomial marked B, and the input corresponds to C, the quantity which is brought down. After the seventh shift the contents of the shift register match the polynomial marked D. The feedback matches E; the F term brought down is the same as the input; and after the eighth shift the shift register contents match G. The process continues until after fourteen shifts, one for each coefficient in the dividend, the shift register contains the remainder, and all the quotient coefficients have appeared at the output.

In this circuit, the coefficient of X^j in the quotient appears at the same time as the coefficient of X^j appears at the input. Thus, input and quotient are synchronized.

A single shift-register circuit that multiplies by $h(X)$ and then divides by $g(X)$ can be made by combining the multiplication circuit of Figure 7.3 and the division circuit of Figure 7.6, as shown in Figure 7.8. In this circuit it is assumed that the degree of $h(X)$ is no greater than the degree of $g(X)$. (See the example that follows.)

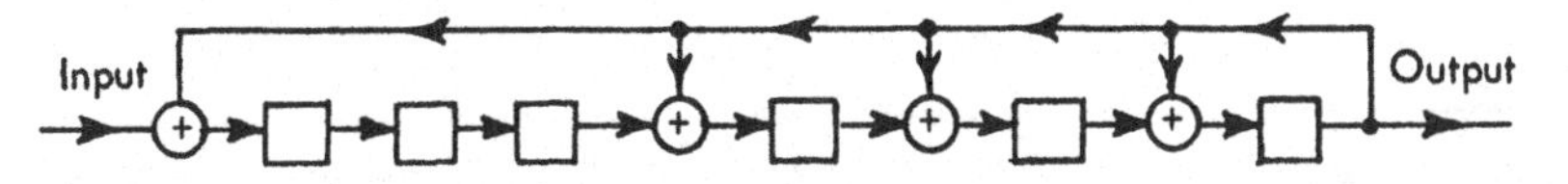

Figure 7.7. A circuit for dividing by $X^6 + X^5 + X^4 + X^3 + 1$.

Table 7.1. Comparison of Long Division and the Division Circuit

(a) Long Division

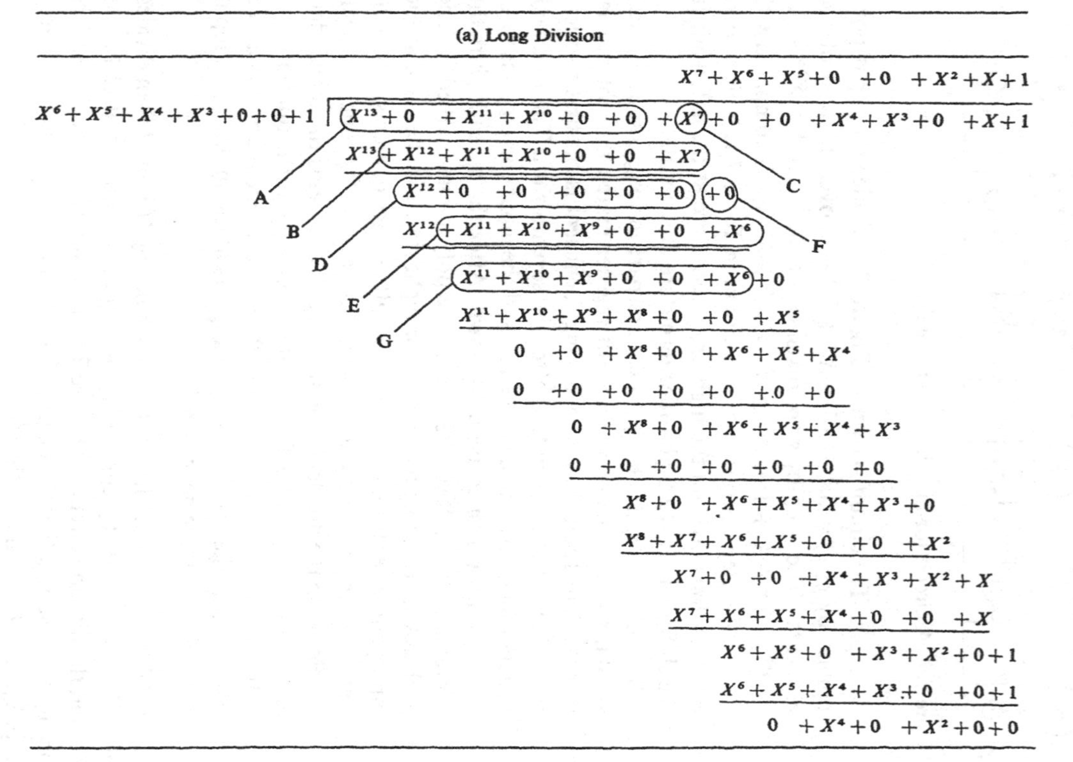

Table 7.1. Comparison of Long Division and the Division Circuit (cont.)

(b) Step-by-Step Operation of the Division Circuit

j	Shift Register Contents after jth Shift	Output Symbol after jth Shift	Feedback on jth Shift	Input Symbol on jth Shift
0	000000	0	—	—
1	100000	0	000000	1
2	010000	0	000000	0
3	101000	0	000000	1
4	110100	0	000000	1
5	011010	0	000000	0
6	001101	1	000000	0
7	000001	1	100111	1
8	100111	1	100111	0
9	110100	0	100111	0
10	111010	0	000000	1
11	111101	1	000000	1
12	111001	1	100111	0
13	011011	1	100111	1
14	001010	0	100111	1

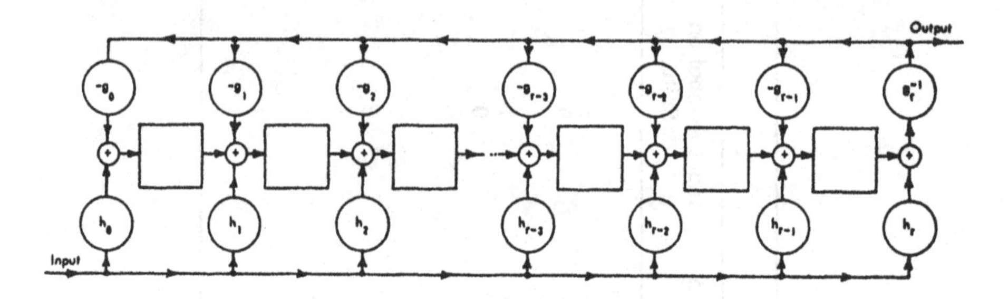

Figure 7.8. A circuit for multiplying by $h(X)$ and dividing by $g(X)$.

Example. A shift-register circuit for multiplying an input polynomial by $X^5 + X + 1$ and then dividing by $X^6 + X^5 + X^4 + X^3 + 1$ is shown in Figure 7.9. The shift register contains the part of the dividend which is being processed. The input connections add into the shift register the product of $X^5 + X + 1$ and the input symbol, instead of simply adding the input symbol as in the division circuit, Figure 7.6.

If the constant factor has higher degree than the divisor, then stages should be added at the low-order end of the shift register, and as many extra shifts with 0 input as added stages are required to complete the division. An example is shown in Figure 7.10, in which the input polynomial is multiplied by $X^{10} + X^9 + X^5 + 1$ and divided by $X^6 + X^5 + X^4 + X^3 + 1$. In this case, four shifts with 0 input are required after the coefficient of the zero-degree term in the input to complete the calculation of the quotient and the remainder.

7.3 Computations in Polynomial Algebras and Galois Fields

The circuits described in the preceding sections can be adapted for use in computations in the algebra of polynomials modulo $g(X)$, a given polynomial.

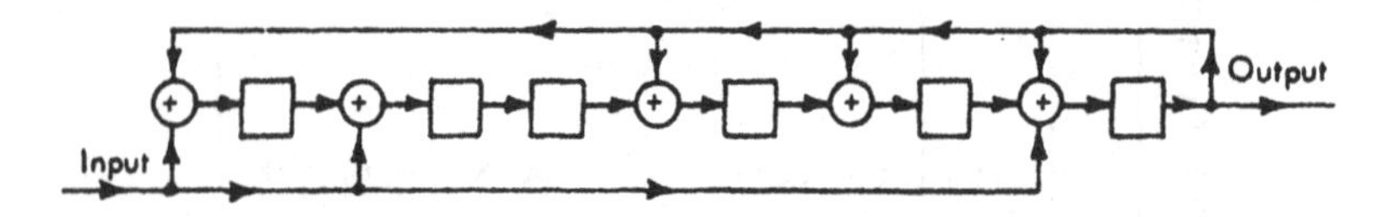

Figure 7.9. A circuit for simultaneously multiplying by $X^5 + X + 1$ and dividing by $X^6 + X^5 + X^4 + X^3 + 1$.

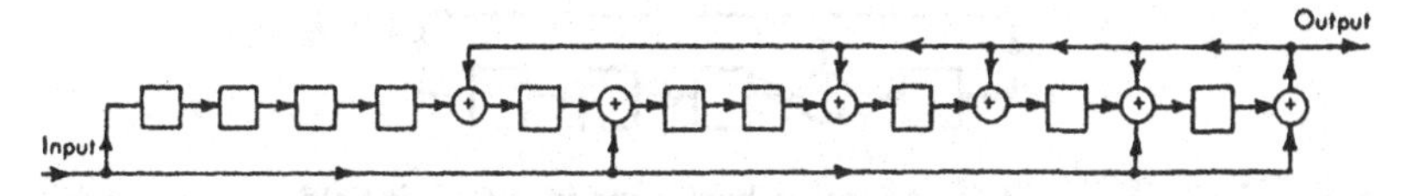

Figure 7.10. A circuit for simultaneously multiplying by $X^{10} + X^9 + X^5 + 1$ and dividing by $X^6 + X^5 + X^4 + X^3 + 1$.

The shift register of r storage devices in Figure 7.6 stores field elements that can be considered to be the coefficients of a polynomial

$$b(X) = b_{r-1}X^{r-1} + b_{r-2}X^{r-2} + \cdots + b_0$$

which has degree $r - 1$ or less. If the register is shifted right once, the contents become

$$b'(X) = b_{r-2}X^{r-1} + b_{r-3}X^{r-2} + \cdots + b_1X^2 + b_0X - b_{r-1}(g_r^{-1}g(X) - X^r).$$

The last term is the result of the feedback connections. This can be rearranged to give

$$b'(X) = Xb(X) - b_{r-1}g_r^{-1}g(X). \tag{7.1}$$

Thus, $b'(X)$ is in the same residue class modulo $g(X)$ as $Xb(X)$, and because $b'(X)$ has degree less than r, it must be the unique polynomial in the residue class $\{Xb(X)\}$ that has degree less than r.

This can be restated as follows: If S designates the residue class containing X, then $\{b(X)\} = b(S)$ and $\{Xb(X)\} = Sb(S)$. Shifting right once thus corresponds to multiplying by S, and the contents of the shift register always are the coefficients of the unique polynomial in S of degree less than r.

The idea will be illustrated using the polynomial $g(X) = X^4 + X + 1$ and the field of two elements. This polynomial is primitive, and therefore $\{X\} = \alpha$, which is a root of $X^4 + X + 1$, is a primitive element of $GF(2^4)$. The corresponding shift register is shown in Figure 7.11. If a 1 is placed in the low-order storage device and 0's in the others, successive shifts will give representations of successive powers of α, in exactly the same form as they appear in Table 6.1. Note that a 1 shifted out of the high-order position corresponds to α^4 and is in effect replaced by its equal $\alpha + 1$ by the feedback connections.

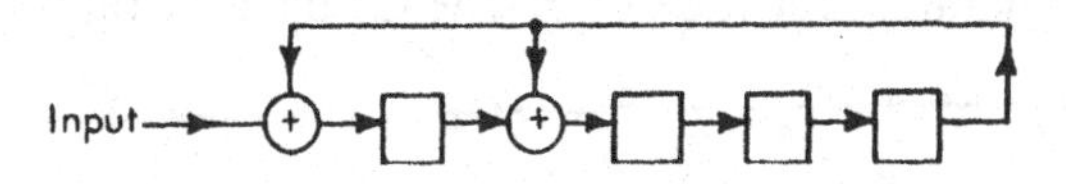

Figure 7.11. A circuit for counting in a Galois field.

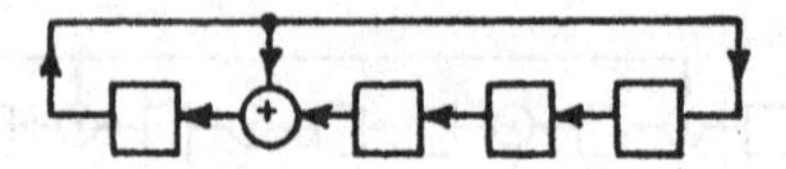

Figure 7.12. A circuit for counting backward in a Galois field.

A variation of this circuit is shown in Figure 7.12. A left shift corresponds to division by α and a 1 shifted out of the low-order end, α^{-1}, is replaced by its equivalent $\alpha^3 + 1$. Thus this device can count down or give Galois field elements in reverse order. A multiplier can be mechanized by putting one factor in a device A such as that shown in Figure 7.11, the other in a device B such as that shown in Figure 7.12. Then both devices are shifted until the code for 1 appears in device B. The product then appears in A. Division can be made in an analogous manner.

Multiplication can also be accomplished in a manner analogous to the method ordinarily used in a digital computer,* with a shift register of the type shown in Figure 7.11 used as an accumulator. This method applies in general to the algebra of polynomials modulo a polynomial $g(X)$ and in particular to Galois fields. As an example, consider multiplying α^{10} and α^7 as elements of $GF(2^4)$ as represented in Table 6.1. The contents of the "accumulator" are now shown after each operation. Note that vector addition is used and that the α^0 bit is on the left:

Multiplier		Accumulator Contents
① ① ⓪ ①		0000
	Add 1(1 1 1 0)	1110
	Shift	0111
	Add 0(1 1 1 0)	0111
	Shift	1111
	Add 1(1 1 1 0)	0001
	Shift	1100
	Add 1(1 1 1 0)	0010 (Answer)

The value of a polynomial $r(X)$ when the field element α is substituted for X can be found also using the device shown in Figure 7.6, by taking $g(X)$ as the minimum function of α. The Galois field representation of

$$r(\alpha) = r_{n-1}\alpha^{n-1} + r_{n-2}\alpha^{n-2} + \cdots + r_0$$

* See, for example, Richards (1955) or Gschwind (1967).

can be calculated by eliminating terms of degree higher than k in α by using the relation $g(\alpha) = 0$. This is exactly what will result if the vector $(r_0, r_1, \ldots, r_{n-1})$ is shifted into the device shown in Figure 7.6.

Example. Let α be a primitive element of $GF(2^4)$ as shown in Table 6.1. The Galois field representation of

$$r(\alpha) = r_{n-1}\alpha^{n-1} + r_{n-2}\alpha^{n-2} + \cdots + r_0$$

can be calculated by shifting $r_0, \ldots, r_{n-1}$ into the circuit shown in Figure 7.11.

To calculate $r(\alpha^j)$ for $j \neq 1$ (or 0) is more complicated if the result must be expressed in terms of a polynomial of lowest degree in α. One method uses a shift register that automatically multiplies by α^j. An example with $j = 5$ should make the principles clear. Note that, from Table 6.1,

$$\begin{aligned} 1\alpha^5 &= \alpha^5 = \alpha^2 + \alpha \\ \alpha\alpha^5 &= \alpha^6 = \alpha^3 + \alpha^2 \\ \alpha^2\alpha^5 &= \alpha^7 = \alpha^3 + \alpha + 1 \\ \alpha^3\alpha^5 &= \alpha^8 = \alpha^2 + 1 \end{aligned}$$

so that

$$\begin{aligned} \alpha^5(a_3\alpha^3 + a_2\alpha^2 + a_1\alpha + a_0) &= a_3(\alpha^2 + 1) + a_2(\alpha^3 + \alpha + 1) \\ &\quad + a_1(\alpha^3 + \alpha^2) + a_0(\alpha^2 + \alpha) \\ &= (a_1 + a_2)\alpha^3 + (a_0 + a_1 + a_3)\alpha^2 \\ &\quad + (a_0 + a_2)\alpha + (a_2 + a_3). \end{aligned}$$

Thus, the new value of a_0 is the old $a_2 + a_3$, the new a_1 is the old $a_0 + a_2$, and so on. A shift register with feedback connection shown in Figure 7.13 gives this result. If the received vector $(r_{2^m-2}, \ldots, r_1, r_0)$ is shifted into this device, after fifteen shifts the result $r(\alpha^5)$ will remain in the register.

A second method of calculating $r(X^j)$ and expressing it in terms of a polynomial of lowest degree in α has been proposed by Chien (1964*b*). In this method the polynomial $r(X^j)$ is formed by inserting $j - 1$ zeros between successive digits of $r(X)$. Then the value of this new polynomial with α substituted for X can be found with the circuit of Figure 7.6. This method employs somewhat simpler circuitry than the previous one but requires j times as many shifts.

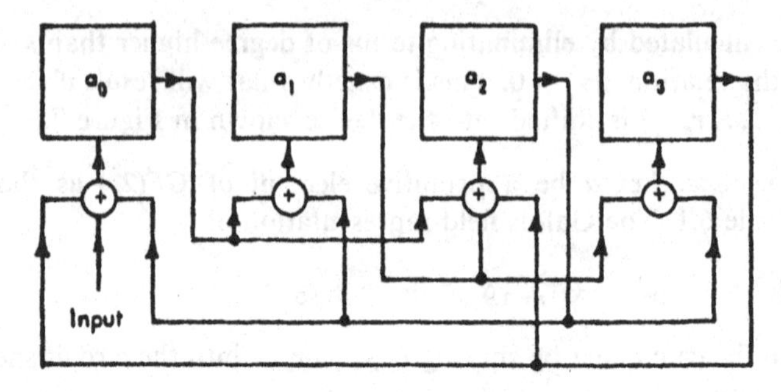

Figure 7.13. A circuit for multiplying by X^5 in $GF(2^4)$.

7.4 Linear Recurrence Relations and Shift-Register Generators

Consider the recurrence relation or difference equation

$$\sum_{j=0}^{k} h_j a_{i+j} = 0 \tag{7.2a}$$

or

$$a_{i+k} = -\sum_{j=0}^{k-1} h_j a_{i+j} \tag{7.2b}$$

where $h_0 \neq 0$ and $h_k = 1$, and each h_j is an element of $GF(q)$. A solution of these equations is a sequence $a_0, a_1, a_2, \ldots$ of elements of $GF(q)$. Equation 7.2*b* is a rule for determining a_k given the values of $a_0, a_1, \ldots, a_{k-1}$. From knowledge of $a_1, a_2, \ldots, a_k$ the value of a_{k+1} can be found, and so forth. Because the equations are linear, any linear combination of solutions is a solution, and the solutions form a vector space. The k solutions, for which one of the symbols $a_0, a_1, \ldots, a_{k-1}$ is 1 and the rest are 0, span the space; therefore the space of solutions has dimension no greater than k. Since $a_0, a_1, \ldots, a_{k-1}$ are arbitrary, the space has dimension at least k. Therefore, the dimension is exactly k.

A linear sequential switching circuit that calculates the sum indicated in Equation 7.2*b* and hence calculates a_i from the previous k values in the sequence is shown in Figure 7.14. The initial values $a_0, a_1, \ldots, a_{k-1}$ are placed in the storage devices. Successive shifts calculate successive symbols, and the output after i shifts is always a_i. This device is called a *shift-register generator*.

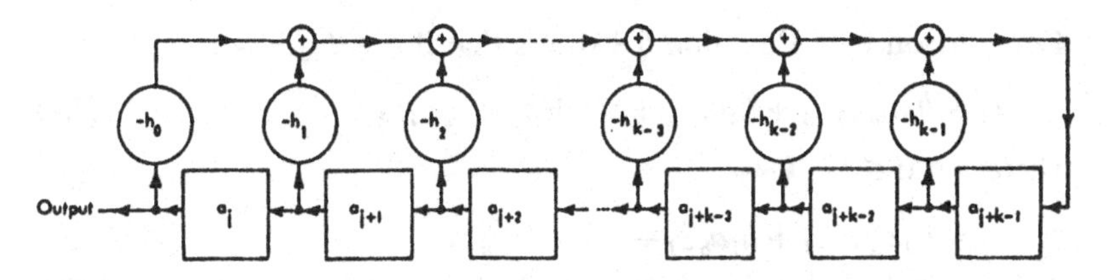

Figure 7.14. A shift-register generator.

The solutions of a linear recurrence relation are characterized in the following theorem:

THEOREM 7.1. *Let* $h(X) = \sum_{j=0}^{k} h_j X^j$, $h_0 \neq 0$, $h_k = 1$, *and let* n *be the smallest positive integer for which* $X^n - 1$ *is divisible by* $h(X)$. *Let* $g(X) = (X^n - 1)/h(X)$. *Then the solutions of the recurrence Relation* 7.2*a*,

$$0 = \sum_{j=0}^{k} h_j a_{i+j},$$

are periodic of period n, *and the set made up of the first period of each possible solution, considered as polynomials modulo* $X^n - 1$,

$$a(X) = a_0 X^{n-1} + a_1 X^{n-2} + \cdots + a_{n-2} X + a_{n-1},$$

is the ideal generated by $g(X)$ *in the algebra of polynomials modulo* $X^n - 1$. *Note that with* $a(X)$ *defined in this manner, if* $a_0, a_1, \ldots$ *are generated in order of increasing index, the coefficients of* $a(X)$ *are generated high order first in accordance with the convention stated in Section* 7.1.

Proof. First it will be shown that, if $\{a(X)\}$ is in the ideal generated by $g(X)$, then the sequence of period n

$$a_0, a_1, \ldots, a_{n-1}, a_0, a_1, \ldots \tag{7.3}$$

is a solution of Equation 7.2*a*. Consider the product

$$\{a(X)\}\{h(X)\} = \{c(X)\},$$

where

$$a(X) = a_0 X^{n-1} + a_1 X^{n-2} + \cdots + a_{n-2} X + a_{n-1},$$
$$h(X) = h_k X^k + h_{k-1} X^{k-1} + \cdots + h_0,$$

and

$$c(X) = c_{n-1} X^{n-1} + c_{n-2} X^{n-2} + \cdots + c_0.$$

Comparison with Equation 6.8 shows that if $k \leqq l \leqq n-1$,

$$c_l = h_0 a_{n-1-l} + h_1 a_{n-l} + \cdots + h_k a_{n-1-l+k}; \tag{7.4}$$

whereas if $0 \leqq l < k$,

$$c_l = h_0 a_{n-1-l} + h_1 a_{n-l} + \cdots + h_l a_{n-1} + h_{l+1} a_0 + h_{l+2} a_1 + \cdots + h_k a_{k-l-1}. \tag{7.5}$$

By Theorem 6.12, if $\{a(X)\}$ is in the ideal $\{g(X)\}$, $\{a(X)\}\{h(X)\} = 0$, and therefore every $c_l = 0$.

Now consider the sequence given in Equation 7.3. In it, $a_i = a_{i+n}$ for all $i \geqq 0$. This makes the recurrence relation, Equation 7.2*a*, exactly equivalent to one or the other of Equations 7.4 or 7.5, and thus if $\{a(X)\}$ is in the ideal generated by $g(X)$, the sequence in Equation 7.3 is a solution of the recurrence relation, Equation 7.2.

Since $g(X) = (X^n - 1)/h(X)$ has degree $n-k$, the ideal $\{g(X)\}$ has dimension k, by Theorem 6.11. This is the same as the dimension of the space of solutions and therefore by Theorem 2.9 must include all solutions.

Some of the solutions may have period less than n, but there must be some that do not. In particular, the solution obtained from $\{g(X)\}$ has period exactly n. This can be shown as follows. If it has period m less than n, then certainly n is a multiple of m, and each block of n symbols consists of n/m identical blocks of m symbols. For this to be the case, it must be that

$$\begin{aligned} g(X) &= q(X)(X^{n-m} + X^{n-2m} + \cdots + X^m + 1) \\ &= q(X)(X^n - 1)/(X^m - 1). \end{aligned}$$

Then,

$$(X^n - 1)(X^m - 1) = h(X)\,g(X)(X^m - 1) = h(X)\,q(X)(X^n - 1)$$

and

$$(X^m - 1) = h(X)\,q(X),$$

which contradicts the assumption that n is the smallest integer for which $X^n - 1$ is divisible by $h(X)$. Q.E.D.

Example. Over $GF(2)$ determine the period of solutions of the difference equation corresponding to $h(X) = X^4 + X^3 + X + 1 = (X+1)^2(X^2+X+1)$. The factor $X^2 + X + 1$ divides $X^3 + 1$, and so does $X + 1$, but in order for $X^n + 1$ to be divisible by

$X^2 + X + 1$ and $(X + 1)^2$, n must be taken to be 6. The period must therefore be 6. Some solutions will have period less than 6, but there must be at least one solution that has period 6. The generator of the ideal from which the solutions are formed is $g(X) = (X^6 - 1)/h(X) = X^2 + X + 1$, and this corresponds to the solution 1 1 1 0 0 0. The other solutions are all vectors in the row space of

$$G = \begin{bmatrix} 111000 \\ 011100 \\ 001110 \\ 000111 \end{bmatrix} \tag{7.6}$$

In particular, the sum of the first two rows, 1 0 0 1 0 0, actually has period 3, and the sum of the first three rows, 1 0 1 0 1 0, actually has period 2.

As a further example, the binary shift-register generator corresponding to the polynomial $h(X) = X^8 + X^6 + X^5 + X^3 + 1$ is shown in Figure 7.15. This polynomial is primitive, and therefore divides $X^{255} - 1$ but does not divide $X^n - 1$ for any smaller n. Thus the period of the shift-register output sequence is 255, which is the maximum length possible for an 8-stage shift-register generator. (See Section 8.5 for further details.)

For the purpose of studying cyclic codes, Theorem 7.1 gives the essential facts in the most convenient form. Furthermore, by the use of this theorem, the possible periods of sequences for a given shift register can be determined easily, as illustrated in the preceding example. Also synthesis of a shift register for sequences of a specified period can be carried out easily using this result. Other ways of studying linear recurrence relations will be described only briefly.

Consider the recurrence relation corresponding to $h(X)$, as described in Theorem 7.1. Let α be any root of $h(X)$, perhaps in an extension field. Then the sequence

$$1, \alpha, \alpha^2, \alpha^3, \ldots \tag{7.7}$$

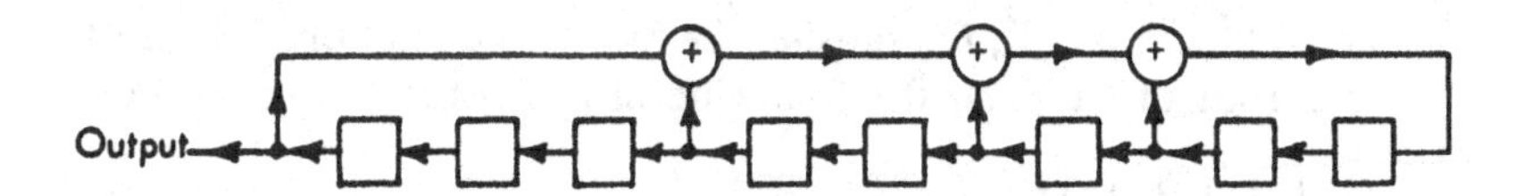

Figure 7.15. A shift-register generator for maximum-length sequences.

obviously satisfies the recurrence relation. Since the recurrence relation is linear, any linear combination of sequences of ascending powers of roots is a solution:

$$R_i = Y_1\alpha_1^i + Y_2\alpha_2^i + \cdots + Y_k\alpha_k^i, \tag{7.8}$$

where $\alpha_1, \alpha_2, \ldots, \alpha_k$ are the k roots of $h(X)$ and $Y_1, Y_2, \ldots, Y_k$ are arbitrary constants. (This assumes that all roots are distinct.) As it is known that the space of solutions has dimension k and as there are k arbitrary constants here, this must be a complete set of solutions. This is, of course, analogous to the classical method for solution of linear differential equations, and there is a close parallel with transform methods, with the roots of $h(X)$ playing the role of roots of the characteristic function or poles of the output function of an ordinary linear system.

Now suppose that $h_1(X)$ is an irreducible factor of $h(X)$ of degree k_1. Let α be a root of $h_1(X)$. Over $GF(q)$, then, α and its powers can be written as vectors with k_1 components. Clearly, each component in Sequence 7.7 must satisfy the recurrence relation. This corresponds to the fact in the study of linear differential equations that, if a complex-valued function satisfies an equation with real coefficients, both the real and imaginary parts of the complex solution are real solutions.

Example. Let α be a root of $X^3 + X^2 + 1$ over $GF(2)$. Then the field elements in the extension field $GF(2^3)$ can be represented by column vectors with three components from $GF(2)$,

$$(1, \alpha, \alpha^2, \alpha^3, \alpha^4, \alpha^5, \alpha^6) = \begin{bmatrix} 1001110 \\ 0100111 \\ 0011101 \end{bmatrix} \tag{7.9}$$

Each row of this matrix satisfies the recurrence relation

$$0 = \alpha_i + \alpha_{i+2} + \alpha_{i+3}$$

corresponding to the polynomial $h(X) = X^3 + X^2 + 1$.

Now consider the polynomial $h(X) = (X + 1)(X^3 + X + 1) = X^4 + X^3 + X^2 + 1$ and the corresponding recurrence relation $0 = a_i + a_{i+2} + a_{i+3} + a_{i+4}$. If β is a root of $X^3 + X + 1$, then $(1, \beta, \beta^2, \beta^3, \beta^4, \beta^5, \beta^6)$ satisfies the recurrence relation. Because 1 is a root of $(X + 1)$, the following also satisfies the recurrence:

$$(1, 1, 1, 1, 1, 1, 1).$$

With use of the representation of $GF(2^3)$ given by polynomials modulo $X^3 + X + 1$, the successive powers of β give the top three rows of the matrix $\mathbf{M}$, and the last row is the row of powers of 1. Thus each row is a solution, and the set of all solutions is the row space of $\mathbf{M}$:

$$\mathbf{M} = \begin{bmatrix} 1001011 \\ 0101110 \\ 0010111 \\ 1111111 \end{bmatrix} \tag{7.10}$$

Alternatively, consider the algebra of polynomials modulo $X^4 + X^3 + X^2 + 1$, and let S denote the residue class that contains X. Then because $S^4 + S^3 + S^2 + 1 = 0$,

$$(1, S, S^2, S^3, S^4, S^5, S^6)$$

satisfies the recurrence relation. (Note that S is not a field element.) Then each element of the algebra can be represented by a vector:

$$\begin{aligned}
1 &= \{1\} &&= (0001) \\
S &= \{X\} &&= (0010) \\
S^2 &= \{X^2\} &&= (0100) \\
S^3 &= \{X^3\} &&= (1000) \\
S^4 &= \{X^3 + X^2 + 1\} &&= (1101) \\
S^5 &= \{X^2 + X + 1\} &&= (0111) \\
S^6 &= \{X^3 + X^2 + X\} &&= (1110)
\end{aligned}$$

and writing $1, S, S^2, S^3, S^4, S^5, S^6$ as column vectors gives a matrix

$$\begin{bmatrix} 1000110 \\ 0100011 \\ 0010111 \\ 0001101 \end{bmatrix} \tag{7.11}$$

Now every row of this matrix is a solution of the recurrence relation, and every solution is in the row space of this matrix.

Still another approach is to employ the concept of a "quotient field" of polynomials. The rigorous treatment is given by Zierler (1959) and only a statement of the main theorem and an example will be given here. Zierler's theorem states that if any polynomial $f(X)$ degree $k - 1$ or less is divided formally by long division by $h^*(X) = h_0 X^k + h_1 X^{k-1} + \cdots$

$+ h_k$, the coefficients of the resulting nonterminating quotient satisfy the recurrence relation

$$0 = h_0 a_i + h_1 a_{i+1} + \cdots + h_k a_{i+k}.$$

Example. Let $h^*(X) = 1 + X + X^3$. Then, by long division,

$$1/(1 + X + X^3) = 1 + X + X^2 + X^4 + X^7 + X^8 + X^9 + X^{11} + \cdots$$

and the sequence of coefficients, 11101001110100... agrees with each row in Equation 7.9.

The circuits described in this section and Section 7.2 are analogous to linear filters and feedback systems. They are, in fact, sampled-data systems, the only important difference from conventional systems being that the quantities are elements of a finite field here and are real numbers in conventional systems. The transform methods used for sampled-data systems apply here, and the mathematics involved is that discussed in the preceding paragraphs. These ideas are pursued further in the following section.

Methods for synthesis of a shift-register generator with a specified or partially specified output sequence are also given in the next section. If only the period is specified, Theorem 7.1 gives sufficient information for easy synthesis.

7.5 Z-Transforms, Transfer Functions, and Synthesis

In this section it is shown that the input-output and transient characteristics of the circuits described in Section 7.2 can be characterized by a transfer function. In Section 7.6 it is shown that this is true for an arbitrary linear sequential circuit. Thus, every linear sequential circuit has a transfer function, and two different circuits with the same transfer function are indistinguishable from the outside, that is, if only inputs and outputs, not internal states, are examined. Furthermore, it is shown that, given any ratio of polynomials, there is a circuit of the type described in Section 7.2 which has that as its transfer function, and thus the transfer function synthesis problem is solved. The problem of finding a transfer function for a specified impulse or transient response is also solved in this section.

The sequences of input or output symbols are designated

$$a_0, a_1, a_2, \ldots$$

with a_0 as the first symbol. (The fact that here the subscript increases with time, whereas in dealing with polynomials the high-order coefficients come first, is an annoyance, but any other convention would also lead to minor difficulties.)

Results are more simply stated in terms of the Z-transform of the sequence

$$a(D) = a_0 + a_1 D + a_2 D^2 + \cdots. \tag{7.12}$$

This can be considered also as a formal power series, or merely a way of representing the sequence. (Frequently, the notation Z is used in place of D.)

Multiplying this transform by D, one has

$$Da(D) = a_0 D + a_1 D^2 + a_2 D^3 + \cdots$$

which corresponds to the same sequence delayed one symbol. Thus, D can be considered as a delay operator. In dealing with polynomials, multiplication by X advances the coefficients one position, and multiplication by X^{-1} delays them one position. Thus, in a sense, $D = X^{-1}$.

Direct analysis of the operation of the multiplying circuits shown in Figures 7.2 and 7.3 shows that for either of them the relationship between the input sequence $a(D)$ and the output sequence $b(D)$ is given by the difference equation

$$\begin{aligned} b(D) &= h_r a(D) + h_{r-1} Da(D) + h_{r-2} D^2 a(D) + \cdots + h_0 D^r a(D) \\ &= h^*(D)a(D), \end{aligned} \tag{7.13}$$

where $h^*(X) = h_r + h_{r-1}X + \cdots + h_0 X^r$ is the reciprocal polynomial of $h(X) = h_r X^r + h_{r-1}X^{r-1} + \cdots + h_0$. (This assumes that the storage devices contained 0's initially.) Thus, this circuit simply multiplies the input sequence by $h^*(D)$, and $h^*(D)$ is called the *transfer function* of the circuit. Of course this circuit was designed to multiply. The reason that the circuit multiplies by the reciprocal polynomial $h^*(D)$ is that $D = X^{-1}$.

Similarly, for the circuit shown in Figure 7.4, the inputs $a_1(D)$ and $a_2(D)$ are related to the output $b(D)$ by the difference equation

$$b(D) = h^*(D)a_1(D) + k^*(D)a_2(D). \tag{7.14}$$

Example. If the input to either of the circuits shown in Figure 7.5 is the sequence 1 1 0 1 0 1 1 1 0 0 1 ..., formal multiplication of the input sequence transform

$$a(D) = 1 + D + D^3 + D^5 + D^6 + D^7 + D^{10} + \cdots$$

by the transfer function $h^*(D) = 1 + D + D^2 + D^3 + D^6$ gives

$$a(D)h^*(D) = 1 + D^3 + D^8 + D^9 + 0D^{10} + \cdots$$

and this is as far as the product can be determined from the given symbols of the input sequence. This is the transform of the circuit output.

The circuit in Figure 7.6 is designed to divide, and it does so even with an infinitely long input sequence. If the transform of the input is divided formally by $g(D^{-1}) = D^{-r}g^*(D)$, the result is the transform of the output sequence. Similarly, a circuit designed to multiply polynomials by $h(X)$ and then divide by $g(X)$ gives the same results as formal multiplication by $h^*(D)$ and division by $g^*(D)$, except for a possible delay.

Example. If the input to the circuit shown in Figure 7.7 is 10110010011011..., the output is 00000011100111.... This can be verified by examination of the circuit, and can be obtained also by formal long division of the input transform, $a(D) = 1 + D^2 + D^3 + D^6 + D^9 + D^{10} + D^{12} + D^{13} + \cdots$ by $D^{-6}g^*(D) = D^{-6}(1 + D + D^2 + D^3 + D^6)$. This should be compared with the example accompanying Figure 7.7, where the same input sequence is used in a different context.

The behavior of the division circuit is also governed by a difference equation. The equation can be derived from that for the multiplication circuits as follows. The two-input multiplication circuit, Figure 7.4, becomes a division circuit, Figure 7.8, if

$$k(X) = -g(X) + g_r X^r \tag{7.15}$$

and if the output is multiplied by g_r^{-1} and used both as the quotient and the input $a_2(X)$. Then Equation 7.14 becomes

$$b(D) = g_r^{-1}\{h^*(D)a_1(D) + [-g^*(D) + g_r]a_2(D)\} \tag{7.16}$$

and

$$a_2(D) = b(D). \tag{7.17}$$

Substituting Equation 7.17 into Equation 7.16 and rearranging, one has

$$h^*(D)a_1(D) = g^*(D)b(D), \tag{7.18}$$

which is the desired difference equation. Formally dividing by $g^*(D)$ to solve for $b(D)$, one has

$$b(D) = \frac{h^*(D)}{g^*(D)}\, a_1(D). \tag{7.19}$$

The ratio $h^*(D)/g^*(D)$ is the *transfer function* of this circuit. It should be noted that the circuit shown in Figure 7.8 requires the degree of $h(X)$ and $g(X)$ both to equal r_0. Equations 7.18 and 7.19 hold for other cases as long as $g^*(X)$ is taken as $X^r g(X^{-1})$ and $h^*(X)$ as $X^r h(X^{-1})$.

Example. The transfer function of the circuit shown in Figure 7.7 is

$$\frac{D^6(1)}{D^6(1 + D^{-3} + D^{-4} + D^{-5} + D^{-6})} = \frac{D^6}{D^6 + D^3 + D^2 + D + 1}.$$

For the circuit of Figure 7.9, the transfer function is

$$\frac{D^6(1 + D^{-1} + D^{-5})}{D^6(1 + D^{-3} + D^{-4} + D^{-5} + D^{-6})} = \frac{D^6 + D^5 + D}{D^6 + D^3 + D^2 + D + 1},$$

and for Figure 7.10,

$$\frac{D^{10}(1 + D^{-5} + D^{-9} + D^{-10})}{D^{10}(D^{-4} + D^{-7} + D^{-8} + D^{-9} + D^{-10})} = \frac{D^{10} + D^5 + D + 1}{D^6 + D^3 + D^2 + D + 1}.$$

Since the circuit shown in Figure 7.8 can be constructed for arbitrary polynomials $h(X)$ and $g(X)$, it is possible to construct such a circuit for any given transfer function. This solves the problem of synthesis for an arbitrary transfer function.

It is possible for a circuit to have an output when the input sequence is all 0's if the storage devices contain nonzero elements initially. Such a sequence is analogous to the transient response of an electrical network. The transient response of a linear sequential circuit with transfer function $h^*(D)/g^*(D)$ is characterized as follows. Let

$$\frac{h^*(D)}{g^*(D)} = \frac{(h_0 D^s + h_1 D^{s-1} + \cdots + h_s)}{(g_0 D^s + g_1 D^{s-1} + \cdots + g_s)}.$$

Then the input $a(D)$ and the output $b(D)$ of this circuit are related by the equation

$$g^*(D)\, b(D) = h^*(D)\, a(D), \tag{7.20}$$

and because the input is the all-zero sequence,

$$g^*(D)\, b(D) = 0.$$

The coefficient of each power of D in this product must be 0. Thus, for D^{i+r},

$$\sum_{j=0}^{r} g_j b_{i+j} = 0. \tag{7.21}$$

The solutions of this equation are characterized in Theorem 7.1, Section 7.4. The particular solution represented by $b(D)$ is determined by the initial conditions of the storage devices.

Example. It is easily verified that the circuit shown in Figure 7.7, with the initial conditions 100111 and with no input, gives the sequence 100111001000001... as its output.

With initial conditions 000001 and again with $a(D) = 0$, the output sequence is 1100111001000001.... (Note that both of these output sequences, as well as their sum, are solutions to Equation 7.21.)

For a circuit with given initial conditions, there may be an input sequence that results in an output sequence of all 0's. Such an input sequence is called a *null sequence* of that circuit. Assume again that the circuit has the transfer function $h^*(D)/g^*(D)$; then the input and output are related by the difference equation given in Equation 7.20. For a null sequence, $b(D) = 0$, and therefore,

$$h^*(D)\,a(D) = 0 \tag{7.22}$$

or

$$\sum_{j=0}^{s} h_j a_{i+j} = 0. \tag{7.23}$$

Furthermore, if $h^*(D)\,a(D) = 0$, then $g^*(D)\,b(D) = 0$ also, and the output sequence is a transient response for the circuit. It can be shown that there exists a set of initial conditions corresponding to each solution of Equation 7.23 for which the output is all 0's. Thus, the null sequences are the solutions of Equation 7.23. Solutions of this equation are characterized by Theorem 7.1, Section 7.4.

Example. In practice it is easier to find a null sequence corresponding to a given set of initial conditions than to find the initial conditions corresponding to a given null sequence. Consider the circuit shown in Fig. 7.5a, with initial conditions (100000). Then if the output is to be 0, the first input must be 1, and after a shift the storage devices contain 110000. Now for the output to be 0, the next input must be 0, and the storage devices contain 011000 after the shift. Similarly, it can be verified that the null sequence must be 100111001000001..., and it repeats this pattern with period 15. This is the same sequence as was found in the preceding example. This agrees with the fact that both must satisfy the same difference equation.

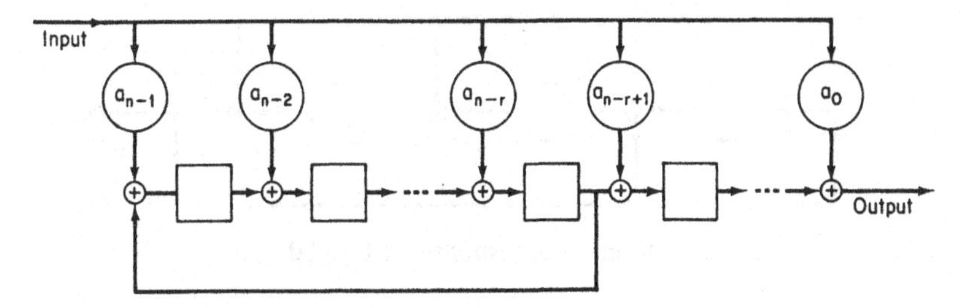

Figure 7.16. Circuit with impulse response $a_0 a_1 \ldots a_{n-r} \ldots a_{n-1} \ldots$.

By analogy to conventional linear circuits, the *impulse response* of a linear finite state circuit can be defined as the output sequence produced by the input sequence 10000.... (All memory devices are assumed to contain zeros initially.)

If the impulse response of a linear sequential circuit is given, then the transfer function can be determined and hence a circuit synthesized in the following manner: Since the circuit is assumed to have a finite number of elements and hence a finite number of states, sooner or later a state will repeat, and then the sequence will be periodic from that point. Thus, the impulse response must have the form

$$a_0 a_1 \ldots a_{n-r} a_{n-r+1} \ldots a_{n-1} \ldots a_{n-r} \cdots a_{n-1} \cdots,$$

where the last r symbols then repeat with period r. The circuit in Figure 7.16 has this as its impulse response. This may not be the simplest form, however. The transfer function for this network is

$$h(D) = a_0 + a_1 D + \cdots + a_{n-r} D_{n-r} + \frac{a_{n-r+1} D^{n-r+1} + \cdots + a_{n-1} D^{n-1}}{D^r - 1}.$$

If the numerator and denominator have a common factor, this can be canceled out, and the resulting $h(D)$ will have the same impulse response and will require the minimum number of shift-register stages.

Example. A binary circuit whose impulse response is periodic with period 7, and whose first period is 1110010..., has as its transfer function

$$h(D) = \frac{1 + D + D^2 + D^5}{1 + D^7} = \frac{1 + D}{1 + D^2 + D^3}.$$

The circuit is shown in Figure 7.17.

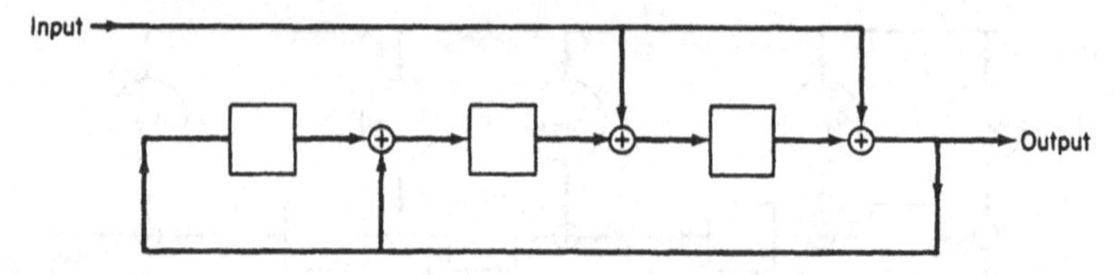

Figure 7.17. A circuit with impulse response 1 1 1 0 0 1 0....

A similar procedure can be used to synthesize a feedback shift register with a specified output sequence. In fact, it can be done by synthesizing a circuit whose impulse response is the desired sequence, then omitting the input to the circuit and setting initial conditions to match what the input circuit would insert when a single 1 is applied.

Example. A shift-register generator whose output is periodic with period 7 and whose first period is 1 1 1 0 0 1 0... can be derived from the circuit in Figure 7.17 by removing the input circuit and placing 1's in the shift-register stages whose outputs appear where the input circuit was connected, as shown in Figure 7.18.

Suppose now that a sequence is partially specified — the first s symbols are given — and it is desired to construct a circuit with these as the first s symbols of its impulse response or, in other words, a shift-register generator with these as the first s symbols of its output. There are many circuits that will produce a given set of s symbols, and if no additional constraints are imposed, the technique described in the previous paragraph can be used to design a suitable circuit. However if it is necessary to find a recurrence relation like that in Equation 7.2 with the order k minimized, then the problem is more difficult (Massey, 1969). Let the specified sequence be

$$S_0, S_1, S_2, \ldots, S_s$$

and let

$$h(X) = \sum_{j=0}^{k} h_j X^j.$$

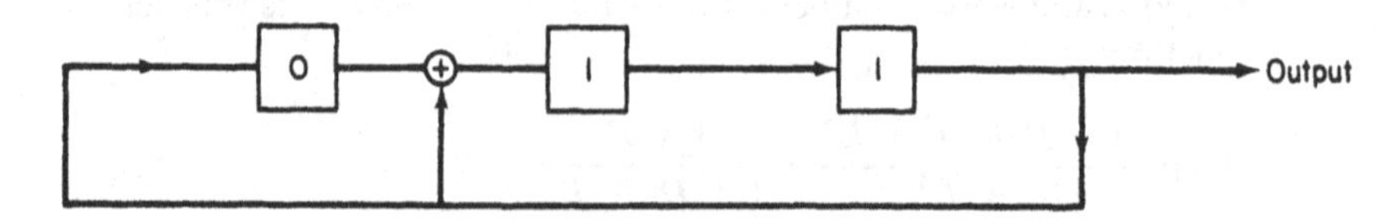

Figure 7.18. A shift-register generator with output 1 1 1 0 0 1 0....

Define $X_1, X_2, X_3, \ldots, X_k$ as the roots of $h(X)$ in an extension field in which $h(X)$ can be factored. Then by Equation 7.8, if the given sequence $S_0, S_1, \ldots, S_s$ satisfies the recurrence relation, Equation 7.2, then there exist values of $Y_1, Y_2, \ldots, Y_k$ such that

$$\sum_{i=1}^{k} Y_i X_i^0 = S_0, \sum_{i=1}^{k} Y_i X_i^1 = S_1, \ldots, \sum_{i=1}^{k} Y_i X_i^s = S_s. \tag{7.24}$$

In these equations $S_0, S_1, \ldots, S_s$ are given and the X_i and Y_i can be considered as unknowns. From a solution for the X_i and Y_i for which k is a minimum, an entire sequence $S_0, S_1, \ldots, S_s, S_{s+1}, \ldots$ can be computed using the formula

$$S_j = \sum_{i=1}^{k} Y_i X_i^j,$$

and a circuit with this as its impulse response or a shift-register generator with this as its output sequence can be synthesized by the methods already given. The denominator in the transfer function will be $h(D)$, where $h(X) = (X - X_1)(X - X_2) \cdots (X - X_k)$, and this will have minimal degree.

The remaining question is how to solve the nonlinear Equations 7.24. Strangely enough, these equations are identical to equations that arise in the error-correction procedures for Bose-Chaudhuri-Hocquenghem (BCH) codes. Techniques for solving them are presented in Sections 9.4 through 9.7.

7.6 Analysis of a General Linear Finite-State Switching Circuit

A general description of an arbitrary linear finite-state switching circuit is given in the following paragraphs. The principal result in this section is that every such circuit has a transfer function of the type discussed in the preceding section; thus, if the circuit is treated as a black box with only the input and output accessible, any linear finite-state switching circuit is indistinguishable from one of the type described in Section 7.2. More specifically, by a linear change in state-variable assignment, the original circuit is changed into an equivalent circuit which is of the type described in Section 7.2, or possibly a combination of several such circuits. The required change in state assignment corresponds to the similarity transform on a matrix that puts it into rational canonical form, and therefore the method of carrying out the change is well known.

Consider an arbitrary linear switching circuit with r storage devices, s input lines, and t output lines. Then the output of the r storage devices at time i is an r-component vector $\mathbf{v}_i$, and the input to the storage devices at time i is the next output $\mathbf{v}_{i+1}$. The vector $\mathbf{v}_i$ is called the *state* of the circuit. Similarly, the circuit input is an s-component vector $\mathbf{u}_i$, and the output is a t-component vector $\mathbf{w}_i$. The input $\mathbf{v}_{i+1}$ to the storage devices is a function of the output $\mathbf{v}_i$ of the storage devices and the circuit input $\mathbf{u}_i$. Since the circuit is made up only of adders and constant multipliers, the function must be linear and can therefore be expressed in matrix form:

$$\mathbf{v}_{i+1} = \mathbf{v}_i\mathbf{T} + \mathbf{u}_i\mathbf{U}, \tag{7.25}$$

where $\mathbf{T}$ is an $r \times r$ matrix and $\mathbf{U}$ is an $s \times r$ matrix. Similarly, the output $\mathbf{w}_i$ is a linear function of the input and the contents of the storage devices:

$$\mathbf{w}_i = \mathbf{v}_i\mathbf{R} + \mathbf{u}_i\mathbf{S}, \tag{7.26}$$

where $\mathbf{R}$ is an $r \times t$ matrix and $\mathbf{S}$ is an $s \times t$ matrix.

Example. The matrices for the circuit of Figure 7.5a are

$$\mathbf{T} = \begin{bmatrix} 010000 \\ 001000 \\ 000100 \\ 000010 \\ 000001 \\ 000000 \end{bmatrix} \qquad \begin{aligned} \mathbf{U} &= [100000] \\ \mathbf{R}^T &= [111001] \\ \mathbf{S} &= [1] \end{aligned}$$

where the components of $\mathbf{v}_i$ are the contents of the storage devices in the same order as Figure 7.5a (the symbol $\mathbf{R}^T$ denotes the transpose of the matrix $\mathbf{R}$). For Figure 7.5b, $\mathbf{T}$ and $\mathbf{S}$ are the same, but

$$\begin{aligned} \mathbf{U} &= [100111] \\ \mathbf{R}^T &= [000001] \end{aligned} \tag{7.27}$$

For Figure 7.7,

$$\mathbf{T} = \begin{bmatrix} 010000 \\ 001000 \\ 000100 \\ 000010 \\ 000001 \\ 100111 \end{bmatrix} \qquad \begin{aligned} \mathbf{U} &= [100000] \\ \mathbf{R}^T &= [000001] \\ \mathbf{S} &= [0] \end{aligned} \tag{7.28}$$

In Figure 7.9, only $\mathbf{U}$ is different:

$$\mathbf{U} = [1\,1\,0\,0\,0\,1] \tag{7.29}$$

In each case the matrices completely describe the circuit connections.

Let $\mathbf{A}$ be a nonsingular $r \times r$ matrix and let

$$\mathbf{v}_i' = \mathbf{v}_i\mathbf{A}, \quad \mathbf{v}_i = \mathbf{v}_i'\mathbf{A}^{-1} \tag{7.30}$$

Then if $\mathbf{v}_i$ is known, $\mathbf{v}_i'$ can be found, and vice versa, and so each contains the same information. The vector $\mathbf{v}_i'$ can be considered as representing $\mathbf{v}_i$ in a different coordinate system. A switching circuit for which the successive states are $\mathbf{v}_i'$ instead of $\mathbf{v}_i$ can be formed by substituting Equation 7.30 for $\mathbf{v}_i$ in Equations 7.25 and 7.26:

$$\mathbf{v}_{i+1}'\mathbf{A}^{-1} = \mathbf{v}_i'\mathbf{A}^{-1}\mathbf{T} + \mathbf{u}_i\mathbf{U}$$

or after multiplication on the right by $\mathbf{A}$,

$$\mathbf{v}_{i+1}' = \mathbf{v}_i'\mathbf{A}^{-1}\mathbf{T}\mathbf{A} + \mathbf{u}_i\mathbf{U}\mathbf{A} = \mathbf{v}_i'\mathbf{T}' + \mathbf{u}_i\mathbf{U}' \tag{7.31}$$

and

$$\mathbf{w}_i = \mathbf{v}_i'\mathbf{A}^{-1}\mathbf{R} + \mathbf{u}_i\mathbf{S} = \mathbf{v}_i'\mathbf{R}' + \mathbf{u}_i\mathbf{S}'. \tag{7.32}$$

The new circuit will for a given input have the same output as the old circuit, though the internal connections are different and the state vectors are different. Thus the matrices for the new circuit are

$$\mathbf{T}' = \mathbf{A}^{-1}\mathbf{T}\mathbf{A}, \quad \mathbf{U}' = \mathbf{U}\mathbf{A}, \quad \mathbf{R}' = \mathbf{A}^{-1}\mathbf{R}, \quad \mathbf{S}' = \mathbf{S}. \tag{7.33}$$

The relationship between $\mathbf{T}$ and $\mathbf{T}'$ given in Equation 7.33 is of great importance in the theory that follows. Matrices $\mathbf{T}$ and $\mathbf{T}'$ related by the equation $\mathbf{T}' = \mathbf{A}^{-1}\mathbf{T}\mathbf{A}$ are called *similar* matrices (Albert 1956, page 83; Birkhoff and MacLane, 1941, page 297).

Example. Consider the matrices corresponding to the circuit in Figure 7.7 and given in Equation 7.28, and let

$$\mathbf{A} = \begin{bmatrix} 000001 \\ 000011 \\ 000110 \\ 001100 \\ 011001 \\ 110011 \end{bmatrix} \qquad \mathbf{A}^{-1} = \begin{bmatrix} 001111 \\ 011110 \\ 111100 \\ 111000 \\ 110000 \\ 100000 \end{bmatrix}$$

Then

$$\mathbf{T}' = \mathbf{A}^{-1}\mathbf{T}\mathbf{A} = \begin{bmatrix} 000001 \\ 100000 \\ 010000 \\ 001001 \\ 000101 \\ 000011 \end{bmatrix} \quad \begin{aligned} \mathbf{U}' &= \mathbf{U}\mathbf{A} &&= [000001] \\ (\mathbf{R}')^T &= (\mathbf{A}^{-1}\mathbf{R})^T &&= [100000] \\ \mathbf{S}' &= \mathbf{S} &&= [0] \end{aligned}$$

The corresponding circuit is shown in Figure 7.19. This circuit can be used to divide polynomials, just as the one in Figure 7.7. The quotient will be correct, since the output is the same for either circuit. However, the contents of the storage devices after division will not be the remainder, since the contents of the storage devices differ in this circuit according to Equation 7.30.

Consider now the behavior of a circuit with no input, which is sometimes called the *autonomous* behavior. Then $\mathbf{u}_i = \mathbf{0}$, and Equation 7.25 gives $\mathbf{v}_{i+1} = \mathbf{v}_i\mathbf{T}$, $\mathbf{v}_{i+2} = \mathbf{v}_{i+1}\mathbf{T} = \mathbf{v}_i\mathbf{T}^2$, and in general,

$$\mathbf{v}_{i+j} = \mathbf{v}_i\mathbf{T}^j. \tag{7.34}$$

It is known that every $r \times r$ square matrix satisfies a minimum polynomial with coefficents that are field elements and that has degree no greater than r (Albert 1956, page 83; Birkhoff and MacLane 1941, page 215; MacDuffee 1943, page 77). Thus there exists a polynomial $m(X) = m_s X^s + m_{s-1}X^{s-1} + \cdots + m_1 X + m_0$ such that

$$m(\mathbf{T}) = m_s\mathbf{T}^s + m_{s-1}\mathbf{T}^{s-1} + \cdots + m_0 = 0.$$

Then

$$m_s\mathbf{v}_i\mathbf{T}^s + m_{s-1}\mathbf{v}_i\mathbf{T}^{s-1} + \cdots + m_0\mathbf{v}_i = 0,$$

or

$$m_s\mathbf{v}_{i+s} + m_{s-1}\mathbf{v}_{i+s-1} + \cdots + m_0\mathbf{v}_i = \mathbf{0}. \tag{7.35}$$

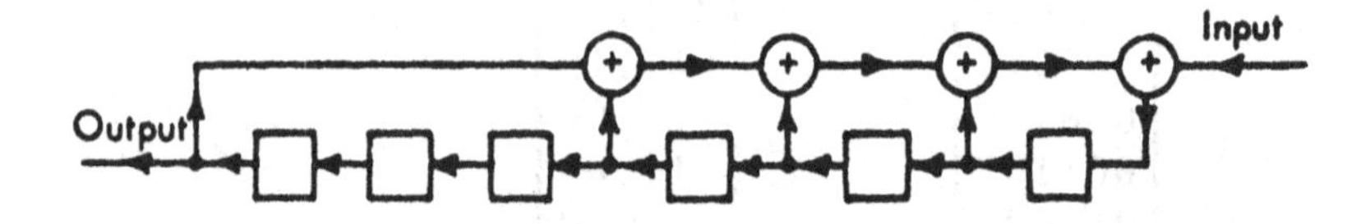

Figure 7.19. A circuit equivalent to the circuit in Figure 7.7.

Thus each component of $\mathbf{v}_i$ (that is, the sequence of contents of each storage device) satisfies a homogeneous difference equation, Equation 7.35. Each output is a linear combination of the contents of storage devices, and therefore each output is also a solution of Equation 7.35. Solutions of this equation are characterized in Theorem 7.1, Section 7.4.

Example. Let

$$\mathbf{T} = \begin{bmatrix} 00100001 \\ 10000000 \\ 01000000 \\ 00100000 \\ 00010000 \\ 00001000 \\ 00000101 \\ 00000010 \end{bmatrix}$$

with elements from the field of two elements. Then the characteristic polynomial of $\mathbf{T}$ is

$$\det[\mathbf{I}X - \mathbf{T}] = X^8 + X^6 + X^5 + X^3 + 1,$$

which is primitive and hence irreducible. The minimum polynomial must divide the characteristic polynomial, and therefore this must also be the minimum polynomial (Albert 1956, page 84; MacDuffee 1943, page 79). This matrix corresponds to the circuit shown in Figure 7.20. It has the same possible output sequence as the circuit shown in Figure 7.15, because it is governed by the same difference equation, but it requires one less adder and otherwise the same number of components.

For any monic polynomial $g(X) = X^r + g_{r-1}X^{r-1} + \cdots + g_0$, there is a *companion matrix*

$$\mathbf{T}_c = \begin{bmatrix} 0 & 1 & 0 & \cdots & 0 \\ 0 & 0 & 1 & \cdots & 0 \\ \vdots & \vdots & \vdots & & \vdots \\ 0 & 0 & 0 & & 1 \\ -g_0 & -g_1 & -g_2 & \cdots & -g_{r-1} \end{bmatrix} \tag{7.36}$$

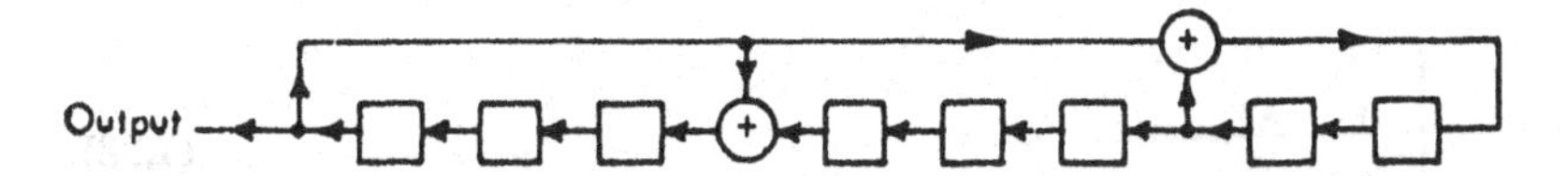

Figure 7.20. A circuit equivalent to the circuit in Figure 7.15.

(Albert 1956, page 85; Birkhoff and MacLane 1941, page 308). Sometimes the companion matrix is defined as the transpose of Equation 7.36 (MacDuffee 1943, page 81):

$$\mathbf{T}_0 = \begin{bmatrix} 0 & 0 & \cdots & 0 & -g_0 \\ 1 & 0 & \cdots & 0 & -g_1 \\ 0 & 1 & \cdots & 0 & -g_2 \\ \vdots & \vdots & & \vdots & \vdots \\ 0 & 0 & \cdots & 1 & -g_{r-1} \end{bmatrix} \tag{7.37}$$

It can be shown that $g(X)$ is the minimum polynomial of both $\mathbf{T}_c$ and $\mathbf{T}_0$. The matrix $\mathbf{T}_c$ given in Equation 7.36 corresponds to the circuit shown in Figure 7.6 with the input omitted, while the matrix $\mathbf{T}_0$ corresponds to the circuit shown in Figure 7.14. The difference equations given previously (Equations 7.21 and 7.2, respectively) agree with Equation 7.35.

If $\mathbf{T}$ is an $r \times r$ matrix and if the degree of its minimum polynomial $m(X)$ is r, then $\mathbf{T}$ is said to be *nonderogatory*. Every nonderogatory matrix is similar to the companion matrix of its minimum function (MacDuffee 1943, page 123). That is, if $\mathbf{T}$ is nonderogatory, there exists a matrix $\mathbf{A}$ such that $\mathbf{A}^{-1}\mathbf{T}\mathbf{A} = \mathbf{T}_c$, where $\mathbf{T}_c$ is the companion matrix of $m(X)$, the minimum polynomial of $\mathbf{T}$. Then the circuit corresponding to $\mathbf{T}_c$ and the one corresponding to $\mathbf{T}$ satisfy the same difference equation. These circuits are equivalent — they differ only in the way the state is represented.

Example. In the example following Equation 7.33, the matrix $\mathbf{A}$ transforms the matrix $\mathbf{T}$ into $\mathbf{T}'$, which matches the companion matrix in Equation 7.37 in form. Note that if the circuit in Figure 7.19 is loaded with initial conditions matching the first row in $\mathbf{A}$, the successive contents of the storage devices are the other rows. This method of finding the matrix $\mathbf{A}$ to transform a given nonderogatory matrix to canonical form is given in MacDuffee (1943, page 122).

Every derogatory matrix $\mathbf{T}$ is similar to a matrix of the following form:

$$\begin{bmatrix} \mathbf{M}_1 & 0 & \cdots & 0 \\ 0 & \mathbf{M}_2 & \cdots & 0 \\ \vdots & \vdots & & \vdots \\ 0 & 0 & \cdots & \mathbf{M}_m \end{bmatrix} \tag{7.38}$$

where $\mathbf{M}_m$ is the companion matrix of the minimum function of $\mathbf{T}$, and each other $\mathbf{M}_i$ is the companion matrix of a polynomial $p_i(X)$. Furthermore, each $p_i(X)$ divides $p_{i+1}(X)$. This is called the *rational canonical form* (Albert 1956, page 86; MacDuffee 1943, Chapter 6).

In the corresponding circuit, there are no interconnections between storage devices corresponding to columns in different matrices $\mathbf{M}_i$ and $\mathbf{M}_j$. Thus the circuit consists of isolated parts corresponding to $\mathbf{M}_1, \mathbf{M}_2, \ldots, \mathbf{M}_m$. Each output is a linear combination of contents of storage devices possibly in several or all of the isolated parts. Furthermore, every $p_i(X)$ must divide the minimum polynomial $p_m(X)$ of $\mathbf{T}$, and therefore, by Theorem 7.1, every possible output of each part of the circuit is a solution of the equation $p_m(D)\mathbf{W}_i = \mathbf{0}$. It follows that every output sequence is a possible output sequence of the circuit corresponding to the matrix $\mathbf{M}_m$ alone.

Thus every autonomous linear sequential switching circuit is equivalent either to a circuit of the type shown in Figure 7.6 (in the nonderogatory case) or to a collection of several such isolated circuits, except that their outputs may be combined (in the derogatory case). In the derogatory case, the circuit described by $\mathbf{M}_m$ alone is equivalent to the original circuit in the sense that it can produce the same outputs. Thus circuits corresponding to derogatory matrices have redundant components.

The preceding development can be generalized to include nonzero inputs, though it is more cumbersome for this case:

$$\begin{aligned}
\mathbf{v}_{i+1} &= \mathbf{v}_i\mathbf{T} + \mathbf{u}_i\mathbf{U} \\
\mathbf{v}_{i+2} &= \mathbf{v}_{i+1}\mathbf{T} + \mathbf{u}_{i+1}\mathbf{U} = (\mathbf{v}_i\mathbf{T} + \mathbf{u}_i\mathbf{U})\mathbf{T} + \mathbf{u}_{i+1}\mathbf{U} \\
&= \mathbf{v}_i\mathbf{T}^2 + \mathbf{u}_i\mathbf{U}\mathbf{T} + \mathbf{u}_{i+1}\mathbf{U}
\end{aligned}$$

and in general,

$$\mathbf{v}_{i+j} = \mathbf{v}_i\mathbf{T}^j + \mathbf{u}_i\mathbf{U}\mathbf{T}^{j-1} + \mathbf{u}_{i+1}\mathbf{U}\mathbf{T}^{j-2} + \cdots + \mathbf{u}_{i+j-1}\mathbf{U}. \tag{7.39}$$

If $m(X) = m_r X^r + m_{r-1}X^{r-1} + \cdots + m_0$ is the minimum polynomial of the matrix $\mathbf{T}$, then $m(\mathbf{T}) = 0$, and

$$\begin{aligned}
m_0\mathbf{v}_i &+ m_1\mathbf{v}_{i+1} + \cdots + m_r\mathbf{v}_{i+r} \\
&= \mathbf{v}_i m(\mathbf{T}) + \mathbf{u}_i(m_1\mathbf{U} + m_2\mathbf{U}\mathbf{T} + \cdots + m_r\mathbf{U}\mathbf{T}^{r-1}) \\
&\quad + \mathbf{u}_{i+1}(m_2\mathbf{U} + m_3\mathbf{U}\mathbf{T} + \cdots + m_r\mathbf{U}\mathbf{T}^{r-2}) \\
&\quad + \cdots + \mathbf{u}_{i+r-1}m_r\mathbf{U},
\end{aligned}$$

$$m(D)\mathbf{v}_i = \mathbf{u}_i\mathbf{U}_0 + \mathbf{u}_{i+1}\mathbf{U}_1 + \cdots + \mathbf{u}_{i+r-1}\mathbf{U}_{r-1}, \tag{7.40}$$

where each $\mathbf{U}_i$ is an $s \times r$ matrix:

$$\begin{aligned} \mathbf{U}_0 &= (m_1 \mathbf{U} + m_2 \mathbf{UT} + \cdots + m_r \mathbf{UT}^{r-1}), \\ \mathbf{U}_1 &= (m_2 \mathbf{U} + m_3 \mathbf{UT} + \cdots + m_r \mathbf{UT}^{r-2}), \\ &\vdots \\ \mathbf{U}_{r-1} &= m_r \mathbf{U}. \end{aligned} \tag{7.41}$$

Then by Equation 7.26,

$$\begin{aligned} \sum_{j=0}^{r} m_j \mathbf{w}_{i+j} &= \sum_{j=0}^{r} m_j \mathbf{v}_{i+j} \mathbf{R} + \sum_{j=0}^{r} m_j \mathbf{u}_{i+j} \mathbf{S} \\ &= \mathbf{u}_i \mathbf{U}_0 \mathbf{R} + \mathbf{u}_{i+1} \mathbf{U}_1 \mathbf{R} + \cdots + \mathbf{u}_{i+r-1} \mathbf{U}_{r-1} \mathbf{R} \\ &\quad + \sum_{j=0}^{r} m_j \mathbf{u}_{i+j} \mathbf{S}. \end{aligned} \tag{7.42}$$

This can be rewritten

$$m^*(D)\mathbf{w}_i = \mathbf{h}(D)\mathbf{u}_i \tag{7.43}$$

where $m^*(D)$ is the reciprocal polynomial of the minimum function of $\mathbf{T}$ and

$$\mathbf{h}(D) = \sum_{j=0}^{r-1} \mathbf{U}_j \mathbf{R} D + \mathbf{S} m^*(D). \tag{7.44}$$

In these expressions, $m^*(D)$ is an ordinary polynomial, but because $\mathbf{U}_j \mathbf{R}$ and $\mathbf{S}$ are $s \times t$ matrices, $\mathbf{h}(D)$ is a polynomial with $s \times t$ matrices as coefficients. Alternatively, $\mathbf{h}(D)$ may be thought of as an $s \times t$ matrix whose elements are ordinary polynomials $h_{jk}(D)$. The input at time i, u_i, is a vector with s components u_{ij}, $j = 1, 2, \ldots, s$, and $\mathbf{w}_i$, the output at time i, is a vector with t components w_{ik}, $k = 1, 2, \ldots, t$. Then

$$m^*(D)\mathbf{w}_{ik} = \sum_{k=1}^{s} h_{jk}(D) u_{ik}, \tag{7.45}$$

which can be written

$$w_{ik} = \sum_{k=1}^{s} \frac{h_{jk}(D)}{m^*(D)} u_{ik}. \tag{7.46}$$

Equations 7.43, 7.44, 7.45, and 7.46 are forms of the input-output relation that applies to a completely arbitrary, multiple-input and output, linear sequential switching circuit.

It is shown in Section 7.5 that given a transfer function of this form, a circuit can be synthesized that consists of t separate parts, each of which has r shift-register stages. If $t = 1$, this will be the minimum number of shift-register stages possible for realizing this transfer function, but for $t > 1$, this is not necessarily the case, and the number tr of stages required for synthesis by this method might be either more or less than the number of stages in the original circuit described by Equations 7.45 and 7.46, from which the transfer function in Equation 7.46 was derived.

In the case of a circuit with a single input and a single output, $\mathbf{S}$ is a 1×1 matrix, that is, a scalar, and so is $\mathbf{U}_j\mathbf{R}$ for each j. Then Equations 7.45 and 7.46 have the same forms as Equations 7.18 and 7.19, respectively; thus the input-output relationship is characterized, in the general case, by a transfer function.

Again the matrix $\mathbf{T}$ plays the key role, since it describes the interconnections among the storage devices. Again the "change of coordinates" described in Equation 7.30 can be used to find a matrix $\mathbf{T}'$ similar to $\mathbf{T}$ but in a special canonical form. If $\mathbf{T}$ is nonderogatory, then $\mathbf{T}'$ is the companion matrix of the minimum polynomial of $\mathbf{T}$. The circuit corresponding to $\mathbf{T}'$ has basic feedback connections like those of Figure 7.6 if the companion matrix of Equation 7.36 is used, or like those of Figure 7.14 if the companion matrix of Equation 7.37 is used. Connections may be made from any input line to any storage device, and from any storage device to any output line. If $\mathbf{T}$ is nonderogatory, the number of shift register stages is the minimum possible for realizing the given transfer function.

In the derogatory case, the matrix $\mathbf{T}'$ has the form given in Equation 7.38 and, as in the autonomous case, the circuit consists of a collection of circuits of the type shown in Figure 7.6 or Figure 7.14. Again connections may be made from any input line to any storage device and from any storage device to any output line, but otherwise there is no connection between the individual circuits corresponding to the individual matrices on the diagonal of Equation 7.38.

It should be noted that if there is a single input and single output, it is always possible to realize a circuit with a given transfer function using a number of stages equal to the larger of the degrees of the numerator and denominator of the transfer function. In such a realization, $\mathbf{T}$ is nonderogatory, and a circuit with a derogatory matrix has more components than are necessary to realize its transfer function. With multiple inputs and outputs this is not necessarily the case.

Notes

The linear filter viewpoint in the study of linear switching circuits originated with Huffman (1956*a*, 1956*b*). Section 7.5 is based entirely on his work, and the circuits described in Section 7.2 appear in Huffman (1956*a*). Simultaneously, Zierler (1955, 1959), Golomb (1955), Blankenship, Albert, and perhaps others became interested in shift-register generators as a means of generating pseudo-random sequences. More recently the connection of shift-register generators with error-correcting codes (Huffman 1956*b*) has given further impetus to their study (Elspas 1959; Fitzpatrick 1960; Fitzpatrick and Stern 1959; Hartmanis 1959; Young 1958). Theorem 7.1 appears in Peterson (1960*a*), and is very similar to results of Hall (1938). The method for synthesizing a shift-register generator of minimum complexity for a partially specified output sequence is due to Massey (1969).

The matrix methods of analysis used in Section 7.6 are the same as those used by Birdsall and Ristenbatt (1958) and Elspas (1959) in the analysis of autonomous linear switching circuits. It is a very natural method, and in fact some of the basic work on cyclic codes has been done in this context, rather than in terms of polynomial algebra, the viewpoint used in this book. Albert (1956, page 85), in the course of introducing the companion matrix of a polynomial, gives an interesting comparison of these two approaches.

Problems

7.1. Devise three shift-register circuits like that in Figure 7.14 with periods 7, 21, and 63. (Answer: Period 21 can be achieved with polynomials $X^6 + X^4 + X^2 + X + 1$ or $(X^2 + X + 1)(X^3 + X + 1)$ or their reciprocal polynomials.)

7.2. Show that if $h(X)$ is irreducible, all the sequences generated by the corresponding shift-register generater have the same period.

7.3. Let $\mathbf{H}_1 = [1, a_1, a_1^2, \ldots, a_1^{n-1}]$ and $\mathbf{H}_2 = [1, a_2, a_2^2, \ldots, a_2^{n-1}]$, where a_1 and a_2 are elements of an extension field and $a_1^n = a_2^n = 1$. If these field elements are expressed as vectors of m_1 and m_2 components, respectively, over $GF(q)$, then $\mathbf{H}_1$ is an $m_1 \times n$ matrix and $\mathbf{H}_2$ is an $m_2 \times n$ matrix. Show that if a_1 and a_2 have the same minimum function, the row spaces of $\mathbf{H}_1$ and $\mathbf{H}_2$ are the same, but if the minimum functions are different, no nonzero vector in the row space of $\mathbf{H}_1$ is in the row space of $\mathbf{H}_2$, and vice versa. (Hint: Use Theorem 7.1.)

7.4. (Reed and Solomon 1960) Let a_i be any maximal length sequence of period $q^m - 1$ over $GF(q)$. Define multiplication of vectors as follows:

a. $\mathbf{0v} = \mathbf{v0} = \mathbf{0}$.

b. Denote by $\mathbf{a}_j$ the vector $(a_j, a_{j+1}, \ldots, a_{j+m-1})$ and then $\mathbf{a}_j \mathbf{a}_k = \mathbf{a}_{j+k}$, $\mathbf{a}_j \neq \mathbf{0} \neq \mathbf{a}_k$.

Show that with this definition the vectors form a field. (With this definition of field elements, successive powers of a appear upon successive shifts in a shift register of the type shown in Figure 7.14. It can be adapted for calculating $r(a)$ also in a manner analogous to that described in Section 7.3.)

7.5. Devise a circuit for squaring a field element and a circuit for taking the square root of a field element in $GF(2^4)$ as it is represented in Table 6.1. Note that in $GF(q^m)$ the qth power and hence the qth root are linear operations, by Theorem 6.14. Use a method similar to that given on page 181 for automatic multiplication by α^j, which is also a linear operation.

7.6. Given a multiplier circuit and a squarer circuit, devise a division procedure which is both fast and simple.

7.7 Synthesize a binary sequential switching circuit to realize the transfer function $h(D) = (1 + D + D^4)/(1 + D + D^3)$.

7.8. Synthesize a binary sequential switching circuit which has as its impulse response

a. 010111001011100101110...
b. 0001110010111001011100101110...

7.9. Synthesize a binary sequential switching circuit with two inputs $\mathbf{u}_i$ and $\mathbf{v}_i$ and one output $\mathbf{w}_i$, for which

$$\mathbf{w}_i = \frac{1 + D}{1 + D + D^3}\mathbf{u}_i + \frac{1 + D^2}{1 + D + D^3}\mathbf{v}_i.$$

7.10. a. Give an example of a transfer function of the form given in Equation 7.46 for two inputs and two outputs, with $m^*(D) = 1 + D + D^2$, which cannot be realized with fewer than four delay elements.

b. Give an example of a transfer function for a two-input, two-output circuit with $m^*(D) = 1 + D + D^2$, which requires only two delay elements.

8 Cyclic Codes

The codes discussed in this chapter can be implemented relatively easily and possess a great deal of well-understood mathematical structure. In addition to, or perhaps because of, these facts, many of the important linear block codes described in Chapter 5 are equivalent to cyclic codes.

Three types of results are presented in this chapter. First, the basic mathematical properties of cyclic codes are explored. Then their properties are used to devise simple encoding, parity checking, and, in some cases, decoding circuits. Finally, several classes of cyclic codes and codes related to cyclic codes are described. These serve as an introduction to the important cyclic codes presented in subsequent chapters.

8.1 Cyclic Codes and Ideals

A subspace V of n-tuples is a called a *cyclic subspace* or a *cyclic code* if for each vector $\mathbf{v} = (a_{n-1}, a_{n-2}, \ldots, a_0)$ in V, the vector $\mathbf{v}' = (a_0, a_{n-1}, a_{n-2}, \ldots, a_1)$ obtained by shifting the components of $\mathbf{v}$ cyclically one unit to the right is also in V.

In this chapter, n-tuples will be considered to be elements of the algebra A_n of polynomials modulo $X^n - 1$. The elements of the algebra are residue classes of polynomials, and here they will be designated $\{f(X)\}$. Unless there is a specific statement to the contrary, $f(X)$ *will always be taken as the polynomial of smallest degree* in the equivalence class. Then $f(X)$ always has degree less than n, and every distinct polynomial of degree less than n is in a distinct residue class; that is, there is a one-to-one correspondence between polynomials of degree less than n and residue classes. Given a polynomial $a(X)$ of degree greater than n, the polynomial of smallest degree in the same equivalence class is found by dividing $a(X)$ by $X^n - 1$. The remainder is the desired polynomial.

Corresponding to each n-tuple $(a_{n-1}, a_{n-2}, \ldots, a_0)$ there is a polynomial of degree less than n, $f(X) = a_{n-1}X^{n-1} + a_{n-2}X^{n-2} + \cdots + a_0$ and hence a residue class $\{a_{n-1}X^{n-1} + a_{n-2}X^{n-2} + \cdots + a_0\}$. The residue class and the vector will be considered as simply different ways of representing the same thing, namely, an element of the algebra A_n of polynomials modulo $X^n - 1$.

The following theorem gives an algebraic characterization of cyclic codes:

THEOREM 8.1. *In the algebra of polynomials modulo $X^n - 1$, a subspace is a cyclic subspace if and only if it is an ideal.*

Proof. The key point is that multiplication by $\{X\}$ is the same as a cyclic shift, for

$$X(a_{n-1}X^{n-1} + a_{n-2}X^{n-2} + \cdots + a_0)$$
$$= a_{n-1}(X^n - 1) + a_{n-2}X^{n-1} + \cdots + a_0 X + a_{n-1}$$

and therefore

$$\{X\}\{a_{n-1}X^{n-1} + a_{n-2}X^{n-2} + \cdots + a_0\}$$
$$= \{a_{n-2}X^{n-1} + a_{n-3}X^{n-2} + \cdots + a_0 X + a_{n-1}\}.$$

If the subspace V is an ideal and $\mathbf{v}$ is any element of V, then $\{X\}\mathbf{v}$ is also in V, and since $\{X\}\mathbf{v}$ is the cyclic shift of $\mathbf{v}$, V is a cyclic subspace.

Now let us assume that V is a cyclic subspace. Then for any $\mathbf{v}$ in V, $\{X\}\mathbf{v}$ is in V, and therefore for any j, $\{X\}^j\mathbf{v} = \{X^j\}\mathbf{v}$ is in V. Since V is a subspace, any linear combination

$$c_{n-1}\{X^{n-1}\}\mathbf{v} + c_{n-2}\{X^{n-2}\}\mathbf{v} + \cdots + c_0\mathbf{v}$$
$$= \{c_{n-1}X^{n-1} + c_{n-2}X^{n-2} + \cdots + c_0\}\mathbf{v}$$

is in V. Thus the product of any element of V and any element of the algebra A_n is in V, and V must be an ideal. Q.E.D.

The structure of ideals in A_n is described in Section 6.4. It may be summarized as follows: Let $g(X)$ be the monic polynomial of smallest degree such that $\{g(X)\}$ is in an ideal J. If $f(X)$ is a polynomial of degree less than n which is divisible by $g(X)$, then $\{f(X)\}$ is in J; conversely, if $\{f(X)\}$ is in J, $f(X)$ is divisible by $g(X)$. Also, $g(X)$ divides $X^n - 1$, and every monic polynomial that divides $X^n - 1$ generates a distinct ideal J in A_n. The polynomial $g(X)$ is called the generator of the ideal.

A cyclic code is therefore specified completely by a polynomial $g(X)$ that divides $X^n - 1$. Alternately the code can be specified completely by the statement that it is the null space of the ideal generated by $h(X) = (X^n - 1)/g(X)$. If $g(X)$ has degree r, then by Theorem 6.11 the code has dimension $k = n - r$. The element $\{f(X)\}$ is in the code if and only if $f(X)$ is divisible by $g(X)$.

The polynomial $h(X)$ is referred to as the *parity-check polynomial* of the code C generated by $g(X)$. Since $h(X)$ divides $X^n - 1$, it can be used as the generator of a cyclic code. This latter code is equivalent to the dual code of C and in the context of cyclic codes is usually referred to simply as the *dual* of C.

Example. $X^7 - 1 = (X - 1)(X^3 + X + 1)(X^3 + X^2 + 1)$ over $GF(2)$. The polynomial $g(X) = X^3 + X^2 + 1$ generates a cyclic (7, 4) code. The elements

$$\begin{aligned} \{X^3g(X)\} &= (1101000) \\ \{X^2g(X)\} &= (0110100) \\ \{Xg(X)\} &= (0011010) \\ \{g(X)\} &= (0001101) \end{aligned} \qquad \mathbf{G} = \begin{bmatrix} 1101000 \\ 0110100 \\ 0011010 \\ 0001101 \end{bmatrix} \tag{8.1}$$

can be taken as basis vectors, and therefore $\mathbf{G}$ can be taken as the generator matrix. This code is the null space of the ideal generated by $h(X) = (X - 1)(X^3 + X + 1) = X^4 + X^3 + X^2 + 1$;

$$\begin{aligned} \{X^2h(X)\} &= (1110100), \\ \{Xh(X)\} &= (0111010), \\ \{h(X)\} &= (0011101). \end{aligned}$$

Because polynomial multiplication and inner or dot product of vectors differ, as indicated in Section 6.4, this code is the null space of a matrix $\mathbf{H}$ formed of $\{X^2h(X)\}$, $\{Xh(X)\}$, and $\{h(X)\}$ as vectors with the order of components reversed:

$$\mathbf{H} = \begin{bmatrix} 0010111 \\ 0101110 \\ 1011100 \end{bmatrix} \tag{8.2}$$

It can easily be verified that $\mathbf{GH}^T = \mathbf{0}$. This code is equivalent to the Hamming (7, 4) code, as can be seen from the fact that the columns of $\mathbf{H}$ are distinct.

An alternative specification of a cyclic code can be made in terms of the roots, possibly in an extension field, of the generator $g(X)$ of the ideal. Assume first that there are no repeated roots. Then the following statement uniquely specifies a cyclic code: The vector $\{f(X)\}$ is in the code space if and only if $\alpha_1, \alpha_2, \ldots, \alpha_r$ are roots of $f(X)$. The relation to the previous specification is given by Theorem 6.16. If the minimum function of α_i is $m_i(X)$, then $\{f(X)\}$ is a code vector if and only if $f(X)$ is divisible by $m_1(X), m_2(X), \ldots, m_r(X)$ and hence by their least common multiple. Therefore, the code is the ideal generated by

$$g(X) = \mathrm{LCM}[m_1(X), m_2(X), \ldots, m_r(X)].$$

Since $g(X)$ must divide $X^n - 1$, $\alpha_1, \alpha_2, \ldots, \alpha_r$ must all be roots of $X^n - 1$, and hence the order of each α_i must divide n. Also, n can be taken to be the least common multiple of the orders of the α_i, since then each α_i is a root of $X^n - 1$ and therefore $g(X)$ is a factor of $X^n - 1$ by Theorem 6.16.

If the roots are given as powers of a single element α of order e, that is, if it is specified that $\alpha_i = \alpha^{u_i}$, where u_i is a given integer, then the number of factors and degree of each factor of $g(X)$ can be found from the integers e and u_i as follows. By Theorem 6.26, all the roots of $m_i(X)$ are contained in the sequence $\alpha^{u_i}, \alpha^{u_i q}, \alpha^{u_i q^2}, \alpha^{u_i q^3}, \ldots$, and hence all the roots are all the distinct elements in this sequence. The exponents, then, are the distinct residues modulo e of $u_i, u_i q, u_i q^2, u_i q^3, \ldots$, and the number of distinct residues is the degree r_i of $m_i(X)$. It is quite possible for α^{u_i} and α^{u_j} to have the same minimum function $m_i(X) = m_j(X)$. When all the roots $m_i(X)$ and $m_j(X)$ are listed, the two lists will coincide. Then only one of them is included as a factor of $g(X)$. The set of exponents associated with the polynomial $m_i(X)$ is called its *cycle set*.

Example. The code in the previous example can be specified by stating that every code polynomial must have α as a root, where α is any root of $X^3 + X^2 + 1$. Alternatively, suppose that it is simply stated that every code polynomial should have α as a root, where α is any primitive element of $GF(2^3)$. All the primitive elements of $GF(2^3)$ are roots either of $X^3 + X^2 + 1$ or $X^3 + X + 1$, and hence the code is either the one in the previous example or the equivalent code generated by $X^3 + X + 1$.

A code for which every code vector has α, a root of $X^3 + X^2 + 1$, and 1 as roots is the code generated by $g(X) = (X - 1)(X^3 + X^2 + 1)$.

Example. For a more complex example, let $\beta = \alpha^{89}$, where α is a primitive element of $GF(2^{11})$, and consider the binary cyclic code that has β, β^2, β^3, and β^4 as roots of all code polynomials. Since $89 \times 23 = 2^{11} - 1$, $\beta^{23} = 1$. Let $m(X)$ be the minimum function of β. Then the roots of $m(X)$ are

$$\beta, \beta^2, \beta^4, \beta^8, \beta^{16}, \beta^{32} = \beta^9, \beta^{18}, \beta^{36}$$
$$= \beta^{13}, \beta^{26} = \beta^3, \beta^6, \beta^{12}, (\beta^{24} = \beta).$$

Therefore, $m(X)$ is the minimum function of β, β^2, β^3, and β^4, and a polynomial is in the code space if and only if it is divisible by $m(X)$. Different choices for a primitive element α of $GF(2^{11})$ lead to different values of β, all of which are roots of one of the two polynomials $X^{11} + X^9 + X^7 + X^6 + X^5 + X + 1$ or $X^{11} + X^{10} + X^6 + X^5 + X^4 + X^2 + 1$. The resulting codes are both equivalent to the Golay (23, 12) code of Section 5.2.

Example. Let $q = 2$ and let α be a primitive element of $GF(2^4)$. Then $\alpha^{15} = 1$. Consider a code for which a vector $\{f(X)\}$ is a code vector if and only if α, α^2, α^3, α^4, α^5, and α^6 are roots. Let $m_i(X)$ denote the minimum function of α^i. Then α, α^2, α^4, and α^8 are the roots of $m_1(X)$, and $m_1(X) = m_2(X) = m_4(X) = m_8(X)$. Similarly, α^3, α^6, α^{12}, $\alpha^{24} = \alpha^9$ are the roots of $m_3(X)$. This can be abbreviated by listing only the exponents or cyclic sets:

1	2	4	8	$m_1(X) = m_2(X) = m_4(X)$	(degree 4)
3	6	12	9	$m_3(X) = m_6(X)$	(degree 4)
5	10			$m_5(X)$	(degree 2)

Then $g(X) = m_1(X)m_3(X)m_5(X)$ and so $g(X)$ has degree 10.

Example. Let $q = 2$ and let α be a primitive element of $GF(2^5)$. Then $\alpha^{31} = 1$. Consider a code for which $\{f(X)\}$ is a code vector if and only if $\alpha, \alpha^2, \alpha^3, \ldots, \alpha^{10}$ are roots of $f(X)$. Then, as before,

1	2	4	8	16	$m_1(X) = m_2(X) = m_4(X) = m_8(X)$	(degree 5)
3	6	12	24	17	$m_3(X) = m_6(X)$	(degree 5)
5	10	20	9	18	$m_5(X) = m_{10}(X) = m_9(X)$	(degree 5)
7	14	28	25	19	$m_7(X)$	(degree 5)

All the elements $\alpha, \alpha^2, \alpha^3, \ldots, \alpha^{10}$ are included among the roots of $m_1(X)$, $m_3(X)$, $m_5(X)$, and $m_7(X)$, and therefore

$$g(X) = m_1(X)m_3(X)m_5(X)m_7(X),$$

which has degree 20.

If it is specified that $f(X)$ must have α_i as a root of multiplicity r_i, then the minimum function $m_i(X)$ of α_i must appear in $g(X)$ repeated r_i times. It can be shown that $X^n - 1$ has no repeated roots if n and q are relatively prime.* If $n = q^s n_1$, where n_1 and q are relatively prime, then

$$X^n - 1 = (X^{n_1} - 1)^{q^s}$$

by Theorem 6.14. Thus, $X^n - 1$ always has all its roots repeated the same number of times, q^s, where q^s is the highest power of q that divides n. The value of n can be found for repeated roots as follows: Take n_1 to be the least common multiple of the orders of the elements $\alpha_1, \alpha_2, \ldots, \alpha_r$. Each is a single root of $X^{n_1} - 1$. Let r_m be the maximum multiplicity of any root, and s the smallest integer such that $r_m \leqq q^s$. Then $n = n_1 q^s$.

Two practical ways of finding the minimum function of a given field element are illustrated next for the element α^3, where α is a root of the primitive polynomial $X^4 + X + 1$. (See Table 6.1.)

1. The roots of $m_3(X)$ are α^3, α^6, α^{12}, and α^9, and therefore, $m_3(X) = (X - \alpha^3)(X - \alpha^6)(X - \alpha^{12})(X - \alpha^9)$. Multiplication with the aid of Table 6.1 yields $m_3(X) = X^4 + X^3 + X^2 + X + 1$.
2. It is known that $m_3(X)$ has degree 4. Let $m(X) = a_0 + a_1 X + a_2 X^2 + a_3 X^3 + X^4$. Substituting $\alpha^3 = (1\,0\,0\,0)$ for X, $\alpha^6 = (1\,1\,0\,0)$ for X^2, $\alpha^9 = (1\,0\,1\,0)$ for X^3, and $\alpha^{12} = (1\,1\,1\,1)$ for X^4 gives

$$a_0 \begin{bmatrix} 0 \\ 0 \\ 0 \\ 1 \end{bmatrix} + a_1 \begin{bmatrix} 1 \\ 0 \\ 0 \\ 0 \end{bmatrix} + a_2 \begin{bmatrix} 1 \\ 1 \\ 0 \\ 0 \end{bmatrix} + a_3 \begin{bmatrix} 1 \\ 0 \\ 1 \\ 0 \end{bmatrix} + \begin{bmatrix} 1 \\ 1 \\ 1 \\ 1 \end{bmatrix} = 0$$

or

$$\begin{aligned} a_1 + a_2 + a_3 + 1 &= 0 \\ a_2 \qquad + 1 &= 0 \\ a_3 + 1 &= 0 \\ a_0 \qquad\qquad + 1 &= 0 \end{aligned}$$

and the solution is $a_0 = a_1 = a_2 = a_3 = 1$. Another method is given in Albert (1956), Theorem 5.25.

* In this case, $X^n - 1$ and its formal derivative nX^{n-1} are relatively prime. See, for example, Albert (1956, page 102), or Birkhoff and MacLane (1941, page 80).

8.2 Matrix Description of Cyclic Codes

The most elementary description by matrices has been illustrated in the previous section. If $g(X) = a_r X^r + a_{r-1}X^{r-1} + \cdots + a_0$ is the generator of the code, then $\{X^{n-r-1}g(X)\}, \{X^{n-r-2}g(X)\}, \ldots, \{g(X)\}$ are all code vectors. Thus, all the rows of the following matrix are code vectors:

$$\mathbf{G} = \begin{bmatrix} a_r & a_{r-1} & \cdots & a_0 & 0 & & & 0 \\ 0 & a_r & a_{r-1} & \cdots & a_0 & & 0 & 0 \\ \vdots & & & & & & & \\ 0 & 0 & & a_r & a_{r-1} & \cdots & a_0 & 0 \\ 0 & 0 & & 0 & a_r & & \cdots & a_0 \end{bmatrix} \tag{8.3}$$

Clearly, they are linearly independent, and the rank of $\mathbf{G}$ is $n - r$, which is also the dimension of the code. Therefore, by Theorem 2.9 the row space of $\mathbf{G}$ is the code space.

As earlier, the following convention will be used. The first k symbols, coefficients of $X^{n-1}, X^{n-2}, \ldots, X^{n-k}$, will be taken as information symbols, and the last $n - k$ symbols, coefficients of $X^{n-k-1}, X^{n-k-2}, \ldots 1$, will be taken as parity-check symbols.

The generator matrix for any cyclic code can be put in modified reduced echelon form as follows. Let $r_i(X)$ be the remainder after dividing X^i by $g(X)$:

$$X^i = g(X)\, q_i(X) + r_i(X).$$

Then

$$X^i - r_i(X) = g(X)\, q_i(X)$$

is a code vector. If these polynomials, for $i = n - 1, n - 2, \ldots, n - k$, are taken as rows of the generator matrix, then

$$\mathbf{G} = [\mathbf{I}_k, -\mathbf{R}],$$

where $\mathbf{I}_k$ is a $k \times k$ identity matrix and $-\mathbf{R}$ is a $k \times (n - k)$ matrix whose jth row is the vector of coefficients of $-r_{n-j}(X)$. Then by Theorem 3.3 the code is also the null space of the matrix

$$\mathbf{H} = [\mathbf{R}^T, \mathbf{I}_{n-k}].$$

The jth row of $\mathbf{H}^T$ is the vector of coefficients of $r_{n-j}(X)$, *even for* $j \leqq n - k$.

Example. For the binary cyclic code generated by $f(X) = X^3 + X^2 + 1$,

$$
\begin{aligned}
X^6 &= g(X)(X^3 + X^2 + X) + X^2 + X \\
X^5 &= g(X)(X^2 + X + 1) \qquad + X + 1 \\
X^4 &= g(X)(X + 1) \qquad + X^2 + X + 1 \\
X^3 &= g(X)(1) \qquad + X^2 \qquad + 1 \\
X^2 &= g(X)(0) \qquad + X^2 \\
X^1 &= g(X)(0) \qquad + X \\
X^0 &= g(X)(0) \qquad + 1
\end{aligned}
\qquad
\mathbf{H}_1^T = \begin{bmatrix} 110 \\ 011 \\ 111 \\ 101 \\ 100 \\ 010 \\ 001 \end{bmatrix} \tag{8.4}
$$

and

$$
\mathbf{G}_1 = \begin{bmatrix} 1000110 \\ 0100011 \\ 0010111 \\ 0001101 \end{bmatrix} \tag{8.5}
$$

The matrix **G** given here is row equivalent to the matrix given in Equation 8.1. The code is the same code, not just an equivalent code.

Now consider the dual code that, by Theorem 6.12, is generated by $(X^7 - 1)/g(X) = (X - 1)(X^3 + X + 1) = X^4 + X^3 + X^2 + 1$:

$$
\begin{aligned}
r_6(X) &= X^3 + X^2 + X \\
r_5(X) &= \qquad X^2 + X + 1 \\
r_4(X) &= X^3 + X^2 \qquad + 1 \\
r_3(X) &= X^3 \\
r_2(X) &= \qquad X^2 \\
r_1(X) &= \qquad\qquad X \\
r_0(X) &= \qquad\qquad\quad 1
\end{aligned}
\qquad
\mathbf{H}_2^T = \begin{bmatrix} 1110 \\ 0111 \\ 1101 \\ 1000 \\ 0100 \\ 0010 \\ 0001 \end{bmatrix} \tag{8.6}
$$

and

$$
\mathbf{G}_2 = \begin{bmatrix} 1001110 \\ 0100111 \\ 0011101 \end{bmatrix} \tag{8.7}
$$

The matrices $\mathbf{H}_1$ and $\mathbf{G}_2$ differ in having the order of columns reversed and the rows reversed, and the same is true of $\mathbf{G}_1$ and $\mathbf{H}_2$. The rearrangement of rows does not affect the row space or null space. The rearrangement of columns is a result of the fact that two polynomials multiply to zero only if the dot product of the vectors, with the order of components reversed in one of them, is zero.

Now assume that a polynomial $f(X)$ is in the code space if and only if it has $\alpha_1, \alpha_2, \ldots, \alpha_r$ as roots. If

$$f(X) = f_{n-1}X^{n-1} + f_{n-2}X^{n-2} + \cdots + f_0$$

then for $i = 1, 2, \ldots, r,$

$$0 = f(\alpha_i) = f_{n-1}\alpha_i^{n-1} + f_{n-2}\alpha_i^{n-2} + \cdots + f_0$$

and this can be written as a matrix product:

$$[f_{n-1}, f_{n-2}, \ldots, f_0][\alpha_i^{n-1}, \alpha_i^{n-2}, \ldots, \alpha_i]^T = 0.$$

This is a condition exactly equivalent to the condition that α_i be a root of $f(X)$. In view of Theorem 6.16, this is also exactly the condition that $f(X)$ be divisible by the minimum function $m_i(X)$ of α_i. The condition that a polynomial have $\alpha_1, \alpha_2, \ldots, \alpha_r$ as roots is equivalent to the condition that the corresponding vector be in the null space of the matrix

$$\mathbf{H} = \begin{bmatrix} \alpha_1^{n-1} \alpha_1^{n-2} & \cdots & \alpha_1^1 \alpha_1^0 \\ \alpha_2^{n-1} \alpha_2^{n-2} & \cdots & \alpha_2^1 \alpha_2^0 \\ \vdots & & \\ \alpha_r^{n-1} \alpha_r^{n-2} & \cdots & \alpha_r^1 \alpha_r^0 \end{bmatrix} \tag{8.8}$$

The set of all polynomials that have α_i as a root is the null space of the matrix

$$[\alpha_i^{n-1}, \alpha_i^{n-2}, \ldots, \alpha_i^0] \tag{8.9}$$

and because these are exactly the polynomials that are divisible by $m_i(X)$ of degree m_i, they form an ideal which has dimension $n - m_i$ by Theorem 6.11. Because the null space of the matrix in Equation 8.9 has dimension $n - m_i$, its row space has dimension m_i, by Theorem 6.11 or Theorem 2.15. Note that the coefficients of the code polynomials are in the field $GF(q)$, but α_i is in an extension field unless $m_i = 1$. Elements of the extension field can be considered as vectors with m_i components over the ground field. Therefore, the row space of the matrix in Equation 8.9 has dimension m_i over $GF(q)$. The following example should make this clear.

If α_i and α_j have the same minimum polynomial $m_i(X) = m_j(X)$, their null spaces are the same, and hence their row spaces, as spaces over $GF(q)$, are the same. Therefore, in forming the matrix **H** in Equation 8.8, only one root need be listed for each irreducible factor of $g(X)$.

Example. Consider again the binary cyclic code for which $f(X)$ is a code vector if and only if $\alpha, \alpha^2, \ldots, \alpha^6$ are roots of $f(X)$. The element α is a root of $p(X) = X^4 + X + 1$ and therefore is a primitive element of $GF(2^4)$. Then

$$g(X) = m_1(X)\, m_3(X)\, m_5(X)$$

and it is sufficient to require that every $f(X)$ have α, α^3, and α^5 as roots. Thus, the code is the null space of the matrix $\mathbf{H}$ whose transpose is

$$\mathbf{H}^T = \begin{bmatrix} \alpha^{14} & \alpha^{42} = \alpha^{12} & \alpha^{70} = \alpha^{10} \\ \alpha^{13} & \alpha^{39} = \alpha^{9} & \alpha^{65} = \alpha^{5} \\ \alpha^{12} & \alpha^{36} = \alpha^{6} & \alpha^{60} = 1 \\ \vdots & \vdots & \vdots \\ \alpha^{1} & \alpha^{3} & \alpha^{5} \\ \alpha^{0} = 1 & \alpha^{0} = 1 & \alpha^{0} = 1 \end{bmatrix}$$

or, with the vector representation of the field elements given in Table 6.1,

$$\mathbf{H}^T = \begin{bmatrix} 1001 & 1111 & 0111 \\ 1101 & 1010 & 0110 \\ 1111 & 1100 & 0001 \\ 1110 & 1000 & 0111 \\ 0111 & 0001 & 0110 \\ 1010 & 1111 & 0001 \\ 0101 & 1010 & 0111 \\ 1011 & 1100 & 0110 \\ 1100 & 1000 & 0001 \\ 0110 & 0001 & 0111 \\ 0011 & 1111 & 0110 \\ 1000 & 1010 & 0001 \\ 0100 & 1100 & 0111 \\ 0010 & 1000 & 0110 \\ 0001 & 0001 & 0001 \end{bmatrix}$$

Now

$$X^{15} - 1 = (X - 1)(X^2 + X + 1)(X^4 + X^3 + X^2 + X + 1) \cdot (X^4 + X^3 + 1)(X^4 + X + 1)$$

and it is easily verified that if α is a root of $X^4 + X + 1$, then α^3 is a root of $X^4 + X^3 + X^2 + X + 1$ and α^5 is a root of $X^2 + X + 1$. Therefore, the rank of $(\alpha^{14}, \alpha^{13}, \ldots, \alpha^0)$ is 4, and the rank of $(\alpha^{42}, \alpha^{39}, \ldots, \alpha^0)$ is 4, since both α and α^3 have minimum functions of degree 4. The degree of the minimum function of α^5, however, is 2, and the $(\alpha^{70}, \alpha^{65}, \ldots, \alpha^0)$ should have rank 2. Clearly, it does; in $\mathbf{H}^T$ earlier, the 9th column is $\mathbf{0}$, and the 10th column is a duplicate of the 11th.

If it is required that $f(X)$ have α_i as a root repeated r_i times, then $f(X)$ and its first $r_i - 1$ formal derivatives must have α_i as a root, and therefore if

$$f(X) = a_{n-1}X^{n-1} + a_{n-2}X^{n-2} + \cdots + \alpha_0$$

then

$$f(\alpha) = a_{n-1}\alpha^{n-1} + a_{n-2}\alpha^{n-2} + \cdots + a_0 = 0,$$
$$f'(\alpha) = a_{n-1}(n-1)\alpha^{n-2} + a_{n-2}(n-2)\alpha^{n-3} + \cdots + a_1 + 0 = 0,$$
$$f''(\alpha) = a_{n-1}(n-1)(n-2)\alpha^{n-3} + \cdots + 2a_2 + 0 + 0 = 0,$$

and so on. Thus, every code vector must be in the null space of the following r_i vectors:

$$\begin{array}{llll}(& \alpha^{n-1}, & \alpha^{n-2}, \ldots, & \alpha^2, \alpha, 1), \\ (& (n-1)\alpha^{n-2}, & (n-2)\alpha^{n-3}, \ldots, & 2\alpha, 1, 0), \\ ((n-1)(n-2)\alpha^{n-3}, & & \ldots & , 2, 0, 0),\end{array}$$

and so on.

8.3 Associated-Polynomial Characterization of Cyclic Codes

There is another important way of characterizing cyclic codes (Mattson and Solomon 1961) in which each code vector is obtained as the n-tuple of values of a polynomial associated with this code vector when $1, \alpha, \ldots, \alpha^{n-1}$ are substituted in it. The derivation follows:

For any polynomial with coefficients from $GF(q^m)$,

$$a(X) = a_{n-1}X^{n-1} + a_{n-2}X^{n-2} + \cdots + a_0,$$

consider the vector

$$\mathbf{b} = (a(\alpha^{n-1}), a(\alpha^{n-2}), \ldots, a(1)),$$

where α is an element of $GF(q^m)$ of order n. Now consider the polynomial

$$\begin{aligned} b(X) &= b_{n-1}X^{n-1} + b_{n-2}X^{n-2} + \cdots + b_0 \\ &= a(\alpha^{n-1})X^{n-1} + a(\alpha^{n-2})X^{n-2} + \cdots + a(1) \\ &= X^{n-1}(a_{n-1}\alpha^{(n-1)(n-1)} + a_{n-2}\alpha^{(n-1)(n-2)} + \cdots + a_0) \\ &+ X^{n-2}(a_{n-1}\alpha^{(n-2)(n-1)} + a_{n-2}\alpha^{(n-2)(n-2)} + \cdots + a_0) \\ &+ \cdots \\ &+ 1(a_{n-1} + a_{n-2} + \cdots + a_0) \\ &= a_{n-1}((\alpha^{n-1}X)^{n-1} + (\alpha^{n-1}X)^{n-2} + \cdots + 1) \\ &+ a_{n-2}((\alpha^{n-2}X)^{n-1} + (\alpha^{n-2}X)^{n-2} + \cdots + 1) \\ &+ \cdots \\ &+ a_0(X^{n-1} + X^{n-2} + \cdots + 1). \end{aligned} \tag{8.10}$$

Note that $1, \alpha, \alpha^2, \ldots, \alpha^{n-1}$ are all roots of

$$X^n - 1 = (X - 1)(X^{n-1} + X^{n-2} + \cdots + 1)$$

and therefore all except 1 are roots of $X^{n-1} + X^{n-2} + \cdots + 1$. The value of $1^{n-1} + 1^{n-2} + \cdots + 1$ is n. It follows that $b(\alpha^{-i}) = na_i$. Thus we have the following theorem:

THEOREM 8.2. *Let $a(X)$ be any polynomial of degree less than n over $GF(q^m)$ and let $b(X)$ be the polynomial whose ith coefficient is $a(\alpha^i)$, $i = 0, 1, \ldots, n - 1$, where α is an element of $GF(q^m)$ of order n. Then the ith coefficient of $a(X)$ is determined by*

$$na_i = b(\alpha^{-i}). \tag{8.11}$$

COROLLARY 8.1. *If $(n, p) = 1$, where p is the characteristic of $GF(q)$, then*

$$a_i = n^{-1}b(\alpha^{-i}).$$

Note that corresponding to every root of $a(X)$ there is a coefficient in $b(X)$ that is zero, and if $(n, p) = 1$, corresponding to every root of $b(X)$ a coefficient of $a(X)$ must be zero. In the remainder of this section it will be assumed that $(n, p) = 1$.

Consider the set of polynomials $a(X)$ satisfying the conditions:

1. For each i, $a(\alpha^i)$ is an element of $GF(q)$, where α is an element of order n. That is, the coefficients of $b(X)$ are elements of $GF(q)$.
2. For each $a(X)$ the coefficients $a_{i_1}, a_{i_2}, \ldots, a_{i_r}$ are all zero.

Since any linear combination of polynomials satisfying these conditions also satisfies these conditions, this set of polynomials is a subspace.

Now consider the set of polynomials $b(X)$ associated with the polynomials $a(X)$. A polynomial is in this set if and only if

1. Its coefficients are all in $GF(q)$, and, by Theorem 8.2,
2. $\alpha^{-i_1}, \alpha^{-i_2}, \ldots, \alpha^{-i_r}$ are all roots of $b(X)$.

Thus the set of polynomials $b(X)$ form a cyclic code whose generator polynomial has $\alpha^{-i_1}, \alpha^{-i_2}, \ldots, \alpha^{-i_r}$ as roots.

The restriction that the coefficients of $b(X)$ be in $GF(q)$ places a restriction on the coefficients of the associated polynomial $a(X)$. Since the coefficient b_i is $a(\alpha^i)$, this means that $a(X)$ must be in $GF(q)$ for $X = 1, \alpha, \alpha^2, \ldots, \alpha^{n-1}$. Then

$$[a(X)]^q = a(X) \tag{8.12}$$

or

$$a_{n-1}^q X^{q(n-1)} + a_{n-2}^q X^{q(n-2)} + \cdots + a_0^q = a_{n-1} X^{n-1} + a_{n-2} X^{n-2} + \cdots + a_0.$$

It follows in particular that

$$a_i^q X^{qi} = a_{qi} X^{qi},$$

where in each case qi is reduced modulo n. Thus in general,

$$a_{qi} = (a_i)^q.$$

Furthermore, this is not only necessary but sufficient, since if this condition holds for every coefficient, Equation 8.12 must hold and the values, being roots of $X^q - X$, must be in $GF(q)$ by Theorem 6.18.

THEOREM 8.3. *A polynomial $a(X)$ over $GF(q^m)$ has values in $GF(q)$ for $X = 1, \alpha, \alpha^2, \ldots, \alpha^{n-1}$, where α is an element of order n and $(n, q) = 1$, if and only if for each i,*

$$a_{qi} = (a_i)^q \qquad (qi \text{ reduced modulo } n).$$

Example. Consider the set of all polynomials $a(X)$ with coefficients in $GF(2^4)$ and with degree less than 9, and whose values are in $GF(2)$. Let α be a primitive element of $GF(2^4)$ so $n = 15$. By Theorem 8.3,

$$a_0 = a_0^2,$$
$$a_1^2 = a_2,\ a_2^2 = a_4,\ a_4^2 = a_8,\ a_8^2 = a_1,$$

$a_3^2 = a_6,\ a_6^2 = a_{12},\ a_{12}^2 = a_9,\ a_9^2 = a_3,$

$a_5^2 = a_{10},\ a_{10}^2 = a_5,$

$a_7^2 = a_{14},\ a_{14}^2 = a_{13},\ a_{13}^2 = a_{11},\ a_{11}^2 = a_7.$

Then a_0 must be 0 or 1. Next a_1 may be chosen arbitrarily from $GF(2^4)$, but then a_2, a_4, and a_8 are determined. Because $a(X)$ is required to have degree less than 9, then $a_{12} = 0$, and therefore a_3, a_6, and a_9 are zero. Similarly $a_5 = a_{10} = 0$ and $a_7 = a_{14} = a_{13} = a_{11} = 0$. Thus, $a(X)$ is of the form

$$a(X) = a_1^8 X^8 + a_1^4 X^4 + a_1^2 X^2 + a_1 X + a_0.$$

Now consider the code polynomial $b(X)$ associated with $a(X)$. From Equation 8.10,

$$\begin{aligned} b(X) = a_1^8[(\alpha^8 X)^{n-1} + (\alpha^8 X)^{n-2} + \cdots + (\alpha^8 X)^0] \\ + a_1^4[(\alpha^4 X)^{n-1} + (\alpha^4 X)^{n-2} + \cdots + (\alpha^4 X)^0] \\ + a_1^2[(\alpha^2 X)^{n-1} + (\alpha^2 X)^{n-2} + \cdots + (\alpha^2 X)^0] \\ + a_1[(\alpha X)^{n-1} + (\alpha X)^{n-2} + \cdots + (\alpha X)^0] \\ + a_0[(\alpha^0 X)^{n-1} + (\alpha^0 X)^{n-2} + \cdots + (\alpha^0 X)^0] \end{aligned}$$

The roots of $b(X)$ are all the elements of $GF(4)$ except α^0, α^{-1}, α^{-2}, α^{-4} and α^{-8}. This can be verified directly. Denote $(X^{15} + 1)/(X + 1)$ by $T(X)$; then, for example,

$$\begin{aligned} b(\alpha^{-8}) &= a_1^8 T(1) + a_1^4 T(\alpha^{-4}) + a_1^2 T(\alpha^{-6}) + a_1 T(a^{-7}) + a_0 T(\alpha^{-8}) \\ &= a_1^8 \end{aligned}$$

because all nonzero elements of $GF(4)$ except α^0 are roots of $T(X)$.

There are 16 choices for a_1 and 2 for a_0, and thus there are $32 = 2^5$ polynomials $b(X)$. These form a binary cyclic code with 2^5 code words, that is, a (15, 5) code. This is the code in the previous example, since its generator polynomial has the same roots.

Theorems 8.2 and 8.3 state that for every code word $b(X)$ in a cyclic code over $GF(q)$ there is an associated polynomial $a(X)$ such that the ith coefficient of $a(X)$ is obtained by evaluating the code polynomial $b(X)$ at $X = \alpha^{-i}$, according to Equation 8.11. These theorems are useful in analyzing cyclic product codes (Section 8.12), the majority-logic decodable codes of Chapter 10, and in several other instances.

8.4 Hamming Codes

The binary $(2^m - 1, 2^m - m - 1)$ Hamming codes discussed in Section 5.1 are equivalent to cyclic codes. Let α be a primitive element of $GF(2^m)$ and consider the null space of

$$\mathbf{H} = (\alpha^{2^m-2}, \alpha^{2^m-3}, \ldots, \alpha, 1). \tag{8.13}$$

If the powers of α are represented by column vectors of 1's and 0's, then every nonzero column of length m appears as a column of **H**. Therefore the null space of **H** is a Hamming single-error-correcting code. As a cyclic code it can be characterized by stating that $\{f(X)\}$ is a code vector if and only if α is a root of $f(X)$. The minimum function of α is a primitive polynomial, and therefore the generator polynomial of this code is primitive. Also, any code generated by a primitive polynomial is a Hamming code.

Example. Let $m = 4$ and let α be a root of the primitive polynomial $X^4 + X + 1$. Then the parity-check matrix **H** of the (15, 11) Hamming code generated by this polynomial is

$$\mathbf{H} = (\alpha^{14}, \alpha^{13}, \ldots, \alpha^2, \alpha, 1)$$

$$= \begin{bmatrix} 111101011001000 \\ 011110101100100 \\ 001111010110010 \\ 111010110010001 \end{bmatrix}.$$

(See Table 6.1.)

The $(2^m, 2^m - m - 1)$ code formed by adding an overall parity check to the Hamming code has minimum distance 4, as shown in Section 5.1. It can be regarded as the null space of the matrix

$$\begin{bmatrix} \alpha^{2^m-2} & \alpha^{2^m-3} & \cdots & \alpha\,1\,0 \\ 1 & 1 & \cdots & 1\,1\,1 \end{bmatrix} \tag{8.14}$$

This is not a cyclic code — it is an example of an *extended cyclic code.*

A binary cyclic $(2^m - 1, 2^m - m - 2)$ code with distance 4 can be generated by the polynomial $(X + 1)p(X)$, where $p(X)$ is a primitive polynomial. This single-error-correcting, double-error-detecting Hamming code is the null space of the matrix

$$\mathbf{H} = \begin{bmatrix} \alpha^{2m-2} & \alpha^{2m-3} & \cdots & 1 \\ 1 & 1 & \cdots & 1 \end{bmatrix}. \tag{8.15}$$

This is slightly different from the distance-4 code considered in the preceding paragraph in that a parity check has been added, but the length of the code has not been increased. Thus one information symbol has been eliminated. For this code, $\{f(X)\}$ is a code vector if and only if α and 1 are roots of $f(X)$. The set of code vectors is the set of even-weight code vectors in the original, distance-3 Hamming code.

There are several ways of arriving at a generalized, that is, nonbinary Hamming code in the framework of this chapter. Two of them are described here and one in Problem 8.5.

The most natural generalization over $GF(q)$ is formed by taking $\{f(X)\}$ to be a code vector if and only if it is in the null space of

$$\mathbf{H} = (\beta^{n-1}, \beta^{n-2}, \ldots, \beta, 1) \tag{8.16}$$

that is, if and only if β is a root of $f(X)$, where $\beta = \alpha^{q-1}$ and α is a primitive root of $GF(q^m)$. Then, as $\alpha^{q^m-1} = 1$,

$$\beta^{(q^m-1)/(q-1)} = 1$$

and n is the order of β, that is,

$$n = \frac{q^m - 1}{q - 1}$$

as it should be for a perfect generalized Hamming code. (See Section 5.1.)

THEOREM 8.4. *The null space of* $\mathbf{H} = [\beta^{n-1}, \beta^{n-2}, \ldots, \beta, 1]$, *where* $n = (q^m - 1)/(q - 1)$, *is a code with minimum distance* 3 *if and only if m is relatively prime to* $q - 1$.

Proof. Because $q^j - 1$ is divisible by $q - 1$ for all j, there exists an integer s_j such that

$$q^j = (q - 1)s_j + 1.$$

Therefore,

$$n = \frac{q^m - 1}{q - 1} = q^{m-1} + q^{m-2} + \cdots + 1$$

$$= (q - 1)(s_{m-1} + s_{m-2} + \cdots + s_1) + m$$

and n is relatively prime to $q - 1$ if and only if m is also. Now suppose that one column of $\mathbf{H}$ is a scalar multiple of another column:

$$\beta^i = a\beta^j \tag{8.17}$$

where a is an element of $GF(q)$. Then

$$\beta^{i-j} = a.$$

The nonzero elements of $GF(q)$ must be, by Theorem 6.18, the roots of $X^{q-1} - 1$ and hence must be the first $q - 1$ powers of α^n. Thus,

$$\alpha^{(q-1)(i-j)} = (\alpha^n)^s$$

for some integer s less than $q - 1$, and

$$(q-1)(i-j) = ns. \tag{8.18}$$

But $q - 1$ cannot divide s since $s < q - 1$, and if $q - 1$ is relatively prime to n, then $i - j = 0$ and $a = 1$. Then no two different columns of $\mathbf{H}$ are linearly dependent. On the other hand, if $q - 1$ and n are not relatively prime, there is a nontrivial solution to Equation 8.18 and hence to Equation 8.17. Q.E.D.

Another form of modified Hamming code can be formed by taking the code to be the null space of

$$\mathbf{H} = \begin{bmatrix} 1, 1, \ldots, 1, 1 \\ \alpha^{q^{m-1}-1}, \quad \ldots, \alpha, 1 \end{bmatrix} \tag{8.19}$$

or in other words by taking $\{f(X)\}$ to be a code vector if and only if α and 1 are roots of $f(X)$, where α is a primitive element of $GF(q^{m-1})$. This code corrects single errors, since no two columns of $\mathbf{H}$ can be linearly dependent. It has m parity-check symbols and q^{m-1} symbols rather than the maximum number possible $(q^m - 1)/(q - 1)$. It is shorter by the fraction $(q - 1)/q$, approximately. The generator polynomial for this code is the product of $X - 1$ and $p(X)$, a primitive polynomial of degree $m - 1$.

Encoding for both types of generalized Hamming codes can be performed as explained in Section 8.7, decoding as explained in Section 8.9.

8.5 Maximum-Length-Sequence Codes

Consider now the maximum period possible for a linear feedback shift register of m stages, or equivalently for solutions of a difference equation corresponding to a polynomial of degree m. The sequence will start repeating as soon as the vector stored in the shift register repeats, and therefore there must be a distinct vector in the shift register for each element in one period of the sequence. Furthermore, if the shift register contains all 0's, all outputs will also be 0's. A sequence of length greater than $q^m - 1$, the number of nonzero vectors of length m, would therefore be impossible.

The existence of such sequences can be shown algebraically as follows. Let $h(X)$ be the polynomial of degree m corresponding to the feedback connections. Then, by Theorem 7.1, the period of the sequences is the smallest n such that $h(X)$ divides $X^{q^m-1} - 1$, and hence $n \leqq q^m - 1$. But if $h(X)$ is a primitive polynomial, $h(X)$ divides $X^n - 1$ for no smaller value of n, and therefore the period of the sequences is exactly $q^m - 1$. Examples of shift-register generators that generate maximum-length binary sequences are given in Figures 7.15 and 7.20.

The set of all possible outputs of such a shift register, that is, the set of all solutions of the corresponding difference equations, has dimension m, and therefore there are q^m such solutions. One is the sequence of all 0's. Given any other, all $q^m - 1$ cyclic shifts of it must be solutions also. This is the total number of solutions. Therefore *any two nonzero solutions differ only in that one is a cyclic shift of the other*. The set of vectors that are the first periods of all the solutions forms an ideal and hence a cyclic code. The nonzero solution with the most leading 0's must be the generator polynomial of the code,

$$\{(X^{q^m-1} - 1)/h(X)\}.$$

The vector contained in the shift register consists of m successive elements of the sequence. Since the contents of the shift register must be different for each element in one period, each nonzero vector of m components must appear in m successive positions of a maximum-length sequence in one and only one place. Finally, in the set of all m-component vectors, every field element appears in $1/q$ of the mq^m positions, that is, in mq^{m-1} positions. If the $\mathbf{0}$ vector is omitted, 0 appears only $m(q^{m-1} - 1)$ times. Since every m-component vector appears once and only once in a maximum-length sequence, and in this way each element of the sequence is counted m times, every nonzero element appears in one period of a maximum-length sequence q^{m-1} times, and 0 appears $q^{m-1} - 1$ times. This tells completely the distance structure of these codes.

The parity-check polynomial of the $(2^m - 1, m)$ binary maximum-length-sequence code is a primitive polynomial. Thus this code is the dual of the cyclic Hamming code discussed in the preceding section whose generator polynomial is this primitive polynomial.

8.6 Some Binary Cyclic Codes

Appendix D contains a list of binary cyclic codes of odd length less than or equal to 65 (Chen 1969). Tabulated are n, k, minimum distance, the minimum distance guaranteed by the BCH bound of Section 9.1, and the exponents of the roots of the generator polynomial. [If α^i is a root of $g(X)$, where α is a root of $X^n - 1$ of order n, then the smallest integer in the set (i, $2i$ modulo n, $2^2 i$ modulo n, ...) is listed.]

Codes for which $g(X) = X - 1$ have minimum distance 2 and codes for which $g(X) = (X^n - 1)/(X - 1)$ have minimum distance n. Both of these types of codes exist for all values of n and so are omitted from the table. Also codes of length n for which $g(X)$ divides $X^m - 1$, $m < n$, are omitted; for these codes, $d = 2$.

The permutation

$$X^i \rightarrow X^{ip}$$

transforms a cyclic code into an equivalent cyclic code provided $(n, p) = 1$, that is, provided n and p are relatively prime. (See Problem 8.19.) In the table only one member of each such equivalence class of codes is tabulated.

A few codes of length 63 have more information symbols than the BCH codes with the same minimum distance; such codes are marked with an asterisk in the table. All these codes can be derived from the (63, 46) $d = 7$ code found by Peterson (1967), the (63, 28) $d = 15$ code found by Kasami and Tokura (1969), the (63, 21) $d = 17$ and 18 codes, and the (63, 19) $d = 19$ code. In this latter reference, the authors prove the existence of an infinite but sparse class of codes whose minimum distance is slightly greater than that of the corresponding BCH codes.

8.7 Encoding Procedures

The very simple methods of encoding cyclic codes presented in this section serve to illustrate one of the most important features of cyclic codes — ease of implementation.

Both procedures accept k-symbol blocks of information digits from the source and forward them to the channel with no delay. Following each such block, $n - k$ parity-check symbols are sent; during this time no information can be accepted from the source. Thus these procedures presume a source capable of starting and stopping on command or else require the use of a buffer.

Two ways to encode an information k-tuple into a code word in a cyclic code are described. The first employs a k-stage shift register; the second a register of $n - k$ stages. For codes with more check symbols than information symbols, the first method is generally preferable, while for codes with $k/n > 0.5$ the second method is usually more economical. Both methods give the *same* code word.

Encoding for the (n, k) cyclic code generated by $g(X)$, a polynomial of degree $n - k$, can be accomplished by using the *k-stage shift register* shown in Figure 7.14, with connections corresponding to $h(X) = (X^n - 1)/g(X)$. The information symbols are stored initially in the k storage devices, and then the device is made to shift n times. The first k symbols that come out will be the information symbols, and the last $n - k$ symbols will be a set of check symbols that make the whole n-symbol vector a code vector. That this is true follows immediately from Theorem 7.1.

Example. For the (7, 4) binary Hamming code considered in previous examples, $g(X) = X^3 + X + 1$ and $h(X) = (X^7 + 1)/g(X) = X^4 + X^2 + X + 1$. The shift register shown in Figure 8.1 can be used for encoding. After 4 shifts the 4 data bits are stored in the register. Since the inputs to the binary adder correspond to the nonzero terms of $h(X)$ (see Problem 8.9), its output is the first parity-check digit. On the 5th shift this digit is entered in the right-most stage of the register and the first information bit is shifted out. Now because the code is cyclic, the second parity digit is the sum of the digits in the same positions relative to itself as the first parity digit. Hence, the output of the adder is this second parity digit. The third parity digit is calculated in a similar manner.

Now consider encoding with a *shift register of n − k stages.* A code word can be formed by multiplying a polynomial of degree $k - 1$ or less whose coefficients are arbitrary information symbols by $g(X)$, the generator polynomial of the code. This can be mechanized with the linear circuit shown in Figure 7.2 or the one in Figure 7.3. With this

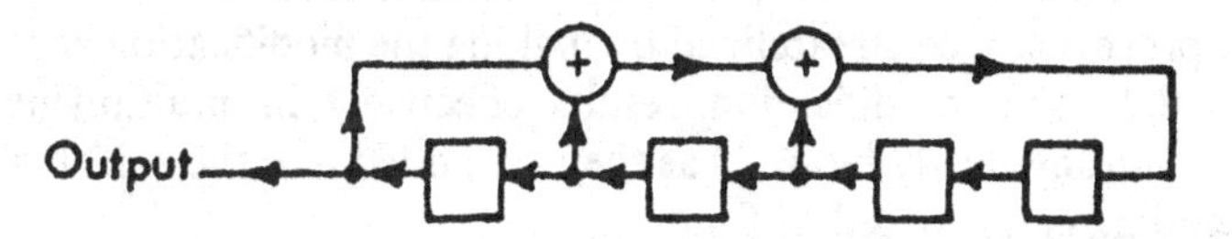

Figure 8.1. A k-stage shift register for encoding the (7, 4) code generated by $X^3 + X + 1$.

method the information symbols do not appear unaltered in the code polynomial but can be recovered from a correct code polynomial by division by $g(X)$, using the circuit in Figure 7.6.

It is generally simpler and more satisfactory to have the code vector consist of the k unaltered information symbols followed by $n - k$ check symbols, that is, to have a systematic code. This can be accomplished for any cyclic code by the following procedure: Let $f_0(X)$ be a polynomial in which the k coefficients of terms involving $X^{n-1}, X^{n-2}, \ldots, X^{n-k}$ are arbitrary information symbols, and the coefficients of terms of degree less than $n - k$ are 0. This corresponds to a vector for which the first k components are arbitrary information symbols, and the last $n - k$ components are 0. Then, by the division algorithm (Equation 6.4),

$$f_0(X) = g(X)\,q(X) + r(X),$$

where $r(X)$ has degree less than $n - k$, the degree of $g(X)$. Then

$$f_0(X) - r(X) = g(X)\,q(X)$$

and hence $\{f_0(X) - r(X)\}$ is a code vector. Since $r(X)$ has degree less than $n - k$, all its terms of degree $n - k$ or greater are 0. Therefore, the high-order terms of $f_0(X) - r(X)$ are the information symbols unaltered, and the low-order terms are the check symbols, $-r(X)$, unaltered. The combined code vector obtained in this way is identical to the one obtained by using a k-stage shift-register generator if the same information symbols are chosen.

The remaining problem is to find a way of implementing the calculation of the remainder after dividing a polynomial $f_0(X)$ by $g(X)$. This can be done with the division circuit shown in Figure 7.6. The polynomial $f_0(X)$ that has information symbols as its k high-order coefficients and 0's as its $n - k$ low-order coefficients is shifted into the circuit, high-order first, until the last coefficient is shifted into the low-order position of the shift register. This requires a total of n shifts, k for the information symbols and $n - k$ for the low-order 0's. Then the remainder $r(X)$ is in the shift register, and the remainder is the additive inverse (negative) of the check symbols. These check symbols can then replace the $n - k$ low-order symbols of $f_0(X)$ to form a code vector.

The process can be streamlined by making the modification shown in Figure 8.2. This modification results effectively in multiplying the symbols automatically by X^{n-k} as they are added into the shift register. Then coding can proceed as follows:

1. Shift the k information symbols into the device shown in Figure 8.2 and simultaneously into the communication channel. As

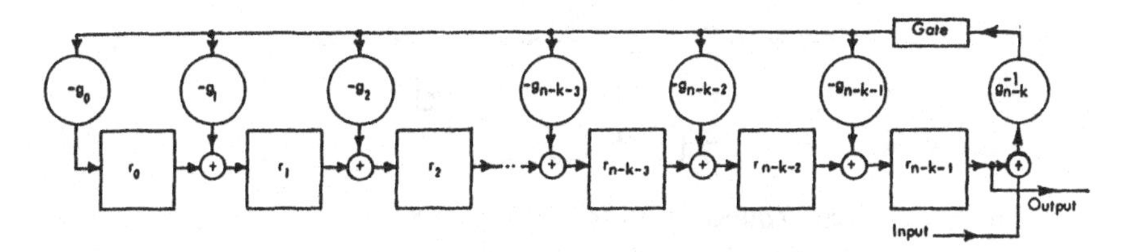

Figure 8.2. An encoder with automatic premultiplication by X^{n-k}.

soon as the k information symbols have entered the shift register, the $n - k$ symbols in the register are the remainder, that is, the negative of the check symbols.

2. Disable the feedback circuit in the shift register, for example by gating it at the point shown on the diagram.
3. Shift the contents of the shift register out, changing the signs of the symbols as they come out, and send them into the communication channel. These $n - k$ check symbols together with the k information symbols make a complete code vector.

Example. For the (7, 4) binary cyclic Hamming code, with $g(X) = X^3 + X + 1$, considered in previous examples the equivalent of Figure 8.2 is shown in Figure 8.3.

Encoding can also be done by a modification of this method by using circuits obtained from the basic division circuit by the transformation given in Equation 7.30. The transformation can be applied to the circuit in Figure 8.2 under both conditions, gate open and gate closed, to yield the correct connections in each case.

Example. The matrices for Figure 8.3 are, for the gate closed,

$$\mathbf{T} = \begin{bmatrix} 0\,1\,0 \\ 0\,0\,1 \\ 1\,1\,0 \end{bmatrix}, \qquad \mathbf{U} = [1\,1\,0], \qquad \mathbf{R}^T = [0\,0\,1], \qquad \mathbf{S} = [1],$$

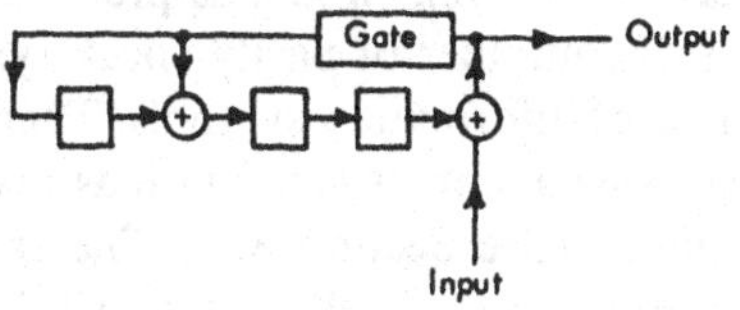

Gate Output

Input

Figure 8.3. An $(n - k)$-stage encoder for a cyclic (7, 4) code generated by $X^3 + X + 1$.

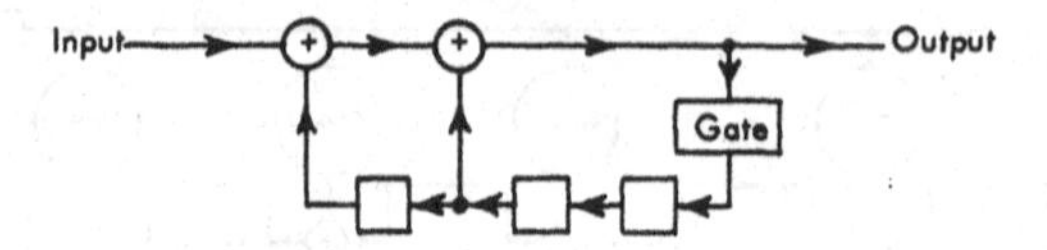

Figure 8.4. A circuit equivalent to that of Figure 8.3.

and for the gate open,

$$\mathbf{T} = \begin{bmatrix} 0\,1\,0 \\ 0\,0\,1 \\ 0\,0\,0 \end{bmatrix}, \qquad \mathbf{U} = [0\,0\,0], \qquad \mathbf{R}^T = [0\,0\,1], \qquad \mathbf{S} = [1].$$

If the transformation

$$\mathbf{A} = \begin{bmatrix} 1\,1\,1 \\ 1\,1\,0 \\ 1\,0\,0 \end{bmatrix} \qquad \mathbf{A}^{-1} = \begin{bmatrix} 0\,0\,1 \\ 0\,1\,1 \\ 1\,1\,0 \end{bmatrix}$$

is applied to this circuit, the result is, for the gate closed,

$$\mathbf{T}' = \begin{bmatrix} 0\,0\,1 \\ 1\,0\,1 \\ 0\,1\,0 \end{bmatrix}, \qquad \mathbf{U}' = [0\,0\,1], \qquad \mathbf{R}'^T = [1\,1\,0], \qquad \mathbf{S}' = [1],$$

and for the gate open,

$$\mathbf{T}' = \begin{bmatrix} 0\,0\,0 \\ 1\,0\,0 \\ 0\,1\,0 \end{bmatrix}, \qquad \mathbf{U}' = [0\,0\,0], \qquad \mathbf{R}'^T = [1\,1\,0], \qquad \mathbf{S}' = [1].$$

The resulting circuit is shown in Figure 8.4.

8.8 Error Detection with Cyclic Codes

Cyclic codes are well suited for error detection, for they can be designed to detect many combinations of likely errors, and implementation of both encoding and error-detecting circuits is practical.

For error detection the number of parity-check symbols will usually be less than the number of information symbols. Then the encoding can be accomplished best using a shift register with as many stages as there are parity-check symbols. (See Section 8.7.) The same device can be used for the detection of a parity-check failure. All that need be done is to subtract (or in the binary case, add) the received parity-check digits and those calculated at the receiver. If the result is zero, the received word is a code word; otherwise it is not. In the binary case this addition is performed automatically by the circuit of Figure 8.2; thus it is only necessary to determine whether the output $(n-k)$-tuple consists of all zeros or not.

Now consider error-detecting capability.

THEOREM 8.5. *No code vector of an (n, k) cyclic code is a burst of length $n-k$ or less. Therefore every (n, k) cyclic code can detect any burst of length $n-k$ or less.*

Proof. Let $\{r(X)\}$ be a burst of length $n-k$ or less and suppose that the code in question is generated by $g(X)$, a polynomial of degree $n-k$. Let the first nonzero coefficient of $r(X)$ be the coefficient of X^j. Then

$$r(X) = X^j r_0(X),$$

where r_0 must have degree less than $n-k$, since $\{r(X)\}$ is a burst of length no greater than $n-k$. Since $g(X)$ divides $X^n - 1$, $g(X)$ is not divisible by X, and X^j and $g(X)$ are relatively prime. Now if $g(X)$ is to divide $r(X)$, it must divide $r_0(X)$, which is impossible since $g(X)$ has degree greater than $r_0(X)$. Therefore, $\{r(X)\}$ cannot be a code vector.

Q.E.D.

A high percentage of longer bursts is detected as well:

THEOREM 8.6. *The fraction of bursts of length $b > n-k$ that can be undetected by a cyclic (n, k) code is $q^{-(n-k-1)}/(q-1)$ if $b = n-k+1$ and $q^{-(n-k)}$ if $b > n-k+1$.*

Proof. Consider bursts of length b starting in the ith and ending in the $(i+b-1)$st symbols. Each has the form $\{r(X)\} = \{X^i r_1(X)\}$, where $r_1(X)$ has degree $b-1$. There are $q-1$ choices for the first coefficient, $q-1$ for the last, and q choices for each coefficient in between, with the result that there are $(q-1)^2 q^{b-2}$ distinct polynomials $r_1(X)$.

The error is undetected if and only if $r_1(X)$ has $g(X)$ as a factor; that is,

$$r_1(X) = g(X)\, Q(X)$$

Since $g(X)$ has degree $n-k$, $Q(X)$ must have degree $b-1-(n-k)$. If $b-1 = n-k$, then $Q(X)$ is a nonzero constant, and there are $q-1$ values it may take. The ratio of undetected bursts to the total number of bursts is $(q-1)/((q-1)^2 q^{b-2}) = q^{-(n-k-1)}/(q-1)$. If $b-1 > n-k$, $Q(X)$ may have any of the $q-1$ nonzero field elements as its first coefficient, any nonzero field element as its last coefficient, and any of the

q field elements for each coefficient in between. There are, therefore, $(q-1)^2 q^{b-1-(n-k)-1}$ choices of $Q(X)$ which give undetected error patterns. The ratio for this case is $q^{-(n-k)}$. Q.E.D.

Theorem 8.6 has some rather surprising consequences. It states that regardless of how long a code is used or how noisy is the channel, the probability of undetected error is proportional to $q^{-(n-k)}$. That is, P_e is determined primarily by the number of parity-check digits. Thus with a binary code, it would be an unusual application that would require more than 30 parity digits and usually half this number would suffice.

Error-detecting ability can be combined with other properties of specific codes. For example, a BCH code of arbitrary distance d can be constructed, and it will then be capable of detecting any combination of $d-1$ or fewer errors or any burst of length $n-k$ or less. A code with the ability to correct any single burst of length b is capable of detecting any combination of two bursts of length b or less or any single burst of length $n-k$ or less.

Examples. It is shown in Section 8.4 that a distance-4 Hamming binary code can be achieved as a cyclic code. Let us take $n = 2^{10} - 1 = 1023$. Then $n - k = 10 + 1 = 11$. This code requires an 11-stage shift register for coding or error detection. It can detect any combination of three or fewer errors or any single burst of length 11 or less.

It is shown in Chapter 9 that a BCH binary code with distance 6 and $n = 1023$ can be constructed using 21 parity checks; therefore, a 21-stage shift register is necessary for encoding and error detection. It can detect any combination of 5 or fewer errors, or any single burst of length 21 or less, and all but 0.00005 percent of all other error patterns.

8.9 Some Simple Error-Correction Procedures For Short Cyclic Codes

In this section several decoding procedures for cyclic codes are presented. These techniques are suitable for decoding burst-correcting and short random-error-correcting cyclic codes. The best-known methods of decoding long random-error-correcting codes, that is, the BCH and majority-logic-decodable codes, are presented in subsequent chapters.

The process of assigning a code word in a linear code to a received n-tuple, that is, decoding, is usually performed in two steps. First, the decoder calculates the syndrome of the received word. Then from the syndrome it determines the coset leader and subtracts it from the received word. The first step in this error-correction process is very simple for cyclic codes; the second is usually much more complex.

The syndrome associated with an n-tuple $\mathbf{v}$ in a linear code is just the $(n-k)$-tuple

$$\mathbf{s} = \mathbf{v}\mathbf{H}^T. \tag{8.20}$$

For a cyclic code this calculation can be performed by dividing the received polynomial by $g(X)$, since the jth row of $\mathbf{H}^T$ is the vector of coefficients in the remainder obtained by dividing X^{n-1-j} by $g(X)$. (See Section 8.7.)

This division operation can be implemented rather simply by the circuit of Figure 7.6. After the received n-tuple has been shifted into the register, the register contains the syndrome. Hereafter the feedback shift register of Figure 7.6 with connections corresponding to $g(X)$ will be referred to as the *syndrome generator* of $g(X)$.

The determination of the error pattern from the syndrome is considerably simplified by the following theorem:

THEOREM 8.7. *Let $s(X)$ denote the syndrome of an n-tuple $r(X)$. The syndrome of a cyclic shift of $r(X)$, that is, of $Xr(X)$, is obtained by shifting the syndrome generator of $g(X)$ once with initial contents $s(X)$.*

Proof. The syndrome $s(X)$ can be obtained as follows:

$$s(X) = r(X) - g(X)\, q_s(X), \tag{8.21}$$

where $q_s(X)$ represents the quotient obtained by dividing $r(X)$ by $g(X)$. The syndrome of $Xr(X)$, denoted $t(X)$, is similarly given by

$$t(X) = Xr(X) - g(X)\, q_t(X).$$

Multiplying Equation 8.21 by X and subtracting the result gives

$$Xs(X) - t(X) = -g(X)[Xq_s(X) - q_t(X)]. \tag{8.22}$$

Now there are two situations to consider. If the degree of $s(X)$ is less than $n-k-1$, then the degree of $Xs(X) - t(X)$ is less than that of $g(X)$, so $Xs(X) - t(X) = 0$. Thus, $t(X)$ is just $s(X)$ shifted right once. On the other hand, if the degree of $s(X)$ is equal to $n-k-1$, then the degree of $Xs(X) - t(X)$ equals that of $g(X)$, so $Xq_s(X) - q_t(X)$ must have degree zero; that is, it must be an element of $GF(q)$. Then,

$$t(X) = Xs(X) - ag(X),$$

where a is an element of $GF(q)$. But since $g(X)$ is monic, the coefficient of X^{n-k-1} in $s(X)$ must be a. Thus, shifting $s(X)$ once in the syndrome generator of $g(X)$ causes $ag(X)$ to be subtracted from the shifted syndrome which yields $t(X)$, as claimed. Q.E.D.

The proof can be extended easily to the case where the syndrome is taken to be $X^{n-k}s(X)$, or indeed the product of the $s(X)$ in Equation 8.20 and any polynomial. Thus, the syndrome can be calculated also by the circuit shown in Figure 8.2, or even as in Figure 8.7 for shortened cyclic codes, with this theorem still true.

A typical decoder for cyclic codes can correct all error patterns $X^i e(X)$, $1 \leq i \leq n-1$ provided it can correct the pattern $e(X)$. Also if $e(X)$ is correctable, its descendants (see Section 3.5) usually are also. Under these conditions Theorem 8.7 states, in effect, that if a decoder can decode the first symbol in a word correctly for all correctable error patterns, then the entire word can be decoded with the same circuitry. This result considerably simplifies the implementation of decoding and is used in all the known decoding processes for cyclic codes.

The preceding theorem provides the basis for the *Meggitt decoder* for cyclic codes shown in Figure 8.5. The syndrome generator employed in this decoder differs slightly from that of Figure 7.6 in that it multiplies the syndrome by X^{n-k}. (See Figure 8.2.) Thus if the input polynomial is $r(X)$, the register contains not $s'(X)$, the syndrome of $r(X)$, but $s(X) = X^{n-k}s'(X)$ modulo $g(X)$. The Meggitt decoder operates as follows:

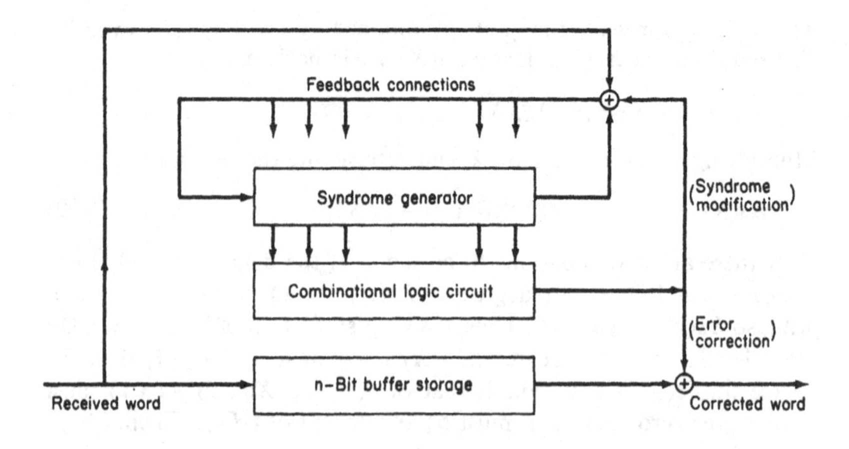

Figure 8.5. A Meggitt decoder for cyclic codes.

1. Assume that for some and possibly all cosets a coset leader is chosen. This would ordinarily be chosen, on the basis of error statistics for the channel, to be the most likely error pattern in the coset. Assume also that for this set of coset leaders every cyclic shift of a coset leader is also a coset leader, and every descendant of a coset leader is a coset leader. (See Section 3.5. The Meggitt decoder is a form of step-by-step decoder.)
2. The received word is shifted into the buffer and simultaneously into the syndrome generator. (In the following description the buffer will be assumed to consist of n stages. In fact, because only the information symbols are ordinarily of interest after decoding, only k stages are really necessary.)
3. There is a one-to-one correspondence between $s(X)$, the contents of the syndrome generator, and the coset leader which must be subtracted from $r(X)$ to remove the error pattern. The combinational logic circuit is designed to produce the ground field element $-a$ at its output if and only if $s(X)$ corresponds to an error pattern with an error of value a in the highest-order symbol, that is, in the symbol about to be read out of the buffer. Thus, if the output of the logical circuit is nonzero, the next symbol to come out of the buffer must be corrected. This is accomplished by reading a symbol out of the buffer and adding to it the output of the logical circuit.
4. At the same time that the symbol is read out of the buffer, the syndrome generator is shifted. If the first symbol coming out of the buffer is corrected, the syndrome must also be altered by adding the output of the logical circuit to the feedback of the syndrome generator. (See Figure 8.5.) This makes the syndrome correspond to the altered received vector, a fact discussed in more detail later.
5. Steps 2 and 3 are repeated until the entire received vector has been read out of the buffer. For each symbol read out of the buffer, both the buffer and syndrome generator are shifted once to the right. By Theorem 8.7, the contents of the syndrome generator after shifting correspond to the syndrome of the shifted error pattern. Thus, the output of the logical circuit indicates at each time the value of the error symbol to be added to the next received symbol.
6. After the received word is read out, the errors will have been corrected if they correspond to a pattern built into the logical circuit, and the syndrome generator will contain all zeros. If

the syndrome generator does not contain all zeros at the end of the process, an error uncorrectable with the given logical circuit has been detected.

As described, the Meggitt decoder is capable of decoding only alternate received words if the decoding circuit is shifted in step with the received symbols, that is, at *line speed*. There are several ways around this problem.

1. Duplicate decoders can be provided; this permits all circuits to operate at line speed.
2. A second n-symbol buffer can be provided. While word B is being corrected, word A is shifted out of and word C shifted into this additional buffer. At the completion of decoding, the roles of the two buffers are interchanged. With this procedure the decoder must operate at not less than twice line speed.
3. Little additional circuitry is needed if a complete word can be decoded in a single symbol-time. In this case the decoder performs n shifts between the arrival of the last symbol of word A and the first symbol of word B.

The fact that adding the correction symbol, say $-a$, to the feedback of the syndrome generator corrects the syndrome can be explained as follows: Originally the syndrome generator contents $s(X)$ correspond to $r(X)$. Correction adds $-a$ (after a shift) to $Xr(X)$. The new register contents then must be $X^{n-k}(Xr(X) - a)$ modulo $g(X)$, since the syndrome of $-a$ is just $-a$. This says that the syndrome generator contents must be modified by adding to it $-aX^{n-k}$ modulo $g(X)$. Adding $-a$ to the feedback accomplishes this with little additional circuitry.

Assume the received message is in the coset of a correctable error pattern. The syndrome is the same for every element of the coset. When the position corresponding to the first nonzero symbol in the coset leader shifts out, the negative of that symbol appears at the output of the combinational circuit and is added to the symbol coming out and to the syndrome generator feedback circuit. Thus, both the received message and syndrome are "corrected" in such a way that they correspond to a coset that contains the original coset leader with its first symbol changed to zero. This being a descendant of the original coset leader is, by the assumptions (1), also a coset leader. Thus, when the position corresponding to its first symbol shifts out of the buffer register, the combinational circuit "corrects" it also. Eventually the syndrome register will contain zero and the received message will have been altered to the code word corresponding to the sum of the received message and the coset leader, as it should.

With the possible exception of the combinational logical circuit, the entire Meggitt decoder is easily implemented. Whether or not this method is practical for decoding a particular code depends entirely on the complexity of this logical circuit. For all the burst-correcting codes discussed in Chapter 11, this circuit is very simple. The majority-logic codes of Chapter 10 are attractive because the combinational circuit can be implemented with a moderate amount of circuitry. On the other hand, for the Bose-Chaudhuri-Hocquenghem (BCH) codes of Chapter 9, it appears that the combinational circuit is quite complex.

An attempt was made to determine the minimum two-level logic circuit for several relatively short BCH codes using the Quine-McCluskey (1965) method of minimization. Among the codes tried were the BCH (15, 7) and (31, 21) double-error-correcting codes and the BCH (15, 5), (31, 16), and the Golay (23, 12) triple-error-correcting codes. The circuits did not simplify a great deal. For example, for the (23, 12) code, the minimum two-level logical circuit had about one-third fewer terms than the original expression. Further factoring reduced the ratio to one-half or a little less. There are 1 single error, 22 double errors, and $22 \times 21 = 462$ triple errors with 1's in their last component, with the result that a total of 485 terms appear in the original expression. Half of this number still requires a costly logical circuit. Fortunately there exists a much more simply implemented method of decoding the BCH codes, explained in the next chapter. Also, the Golay code can be decoded efficiently by "error trapping," which is explained later in this section.

The Hamming codes can be decoded very easily with a Meggitt decoder. The first column of the parity-check matrix $\mathbf{H}$ of a binary Hamming code is α^{n-1}, where α is a primitive element of $GF(2^m)$ and $n = 2^m - 1$. If a single error occurs in the highest-order position, the m-bit syndrome is the binary representation of α^{n-1}; if a single error occurs anywhere else, the syndrome is not α^{n-1}. Because the syndrome generator in the Meggitt decoder multiplies the actual syndrome by $X^{n-k} = X^m$, the register contains α^{m-1}, the syndrome of X^{m-1}. In binary form the syndrome is just the m-tuple $(000\cdots001)$. Thus the combinational circuit for this Meggitt decoder is simply the m-input AND-gate which has a 1 at its output for this and only this syndrome.

Example. The polynomial $g(X) = X^4 + X + 1$ generates a (15, 11) Hamming code. If the error pattern that occurs is X^{14}, the contents of the syndrome generator is $X^4 \cdot X^{14}$ modulo $g(X) = X^3$; the

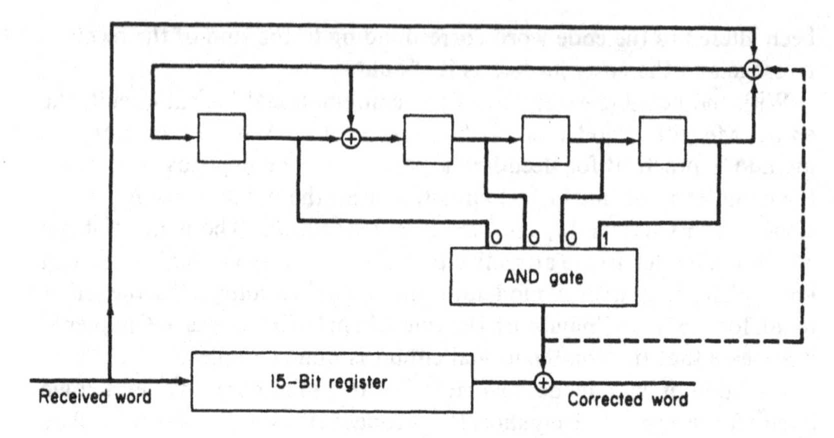

Figure 8.6. A Meggitt decoder for the (15, 11) Hamming code.

binary representation of this syndrome is just 0001. The Meggitt decoder for this code is shown in Figure 8.6.

The nonbinary Hamming codes of Section 8.4 can also be decoded simply with the Meggitt decoder. The combinational circuit for either type must detect the presence of $m-1$ zeros in the low-order syndrome positions. When this occurs, the value of the error is contained in the first stage.

For the syndrome calculation for a received polynomial $r(X)$ performed by an $n-k$-stage shift register as in Figure 8.2, the syndrome* is taken to be

$$s(X) = X^{n-k}r(X) - q(X)\,g(X),$$

where $q(X)$ is the quotient resulting from dividing $X^{n-k}r(X)$ by $g(X)$. Subtracting the syndrome from the high-order part of the received polynomial, one has

$$r(X) - X^k s(X) = r(X) - X^n r(X) + q'(X)\,g(X) = q'(X)\,g(X)$$

since $X^n - 1 = 0$. Thus, subtracting the syndrome from the high-order part of the received polynomial always results in a code polynomial.

Now suppose that all the errors actually lie in the high-order $n-k$ symbols of $r(X)$. Subtracting the syndrome from the high-order part of $r(X)$ results in a code word that matches the low-order k symbols of $r(X)$, and hence of the transmitted polynomial $t(X)$. Thus, $r(X) - X^k s(X)$

* Note that this syndrome differs from that defined earlier because of the premultiplication by X^{n-k}.

$-t(X)$ has zeros as its k lowest order coefficients, and thus is of the form $X^k f(X)$ where $f(X)$ has degree less than $n-k$. But being the difference between two code polynomials, it must be divisible by $g(X)$. This is possible only if $X^k f(X)$ is zero. Thus,

$$r(X) = t(X) + X^k s(X)$$

and since $r(X)$ is the sum of $t(X)$ and the error pattern, $X^k s(X)$ must be the error pattern. Thus the following theorem holds:

THEOREM 8.8. *If the syndrome of $r(X)$ is taken to be the remainder after dividing $X^{n-k} r(X)$ by $g(X)$, and all errors lie in the highest-order $n-k$ symbols of $r(X)$, then the nonzero portion of the error pattern appears in the corresponding positions of the syndrome.*

There is a variation of Meggitt decoding, called *error trapping* (Rudolph and Mitchell 1964), which is based on this theorem. Suppose that every coset leader contains somewhere in it k successive zeros. (The k zeros might be partly at the beginning and partly at the end because of the cyclic nature of the code.) Then, as the received vector and syndrome are shifted together, at some point the zeros line up with the low-order part of the buffer register and the error pattern appears entirely in the high-order part. Then, by Theorem 8.8, it will also appear in the syndrome register. Thus, the combinational circuit of the Meggitt decoder need only detect the presence of a correctable error pattern in the syndrome register with a nonzero symbol in the high-order position.

Actually, at this point a slight deviation from the Meggitt decoder may be more convenient. The combinational circuit need only detect the presence of the correctable error pattern in some position in the syndrome register and then subtract the syndrome register from the high-order part of the buffer.

Note that with error trapping, if the $n-k$ positions containing the error pattern are partly at the high-order end and partly at the low-order end of the buffer initially, the positions at the high-order end will not be corrected during the first n shifts. This difficulty can be obviated by originally calculating the syndrome by dividing $r(X)$ by $g(X)$ without premultiplication by X^{n-k}. Then the syndrome register is shifted $n-k$ times, each time checking for a correctable pattern. If one appears, the errors in the high-order end can be corrected immediately; otherwise, k additional shifts of the syndrome generator and received vector as described in the preceding paragraphs are required.

Error trapping is effective if it is possible to confine all patterns to

$n-k$ consecutive positions. This is obviously true for all single-error-correcting codes and in fact for all burst-correcting codes. For a code that corrects all bursts of length b or less, the combinational circuit can be specified as follows: The output is zero if any of the low-order $n-k-b$ symbols in the syndrome register is nonzero, and otherwise it equals the negative of the high-order symbol in the syndrome register. For the binary case, this is simply an $(n-k-b+1)$-input AND-gate whose inputs are the complements of the first $n-k-b$ symbols and the true value of the last symbol in the syndrome register.

For correction of random errors, it can be shown that a necessary and sufficient condition for all error patterns of t or fewer errors to contain at least k successive zeros is

$$t < \frac{1}{R}, \tag{8.23}$$

where R is the code rate, k/n. (See Problem 8.10.)

A number of modifications to error-trapping decoding have been proposed to extend its usefulness. The following variation provides a good way to decode many short cyclic codes, including the Golay (23, 12) code, which is discussed in the example below. Consider a pattern of three errors; imagine the pattern arranged in a circle — three 1's with three spacings of 0's of length S_1, S_2, and S_3. Then, $S_1 + S_2 + S_3 = 20$, the total number of 0's. Now assume $S_3 \geqq S_2 \geqq S_1$. For those error patterns that cannot be corrected by simple error trapping, $S_3 < k = 12$, and therefore $S_1 + S_2 > 8$. But since $S_2 \geqq S_1$, then $2S_2 > 8$, and $S_2 > 4$, so $S_2 \geqq 5$. If $S_2 = 5$, since $S_1 \leqq S_2$, it follows that $S_3 \geqq 10$. Thus, one of the three 1's in the error pattern has at least 5 0's on one side of it and at least 6 on the other side. Therefore, at some time or other during the shifting, that 1 appears either in the 6th or the 7th position in the buffer and simultaneously both other errors lie in the last $n-k$ positions. An error in the ith position adds into the syndrome register the remainder after dividing $X^{i-1}X^{n-k}$ by $g(X)$. Let us call this remainder $r_i(X)$. Then, correction can be done for the Golay code as follows:

1a. If the weight of the syndrome is 3 or less, use this as the error pattern and add it to the high-order part of the received vector in the buffer.

1b. Add $r_5(X)$ to the syndrome. If the resulting weight is 2 or less, add the syndrome to the high-order part of the received vector in the buffer and in addition invert the 6th symbol in the buffer.

1c. Add $r_6(X)$ to the syndrome. If the resulting weight is 2 or less, add the syndrome to the high-order part of the received vector and also invert the 7th symbol in the buffer.

2. Shift the received vector and the syndrome register and repeat step 1 a total of $2n$ times.

The additional positions that must be checked, positions 6 and 7 for the Golay code, are referred to as *windows*. There does not appear to be a straightforward way to choose windows except for double-error-correcting codes. Kasami (1964) gives choices for the triple-error-correcting BCH (31, 16) and (63, 45) codes, the four-error-correcting quadratic-residue (41, 21) code and the five-error-correcting (31, 11) BCH code as well as for the Golay code.

Another variation of error trapping, known as *permutation decoding* (MacWilliams 1964), makes use of code-preserving permutations other than the cyclic permutation. (See Section 8.11.) Suppose correction of every combination of t or fewer errors by a code with minimum distance $d \geqq 2t + 1$ is required. Also suppose that a set of code-preserving permutations $\mathbf{P}_1, \mathbf{P}_2, \ldots, \mathbf{P}_e$ can be found such that for every pattern $\mathbf{v}$ of t errors, at least one of the vectors $\mathbf{v}, \mathbf{vP}_1, \mathbf{vP}_2, \ldots, \mathbf{vP}_e$ has k successive errors. Then the following procedure will achieve correction: First apply error trapping to $\mathbf{v}$. If it corrects, the process is complete. If not, apply error trapping to $\mathbf{vP}_1$. If it corrects, giving $\mathbf{v}'$, then $\mathbf{v}'\mathbf{P}_1^{-1}$ is the desired result. If not, then apply error trapping to $\mathbf{vP}_2$, and so on.

In order to correct, say, all error patterns of weight t or less with permutation decoding, it is necessary to determine a set of code-preserving permutations which map every correctable pattern onto one with at least k consecutive correct digits. There are several code-preserving permutations for every cyclic code. For example, for any cyclic code with symbols from $GF(q)$, the permutations

$$X^j \rightarrow (X^j)^{q^i}, \qquad j = 0, 1, 2, \ldots, n-1,$$
$$i = 1, 2, \ldots$$

map each code word onto another, provided $(n, q) = 1$. (See Theorem 8.13.) For many individual codes it is also possible to find other code-preserving permutations. (See Section 8.11 for examples.) However, it is not known, in general, how to choose a set of permutations for given values of n, k, and t, or even if such a set exists. Thus, although permutation decoding is applicable to some codes that cannot be corrected by simple error trapping, at present it seems limited to relatively short codes or codes with low rate.

It is possible to decode using permutations which do not preserve the code. However, the decoder must have the ability to correct error patterns in the equivalent codes used. Clearly the decoder can correct an error pattern in any code when all errors lie in the "parity" section of the word. The difficult problem of how to choose the set of permutations has been approached in an interesting way by Omura (1969a). His computer results indicate that a surprisingly small number of randomly selected permutations yields a high probability of decoding correctly, even for codes several hundred bits long. In this regard see Problem 8.24.

Still another way of using error trapping to correct slightly more than $1/R$ errors is known. However, this *trial-and-error* technique also seems to be limited to relatively short codes. (See Problem 8.15.) Suppose a binary code can correct all patterns of t errors but that it can be guaranteed only that $t-1$ of these can be cyclically shifted into some $(n-k)$-symbol section of the word. Any pattern of weight t or less can be corrected as follows. Invert the first bit and attempt to decode using error trapping. In this case, the single threshold gate has a 1 at its output if and only if $t-1$ or fewer of its inputs are 1's. If unsuccessful, reinvert the bit, invert the next bit, and again attempt to decode. (For a code with symbols from $GF(q)$ it is necessary to try all $q-1$ possible error values at each stage.) Eventually some incorrect bit will be inverted which enables the other $t-1$ errors to be cyclically shifted into an $(n-k)$-bit section of the word. Then error-trapping decoding can be used to correct the remaining errors.

If t or fewer errors occurred initially, adding one more error leaves the received word at least distance t from any other code word. Because the threshold is set to $t-1$, incorrect decoding cannot result.

The generalization of this technique to inverting bits 2 at a time, 3 at a time, and so on, is immediate, and little hardware is required in any case. Unfortunately, the amount of time required for decoding grows very rapidly with the number of "extra" errors to be corrected. Thus, like error trapping and the modifications thereof just described, it is somewhat limited in applicability.

8.10 Shortened Cyclic Codes

Because cyclic codes are generated by divisors of $X^n - 1$, there are relatively few codes for most values of n and k. Thus it is natural to look for linear codes that, though not actually cyclic, share the mathematical structure and ease of implementation of cyclic codes. Two such classes of codes are presented in this section and in Section 8.14.

Given an (n, k) linear code, it is always possible to form an $(n - i, k - i)$ linear code by making the i leading information symbols identically 0 and omitting them from all code vectors. In the case of cyclic codes, this corresponds to omitting the first i rows and columns of the generator matrix, or the first i columns from the parity-check matrix. The resulting code is not a cyclic code, however, because it is no longer true in every case that the vector formed by shifting a code vector cyclically is also a code vector. Such a code is called a *shortened cyclic code*.

Example. If the leading information symbol is dropped from the (7, 4) code in the example in Section 8.2, the resulting (6, 3) code has the following generator matrix **G** and parity-check matrix **H**:

$$\mathbf{G} = \begin{bmatrix} 100011 \\ 010111 \\ 001101 \end{bmatrix}, \qquad \mathbf{H} = \begin{bmatrix} 011100 \\ 110010 \\ 111001 \end{bmatrix}$$

The vectors (0 0 1 1 0 1), (0 1 1 0 1 0), and (1 1 0 1 0 0) are code vectors, but one more cyclic shift results in (1 0 1 0 0 1), which is not in the null space of **H**.

A shortened code has at least as great a minimum distance as the code from which it is derived, and it can correct any burst-error pattern that the original code could correct. In fact, since the number of cosets remains unchanged by shortening, the shortened code can correct an appropriately shortened version of any error pattern correctable with the original code. Furthermore, the same circuitry can be used to decode both codes provided only that each shortened received word is always prefixed with i zeros.

Theorem 8.1 states that cyclic codes are ideals in the algebra of polynomials modulo $X^n - 1$. A natural generalization is to construct codes that are ideals modulo some other polynomial $f(X)$. Such a code is called a *pseudo-cyclic code*. The following two theorems show that, as classes, the shortened cyclic codes and the pseudo-cyclic codes are the same.

THEOREM 8.9. *Every pseudo-cyclic code with minimum weight greater than 2 is a shortened cyclic code.*

Proof. Let $f(X)$ be a polynomial of degree n and consider an ideal in the algebra of polynomials modulo $f(X)$, that is, a pseudo-cyclic code. Then, by Theorems 6.9 and 6.10, there is a monic polynomial $g(X)$ that is the generator of the ideal, and a vector $(a_{n-1}, a_{n-2}, \ldots, a_0)$ is in the ideal if and only if $a(X) = a_{n-1}X^{n-1} + a_{n-2}X^{n-2} + \cdots + a_0$ is divisible by $g(X)$. Let n' be the smallest integer for which $X^{n'} - 1$ is divisible by $g(X)$. Then, $n' > n$, for otherwise $X^{n'} - 1$ would be a code vector of weight 2. Then, $g(X)$ generates a cyclic code of length n', and in this code a vector $(a_{n'-1}, a_{n'-2}, \ldots, a_0)$ is a code vector if and only if $f(X) = a_{n'-1}X^{n'-1} + a_{n'-2}X^{n'-2} + \cdots + a_0$ is divisible by $g(X)$. If this cyclic code is shortened by including only those code vectors for which $a_n, a_{n+1}, \ldots, a_{n'-1}$ are all 0 and dropping those components, the code vectors are exactly those of the pseudo-cyclic code. Q.E.D.

THEOREM 8.10. *Every shortened cyclic code is a pseudo-cyclic code.*

Proof. Suppose that $g(X)$ generates a cyclic code of length n' and consider the shortened cyclic code of length n obtained from this code. By Equation 6.4,

$$X^n = g(X)\,q(X) + r(X), \tag{8.24}$$

where $r(X)$ has degree less than the degree of $g(X)$. Let $f(X) = X^n - r(X)$, and consider the algebra of polynomials modulo $f(X)$. It can be seen from Equation 8.24 that $g(X)$ divides $f(X)$. By Theorem 6.10, $g(X)$ generates an ideal, and hence a pseudo-cyclic code, that can be seen to be the same as the shortened cyclic code. Q.E.D.

It is worth noting that most of the best known random-error-correcting codes are shortened cyclic codes. (See, for example, Table 5.4.)

A cyclic code shortened by i symbols can be decoded by the circuitry used to decode the original code; it is necessary only to prefix the shortened words by i zeros. However, decoding can be accomplished more quickly if, instead of calculating the syndrome of $X^{n-k}r(X)$ as would be done for a cyclic code, the syndrome of $X^{n-k+i}r(X)$ is calculated. In a Meggitt decoder (Figure 8.5) this has the effect of making the first received symbol, X^{n-i-1}, the first symbol to be corrected by the combinational logic circuit.

Let $s(X)$ denote the syndrome of $X^{n-k+i}r(X)$. Then

$$s(X) = X^{n-k+i}r(X) + g(X)\,q_1(X). \tag{8.25}$$

Now let the polynomial $f(X)$ be chosen as

$$f(X) = X^{n-k+i} + g(X)\,q_2(X), \tag{8.26}$$

where $f(X)$ has degree less than that of $g(X)$. Then from Equations 8.25 and 8.26,

$$r(X)f(X) = s(X) + g(X)\,q_3(X). \tag{8.27}$$

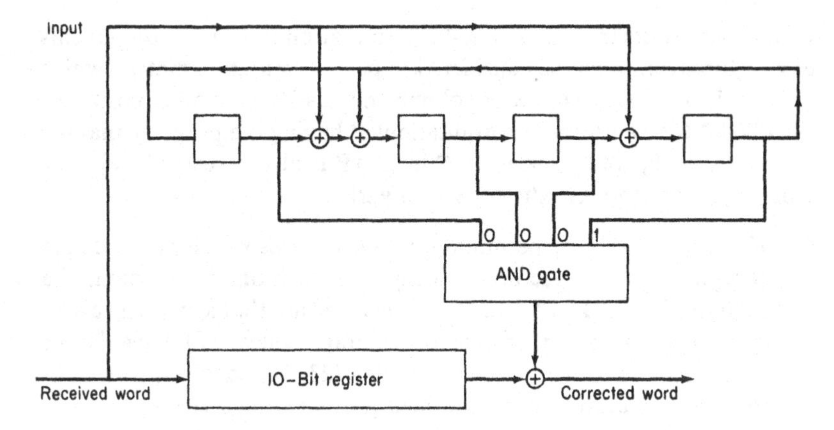

Figure 8.7. A Meggitt decoder for a (10, 6) shortened Hamming code.

Thus premultiplication by X^{n-k+i} can be accomplished simply by multiplying the received polynomial by $f(X)$ as it is shifted into the syndrome register.

Example. The polynomial $g(X) = X^4 + X + 1$ generates a binary (15, 11) single-error-correcting Hamming code. Suppose it is necessary to shorten this code by 5 bits to give a (10, 6) code. The remainder obtained by dividing $X^{n-k+5} = X^9$ by $g(X)$ is

$$f(X) = X^3 + X = X^9 + (X^5 + X^2 + X)(X^4 + X + 1).$$

A circuit that multiplies the received 10-tuple by $f(X)$, calculates the syndrome, and corrects a single error using the error-trapping technique described in the preceding section is shown in Figure 8.7. (See Figure 8.6 and the associated example.)

8.11 Code Symmetry

For cyclic codes, a cyclic permutation of any code word gives another code word, and hence a cyclic permutation of the collection of all code words results in the same collection of code words. Thus, cyclic codes are invariant under the cyclic permutation. Other codes are invariant under other permutations, and some cyclic codes are invariant under other than cyclic permutations. Some general theory of this kind of code symmetry is presented in this section.

Let V_1 denote an (n, k) group code, let V_2 denote the null space of V_1. Let $\mathbf{P}$ denote a permutation on n symbols, and let $\mathbf{v}_1\mathbf{P}$ denote the vector that results from applying the permutation $\mathbf{P}$ to the n components of $\mathbf{v}_1$. Moreover, $\mathbf{P}$ can be considered to be a permutation matrix, which has one 1 in each row and each column and has 0's in all other positions. Finally, let G be a group of permutations $\mathbf{P}$ having the property that if $\mathbf{v}$ is a vector in V_1, then, for every $\mathbf{P}$ in G, $\mathbf{vP}$ is also a vector in V_1. The group G is said to leave the code V_1 invariant.

> *Example.* If $\mathbf{P}$ is the permutation on n symbols which permutes the components of a vector cyclically one position to the right, the permutations $\mathbf{1}, \mathbf{P}, \mathbf{P}^2, \ldots, \mathbf{P}^{n-1}$ form a group that leaves any cyclic (n, k) code invariant. Quite commonly, codes will have larger symmetry groups — the binary Golay (23, 12) code can be shown to be left invariant by the Mathieu group (Prange 1959).

THEOREM 8.11. *If V_1 is invariant under a group G of permutations* $\mathbf{P}$, *then the null space V_2 of V_1 is also invariant under G.*

Proof. Note that for any two vectors $\mathbf{v}_1$ and $\mathbf{v}_2$ and any permutation $\mathbf{P}$,

$$\mathbf{v}_1 \cdot \mathbf{v}_2 = (\mathbf{v}_1\mathbf{P}) \cdot (\mathbf{v}_2\mathbf{P}), \tag{8.28}$$

since each side is the sum of products of corresponding components of $\mathbf{v}_1$ and $\mathbf{v}_2$, the right differing from the left only in having the terms rearranged according to the permutation $\mathbf{P}$. This certainly does not affect the sum, and therefore the two sides are equal.

Let $\mathbf{v}_2$ be a vector in V_2 and $\mathbf{v}_1$ any vector in V_1. Then,

$$(\mathbf{v}_2\mathbf{P}) \cdot \mathbf{v}_1 = \mathbf{v}_2\mathbf{P} \cdot (\mathbf{v}_1\mathbf{P}^{-1}\mathbf{P}) = \mathbf{v}_2 \cdot (\mathbf{v}_1\mathbf{P}^{-1})$$

by Equation 8.28. But $\mathbf{P}^{-1}$ is in G since G is a group. So $\mathbf{v}_1\mathbf{P}^{-1}$ is a vector in V_1. Since $\mathbf{v}_2$ is in the null space of V_1,

$$(\mathbf{v}_2\mathbf{P}) \cdot \mathbf{v}_1 = \mathbf{v}_2 \cdot (\mathbf{v}_1\mathbf{P}^{-1}) = 0.$$

Thus $\mathbf{v}_2\mathbf{P}$ is orthogonal to any $\mathbf{v}_1$ in V_1, and it follows that $\mathbf{v}_2\mathbf{P}$ is in V_2.

Q.E.D.

THEOREM 8.12. *If U is a coset of V_1 and V_2 is left invariant by* $\mathbf{P}$, *then the set $U\mathbf{P}$ of all vectors formed by applying* $\mathbf{P}$ *to a vector in U is also a coset of V_1.*

Proof. Let $\mathbf{u}_1$ and $\mathbf{u}_2$ be any two vectors in U. Then $U\mathbf{P}$ is a coset if and only if $\mathbf{u}_1\mathbf{P} - \mathbf{u}_2\mathbf{P}$ is a code vector, that is, a vector in V_1. But

$$\mathbf{u}_1\mathbf{P} - \mathbf{u}_2\mathbf{P} = (\mathbf{u}_1 - \mathbf{u}_2)\mathbf{P}, \tag{8.29}$$

and since U is a coset, $\mathbf{u}_1 - \mathbf{u}_2$, and therefore $(\mathbf{u}_1 - \mathbf{u}_2)\mathbf{P}$, are code vectors. The truth of Equation 8.29 can be seen by noting that it does not matter whether one permutes first and then subtracts, or vice versa. Alternatively, if the permutations are written as matrices, Equation 8.29 follows from the distributive law for matrix multiplication. Q.E.D.

A group G of permutations on n symbols divides the space V of all n-component vectors into classes, with two vectors $\mathbf{v}_1$ and $\mathbf{v}_2$ in the same class whenever there is a permutation $\mathbf{P}$ in G for which $\mathbf{v}_1\mathbf{P} = \mathbf{v}_2$: If a code V_1 is left invariant by G, then V_1 must consist of a number of complete classes of V. Theorem 8.11 states that the null space also consists of a number of complete classes.

For a given code V_1, two cosets U_1 and U_2 are said to be *equivalent* if there is a $\mathbf{P}$ in G such that $U_1\mathbf{P} = U_2$. The cosets then divide into classes also, with U_1 and U_2 in the same class if and only if they are equivalent. If U_1 and U_2 are equivalent, a permutation of a minimum weight element of U_1 appears in U_2, and vice versa, and therefore U_1 and U_2 have the same minimum weight.

Example. Consider the set of all 7-component vectors over $GF(2)$ and the group $\mathbf{1}$, $\mathbf{P}$, $\mathbf{P}^2$, ..., $\mathbf{P}^6$ of cyclic permutations. The 128 vectors fall into 20 classes. One vector of each class is listed in Table 8.1. The others are cyclic shifts of these. The vectors of all 1's and all 0's each form a class of one element. The others have 7 vectors in each class, which are the 7 cyclic shifts of the given vector. The cyclic (7, 4) code given in the example in Section 8.1 is made up of classes A, G, L, and P, a total of 16 vectors. The null

Table 8.1. Classes of 7-Component Binary Vectors

A 0000000	*F* 1110000	*K* 0001111	*P* 1111111
B 1000000	*G* 1101000	*L* 0010111	*Q* 0111111
C 1100000	*H* 1100100	*M* 0011011	*R* 0011111
D 1010000	*I* 1100010	*N* 0011101	*S* 0101111
E 1001000	*J* 1010100	*O* 0101011	*T* 0110111

space consists of the vector $\mathbf{0}$ and the class L only, a total of 8 vectors. There are only two classes of cosets, one being the code itself and the other consisting of the seven cosets whose leaders are in class B. It is true in general that the number of classes in the null space equals the number of classes of cosets; a proof is given in Peterson 1961, p. 211.

THEOREM 8.13. *Every cyclic code of length n is invariant under the permutation* **P** *which for each i permutes the symbol in position i to position qi modulo n provided* $(n, q) = 1$.

Proof. If $f(X)$ is a code polynomial, then permuting the symbols in $f(X)$ by P results in a polynomial $f(X^q)$ reduced modulo $X^n - 1$. But $f(X^q) = (f(X))^q$. If $g(X)$ is the generator polynomial for the code, $f(X)$ and $X^n - 1$ are divisible by $g(X)$. Therefore, $f(X^q)$ reduced modulo $X^n - 1$ is also divisible by $g(X)$ and hence is a code vector. Q.E.D.

A group of permutations is said to be *transitive* if for any two symbols in a code vector there exists a permutation that interchanges them, possibly rearranging other symbols at the same time. Let A_i denote the number of code words of weight i in a code V_1.

THEOREM 8.14. *If a code is invariant under a transitive group of permutations,* iA_i *is divisible evenly by n.*

Proof. Arrange all code vectors of weight i in a column. Next, apply to all these code vectors the permutation that interchanges the first column and the jth column. All the resulting vectors have weight i, and all are distinct. Thus, as a collection of vectors they are the same as the original set, but they may be rearranged. This, however, does not affect the number of nonzero components in the first column, and the number of nonzero components in the jth column must be the same as the number of nonzero components in the first column. Denote this column weight a_i. Then, the total number of nonzero components in the entire collection is n times the column weight, or A_i times the row weight. Thus,

$$na_i = iA_i. \tag{8.30}$$

Q.E.D.

THEOREM 8.15. *Let V be an* (n, k) *code formed by dropping the first symbol in an* $(n + 1, k)$ *code* V_1 *which is invariant under a transitive group and has no vectors of weight* $i - 1$. *Then if* B_i *denotes the number of code vectors of weight i in V,*

$$iB_i = (n + 1 - i)B_{i-1}, \qquad \textit{for } i \textit{ even}.$$

Proof. If A_i denotes the number of code words of weight i in the original code, then as the proof of Theorem 8.14,

$$(n + 1)B_{i-1} = iA_i \tag{8.31}$$

because the number of code vectors of weight $i-1$ in V must be the number of code vectors of weight i having a nonzero element in the first column. Furthermore,

$$B_i + B_{i-1} = A_i \tag{8.32}$$

and substituting Equation 8.32 in Equation 8.31 to eliminate A_i gives the desired result. Q.E.D.

Many cyclic codes of length n can be derived by dropping the first symbol from each code word of a code of length $n+1$ which is invariant under a doubly-transitive group of permutations. (A *doubly transitive group* is one for which for any distinct positive integers i, j, k, l less than or equal to n there is a permutation that interchanges the symbols in positions i and j and simultaneously those in positions k and l.) This is true of the Golay code, all quadratic residue codes (Peterson and Prange 1964) and all primitive BCH codes (Section 9.3), and primitive cyclic Reed-Muller codes (Section 10.2). For all these codes, both Theorems 8.14 and 8.15 apply.

There is a large class of cyclic codes of length $q^m - 1$ which, when extended by the addition of an overall parity-check symbol, are invariant under the doubly transitive affine group. An *affine transformation* with parameters a and b, $a \neq 0$, a and b elements of $GF(q^m)$, is a permutation that carries the symbol in position X to the position $aX + b$. A code will be called *invariant under the affine group* if every affine permutation carries every code word into another code word. These codes are characterized in the next theorem; the definitions of the primitive BCH codes with $m_0 = 1$ and the primitive generalized Reed-Muller codes show that these codes belong to this class.

Let i be a positive integer less than q^m. Then i can be expressed in radix-p form, where p is the characteristic of the field and $q = p^l$:

$$i = \sum_{t=0}^{ml-1} \delta_t p^t, \tag{8.33}$$

where

$$0 \leqq \delta_t \leqq p-1 \qquad \text{for} \qquad 0 \leqq t \leqq ml-1. \tag{8.34}$$

For any given i, let $J(i)$ denote the set of all nonzero integers j such that

$$j = \sum_{t=0}^{ml-1} \sigma_t p^t, \tag{8.35}$$

where

$$0 \leqq \sigma_t \leqq \delta_t \qquad \text{for} \qquad 0 \leqq t \leqq ml-1.$$

That is, $J(i)$ consists of i and all of its descendants (Section 3.5).

Let α be a primitive element of $GF(q^m)$. Consider a q-ary cyclic code C of length $q^m - 1$, with symbols from $GF(q)$, generated by the polynomial $g(X)$. A code C_e can be constructed by appending an overall parity check to C and taking this sum as its first digit. Now number the components of the code vector of C_e as follows: The first component is numbered 0, the second is numbered 1, and for $i > 2$, the ith component is numbered α^{i-2}.

THEOREM 8.16. *The extended code C_e is invariant under the affine group of permutations if and only if, for every α^i that is a root of the generator polynomial $g(X)$, for every j in $J(i)$, α^j is also a root of $g(X)$, and $g(1) \neq 0$.*

Proof. Let $X_1, X_2, \ldots, X_w$ be the location numbers of the nonzero components of a vector $\mathbf{v}$, and $Y_1, Y_2, \ldots, Y_w$ the values of the nonzero components, where $X_h \in GF(q^m)$ and Y_h is an element of $GF(q)$. Then, $\mathbf{v}$ is a code vector if and only if for each root α^i of $g(X)$,

$$S_i = \sum_{h=1}^{w} Y_h X_h^i = 0.$$

Let T be any element of the affine group of permutations, and let its parameters be a and b. For any code vector $\mathbf{v}$ in C_e, then, $\mathbf{v}' = \mathbf{T}\mathbf{v}$ has nonzero components Y_h in locations $aX_h + b$, for $1 \leq h \leq w$. Then, $\mathbf{v}'$ is in C_e if and only if

$$S_i' = \sum_{h=1}^{w} Y_h(aX_h + b)^i = 0 \tag{8.36}$$

for each i.

The binomial expansion gives

$$(aX + b)^i = \sum_{j=0}^{i} \binom{i}{j} a^j b^{i-j} X^j.$$

Lucas (1878) has shown that

$$\binom{i}{j} = \prod_{t=0}^{ml-1} \binom{\delta_t}{\sigma_t} (\text{mod } p)$$

where δ_t and σ_t are defined in Equations 8.33 and 8.35. A proof is included in Berlekamp (1968). This product is nonzero if and only if each factor is nonzero, and this will be the case if and only if each $\sigma_t \leq \delta_t$. (In this regard, see Lemma 10.2.) Therefore, $\binom{i}{j} \neq 0$ if and only if j is in $J(i)$.

Now Equation 8.36 becomes

$$S'_i = \sum_{h=1}^{w} \sum_{j \in J(i)} Y_h K_j a^j b^{i-j} X_h^j = \sum_{j \in J(i)} K_j a^j b^{i-j} S_j, \tag{8.37}$$

where every remaining $K_j = \binom{i}{j}$ is nonzero.

Denote the number of elements in $J(i)$ by N, and the elements themselves by $j_1, j_2, \ldots, j_N$. Since $N \leq q^m - 1$, it is possible to choose N distinct nonzero elements of $GF(q^m)$: $a_1, a_2, \ldots, a_N$. Now let us form vectors $\mathbf{v}_l$ from $\mathbf{v}$ by applying to $\mathbf{v}$ the affine permutation $\mathbf{T}_l$ that carries the component in location X to location $a_l X + 1$, where $1 \leq l \leq N$. Let $S'_i(l)$ denote the value of S'_i for the vector $\mathbf{v}_l$. Then, by Equation 8.37,

$$S'_i(l) = \sum_{t=1}^{N} K_{j_t} a_l^{j_t} S_{j_t}. \tag{8.38}$$

We can write Equation 8.38 in matrix form:

$$\begin{bmatrix} S'_i(1) \\ S'_i(2) \\ S'_i(3) \\ \vdots \\ S'_i(N) \end{bmatrix} = \begin{bmatrix} a_1^{j_1} & a_1^{j_2} & \cdots & a_1^{j_N} \\ a_2^{j_1} & a_2^{j_2} & \cdots & a_2^{j_N} \\ a_3^{j_1} & a_3^{j_2} & \cdots & a_3^{j_N} \\ \vdots & & & \\ a_N^{j_1} & a_N^{j_2} & \cdots & a_N^{j_N} \end{bmatrix} \cdot \begin{bmatrix} K_{j_1} S_{j_1} \\ K_{j_2} S_{j_2} \\ K_{j_3} S_{j_3} \\ \vdots \\ K_{j_N} S_{j_N} \end{bmatrix}$$

The matrix $\{a_k^{j_t}\}$ is a Van der Monde matrix and hence is nonsingular. (See Section 9.2.) Thus $S'_i(t) = 0$ for $1 \leq t \leq N$ if and only if $K_{j_t} S_{j_t} = 0$ for $1 \leq t \leq N$. Since the K_{j_t} are nonzero, it follows that $S'_i(t) = 0$ for $1 \leq t \leq N$ if and only if $S_{j_t} = 0$ for j_t in $J(i)$. This implies that $S'_i = 0$ if and only if $S_j = 0$ for j in $J(i)$. Thus, for any $\mathbf{v}$ in C_e and any permutation $\mathbf{T}$, $\mathbf{T}\mathbf{v}$ is in C_e if and only if $S_j = 0$ for j in $J(i)$. Since for any $\mathbf{v}$ in C_e, $S_j = 0$, it follows that α^j is a root of $g(X)$. Q.E.D.

THEOREM 8.17. *If a code C of length $n = q^m$ is invariant under the doubly transitive affine group of permutations, then the code C′ obtained by deleting the first digit of C is cyclic.*

This follows from the fact that the permutation $X' = \alpha X$ does not affect the first symbol in the extended code but permutes the others cyclically.

The results of this section will be useful in determining the true minimum distance of BCH codes (Section 9.3).

8.12 Cyclic Product Codes

Let C_1 and C_2 be cyclic codes of lengths n_1 and n_2, respectively, with symbols in $GF(q)$. Then, a two-dimensional array of symbols

$$\begin{bmatrix} a_{00} & a_{01} & \cdots & a_{0(n_1-1)} \\ a_{10} & a_{11} & \cdots & a_{1(n_1-1)} \\ \vdots & & & \\ a_{(n_2-1)0} & a_{(n_2-1)1} & \cdots & a_{(n_2-1)(n_1-1)} \end{bmatrix} \tag{8.39}$$

is a code word in the product code if each row is a code vector in C_1 and each column is a code vector in C_2. It will be shown in this section that the vectors formed by taking symbols diagonally from matrix 8.39 form a cyclic code. (The generator polynomial for this code is characterized in Theorem 8.19.)

THEOREM 8.18. *Let $[\mathbf{a}_{ij}]$ be a code word in the product of two cyclic codes over $GF(q)$ of relatively prime lengths n_1 and n_2. Let i_1 be the residue modulo n_1 of i and i_2 the residue modulo n_2 of i, for $i = 0, 1, \ldots, n_1n_2 - 1$. Then, the $n = n_1n_2$-dimensional vectors $[\mathbf{b}_i]$, where $b_i = a_{i_2i_1}$, form a cyclic code.*

The method of forming the vector $[\mathbf{b}_i]$ is shown by the following example. Suppose $n_1 = 5$ and $n_2 = 3$,

$$[a_{ij}] = \begin{bmatrix} a_{00} & a_{01} & a_{02} & a_{03} & a_{04} \\ a_{10} & a_{11} & a_{12} & a_{13} & a_{14} \\ a_{20} & a_{21} & a_{22} & a_{23} & a_{24} \end{bmatrix}$$

and $[\mathbf{b}_i] = (a_{00}, a_{11}, a_{22}, a_{03}, a_{14}, a_{20}, a_{01}, a_{12}, a_{23}, a_{04}, a_{10}, a_{21}, a_{02}, a_{13}, a_{24})$.

Proof. The mapping $[\mathbf{a}_{ij}]$ onto $[\mathbf{b}_i]$ is one-to-one provided $(n_1, n_2) = 1$. For then $[\mathbf{b}_i] = [\mathbf{b}_i']$ implies that $i_1 = i_1'$ and $i_2 = i_2'$. Now shift each row of the array cyclically one place to the right and shift each column cyclically one place downward. In other words,

$$i_1' = i_1 + 1 \bmod n_1,$$

$$i_2' = i_2 + 1 \bmod n_2.$$

From the definition of i_1 and i_2,

$$i_1' = (i + 1) \bmod n_1,$$

$$i_2' = (i + 1) \bmod n_2.$$

so the result of shifting rows and columns is to shift the n-dimensional vector $[\mathbf{b}_i]$ cyclically one place to the right. It follows that the vectors $[\mathbf{b}_i]$ form a cyclic code. Q.E.D.

In dealing with cyclic codes, polynomial notation has proved useful. The two-dimensional structure of cyclic product codes suggests considering code words as polynomials in two indeterminates (Elspas 1967).

Consider the polynomial

$$f(X, Y) = \sum_{i=0}^{n_2-1} \sum_{j=0}^{n_1-1} a_{ij} X^i Y^j. \tag{8.40}$$

Let α_1 and α_2 be elements of order n_1 and n_2, respectively. Now consider the polynomial

$$S(Z, Y) = \sum_{i=0}^{n_1-1} f(\alpha_1^i, Y) Z^i. \tag{8.41}$$

Applying the corollary to Theorem 8.2 to the coefficients of Y^j for each j gives

$$f(X, Y) = n_1^{-1} \sum_{i=0}^{n_1-1} S(\alpha_1^{-i}, Y) X^i \tag{8.42}$$

provided $(n_1, p) = 1$, where p is the characteristic of $GF(q)$. Similarly, let

$$F(Z, W) = \sum_{j=0}^{n_2-1} S(Z, \alpha_2^j) W^j. \tag{8.43}$$

Then applying the corollary to the coefficients of Z^i for each i gives

$$S(Z, Y) = n_2^{-1} \sum_{j=0}^{n_2-1} F(Z, \alpha_2^{-j}) Y^j \tag{8.44}$$

provided $(n_2, p) = 1$. Substituting Equation 8.41 into Equation 8.43 gives the result that

$$F(Z, W) = \sum_{i=0}^{n_2-1} \sum_{j=0}^{n_1-1} f(\alpha_1^i, \alpha_2^j) Z^i W^j \tag{8.45}$$

and substituting Equation 8.44 into Equation 8.42 gives

$$f(X, Y) = n^{-1} \sum_{i=0}^{n_2-1} \sum_{j=0}^{n_1-1} F(\alpha_1^{-i}, \alpha_2^{-j}) X^i Y^j \tag{8.46}$$

where $n = n_1 n_2$.

Since n_1 and n_2 are assumed relatively prime, $\alpha = \alpha_1\alpha_2$ is an element of order n, and the elements $1, \alpha, \alpha^2, \ldots, \alpha^{n-1}$ are distinct. They are simply an arrangement of the elements $\alpha_1^i\alpha_2^i$, $0 \leq i \leq n_1 - 1$, $0 \leq j \leq n_2 - 1$. In fact, $\alpha^i = \alpha_1^i\alpha_2^i$, and the exponents of α_1 can be reduced modulo n_1, because $\alpha_1^{n_1} = 1$, and similarly the exponent of α_2 can be reduced modulo n_2. Now consider the vector $(b_0, b_1, \ldots, b_{n-1})$ whose components are

$$b_i = n^{-1}F(\alpha_1^{-i}, \alpha_2^{-i}) \tag{8.47}$$

and the corresponding polynomial

$$b(X) = n^{-1}\sum_{i=0}^{n-1} F(\alpha_1^{-i}, \alpha_2^{-i})X^i. \tag{8.48}$$

By Equation 8.46 the coefficients b_i aie simply a rearrangement of all the symbols in Matrix 8.39, and therefore, in particular, are elements of $GF(q)$. Now ask whether a cyclic shift of the vector $(b_0, b_1, \ldots, b_{n-1})$ is a code word in the original product code of C_1 and C_2. Suppose all the rows of Matrix 8.39 are shifted cyclically one place to the right and all the columns simultaneously are shifted cyclically down one place. Call the resulting matrix a'_{ij}. Then,

$$\begin{aligned} f'(X, Y) &= \sum_{i=0}^{n_2-1}\sum_{j=0}^{n_1-1} a'_{ij}X^iY^j \\ &= \sum_{i=0}^{n_2-1}\sum_{j=0}^{n_1-1} a_{ij}X^{i+1}Y^{j+1} \bmod X^{n_1} - 1 \quad \text{and} \quad Y^{n_2} - 1 \\ &= XYf(X, Y) \bmod X^{n_1} - 1 \quad \text{and} \quad Y^{n_2} - 1. \end{aligned} \tag{8.49}$$

Then,

$$\begin{aligned} F'(Z, W) &= \sum_{i=0}^{n_2-1}\sum_{j=0}^{n_1-1} f'(\alpha_1^i, \alpha_2^j)Z^iW^j \\ &= \sum_{i=0}^{n_2-1}\sum_{j=0}^{n_1-1} f(\alpha_1^i, \alpha_2^j)\alpha_1^i\alpha_2^j Z^iW^j \\ &= F(\alpha_1 Z, \alpha_2 W). \end{aligned} \tag{8.50}$$

Finally,

$$b'_i = F'(\alpha_1^{-i}, \alpha_2^{-i}) = F(\alpha_1^{-i+1}, \alpha_2^{-i+1}) = b_{i-1}.$$

Thus, the result of shifting Matrix 8.39 cyclically one place to the right and simultaneously one place down is that b_i is shifted cyclically one place. It follows that the vectors b_i form a cyclic code of length n.

Theorem 8.19 characterizes the generator polynomial of C in the case when $(n, p) = 1$.

THEOREM 8.19. *Suppose C_1 and C_2 are cyclic codes with relatively prime lengths n_1 and n_2 and generator polynomials $g_1(X)$ and $g_2(X)$, and C is the cyclic product code of length n and with generator polynomial $g(X)$. Assume that $(n, p) = 1$. Then, α^i is a root of $g(X)$ if and only if either α_1^i is a root of $g_1(X)$, or α_2^i is a root of $g_2(X)$, or both.*

Proof. From Equations 8.46 and 8.48, $b(X) = f(X, X)$, therefore

$$b(\alpha^i) = f(\alpha^i, \alpha^i).$$

Because the rows of Matrix 8.39 are code vectors in $C_1, f(\alpha^i, Y) = 0$ for all choices of Y if α^i is a root of $g_1(X)$. Similarly, because the columns are code vectors in $C_2, f(X, \alpha^i) = 0$ for all choices of X if α^i is a root of $g_2(X)$. Thus, $b(X) = 0$ if either α_1^i is a root of $g_1(X)$ or α_2^i is a root of $g_2(X)$. By Theorem 8.18 the number of roots of $g(X)$ is $n_1n_2 - k_1k_2$, while the number of elements $\alpha_1^i\alpha_2^i$ is $(n_1 - k_1)k_2 + (n_2 - k_2)k_1 + (n_1 - k_1)(n_2 - k_2) = n_1n_2 - k_1k_2$. Thus, there are no other roots.

Q.E.D.

COROLLARY. *If C_1 and C_2 are cyclic codes of relatively prime lengths n_1 and n_2 with parity-check polynomials $h_1(X)$ and $h_2(X)$, and if $h(X)$ is the parity-check polynomial of the product code, then α^i is a root of $h(X)$ if and only if α_1^i is a root of $h_1(X)$ and α_2^i is a root of $h_2(X)$, where α_1 is an element of order n_1, α_2 is an element of order n_2, and $\alpha = \alpha_1\alpha_2$.*

Proof. This follows directly from Theorem 8.19 and the fact that, since $h(X) = (X^n - 1)/g(X)$, α^i is a root of $h(X)$ if and only if it is not a root of $g(X)$.

Q.E.D.

Theorem 8.19 and its corollary can be proved without assuming that n is not divisible by p. (Burton and Weldon 1965; Lin and Weldon 1970; and Problem 8.16.) Also, the generalization of these results to product codes of higher dimension is immediate, since the product of a 2-dimensional cyclic product code and another cyclic code is a 3-dimensional product code.

The results of this section and the fact that $d = d_1d_2$ for any product code provide some information about the minimum distance of certain cyclic codes (Goethals 1967). See Theorem 9.3, for example.

8.13 Quadratic Residue Codes

In this section a class of cyclic codes with interesting mathematical properties is discussed. Although most of the results generalize, only binary codes are considered here.

An integer i is a quadratic residue of a prime p provided there exists an integer X such that

$$X^2 \equiv i \bmod p.$$

For example, 1 is a quadratic residue of all primes. Let g be a primitive element of $GF(p)$. If r is a quadratic residue of p, then

$$r^{(p-1)/2} \equiv X^{p-1} \equiv 1 \bmod p$$

since the order of every element of the multiplicative group $GF(p)$ divides $p - 1$. It follows that if

$$n^{(p-1)/2} \not\equiv 1 \bmod p$$

then the number is a nonresidue. Clearly, the even powers of g are quadratic residues, and since for every odd i, $(g^i)^{(p-1)/2} = g^{(p-1)/2} \neq 1$, all the odd powers of g are nonresidues.

Now if p is of the form $8m \pm 1$, then it can be shown that 2 is a quadratic residue of p. (See Berlekamp 1968b, p. 158, for example.) It follows that, for these primes, g^i is a quadratic residue if and only if $2g^i$, $4g^i$, $8g^i$, ... are also, and the set of quadratic residues (nonresidues) consists of one or more complete cycle sets. This implies that the polynomial $X^p - 1$ factors into $(X - 1)g_r(X)\, g_n(X)$, where the roots of $g_r(X)$ are quadratic residues of p and the roots of $g_n(X)$ are quadratic nonresidues. The cyclic codes generated by $g_r(X)$, $(X - 1)g_r(X)$, $g_n(X)$, and $(X - 1)g_n(X)$ are referred to as *quadratic residue codes.*

Now consider the mapping $i \to ri$. Since r is a nonzero element of $GF(p)$, this permutes all the field elements. Thus, the mapping $X^i \to X^{ri}$ permutes the elements of code polynomials. Consider the code resulting from applying this permutation to all the polynomials in a quadratic residue code. If $f(X)$ is a code word in the quadratic residue code, then $f(X^r)$ is a code word in the derived code. Let α^{e_i} be a root of the generator polynomial of the original code, $i = 1, 2, \ldots (p \pm 1)/2$; then α^{re_i} is also a root since r is a quadratic residue. Thus,

$$f(X^r)\Big|_{X=\alpha^{e_i}} = 0 = f(X)\Big|_{X=\alpha^{re_i}}; \qquad i = 1, 2, \ldots, \frac{p \pm 1}{2},$$

and so the derived code is identical to the original.

By a similar argument it follows that the transformation $X^i \to X^{ni}$, n a nonresidue of p, maps the codes generated by $g_r(X)$, $g_n(X)$, $(X-1)g_r(X)$, and $(X-1)g_n(X)$ onto those generated by $g_n(X)$, $g_r(X)$, $(X-1)g_n(X)$, and $(X-1)g_r(X)$, respectively.

If p is of the form $8m+1$, then $(p-1)/2$ is even, and it follows that -1 is a quadratic residue. Similarly, if $p = 8m-1$, that is, $(p-1)/2$ is odd, then -1 is a nonresidue. Thus in this case

$$g_n(X) = g_r(X^{-1})$$

and

$$g_r(X) = g_n(X^{-1}).$$

Now consider a polynomial $p(X)$ of minimum weight d in the quadratic residue code generated by $g_n(X)$ (or $g_r(X)$). It can be shown that d is odd (Assmus, Mattson, and Turyn 1966). The product $p(X^r)p(X^n)$ is divisible by both $g_n(X)$ and $g_r(X)$ but not by $X-1$ and so is a multiple of $X^{n-1} + X^{n-2} + \cdots + X + 1$. Consequently, there must be at least n terms in the product. Therefore, since the weight of each multiplier is d, and since n is prime,

$$d^2 > n. \tag{8.51}$$

If $p = 8m-1$, then the term X^0 appears in the product $p(X)p(X^{-1})$ exactly d times. Therefore, for these codes

$$d(d-1) \geqq n-1. \tag{8.52}$$

Several slight improvements have been made on this result. In particular it has been shown (Assmus, Mattson, and Turyn 1966) that all code words have weight of the form $4l-1$ or $4l$ in quadratic residue codes generated by $g_r(X)$ or $g_n(X)$ and of the form $4l$ in codes generated by $(X-1)g_r(X)$ or $(X-1)g_n(X)$.

Equations 8.51 and 8.52 provide a lower bound on the minimum distance of quadratic residue codes. Another lower bound is provided by the BCH bound (Section 9.1), which states that d is greater than the largest number of consecutive roots in the generator polynomial. Neither of these results seems to be especially tight for quadratic residue codes, however, and in most cases where it has been determined explicitly, d exceeds the bounds.

Table 8.2 contains a list of some $[n, (n+1)/2]$ quadratic residue codes for which d is known. Additional codes for which only an upper bound on d is known are given by Berlekamp (1968*b*).

Table 8.2. Some Quadratic Residue Codes

n	d	Reference
7	3	Hamming code
17	5	Prange (1958)
23	7	Golay code
31	7	MacWilliams (1963*b*)
41	9	Assmus and Mattson (1962)
47	11	Gleason (1961)
71	11	Pless (1964)
79	15	Karlin (1969)
89	17	Karlin (1969)
103	19	Karlin (1969)
113	15	Karlin (1969)
151	19	Karlin (1969)

It has been shown that all quadratic residue codes are invariant under the transformation

$$X \to X^r; \qquad r \text{ a quadratic residue.}$$

This suggests the possibility of decoding quadratic residue codes with permutation decoding. (See Section 8.9.) Since the codes are invariant under a considerably larger permutation group than are cyclic codes in general, it should be possible to "collect" a relatively large number of errors into $n - k$ consecutive positions. Little theoretical progress has been made on this problem; however computer analysis has shown that it is possible to correct all patterns of weight $(d-1)/2$ with this method for all of the codes listed in Table 8.2 with $n \leq 47$ (MacWilliams 1963*b*).

Quadratic residue and, more generally, eth-power residue codes have been shown to be closely related to the quasi-cyclic codes of Section 8.14 (Karlin 1969; Chen, Peterson, and Weldon 1969).

8.14 Quasi-Cyclic Codes

Cyclic codes can be implemented with attractively simple circuits primarily because they are invariant under a large group of permutations, that is, the cyclic group of order n. In attempting to construct other classes of simply implemented codes, it is natural to consider classes of linear codes which are invariant under relatively large permutation groups. Quasi-cyclic codes form one such class.

Number the positions in a linear (mn_0, mk_0) block code 1, 2, ..., $n = mn_0$. If the code is invariant under the permutation

$$i \to i + n_0 \bmod mn_0, \qquad i = 1, 2, \ldots, n \tag{8.53}$$

that is, if a cyclic shift of n_0 digits always produces another code word, then it is said to be *quasi-cyclic*.

With this definition, cyclic codes for which an integer $m \neq 1$ divides both n and k are quasi-cyclic. For example, the (15, 5) BCH code is quasi-cyclic with $m = 5$. However these cyclic codes are not of primary interest here.

The row space of the following matrix is invariant under the Permutation (8.53) and hence is a quasi-cyclic (mn_0, mk_0) code,

$$\mathbf{G} = \begin{bmatrix} \mathbf{IP}_0 & \mathbf{OP}_1 & \cdots & \mathbf{OP}_{m-1} \\ \mathbf{OP}_{m-1} & \mathbf{IP}_0 & \cdots & \mathbf{OP}_{m-2} \\ \vdots & \vdots & & \vdots \\ \mathbf{OP}_1 & \mathbf{OP}_2 & \cdots & \mathbf{IP}_0 \end{bmatrix} \tag{8.54}$$

where **I** and **O** represent, respectively, the identity and all-zero matrices of order k_0, and $\mathbf{P}_i$ is an arbitrary $k_0 \times (n_0 - k_0)$ matrix. Each code word consists of m blocks of k_0 unaltered information symbols followed by $n_0 - k_0$ parity-check symbols. (Note the similarity between Equation 8.54 and Equation 3.13, the generator matrix of an (mn_0, mk_0) convolutional code.) The parity-check matrix associated with Equation 8.54 is

$$\mathbf{H} = \begin{bmatrix} \mathbf{P}_0^T\mathbf{I} & \mathbf{P}_{m-1}^T\mathbf{O} & \cdots & \mathbf{P}_1^T\mathbf{O} \\ \mathbf{P}_1^T\mathbf{O} & \mathbf{P}_0^T\mathbf{I} & \cdots & \mathbf{P}_2^T\mathbf{O} \\ \vdots & & & \\ \mathbf{P}_{m-1}^T\mathbf{O} & & \cdots & \mathbf{P}_0^T\mathbf{I} \end{bmatrix}$$

where **I** and **O** represent the identity and all-zero matrices of order $n - k$.

A more general class of quasi-cyclic codes in which the identity and zero matrices of Matrix 8.54 are replaced by arbitrary square matrices of order k_0 has also been studied (Chen 1969; Karlin 1969).

It is possible to encode a quasi-cyclic code with a k-stage shift register in a manner exactly analogous to that for encoding cyclic codes. This is illustrated now for a binary (12, 4) code.

Example. The best binary (12, 4) code has minimum distance 6. (See Table 5.4.) There exists a quasi-cyclic code with these parameters; its generator matrix is

$$\mathbf{G} = \begin{bmatrix} 111 & 011 & 000 & 001 \\ 001 & 111 & 011 & 000 \\ 000 & 001 & 111 & 011 \\ 011 & 000 & 001 & 111 \end{bmatrix}$$

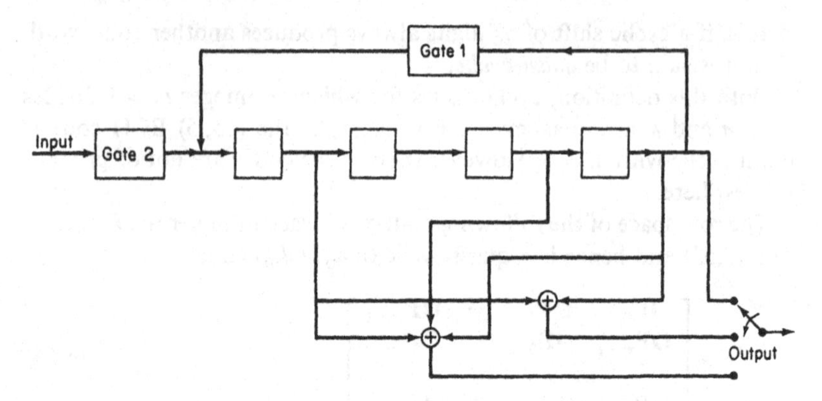

Figure 8.8. A k-stage encoder for a (12, 4) quasi-cyclic code.

This can be encoded with the $k = 4$-stage shift register shown in Figure 8.8. This register operates as follows: After the four information digits have been shifted into the register, gate 2 is closed, gate 1 is opened, and the outputs of the two binary adder circuits are the two parity digits in the first 3-bit block of the code word. The digits of this block are then read out to the channel in the usual order — first information, then parity. Next, the register is shifted once and the process repeated. Because of the quasi-cyclic property, the next two parity digits again appear at the outputs of the adders. Encoding is completed when the last information digit has been read out, in this case after 4 shifts.

Because the quasi-cyclic code is not in systematic form, this encoder usually requires an additional k-stage register to store the information symbols of the next block until encoding is completed. This difficulty can be avoided by using an equivalent systematic code. A quasi-cyclic code can also be encoded with a register of $n - k$ stages. (See Problem 8.18.)

The generator matrix of the (mn_0, mk_0) quasi-cyclic code of Equation 8.54 can be put in reduced echelon form by means of column permutations. For example, the generator matrix of the (15, 5) BCH code generated by $X^{10} + X^8 + X^5 + X^4 + X^2 + X + 1$ can be written in the form

$$\mathbf{G} = \begin{bmatrix} 100 & 001 & 010 & 011 & 011 \\ 011 & 100 & 001 & 010 & 011 \\ 011 & 011 & 100 & 001 & 010 \\ 010 & 011 & 011 & 100 & 001 \\ 001 & 010 & 011 & 011 & 100 \end{bmatrix}$$

Columns 1, 4, 7, 10, and 13, columns 2, 5, 8, 11, and 14, and columns 3, 6, 9, 12, and 15 form three circulant matrices as shown here:

$$\begin{bmatrix} 10000 & 00111 & 01011 \\ 01000 & 10011 & 10101 \\ 00100 & 11001 & 11010 \\ 00010 & 11100 & 01101 \\ 00001 & 01110 & 10110 \end{bmatrix} = [\mathbf{I}_k \mathbf{C}_1 \mathbf{C}_2].$$

Quasi-cyclic codes in this form have been investigated by several authors, and some rather powerful random-error-correcting codes have been discovered. Table 8.3 contains a list of quasi-cyclic $(n, n/2)$ codes which have the largest minimum distance of any quasi-cyclic code, for various values of n (Chen 1969). In addition to n, k, and d, the top row of the circulant matrix, which completely specifies **G**, is given in octal form. It is worth noting that in all cases where they have been examined, these rate-½ codes attain the largest known value of minimum distance for any linear code with the same values of n and k.

Table 8.3. Some $(n, n/2)$ Binary Quasi-Cyclic Codes. Each Code Listed Has the Largest Value of d for Any Quasi-Cyclic Code of That Length with $R = 0.5$

Length n	Generator of Circulant (in Octal)	Minimum Distance d
6	3	3
8	7	4
10	7	4
12	7	4
14	7	4
16	27	5
18	117	6
20	57	6
22	267	7
24	573	8
26	653	7
28	727	8
30	2167	8
32	557	8
34	557	8
36	573	8
38	557	8
40	5723	9
42	14573	10

In light of this last remark it would be desirable to present here techniques for constructing quasi-cyclic codes; unfortunately, only one method of constructing quasi-cyclic codes has been devised at this writing. Although these codes, the self-orthogonal quasi-cyclic codes (Townsend and Weldon 1967), can be decoded very simply with majority-logic decoding, they have relatively low minimum distance.

The existence of very, but not arbitrarily long, binary, quasi-cycic codes that meet the Gilbert bound has been demonstrated (Chen, Peterson, and Weldon 1969). These codes, for which the circulant matrices must be nonsingular, also meet the expurgated random-coding bound on the probability of error. (See Section 4.2.)

Quasi-cyclic codes have an interesting polynomial representation. Consider a $(2k, k)$ quasi-cyclic code in systematic form and let $\mathbf{C}$ be the circulant matrix that specifies the code. If $\mathbf{i}$ denotes the information vector to be encoded, then

$$\mathbf{v} = \mathbf{i}\mathbf{G} = [\mathbf{i} \quad \mathbf{i}\mathbf{C}].$$

Now let $i(X)$ denote the information vector in polynomial form and let $c(X)$ denote the top row of the circulant matrix $\mathbf{C}$. Clearly, the other rows of $\mathbf{C}$ are

$$Xc(X) \bmod X^k - 1, X^2c(X) \bmod X^k - 1, \ldots, X^{k-1}c(X) \bmod X^k - 1.$$

It is easily verified that the algebra of $m \times m$ circulant matrices is isomorphic to the algebra of polynomials modulo $X^m - 1$ and that multiplying the vector $\mathbf{i}$ by the circulant matrix $\mathbf{C}$ is identical to the polynomial product $i(X)c(X) \bmod X^k - 1$. Therefore, $v(X)$ has the form

$$[i(X), i(X)c(X)]. \tag{8.55}$$

Thus the code word in the quasi-cyclic code can be considered as an information polynomial followed by a code word in the cyclic code of length k generated by $\text{GCD}[c(X), X^k - 1]$.

Some cyclic codes are closely related to quasi-cyclic codes. Consider, for example, the $(17, 9)$ quadratic residue code that has minimum distance 5. Let α be a root of $X^8 + X^7 + X^6 + X + 1$. Choose $\beta = \alpha^{15}$. Then $g(X) = m(\beta) = X^8 + X^7 + X^6 + X^4 + X^2 + X + 1$. The parity-check matrix of the code can be written

$$\mathbf{H} = [\beta^{16}\beta^{15}\beta^{14}\beta^{13}\beta^{12}\beta^{11}\beta^{10}\beta^{9}\beta^{8}\beta^{7}\beta^{6}\beta^{5}\beta^{4}\beta^{3}\beta^{2}\beta^{1}\beta^{0}].$$

From Appendix C, α and its conjugates $\alpha^2, \alpha^{2^2}, \alpha^{2^3}, \ldots, \alpha^{2^7}$ are linearly independent. Thus β can be written in terms of this *normal basis*, as it is called, as

$$\beta = 0 + \alpha^{2^6} + \alpha^{2^5} + \alpha^{2^4} + \alpha^{2^3} + 0 + \alpha^{2^1} + 0$$

and by Theorem 6.14, its conjugates are cyclic shifts of this polynomial; that is,

$$\beta^2 = \alpha^{2^7} + \alpha^{2^6} + \alpha^{2^5} + \alpha^{2^4} + 0 + \alpha^{2^2} + 0 + 0,$$
$$\vdots$$
$$\beta^{2^7} = \beta^9 = 0 + 0 + \alpha^{2^5} + \alpha^{2^4} + \alpha^{2^3} + \alpha^{2^2} + \alpha^{2^1} + \alpha^{2^0}.$$

With some effort it can be shown that $\beta^3 = \alpha^{2^5} + \alpha^{2^0}$. Then the conjugates of β^3 consist of cyclic shifts of the 8-tuple 00100001. The root β^0 can be shown to equal $\alpha^{2^7} + \alpha^{2^6} + \alpha^{2^5} + \alpha^{2^4} + \alpha^{2^3} + \alpha^{2^2} + \alpha^{2^1} + \alpha^{2^0}$. (See Problem 8.23.) Thus, the matrix **H** can be rearranged to give

$$\mathbf{H} = [[\beta^9\beta^{13}\beta^{15}\beta^{16}\beta^8\beta^4\beta^2\beta^1][\beta^{10}\beta^5\beta^{11}\beta^{14}\beta^7\beta^{12}\beta^6\beta^3]\beta^0]$$

$$= \left[\begin{bmatrix} 01011110 \\ 00101111 \\ 10010111 \\ 11001011 \\ 11100101 \\ 11110010 \\ 01111001 \\ 10111100 \end{bmatrix}\begin{bmatrix} 10000100 \\ 01000010 \\ 00100001 \\ 10010000 \\ 01001000 \\ 00100100 \\ 00010010 \\ 00001001 \end{bmatrix}\begin{matrix} 1 \\ 1 \\ 1 \\ 1 \\ 1 \\ 1 \\ 1 \\ 1 \end{matrix}\right] = [\mathbf{C}_1\mathbf{C}_2].$$

Therefore, the (17, 9) code with one information symbol deleted is equivalent to a (16, 8) quasi-cyclic code. Because $\mathbf{C}_2$ is nonsingular, the matrix $[\mathbf{C}_1\ \mathbf{C}_2]$ can be put in echelon canonical form by multiplying it on the left by the inverse of $\mathbf{C}_1$.

It is known that every finite field has a normal basis (Albert 1956, p. 119). Thus, the generator matrix of every cyclic code can be decomposed into circulants, although many will be trivial. Then, removing columns corresponding to elements of order less than n will give the generator matrix of a quasi-cyclic code. It may not be possible to put such a code in systematic form, however.

8.15 Codes Based on the Chinese Remainder Theorem

Let $i(X)$ denote a polynomial of degree $k - 1$ or less with symbols from $GF(q^m)$. Let $m_i(X)$ denote a polynomial of degree d_i with symbols from the same field. An interesting class of codes can be constructed from the following version of the Chinese Remainder Theorem (Stone 1963).

THEOREM 8.20. *The polynomial $i(X)$ can be reconstructed from the remainders*

$$r_i(X) \equiv i(X) \bmod m_i(X) \qquad i = 1, 2, \ldots, n, \tag{8.56}$$

provided the $m_i(X)$ are relatively prime in pairs and that

$$\sum_{i=1}^{n} d_i > k - 1. \tag{8.57}$$

Proof. Any two solutions $i_1(X)$ and $i_2(X)$ to the set of congruences (8-56) are congruent modulo $m(X) = \prod_{i=1}^{n} m_1(X)$; for $i_1(X) - i_2(X)$ is divisible by $m(X)$ if and only if it is divisible by each $m_i(X)$. Since there is exactly one polynomial of degree less than k in each residue class modulo $m(X)$, there is exactly one solution for the set of congruences (8.56), and this must be the correct solution. Q.E.D.

This theorem can be used to construct a class of random-error-correcting codes with symbols from $GF(q^m)$ as follows: Choose as the $m_i(X)$ the factors of $X^{q^m-1} - 1$ in $GF(q^m)$. Since this polynomial splits completely in $GF(q^m)$,

$$m_i(X) = (X - \alpha^i), \qquad i = 0, 1, \ldots, q^m - 2,$$

where α is a primitive element of $GF(q^m)$.

Now calculate the $n = q^m - 1$ residues of the information polynomial $i(X)$ which has degree less than k. The set of these polynomials forms an (n, k) linear code with symbols from $GF(q^m)$.

Decoding can be performed as follows: Suppose t errors occur so that $n - t$ of the residues are received correctly. Now, $i(X)$ is determined by any set of k correct residues. Thus, of the $\binom{n}{k}$ ways of determining $i(X)$, exactly $\binom{n-t}{k}$ will agree and give the correct polynomial $i(X)$. It is possible that $t - 1$ transmitted residues have been changed so as to be the residues of some other polynomial $j(X)$ of degree $k - 1$ or less which is determined by $k - 1$ correct residues and one incorrect residue. There are

$$\binom{k-1+t}{k}$$

determinations which will give the same incorrect answer.

Now if $n - t > k - 1 + t$, then the number of correct determinations exceeds the number of incorrect ones, so $i(X)$ can be reconstructed correctly. That is, if t is chosen such that

$$2t + 1 = n - k + 1$$

for a particular code, then all t errors can be corrected. Since the minimum distance is not less than $2t + 1$, and since $d \leqq n - k + 1$ for any linear code, it follows that for these codes,

$$d = n - k + 1.$$

It turns out that these codes can be put in a cyclic form. The residue of $i(X) = i_{k-1}X^{k-1} + i_{k-2}X^{k-2} + \cdots + i_1X + i_0 \bmod(X - \alpha^i)$, which is an element of $GF(q^m)$, is given by

$$i(X) = r_i + g_i(X)(X - \alpha^i).$$

Thus

$$r_i = i(X)\,|_{X=\alpha^i} = i(\alpha^i).$$

Let the generator matrix of an (n, k) code with symbols in $GF(q^m)$ be

$$\mathbf{G} = \begin{bmatrix} (\alpha^{k-1})^{n-1} & (\alpha^{k-1})^{n-2} & \cdots & \alpha^{k-1} & \alpha^0 \\ (\alpha^{k-2})^{n-1} & (\alpha^{k-2})^{n-2} & \cdots & \alpha^{k-2} & \alpha^0 \\ \vdots & & \cdots & & \vdots \\ \alpha^{n-1} & \alpha^{n-2} & \cdots & \alpha^1 & \alpha^0 \end{bmatrix} \tag{8.58}$$

Multiplying $\mathbf{G}$ by the information vector $= (i_{k-1}i_{k-2} \cdots i_0)$ gives the n-tuple

$$[i(X)|_{X=\alpha^{n-1}}, i(X)|_{X=\alpha^{n-2}}, \ldots, i(X)|_{X=\alpha}, i(X)|_{X=1}]$$
$$= [r_{n-1}, r_{n-2}, \ldots, r_1, r_0], \tag{8.59}$$

which is a code word in the code based on the Chinese Remainder Theorem.

But $\mathbf{G}$ is the generator matrix of the cyclic (n, k) code for which $h(X)$ has roots $\alpha^1, \alpha^2, \ldots, \alpha^{k-1}$. In fact, this is a Reed-Solomon code and is discussed at length in the next chapter.

The decoding procedure presented here for these codes is clearly impractical for all but the shortest codes. It requires that the decoder perform $\binom{n}{k}$ operations for each decoding. Fortunately a more easily mechanized method of decoding these very powerful codes has been found; it too is discussed in Chapter 9.

Since a symbol in $GF(q^m)$ can be represented as an m-tuple over $GF(q)$, these codes are ideally suited to multiple burst-error correction. This is discussed in Chapter 11.

It is not necessary to consider linear factors in an extension field; polynomials of higher degree over $GF(q)$ also yield interesting codes.

However these codes are not as powerful as the codes based on linear factors, that is, the Reed-Solomon codes.

Example. There are 6 binary polynomials of degree 4 which are relatively prime in pairs. Choose $k = 8$ and assume that 2 or fewer errors occur. The number of correct determinations of $r(X)$ is at least

$$\binom{6-2}{8/4} = 6.$$

while the number of determinations of a particular incorrect information polynomial is at most

$$\binom{8/4 + 2 - 1}{8/4} = 3.$$

Hence this (24, 8) code has $d \geqq 5$. Note also that if the residues are transmitted in blocks, a burst of errors of length 5 or less can affect at most 2 blocks, so this code has burst-correcting capability of at least 5.

Notes

The study of cyclic codes originated with Prange (1957, 1959). Many references on specific cyclic codes are cited in the next three chapters, and a number of the ideas presented in this chapter come directly or indirectly from those sources. The equivalence of cyclic codes with ideals was noticed independently by Prange, Peterson (1960*a*), and Kasami (1960). The associated-polynomial approach is due to Mattson and Solomon (1961). The results in Section 8.6 were collected by Chen (1969). The method of encoding using a k-stage register is essentially equivalent to the idea of using shift-register-generated sequences as code vectors and appears in Green and San Soucie (1958) and in Prange (1958). The encoder that uses an $(n - k)$-stage shift register was found by Peterson (1960*a*) and the fact that it can be modified for use with circuits equivalent to the division circuit was discovered by Meggitt and Abramson. Theorem 8.7 and the implications of Theorem 8.6 with respect to error-detection by cyclic codes were both pointed out by Brown (1961). An application of these ideas to a practical error detection problem is described in Fontaine and Gallager (1960). Green and San Soucie (1958) proposed the use of maximal length sequences for error-correction, and Zierler (1958) pointed out their connection with Reed-Muller codes.

Hamming codes have been previously studied by Abramson (1960*a*), Elspas (1960), and Stern and Friedland (1959) as cyclic codes. Stern and Friedland use a linear-circuit viewpoint and arrive at a different way of mechanizing the code described in Problem 8.5. In their system, the coding is not "systematic"; that is, the information symbols do not appear unchanged in the coded vector. This necessitates the use of a "decoding filter" in addition to error correction. There does not seem to be any fundamental reason why the approach used in this chapter should lead to a better decoding method in every case. The basic decoder of Section 8.9 was first described by Meggitt (1960). Error trapping was probably first devised by Prange; he also introduced permutation decoding as a variation of error trapping. This decoding procedure was developed independently by MacWilliams (1964). Error trapping with windows was conceived independently by Kasami (1964) and Mitchell et al. (1961).

Section 8.10 is based on the work of Shatz. The material on code symmetry originated for the most part with Prange. The theorems on the affine permutations are due to Kasami (Kasami, Lin, and Peterson 1966). The first proof that the product of cyclic codes could be cyclic is due to Burton and Weldon (1965) and was suggested by Problem 11.2. The elegant treatment of cyclic product codes, and in particular Theorem 8.19, is due to Lin (1970). Quadratic residue codes were first considered by Prange (1958) and significant further results were obtained by Gleason (1961), Pless (1963), and Assmus, Mattson, and Turyn (1966). Quasi-cyclic codes were first treated by Townsend and Weldon (1967), and further studies have been made by Karlin (1969), Chen (1969), and Hoffner and Reddy (1970). Section 8.15 is based entirely on a paper by Stone (1963).

Problems

8.1. A cyclic code is generated by $g(X) = X^8 + X^7 + X^6 + X^4 + 1$.

a. Show that its length is 15.
b. Find the generator matrix and parity-check matrix in modified-echelon canonical form for this code.
c. Devise a linear switching circuit for encoding using $k = 7$ stages and one using $n - k = 8$ stages.
d. Show that α, α^2, α^3, and α^4 are roots of $g(X)$, where α is a root of $X^4 + X + 1$. (Compare Table 6.1.)
e. Devise circuits for calculating $r(1)$, $r(\alpha)$, and $r(\alpha^3)$ for any received vector $\{r(X)\}$.

8.2. Show that the binary cyclic code of length n generated by $g(X)$ has minimum weight at least 3 if n is the smallest integer for which $g(X)$ divides $X^n - 1$. Is this statement true for nonbinary codes?

8.3. Suppose that $g(X)$ generates a cyclic code of length n over $GF(q)$ and suppose that $(n, q) = 1$. Show that a vector consisting of all 1's is a code vector if and only if $g(X)$ is not divisible by $X - 1$.

8.4. Let $g^*(X)$ denote the reciprocal polynomial of $g(X)$.

a. Show that codes generated by $g(X)$ and $g^*(X)$ are equivalent.
b. Show that if $g(X) = g^*(X)$, the code generated by $g(X)$ has the property that if $\mathbf{v} = (a_0, a_1, \ldots, a_{n-1})$ is a code vector, so is $\mathbf{v}^* = (a_{n-1}, a_{n-2}, \ldots, a_0)$.

8.5. Let α be a primitive element of $GF(q^m)$ and let $n = (q^m - 1)/(q - 1)$. (Show that α is a primitive root of $GF(q)$.) Consider the matrix

$$\mathbf{H} = [\alpha^{n-1}, \alpha^{n-2}, \ldots, \alpha, 1]$$

and the code that is its null space. (The null space of **H** is a shortened cyclic code, since $\alpha^n \neq 1$. It is a cyclic code of length $q^m - 1$ in which only the n lowest order components are used.) Show that the null space of **H** has minimum distance at least 3. Devise an m-stage shift register for encoding. Devise a system similar to those given in Section 8.9 for decoding and show the required shift-register circuits.

8.6. Show that for a binary cyclic code with n odd, the sequence of all 1's is not a code word if the code has an overall parity check. Also show that it is a code word if the code does not have an overall parity check.

8.7. Using the concepts of a normal basis (Section 8.14), construct the (6, 3) quasi-cyclic code of Table 8.3 from the (7, 4) Hamming code.

8.8. Let α be a primitive element of $GF(q^m)$ and $\beta = \alpha^{q-1}$. Then the order of β is $n = (q^m - 1)/(q - 1)$. (See Section 6.6.) Let $h(X)$ be the minimum function of β and $g(X) = (X^n - 1)/(h(X)$.

a. Show that if **v** is a code vector in the code generated by $g(X)$, for distinct pairs (j, γ), $0 \leqq j < n$ and $\gamma \varepsilon GF(q)$, the vectors resulting from shifting **v** cyclically j places and multiplying the resulting vector by the scalar γ are distinct code words.
b. Using the result of Part a show that all nonzero code words in this code have the same weight.

This is the null space of the Hamming codes. From this result and MacWilliams's identity, the weight distribution of the Hamming codes can be found. (See Problem 3.22.)

8.9. Let $\mathbf{G} = [\mathbf{IP}]$ be the generator matrix of a cyclic code. If

$$h(X) = X^k + h_{k-1} X^{k-1} + \cdots + h_1 X + 1$$

is the parity-check polynomial of the code, show that the first column of the matrix **P** is $(1, h_1, h_2, \ldots, h_{k-1})^T$.

8.10. Show that if $t < n/k$ then every n-symbol pattern of weight t or less will contain a sequence of at least k successive zeros. Show that if $t \geqq n/k$ then there is at least one pattern of weight t which does not contain k successive zeros.

8.11. Using Appendix D and the preceding problem, list each multiple error-correcting cyclic code that can be decoded up to its error-correcting ability t by error trapping. List only one code for a given value of n and k.

8.12. The (31, 21) binary cyclic code listed in Appendix D cannot be decoded with error trapping if it is necessary to correct all error patterns of weight 2 or less. (See Problem 8.10.) Show that by using the permutation $X^i \rightarrow X^{2i}$ it is possible to map every pattern of weight $\leqq 2$ onto another pattern in which the 1's lie within 10 consecutive digits. This proves that the code can be decoded with permutation decoding.

8.13. For any m there exists a binary double-error-correcting $(2^m - 1, 2^m - 1 - 2m)$ BCH code. (See Chapter 9.) For which values of m can these codes be decoded with permutation decoding using the permutation $X^i \to X^{2i}$? (Do Problem 8.12 first.)

8.14. Given an (n, k) double-error-correcting cyclic code, show that for error-trapping decoding with windows, the number of windows required is the smallest integer equal to or greater than $[(n/2) + 1]/(n - k) - 1$.

8.15. Derive an expression similar to Equation 8.23 for the error-correcting ability of the trial-and-error modification of error trapping described in Section 8.9. Which codes of length $\leqq 31$ in Appendix D can be decoded up to their random-error-correcting ability with this procedure?

8.16. (Burton and Weldon 1965) Prove that Theorem 8.19 holds even when p divides n_1 or n_2.

8.17. Modify the encoder for the (12, 4) quasi-cyclic code shown in Figure 8.8 so that it can be used to encode when the code is in systematic form. Compare with the k-stage encoder for cyclic codes presented in Section 8.7.

8.18. Devise an $(n - k)$-stage encoder for a quasi-cyclic code in systematic form.

8.19. The permutation

$$X^i \to X^{pi}$$

permutes the symbol in the ith position in a cyclic code of length n into the pith position. Show that if $(n, p) = 1$, the code is mapped onto an equivalent cyclic code.

In Problems 8.20, 8.21, and 8.23, assume that C_1 and C_2 are cyclic codes of relatively prime lengths n_1 and n_2, respectively. The generator polynomials are $g_1(X)$ and $g_2(X)$, respectively, and the parity-check polynomials are $h_1(X)$ and $h_2(X)$. Here C is the cyclic product code of length $n = n_1 n_2$ and with generator and parity-check polynomials $g(X)$ and $h(X)$, respectively. Let a and b be defined by $an_1 + bn_2 = 1$.

8.20. Show that $g(X) = \text{GCD}[g_1(X^{bn_2}), g_2(X^{an_1}), X^n - 1]$.

8.21. Show that

$$g(X) = \text{LCM}\{\text{GCD}[g_1(X^{bn_2}],\ X^n - 1),\ \text{GCD}[g_2(X^{an_1}), X^n - 1]\}$$

8.22. Show that $h(X) = \text{GCD}[h_1(X^{bn_2}), h_2(X^{an_1}), X^n - 1]$

8.23. In the example on page 260 in Section 8.14, show that

$$\sum_{i=0}^{7} \alpha^{2^i} = 1 = \beta^0.$$

Hint: Consider the product

$$\sum_{j=0}^{7} (X - \alpha^{2^j}) = m(\alpha).$$

8.24. Consider an (n, k) code with minimum distance $d=2t+1$. To correct all error patterns of weight t or less by randomized permutation decoding (Omura 1969*a*), N permutations are necessary. Show that

$$N \geq \frac{\sum_{i=1}^{t} \binom{n}{i}}{\sum_{i=1}^{t} \binom{n-k}{i}} \approx \left(\frac{1}{1-R}\right)^{t} \text{ for } n \text{ large,}$$

where R is the code rate. Experimental evidence (Omura 1969*a*) for values of n on the order of several hundred indicates that this bound is reasonably tight. Discuss.

9 Bose-Chaudhuri-Hocquenghem Codes

The codes described in this chapter are a remarkable generalization of Hamming codes for correcting multiple errors. They are as a class the best, known, constructive (that is, nonrandom) codes for channels in which errors affect successive symbols independently. Furthermore, a simply implemented decoding procedure has been devised for these codes.

9.1 The BCH Bound

The lower bound on minimum distance presented in this section applies to all cyclic codes. The Bose-Chaudhuri-Hocquenghem (BCH) codes are a class of cyclic codes whose generator polynomials are chosen to make the minimum distance guaranteed by this bound large.

THEOREM 9.1. *Let $g(X)$ be the generator polynomial of a cyclic code of length n over $GF(q)$ and let $\alpha^{e_1}, \alpha^{e_2}, \ldots \alpha^{e_{n-k}}$ be the roots of $g(X)$, possibly in an extension field, where α is an element of order n. The minimum distance of the code is greater than the largest number of consecutive integers modulo n in the set $e = (e_1, e_2, \ldots, e_{n-k})$.*

Proof. Let $m_0, m_0 + 1, \ldots, m_0 + d_0 - 2$ denote the largest set of consecutive integers modulo n in the set e. As indicated in Section 8.2, a cyclic code with roots $\alpha^{e_1}, \alpha^{e_2}, \ldots, \alpha^{e_{n-k}}$ is the null space of the matrix.

$$\mathbf{H} = \begin{bmatrix} (\alpha^{e_1})^{n-1} & (\alpha^{e_1})^{n-2} & \cdots & \alpha^{e_1} & 1 \\ (\alpha^{e_2})^{n-1} & (\alpha^{e_2})^{n-2} & \cdots & \alpha^{e_2} & 1 \\ \vdots & \vdots & & \vdots & \vdots \\ (\alpha^{e_{n-k}})^{n-1} & (\alpha^{e_{n-k}})^{n-2} & \cdots & \alpha^{e_{n-k}} & 1 \end{bmatrix} \tag{9.1}$$

Now if no linear combination of $d_0 - 1$ columns of the (sub)matrix

$$\begin{bmatrix} (\alpha^{m_0})^{n-1} & (\alpha^{m_0})^{n-2} & \cdots & \alpha^{m_0} & 1 \\ (\alpha^{m_0+1})^{n-1} & (\alpha^{m_0+1})^{n-2} & \cdots & \alpha^{m_0+1} & 1 \\ \vdots & \vdots & & \vdots & \vdots \\ (\alpha^{m_0+d_0-2})^{n-1} & (\alpha^{m_0+d_0-2})^{n-2} & \cdots & \alpha^{m_0+d_0-2} & 1 \end{bmatrix} \tag{9.2}$$

is zero, then clearly no linear combination of $d - 1$ columns of $\mathbf{H}$ is zero, and by Corollary 3.1 the code has minimum distance d_0 or greater.

That Matrix 9.2 has the requisite property can be seen by examining the determinant of any set of $d_0 - 1$ of its columns.

$$D = \begin{vmatrix} (\alpha^{m_0})^{j_{d_0-1}} & (\alpha^{m_0})^{j_{d_0-2}} & \cdots & (\alpha^{m_0})^{j_1} \\ (\alpha^{m_0+1})^{j_{d_0-1}} & (\alpha^{m_0+1})^{j_{d_0-2}} & \cdots & (\alpha^{m_0+1})^{j_1} \\ \vdots & \vdots & & \vdots \\ (\alpha^{m_0+d_0-2})^{j_{d_0-1}} & (\alpha^{m_0+d_0-2})^{j_{d_0-2}} & \cdots & (\alpha^{m_0+d_0-2})^{j_1} \end{vmatrix}$$

Factoring $\alpha^{m_0 j_i}$ out of the ith column for every i gives

$$\alpha^{m_0(j_1+j_2+\cdots j_{d_0-1})} \begin{vmatrix} 1 & 1 & \cdots & 1 \\ \alpha^{j_{d_0-1}} & \alpha^{j_{d_0-2}} & \cdots & \alpha^{j_1} \\ (\alpha^{j_{d_0-1}})^2 & (\alpha^{j_{d_0-2}})^2 & \cdots & (\alpha^{j_1})^2 \\ \vdots & \vdots & & \vdots \\ (\alpha^{j_{d_0-1}})^{d_0-2} & (\alpha^{j_{d_0-2}})^{d_0-2} & \cdots & (\alpha^{j_1})^{d_0-2} \end{vmatrix} \tag{9.3}$$

and this is a Vandermonde determinant:

$$\begin{vmatrix} 1 & 1 & \cdots & 1 \\ X_1 & X_2 & \cdots & X_s \\ X_1^2 & X_2^2 & \cdots & X_s^2 \\ \vdots & \vdots & \cdots & \vdots \\ X_1^{s-1} & X_2^{s-1} & \cdots & X_s^{s-1} \end{vmatrix} = \prod_{i>j} (X_i - X_j). \tag{9.4}$$

Equation 9.4 can be verified by direct calculation or in the following way:

1. If $X_i = X_j$, the determinant is 0; therefore $X_i - X_j$ is a factor of the left side for all i and j, and consequently the right side must divide the left side.
2. Since both sides are polynomials of the same degree, they must differ by a constant factor.

3. The constant factor must be 1, since the coefficient of $1 X_2 X_3^2 \cdots X_s^{s-1}$ is the same on both sides. It follows from Equation 9.3 that as long as no two columns are identical, the determinant D is certainly not 0, and hence no combination of $d_0 - 1$ or fewer columns of **H** is linearly dependent. By Corollary 3.1, the code that is the null space of **H** has minimum distance at least d_0. Q.E.D.

COROLLARY 9.1. *A cyclic code with roots $\alpha^e, \alpha^{e+j}, \ldots, \alpha^{e+j(d_0-2)}$, and possibly others, where α is an element of order n, has minimum distance d_0 or greater provided $(j, n) = 1$.*

Proof. Let $\beta = \alpha^j$. Then since $(j, n) = 1$, β also has order n, and α^e can be expressed as a power of β, $\alpha^e = \beta^{m_0}$. Then, the roots include β^{m_0}, $\beta^{m_0+1}, \ldots, \beta^{m_0+d_0-2}$, and the corollary follows from Theorem 9.1.

The BCH bound can also be proved in a straightforward manner using the properties of the associated polynomial presented in Section 8.3. Recall that for any code word $\mathbf{b} = (b_{n-1}, b_{n-2}, \ldots, b_0)$ in a cyclic code over $GF(q)$ there exists an associated polynomial $a(X)$ with coefficients in $GF(q^m)$ such that

$$b_i = a(\alpha^i); \qquad i = 0, 1, \ldots n - 1 \tag{9.5}$$

Theorem 8.2 shows that the nonzero terms of $a(X)$ correspond to roots of $h(X)$, the parity-check polynomial of the code. That is, if $\alpha^{-e_1}, \alpha^{-e_2}, \ldots, \alpha^{-e_{n-k}}$ are roots of $g(X)$, then the coefficients of X^{e_1}, $X^{e_2}, \ldots X^{e_{n-k}}$ in $a(X)$ are zero. Now if $\alpha^{m_0}, \alpha^{m_0+1}, \ldots, \alpha^{m_0+d_0-2}$ but not $\alpha^{m_0+d_0-1}$ are roots of $g(X)$, then using the fact that $\{X^n\} = \{1\}, a(X)$ can be factored into

$$\{a(X)\} = \{X^{m_0+d_0-1}\}\{a'(X)\}$$

where $a'(X)$ has degree $n - d_0$ or less. Thus $a(X)$ has at most $n - d_0$ roots in the set $(1, \alpha, \ldots, \alpha^{n-1})$. It follows from Equation 9.5 that the code word $b(X)$ has at least $n - (n - d_0) = d_0$ nonzero components. This completes the second proof of the BCH bound.

The remarkable bound of Theorem 9.1 applies to all cyclic codes. For some, and in particular for the BCH codes, it is rather tight. In Section 9.3 it is shown to give the true minimum distance for several large classes of BCH codes.

9.2 Definition of the Codes

Let α be an element of $GF(q^m)$. For any specified m_0 and d_0, the code generated by $g(X)$ is a BCH code if and only if $g(X)$ is the polynomial of lowest degree over $GF(q)$ for which $\alpha^{m_0}, \alpha^{m_0+1}, \ldots, \alpha^{m_0+d_0-2}$ are roots.

The length of the code is the least common multiple of the orders of the roots. Except for the trivial case when only one root, α^{m_0}, is specified, the length n of the code is the order e of α. For

$$(\alpha^{m_0})^n = \alpha^{m_0 n} = 1 \quad \text{and} \quad (\alpha^{m_0+1})^n = \alpha^{m_0 n+n} = 1$$

and therefore $\alpha^n = 1$, e divides n, and n could be no less than e, the order of α. On the other hand, if $\alpha^e = 1$, $(\alpha^j)^e = 1$, so that the order of every element α divides e, then n is no greater than e, and hence $n = e$.

The number of parity-check symbols and the number of information symbols can be found by the method given in Section 8.1 or by using the procedure in Chapter 12, Berlekamp (1968*b*). By Theorem 9.1, the minimum distance of the codes is at least d_0, and d_0 is called the *designed distance.*

The most important BCH codes are the binary codes obtained by letting α be a primitive element of $GF(2^m)$ and letting $m_0 = 1$ and $d_0 = 2t_0 + 1$.* Then $\{f(X)\}$ is a code vector if and only if

$$\alpha, \alpha^2, \alpha^3, \ldots \alpha^{2t_0}$$

are roots of $f(X)$. However, every even power of α is a root of the same minimum function as some previous odd power of α. For example, if $m_j(X)$ denotes the minimum function α^j, then α^2 and α^4 are roots of $m_1(X)$, α^6 is a root of $m_3(X)$, α^8 is a root of $m_1(X)$, α^{10} is a root of $m_5(X)$, and so forth. Therefore, an equivalent statement is that $\{f(X)\}$ is a code vector if and only if

$$\alpha, \alpha^3, \ldots, \alpha^{2t_0-1}$$

are roots of $f(X)$. Thus, the generator polynomial of the code is

$$g(X) = LCM(m_1(X), m_3(X), \ldots, m_{2t_0-1}(X)) \tag{9.6}$$

and each $m_i(X)$ has degree no greater than m by Theorems 6.16 and 6.24. Therefore, $g(X)$ has degree at most mt_0, and the code has at most mt_0 parity checks. These results can be summarized as follows:

THEOREM 9.2. *For any positive integers m and $t_0 < n/2$, there is a BCH binary code of length $n = 2^m - 1$ which corrects all combinations of t_0 or fewer errors and has no more than mt_0 parity-check symbols.*

All BCH codes with $g(X)$ given by Equation 9.6 with length no greater than 1023 are listed in Table 9.1, with the actual number of information symbols indicated. The tabulated parameter t_o is the designed error-correcting ability, $[(d_0 - 1)/2]$. For many of the codes, the designed distance can be proved to be equal to the minimum distance

* These codes have been called "narrow-sense" BCH codes.

by means of the theorems of Section 9.3. Berlekamp (1968*b*, Chapter 12) using results of Mann (1962), has developed an algebraic procedure for determining the number of information symbols in a BCH code.

In Table 9.1 all the codes of length 15 or less are optimal (Peterson 1960*a*) and all the double-error-correcting codes are quasi-perfect and hence optimal also. The shortest code for which a better linear code has been found is the (31, 16) $d = 7$ code; in Karlin (1969) a noncyclic (31, 16) code with $d = 8$ is presented.

Only a handful of the 8000 or so cyclic codes of length 63 are better than the BCH codes; see Appendix D. Most of these are members of a small infinite class of cyclic codes known to have larger minimum distance than the corresponding BCH codes (Kasami and Tokura 1969).

In Figure 9.1 the parameters k/n and t/n are plotted for BCH codes up to length 65,535. It is interesting to consider the behavior of these codes as n becomes very large. Examination of Figure 9.1 shows that if the ratio k/n is kept fixed, the lower bound on t/n appears to approach zero as n becomes large. In fact this is true and is proved in Peterson (1960*a*) and Berlekamp (1968*b*). Also Theorem 9.8 demonstrates that

$$d \leqq 2d_0 \tag{9.7}$$

This and the fact that the ratio d_0/n approaches zero for fixed k/n as n increases guarantee that the ratio of actual minimum distance to length also approaches zero. Thus these best known constructive codes are actually very weak for n large.

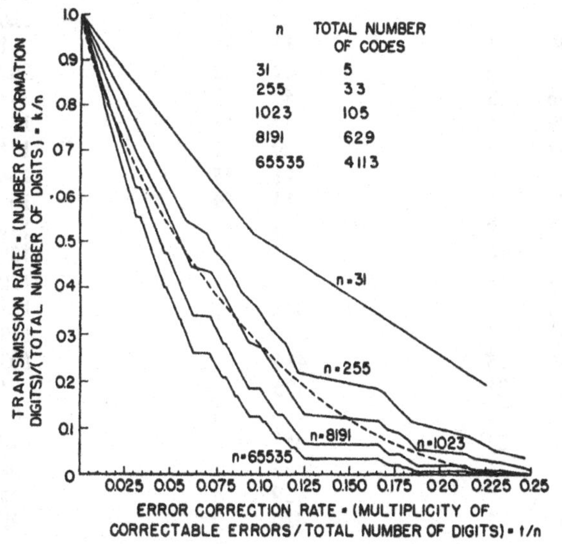

Figure 9.1. Error-correcting ability of some binary BCH codes.

Table 9.1. Binary Narrow-Sense BCH Codes Generated by Primitive Elements of Order Less than 2^{10}

n	k	t_0	n	k	t_0	n	k	t_0
7	4	1	255	239	2	511	421	10
				231	3		412	11
15	11	1		223	4		403	12
	7	2		215	5		394	13
	5	3		207	6		385	14
				199	7		376	15
31	26	1		191	8		367	16
	21	2		187	9		358	18
	16	3		179	10		349	19
	11	5		171	11		340	20
	6	7		163	12		331	21
				155	13		322	22
63	57	1		147	14		313	23
	51	2		139	15		304	25
	45	3		131	18		295	26
	39	4		123	19		286	27
	36	5		115	21		277	28
	30	6		107	22		268	29
	24	7		99	23		259	30
	18	10		91	25		250	31
	16	11		87	26		241	36
	10	13		79	27		238	37
	7	15		71	29		229	38
				63	30		220	39
127	120	1		55	31		211	41
	113	2		47	42		202	42
	106	3		45	43		193	43
	99	4		37	45		184	45
	92	5		29	47		175	46
	85	6		21	55		166	47
	78	7		13	59		157	51
	71	9		9	63		148	53
	64	10					139	54
	57	11					130	55
	50	13	511	502	1		121	58
	43	14		493	2		112	59
	36	15		484	3		103	61
	29	21		475	4		94	62
	22	23		466	5		85	63
	15	27		457	6		76	85
	8	31		448	7		67	87
				439	8		58	91
255	247	1		430	9		49	93

Table 9.1. (*Cont.*) Binary Narrow-Sense BCH Codes Generated by Primitive Elements of Order Less than 2^{10}

n	k	t_0	n	k	t_0	n	k	t_0
511	40	95	1023	698	35	1023	338	89
	31	109		688	36		328	90
	28	111		678	37		318	91
	19	119		668	38		308	93
	10	127		658	39		298	94
				648	41		288	95
1023	1013	1		638	42		278	102
	1003	2		628	43		268	103
	993	3		618	44		258	106
	983	4		608	45		248	107
	973	5		598	46		238	109
	963	6		588	47		228	110
	953	7		578	49		218	111
	943	8		573	50		208	115
	933	9		563	51		203	117
	923	10		553	52		193	118
	913	11		543	53		183	119
	903	12		533	54		173	122
	893	13		523	55		163	123
	883	14		513	57		153	125
	873	15		503	58		143	126
	863	16		493	59		133	127
	858	17		483	60		123	170
	848	18		473	61		121	171
	838	19		463	62		111	173
	828	20		453	63		101	175
	818	21		443	73		91	181
	808	22		433	74		86	183
	798	23		423	75		76	187
	788	24		413	77		66	189
	778	25		403	78		56	191
	768	26		393	79		46	219
	758	27		383	82		36	223
	748	28		378	83		26	239
	738	29		368	85		16	247
	728	30		358	86		11	255
	718	31		348	87			
	708	34						

The problem of determining the actual minimum distance of BCH codes is discussed in the succeeding section.

Examples. The last two examples in Section 8.1 are binary BCH codes. The latter one is defined by the specification that $\{f(X)\}$ is a code vector if and only if $\alpha, \alpha^2, \ldots, \alpha^{10}$ are roots of $f(X)$, where α is a primitive element of $GF(2^5)$. Then, $g(X)$ is shown to have degree 20. Therefore this code, which has minimum distance 11 and is capable of correcting all patterns of 5 or fewer errors, has length $2^5 - 1 = 31$, requires 20 parity-check symbols, and so has 11 information symbols.

The other code, that is, the binary (15, 5) code is used for a detailed illustration of the error-correction procedures described later in the chapter. Therefore, it is described in more detail here. For it, $\{f(X)\}$ is a code vector if and only if $\alpha, \alpha^2, \ldots, \alpha^6$ are roots of $f(X)$, where α is a primitive root of $GF(2^4)$. Earlier it was found that for this code

$$g(X) = m_1(X)\, m_3(X)\, m_5(X)$$

If α is taken to be a root of $X^4 + X + 1$, as in Table 6.1, then $m_1(X) = X^4 + X + 1$, and it can be verified that $m_3(X) = X^4 + X^3 + X^2 + X + 1$ and $m_5(X) = X^2 + X + 1$. Thus,

$$g(X) = (X^4 + X + 1)(X^4 + X^3 + X^2 + X + 1)(X^2 + X + 1)$$
$$= X^{10} + X^8 + X^5 + X^4 + X^2 + X + 1$$
$$h(X) = \frac{(X^{15} + 1)}{g(X)} = X^5 + X^3 + X + 1$$

Other interesting binary BCH codes can be found by taking α to be a nonprimitive root of $GF(2^m)$ and taking $m_0 = 1$.

Example. Let α be the cube of a primitive element of $GF(2^6)$. Then α has order 21. If the minimum function of α^j is denoted $m_j(X)$, then $\alpha^{21} = 1$, and

$$\alpha, \alpha^2, \alpha^4, \alpha^8, \alpha^{16}, \alpha^{32} = \alpha^{11} \text{ are roots of } m_1(X) \quad \text{(degree 6)}$$
$$\alpha^3, \alpha^6, \alpha^{12} \text{ are roots of } m_3(X) \quad \text{(degree 3)}$$

and therefore,

$$g(X) = m_1(X)m_3(X) \quad \text{(degree 9)}$$

has α, α^2, α^3, and α^4 as roots, and the code generated by $g(X)$ is a

BCH code that corrects all double errors. It has $n = 21, n - k = 9$, and therefore $k = 12$.

In Appendix D the true minimum distance and the minimum distance guaranteed by the BCH bound that is, the designed distance, are tabulated for all binary cyclic codes of length 65 or less. The typical wide discrepancy between d and d_0 for nonprimitive BCH codes stands in contrast to the case of the primitive codes, where in most cases in which d is known, $d = d_0$. (See Section 9.3.)

Most of the codes described in this section have a minimum distance shown to be at least $2t_0 + 1$ for some t_0. The bound on distance can be increased to $2t_0 + 2$ by including 1 as a root. The minimum function of 1 is $X - 1$, and hence this adds one parity check, which can easily be seen to be simply a parity check on all symbols. Let C_1 be a cyclic code generated by a $g(X)$ not divisible by $X - 1$ and let C_2 be the code generated by $(X - 1)g(X)$. Then a polynomial belongs to C_2 if and only if it is divisible by $g(X)$ and by $X - 1$, that is, if and only if it is a polynomial of C_1 for which the sum of the coefficients is 0.

Another very important subclass of the class of BCH codes, the *Reed-Solomon codes*, is obtained by setting $m = m_0 = 1$. Let α be an element of $GF(q)$, and let n be the order of α. (If α is primitive, n is $q - 1$, the largest possible value.) Let $\{f(X)\}$ be a code vector if and only if $\alpha, \alpha^2, \ldots, \alpha^{d-1}$ are roots of $f(X)$. The minimum function of α^j is simply $X - \alpha^j$, and thus

$$g(X) = (X - \alpha)(X - \alpha^2)\cdots(X - \alpha^{d-1}) \tag{9.8}$$

and $g(X)$ has degree $d - 1$, and the result is a code with n symbols, $d - 1$ parity-check symbols, and minimum distance d.

Since $d = n - k + 1$ for Reed-Solomon codes, these codes are maximum-distance separable (Section 3.9). Thus their weight distributions are given by Equation 3.44.

Let $q = p^m$; then each q-ary symbol can be expressed as an m-tuple over $GF(p)$. Consequently a t-error-correcting $(q^m - 1, q^m - 1 - 2t)$ Reed-Solomon code over $GF(q)$ can be regarded as an

$$(m(q^m - 1), m(q^m - 1 - 2t))$$

code over $GF(p)$ capable of correcting any error pattern whose nonzero digits are confined to t m-symbol blocks. Some of the most powerful known burst-correcting codes and burst-and-random-correcting codes can be constructed using this idea, as discussed in Chapter 11.

Note that the dual of a Reed-Solomon code is also a Reed-Solomon code, but that this is not true in general for BCH codes.

9.3 The True Minimum Weight for BCH Codes

The BCH bound (Theorem 9.1) gives a lower bound on the minimum weight in BCH codes. Figure 9.1 seems to indicate that for any fixed rate the ratio of designed distance to code length approaches zero for primitive-length BCH codes as the code length approaches infinity. A natural question then is, is this true of the actual minimum weight, or are BCH codes significantly better than the BCH bound indicates? A number of theorems establishing minimum weight in BCH codes and other codes have been discovered recently (Kasami, Lin, and Peterson 1966; Berlekamp 1968*b*; Kasami and Tokura 1969; Peterson 1967; Lin and Weldon 1970; Chen and Lin 1969). Several key theorems are presented in this section; they are sufficient to answer the questions raised here.

The general method for establishing the minimum weight in a code is to exhibit or show the existence of a code word whose weight equals the known lower bound on minimum weight. One variation of this method is to find a cyclic product code which is a subcode of the given code and which contains a minimum-weight code word. (Cyclic product codes are discussed in Section 8.12.) The following theorem is based on this idea.

THEOREM 9.3. *Let n_1 and n_2 be relatively prime and a be a factor of n_1. If a BCH code of length n_2 and designed distance d over $GF(q)$ has minimum distance exactly d, then the BCH code of length n_1n_2 and designed distance ad has minimum distance exactly ad.*

Proof. Let C_2 be the code of length n_2 in the theorem, and let C_1 be the code of length n_1 for which $g_1(X) = (X^{n_1} - 1)/(X^a - 1)$, $h_1(X) = X^a - 1$. If α_1 is an element of order n_1, then $\alpha_1, \alpha_1^2, \alpha_1^3, \ldots, \alpha_1^{b-1}$ are roots of $g_1(X)$, where $b = n_1/a$, but α_1^b is a root of $h_1(X)$. By the BCH bound, C_1 has minimum weight at least b. However $g(X)$ itself has weight b, so the minimum weight of C_1 must be exactly b. For this code, $1, \alpha_1^b, \alpha_1^{2b}, \ldots, \alpha_1^{n_1-b}$ are roots of $h(X)$ and all other powers of α_1 are roots of $g(X)$.

Let α_2 be an element of order n_2 and let C_2 be the code generated by $g_2(X)$ which has $\alpha_2^a, \alpha_2^{2a}, \alpha_2^{3a}, \ldots, \alpha_2^{(d-1)a}$ but not α_2^{da} as roots. Since a is relatively prime to n_2, α_2^a is a primitive n_2th root of unity and can be used to define $g(X)$ in this manner.

Next consider the cyclic product code of C_1 and C_2. Since n_1 and n_2 are relatively prime, $\alpha = \alpha_1\alpha_2$ has order $n = n_1n_2$, and of the elements

$\alpha, \alpha^2, \alpha^3, \ldots$ the first one that is an element of $h(X)$ for the product code is α^{ad}, by the corollary to Theorem 8.19. Thus, $\alpha, \alpha^2, \ldots, \alpha^{ad-1}$ are roots of $g(X)$, and the product code is a subcode of the BCH code of length $n = n_1 n_2$ and designed distance ad. But since a code word of weight a exists in C_1, and by hypothesis one of weight d exists in C_2, one of weight ad must exist in the product code and hence in the BCH code that contains it, and ad must be the true minimum weight in the BCH code. Q.E.D.

The following corollaries result from taking $a = 1$ and $a = n_1$, respectively:

COROLLARY 9.2. *If n_1 and n_2 are relatively prime and a BCH code of designed distance d and length n_2 has minimum distance exactly d, then a BCH code of length $n_1 n_2$ and designed distance d has minimum distance exactly d.*

COROLLARY 9.3. *If n_1 and n_2 are relatively prime and a BCH code of designed distance d and length n_2 has minimum distance exactly d, then a BCH code of length $n_1 n_2$ and designed distance $n_1 d$ has minimum distance exactly $n_1 d$.*

Finally, the code consisting of n_2 repetitions of a single information symbol, with n_2 relatively prime to q, is a degenerate case of a BCH code of designed distance n_2 and true distance n_2. For that case the two corollaries reduce to the following:

COROLLARY 9.4. *If $n = n_1 n_2$, then a BCH code of length n and designed distance n_2 has minimum distance exactly n_2.*

Theorems 9.4 and 9.5 specify additional subclasses of BCH codes with known minimum weight. These results use ideas developed in Section 9.4.

LEMMA 9.1. *The power-sum symmetric functions S_h are zero for $1 \leqq h \leqq j$ if and only if the elementary symmetric functions σ_h are zero for all h which do not exceed j and are not divisible by p, the characteristic of the field.*

Proof. The "*only if*" part follows directly from Newton's identities, Equation 9.54. The "*if*" part is proved by induction using Newton's identities. Since $S_1 = \sigma_1$, it is certainly true for $j = 1$. Assume it is true for $j = j_0$. If $\sigma_i = 0$ for each i which is less than $j_0 + 1$ and not divisible by p, then by the induction hypothesis, $S_1, S_2, \ldots, S_{j_0}$ are all zero. It follows then from the first Newton identity which involves S_{j_0+1} that S_{j_0+1} is also zero. Q.E.D.

LEMMA 9.2. *The roots of $p(X) = X^j + a_1 X^{j-1} + \cdots + a_j$ are the location numbers of a code word of weight j in a BCH code of designed distance d and length n if and only if*

1. *$p(X)$ has j distinct roots in $GF(q^m)$*
2. *Each root has order n, and*
3. *$a_i = 0$ for each i less than d and relatively prime to p, the characteristic of the field.*

Proof. If these three conditions are met, the power-sum symmetric functions $S_1, S_2, \ldots, S_{d-1}$ of the roots are zero, by Lemma 9.1, and hence these are the location numbers of a code word. Conversely, if the roots of $p(X)$ are the location numbers of a code word, (1) and (2) are obviously satisfied, and since for any code word $S_1, S_2, \ldots, S_{d-1}$ must be zero, (3) follows from Lemma 9.1.

THEOREM 9.4. *For any h, $1 \leq h < m$, a primitive BCH code of length $n = q^m - 1$ and designed distance $d = q^h - 1$ has minimum distance exactly $q^h - 1$.*

Proof. Let $0, X_1, \ldots, X_{q^h-1}$ be any subspace of $GF(q^m)$ over $GF(q)$. Then, by Corollary 6.2, $p(X) = X(X - X_1) \cdots (X - X_{q^h-1})$ has the form $p(X) = X^{q^h} + a_1 X^{q^h-1} + \cdots + a_n X$. Therefore, $p(X)/X$ satisfies the hypotheses of Lemma 9.2 and there exists a code word of weight $q^h - 1$. Q.E.D.

This theorem is also a direct consequence of Theorems 10.9 and 10.10, which state that the generalized Reed-Muller codes are subcodes of BCH codes and have minimum distance that equals the BCH bound.

THEOREM 9.5. *Suppose that a primitive BCH code of length $q^m - 1$ and designed distance d_0 over $GF(q)$ has minimum weight exactly d_0, and suppose $d_0 + 1$ is divisible by p, the characteristic of the field. Then a primitive BCH code of length $q^m - 1$ and designed distance $(d_0 + 1)q^{m-h} - 1$ with $h \geq d_0$ has minimum weight exactly $(d_0 + 1)q^{m-h} - 1$. (Note that the condition that $d_0 + 1$ be divisible by p is satisfied for all binary primitive BCH codes.)*

Proof. By hypothesis and Lemma 9.2 there exists a polynomial $a(X) = a_0 + a_1X + \cdots + a_{d_0}X_{d_0}$ with d_0 roots in $GF(q^m)$ and for which $a_i = 0$ for each i less than d_0 and relatively prime to p, the characteristic of the field. Let U be any h-dimensional subspace of $GF(q^m)$ containing all the roots of $a(X)$. Since there are d_0 roots and $d_0 \leq h$, there certainly exist such subspaces. For this U, form the polynomial $\bar{g}(X)$ of Theorem 6.30. Note that because of the form of $\bar{g}(X)$, it is a linear mapping. The set of elements mapped into zero is therefore a subspace V of dimension $m - h$, and the set of elements mapped into each element of U is a distinct coset of V.

Now consider $a(\bar{g}(X))$. Each element of each of the d_0 cosets which $\bar{g}(X)$ maps into a root of $a(X)$ is a root of $a(\bar{g}(X))$. Therefore, $a(\bar{g}(X))$ has at least d_0q^{m-h} roots. But the degree of $a(\bar{g}(X))$ is d_0q^{m-h}, and therefore $a(\bar{g}(X))$ splits completely in $GF(q^m)$. Now, $Xa(X)$ has a linear term, and all other nonzero terms have exponents which are divisible by p, the characteristic of $GF(q)$. The same is true of $\bar{g}(X)$, and it follows that the same is true of $\bar{g}(X)a(\bar{g}(X))$. Therefore,

$$\bar{g}(X)a(\bar{g}(X))/X = X^j + b_1X^{j-1} + \cdots + b_j$$

where $j = (d_0 + 1)q^{m-h} - 1$, and $b_i = 0$ if i is not divisible by p. Furthermore, $\bar{g}(X)/X$ and $a(\bar{g}(X))$ both split completely. The roots of $\bar{g}(X)/X$ are the nonzero elements of V, and the roots of $a(\bar{g}(X))$ are d_0 cosets of V. Therefore, $\bar{g}(X)a(\bar{g}(X))$ splits completely and all its roots are distinct. The theorem then follows from Lemma 9.2. Q.E.D.

The following simple theorem covers many cases of minimum weight for BCH codes that correct relatively few errors:

THEOREM 9.6. (*Farr*) *If* $m > 1 + \log_2(t + 1)!$, *then a primitive binary BCH code of length* $2^m - 1$ *and designed distance* $2t + 1$ *has minimum weight exactly* $2t + 1$.

Only an outline of the proof will be given. It can be shown with some elementary but not simple algebraic manipulation that if $m > 1 + \log_2(t + 1)!$ then

$$\sum_{i=0}^{t+1} \binom{2^m - 1}{i} > \binom{2^m - 1}{t + 1} > 2^{mt}. \tag{9.9}$$

The left side is the number of error patterns or $t + 1$ or fewer errors, while the right side is an upper bound on the number of cosets in a BCH code of design distance $2t + 1$. Since a $(t + 1)$-error-correcting code must have every pattern of $t+1$ or fewer errors in a different coset, there are not enough cosets for the t-error-correcting code to correct $t+1$ errors. Thus the minimum distance for the code is less than $2(t+1)+1=2t+3$. It may be $2t+2$ or $2t+1$. Since the BCH codes of primitive length are invariant under the affine group, it follows from Theorem 8.15 that the minimum weight is odd.

Theorem 9.5 and Farr's Theorem can be combined to give a stronger theorem:

THEOREM 9.7. *If* $m > 1 + \log_2[(d_0+1)/2]!$ *and* $h \geqq d_0$, *then a primitive binary BCH code of length* $2^m - 1$ *and designed distance* $(d_0+1)2^{m-h} - 1$ *has minimum distance exactly* $(d_0+1)2^{m-h} - 1$.

Finally, the question of whether long BCH codes are significantly better than the BCH bound indicates is answered by the following theorem:

THEOREM 9.8. *The true minimum weight of a primitive BCH code with symbols from* $GF(q)$ *does not exceed* $qd_0 + q - 2$, *where* d_0 *is the designed distance.*

Proof. Let h be chosen so that $q^h - 1 \geqq d_0$ but $q^{h-1} - 1 < d_0$. Then, by Theorem 9.5, the BCH code of designed distance $q^h - 1$ has minimum distance exactly $q^h - 1$. But this code is contained in the code of designed distance d_0, and therefore the code of designed distance d_0 has in it code words of weight $q^h - 1$. Then its true minimum weight d does not exceed $q^h - 1$. Thus

$$d \leqq q^h - 1 = q(q^{h-1} - 1) + q - 1 < qd_0 + q - 1. \tag{9.10}$$

Q.E.D.

In the binary case, Theorem 9.8 implies that the BCH of designed distance d_0 has minimum weight no greater than $2d_0$. It appears in Figure 9.1 that the BCH bound approaches zero at a fixed rate as the code length approaches infinity. Mann (1962) has derived an expression for the number of information symbols in a binary BCH code with designed distance d_0. Examination of this formula shows that, in fact, the BCH bound does approach zero with increasing code length. It follows from Theorem 9.8 that for any fixed code rate, the rate of the minimum distance to code length approaches zero as n increases.

9.4 An Error-Correction Procedure

An error-correction procedure is described here for an arbitrary Bose-Chaudhuri-Hocquenghem code as described in Section 9.1. It will correct any combination of t_0 or fewer errors if $d_0 \geqq 2t_0 + 1$.

The first step in deriving an error-correction procedure is to describe what information the parity checks, which are the syndrome, give about the errors. Suppose that a code vector $f(X)$ is transmitted, and errors occur which result in a received vector $r(X) = f(X) + e(X)$. Then, consider the results of substituting $\alpha^{m_0}, \alpha^{m_0+1}, \ldots, \alpha^{m_0+2t_0-1}$ in the polynomial $r(X)$. Since $f(X)$ is a code vector and therefore has these elements as roots, the result is $e(\alpha^{m_0}), e(\alpha^{m_0+1}), \ldots, e(\alpha^{m_0+2t_0-1})$.

The error pattern $e(X)$ can be described by a list of values and locations of its nonzero components. The location will be given in terms of an *error-location number*, which is simply α^j for the $(n-j)$th symbol. Thus, each nonzero component of $e(X)$ is described by a pair of field elements, Y_i (the magnitude of the error), and X_i (the error-location number); Y_i is an element of $GF(q)$ and X_i an element of $GF(q^m)$. If v errors occur, there are v nonzero components of $e(X)$, and hence v pairs (X_i, Y_i) are required to describe the errors.

Then, in terms of the pairs (X_i, Y_i),

$$e(\alpha^j) = \sum_{i=1}^{v} Y_i X_i^j = S_j \tag{9.11}$$

and the values of $S_j = e(\alpha^j)$ are given by parity-check calculations for $m_0 \leqq j \leqq m_0 + 2t_0 - 1$. Note that

$$(S_j)^q = \left(\sum_{i=1}^{v} Y_i X_i^j\right)^q = \sum_{i=1}^{v} Y_i^q X_i^{jq} = \sum_{i=1}^{v} Y_i X_i^{jq} = S_{(jq)} \tag{9.12}$$

by Theorems 6.14 and 6.18.

There is a simplification in the binary case. Since Y_i is not 0, it must be 1. The location of the error is all one needs to know in order to correct it, and thus the error pattern is described completely by a list of error-location numbers.

The $2t_0$ quantities S_j, $m_0 \leqq j \leqq m_0 + 2t_0 - 1$, are calculated from the received vector, and in order to correct the errors, the pair (Y_i, X_i) must be found for each of the t_0 or fewer errors. The known and the desired quantities are related by the $2t_0$ equations

$$S_j = \sum_i Y_i X_i^j; \quad m_0 \leqq j \leqq m_0 + 2t_0 - 1 \tag{9.13}$$

and any method of solving these equations is the basis for an error-correction procedure.

The equations are nonlinear, and at first glance there appears to be no hope of a direct solution. There are only a finite number of possible solutions, and the correct solution could be found by simply trying all possible solutions. In interesting cases, however, there are simply too many possible solutions for this to be an effective method. There is, however, an effective compromise.

Suppose that $v \leqq t_0$ errors actually occur. These are described by v pairs (Y_i, X_i), for which neither Y_i nor X_i is 0. Then let the equation

$$(X + X_1)(X + X_2) \cdots (X + X_v) = X^v + \sigma_1 X^{v-1} + \cdots + \sigma_{v-1} X + \sigma_v \quad (9.14)$$

define the quantities $\sigma_1, \sigma_2, \ldots, \sigma_v$. These are the *elementary symmetric functions* of the X_i. Note that if $-X_i$ is substituted for X in Equation 9.14, both sides become zero. It turns out that the quantities S_j and σ_i are related by a set of linear equations, and thus it is feasible to solve for the σ_i. The X_i can then be found by substituting all field elements into Equation 9.14. Given the values of the X_i, the Equations 9.11 are linear in the Y_i, and can be solved.

The next step is to derive the relationship between the S_j and the σ_i, and to prove that a solution always exists. If both sides of Equation 9.14 are multiplied by $Y_i X_i^j$ and then $-X_i$ is substituted for X, the following equation results

$$Y_i X_i^j \sigma_v + Y_i X_i^{j+1} \sigma_{v-1} + \cdots + Y_i X_i^{j+v-1} \sigma_1 + Y_i X_i^{j+v} = 0 \quad (9.15)$$

Summing these equations for $1 \leqq i \leqq v$ and substituting from Equation 9.11 yield the relationship between the σ_i and S_j,

$$S_j \sigma_v + S_{j+1} \sigma_{v-1} + \cdots + S_{j+v-1} \sigma_1 + S_{j+v} = 0 \quad (9.16)$$

and all S are known for $m_0 \leqq j \leqq m_0 + 2t_0 - 1 - v$.

The question of whether or not Equations 9.16 can be solved is answered by the following theorem:

THEOREM 9.9. *The matrix*

$$\mathbf{M} = \begin{bmatrix} S_{m_0} & S_{m_0+1} & \cdots & S_{m_0+v-1} \\ S_{m_0+1} & S_{m_0+2} & \cdots & S_{m_0+v} \\ \vdots & \vdots & & \vdots \\ S_{m_0+v-1} & S_{m_0+v} & \cdots & S_{m_0+2v-2} \end{bmatrix} \quad (9.17)$$

is nonsingular if the quantities S_j are formed from exactly v nonzero *distinct pairs (Y_i, X_i). This matrix* **M** *is singular if it is formed from fewer than v nonzero pairs (Y_i, X_i).*

Proof. It may be checked by comparing with Equations 9.11 that

$$\mathbf{M} = \begin{bmatrix} 1 & 1 & \cdots & 1 \\ X_1 & X_2 & \cdots & X_v \\ \vdots & \vdots & & \vdots \\ X_1^{v-1} & X_2^{v-1} & \cdots & X_v^{v-1} \end{bmatrix}$$

$$\times \begin{bmatrix} Y_1 X_1^{mo} & 0 & \cdots & 0 \\ 0 & Y_2 X_2^{mo} & & 0 \\ \vdots & \vdots & \ddots & \vdots \\ 0 & 0 & & Y_v X_v^{mo} \end{bmatrix} \begin{bmatrix} 1 & X_1 & \cdots & X_1^{v-1} \\ 1 & X_2 & \cdots & X_2^{v-1} \\ \vdots & \vdots & & \vdots \\ 1 & X_v & \cdots & X_v^{v-1} \end{bmatrix} \tag{9.18}$$

The matrix **M** is nonsingular if and only if each of the matrices on the right side of Equation 9.18 is nonsingular. The first and last are Vandermonde matrices, and Equation 9.4 shows that they are nonsingular if and only if $X_1, X_2, \ldots, X_v$ are distinct. The middle factor is a diagonal matrix and is nonsingular if and only if each of the X_1 and Y_1 is nonzero. Thus, **M** is nonsingular if and only if the pairs (Y_i, X_i) are distinct and contain no zeros. Q.E.D.

In order to determine the error magnitudes Y_i from the power sums and error locations, it is necessary that v of the Equations 9.11 be linearly independent. Consider the first v equations

$$\begin{aligned} Y_1 X_1^{mo} + Y_2 X_2^{mo} + \cdots + Y_v X_v^{mo} &= S_{mo} \\ Y_1 X_1^{mo+1} + Y_2 X_2^{mo+1} + \cdots + Y_v X_v^{mo+1} &= S_{mo+1} \\ \vdots \\ Y_1 X_1^{mo+v-1} + Y_2 X_2^{mo+v-1} + \cdots + Y_v X_v^{mo+v-1} &= S_{mo+v-1} \end{aligned} \tag{9.19}$$

The determinant of the coefficients of the Y's is

$$\begin{vmatrix} X_1^{mo} & X_2^{mo} & \cdots & X_v^{mo} \\ X_1^{mo+1} & X_2^{mo+1} & \cdots & X_v^{mo+1} \\ \vdots \\ X_1^{mo+v-1} & X_2^{mo+v-1} & \cdots & X_v^{mo+v-1} \end{vmatrix}$$

$$= X_1^{mo} X_2^{mo} \cdots X_v^{mo} \begin{vmatrix} 1 & 1 & \cdots & 1 \\ X_1 & X_2 & \cdots & X_v \\ \vdots \\ X_1^{v-1} & X_2^{v-1} & \cdots & X_v^{v-1} \end{vmatrix} \tag{9.20}$$

and the determinant on the right is a Vandermonde determinant as in Equation 9.4. Therefore the right-hand side is nonzero as long as all the X_i are distinct and nonzero, which is clearly the case here. Consequently the Equations 9.19 are linearly independent and can be solved for the unknowns $Y_1, Y_2, \dots Y_v$, after $X_1, X_2, \dots X_v$ have been found. Equation 9.20 shows that these error values can be determined by means of a matrix inversion.

The error-correction procedure can be outlined as follows:

1. Calculate the quantities S_j, $m_0 \leqq j \leqq m_0 + 2t_0 - 1$ from the received vector. This amounts to a parity-check calculation.
2. Determine the maximum number of successive equations that are linearly independent. This is the number v of errors that actually occurred.
3. Set $\sigma_{v+1}, \sigma_{v+2}, \dots, \sigma_t$ all equal to zero and solve the first v equations for $\sigma_1, \sigma_2, \dots, \sigma_v$.
4. Substitute each of the nonzero elements of GF(q^m) in the polynomial

$$X^v - \sigma^1 X^{v-1} + \dots + \sigma_v \tag{9.21}$$

   The roots are the error-location numbers $X_1, X_2, \dots, X_v$.
5. (This step is unnecessary in the binary case.) Substitute the error-location numbers found in Step 4 into the first v Equations 9.11 and solve for the corresponding values of Y_i. The determinant of the matrix of coefficients has the same general form as Equation 9.4 and is therefore not zero. Thus, these equations are linearly independent. Knowledge of the values of X_i and Y_i is sufficient for correction.

Example. The binary Bose-Chaudhuri (15,5) code that corrects all combinations of three or fewer errors was considered in the previous example. Now suppose that two errors occur, in the positions corresponding to α^3 and α^{10}. Then the parity-check calculation for the received vector $\{r(X)\}$ gives (from Table 6.1)

$$\begin{aligned} S_1 &= r(\alpha) = (1\,1\,1\,1) = \alpha^{12} \\ S_3 &= r(\alpha^3) = (1\,1\,0\,1) = \alpha^7 \\ S_5 &= r(\alpha^5) = (0\,1\,1\,1) = \alpha^{10} \end{aligned} \tag{9.22}$$

and

$$\begin{aligned} S_2 &= S_1^2 = \alpha^9 = (1\,0\,1\,0) \\ S_4 &= S_2^2 = \alpha^3 = (1\,0\,0\,0) \\ S_6 &= S_3^2 = \alpha^{14} = (1\,0\,0\,1) \end{aligned} \tag{9.23}$$

Equations 9.16 become

$$\begin{aligned} \alpha^{12}\sigma_3 + \alpha^9\sigma_2 + \alpha^7\sigma_1 &= \alpha^3 \\ \alpha^9\sigma_3 + \alpha^7\sigma_2 + \alpha^3\sigma_1 &= \alpha^{10} \\ \alpha^7\sigma_3 + \alpha^3\sigma_2 + \alpha^{10}\sigma_1 &= \alpha^{14} \end{aligned} \tag{9.24}$$

Multiplying the first equation by $\alpha^8 = \alpha^{-7}$, the second by $\alpha^{12} = \alpha^{-3}$, and the third by $\alpha^5 = \alpha^{-10}$ yields

$$\alpha^5\sigma_3 + \alpha^2\sigma_2 + \sigma_1 = \alpha^{11}$$

$$\alpha^6\sigma_3 + \alpha^4\sigma_2 + \sigma_1 = \alpha^7$$

$$\alpha^{12}\sigma_3 + \alpha^8\sigma_2 + \sigma_1 = \alpha^4$$

Adding the first equation to each of the others then gives two equations with σ_1 eliminated:

$$\begin{aligned} (1010)\sigma_3 + (0111)\sigma_2 = (0101) \quad &\text{or} \quad \alpha^9\sigma_3 + \alpha^{10}\sigma_2 = \alpha^8 \\ (1001)\sigma_3 + (0001)\sigma_2 = (1101) \quad &\text{or} \quad \alpha^{14}\sigma_3 + \sigma_2 = \alpha^{13} \end{aligned} \tag{9.25}$$

These equations differ only by a factor α^5, and hence the latter is dependent on the former. Therefore, the last of the original three of Equations 9.23 must have been dependent on the first two, and there must have been only two errors. Setting $\sigma_3 = 0$ in Equations 9.25 gives $\alpha^{10}\sigma_2 = \alpha^8$, or $\sigma_2 = \alpha^{13}$. From any of Equations 9.24 σ_1 is found to be α^{12}, and the error-location numbers are roots of

$$X^2 + \alpha^{12}X + \alpha^{13} = 0 \tag{9.26}$$

It is easily verified that the elements α^3 and α^{10}, and only these, satisfy Equation 9.26. Since this is a binary code, knowledge of the error locations alone suffices for error correction—the erroneous symbols simply need to be changed.

As a second example, consider a Reed-Solomon code over the field GF(2^4), using the representation of the field given in Table 6.1. Suppose that an error equal to α^7 occurs in the location corresponding to the location α^3 and an error α^{11} in the location corresponding to α^{10}. Then

$$S_1 = \alpha^7\alpha^3 + \alpha^{11}\alpha^{10} = (1011) = \alpha^7$$

$$S_2 = \alpha^7\alpha^6 + \alpha^{11}\alpha^{20} = (1111) = \alpha^{12}$$

$$S_3 = \alpha^7\alpha^9 + \alpha^{11}\alpha^{30} = (1100) = \alpha^6$$

$$S_4 = \alpha^7\alpha^{12} + \alpha^{11}\alpha^{40} = (1111) = \alpha^{12}$$

$$S_5 = \alpha^7\alpha^{15} + \alpha^{11}\alpha^{50} = (1001) = \alpha^{14}$$

$$S_6 = \alpha^7\alpha^{18} + \alpha^{11}\alpha^{60} = (1001) = \alpha^{14}$$

and Equations 9.16 become

$$\begin{aligned} \alpha^7\sigma_3 + \alpha^{12}\sigma_2 + \alpha^6\sigma_1 &= \alpha^{12} \\ \alpha^{12}\sigma_3 + \alpha^6\sigma_2 + \alpha^{12}\sigma_1 &= \alpha^{14} \\ \alpha^6\sigma_3 + \alpha^{12}\sigma_2 + \alpha^{14}\sigma_1 &= \alpha^{14} \end{aligned} \tag{9.27}$$

Multiplying the first by $\alpha^9 = \alpha^{-6}$, the second by $\alpha^3 = \alpha^{-12}$, and the third by $\alpha = \alpha^{-14}$ yields

$$\alpha\sigma_3 + \alpha^6\sigma_2 + \sigma_1 = \alpha^6$$

$$\sigma_3 + \alpha^9\sigma_2 + \sigma_1 = \alpha^2$$

$$\alpha^7\sigma_3 + \alpha^{13}\sigma_2 + \sigma_1 = 1$$

and adding the first to each of the last two gives

$$\begin{aligned} (0011)\sigma_3 + (0110)\sigma_2 = (1000), &\quad \text{or} \quad \alpha^4\sigma_3 + \alpha^5\sigma_2 = \alpha^3 \\ (1001)\sigma_3 + (0001)\sigma_2 = (1101), &\quad \text{or} \quad \alpha^{14}\sigma_3 + \sigma_2 = \alpha^{13} \end{aligned} \tag{9.28}$$

Again these are dependent, so that fewer than three errors must have occurred. Setting $\sigma_3 = 0$ gives $\sigma_2 = \alpha^{13}$, and σ_1 is again easily found to be α^{12}. The error-location numbers satisfy

$$X^2 + \alpha^{12}X + \alpha^{13} = 0$$

as before, and the error locations are the two roots α^3 and α^{10}.

The error values Y_i are found from Equations 9.11,

$$Y_1X_1 + Y_2X_2 = S_1, \quad \text{or} \quad \alpha^3Y_1 + \alpha^{10}Y_2 = \alpha^7$$

$$Y_1X_1^2 + Y_2X_2^2 = S_2, \quad \text{or} \quad \alpha^6Y_1 + \alpha^{20}Y_2 = \alpha^{12}$$

and these equations can be solved easily to give $Y_1 = \alpha^7$ and $Y_2 = \alpha^{11}$.

9.5 Refinements of the Error-Correction Procedure

It is shown in Section 9.4 that error correction can be accomplished by a four-step procedure:

1. Calculation of the syndrome $S_1, S_2, \ldots, S_{2t_0}$.
2. Calculation of the $\sigma_1, \sigma_2, \ldots, \sigma_{t_0}$ from the S_j.
3. Calculation of the error locations X_i from the σ_i.
4. Calculation of the error values Y_i from the X_i and S_j.

Refinements of these computations for the last three steps have been found which greatly reduce the amount and complexity of the computation. They are described in this section for the general case. For the binary case, the fourth step is always unnecessary. The first and third steps simplify only because binary circuits are simpler to construct than are nonbinary, and the methods presented in this section for the case of $m_0 = 1$ are the best so far found. Step 2 simplifies significantly in the binary case. This is described in the next section.

Step 2, Calculation of the σ_1: (Berlekamp 1968*a*, Massey 1969)
The decoder is confronted with the problem of determining from Eq. (9.16) the σ_i, $1 \leqq i \leqq v \leqq t_0$, given the S_j, $1 \leqq j \leqq 2t_0$. This can be accomplished in an iterative fashion. At the nth step in the iteration the decoder considers only the first n power sums and attempts to determine a set of l_n values $\sigma_i^{(n)}$ such that the $n - l_n$ equations

$$\begin{aligned} S_n \quad &+ S_{n-1}\sigma_1^{(n)} + \cdots + S_{n-l_n}\sigma_{l_n}^{(n)} \quad = 0 \\ S_{n-1} &+ S_{n-2}\sigma_1^{(n)} + \cdots + S_{n-l_n-1}\sigma_{l_n}^{(n)} = 0 \\ &\vdots \qquad\qquad\qquad \vdots \\ S_{l_n+1} &+ S_{l_n}\sigma_1^{(n)} \quad + \cdots + S_1\sigma_{l_n}^{(n)} \qquad = 0 \end{aligned} \tag{9.29}$$

are satisfied and l_n is as small as possible, and hence the number of equations is maximized. [The superscript (n) serves to distinguish the solutions at the various stages.] It may be impossible at stage n to satisfy even one equation of the form of Equations 9.29. In this case, consider $n - l_n = 0$, that is, $n = l_n$, and consider any set of l_n σ's to be a solution.

It is convenient to represent this set of σ_i by the polynomial

$$\sigma(X)^{(n)} = \sigma_0^{(n)} + \sigma_1^{(n)}X + \sigma_2^{(n)}X^2 + \cdots + \sigma_{l_n}^{(n)}X^{l_n}$$

where $\sigma_0^{(n)} = 1$. This polynomial has degree l_n or less, and it is possible that $\sigma_{l_n}^{(n)}$ may be zero, and thus the true degree of $\sigma^{(n)}(X)$ may be less than l_n. At first sight it might appear that l_n could always be taken to be the degree of the minimal $\sigma^{(n)}(X)$. An example is given in this section of a minimal solution for $n = 3$ and $l_n = 2$, in which $\sigma(X)$ has degree $1 < l_n$. In this case, l_3 cannot be taken to be 1 because, although

$$S_3 + S_2\sigma^{(3)} = 0$$

it turns out that

$$S_2 + S_1\sigma_1^{(3)} \neq 0$$

Now, suppose that at the nth stage the decoder has determined $\sigma^{(n)}(X)$, with minimal l_n such that Equation 9.29 holds. At the $(n+1)$th stage, the decoder seeks to find the polynomial $\sigma^{(n+1)}(X)$ of lowest degree such that the equations

$$\sum_{i=0}^{l_{n+1}} S_{j-i}\sigma_i^{(n+1)} = 0; \qquad l_{n+1} + 1 \leqq j \leqq n + 1 \tag{9.30}$$

hold. Define the *nth discrepancy* d_n as

$$S_{n+1} + S_n\sigma_1^{(n)} + \cdots + S_{n+1-l_n}\sigma_{l_n}^{(n)} = d_n \tag{9.31}$$

If $d_n = 0$, then Equation 9.30 holds with $\sigma^{n+1}(X) = \sigma^n(X)$. And, since $\sigma^n(X)$ is presumably a minimal solution at the nth stage, it is certainly a minimal solution at the $(n+1)$th stage. Usually, however, $d_n \neq 0$ and the determination of $\sigma^{(n+1)}(X)$ from $\sigma^{(n)}(X)$ is not so straightforward. The following two lemmas are helpful in determining $\sigma^{(n+1)}(X)$.

Lemma 9.3. *Suppose that $\sigma^{(n)}(X)$ is a minimal polynomial solution for the first n power sums (that is, such that Equation 9.29 holds) and has next discrepancy $d_n \neq 0$. Let*

$$\sigma^{(m)}(X) = 1 + \sigma_1^{(m)}X + \sigma_2^{(m)}X^2 + \cdots + \sigma_{l_m}^{(m)}X^{l_m}$$

be any polynomial solution for the first m power sums, $1 \leqq m < n$, with next discrepancy $d_m \neq 0$. Then the polynomial

$$\sigma^{(n)}(X) - d_n d_m^{-1} X^{(n-m)}\sigma^{(m)}(X) = \sigma^{(n+1)}(X)$$

is a solution for the first $n+1$ power sums. Moreover,

$$l_{n+1} = \max\,[l_n, l_m + n - m].$$

Proof. Since $\sigma^{(n)}(X)$ is a solution for the first n power sums, Equation 9.29 holds. That is,

$$\begin{aligned}\sum_{i=0}^{l_n} S_{j-i}\sigma_i^{(n)} &= 0; \qquad l_n + 1 \leqq j \leqq n \\ &= d_n \neq 0; \qquad j = n + 1.\end{aligned} \tag{9.32}$$

Similarly, since $\sigma^{(m)}(X)$ is a solution for the first m power sums,

$$\begin{aligned}\sum_{i=0}^{l_m} S_{j-i}\sigma_i^{(m)} &= 0; \qquad l_m + 1 \leqq j \leqq m < n \\ &= d_m \neq 0; \qquad j = m + 1.\end{aligned} \tag{9.33}$$

If $\sigma^{(n+1)}(X) = \sigma^{(n)}(X) - d_n d_m^{-1} X^{n-m} \sigma^{(m)}(X)$ is to be a solution for the first $n + 1$ power sums, then it must be that

$$\sum_{i=0}^{l_{n+1}} S_{j-i} \sigma_i^{(n+1)} = 0; \qquad l_{n+1} + 1 \leqq j \leqq n + 1. \tag{9.34}$$

This sum has the form

$$\sum_{i=0}^{l_{n+1}} S_{j-i}(\sigma_i^{(n)} - d_n d_m^{-1} \sigma_{i-(n-m)}^{(m)}). \tag{9.35}$$

Since $\sigma_i^{(n)} = 0$ for $i < 0$ and $i > l_n$, and since $\sigma_i^{(m)} = 0$ for $i < 0$ and $i > l_m$, Sum 9.35 can be written as

$$\sum_{i=0}^{l_n} S_{j-i} \sigma_i^{(n)} - d_n d_m^{-1} \sum_{i=n-m}^{l_m+n-m} S_{j-i} \sigma_{i-(n-m)}^{(m)}. \tag{9.36}$$

For $j = n + 1$, the first sum has the value d_n and the second has the value d_m. Equation 9.36 reduces to $d_n - d_n d_m^{-1}(d_m) = 0$ and thus is true. By Equation 9.32, the first sum in Equation 9.36 has the value zero provided $l_n + 1 \leq j \leq n$. By Equation 9.33 the second sum in Equation 9.36 has the value zero provided $n = m + l_m + 1 \leq j \leq n - m + m = 1$. Thus Equation 9.36 is satisfied provided that

$$\max(l_n, n - m + l_m) + 1 \leq j \leq n + 1.$$

Since $n + 1 - \max(l_n,\ n - m + l_m)$, Equations 9.29 are satisfied by $\sigma^{(n+1)}(X)$; its degree is given formally by $l_{n+1} = \max(l_n, n - m - l_m)$. Note that the high-order coefficients of $\sigma^{(n+1)}(X)$ may be 0, therefore additional Equations 9.29 may be satisfied. That is, $\sigma^{n+1}(X)$ may not be minimal.

Q.E.D.

LEMMA 9.4. *Let* $\sigma^{(n)}(X)$, l_n *and* $d_n \neq 0$ *be defined as in Lemma 9.3. Suppose that* $\sigma^{(n+1)}(X)$ *is any solution polynomial of Equations 9.29 satisfying* $n + 1 - l_{n+1}$ *equations. Then let*

$$\sigma^{(n+1)}(X) - \sigma^{(n)}(X) = aX^{n-m}\sigma^{(m)}(X) \tag{9.37}$$

where $a \neq 0$ *and* $\sigma_0^{(m)} = 1$. *Then the polynomial* $\sigma^{(m)}(X)$ *is a solution polynomial for the first* $m - l_m$ *Equations 9.29 and has next discrepancy* $d_m \neq 0$, *and*

$$l_m = l_{n+1} - (n - m).$$

Proof. By hypothesis

$$\sum_{i=0}^{l_{n+1}} S_{j-i}\sigma_i^{(n+1)} = 0; \qquad l_{n+1}+1 \leqq j \leqq n+1 \tag{9.38}$$

and

$$\begin{aligned} \sum_{i=0}^{l_n} S_{j-i}\sigma_i^{(n)} &= 0; \qquad l_n+1 \leqq j \leqq n \\ &= d_n \neq 0; \qquad j = n+1 \end{aligned} \tag{9.39}$$

Since $\sigma^{(n)}(X)$ is a minimal solution, $l_{n+1} \geqq l_n$. Subtracting Equations 9.39 from 9.38 for $l_{n+1} \leqq j \leqq n+1$ gives

$$\begin{aligned} \sum_{i=0}^{l_{n+1}} S_{j-i}(\sigma_i^{(n+1)} - \sigma_i^{(n)}) &= 0; \qquad l_{n+1} \leqq j \leqq n \\ &= -d_n; \qquad j = n+1. \end{aligned} \tag{9.40}$$

Now, denote the first nonzero coefficient of S_{j-i} in Equation 9.40 by a, where the first $n-m$ coefficients are zero. (Note that since $\sigma_0^{(n+1)} = \sigma_0^{(n)} = 1$, $n > m$.) Then, Equation 9.40 reduces to

$$\begin{aligned} \sum_{i=n-m}^{l_{n+1}} S_{j-i}(\sigma_i^{(n+1)} - \sigma_i^{(n)}) &= 0; \qquad l_{n+1}+1 \leqq j \leqq n \\ &= -d_n; \qquad j = n+1. \end{aligned} \tag{9.40a}$$

Letting $j' = j - (n-m)$, $i' = i - (n-m)$, and $l_m = l_{n+1} - (n-m)$ gives

$$\begin{aligned} \sum_{i=0}^{l_m} S_{j'-i'}(\sigma_{i'+n-m}^{(n+1)} - \sigma_{i'+n-m}^{(n)}) &= 0; \qquad l_m+1 \leqq j' \leqq m \\ &= -d_n \neq 0; \qquad j' = m+1. \end{aligned} \tag{9.40b}$$

Finally, define the polynomial $\sigma^{(m)}(X)$ by $\sigma_{i'}^{(m)} = (\sigma_{i'+n-m}^{(n+1)} - \sigma_{i'+n-m}^{(n)})a^{-1}$. Thus,

$$\begin{aligned} \sum_{i=0}^{l_m} S_{j'-i'}\sigma_{i'}^{(m)} &= 0; \qquad l_m+1 \leqq j' \leqq m \\ &= d_n a^{-1} = d_m \neq 0; \qquad j' = m+1. \end{aligned} \tag{9.41}$$

By Equations 9.41, $\sigma^{(m)}(X)$ is a solution to the first $m - l_m$ Equations 9.29 and has next discrepancy $d_m \neq 0$. The degree of $\sigma^{(m)}(X)$ is given formally by its definition, $l_m = l_{n+1} - (n-m)$. Note that the high-order coefficients of $\sigma^{(m)}(X)$ may be 0 and that some Equations 9.29 not included in Equations 9.40b may also be satisfied. That is, $\sigma^{(m)}(X)$ may not be minimal. In any case the degree of $\sigma^{(m)}(X)$ can be taken to be $l_{n+1} - (n-m)$. Q.E.D.

THEOREM 9.10. *Let $\sigma^{(n)}(X)$ be a minimal solution at the nth stage; let $\sigma^{(m)}(X)$ be one of the prior minimal solutions, $1 \leqq m \leqq n$, with $d_m \neq 0$, such that $m - l_m$ has the largest value. Then a minimal solution at stage $n + 1$ is $\sigma^{(n+1)}(X)$, where*

$$\sigma^{(n+1)}(X) = \sigma^{(n)}(X) \text{ and } l_{n+1} = l_n; \qquad d_n = 0 \tag{9.42a}$$

$$\sigma^{(n+1)}(X) = \sigma^{(n)}(X) - d_n d_m^{-1} X^{n-m} \sigma^{(m)}(X) \tag{9.42b}$$

and

$$l_{n+1} = \max[l_n, l_m + n - m]; \qquad d_n \neq 0. \tag{9.43}$$

Proof. If $d_n = 0$, clearly $\sigma^{(n+1)}(X) = \sigma^{(n)}(X)$ since the latter is a minimal solution. Now consider the case where $d_n \neq 0$. Since $\sigma^{(m)}(X)$ and $\sigma^{(n)}(X)$ are known to the decoder, so is $\sigma^{(n+1)}(X)$ in Equation 9.42b. By Lemma 9.3, $\sigma^{(n+1)}(X)$ is a solution polynomial with degree given by Equation 9.43. It remains to show that this is a minimal solution. If $m - l_m \geqq n - l_n$, then $l_{n+1} = l_n$ by Lemma 9.3, and $\sigma^{(n+1)}(X)$ is a minimal solution at stage $n + 1$. If, on the other hand, $m - l_m < n - l_n$, then $l_{n+1} = \max[l_n, l_m + n - m] = l_m + n - m > l_n$. Assume that there exists a polynomial $D^{(n+1)}(X)$ of degree d where $l_n \leqq d < l_m + n - m$. There are two cases to consider. If $d = l_n$, then by Lemma 9.4, there is a solution $\sigma^{(m')}(X)$ with $m' - l_{m'} \geqq n - l_n$. But $m - l_m < n - l_n$, and $m - l_m$ was chosen to be the largest of the values $k - l_k$ for the previous solutions. On the other hand, if $d > l_n$, by Lemma 9.4, $d = l_{m'} + n - m'$. But since $m - l_m \geqq m' - l_{m'}$, $d = n - (m' - l_{m'}) \geqq n - (m - l_m) = l_{n+1} > d$, which is a contradiction. Thus, $\sigma^{(n+1)}(X)$ is a minimal solution.

Q.E.D.

Theorem 9.10 provides a means of determining a minimal solution at stage $n + 1$ given the solutions for all previous stages, provided at least one of the previous discrepancies is nonzero. To complete the algorithm, then, it is necessary to find one solution $\sigma^{(i)}(X)$ such that $d_i \neq 0$.

Take $\sigma^{(0)}(X) = 1$. If no errors occurred, this is the solution at every stage. If i, $1 \leq i \leq (d-1)/2$, errors occurred, then not all the S_j, $1 \leqq j \leqq 2t$, can be zero, because the resulting vector cannot be a code vector. Let v be the lowest value of j for which $S_j \neq 0$. Then, $\sigma^{(0)}(X) = \sigma^{(1)}(X) = \cdots = \sigma^{(v-1)}(X)$, but $d_{v-1} = S_v \neq 0$. Furthermore $l_0 = l_1 = \cdots = l_{v-1} = 0$. However no polynomial $\sigma^{(v)}(X)$ satisfies the equation

$$S_v + S_{v-1}\sigma_1^{(n)} + \cdots = 0$$

because $S_v \neq 0$, but $S_{v-1} = S_{v-2} = \cdots = 0$. Therefore, $v - l_v = 0$ equations are satisfied at the vth stage, l_v must be taken to be zero, and

$\sigma^{(v)}(X)$ is an arbitrary polynomial of degree $l_v = v$ or less. A satisfactory choice is $\sigma^{(v)}(X) = 1$. Given

$$\begin{aligned} &\sigma^{(v-1)}(X) = 1, \qquad l_{v-1} = 0, \qquad d_{v-1} = S_v \neq 0 \\ &\sigma^{(v)}(X) = 1, \qquad l_v = v, \qquad d_v = S_{v+1} \end{aligned} \tag{9.44}$$

it is possible to apply Theorem 9.10. Furthermore, since the first $v - 1$ power sums are zero, the error pattern has weight at least v by the BCH bound, and therefore the final solution cannot occur for $n < 2v$, and therefore some application of Theorem 9.10 will give the solution.

Consider the following rather artificial definitions:

$$\begin{aligned} &\sigma^{(-1)}(X) = 1, \qquad l_{-1} = 0, \qquad d_{-1} = 1 \\ &\sigma^{(0)}(X) = 1, \qquad l_0 = 0, \qquad d_0 = S_1. \end{aligned} \tag{9.45}$$

Assume again that $S_v \neq 0$ but $S_i = 0$ for $i < v$. Then applying Theorem 9.10 gives $\sigma^{(0)}(X) = \sigma^{(1)}(X) = \cdots = \sigma^{(v-1)}(X)$, and $d_{v-1} = S_v \neq 0$. Also, $l_0 = l_1 = \cdots = l_{v-1} = 0$ and

$$\begin{aligned} \sigma^{(v)}(X) &= \sigma^{(v-1)}(X) - d_{v-1} d_{-1}^{-1} X^{(v-1)-(-1)} \sigma^{(-1)}(X) \\ &= 1 - S_v X^v \end{aligned} \tag{9.46}$$

which, according to the preceding paragraph, is an acceptable choice for $\sigma^{(v)}(X)$. It also gives

$$l_v = \max\,(l_{v-1}, (v-1) - (-1) + l_{-1}) = v$$

which is the correct value for l_v. Proceeding from here using Theorem 9.10 then will give correct solutions at each stage. The initial conditions of Equations 9.45 may be easier to program, since no test is required to determine which S_i are zero.

Example. First let us consider the decoding of the Reed-Solomon code used as an example in Section 9.4. For the case considered there, $S_1 = \alpha^7$, $S_2 = \alpha^{12}$, $S_3 = \alpha^6$, $S_4 = \alpha^{12}$, $S_5 = \alpha^{14}$, and $S_6 = \alpha^{14}$. Starting with Equation 9.45

$$\sigma^{(-1)}(X) = 1, \qquad l_{-1} = 0, \qquad d_{-1} = 1$$

$$\sigma^{(0)}(X) = 1, \qquad l_0 = 0, \qquad d_0 = S_1 = \alpha^7 \neq 0$$

and applying Theorem 9.10 gives

$$\sigma^{(1)}(X) = 1 + \alpha^7 X, \qquad l_1 = 1$$

and

$$d_1 = S_2 \cdot 1 + S_1 \cdot \alpha^7 = \alpha^5.$$

Next taking $n = 1$, $m = 0$, and applying Theorem 9.10 again gives

$$\sigma^{(2)}(X) = 1 + \alpha^7 X + \alpha^5 \alpha^{-7} X = 1 + \alpha^5 X$$

and

$$l_2 = \max(l_1, 1 - 0 + l_0) = 1, \qquad d_2 = \alpha^3.$$

Since $1 - l_1 = 0 - l_0$, $m = 1$ and $m = 0$ are equally acceptable choices at the next stage, and the first gives

$$\sigma_a^{(3)}(X) = 1 + \alpha^5 X + \alpha^{11} X^2 \qquad d_3 = \alpha^2$$

while the second gives

$$\sigma_b^{(3)}(X) = 1 + \alpha^7(X) + \alpha^5 X^2 \qquad d_3 = \alpha^5$$

For either, $l_3 = \max(l_2, l_m + 2 - m) = 2$. And for either, at the next stage $n = 3$, $m = 2$, $l_4 = 2$, and

$$\sigma^{(4)}(X) = 1 + \alpha^{12} X + \alpha^{13} X^2$$

and $d_4 = d_5 = 0$. This is the correct $\sigma(X)$, the same as was found in Section 9.4.

Since the Equations 9.29 are linear, any linear combination $a\sigma_a^{(3)}(X) + b\sigma_b^{(3)}(X)$ is a solution, provided that $a + b = 1$ so that the constant term in the result is 1. It is possible to choose a and b so that the higher order coefficients cancel. Thus

$$\alpha^2 \sigma(_a^{(3)} X) + \alpha^8 \sigma_b^{(3)}(X) = 1 + \alpha^9 X = \sigma_c^{(3)}(X).$$

This is also a solution with $l_3 = 2$, for $S_3 + \alpha^9 S_2 = 0$, but $S_2 + \alpha^9 S_1 \neq 0$.

Finally, let us try an alternative set of initial conditions, Equation 9.44;

$$\sigma^{(0)}(X) = 1, \qquad l_0 = 0, \qquad d_0 = S_1 = \alpha^7 \neq 0$$

$$\sigma^{(1)}(X) = 1, \qquad l_1 = 1, \qquad d_1 = S_2 = \alpha^{12}$$

Then the next application of Theorem 9.10 gives for $n = 1$, $m = 0$,

$$\sigma^{(2)}(X) = 1 + \alpha^5 X, \qquad l_2 = 1, \qquad d_2 = \alpha^3.$$

Again there are two choices, $n = 2$, $m = 0$ or $n = 2$, $m = 1$. The first choice gives, as before,

$$\sigma^{(3)}(X) = 1 + \alpha^5 X + \alpha^{11} X^2, \qquad d_3 = \alpha^2, \qquad l_3 = 2$$

while the second gives

$$\sigma^{(3)}(X) = 1 + \alpha^9 X, \qquad d_3 = \alpha^{11}, \qquad l_3 = 2$$

which is the third solution for $\sigma^{(3)}(X)$ just shown. Either of these choices of $\sigma^{(3)}X$ leads to the unique correct $\sigma^{(4)}X$ which is the final answer.

Step 3, Determination of the error locations:
Given the σ_i, $1 \leqq i \leqq \nu \leqq t$, where ν equals the number of errors which actually occurred, it is a relatively simple matter to determine the ν error locations from Equation 9.14. It is necessary merely to substitute all n possible nonzero error locations for X. If

$$\sigma_\nu + \sigma_{\nu-1}X + \cdots + \sigma_1 X^{\nu-1} + X^\nu \Big|_{X=\alpha^l} = 0 \tag{9.47}$$

then α^l is an error location; otherwise it is not. This procedure can be implemented in a straightforward manner by means of a *Chien search* (Chien 1964*b*).

Since code words are transmitted high-order digit first, it is convenient to perform the first test on location α^{n-1}. Now α^{n-1} is a root of

$$\sigma_\nu + \sigma_{\nu-1}X + \cdots + \sigma_1 X^{\nu-1} + X^\nu, \tag{9.48}$$

if and only if 1 is a root of the polynomial

$$\alpha^\nu\sigma_\nu + \alpha^{\nu-1}\sigma_{\nu-1}X + \cdots + \alpha\sigma_1 X^{\nu-1} + X^\nu \tag{9.49}$$

Thus, to test position α^{n-1} the decoder forms the coefficients $\alpha^\nu\sigma_\nu$, $\alpha^{\nu-1}\sigma_{\nu-1}, \ldots, \alpha\sigma_1$ and then adds them. If they add to the unity, α^{n-1} is an error location; otherwise it is not.

To test location α^{n-2}, each coefficient $\alpha^i\sigma_i$ must be multiplied by α^i. Then, the new coefficients are added, and if they add to 1, α^{n-2} is an error location. If they do not, the second received digit is correct.

In general, α^{n-j} is an error location if and only if

$$\sum_{i=0}^{\nu} \alpha^{ij}\sigma_i = 1.$$

Thus, at each step it is necessary only to multiply the ith coefficient $\alpha^{ij}\sigma_i$ by α^i for $1 \leqq i \leqq \nu$ in order to obtain the next set of coefficients. This computation can be implemented quite readily with shift registers of the type described in Section 7.2. The details are given in Chien (1964*b*).

Step 4, Calculation of the Error Magnitudes (Forney 1965)
The error values Y_i can be calculated efficiently using equations derived

in this section. Define the elementary symmetric functions σ_{jl} of the error-location numbers $X_1, X_2, \cdots, X_{j-1}, X_{j+1}, \cdots, X_v$ by

$$\prod_{l\neq j}(X - X_l) = \sum_{l=0}^{v-1}(-1)^l \sigma_{jl} X^{v-1-l}, \tag{9.50}$$

Equation 9.14 can be written as

$$\prod_{i=1}^{v}(X - X_i) = \sum_{l}^{v}(-1)^l \sigma_l X^{v-l} \tag{9.51}$$

where σ_0 is always equal to unity. These two equations give

$$(X - X_j)\sum_{l=0}^{v-1}(-1)^l \sigma_{jl} X^{v-1-l} = \sum_{i=0}^{v} \sigma_i X^{v-i}$$

and upon equating coefficients

$$\sigma_l = \sigma_{jl} - X_j \sigma_{j(l+1)}. \tag{9.52}$$

This permits the determination of the σ_{jl} recursively from the known X_l and σ_l, because $\sigma_{j0} = 1$. Now

$$\sum_{l=0}^{v-1}(-1)^l \sigma_{jl} S_{v-l} = \sum_{l=0}^{v-1}(-1)^l \sigma_{jl} \sum_{i=1}^{v} Y_i X_i^{v-l}$$

$$= \sum_{i=1}^{v} Y_i X_i \sum_{l=0}^{v-1}(-1)^l \sigma_{jl} X_i^{v-l}$$

which, by Equation 9.50 gives

$$\sum_{l=0}^{v-1}(-1)^l \sigma_{jl} S_{v-l} = \sum_{i=1}^{v} Y_i X_i \prod_{m\neq j}(X_i - X_m).$$

In the sum on the right, only the term for which $i = j$ is nonzero, and therefore,

$$\sum_{l=0}^{v-1}(-1)^l \sigma_{jl} S_{v-l} = Y_j X_j \prod_{m\neq j}(X_j - X_m)$$

and by Equation 9.50 again

$$\sum_{l=0}^{v-1}(-1)^l \sigma_{jl} S_{v-l} = Y_j \sum_{l=0}^{v-1}(-1)^l \sigma_{jl} X_j^{v-l}.$$

Thus the error magnitudes can be computed from the formula

$$Y_j = \frac{\sum_{l=0}^{v-1}(-1)^l \sigma_{jl} S_{v-l}}{\sum_{l=0}^{v-1}(-1)^l \sigma_{jl} X_j^{v-l}}. \tag{9.55}$$

Example. For the example of decoding a Reed-Solomon code in Section 9.4, $S_1 = \alpha^7$, $S_2 = \alpha^{12}$, $\sigma_1 = \alpha^{12}$, $\sigma_2 = \alpha^{13}$, $X_1 = \alpha^3$, and $X_2 = \alpha^{10}$. From Equation 9.52, $\sigma_{10} = \sigma_{20} = 1$, $\sigma_{11} = \sigma_1 + X_1 = \alpha^{10}$, and $\sigma_{21} = \sigma_1 + X_2 = \alpha^3$. Then, from Equation 9.53,

$$Y_1 = \frac{\sigma_{10} S_2 + \sigma_{11} S_1}{\sigma_{10} X_1^2 + \sigma_{11} X_1} = \alpha^7, \qquad Y_2 = \frac{\sigma_{20} S_2 + \sigma_{21} S_1}{\sigma_{20} X_2^2 + \sigma_{21} X_2} = \alpha^{11}.$$

It is important to determine, at least approximately, the complexity of the machine necessary to decode BCH codes. Step 1, the calculation of the weighted power sums, requires $2t_0$ m-stage q-ary feedback shift registers. The calculation, which is customarily performed as the word enters the decoder, takes n clock cycles to complete.

Step 2, the determination of the normalized elementary symmetric functions, is performed in $2t_0$ stages. At each stage it is necessary, in general, to calculate a new solution polynomial from the previous solution and one prior solution. Each polynomial has degree t_0 or less. Thus, in addition to a central arithmetic unit capable of dividing,* adding, subtracting, and multiplying in $GF(q^m)$, t_0 auxiliary arithmetic units capable only of adding and multiplying are necessary. Thus, roughly $4mt_0$ additional stages of shift register are required. Each stage requires one multiply-add operation, so a total of $2mt_0$ clock cycles are needed for Step 2.

Step 3, the calculation of the error locations, is performed in n stages (or perhaps only k stages if only information symbols are corrected). Each stage involves t_0 fixed-element multiplications and an addition. Thus, the total time required is roughly mn clock cycles. A total of t_0 registers are necessary for this step.

Step 4, the calculation of the error magnitudes involves first determining the σ_{jl} from Equation 9.50, and then determining the error values from Equation 9.53. Since t_0 arithmetic units are available, the first of these two operations requires $2mt_0$ clock cycles for each error; the second, $4mt_0$. Thus a total of $6mt_0$ clock cycles are necessary in all. Also t_0 additional m-stage shift registers must be used. Table 9.2 summarizes the foregoing estimates.

For a primitive BCH code, $m \approx \log_q n$. If t_0 is taken as an, $0 < a < 0.25$, then

$$\text{Number of register stages} = n(2 + 7a \log_q n)$$

$$\text{Number of clock cycles} = n(1 + \log_q n\,(1 + 8a))$$

* A recent paper by Burton (1970) shows that in the binary case at least, division is unnecessary.

Table 9.2. Complexity of Major Steps in BCH Decoding Using a Special-Purpose Computer

Operation	Register Stages	Clock Cycles
Step 1: Calculate S_j	$2mt_0$	n
Step 2: Calculate σ_i	$4mt_0$	$2mt_0$
Step 3: Calculate X_i	mt_0	mn
Step 4: Calculate Y_i	mt_0	$6mt_0$
Word Store	$2n$	—
Totals	$2n + 8mt_0$	$(1 + m)n + 8mt_0$

Thus, both the speed and size of the decoder increase as $n \log_q n$. For large n then, complexity increases only slightly faster than linearly with block length.

The previous calculations have assumed a machine with t_0 arithmetic units. If a general rather than special-purpose computer is employed, the one arithmetic unit must do the work of t_0, and so operating speed must increase as $n^2 \log_q n$.

9.6 Simplifications in the Binary Case

Decoding binary BCH codes is simpler in three ways than decoding nonbinary codes. First of all, the circuitry employed is simpler since digital circuits use two-valued logic. Second, Step 4 in the algorithm is unnecessary because all errors have magnitude one. Finally, Step 2 can be performed in t_0 rather than $2t_0$ steps. The remainder of this section is devoted to proving this last assertion.

The equations relating the syndrome and the error locations and magnitudes, Equation 9.11, simplify in the binary case because every Y_i must equal 1. Thus, when $m_0 = 1$,

$$S_j = \sum X_i^j, \qquad 1 \leqq j \leqq 2t_0.$$

The S_j are symmetric functions in the X's, known as "power-sum symmetric functions." Thus the syndrome gives the first $2t_0$ power-sum symmetric functions. The elementary symmetric functions σ_i are related to the power-sum symmetric functions S_j by Newton's identities.*

* See, for example, Muir and Metzler (1930); Riordan (1958); and van der Waerden (1949).

$$\begin{aligned}
&S_1 - \sigma_1 = 0 \\
&S_2 - S_1\sigma_1 + 2\sigma_2 = 0 \\
&S_3 - S_2\sigma_1 + S_1\sigma_2 - 3\sigma_3 = 0 \\
&S_4 - S_3\sigma_1 + S_2\sigma_2 - S_1\sigma_3 + 4\sigma_4 = 0 \\
&\qquad\vdots
\end{aligned} \tag{9.54}$$

Thus, for the binary case, the second step in the decoding procedure might be accomplished by solving these equations, if that is possible. Now if $v \leq t_0$ errors occurred, then $\sigma_i = 0$ for $i > v$. Then, the following theorem shows that Equations 9.43 can be solved for the σ_i given the S_j.*

THEOREM 9.11. *The $v \times v$ matrix*

$$\mathbf{M}_v = \begin{bmatrix} 1 & 0 & 0 & 0 & \cdots & 0 \\ S_2 & S_1 & 1 & 0 & \cdots & 0 \\ S_4 & S_3 & S_2 & S_1 & \cdots & 0 \\ \vdots & \vdots & \vdots & \vdots & & \vdots \\ S_{2v-4} & S_{2v-5} & S_{2v-6} & S_{2v-7} & \cdots & S_{v-3} \\ S_{2v-2} & S_{2v-3} & S_{2v-4} & S_{2v-5} & \cdots & S_{v-1} \end{bmatrix} \tag{9.55}$$

is nonsingular if the power-sum symmetric functions S_j are power sums of v or $v-1$ distinct field elements and is singular if the S_j are sums of fewer than $v-1$ distinct field elements.

The proof requires the following two lemmas:

LEMMA 9.5. *If the S_j are power sums of fewer than v distinct field elements, M_v is singular.*

Proof.

$$\mathbf{M}_v \begin{bmatrix} 0 \\ 1 \\ \sigma_1 \\ \vdots \\ \sigma_{v-2} \end{bmatrix} = \begin{bmatrix} 0 \\ 0 \\ 0 \\ \vdots \\ 0 \end{bmatrix}$$

by Newton's identities, Equation 9.54, and thus $\mathbf{M}_v$ must be singular.

Q.E.D.

LEMMA 9.6. *If the S_j are power sums of v indeterminants $X_1, \ldots, X_v$, then the determinant*

$$|\mathbf{M}_v| = \prod_{j<i} (X_i + X_j)$$

* Similar results for a real field appear, for example in Foulkes, 1956.

Proof. If $X_i = X_j$, all of the power sums contain two identical terms, which cancel because the field has characteristic 2. Then, it is just as if there were no more than $\nu - 2$ distinct elements used in forming the power sums, and, by Lemma 9.5, the determinant is zero. Therefore, X_i X_j is a factor of the determinant for all i and j, and the left-hand side must be divisible by the right-hand side. The left-hand side is homogeneous of degree $\nu(\nu - 1)/2$, the same as the right-hand side, and therefore they must differ at most by a constant factor.

To determine the constant factor, a single special case suffices. If ν is odd, let the X_i be the roots of the equation

$$X^\nu - 1 = 0$$

Then

$$\begin{aligned} \sum X_i^j = S_j &= 0 \qquad \text{if } j \not\equiv 0 \bmod \nu \\ &= 1 \qquad \text{if } j \equiv 0 \bmod \nu \end{aligned}$$

There is exactly one 1 in each row and each column in Equation 9.55, and it follows that $|\mathbf{M}_\nu| = 1$ in this case. For ν even, letting the X_i be all of the roots of the equation

$$X^\nu - X = 0$$

gives the same result. The constant factor, which could be only 0 or 1, must be 1. Q.E.D.

Now Theorem 9.11 follows from the fact that if the determinant $|\mathbf{M}_\nu|$ is zero, it must be that some $X_i = X_j$. Since all the nonzero X_i must be distinct, $X_i = X_j = 0$, and there are fewer than $\nu - 1$ errors.

Q.E.D.

This result shows that the σ_i can be calculated from the S_j provided t_0 or fewer errors occurred, by attempting to solve the first t_0 Equations 9.54. If t_0 or $t_0 - 1$ errors occur, a solution will be obtained by inverting $\mathbf{M}_{t_0}$; otherwise, the number of equations is reduced by 2 and the procedure is repeated. Ultimately, a solution will be obtained in this manner.

Fortunately, a version of the iterative algorithm of Section 9.5 applies to Equations 9.54 and the need for successive attempts to solve these equations is eliminated. Consider the first t_0 equations

$$\begin{aligned} &S_1 \sigma_0 + \sigma_1 = 0 \\ &S_3 \sigma_0 + S_2\sigma_1 + S_1\sigma_2 + \sigma_3 = 0 \\ &\vdots \\ &S_{2t_0-3}\sigma_0 + S_{2t_0-4}\sigma_1 + \cdots + S_{2t_0-3-\nu}\sigma_\nu = 0 \\ &S_{2t_0-1}\sigma_0 + S_{2t_0-2}\sigma_1 + \cdots + S_{2t_0-1-\nu}\sigma_\nu = 0 \end{aligned} \qquad (9.56)$$

where $\sigma_0 = 1$. In general, these equations have many solutions if v is allowed to be arbitrarily large. When v is restricted to be not greater than t_0 however, Theorem 9.11 shows that there is only one solution; that is, all other solutions involve more than t_0, and in fact more than $2t_0 - v$, elements σ_i.

It is convenient to represent the σ_i by means of the polynomial

$$\sigma(X) = \sigma_0 + \sigma_1 X + \sigma_2 X^2 + \cdots + \sigma_l X^l$$

Thus, the decoder's problem is to find the lowest-degree polynomial $\sigma(X)$ such that Equations 9.56 hold with $\sigma_0 = 1$. This can be done iteratively; at stage n the decoder considers only the first n equations and determines a polynomial of minimum degree

$$\sigma^{(n)}(X) = \sigma_0 + \sigma_1^{(n)} X + \sigma_2^{(n)} X^2 + \cdots + \sigma_{l_n}^{(n)} X^{l_n}$$

such that these equations hold. The degree l_n is not greater than n. At stage $n + 1$, this result and previous minimal solutions are used to find $\sigma^{(n+1)}(X)$, the next minimal solution. Upon reaching state v, *the* minimal solution is obtained, for by Theorem 9.11 there is only one solution of degree v. This solution remains unchanged for n greater than v and less than or equal to t_0.

The following lemmas are useful in proving the preceding assertions.

LEMMA 9.7. *Let $\sigma^{(n)}(X)$ be a minimal solution of degree $l_n \leqq n$ to the first n Equations* 9.56 *and let $d_n \neq 0$ be the value of the left side of the* $(n + 1)$*th equation; call this quantity the nth discrepancy. Let $\sigma^{(m)}(X) = 1 + \sigma_1^{(m)} X + \cdots + \sigma_{l_m}^{(m)} X^{l_m}$ be any solution to the first $m < n$ equations with mth discrepancy $d_m \neq 0$. Then the polynomial*

$$\sigma^{(n)}(X) + d_n d_m^{-1} X^{2(n-m)} \sigma^{(m)}(X) = \sigma^{(n+1)}(X) \tag{9.57}$$

is a solution for the first $n + 1$ power sums. Moreover, the degree of $\sigma^{(n+1)}(X)$ is

$$l_{n+1} = \max [l_n, l_m + 2(n - m)].$$

Proof. Since $\sigma^{(n)}(X)$ is a solution for the first n Equations 9.56

$$\begin{aligned} \sum_{i=1}^{2j-1} S_i \sigma_{2j-1-i}^{(n)} + \sigma_{2j-1}^{(n)} &= 0; \qquad j = 1, 2, \ldots, n \\ &= d_n; \qquad j = n + 1 \end{aligned} \tag{9.58}$$

where $\sigma_i^{(n)} = 0$ if $i > l_n$ and $\sigma_0^{(n)} = 1$. Similarly, since $\sigma^{(m)}(X)$ is a solution for the first m equations with $d_m \neq 0$,

$$\begin{aligned} \sum_{i=1}^{2j-1} S_i \sigma_{2j-1-i}^{(m)} + \sigma_{2j-1}^{(m)} &= 0; \qquad j = 1, 2, \ldots, m \\ &= d_m; \qquad j = m + 1 \end{aligned} \tag{9.59}$$

where $\sigma^{(m)} = 0$ if $i > l_m$. Now consider

$$\sum_{i=1}^{2j-1} S_i \sigma_{2j-1-i}^{(n+1)} + \sigma_{2j-1}^{(n+1)}$$

$$= \sum_{i=1}^{2j-1} S_i(\sigma_{2j-1-i}^{(n)} + d_n d_m^{-1} \sigma_{2j-2(n-m)-1-i}^{(m)})$$

$$+ \sigma_{2j-1}^{(n)} + d_n d_m^{-1} \sigma_{2j-1-2(n-m)}^{(m)}$$

$$= \sum_{i=1}^{2j-1} S_i \sigma_{2j-1-i}^{(n)} + \sigma_{2j-1}^{(n)}$$

$$+ d_n d_m^{-1} \left(\sum_{i=1}^{2j-1} S_i \sigma_{2j-2(n-m)-1-i}^{(m)} + \sigma_{2j-1-2(n-m)}^{(m)} \right)$$

Since $\sigma_i^{(m)} = 0$ for $i < 0$, by Equations 9.58 and 9.59 this is zero for $j = 1, 2, \ldots, n$, and also for $j = n + 1$; thus, it is a solution of the first $n + 1$ Equations 9.56.

In Equation 9.57 the degree of the first term is l_n, and the degree of the second is $l_m + 2(n - m)$. If $l_m + 2(n - m) > l_n$, clearly the degree of $\sigma^{(n+1)}(X)$ is $l_m + 2(n - m)$; and if $l_m + 2(n - m)$ is less than l_n, the degree is l_n. In the case of equality the degree does not exceed l_n, but since $\sigma^{(n)}(X)$ is a solution of minimum degree, the degree of $\sigma^{(n+1)}(X)$ can not be less than l_n. Q.E.D.

LEMMA 9.8. *Let $\sigma^{(n)}(X)$ be a minimal solution of degree l_n and with $d_n \neq 0$. Suppose $\sigma^{(n+1)}(X)$ is any solution polynomial of Equations 9.56 satisfying the first n equations. Let*

$$\sigma^{(n+1)}(X) - \sigma^{(n)}(X) = aX^{n-m}\sigma^{(m)}(X)$$

where $a \neq 0$ and $\sigma_0^{(m)} = 1$. Then the polynomial $\sigma^{(m)}(X)$ is a solution polynomial for the first m equations and has next discrepancy $d_m \neq 0$, and

$$l_m = l_{n+1} - 2(n - m), \text{ if } l_{n+1} > l_n$$

$$l_m < l_n - 2(n - m), \text{ if } l_{n+1} = l_n.$$

Proof. By hypothesis,

$$\sum_{i=1}^{2j-1} S_i \sigma_{2j-1-i}^{(n+1)} + \sigma_{2j-1}^{(n+1)} = 0; \qquad = 1, 2, \ldots, n + 1$$

$$\sum_{i=1}^{2j-1} S_i \sigma_{2j-1-i}^{(n)} + \sigma_{2j-1}^{(n)} = 0; \qquad j = 1, 2, \ldots, n$$

$$= d_n \neq 0; \qquad j = n + 1$$

Subtracting gives

$$\sum_{i=1}^{2j-1} S_i[\sigma_{2j-1-i}^{(n+1)} - \sigma_{2j-1-i}^{(n)}] + \sigma_{2j-1}^{(n+1)} - \sigma_{2j-1}^{(n)} = 0; \qquad j = 1, 2, \ldots, n$$
$$= d_n \neq 0; \qquad j = n + 1. \tag{9.60}$$

Therefore, the set of numbers

$$\sigma_i = \sigma_i^{(n+1)} - \sigma_i^{(m)}$$

satisfies the Equations 9.56 at stage n with nonzero discrepancy, except that $\sigma_0 = \sigma_0^{(n+1)} - \sigma_0^{(n)} = 0$. In general, if the first l coefficients are zero and l is odd, Equation 9.56 requires that the $(l + 1)$st coefficient be zero also. Let m be the smallest integer such that the first $2(n - m)$ coefficients σ_i are zero, and let a denote the first nonzero coefficient. Then Equation 9.60 can be written

$$\sum_{i=1}^{2j-1-2(n-m)} S_i\sigma_{2j-1-i} + \sigma_{2j-1} = 0; \qquad j = n - m + 1, n - m + 2, \ldots, n$$
$$= d_n \neq 0; \qquad j = n + 1 \tag{9.61}$$

Now define

$$\sigma_i^{(m)} = a^{-1}\sigma_i + (n - m)$$
$$d_m = a^{-1}d_n$$

and set $j = j - (n - m)$ in Equation 9.61. The result is

$$\sum_{i=1}^{2j-1} S_i\sigma_{2j-1-i}^{(m)} + \sigma_{2j-1}^{(m)} = 0; \qquad j = 1, 2, \ldots, m$$
$$= d_m \neq 0; \qquad j = m + 1$$

Now if $l_{n+1} > l_n$, then clearly $l_m = l_{n+1} - 2(n - m)$. If $l_{n+1} = l_n$ and if then the high-order coefficients of $\sigma^{(n)}(X)$ and $\sigma^{(n+1)}(X)$ are different, then a linear combination of these two solutions yields another solution of degree less than l_n, which is impossible. Thus, if $l_{n+1} = l_n$, $l_m < l_n - 2(n - m)$. Q.E.D.

THEOREM 9.12. *Let $\sigma^{(n)}(X)$ be a minimal solution at the nth stage; let $\sigma^{(m)}(X)$ be one of the prior minimal solutions, $1 \leqq m < n$, with*

$d_m \neq 0$ such that $2m - l_m$ has the largest value. Then a minimal solution at stage $n + 1$ is given by

$$\sigma^{(n+1)}(X) = \sigma^{(n)}(X); \qquad d_n = 0$$

$$= \sigma^{(n)}(X) + d_n d_m^{-1} X^{2(n-m)} \sigma^{(m)}(X); \qquad d_n \neq 0 \tag{9.62}$$

In the latter case, $\sigma^{(n+1)}(X)$ has degree

$$l_{n+1} = \max\,[l_n, l_m + 2(n - m)] \tag{9.63}$$

Proof. If $d_n = 0$, clearly $\sigma^{(n+1)}(X)$ is a minimal solution, since $\sigma^{(n)}(X)$ is minimal.

If $d_n \neq 0$, then by Lemma 9.7, $\sigma^{(n+1)}(X)$ is a solution with degree l_{n+1} given by Equation 9.63. It remains to show that this is a minimal solution.

If $l_n \geqq l_m + 2(n - m)$, then by Lemma 9.7, $l_{n+1} = l_n$ and $\sigma^{(n+1)}(X)$ is clearly minimal.

If $l_n < l_m + 2(n - m)$, then $l_{n+1} = l_m + 2(n - m)$. Assume that there exists a polynomial $D^{(n+1)}(X)$ of degree d where $l_n \leqq d < l_m + 2(n - m)$, or $2n - d > 2m - l_m$. Now if $d = l_n$, then by Lemma 9.8 there is a solution at some stage m' with $2m' - l_{m'} > 2n - l_n$. But $2m' - l_{m'} < 2n - l_n$ since by hypothesis, m was chosen to make $2m - l_m$ the largest such value for all prior solutions. Thus, $d \neq l_n$.

Now, if $d > l_n$, then by Lemma 9.8, $d = l_{m'} + 2(n - m')$, or $2n - d = 2m' - l_{m'}$. This implies that $2m' - l_{m'} > 2m - l_m$, contradicting the hypothesis that m was chosen to maximize $2m - l_m$. Thus, no polynomial $D^{(n+1)}(X)$ exists and the theorem is proved. Q.E.D.

9.7 Correction of Erasures and Errors

In some situations it is desirable for the decoder to correct erasures in addition to errors. If the code has designed distance d_0 and e erasures occur and if

$$d_0 = 2t + e + 1, \tag{9.64}$$

then these erasures and up to t errors can be corrected. (See Problem 1.5.)

To the decoder, an erasure is just an error whose location is known and whose magnitude may or may not be zero. For binary codes, combined error and erasure correction is straightforward. First, the decoder attempts to decode the received word with arbitrary values, say zeros, substituted for the e erasures. Then it complements these values and again attempts to decode. Suppose f, $0 \leqq f \leqq e$, of the initial guesses were incorrect; then $e - f$ of their complements will be incorrect.

Since min $(f, e-f) \leqq e/2$, in one of the two cases the total number of errors will not be greater than $(d_0 - 1)/2$. Thus, this error pattern is correctable with the procedure described in Section 9.4.

Now in the other case, a total of $t + \max[e, e-f]$ errors must be corrected. If it happens that this does not exceed $(d_0 - 1)/2$, then correct decoding results here as well. Otherwise the total number of errors exceeds the correction capability of the decoder, and since $2t + e < d_0$, a legitimate code word cannot result.

This technique does not generalize in a simple way to nonbinary codes however, for each erasure magnitude can take on $q > 2$ values and a substantial number of guesses is required to guarantee that at least half are correct. (See Problem 9.9.) However, the algorithm of Section 9.4 can be modified to correct both erasures and errors.

Suppose that $v \leqq t$ errors occur in positions $X_1, X_2, \ldots, X_v$ with respective nonzero magnitudes $Y_1, Y_2, \ldots, Y_v$. Suppose further that e erasures occur in positions $U_1, U_2, \ldots, U_e$ with respective magnitudes $V_1, V_2, \ldots, V_e$. Now e and the U_i are known to the decoder, and the V_i may or may not be zero. Furthermore, the decoder may assume that Equation 9.64 holds.

The first step in decoding is to calculate the power-sum symmetric functions from the received polynomial $r(X)$.

$$S_j = r(\alpha^j) = \sum_{i=1}^{v} Y_i X_i^j + \sum_{i=1}^{e} V_i U_i^j; \qquad m_0 \leqq j \leqq m_0 + d_0 - 2. \tag{9.65}$$

Again, as in Section 9.5, m_0 will be taken to be unity although the results can be generalized in a straightforward manner.

Let

$$\prod_{i=1}^{e}(U - U_i) = \sum_{k=0}^{e}(-1)^k \sigma_k U^{e-k} \tag{9.66}$$

define the elementary symmetric functions of the known erasure locations. Now define the modified syndromes as

$$T_j = \sum_{k=0}^{e}(-1)^k \sigma_k S_{j-k}; \qquad j = e+1, e+2, \ldots, d-1$$

Substituting Equations 9.65 and 9.66 into this result gives

$$\begin{aligned} T_j &= \sum_{k=0}^{e}(-1)^k \sigma_k \sum_{i=1}^{v} Y_i X_i^{j-k} + \sum_{k=0}^{e}(-1)^k \sigma_k \sum_{i=1}^{e} V_i U_i^{j-k} \\ &= \sum_{i=1}^{v} Y_i X_i^{j-e} \sum_{k=0}^{e}(-1)^k \sigma_k X_i^{e-k} + \sum_{i=1}^{e} V_i U_i^{j-e} \sum_{k=0}^{e}(-1)^k \sigma_k U_i^{e-k} \end{aligned}$$

From Equation 9.66,

$$\sum_{k=0}^{e}(-1)^k \sigma_k U_i^{e-k} = 0; \qquad i = 1, 2, \ldots, e,$$

therefore,

$$T_j = \sum_{i=1}^{v} E_i X_i^j; \qquad j = e+1, e+2, \ldots, d-1, \tag{9.67}$$

where

$$E_i = Y_i X_i^{-e} \sum_{k=0}^{e} (-1)^k \sigma_k X_i^{e-k}.$$

Since $X_i \neq 0$, and $X_i \neq U_i$, it follows that $E_i \neq 0$.

The Equations 9.67 are a set of $d_0 - e - 1 > 2v$ known power sums in the v unknowns X_i. In Steps 2 and 3 of the general decoding procedure of Sections 9.4 and 9.5, an elegant and easily implemented method of solving these equations for the X_i was presented.

With the X_i known, all that remains is the calculation of the v nonzero magnitudes Y_i and the e possibly zero magnitudes V_i. These magnitudes are related to the known locators and power sums by the linear Equations 9.65. In Step 4 of the error-correction algorithm of Section 9.5, it is shown that the first v equations can be solved in a simple manner for the v error values given the locators and power sums. The analysis presented there carries over directly with v being replaced by $v + e$. Thus, any pattern of v errors and e erasures can be corrected with this modification of the iterative algorithm provided that the BCH code has designed distance $d_0 \geqq 2v + e$.

The complexity of the decoder necessary to perform this erasure and error correction is slightly greater than that required for error correction only. It too grows as $n \log_q n$, however.

9.8 Negacyclic Codes

Virtually all research on error-correcting codes has been based on the Hamming metric. One notable exception are the "negacyclic" codes of Berlekamp (1968*a*) which employ the Lee metric (See Section 3.1). These are a form of BCH code.

A BCH code, or for that matter any type of code with Hamming distance d has Lee distance $d_L \geqq d$. If a BCH code of length $2n$ and rate $> 1/2$ over $GF(p)$, p a prime $\geqq 5$, with roots $\alpha^1 \alpha^2 \cdots \alpha^{d-1}$, is shortened to half its natural length, then the new code has a Lee distance of at least d. Berlekamp (1968*a*) has shown that, if the even powers of α are eliminated as roots of $g(X)$, then the resulting code is an ideal in the algebra of polynomials modulo $X^n + 1$ and has Lee distance d, provided $d \leqq p$. (See Problem 9.10.) In brief, the Lee distance is twice as large as the Hamming distance guaranteed by the BCH bound. Furthermore, Berlekamp (1968*a*) has devised a decoding algorithm for these codes which is similar to that used to decode the BCH codes (Sections 9.4 to 9.6).

These codes are superior to codes employing Hamming distance on channels in which adjacent symbol transitions occur much more frequently than do other types of errors.

Notes

The codes described in this chapter were discovered independently by Hocquenghem (1959) and by Bose and Ray-Chaudhuri (1960*a*; 1960*b*). The codes discovered earlier by Reed and Solomon (1960) and described in Section 9.2 turn out in an interesting way to be a special case of BCH codes. The results on the true minimum weight of BCH codes are based largely on the work of Kasami, Lin, Peterson (1966).

The first error-correction procedure found was that described at the beginning of Section 9.6. Most codes, coding, and correction techniques generalize in a trivial way, but this correction scheme depends strongly on the fact that the syndrome gives certain symmetric functions in the binary case. Thus, the discovery by Zierler and Gorenstein of the decoding scheme described in Section 9.4 was quite surprising. Mathematically the method is closely related to an interpolation problem (Wolf 1967). The iterative algorithms presented in Sections 9.5 and 9.6 were discovered by Berlekamp (1968*b*), algorithms for a similar set of equations over the real field was used earlier by Trench (1964.) The presentation here follows Massey (1969). The simplifications of Steps 3 and 4 presented in Section 9.6 were found by Chien (1964*b*) and Forney (1965), respectively.

The ideas in Section 9.7 are based on the work of Blum and Weiss (1960) and of Forney (1965). Negacyclic codes were discovered by Berlekamp (1968*a*).

Problems

9.1. Show that any binary code generated by $g(X) = g^*(X)$ which has 1 as a root is a BCH code of minimum distance at least 6. Show that this applies to either of the two (17, 8) binary cyclic codes.

9.2. Show that if α in the definition of BCH codes is replaced by any other element α' of the same order, an equivalent code results. (Hint: First show that α and α' can each be expressed as a power of the other.)

9.3. Show that the Reed-Solomon code with symbols from $GF(q)$ generated by

$$g(X) = (X - \alpha)(X - \alpha^2) \cdots (X - \alpha^{d-1})$$

where a is a primitive root of $GF(q)$, has minimum distance exactly d.

9.4. Let C_1 be a binary cyclic (n, k) code with designed distance $2t_1$ and suppose that $(X+1)$ does not divide $g_1(X)$, the generator of C_1. Now let C_2 be the cyclic $(n, k-1)$ code generated by $(X+1)g_1(X)$ and suppose this code has designed distance $2t_2 > 2t_1$. Show that the actual minimum distance of C_1 is at least $2t_1 + 1$.

9.5. Use the results of the previous problem to prove that the (17, 9) and (65, 53) BCH codes have distance 5.

9.6. Use the results of the previous two problems to show that all cyclic $(2^m+1, 2^m+1-2m)$ codes have distance 5. Note that these codes are slightly better than the primitive BCH codes with the same minimum distance and number of parity checks.

9.7. A data communications system operating at 10,000 bits/second calls for the use of a binary BCH code of length $65{,}535 = 2^{16} - 1$ or fewer with rate $R = 0.75 (k = 49{,}151)$. Such a code can correct all patterns of (approximately) 1,050 or fewer errors. Determine the speed at which the logic circuitry must operate. Determine the cost of the machine assuming that for each flip-flop 4 gates must also be used and assuming that gates cost $1 and flip-flops cost $2. (A limited-access store for two received words is available and costs $5,000.)

9.8. The large, general-purpose digital computer with which you are most familiar is to be used to decode the code in the preceding problem. Calculate the number of computations required for each step in the decoding procedure, and determine the maximum data rate which the machine can handle. Keep in mind that only one arithmetic unit is available.

9.9. Consider a q-ary cyclic code with minimum distance d. A total of $e < d$ symbols are erased by the channel. Decoding is to be performed as follows. The decoder guesses at the e erased symbols and attempts to correct these errors (perhaps by using the procedure of Section 9.4 if the code is a BCH code). If a correct code word results, decoding is finished. Otherwise, a second guess is made and error correction is again attempted.

Show that at least $2(q/2)^e$ guesses must be made to guarantee that all erasure patterns can be corrected in this manner.

9.10. Let p be an odd prime and consider a $(2n, k)$ code over $GF(p)$. Show that shortening the code to length n produces a code which is an ideal in the algebra of polynomials modulo $X^n + 1$ provided all roots of the generator polynomial of the original code are odd powers of some root of order $2n$.

9.11. For the iterative algorithm for binary codes, Theorem 9.12, shows that if $2n - l_n$ is even, $2(n+1) - l_{n+1}$ is either the next even number (if $l_n = l_{n+1}$) or else it is the smallest previously unused odd number (if $l_n \neq l_{n+1}$). Similarly, if $2n - l_n$ is odd, either $2(n+1) - l_{n+1}$ is the next odd number or the smallest previously unused even number. Thus, at each step $m - l_m$ has a different value, and there is a unique previous step for which $m - l_m$ is maximum.

9.12. Show that for the iterative algorithm for binary codes, no two minimal solutions at different stages $\sigma^{(n)}(X)$ and $\sigma^{(m)}(X)$ can have $2n - l_n = 2m - l_m$. Show also that two solutions at the same stage n have their highest-order coefficients $\sigma_{l_n}^{(n)}$ equal.

10 Majority-Logic Decodable Codes

Like the BCH codes, the codes discussed in this chapter are cyclic random-error-correcting codes over $GF(q)$. They can be decoded rather simply in most cases, but seem to be somewhat less powerful than BCH codes for many interesting values of n, k, and d. Thus, from a practical point of view, the two types of codes are competitive in many situations.

10.1 Majority-Logic Decoding

As usual, the first step in decoding is to calculate the syndrome of the received n-tuple. Each digit of the syndrome and, in fact, any linear combination of syndrome digits, is a linear combination of a subset of the received digits. Because the syndrome of every code word is zero, the decoder knows the value of q^{n-k} linear combinations of certain subsets of the n error digits. Majority-logic decoding (Reed 1954, Massey 1963) is a simple method of determining the error digits from these parity check sums.

The concept of orthogonal parity-check sums is central to majority logic decoding. Let $s_1, s_2, \ldots, s_j$ denote check sums of various noise digits. Now if a particular error digit e_1, weighted by a coefficient a from $GF(q)$, is involved in every sum in the set and no other error digit is checked by more than one sum, then the sums are said to be *orthogonal** on e_1. More generally, if every sum checks $e_1, e_2, \ldots, e_l$ with coeffi-

* In this chapter the meaning of *orthogonal* is entirely different than its usual dot-product meaning (Section 2.5). In fact, two vectors orthogonal on a single digit (here) are not orthogonal (there).

cients $a, b, \ldots, j$ and no other error digits appear in more than one sum, then the check sums are orthogonal on the sum $ae_1 + be_2 + \cdots + je_i$. For example, in Equation 10.1, s_1, s_2, and s_3 are orthogonal on the sum $ae_1 + be_2$,

$$\begin{aligned} s_1 &= ae_1 + be_2 \\ s_2 &= ae_1 + be_2 + ce_3 \\ s_3 &= ae_1 + be_2 \qquad + de_4 + fe_5 . \end{aligned} \tag{10.1}$$

Of course, if the sums are orthogonal on only one digit, it is possible to choose its coefficients to be unity, since the code forms a vector space over $GF(q)$. The following theorem is the reason for considering orthogonal check sums.

THEOREM 10.1 *If in a linear code there are at least $d-1$ check sums orthogonal on each digit, then the code has minimum distance at least d.*

Proof. In order to show that every nonzero code word has weight at least d, consider one of the nonzero digits in a code word. Call this the ith digit and denote the first $d-1$ check sums orthogonal on it by $s_{i1}, s_{i2}, \ldots, s_{i(d-1)}$. Now all these sums are zero because the word is a code word. Yet each equation has a nonzero entry so there must be at least one other nonzero digit in each sum. Because the sums are orthogonal, there must be at least $d-1$ nonzero digits beside the ith.

COROLLARY 10.1. *If it is possible to construct a set of $d-1$ check sums orthogonal on any digit in a cyclic code, then the code has minimum distance at least d.*

A slightly different interpretation of the orthogonal sums of Eq. 10.1 can be given as follows. Assume that there are $d-1$ check sums orthogonal on some sum of error digits, e. Denote these sums $s_1, s_2, \ldots, s_{d-1}$, where $s_i = e + e_i$. Let

$$r = c + e$$

where r and c denote respectively the received and transmitted digits in the positions corresponding to the digits of e. Then the d sums

$$\begin{aligned} r &= c + e \\ s_1 + r &= c + e_1 \\ s_2 + r &= c + e_2 \\ &\vdots \\ s_{d-1} + r &= c + e_{d-1} \end{aligned}$$

are said to be *orthogonal estimates* (Rudolph 1967) of the sum of transmitted digits c. This idea generalizes directly to the case where the check sums are orthogonal on a linear combination of error digits.

Orthogonal check sums have another function in addition to providing a lower bound on minimum distance; they can be used to decode the code with a version of the Meggitt decoder discussed in Chapter 8. Consider a linear code in which there are at least $d-1$ check sums orthogonal on each digit and assume that $[(d-1)/2]$ or fewer errors occur. If the ith error digit is 0, then at least $d-1-[(d-1)/2]$ or at least half of the sums orthogonal on it will be 0. Because the code is over $GF(q)$ it is always possible to choose the coefficient of the ith digit to be 1. If, on the other hand, the digit has value $v \neq 0$, then at least $d-1-\{[(d-1)/2]-1\}$ or at least half of the sums will have value v. For the other $[(d-1)/2]-1$ errors can affect only $[(d-1)/2]-1$ or fewer of the orthogonal sums. Thus, the value of each noise digit is given by the value assumed by a clear majority of the check sums orthogonal on it; if no value is assumed by a clear majority, the noise digit is zero. Stated differently the value of each transmitted digit is the value given by the majority of its orthogonal estimaters.

Figure 10.1 shows a version of the Meggitt decoder of Figure 8.5. This decoder can be used to decode a cyclic code which has $d-1$ orthogonal check sums on each digit. Here the combinational logic circuit of the Meggitt decoder has been implemented as a set of $GF(q)$ multipliers and a single $(d-1)$-input majority gate.

The $(n-k)$-stage feedback shift register in Figure 10.1 is identical in form to that of Figure 8.2. It premultiplies the received word by X^{n-k} and then divides the result by $g(X)$. The remainder after division is a shifted version of the syndrome and is stored in the register. (In this chapter this remainder will be referred to as the syndrome unless otherwise stated.) The $d-1$ check sums orthogonal on the first error digit with coefficient unity are formed by the $d-1$ $GF(q)$ adders and their scalar multipliers. The majority gate produces at its output the value assumed by the majority of its inputs, or 0 if a clear majority is assumed by no element of $GF(q)$. This value is then subtracted from the first received information digit as the information register and syndrome generator are shifted once. By Theorem 8.4, the syndrome generator, after shifting, contains the syndrome of the received word shifted one place to the right. Thus, the new inputs to the majority gate are the check sums orthogonal on the second received digit, so this digit can be corrected exactly as was the first one. Clearly, a total of $k-1$ shifts are necessary to correct all the errors in the information section of the

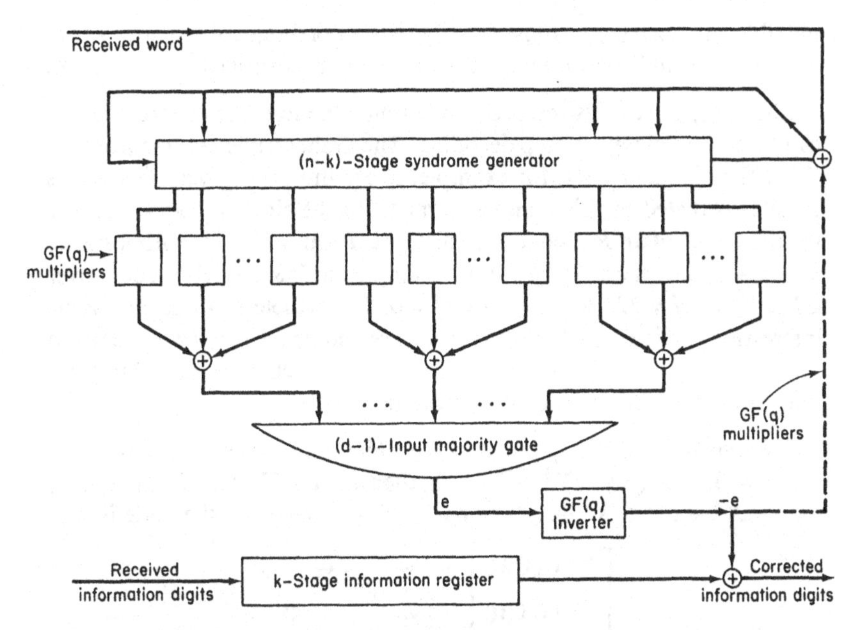

Figure 10.1. A one-step majority-logic decoder for a cyclic (n, k) code.

received word. Errors in the parity section can be corrected in this manner also if desired. This type of decoding has been referred to as *1-step decoding* since only one level of majority logic is necessary.

It should be clear that each of the q^{n-k} parity-check sums known to the decoder corresponds to one of the n-tuples in the null space of the code. The problem considered in Sections 10.2 and 10.3 is the construction of cyclic codes with large sets of orthogonal vectors in their null spaces. The following theorem gives a necessary condition for 1-step decoding an (n, k) code.

THEOREM 10.2. *Let $\bar{d}$ denote the minimum distance of the dual code of an (n, k) code. Then the number of errors which can be corrected by* 1-*step majority logic decoding, t_1, is bounded by*

$$t_1 \leqq \frac{n-1}{2(\bar{d}-1)} \tag{10.2}$$

Proof. Because the minimum weight in the null space is $\bar{d}$, there must be at least $\bar{d}$ digits in each sum. One of these appears in all; the other $\bar{d}-1$ appear in only one of the sums. Since there are $n-1$ error digits in addition to the one on which the equations are orthogonal, it is possible to construct at most $(n-1)/(\partial - 1)$ orthogonal equations. But t_1 is at most half this number so the theorem is proved. Q.E.D.

For many codes this result severely limits the number of errors which can be corrected with 1-step decoding. The Golay triple-error-correcting (23, 12) code has $t_1 = 1$, for example. More important, very few errors can be corrected in this manner in most Reed-Solomon codes, because the dual code of an *R-S* code with distance d is an *R-S* code with distance $n - d + 2$, a large number. For example, a (63, 32) *R-S* code over $GF(2^6)$ has $d = 32$, $\partial = 33$, but $t_1 = 0$. Nevertheless, there are some interesting cyclic codes for which t_1 is large compared to $[(d - 1/2)]$ and these will be examined shortly. Codes for which $t_1 = [(d-1)/2]$ are said to be *completely orthogonalizable* in one step.

Example. The (7, 3) binary cyclic Hamming code has $d = 4$ and $\partial = 3$. Let $h(X) = X^3 + X^2 + 1$; then $g(X) = (X + 1)(X^3 + X + 1) = X^4 + X^3 + X^2 + 1$. The parity-check matrix of the code is

$$\mathbf{H} = [\mathbf{P}^T\mathbf{I}_4] = \begin{bmatrix} 1011000 \\ 1110100 \\ 1100010 \\ 0110001 \end{bmatrix} \begin{matrix} \leftarrow \; \leftarrow \qquad\quad \leftarrow \\ \qquad \oplus \\ \quad\;\; \leftarrow \qquad\quad \oplus \\ \qquad\qquad\quad \leftarrow \\ \qquad\qquad\quad \leftarrow \end{matrix}$$

An error in the highest-order position will contribute (1 0 0 0) to the syndrome since the pattern is multiplied by X^4 before the syndrome is calculated. The checks corresponding to the first row, the sum of the first and second and the sum of the first, third, and fourth, are orthogonal on the first information digit. Thus, $t_1 = [(d-1)/2] = 1$ and the code is completely orthogonalized. The decoder for this code is shown in Figure 10.2. This code is an example of the Projective Geometry codes presented in Section 10.3.

Note that the first digit of the syndrome is involved in each of the orthogonal check sums. Adding a fixed element of $GF(q)$ to every input of a majority gate is equivalent to adding it to the output. For $q = 2$, by De Morgan's theorem, $\text{maj}(\bar{X}_1, \bar{X}_2, \bar{X}_3) = \overline{\text{maj}(X_1, X_2, X_3)}$, where the overbar denotes complementation. Of course, the latter operation is simpler, and therefore the decoder of Figure 10.1 can sometimes be simplified slightly. The simplified decoder for the (7, 3) code of the preceding example is shown in Figure 10.3.

If a set of at least $d - 1$ orthogonal check sums can be formed on a linear combination of error digits e, then by an argument identical to

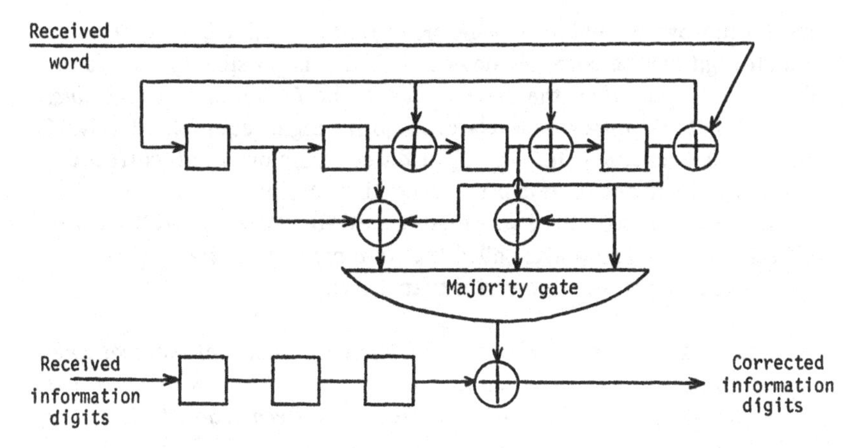

Figure 10.2. A one-step majority logic decoder for the (7, 3) binary cyclic Hamming code.

the proof of Theorem 10.1, the value of e is given by the value assumed by a majority of the check sums (or zero if no element of $GF(q)$ has a clear majority), provided $[(d-1)/2]$ or few errors occurred. If a number of linear combinations of noise digits can be found in this way, then together with the q^{n-k} original check sums and linear combination thereof, these form a larger set of known check sums. This new set is a vector space that contains the null space of the code as a proper subspace.

Now if it is possible to carry out this procedure several times — each time obtaining at least $d-1$ orthogonal check sums — until a set of

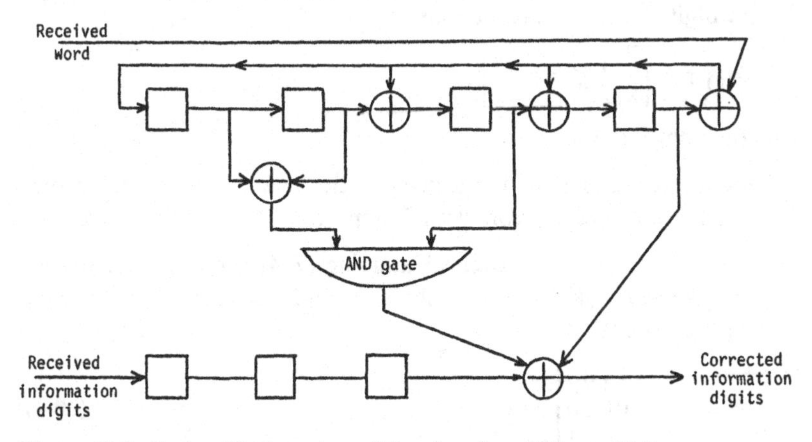

Figure 10.3. A simplified version of the decoder of Figure 10.2.

check sums orthogonal on a single error digit is obtained, then the value of that digit can be correctly determined. If it is possible to do this for all n error digits, then the code is said to be L-step *orthogonalizable*, where L is the number of levels of majority logic required. Clearly, if the code is cyclic, and $[(d-1)/2]$ or fewer errors occurred, correct decoding results if one digit can be decoded correctly.

This decoding procedure was first devised for the Reed-Muller codes of Section 5.5 and so is also called the *Reed algorithm*. Not surprisingly, L-step decoding is more powerful than 1-step.

THEOREM 10.3. *Let* $\bar{d}$ *denote the minimum distance of the dual code of an* (n, k) *code. Then the number of errors that can be corrected with L-step majority-logic decoding (the Reed algorithm),* t_L, *is bounded by*

$$t_L \leqq \frac{n}{\bar{d}} - \frac{1}{2}; \qquad \bar{d} \text{ even}$$
$$\leqq \frac{n+1}{\bar{d}+1} - \frac{1}{2}; \qquad \bar{d} \text{ odd}. \tag{10.3}$$

Proof. In order to correct t_L errors it must be possible to construct at least $2t_L$ check sums orthogonal on a set of digits common to each sum. Call the number of digits in this set B. Clearly, $B \leqq [\bar{d}/2]$. For otherwise, the sum of the vectors corresponding to two sums orthogonal on the set of B digits, which is also in the null space of the code, would have weight less than $\bar{d}$.

Since the $2t_L$ equations have at most $[\bar{d}/2]$ digits in common and at least $\bar{d}$ digits in all, it must be that

$$2t_L\left(\bar{d} - \left[\frac{\bar{d}}{2}\right]\right) \leqq n - \left[\frac{\bar{d}}{2}\right].$$

The theorem follows. Q.E.D.

This result states that, for a given code, one can hope to correct roughly twice as many errors with L-step decoding as with 1-step.

Example. The binary cyclic Hamming (7, 4) code is decodable in two steps. If $g(X)$ is taken as $X^3 + X^2 + 1$, the parity-check matrix of the code is

$$H = \begin{bmatrix} 1011100 \\ 1110010 \\ 0111001 \end{bmatrix} \tag{10.4}$$

Denote the error digits $(e_6, e_5, \ldots, e_0)$. The check sums corresponding to row 1 and the sum of rows 1 and 2 are orthogonal on the sum $e_6 + e_0$; call the sum s_1. The sums corresponding to the sum of rows 1, 2, and 3 and the sum of rows 1 and 3 are orthogonal on $e_6 + e_4 = s_2$. (Recall the premultiplication by X^3.) Then, if one or fewer errors occurred, s_1 and s_2 can be determined correctly. However,

$$s_1 = e_6 + e_0$$
$$s_2 = e_6 + e_4$$

these sums are orthogonal on e_6 so this error digit can be determined by a second level of majority logic. The decoder for this code is shown in Figure 10.4. This code is an example of the Euclidean geometry codes discussed in Section 10.2.

Again as in 1-step decoding, the majority-logic circuitry can be simplified somewhat by noting that the first digit of the syndrome is involved in each of the orthogonal check sums.

Theorems 10.2 and 10.3 show that the power and range of application of majority-logic decoding is rather limited. In an effort to circumvent these difficulties, several modifications of the basic algorithm have been devised. These are presented in Section 10.4.

10.2 Euclidean Geometry Codes

The Reed-Muller codes presented in Section 5.5 have an interesting geometric interpretation. The 2^m digits can be associated uniquely with the 2^m points in an m-dimensional Euclidean geometry over $GF(2)$, that is EG(m, 2)*. The rth-order Reed-Muller code is the row space of the matrix whose rows are all r-fold vector products of the m original vectors. Furthermore, the null space of this code is the $(m - r - 1)$th-order Reed-Muller code.

Now the points corresponding to the nonzero positions in each of the original m vectors can be seen to form a Euclidean geometry of dimension $m - 1$ in EG(m, 2), that is, an $(m - 1)$-flat. The intersection of two different $(m - 1)$-flats is an $(m - 2)$-flat or is empty. But the vector product used in the formulation of the Reed-Muller codes corresponds to taking the intersection of the flats corresponding to the vectors. As a result, the rth-order Reed-Muller code has in its null space the vectors

* Euclidean geometries are discussed in Carmichael (1937), p. 329 and Blumenthal (1961).

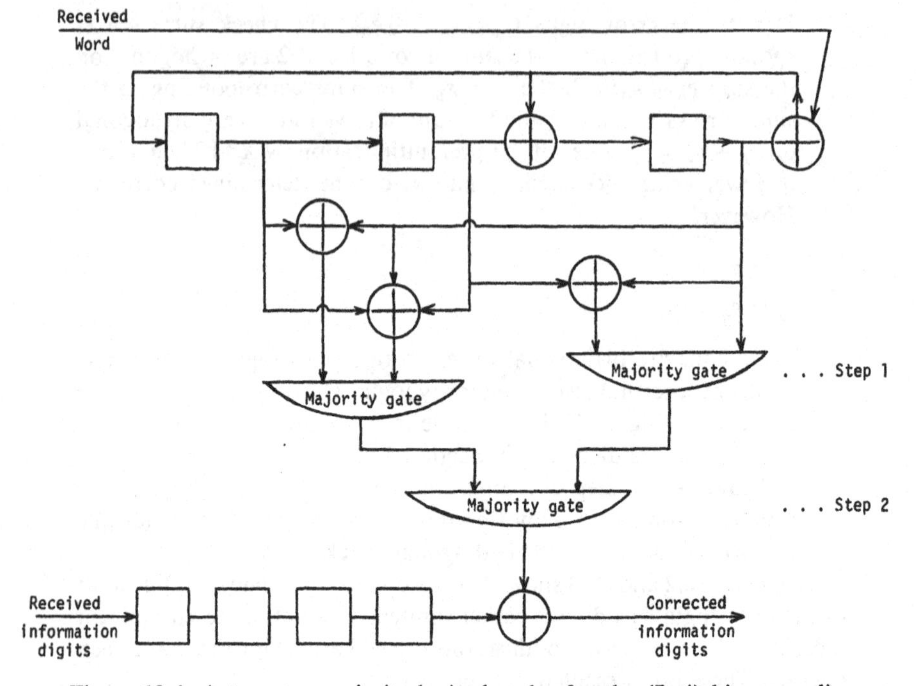

Figure 10.4. A two-step majority-logic decoder for the (7, 4) binary cyclic Hamming code.

corresponding to all $(r + 1)$-flats of EG$(m, 2)$. These flats are used in decoding with the Reed algorithm and also provide a means of lower-bounding the minimum distance of the codes. These notions will be made more precise shortly.

The Reed-Muller codes can be seen to be cyclic codes with an overall parity check added, for the generator matrix of the first-order code is just the generator matrix of the dual of a Hamming code with an overall check digit added. Then let S denote the operation: cyclically shift all digits except the overall parity check. If V_1 and V_2 are two vectors in the first-order code, then let

$$V_1 \times V_2 = V_{12}.$$

Clearly,

$$SV_1 \times SV_2 = SV_{12}$$

and so a cyclic shift of any code word in the second-order code is also a code word. It is not difficult to see that all Reed-Muller codes are equivalent to cyclic codes with an overall check digit.

Euclidean geometry (EG) codes are a natural generalization of the cyclic Reed-Muller codes. Actually, three generalizations are involved. First, one can consider codes with symbols from $GF(p)$, p prime, having length $p^{m'}$. Second and more important, one can associate the $p^{m'}$ code points with different geometries. For example, if $m' = sm$, $s \neq 1$, and $m \neq 1$, then the geometries EG(m', p), EG(m, p^s) and EG(s, p^m) can be used to construct majority-logic decodable, extended cyclic codes of length $p^{m'}$. Third, one can construct codes with symbols from $GF(q)$, q a prime power. It happens that the q-ary codes can be constructed from the p-ary codes, so this last generalization will be considered after the p-ary codes have been presented.

Let α be a primitive element of $GF(p^{sm})$. Then any field element α^j can be expressed as

$$\alpha^j = a_{0j} + a_{1j}\alpha + \cdots + a_{(m-1)j}\alpha^{m-1}$$

where a_{ij} is an element of $GF(p^s)$. For the purposes of this section, it is convenient to regard this vector space as an m-dimensional Euclidean geometry over $GF(p^s)$, that is, as EG(m, p^s). This geometry contains p^{sm} points α^j, each of which can be represented by a coordinate vector $\mathbf{a}_j = (a_{0j}, a_{1j}, \ldots, a_{m-1})_j$.

Let b denote an element of $GF(p^s)$. Then the product $b\mathbf{a}_j$ is defined in the usual way as $(ba_{0j}, ba_{1j}, \ldots, ba_{(m-1)j})$. There are p^s points whose coordinate vectors have the form $\mathbf{a}_k + b\mathbf{a}_j$ for two given vectors $\mathbf{a}_k$ and $\mathbf{a}_j$. This collection of points is referred to as a line or *1-flat*. If $\mathbf{a}_0$, $\mathbf{a}_1$, and $\mathbf{a}_2$ are linearly independent, that is, they do not all lie in the same line, then the set of p^{2s} points whose coordinate vectors have the form $\mathbf{a}_0 + b_1\mathbf{a}_1 + b_2\mathbf{a}_2$ form a 2-flat or plane in EG(m, p^s). More generally, the set of points linearly dependent on $r + 1$ points not in a $(r - 1)$-flat forms an r-flat.

Now the nonzero elements of $GF(p^{sm})$ can be considered as the location numbers of a cyclic code of length $p^{sm} - 1$ over $GF(p)$. An r-flat in EG(m, p^s) which does not contain the zero point (which corresponds to the overall parity check) can be associated with a polynomial in the algebra of polynomials modulo $x^{p^{sm}-1} - 1$. This polynomial will be taken to have coefficient 1 in positions corresponding to the p^{sr} points of the flat and 0 elsewhere.

A Euclidean Geometry (EG) cyclic code of order r and length $p^{sm} - 1$ with symbols from $GF(p)$ is defined as the largest cyclic code whose null space contains the polynomials corresponding to all $(r + 1)$-flats of EG(m, p^s) which do not pass through the origin. These flats are useful for correcting random errors, as will be seen shortly.

Several important questions can be asked about an *EG* code: What is its generator polynomial? What is its minimum distance? How is it decoded? Answers to these questions are given in the following paragraphs.

The generator polynomial of a cyclic code is known if the roots of $h(X)$, the parity-check polynomial, can be determined. Let α be a primitive element of $GF(p^{sm})$. If $\gamma_1, \gamma_2, \ldots, \gamma_k$ can be shown to be roots of every $(r+1)$-flat polynomial, then each of these is a root of $h(X)$, and $g(X)$ can be taken to be

$$g(X) = \frac{X^{p^{sm}-1} - 1}{\prod_{i=1}^{k} (X - \gamma_i)}. \tag{10.5}$$

An $(r+1)$-flat consists of the $p^{s(r+1)}$ points whose location numbers satisfy

$$\alpha^j = \alpha^{e_0} + \beta^{i_1}\alpha^{e_1} + \beta^{i_2}\alpha^{e_2} + \cdots + \beta^{i_{r+1}}\alpha^{e_{r+1}} \tag{10.6}$$

$$\begin{aligned} i_1 &= 0, 1, \ldots, p^s - 1 \\ i_2 &= 0, 1, \ldots, p^s - 1 \\ &\vdots \\ i_{r+1} &= 0, 1, \ldots, p^s - 1 \end{aligned}$$

where β is a primitive element of $GF(p^s)$ and the α^{e_i} are linearly independent elements of $GF(p^{sm})$, as explained earlier. In what follows, it will be assumed that the flat does not contain the origin. Let $f(X)$denote the polynomial associated with this flat. If α^t is a root of $f(X)$, then

$$f(\alpha^t) = \sum (\alpha^t)^j = 0 \tag{10.7}$$

where the sum is over all $p^{s(r+1)}$ values of j for which Equation 10.6 is satisfied. Now consider the sum

$$f(\alpha^t) = \sum_{i_1, i_2, \ldots, i_{r+1}} (\alpha^{e_0} + \beta^{i_1}\alpha^{e_1} + \cdots + \beta^{i_{r+1}}\alpha^{e_{r+1}})^t. \tag{10.8}$$

Upon expanding in a multinomial expansion, this gives

$$f(\alpha^t) = \sum_i \sum_h \frac{t!}{h_0!\,h_1! \cdots h_{r+1}!} (\alpha^{e_0})^{h_0} (\beta^{i_1}\alpha^{e_1})^{h_1} \cdots (\beta^{i_{r+1}}\alpha^{e_{r+1}})^{h_{r+1}} \tag{10.9}$$

where

$$h_0 + h_1 + \cdots h_{r+1} = t \tag{10.10}$$

This formidable-looking expression can be simplified considerably with the help of the following lemma.

LEMMA 10.1. *Let β be a primitive element of $GF(p^s)$. Then,*

$$\sum_{i=0}^{p^s-2,\,\infty} \beta^{ih} = -1; \qquad h = k(p^s - 1), \qquad h \neq 0$$

$$= \quad 0; \qquad \textit{otherwise}$$

where the symbol β^∞ denotes the zero element of $GF(p^s)$.

Proof. Since $\beta^{p^s-1} = 1$, clearly,

$$\sum_{i=0}^{p^s-2,\,\infty} \beta^{ih} = p^s - 1 = -1; \qquad h = k(p^s - 1), h \neq 0$$

$$= 0; \qquad\qquad h = 0$$

because $(\beta^\infty)^0 = (0)^0 = 1$. If on the other hand, $GCD(h, p^s - 1) = a < p^s - 1$, the order of β^h, say n, divides $p^s - 1$. then,

$$\sum_{i=0}^{p^s-1,\,\infty} \beta^{ih} = \left(\frac{p^s - 1}{n}\right) \sum_{i=0}^{n-1} \beta^{ih} \tag{10.11}$$

But this last sum is just the coefficient of X^{n-1} in the product of all the factors $(X - \beta^{ih})$, that is, the coefficient of X^{n-1} in the polynomial $X^n - 1$, or in other words, zero. This proves the lemma. Q.E.D.

Now if the order of summation is reversed in Equation 10.9, then it can be seen that $f(\alpha^t) = 0$ unless all the h's except possibly h_0 are multiples of $p^s - 1$; that is,

$$h_v = k_v(p^s - 1); \qquad 1 \leqq v \leqq r + 1.$$

Then Equation 10.9 reduces to

$$f(\alpha^t) = (-1)^{r+1} \sum_k \frac{t!}{h_0!\{k_1(p^s - 1)\}! \cdots \{k_{r+1}(p^s - 1)\}!} \cdot \alpha^{e_0 h_0} \alpha^{e_1 k_1 (p^s - 1)} \cdots \alpha^{e_{r+1} k_{r+1} (p^s - 1)} \tag{10.12}$$

At this point another lemma is necessary.

LEMMA 10.2. *Let* $n = n_0 + n_1 p + n_2 p^2 + \cdots$ and $k = k_0 + k_1 p + k_2 p^2 + \cdots$ *where* $0 \leqq n_i \leqq p - 1$ *and* $0 \leqq k_i \leqq p - 1$. *Then*

$$\binom{n}{k} \not\equiv 0 \quad \mod p$$

if and only if $n_i \geqq k_i$ *for all* i.

Proof. It can be shown, by induction on n for example, that the largest power of p which divides $n!$ is

$$e_n = \sum_{i=1}^{\infty} \left[\frac{n}{p^i}\right] = \sum_{i=1}^{\infty} \sum_{j=0}^{i-1} n_i p^j$$

Summing on j and multiplying both numerator and denominator by $p - 1$ give

$$e_n = \frac{1}{p-1} \sum_{i=1}^{\infty} n_i(p^i - 1) = \frac{1}{p-1}(n - w_n)$$

where $w_n = \sum_{i=0}^{\infty} n_i$ denotes the weight of n in radix-p form.

Now $\binom{n}{k} \equiv 0 \bmod p$ if and only if p divides $n!$ more times than it divides $k! \cdot (n-k)!$ Thus, $\binom{n}{k} \equiv 0$ if and only if

$$(n - w_n) > (k - w_k) + (n - k - w_{n-k})$$

or in other words, if and only if

$$w_n < w_k + w_{n-k}.$$

But $w_n < w_k + w_{n-k}$ implies and is implied by $n_i < k_i$ for some i. Therefore, for $\binom{n}{k}$ to be nonzero mod p, it is necessary and sufficient that $n_i \geqq k_i$ for all i. In the language of Section 3.5, $\binom{n}{k} \not\equiv 0 \bmod p$ if and only if k is a descendant of n when expanded in radix-p form.

Q.E.D.

Now the multinomial coefficient in Equation 10.12 can be expressed as

$$\binom{t}{h_0}\binom{t-h_0}{k_1(p^s-1)}\binom{t-h_0-k_1(p^s-1)}{k_2(p^s-1)}\cdots \times \binom{t - h_0 - \sum_{i=1}^{r} k_i(p^s-1)}{k_{r+1}(p^s-1)} \tag{10.13}$$

This product is nonzero mod p if and only if each factor is nonzero. Thus, for α^t to be a root of $g(X)$, when written in radix-p form, t must be the sum of at least $r + 1$ multiples of $p^s - 1$ with no carries in the sum. For otherwise, $k_j(p^s - 1)$ will not be a descendant of $t - h_0 - \sum_{i=1}^{j} k_i(p^s - 1)$ for some j, and by Lemma 10.2 the $(j + 1)$th factor in Equation 10.13 will be zero, and α^t will be a root of $h(X)$. Q.E.D.

THEOREM 10.4. *Let α denote a primitive element of $GF(p^{sm})$. The parity-check polynomial, $h(X)$, of an order-r Euclidean geometry code has α^t as a root provided $w_s(t) \leq r$. The s-weight of t [denoted $w_s(t)$] is defined as the largest number of multiples of $p^s - 1$ contained in the radix-p expansion of t.*

Example. For $p = s = 2$ and $m = 3$, the 2-weights of various values of t are given in the accompanying table:

t	Binary Representation	$w_2(t)$
3	000011	1
5	000101	0
7	000111	1
9	001001	1
15	001111	2
21	010101	1
27	011011	2

This result guarantees that certain roots of $X^{p^{sm}-1} - 1$ are roots of $h(X)$. It does not say that other roots of $X^{p^{sm}-1} - 1$ are not also roots of $h(X)$; however in Section 10.6 it is shown that $h(X)$ has no other roots.

Theorem 10.4 provides a method of determining k, the number of information symbols in an EG code. It has proved difficult to obtain a combinatorial expression for this bound. However, for $r = m - 2$, the following result has been proved by several investigators including Smith (1967) and MacWilliams and Mann (1967):

$$k = n - \left[\binom{m + p - 1}{m}\right]^s + 1.$$

Here k denotes the lower bound on k discussed earlier.

In Section 5.5, the Reed-Muller codes were presented. The rth order code was defined as the row space of a matrix whose k rows were the incidence vectors of certain $(m - r)$-flats of EG$(m, 2)$. It was shown that since an $(m - r)$-flat and an $(r + 1)$-flat intersect in either no points or at least two, every $(r + 1)$-flat is in the null space of the code that has dimension $n-k$. Thus, the Reed-Muller codes with the digit corresponding to the origin removed are equivalent to EG codes with $s=1$ and $p=2$. For these codes,

$$k=\sum_{i=0}^{r}\binom{m}{i}.$$

A lower bound on the minimum distance of EG codes is provided by the BCH bound. Every element of $GF(p^{sm})$, α^t, for which the radix-p expansion of t contains $r+1$ or more multiples of p^s-1 is a root of $g(X)$. Now expand t in radix-p notation. Then the number

$$\begin{array}{llll} (p-1)p^{s(m-r-1)-1} & +\cdots+(p-1)p^{s(m-r-2)+1} & +\,0 & \\ +\,(p-1)p^{s(m-r)-1} & +\cdots+(p-1)p^{s(m-r-1)+1} & +\,(p-2)p^{s(m-r-1)} & \\ +\,(p-1)p^{s(m-r+1)-1} & +\cdots+(p-1)p^{s(m-r)+1} & +\,(p-1)p^{s(m-r)} & \\ \quad\vdots & & \quad\vdots & \\ +\,(p-1)p^{sm-1} & +\cdots & +\,(p-1)p^{s(m-1)} & \\ & =p^{sm}-p^{s(m-r-1)}-p^{s(m-r-2)+1} & & (10.14) \end{array}$$

has s-weight exactly r. Each of the last r rows in the array is a multiple of p^s-1, and the other two rows do not contain another multiple. Were any coefficient of p^i, $0\leq i\leq s(m-r-2)$, nonzero, however, the s-weight would be at least $r+1$. Accordingly, this term and the upper two rows of the array, Equation 10.14, would contain at least one multiple of p^s-1. This follows directly from Lemma 10.3.

LEMMA 10.3. (Lin 1968). *Let* $a=a_0+a_1p^s+a_2p^{2s}+\cdots+a_vp^{vs}$. *Denote the* p^s*-weight of* a *by*

$$w_{p^s}(a)=\sum_{i=0}^{V}a_i$$

Then p^s-1 *divides* a *if and only if* p^s-1 *divides* $w_{p^s}(a)$.

Proof.

$$a-w_{p^s}(a)=a_1(p^s-1)+a_2(p^{2s}-1)+\cdots+a_v(p^{vs}-1) \qquad (10.15)$$

The lemma follows directly: If p^s-1 divides either of the terms on the left side of Equation 10.14, it divides the other as well. Q.E.D.

Thus, in this case it is always possible to find a number a which is a descendant of the added term and the upper two rows of the Array 10.14 and which is divisible by p^s-1.

Since $p^{sm} - p^{s(m-r-1)} - p^{s(m-r-2)+1}$ is the largest root in $h(X)$, then $g(X)$ must have $p^{s(m-r-1} + p^{s(m-r-2)+1} - 2$ consecutive roots; therefore for the EG code of order r and length $p^{sm} - 1$ over $GF(p)$,

$$d \geqq d_{\text{BCH}} = p^{s(m-r-1)} + p^{s(m-r-2)+1} - 1 \qquad (10.16)$$

It is not known, in general, whether this result holds with equality. For many short binary codes and for the Reed-Muller codes it does, however.

It is possible to correct nearly $[(d_{\text{BCH}} - 1)/2]$ random errors with EG codes using an $(r + 1)$-step majority-logic decoder that employs the Reed algorithm developed for the Muller codes. The key point is that the check sums corresponding to the $(r + 1)$-flats intersecting on a given r-flat are orthogonal on the check sum corresponding to this r-flat. Since the check sums corresponding to all $(r + 1)$-flats are known to the decoder, it can determine all check sums corresponding to r-flats with one level of majority logic.

Consider, temporarily, the entire EG(m, p^s) including the origin, and let $J + 1$ denote the number of $(r + 1)$-flats intersecting on a particular r-flat. There are p^{sm} points in this space and p^{sr} points in an r-flat. There are $p^{s(r+1)} - p^{sr}$ points in each of the $(r + 1)$-flats intersecting on a given r-flat which are outside the r-flat itself. No point outside the r-flat can lie in more than one of these $(r + 1)$-flats, for otherwise two flats would be identical. Furthermore, every point must lie in one $(r + 1)$-flat since that point and the "central" r-flat determine completely an $(r + 1)$-flat that contains the r-flat. Thus, $(J + 1)(p^{s(r+1)} - p^{sr})$ must equal $p^{sm} - p^{sr}$, the number of points in the space outside the "central" r-flat. One of these $(r + 1)$-flats passes through the origin and so is not in the null space of the EG code. Letting $d_{\text{ML}} = J + 1$ gives

$$J + 1 = d_{\text{ML}} = \frac{p^{s(m-r)} - 1}{p^s - 1} = p^{s(m-r-1)} + p^{s(m-r-2)} + \cdots + p^s + 1 \qquad (10.17)$$

It follows from Theorem 10.1 that if $[(d_{\text{ML}} - 1)/2]$ or fewer errors occurred, then the decoder can correctly determine the check sums corresponding to all r-flats. The parameter J can be viewed as a function of the dimension of the central flat; Equation 10.17 shows that it is a monotone decreasing function of this dimension. Thus, the decoder can find at least $J + 1$ r-flats orthogonal on each $(r - 1)$-flat, at least $J + 1$ $(r - 1)$-flats orthogonal on each $(r - 2)$-flat, and so on. Provided

$[(d_{ML}-1)/2]$ or fewer errors occurred, all decisions will be correct and the 0-flats, that is, error digits, will be determined with $r+1$ levels of majority logic.

THEOREM 10.5. *A Euclidean Geometry cyclic code of length p^{sm} and order r [whose null space contains all $(r+1)$-flats of EG(m, p^s)] can be $(r+1)$-step majority-logic decoded provided $[(d_{ML}-1)/2]$ or fewer errors occurred, where*

$$d_{ML} = \frac{p^{s(m-r)} - 1}{p^s - 1} \tag{10.18}$$

For $p = 2$ and $r = m - 2$ or for $p = 2$ and $s = 1$, $d_{ML} = d_{BCH}$. For all other values of the parameters, $d_{ML} < d_{BCH}$, although the difference is relatively small.

A list of binary Euclidean Geometry codes is given in Table 10.1 for $n \leqq 63$. In Section 10.4 several modifications of the basic majority logic decoding algorithm described above which apply to the EG codes are presented.

Table 10.1. Parameters of Binary Euclidean Geometry Cyclic Codes with $n \leqq 63$. All $(r+1)$-flats are in the null space of an order-r code. All codes with $s=1$ are equivalent to Reed-Muller codes with a digit omitted. All codes with $n \leqq 31$ are BCH codes. For all codes listed, k equals the lower bound of Theorem 10.4.

n	k	d_{BCH}	d_{ML}	Geometry EG$(m, 2^s)$	Order r
7	4	3	3	EG(3, 2)	1
	1	7	7	EG(3, 2)	0
15	11	3	3	EG(4, 2)	2
	7	5	5	EG(2, 2)	0
	5	7	7	EG(4, 2)	1
	1	15	15	EG(4, 2)	0
31	26	3	3	EG(5, 2)	3
	16	7	7	EG(5, 2)	2
	6	15	15	EG(5, 2)	1
	1	31	31	EG(5, 2)	0
63	57	3	3	EG(6, 2)	4
	48	5	5	EG(3, 2^2)	1
	42	7	7	EG(6, 2)	3
	37	9	9	EG(2, 2^3)	0
	22	15	15	EG(6, 2)	2
	13	23	21	EG(3, 2^2)	0
	7	31	31	EG(6, 2)	1
	1	63	63	EG(6, 2)	0

Example. The (7, 4) binary Hamming code is an EG code; the associated geometry is EG(3, 2) and the code has order $r = 1$. Let α denote a root of $X^3 + X + 1$. The nonzero field elements are

	α^2	α^1	α^0
$\alpha^0 =$	0	0	1
$\alpha^1 =$	0	1	0
$\alpha^2 =$	1	0	0
$\alpha^3 =$	0	1	1
$\alpha^4 =$	1	1	0
$\alpha^5 =$	1	1	1
$\alpha^6 =$	1	0	1

$\alpha^7 = \alpha^0$

The code has all 2-flats in its null space, and by Theorem 10.4 $h(X)$ contains all roots α^i such that the weight of i, when expanded in binary, is 0 or 1. Thus, $h(X)$ has roots α^0, α^1, α^2, and α^4; that is $h(X) = X^4 + X^3 + X^2 + 1$.

By Theorem 10.5, the code can be decoded in two steps. To execute the second step, two 1-flats orthogonal on the error digit in the position corresponding to X^2 must be determined. (Recall that the decoder premultiplies by X^3.) These can be found if it is possible to construct two 2-flats orthogonal on each of these 1-flats. The null space of the code contains eight 7-tuples and seven of them are 2-flats:

Flats	Points						
	Information				Parity		
	α^0	α^1	α^2	α^3	α^4	α^5	α^6
1	1	0	1	1	1	0	0
2	0	1	0	1	1	1	0
3	0	0	1	0	1	1	1
4	1	0	0	1	0	1	1
5	1	1	0	0	1	0	1
6	1	1	1	0	0	1	0
7	0	1	1	1	0	0	1

Flats numbered 1 and 2 intersect on the line through the points α^3 and α^4. Flats 3 and 5 intersect on the line through the points α^4 and α^6. These two lines, of course, intersect on the point α^4, which corresponds to the error digit in the first information symbol as a result of the premultiplication by X^3. It follows that $d_{ML} = 3$.

The decoder for this code is discussed in the example following Theorem 10.3 and is depicted in Figure 10.3.

Throughout the derivation on the preceding pages, codes have been taken to have symbols from $GF(p)$ rather than the more general $GF(q)$. The q-ary case is treated in Section 10.6.

10.3 Projective Geometry Codes

In a Euclidean geometry two lines or flats can be parallel. It is possible to arrange the elements of $GF(p^t)$ in an entirely different manner to produce a geometry in which parallel lines do not occur. A *projective geometry* (PG) of dimension m over $GF(p^s)$, namely PG(m, p^s), can be constructed from $GF(p^{(m+1)s})$ as follows. Associated with a point of the geometry (α) is the set of nonzero field elements

$$(\alpha) = \alpha,\ \alpha\beta,\ \alpha\beta^2, \ldots, \alpha\beta^{p^s-2}$$

where α is a nonzero element of $GF(p^{(m+1)s})$ and β is a primitive element of $GF(p^s)$.* The number of points defined in this manner is

$$\frac{p^{(m+1)s} - 1}{p^s - 1} = p^{ms} + p^{(m-1)s} + \cdots + p^s + 1. \tag{10.19}$$

Let α denote a primitive element of $GF(p^{s(m+1)})$. If (α^{e_0}) and (α^{e_1}) denote any two distinct points of the geometry, then a line (1-flat) is defined as the set of points $(\beta^{i_0}\alpha^{e_0} + \beta^{i_1}\alpha^{e_1})$, where β^{i_0} and β^{i_1} take on all possible pairs of values in $GF(p^s)$ except $\beta^{i_0} = \beta^{i_1} = 0$. Exactly $p^{2s} - 1$ elements of $GF(p^{s(m+1)})$ are assumed, and $p^s - 1$ of these always represent one point. Thus, a line has $p^s + 1$ points. Similarly, a 2-flat consists of the points $(\beta^{i_0}\alpha^{e_0} + \beta^{i_1}\alpha^{e_1} + \beta^{i_2}\alpha^{e_2})$, provided the points (α^{e_0}), (α^{e_1}), and (α^{e_2}) do not all lie on the same 1-flat, that is, are linearly independent. Again, the β^i cannot all be simultaneously zero.

In general, an r-flat is defined as the set of points $(\beta^{i_0}\alpha^{e_0} + \beta^{i_1}\alpha^{e_1} + \cdots + \beta^{i_r}\alpha^{e_r})$, where the points $(\alpha^{e_0}), (\alpha^{e_1}), \ldots, (\alpha^{e_r})$ are linearly independent. The β^i can assume exactly $p^{s(r+1)} - 1$ values, since the all-zeros choice is forbidden. It follows that an r-flat has $p^{sr} + p^{s(r-1)} + \cdots + p^s + 1$ points.

In a projective geometry, if A and B are distinct points, there is one and only one line that contains both A and B. Also, if A, B, and C do not all lie on the same line and if a line L contains a point D of the line

* See Carmichael (1937) or Veblen and Young (1910) for a complete treatment of projective geometries.

AB and a point E of the line BC but does not contain A or B or C, then L contains a point F on the line CA. That is, two lines cannot be parallel.

Like the Euclidean Geometry codes, the Projective Geometry codes are a generalization of the Reed-Muller codes. Again, as in Section 10.2, the codes presented will have symbols from $GF(p)$. It is convenient to associate with each of the points of PG(m, p^s) one of the digit positions in a cyclic code of length $n = p^{sm} + p^{s(m-1)} + \cdots + p^s + 1$. In particular, the digit position corresponding to X^i is associated with the point (α^i), $i = 0, 1, 2, \ldots, n-1$. In this context an r-flat can be associated with an n-tuple which has 1's in positions corresponding to points in the flat and 0's elsewhere. As usual, this n-tuple will be represented as a polynomial over $GF(p)$ in the algebra of polynomials modulo $X^n - 1$.

Now every cyclic shift of the polynomial associated with an r-flat produces a polynomial associated with another r-flat. If $\alpha^{e_0}, \alpha^{e_1}, \ldots, \alpha^{e_r}$ are the defining points of the original flat, then $\alpha^{e_0+1}, \alpha^{e_1+1}, \ldots, \alpha^{e_r+1}$ define the new flat. This suggests defining a class of cyclic codes as follows:

A *Projective Geometry* (PG) cyclic code of order r and length $n = p^{sm} + p^{s(m-1)} + \cdots p^s + 1$ with symbols from $GF(p)$ is defined as the largest cyclic code whose null space contains the polynomials corresponding to all r-flats of PG(m, p^s).

The remainder of this section is devoted to determining the generator polynomial of these PG codes and their minimum distance, and to describing a decoding procedure for them. The analysis parallels that of Section 10.2 for EG codes.

Let $f(X)$ denote the polynomial in the algebra of polynomials modulo $X^n - 1$ associated with an r-flat in PG(m, p^s). Let α denote a primitive root in $GF(p^{(m+1)s})$; then for α^u to be a root of $f(X)$, its order must divide n and so $p^s - 1$ must divide u. If $\alpha^{t(p^s-1)}$ is a root of $f(X)$, then

$$f(\alpha^{t(p^s-1)}) = \sum (\alpha^{t(p^s-1)})^j = 0 \tag{10.20}$$

where the sum is over all $p^{s(r)} + p^{s(r-1)} + \cdots + p^s + 1$ values of j which correspond to points in the r-flat. But

$$f(\alpha) = \frac{1}{p^s - 1} \sum_{i_0 i_1 \cdots i_r} (\beta^{i_0}\alpha^{e_0} + \beta^{i_1}\alpha^{e_1} + \cdots + \beta^{i_r}\alpha^{e_r}) \tag{10.21}$$

since each point corresponds to $p^s - 1$ elements of $GF(p^{s(m+1)})$. Thus, $\alpha^{t(p^s-1)}$ is a root of $f(X)$ if and only if

$$\sum_{i_0 i_1 \cdots i_r} (\beta^{i_0}\alpha^{e_0} + \beta^{i_1}\alpha^{e_1} + \cdots + \beta^{i_r}\alpha^{e_r})^{t(p^s-1)} = 0. \tag{10.22}$$

Upon expanding in a multinomial expansion this sum gives

$$\sum_i \sum_h \frac{(t(p^s - 1))!}{h_0!\,h_1! \cdots h_r!} (\beta^{i_0}\alpha^{e_0})^{h_0}(\beta^{i_1}\alpha^{e_1})^{h_1} \cdots (\beta^{i_r}\alpha^{e_r})^{h_r} \tag{10.23}$$

where

$$h_0 + h_1 + \cdots + h_r = t(p^s - 1).$$

Now by Lemma 10.1 this sum is zero unless for each h_v

$$h_v = k_v(p^s - 1); \qquad 0 \leqq v \leqq r.$$

Equation 10.23 can then be written

$$\sum_k \frac{t(p^s - 1)!}{[k_0(p^s - 1)]!\,[k_1(p^s - 1)]! \cdots [k_r(p^s - 1)]!} \times \alpha^{e_0 k_0(p^s - 1)} \alpha^{e_1 k_1(p^s - 1)} \cdots \alpha^{e_r k_r(p^s - 1)}$$

By Lemma 10.2 and the argument immediately following it, all these multinomial coefficients are zero mod p unless the integer $t(p^s - 1)$, when expanded in radix-p form, is nonzero and is the sum of $r + 1$ or more multiples of $p^s - 1$ with no carries [when $t = 0$, the Sum 10.22 = 1 so α^0 is not a root of $f(X)$]. This can be stated in the form of a theorem.

THEOREM 10.6. *Let α denote a primitive element of $GF(p^{s(m+1)})$. The parity-check polynomial of an order-r Projective Geometry code of length $n = p^{sm} + p^{s(m-1)} + \cdots + p^s + 1$ has $\alpha^{t(p^s-1)}$, $t \neq 0$, as a root, provided $w_s[t(p^s - 1)] \leqq r$.*

In Section 10.6 it is shown that $h(X)$ contains *only* roots of s-weight r or less. Thus Theorem 10.6 provides a means of determining the number of information symbols in a PG code; one need only weigh the n roots of $X^n - 1$. It has proved difficult to devise a combinatorial expression for this bound, however. One exception is the case of $r = m - 1$; for these *difference-set codes*, it has been shown that (Graham and MacWilliams 1966) the bound is satisfied with equality and that

$$n - k = \left[\binom{m + p - 1}{m}\right]^s + 1$$

When $p = 2$ and $s = 1$, the PG codes reduce to a form of cyclic Reed-Muller code. In particular, they are the duals of the cyclic Reed-Muller codes with one digit removed. From Section 5.5,

$$k = \sum_{i=1}^{r} \binom{m + 1}{i}$$

for these codes.

The BCH lower bound on minimum distance applies to PG codes. Every element of $GF(p^{s(m+1)})$ of the form $\alpha^{t(p^s-1)}$ for which the radix-p expansion contains $r+1$ or more multiples of $p^s - 1$ is a root of $g(X)$, as is α^0. Now the number

$$\begin{aligned} v &= (p-1)p^{s(m-r+2)-1} + \cdots + (p-1)p^{s(m-r+1)+1} + (p-1)p^{s(m-r+1)} \\ &+ (p-1)p^{s(m-r+3)-1} + \cdots + (p-1)p^{s(m-r+2)+1} + (p-1)p^{s(m-r+2)} \\ &+ (p-1)p^{s(m+1)-1} + \cdots + (p-1)p^{sm+1} + (p-1)p^{sm} \\ &= (p^{s(m+1)} - 1) - (p^{s(m-r+1)} - 1) \end{aligned}$$

is divisible by $p^s - 1$ and has s-weight r; hence, α^v is a root of $h(X)$. Adding any multiple of $p^s - 1$ to v increases the s-weight to at least $r+1$, for the s-weight of the number added is at least one. Thus, α^v is the largest root in $h(X)$, and if $v < i < p^{s(m+1)}$ and i is a multiple of $p^s - 1$, α^i is a root of $g(X)$. The number of successive roots in this interval is $(p^{s(m-r+1)} - 1)/(p^s - 1)$. Since α^0 is also a root of $g(X)$, it follows that a PG code over $GF(p)$ of order r and length $(p^{s(m+1)} - 1)/(p^s - 1)$

$$d \geqq d_{BCH} = \frac{p^{s(m-r+1)} - 1}{p^s - 1} + 1. \tag{10.24}$$

For binary codes with $n \leqq 73$ and for Reed-Muller codes, this result is known to hold with equality. For longer codes, this is an open question at present.

It is possible to correct $[(d_{BCH} - 1)/2]$ or fewer random errors with a PG code when it is decoded with the Reed algorithm. The key point is that an r-flat and a point not in the flat define an $(r+1)$-flat. This follows directly from the definition of an r-flat.

As earlier for the EG codes, the decoder can determine the check sums corresponding to all r-flats. The set of J sums corresponding to the r-flats which intersect on an $(r-1)$-flat are orthogonal on the sum corresponding to that $(r-1)$-flat. There are $p^{s(r-1)} + p^{s(r-2)} + \cdots + p^s + 1$ points in the $(r-1)$-flat and p^{sr} points in each of the J r-flats which do not lie in this $(r-1)$-flat. Each of these Jp^{sr} points can lie in only one such flat, and every point in the space not in the central $(r-1)$-flat is in one of these r-flats. Hence,

$$(p^{sm} + p^{s(m-1)} + \cdots + p^s + 1) - (p^{s(r-1)} + p^{s(r-2)} + \cdots + p^s + 1) = Jp^{sr}$$

Define $d_{ML} = J + 1$; then

$$d_{ML} = \frac{p^{s(m-r+1)} - 1}{p^s - 1} + 1 = d_{BCH} \tag{10.25}$$

from Equation 10.24.

Since the r-flats are known initially, the $r-1$ flats can be determined with one level of majority logic provided $[(d_{\mathrm{BCH}}-1)/2]$ or fewer errors occurred. The $(r-2)$-flats can be determined similarly; Equation 10.25 shows that the number of orthogonal check sums increases as the dimension decreases. Hence, $r-1$ steps are needed to determine the 0-flats.

THEOREM 10.7. *A Projective Geometry cyclic code of length* $(p^{s(m+1)}-1)/(p^s-1)$ *and order* r *(whose null space contains all* r*-flats of* PG(m, p^s)*) can be* r*-step majority-logic decoded provided* $[(d_{\mathrm{BCH}}-1)/2]$ *or fewer errors occurred, where* d_{BCH} *is given by Equation* 10.25.

Table 10.2. Parameters of Binary Projective Geometry Cyclic Codes with $n \leqq 85$. All r-flats are in the null-space of an order-r code. Codes with $s=1$ are equivalent to duals of Reed-Muller codes with one digit omitted. All codes with $d \leqq 31$ are BCH codes.

n	k	d_{BCH}	Geometry PG$(m, 2^s)$	Order r
7	3	4	PG(2, 2)	1
15	10	4	PG(3, 2)	2
	4	8	PG(3, 2)	1
21	11	6	PG$(2, 2^2)$	1
31	25	4	PG(4, 2)	3
	15	8	PG(4, 2)	2
	5	16	PG(4, 2)	1
63	56	4	PG(5, 2)	4
	41	8	PG(5, 2)	3
	21	16	PG(5, 2)	2
	6	32	PG(5, 2)	1
73	45	10	PG$(2, 2^3)$	1
85	68	6	PG$(3, 2^2)$	2
	24	22	PG$(3, 2^2)$	1

A list of binary Projective Geometry codes is given in Table 10.2 for $n \leqq 85$. Several modified decoding procedures that are applicable to these PG codes are described in Section 10.4.

Example. The (7, 3) binary cyclic code is a PG code based on the projective geometry PG(2, 2). The code has order $r=1$, and so all 1-flats of PG(2, 2) are in the null space of the code.

By Theorem 10.6, the generator polynomial of the code has all roots α^i such that $i = 0$ or that the weight of i, when expanded in binary, is 2 or greater. Thus, α^0, α^3, α^6, and α^5 are roots of $g(X)$. If α is chosen as a primitive root or $X^3 + X^2 + 1$, then $g(X) = X^4 + X^3 + X^2 + 1$ and $h(X) = X^3 + X^2 + 1$.

By Theorem 10.7 the code can be decoded in $r = 1$ step. To construct the decoder it is necessary to construct the $p^{ms} + p^{(m-1)s} + \cdots + p^s + 1 = 7$ one-dimensional flats in the null space. These can be exhibited as follows:

Flats	Points						
	Information			Parity			
	α^0	α^1	α^2	α^3	α^4	α^5	α^6
1	1	0	1	1	0	0	0
2	0	1	0	1	1	0	0
3	0	0	1	0	1	1	0
4	0	0	0	1	0	1	1
5	1	0	0	0	1	0	1
6	1	1	0	0	0	1	0
7	0	1	1	0	0	0	1

It is clear that flats 1, 2, and 4 are orthogonal on the point α^3, which corresponds to the first information symbol due to the pre-multiplication by X^4. It follows that $d_{ML} = d_{BCH} = 4$.
The decoder for this code is shown in Figure 10.2.

Up to this point only codes with symbols from $GF(p)$ have been considered; codes with symbols from the more general $GF(q)$ are treated in Section 10.6.

10.4 Modifications of the Basic Majority-Logic Decoding Algorithm

The algebraic decoding procedure for the BCH codes performs bounded-distance decoding; that is, all error patterns of weight t or less and none of higher weight are corrected. Majority-logic decoding, on the other hand, can also correct many patterns of weight greater than t.

The Use of Feedback.

Suppose a t-error-correcting code is to be majority-logic decoded and $t + 1$ errors occur, one of which is in the first information position. Now it is possible that this first error be corrected. This is easily seen in the case of 1-step decoding; here correct decoding will result if one of the $d-1$ check sums orthogonal on the first digit contains two additional errors. The effect of this error can be immediately removed; thus, only t errors remain and the pattern can be corrected.

An error with magnitude e_{n-1} in the highest order position contributes

$$(0, 0, \ldots, 0, e_{n-1})$$

to the syndrome, since the received word was premultiplied by x^{n-k} before the syndrome was calculated. Now if the quantity $-e_{n-1}$ is added to the feedback path in the syndrome generator, the effect of the error is removed from the syndrome. The dashed-line connection in Figure 10.1 accomplishes this addition as the generator is shifted prior to decoding the second information digit. Obviously, this method works for L-step decoding also.

Variable Threshold Decoding Townsend and Weldon (1967).
Consider binary codes. An m-input majority gate is a special case of an m-input threshold gate. The output of this gate is 1 when T or more of its inputs are 1 and is 0 otherwise. This suggests modifying the 1-step decoding procedure as follows. With the threshold set at its highest value, $d-1$, the decoder attempts to decode each bit of the received word. A given bit is changed if and only if all $d-1$ inputs to the majority gate are one at the appropriate time. If the decoder attempts to decode each of the n-bits of the word and is unsuccessful, the threshold is lowered by one. If another cycle is completed with no changes, the threshold is again lowered by one. When a change is made, the syndrome is modified and the threshold is immediately increased by one. At the completion of every cycle it is decreased by one, and raised by one when a correction is made (except initially when it is set at $d-1$). Thus, the threshold is gradually lowered until it reaches its minimal value, $[(d+1)/2]$, where decoding ceases. Although no analytic results have been derived, computer simulations have shown that this technique permits the correction of many error patterns of weight greater than $[(d-1)/2]$ which are uncorrectable with conventional 1-step decoding. Of course, considerably more time is required to decode.

The Use of Non-Orthogonal Check Sums.
This procedure is an alternative to L-step decoding which applies to both types of finite geometry codes. It is approximately as difficult (or simple) to implement as L-step decoding but corrects somewhat fewer errors.

The method will be explained for the Projective Geometry codes; the results for Euclidean Geometry codes are identical.

Let M denote the number of r-flats in PG(m, p^s). From Mann (1949)

$$M = \frac{(p^{sm} + p^{s(m-1)} + \cdots + p^s + 1)(p^{sm} + p^{s(m-1)} + \cdots + p^s)\cdots(p^{sm} + \cdots + p^{sr})}{(p^{sr} + p^{s(r-1)} + \cdots + p^s + 1)\cdots(p^{s(r-1)} + p^{sr})p^{sr}}$$

Now each r-flat contains $p^{sr} + p^{s(r-1)} + \cdots + p^s + 1$ points. Hence, the number of r-flats passing through a given point is

$$\begin{aligned} N &= \frac{M(p^{sr} + p^{s(r-1)} + \cdots + p^s + 1)}{(p^{sm} + p^{s(m-1)} + \cdots + p^s + 1)} \\ &= \frac{(p^{sm} + p^{s(m-1)} + \cdots + p^s)\cdots(p^{sm} + \cdots + p^{sr})}{(p^{sr} + p^{s(m-1)} + \cdots + p^s)\cdots(p^{sr} + p^{s(r-1)})p^{sr}} \end{aligned} \tag{10.26}$$

Also, each r-flat contains

$$\frac{(p^{sr} + \cdots + p^s + 1)(p^{s(r-1)} + \cdots + p^s + 1)}{(p^s + 1)}$$

lines or 1-flats. Hence, the number of r-flats passing through a given line is

$$\frac{M(p^{sr} + \cdots + p^s + 1)(p^{s(r-1)} + \cdots + p^s + 1)/(p^s + 1)}{(p^{sm} + \cdots + p^s + 1)(p^{s(m-1)} + \cdots + p^s + 1)/(p^s + 1)} = \lambda \tag{10.27}$$

where the denominator is just the number of 1-flats in PG(m, p^s).

Consider the N check sums on a particular digit corresponding to the r-flats passing through a point. Each other digit appears in λ of these sums since the two points define a line and there are λ r-flats on each line.

Note that

$$\frac{N}{\lambda} = \frac{p^{s(m-1)} + \cdots + p^s + 1}{p^{s(r-1)} + \cdots + p^s + 1} = \frac{p^{sm} - 1}{p^{sr} - 1} \tag{10.28}$$

If $[N/2\lambda]$ or fewer errors occurred, then the value of the "central" error digit must be correctly given by the value assumed by the majority of the r-flats, or 0 in the case of a tie. Hence, the codes can be decoded with a single majority gate, albeit one with a very large number of inputs.

For most interesting values of m, p, r, and s, the quantity N/λ given in Equation 10.28 is less than $d_{ML} - 1$, given in Equation 10.25. Especially for long codes some error-correcting ability is sacrificed if this method is used.

By using nonorthogonal check sums and decoding in two steps instead of one, it is possible to correct all patterns of $[(d_{ML} - 1)/2]$ or fewer errors. At Step 1 determine all $(r - 1)$-flats which intersect the high-order digit of the code. In Step 2 the 0-flats are determined from these $(r - 1)$-flats using the method explained in the preceding paragraphs. Now from Equation 10.28, if

$$\frac{p^{sm} - 1}{2(p^{sr} - 1)}$$

or fewer errors occurred, the value of the high-order information digit will be correctly determined by the majority of the nonorthogonal $(r - 1)$-flats on the point corresponding to this digit. It is easily proved that this number is not less than $[(d_{ML} - 1)/2]$. Hence, $[(d_{ML} - 1)/2]$ or fewer errors can be corrected with this method.

Identical results can be proved for Euclidean Geometry codes; partial correction can always be achieved in one step using nonorthogonal flats, but complete correction requires two steps.

It should be pointed out that while any finite geometry code can be decoded in two steps using this modified algorithm, it may be more economical to use the conventional algorithm even if more than two steps are involved. The reason for this is that N in Equation 10.26 can be a very large number even for reasonable values of p, m, and s, and an N-input majority gate is required.

Example. The (7, 4) binary cyclic Hamming code used to illustrate L-step decoding can be decoded in one step. From Equation 10.4,

$$\mathbf{H} = \begin{bmatrix} 1011100 \\ 1110010 \\ 0111001 \end{bmatrix} = \begin{bmatrix} \mathbf{R}_1 \\ \mathbf{R}_2 \\ \mathbf{R}_3 \end{bmatrix}$$

The vectors $\mathbf{R}_1$, $\mathbf{R}_1 + \mathbf{R}_3$, $\mathbf{R}_1 + \mathbf{R}_2$, and $\mathbf{R}_1 + \mathbf{R}_2 + \mathbf{R}_3$ are

1011100
1100101
0101110
0010111.

All four of the sums corresponding to these vectors check e_6, the first error digit, and no other digit appears in more than two sums. Thus, the correct value of e_1 is given by the value assumed by a majority of the sums, or zero in the case of a tie.

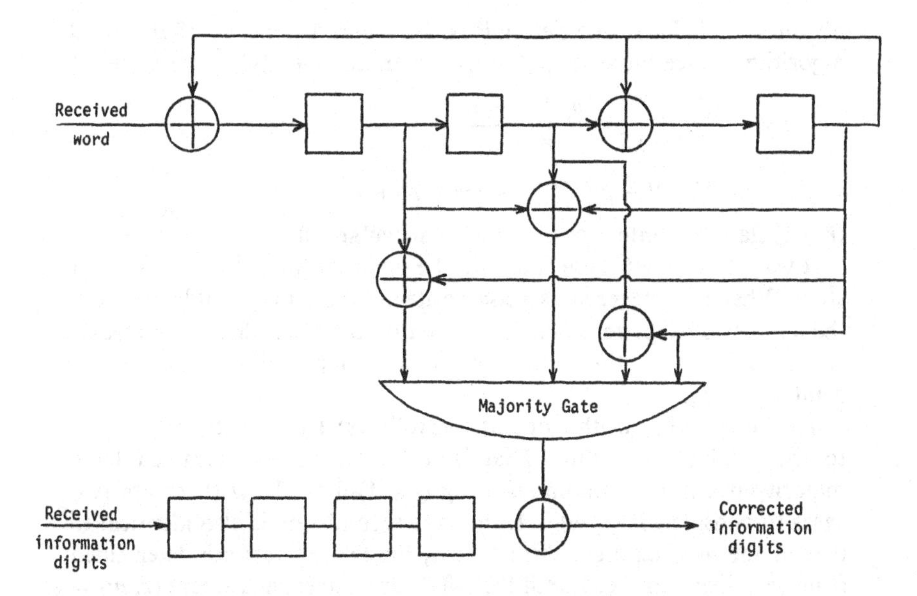

Figure 10.5. A one-step majority-logic decoder for the (7, 4) binary cyclic Hamming code using nonorthogonal check sums.

The decoder for this code is shown in Figure 10.5. Note that this decoder is identical to that of Figure 10.4 with a four-input majority gate replacing the 3 two-input gates. Here no error-correcting ability is sacrificed by using nonorthogonal check sums.

An Improvement in the Reed Algorithm for EG *Codes.*
The Reed algorithm applies to the original Reed-Muller codes and to their two generalizations, the projective geometry and Euclidean geometry codes. The improvement described now is applicable only to the RM and EG codes.

For a prime p, an extended cyclic p-ary Euclidean Geometry code of order r has the following properties:

$$n = p^{ms}$$

$$\begin{array}{c}\text{associated}\\ \text{geometry}\end{array} = \mathrm{EG}(m, p^s)$$

and the additional property that the polynomial associated with every $(r + 1)$-flat in this geometry is in the null space of the code. Now given all the $(r+1)$-flats, one determines the r-flats by means of the Reed algorithm. Since there are $p^{s(r+1)}$ points in an $(r+1)$-flat, there are

$$J = \frac{p^{sm} - p^{sr}}{p^{s(r+1)} - p^{sr}} = \frac{p^{s(m-r)} - 1}{p^s - 1}$$

$$= p^{s(m-r-1)} + p^{s(m-r-2)} + \cdots + p^s + 1$$

$(r+1)$-flats that intersect only on a particular r-flat.

It was shown that these codes can be majority logic decoded in $r+1$ steps. When the integer ms is a composite number, it is possible to reduce the number of steps considerably. Since the cost of the decoder increases very rapidly with L, the number of decoding steps, this can effect a substantial saving.

The improved algorithm operates as follows: The first step is identical to the original algorithm. That is, the r-flats are determined by a majority decision of the intersecting $(r+1)$-flats. Now there are two cases to consider. If $(r, m) = 1$, then the second step is also identical to that of the original algorithm; that is, the $(r-1)$-flats are determined from the r-flats. Proceed until the c-flats are determined where $(c, m) = f \neq 1$. Let $c/f = c'$ and let $m/f = m'$. Now a c'-flat in $\mathrm{EG}(m', p^{sf})$ is also an fc'-flat in $\mathrm{EG}(fm', p^s)$. (The converse is not necessarily true, however.) Thus, one can now consider the geometry $\mathrm{EG}(m', p^{sf})$ which has considerably lower dimension than the original. Since every fc'-flat in $\mathrm{EG}(fm', p^s)$ is known, so is every c'-flat in $\mathrm{EG}(m', p^{sf})$. The number of c'-flats orthogonal on a $(c'-1)$-flat is

$$J' = \frac{p^{sfm'} - p^{sf(c'-1)}}{p^{sfc'} - p^{sf(c'-1)}} = p^{sf(m'-c')} + p^{sf(m'-c'-1)} + \cdots + p^{sf} + 1$$

Since $r+1 > c$, it is not difficult to verify that $J' \geqq J$ for all choices of p, r, c, s, and m. The details are omitted here. The next step is to determine the $(c'-1)$-flats when the c'-flats are known. Because $J' \geqq J$, this is possible even in the presence of $t = [J/2]$ or fewer errors. Therefore, the new algorithm does not decrease the error-correcting capability of the decoder.

Given the $(c'-1)$-flats, it is possible to determine the $(c'-2)$-flats, and so on. Alternately, one can apply the same trick again and so reduce the number of steps still further.

Example. Let $p = 2$, $ms = 12$, and consider the order-10 Reed-Muller code. The associated geometry is $\mathrm{EG}(12, 2)$, and all 11-flats of the geometry are in the null space of the code. Given the 11-flats, we determine the 10-flats in the ordinary way. These can be regarded as 5-flats in EG(6, 2^2) since $f = (10, 12) = 2$. Thus, in the next step the 4-flats of EG(6, 2)^2 (or 8-flats of the original geometry) are determined.

Now again the new c and m are not relatively prime, $(4, 6) = 2$, so the 4-flats of EG(6, 2^2) can be regarded as 2-flats of EG(3, 2^4). Then the third step in decoding consists of determining the 1-flats of EG(3, 2^4) (or the 4-flats of the original geometry). The fourth and last step is to determine the 0-flats of EG(3, 2^4) from the 1-flats. This procedure is depicted in the following chart:

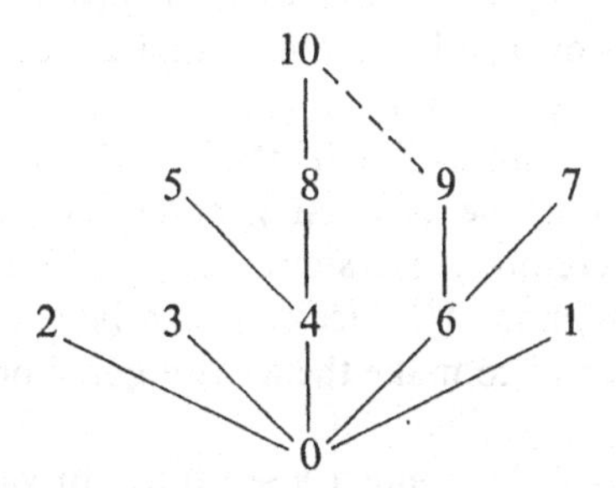

Decoding Chart for EG and RM Codes of Length 4096.

The numbers in the chart represent the dimensions of the various flats in EG(12, 2). The decoding path just described begins with the 11-flats of EG(12, 2), proceeds to the 10-flats, to the 8-flats, 4-flats, and finally 0-flats. Thus, the original 11-step decoding has been reduced to 4 steps. Since the first step in decoding any EG or RM code is always specified, it is not shown in the chart. The other paths represent the decoding procedures for other RM and EG codes. For example, the order-7 RM code, which has 8-flats in its null space, as the path $7 - 6 - 0$.

A Universal Majority Logic Decoding Algorithm for Linear Codes (Gore 1969a, b; Rudolph 1969).

By Corollary 3.1, any $d - 1$ columns in the parity-check matrix of a code with minimum distance d are linearly independent. Thus, in the null space of the code are the $d - 1$ vectors:

$$\begin{matrix} 1 & \beta_{11} & \beta_{12} & \cdots & \beta_{1(n-d)} & \alpha_1 & 0 & \ldots & 0 \\ 1 & \beta_{21} & \beta_{22} & \cdots & \beta_{2(n-d)} & 0 & \alpha_2 & \ldots & 0 \\ \vdots & & & & \vdots & & & & \vdots \\ 1 & \beta_{(d-1)1} & \beta_{(d-1)2} & \cdots & \beta_{(d-1)(n-d)} & 0 & 0 & \ldots & \alpha_{d-1} \end{matrix} \qquad (10.29)$$

where the β's and α's are elements of $GF(q)$. The assignment of n-tuple positions in Matrix 10.29 to digit positions in the code is completely arbitrary because Corollary 3.1 holds for any $d-1$ columns of $\mathbf{H}$.

Now the error digit in position one can be correctly determined provided $[(d-1)/2]$ or fewer errors occurred. From Matrix 10.29 it is possible to determine a generalized parity check on the first digit and any $n-d$ other digits by majority decision. (A *generalized parity-check sum* on a digit γ and $n-d$ other digits is defined as a check sum that gives the value of the error digit at position γ provided no errors occurred in the other $n-d$ positions.) Then from $d-1$ of these generalized parity-check sums on γ and $n-d$ other digits, a generalized parity-check sum on γ and $n-d-1$ other digits can be determined by majority decision, again for any choice of the $n-d-1$ other digits. For the $n-d$ other digits in the original generalized parity-check sums are arbitrary, and therefore these sums can be chosen to have $n-d-1$ other digits in common. The last digit can be chosen to be different in each of the sums so as to make them orthogonal on γ and the $n-d-1$ other digits.

This reduction can be applied $n-d$ times to yield a set of ordinary check sums orthogonal on γ. For a cyclic code this is enough; for an arbitrary linear code the process must be repeated once for each of the k information symbols.

It should be clear that for all but the simplest codes this method is impractical to implement. Since complexity grows exponentially with $n-d$ (and with a large exponent), the procedure is approximately as complex to implement as a trial-and-error search.

10.5 Generalized Reed-Muller Codes

In this section, a generalization of the associated polynomial concept presented in Section 8.3 is given; then in terms of this a natural generalization of the Reed-Muller codes is defined. Theorem 10.9 characterizes these codes in terms of the roots if their generator polynomial, and Theorem 10.10 gives their precise minimum weight. Theorem 10.11 shows that for one important subclass of these codes, the minimum weight code words are the incidence vectors of Euclidean flats, and Theorem 10.12 shows that for another important subclass the minimum weight vectors are the incidence vectors of projective subspaces. These results are used in the next section to show that Euclidean Geometry codes and Projective Geometry codes can be studied in a new and more general theoretical framework.

Let $\mathbf{X}$ denote a vector of indeterminants $(X_0, X_1, \ldots, X_{m-1})$. Represent any integer $i < q^m$, in a radix-q system as

$$i = i_0 + i_1 q + i_2 q^2 + \cdots + i_{m-1} q^{m-1}. \tag{10.30}$$

In order to simplify the appearance of polynomials in the indeterminants $X_1, \ldots, X_m$, the following notation will be used:

$$X^{(i)} = X_0^{i_0} X_1^{i_1} \cdots X_{m-1}^{i_{m-1}}. \tag{10.31}$$

With this notation, an arbitrary polynomial with exponents less than q can be written

$$f(\mathbf{X}) = \sum C_i X^{(i)}. \tag{10.32}$$

Now let us define the q-ary weight of an integer as follows:

$$W_q(i) = i_0 + i_1 + \cdots + i_{m-1}. \tag{10.33}$$

By Lemma 10.3, i is divisible by $q - 1$ if and only if $W_q(i)$ is divisible by $q - 1$.

Let α be a primitive element of $GF(q^m)$. Then every nonzero field element can be written in the form

$$\alpha^j = \sum_{i=0}^{m-1} a_{ij} \alpha^i \tag{10.34}$$

where the elements a_{ij} are in $GF(q)$. Let us denote

$$\mathbf{A}_j = (a_{0j}, a_{1j}, \ldots, a_{(m-1)j}). \tag{10.35}$$

This will be called the coordinate vector of α^j. Every nonzero m-tuple of elements of $GF(q)$ occurs for some j, $0 \leqq j \leqq q^m - 1$. Thus, the vectors $\mathbf{A}_j$ can be substituted for $\mathbf{X} = (X_0, X_1, \ldots, X_{m-1})$ in a polynomial to obtain all possible values of the polynomial.

With this notation the *generalized Reed-Muller codes* can be defined as follows. Let b be a divisor of $q - 1$ and $n = (q^m - 1)/b$. Consider the set $P(m, q, \mu, b)$ of polynomials $f(\mathbf{X}) = \sum C_j X^{(j)}$ that satisfy the following conditions:

1. C_j is an element of $GF(q)$.
2. $j \leqq q^m - 1$.
3. $W_q(j)$ is divisible by b and not greater than μb for every nonzero term.

It can be verified easily that this set of polynomials forms a vector space over $GF(q)$. The dimension of the space is equal to the number of terms that may be nonzero, that is, the number of integers less than $q^m - 1$ whose weight is divisible by b and less than or equal to μb.

Now for each polynomial $f(\mathbf{X})$ the following vector can be formed:

$$\mathbf{v}(f) = [f(\mathbf{A}_0), f(\mathbf{A}_1), f(\mathbf{A}_2), \ldots, f(\mathbf{A}_n)]. \tag{10.36}$$

Since the relationship between $f(\mathbf{X})$ and $\mathbf{v}(f)$ is linear, the set of vectors $\mathbf{v}(f)$ corresponding to all $f(\mathbf{X})$ in the space $P(m, q, \mu, b)$ is also a vector subspace, and this vector subspace is the generalized Reed-Muller code.

The following theorem shows that given $\mathbf{v}(f)$ it is possible to calculate $f(\mathbf{X})$. As a consequence, there is a one-to-one correspondence between the vectors $\mathbf{v}(f)$ and polynomials $f(\mathbf{X})$, and it follows that the two spaces have the same dimension.

THEOREM 10.8. *Let* $f(\mathbf{X}) = \sum_{i=0}^{n-1} C_i X^{(i)}$ *belong to* $P(m, q, \mu, b)$ *and* $\mathbf{v}(f) = [f(\mathbf{A}_0), f(\mathbf{A}_1), \ldots, f(\mathbf{A}_n)] = (v_0, v_1 \ldots, v_{n-1})$, *where* $n = (q^m - 1)/b$. *Then*

$$C_i = \left(\frac{q^m - 1}{n}\right)(-1^m) \sum_{j=0}^{n-1} v_j \mathbf{A}_j^{(q^m - 1 - i)} \tag{10.37}$$

The proof requires three lemmas.

LEMMA 10.4. *Let* α *denote a primitive element of* $GF(q)$. *Then*

$$\sum_{i=0}^{q-2} (\alpha^i)^j = 0; \qquad 0 < j < (q-1)$$

$$= -1; \qquad = q - 1$$

Proof. Recall that

$$X^{q-1} - 1 = (X - 1)(X^{q-2} + X^{q-3} + \cdots + X + 1)$$

and that all nonzero elements of $GF(q)$ are roots of $X^{q-1} - 1$. Then

$$\sum_{i=0}^{q-2} (\alpha^j)^i = X^{q-2} + X^{q-3} + \cdots + X + 1 \Big|_{X = \alpha^j}$$

$$= 0 \qquad \text{if } 0 < j < q - 1.$$

Also,

$$1^{q-2} + 1^{q-3} + \cdots + 1^1 + 1 = -1 \bmod q.$$

Q.E.D.

LEMMA 10.5.

$$\sum_{j=0}^{q^m-2} A_j^{(i)} = 0 \qquad \text{if } i < q^m - 1$$
$$= (-1)^m \qquad \text{if } i = q^m - 1.$$

Proof.

$$\sum_{j=0}^{q^m-2} A_j^{(i)} = \sum_{j=0}^{q^m-2} a_{0j}^{i_0} a_{1j}^{i_1} \cdots a_{(m-1)j}^{i_{m-1}}$$

where $i = i_0 + i_1 q + \cdots + i_{m-1} q^{m-1}$. Because the set of $\mathbf{A}_i$ contains all nonzero vectors, in each component a_{jl} each nonzero element of $GF(q)$ occurs $q^{m-1}(q-1)$ times and zero occurs $q^{m-1} - 1$ times. Dropping the zero terms gives

$$\sum_{j=0}^{q^m-2} A_j^{(i)} = \sum_{a_0}\sum_{a_1}\cdots\sum_{a_{m-1}} a_0^{i_0} a_1^{i_1} \cdots a_{m-1}^{i_{m-1}}$$
$$= \left(\sum_{a_0} a_0^{i_0}\right)\left(\sum_{a_1} a_1^{i_1}\right)\cdots\left(\sum_{a_{m-1}} a_{m-1}^{i_{m-1}}\right)$$

where for each summation a_l is summed over all the nonzero elements of $GF(q)$. By Lemma 10.4, for each individual factor in this last expression

$$\sum_{a_l} a_l^{i_l} = 0 \qquad \text{if } i_l < q - 1$$
$$= -1 \quad \text{if } i_l = q - 1$$

The lemma follows directly. Q.E.D.

LEMMA 10.6. *If $q - 1$ is divisible by b and $n = (q^m - 1)/b$, and if $W_q(i)$ is divisible by b, then*

$$\sum_{j=0}^{n-1} A_j^{(i)} = 0 \qquad \text{if } i < q^m - 1$$
$$\sum_{j=0}^{n-1} A_j^{(i)} = -n(-1)^m \qquad \text{if } i = q^m - 1$$

Proof. If α is a primitive element of $GF(q^m)$, then $(\alpha^{ln})^{(q-1)} = (\alpha^{l(q^m-1)})^{(q-1)/b} = (\alpha^{q^m-1})^{l(q-1)/b} = 1$. Therefore, α^{ln} is an element of $GF(q)$. Since

$$\alpha^{j+ln} = \alpha^{ln}\alpha^j$$

it follows from Equations 10.34 and 10.35 that

$$\mathbf{A}_{j+ln} = \alpha^{ln}\mathbf{A}_j. \tag{10.38}$$

Therefore,

$$\begin{aligned}\sum_{j=0}^{q^m-2} A_j^{(i)} &= \sum_{l=0}^{(q^m-1)/n-1} \sum_{j=0}^{n-1} A_{j+ln}^{(i)} \\ &= \sum_{l=0}^{(q^m-1)/n-1} \sum_{j=0}^{n-1} (A_j\alpha^{ln})^{(i)} \\ &= \sum_{l=0}^{(q^m-1)/n-1} \sum_{j=0}^{n-1} \alpha^{lnW_q(i)} A_j^{(i)}.\end{aligned}$$

But since $W_q(i)$ is assumed divisible by b, then $\alpha^{lnW_q(i)} = 1$, and therefore,

$$\sum_{j=0}^{q^m-2} A_j^{(i)} = \frac{q^m-1}{n} \sum_{j=0}^{n-1} A_j^{(i)}. \tag{10.39}$$

Lemma 10.5 gives the value of the left side of Equations 10.39, and Lemma 10.6 follows. Q.E.D.

Now for the proof of the theorem,

$$\begin{aligned}\sum_{j=0}^{n-1} f(\mathbf{A}_j)A_j^{(q^m-1-i)} &= \sum_l \sum_{j=0}^{n-1} C_l A_j^{(l)} A_j^{(q^m-1-i)} \\ &= \sum_l C_l \sum_{j=0}^{n-1} A_j^{(q^m-1-i+l)}.\end{aligned}$$

Now by Lemma 10.6, the second sum is zero unless $l = i$, in which case it equals $-n(-1)^m$. Therefore,

$$\sum_{j=0}^{n-1} f(\mathbf{A}_j)A_j^{(q^m-1-i)} = -n(-1)^m C_i \tag{10.40}$$

and the theorem follows from the fact that $n[(q^m-1)/n] = q^m - 1 = -1$ in the field. Q.E.D.

THEOREM 10.9. *The generalized Reed-Muller codes are cyclic, and α^h is a root of the generator polynomial of the code with parameters m, q, μ, and b if and only if $W_q(h)$ is divisible by b and $0 < W_q(h) < m(q-1) - \mu b$.*

Proof. Consider the polynomial

$$\begin{aligned}f_h(\mathbf{X}) &= \left(\sum_{i=1}^{m} \alpha^{i-1}X_i\right)^h = \left(\sum_{i=1}^{m} \alpha^{i-1}X_i\right)^{\sum_{l=0}^{m-1} h_l q^l} \\ &= \prod_{l=0}^{m-1} \left(\sum_{i=1}^{m} \alpha^{(i-1)q^l}X_i\right)^{h_l}.\end{aligned} \tag{10.41}$$

The degree of $f_h(X)$ is $W_q(h)$. By Equations 10.34 and 10.35, $\mathbf{v}(f_h) = (1, \alpha^h, \alpha^{2h}, \ldots, \alpha^{(n-1)h})$. For any polynomial $f(X)$ in $P(m, q, \mu, b)$, let $\mathbf{v}(f) = (v_0, v_1, \ldots, v_{n-1})$. Then

$$\mathbf{v}(f)\mathbf{v}(f_h)^T = \sum_{i=0}^{n-1} v_i \alpha^{ih} = \sum_{j=0}^{n-1} f(\mathbf{A}_j) f_h(\mathbf{A}_j). \tag{10.42}$$

Now let us assume that $W_q(h)$ is divisible by b and is less than $m(q-1) - \mu b$. Then, since all the terms of $f(X)$ have degree i whose weight $W_q(i)$ is divisible by b and does not exceed μb, it follows that in $f(X) f_h(X)$ the degree i of every term has weight $W_q(i)$ less than $m(q-1)$. Furthermore, $f(\mathbf{0}) f_h(\mathbf{0}) = 0$, because $f_h(\mathbf{0}) = 0$. Therefore, by Lemma 10.6, every term on the right side of Equation 10.41 sums to zero, and α^h must be a root of the code polynomial

$$v_{m-1}X^{m-1} + v_{m-2}X^{m-2} + \cdots + v_0$$

Since this is true for every $f(X)$ in $P(m, q, b, \mu)$, α^h must be a root of the generator polynomial. The number of such roots equals the dimension of the null space, given with the definition of the codes, and therefore this must be all the roots. Q.E.D.

THEOREM 10.10. *The minimum weight of the generalized Reed-Muller codes is exactly* $[(R+1)q^Q - 1]/b$, *where* Q *and* R *are the quotient and remainder, respectively, resulting from dividing* $m(q-1) - \mu b$ *by* $q-1$, *and the code is a subcode of the* BCH *code of the same designed distance.*

Proof. Every number less than $Rq^Q + q^Q - 1$ has weight less than $m(q-1) - \mu b$, and therefore there are at least $\{[(R+1)q^Q - 1]/b\} - 1$ successive powers of α^b that are roots of $g(X)$. It follows from the BCH bound that the minimum weight is at least $[(R+1)q^Q - 1]/b$.

Let α be a primitive root of $GF(q^m)$ and $\gamma = \alpha^{(q^m-1)/(q-1)}$. Then γ is a primitive root of $GF(q)$. Let $n = (q^m - 1)/b$ and $z = (q-1)/b$. Then $\eta = \alpha^n = \gamma^z$ is a primitive bth root of unity, because $\eta^b = 1$ but no smaller power of η is one. The roots of $X^b - \gamma^{jb}$ then are

$$X = \gamma^j, \eta\gamma^j, \ldots, \eta^{b-1}\gamma^j = \gamma^j, \gamma^{j+z}, \ldots, \gamma^{j+(b-1)z}. \tag{10.43}$$

Consider the polynomial

$$f_0(X_0) = \prod_{j=1}^{(q-1-R)/b} (X_0^b - \gamma^{jb}). \tag{10.44}$$

Its nonroots must include zero and

$$\gamma^j, \eta\gamma^j, \ldots, \eta^{b-1}\gamma^j \text{ for } (q-1-R)/b < j \leqq (q-1)/b.$$

Thus, there are R/b sets of b roots, besides zero, and each set of roots contains all multiples of any one root by powers of η.

Now consider

$$f_{\min}(\mathbf{X}) = f_0(X_0)(X_1^{q-1} - 1)(X_2^{q-1} - 1) \cdots (X_{m-Q-1}^{q-1} - 1). \quad (10.45)$$

Clearly, $f_{\min}(\mathbf{X})$ is an element of $P(m, q, \mu, b)$. The coordinate vectors $\mathbf{A}_j$ which are nonroots are those that have as a_{0j} a nonroot of $f_0(X_0)$, and for which $X_1, X_2, \ldots, X_{m-Q-1}$ are all zero, but $X_{m-Q}, \ldots, X_{m-1}$ are arbitrary. There are $(R+1)q^Q - 1$ such vectors excluding the all-zero vector. They fall in classes of b vectors also, in which each member of the class is a multiple of each other member by a power of η. By Equation 10.38, in each class, for one and only one vector $\mathbf{A}_j$, the j is less than η. Therefore, among the components of the code vector

$$\mathbf{v}(f_{\min}) = [f_{\min}(\mathbf{A}_0), f_{\min}(\mathbf{A}_1), \ldots, f_{\min}(\mathbf{A}_{n-1})],$$

there must be exactly $[(R+1)q^Q - 1]/b$ nonzero components, that is, this is the weight of $\mathbf{v}(f_{\min})$, which is in the code. Q.E.D.

THEOREM 10.11. *In a primitive-length generalized $c(q-1)$-order Reed-Muller code (that is, $b = 1$, and $n = q^m - 1$), the location numbers of a minimum-weight code vector form an $(m-c)$-dimensional linear subspace of $GF(q^m)$ and the component values are all equal, and conversely every vector whose components are all equal and whose location numbers form an $(m-c)$-dimensional subspace of $GF(q^m)$ is a minimum-weight code vector in the $c(q-1)$-order primitive Reed-Muller code.*

Proof. Let V be an $m-c$ dimensional subspace of $GF(q^m)$ over $GF(q)$, and let U be its null space, with the inner product defined in the usual way. That is, if $\mathbf{A} = (a_1, a_2, \ldots, a_m)$ is an element of V and $\mathbf{B} = (b_1, b_2, \ldots, b_m)$ is an element of U, then

$$\mathbf{A} \cdot \mathbf{B} = a_1 b_1 + a_2 b_2 + \cdots + a_m b_m = 0.$$

Let $\mathbf{B}_1, \mathbf{B}_2, \ldots, \mathbf{B}_c$ be a basis for U. Now consider the polynomial

$$f(\mathbf{X}) = C_0 \prod_{i=1}^{c} (1 - (\mathbf{B}_i \cdot \mathbf{X}^T)^{q-1}) \quad (10.46)$$

where C_0 is an element of $GF(q)$. Since $f(\mathbf{X})$ has degree $c(q-1)$, it belongs to $P(m, q, c(q-1), 1)$ and the vector of values $\mathbf{v}(f)$ is a code vector in the $c(q-1)$-order primitive generalized Reed-Muller code.

For every $\mathbf{A}_i$ that is not in V, $f(\mathbf{A}_i) = 0$, but for every $\mathbf{A}_i$ that is in V, $f(\mathbf{A}_i) = C_0$. This proves the second part of the theorem.

Let $X_1, X_2, \ldots, X_{q^{m-c}-1}$ be the location numbers for a minimum-weight code vector, and let $S_1, S_2, \ldots$ be the power-sum symmetric functions and $\sigma_1, \sigma_2, \ldots, \sigma_{q^{m-c}-1}$ be the elementary symmetric functions. By Theorem 10.9, S_i is zero if $w(i) < (m-c)(q-1)$. Of the integers i between 1 and $2(q^{m-c}-1)$, the only ones for which S_i may not be zero are of the form $2q^{m-c}-1-q^l$ for some l. This fact greatly simplifies Newton's identities. The identities numbered $q^{m-c}-1$ through $2q^{m-c}-2-q^{m-c-1}$ become

$$\begin{aligned} S_{q^{m-c}-1} + (q^{m-c}-1)\sigma_{q^{m-c}-1} &= 0 \\ S_{q^{m-c}-1}\sigma_1 &= 0 \\ S_{q^{m-c}-1}\sigma_2 &= 0 \\ &\vdots \\ S_{q^{m-c}-1}\sigma_{q^{m-c}-q^{m-c-1}-1} &= 0 \end{aligned} \tag{10.47}$$

Note that since the X's are not zero, $\sigma_{q^{m-c}-1} \neq 0$. The next equation becomes

$$S_{2q^{m-c}-1-q^{m-c-1}} + S_{q^{m-c}-1}\sigma_{q^{m-c}-q^{m-c-1}} = 0$$

so that $\sigma_{q^{m-c}-q^{m-c-1}}$ may be nonzero. Taking into account Equation 10.47, the next equations become

$$\begin{aligned} S_{2q^{m-c}-1-q^{m-c-1}}\sigma_1 + S_{q^{m-c}-1}\sigma_{q^{m-c}-q^{m-c-1}+1} &= 0 \\ S_{q^{m-c}-1}\sigma_{q^{m-c}-q^{m-c-1}+1} &= 0 \\ S_{q^{m-c}-1}\sigma_{q^{m-c}-q^{m-c-1}+2} &= 0 \\ &\vdots \\ S_{q^{m-c}-1}\sigma_{q^{m-c}-q^{m-c-2}-1} &= 0 \\ S_{2q^{m-c}-1-q^{m-c-2}} + S_{q^{m-c}-1}\sigma_{q^{m-c}-q^{m-c-2}} &= 0 \end{aligned} \tag{10.48}$$

Thus, the next possible nonzero σ is $\sigma_{q^{m-c}-q^{m-c-2}}$. Continuing in the same manner shows that the only possible nonzero σ's are numbered $q^{m-c}-q^l$ for some i less than q^{m-c}. Thus,

$$\begin{aligned} f(X) &= (X-X_1)(X-X_2)\cdots(X-X_{q^{m-c}-1}) \\ &= \sum_{i=0}^{q^{m-c}-1} \sigma_i X^{q^{m-c}-1-i} \\ &= X^{q^{m-c}-1} - \sigma_{q^{m-c}-q^{m-c-1}}X^{q^{m-c-1}-1} \cdots - \sigma_{q^{m-c}-1} \end{aligned} \tag{10.49}$$

and $Xf(X)$ is a linearized polynomial and has as its roots the elements of a linear subspace of $GF(q)$ by Theorem 6.30.

By the second part of the theorem, already proved, given any C_0 and subspace V of $GF(q^m)$, there exists a code vector whose location numbers are the points of the subspace and which has the value C_0 at each location. Suppose there also exists a code vector with the same location numbers but not with the same value for each component. Let C_0 be the value of the first component, and form the code vector with constant values C_0. Subtracting these will give a nonzero code vector of smaller weight. This is impossible. Therefore, every minimum-weight code vector must have all components equal. Q.E.D.

Theorem 10.11 can be generalized to the case in which $b > 1$ as follows:

THEOREM 10.12. *In a generalized Reed-Muller code of nonprimitive length* $n = (q^m - 1)/b$, $b > 1$, *with* $\mu b = c(q - 1)$, *a vector is a minimum-weight code vector if and only if*

1. *The components are all equal.*
2. *The n-bit vector is repeated b times to form an* $nb = (q^m - 1)$*-component vector, the location numbers in this latter vector form an* $(m - c)$*-dimensional subspace of* $GF(q^m)$.

Proof. Suppose the components of a vector are all equal, and the location numbers of the vector repeated b times do form a linear subspace. Then the resulting $nb = (q^m - 1)$ component vector is a minimum weight vector in the $\mu = c(q - 1)$, $b = 1$ Reed-Muller code. It corresponds to a polynomial

$$f(\mathbf{X}) = \sum_{i=0}^{q^m - 1} C_i X^{(i)} \tag{10.50}$$

and by Theorem 10.8,

$$C_i = (-1)^m (q^m - 1) \sum_{j=0}^{q^m - 2} \mathbf{v}_j A_j^{(q^m - 1 - i)} \tag{10.51}$$

Since $\mathbf{v}_j$ is the $(q^m - 1)$-component vector consisting of b repetitions of an n-component vector,

$$C_i = (-1)^m (q^m - 1) \sum_{j=0}^{n-1} \sum_{l=0}^{b-1} \mathbf{v}_{j+nl} A_{j+nl}^{(q^m - 1 - i)}$$

and $\mathbf{v}_{j+nl} = \mathbf{v}_j$; therefore,

$$C_i = (-1)^m (q^m - 1) \sum_{j=0}^{n-1} \mathbf{v}_j \sum_{l=0}^{b-1} A_{j+nl}^{(q^m - 1 - i)}.$$

Next, by Equation 10.38

$$C_i = (-1)^m (q^m - 1) \sum_{j=0}^{n-1} v_j A_j^{(q^m - 1 - i)} \sum_{l=0}^{b-1} \alpha^{ln(q^m - 1 - i)}. \tag{10.52}$$

The last summation is zero unless $ln(q^m - 1 - i)$ is a multiple of $q^m - 1$, that is, unless i is a multiple of b. Therefore, in Equation 10.50, the weight of each exponent is a multiple of b. It follows that this polynomial $f(\mathbf{X})$ corresponds to an n-component vector $\mathbf{v}(f)$ in the generalized Reed-Muller code with $b > 0$. Since the weight of the $(q^m - 1)$-component vector is, by Theorem 10.10, $q^{m-c} - 1$, the weight of the n-component vector is $(q^{m-c} - 1)/b$, which, by Theorem 10.11, is the minimum weight, and thus this is a minimum-weight code vector.

Now assume $\mathbf{v}(f)$ is a minimum-weight code vector in the generalized Reed-Muller code with $b > 1$ and $\mu = c(q-1)/b$. The corresponding polynomial is an element of $P(n, q, b, \mu)$ which is contained in $P(q^m - 1, q, b, \mu)$, and therefore the corresponding $q^m - 1$ component vector is in the primitive generalized Reed-Muller code. By Theorem 10.10, the weight of the n-component vector is $(q^{m-c} - 1)/b$, and from Equation 10.38 it follows that the weight of the $q^m - 1$ component vector is b times as great, or $q^{m-c} - 1$. Therefore, it is a minimum-weight code vector in the primitive-length code, and its components must be constant and its location numbers must form a linear subspace of $GF(q^m)$. Q.E.D.

COROLLARY 10.2. *In a generalized Reed-Muller code of length* $n = (q^m - 1)/(q - 1)$, *with* $b = q - 1$ *and* $\mu = c$, *a code vector is a minimum-weight code vector if and only if the nonzero components are all equal and the location numbers correspond to the points in a projective subspace of dimension* $m - c - 1$.

Proof. By Equation 10.38, $\mathbf{A}_{j+ln} = \alpha^{ln}\mathbf{A}_j$, and since α is a primitive root of $GF(q^m)$, α^n is a primitive root of $GF(q)$. Therefore, the set of vectors $\mathbf{A}_{j+ln}$, $l = 0, 1, \ldots, q-2$, are the set of all nonzero scalar multiples of a single vector, say $\mathbf{A}_j$, $0 \leqq j < n$. This set of $\mathbf{A}$'s then corresponds to a point in projective space, and there is in this sense a point in projective space for each $\mathbf{A}_j$, $0 \leqq j < n$. By Theorem 10.11, for any minimum-weight code vector the nonzero components are equal and the location numbers correspond to a linear subspace of $GF(q^m)$ of dimension $m - c$. It follows directly from the definition of a projective subspace that the location numbers among the first n components form a projective subspace of dimension $m - c - 1$. On the other hand, suppose a code vector of length n has equal nonzero components and location numbers corresponding to a projective subspace of dimension $m - c - 1$. This vector repeated $q - 1$ times then corresponds to a minimum-weight vector in the primitive generalized Reed-Muller code of length $q^m - 1$ with $\mu = c$ and, by Theorem 10.12, this vector is a minimum-weight vector in the nonprimitive code. Q.E.D.

10.6 Polynomial Codes

The class of codes called *polynomial codes* includes as special cases most of the important cyclic codes so far studied: BCH codes, including Hamming codes and Reed-Solomon codes; Reed-Muller codes; Projective Geometry codes; and Euclidean Geometry codes. This large class of codes is treated in the remainder of this chapter. First the notion of a subfield subcode is defined. Then polynomial codes are defined as the subfield subcodes of the generalized Reed-Muller codes. Finally, it is shown that PG and EG codes are polynomial codes, and in this framework additional properties of PG and EG codes are derived.

If V is a code with symbols from $GF(q^s)$, then the *$GF(q)$-subfield subcode* of V is the set of all vectors in V whose components are all elements of $GF(q)$. It is easily verified that this is a subspace.

THEOREM 10.13. *Let $g(X)$ generate a code with symbols from $GF(q^s)$ and $g'(X)$ generate the $GF(q)$ subfield of $GF(q^s)$. Then β is a root of $g'(X)$ if and only if β^{q^i} is a root of $g(X)$ for some i, $0 \leqq i < s$.*

Proof. By the definition of the subcode, $g'(X)$ must belong to the original code, and hence every root of $g(X)$ is also a root of $g'(X)$. In addition, since $g'(X)$ has coefficients from $GF(q)$, if β is a root of $g'(X)$, so is $\beta^q, \beta^{q^2}, \ldots$. Then if β^{q^i} is a root of $g(X)$, β^{q^i} and $(\beta^{q^i})^{q^{s-i}} = \beta^{q^s} = \beta$ are roots of $g'(X)$. On the other hand, the polynomial that has as its roots all β satisfying the condition that for some i β^{q^i} is a root of $g(X)$ has in particular all roots of $g(X)$ as roots and has all real coefficients. Hence, it belongs to the subcode and must be divisible by $g'(X)$, and $g'(X)$ can have no other roots. Q.E.D.

As an example of subfield subcodes, note that every (n, k) BCH code of designed distance d_0 is a subfield subcode of an (n, k') Reed-Solomon code of designed distance d_0, with $k < k'$ if it is a proper subcode.

A polynomial code is defined as the subfield subcode over $GF(q)$ of a generalized Reed-Muller code over $GF(q^s)$. Alternatively, it can be defined as the set of all vectors over $GF(q)$ whose associated polynomials are in $P(m, q^s, \mu, b)$. There are five parameters:

- q The number of elements in the field of code symbols.
- q^s The number of elements in the generalized Reed-Muller code of which this is a subcode.
- m A parameter related to the location numbers and code length. The code vector components are given location numbers from $GF(q^{ms})$, and hence also the code length n is a divisor of $q^{ms} - 1$.
- b A divisor of $q^s - 1$. The code length $n = (q^{ms} - 1)/b$, and every term in the associated polynomials must have degree divisible by b.
- μ The order of the code. The associated polynomials in $\mathbf{X} = (X_0, X_1, \ldots, X_m)$ have degree μb.

The following theorem is a direct consequence of Theorems 10.13 and 10.9:

THEOREM 10.14. *Let α be a primitive element of $GF(q^{ms})$. Then α^h is a root of the generator polynomial $g(X)$ of a polynomial code if and only if b divides h and*

$$\min_{0 \leq l < s} W_{q^s}(hq^l) = jb \quad \text{with} \quad 0 < j < \left\lceil \frac{m(q-1)}{b} \right\rceil - \mu.$$

Also, since polynomial codes are subcodes of generalized Reed-Muller codes, Theorem 10.10 provides a simple lower bound on minimum distance for polynomial codes.

Many codes already studied occur as subcodes of polynomial codes. By definition, the generalized Reed-Muller codes are a subclass, where the subfield is taken to be the whole field of symbols; that is, $s = 1$. The Reed-Solomon codes occur as a special case of generalized Reed-Muller codes with $b = m = 1$. Hence, they are also polynomial codes. The primitive BCH codes are subfield subcodes of Reed-Solomon codes, and therefore they occur as polynomial codes with $b = m = 1$ but with s possibly greater than one. These facts can also be verified by examining the roots of the generator polynomials using Theorem 10.9.

In the remainder of this chapter the relationship between polynomial codes and Euclidean Geometry codes and Projective Geometry codes is discussed.

Consider the case of polynomial codes with $b = 1$ and $\mu = D(q^s - 1)$. It follows immediately from Theorem 10.11 that every vector whose nonzero components are all equal and lie at the locations corresponding to a Euclidean flat of dimension $(m - D)$ through the origin is a code vector, and every minimum-weight code vector is of this form. Furthermore, it follows directly from Theorems 8.16 and 10.14 that the extended polynomial codes are invariant under the affine transformation. By an affine transformation it is possible to permute any flat not through the origin into a flat through the origin, and vice versa. Thus, the flats not through the origin are also code vectors, and the dual codes of the polynomial codes with $b = 1$ and $\mu = D(q^s - 1)$ have all the $(m - D)$-dimensional flats as parity-check vectors. The following theorem shows that in fact these codes are the same as the codes defined in Section 10.2 as Euclidean Geometry codes if q is a prime.

THEOREM 10.15. *The Euclidean Geometry code with order r is the dual code of the polynomial code with parameter $\mu = (m - 1 - r)(p^s - 1)$.*

Proof. By Theorem 10.4, the parity-check polynomial of the Euclidean Geometry code has α^h as a root if and only if $w_s(h) \leqq r$. By Theorem 10.14, the generator of the polynomial code has α^h as a root if and only if

$$\min_{0 \leqq l < s} W_{p^s}(hq^l) < (r + 1)(p^s - 1). \tag{10.53}$$

Thus, it must be shown that these two inequalities imply each other. This can be done with the aid of the following:

LEMMA 10.7. *If $W_{p^s}(h) > p^s - 1$, there exist h_a and h_b such that $h = h_a + h_b$, with $W_{p^s}(h_a) = p^s - 1$, and in the radix-q^s system there are no carries in the addition of h_a and h_b.*

Proof. Let $h = h_0 + h_1 p^s + \cdots + h_{m-1} p^{(m-1)s}$, and let $h_a = h_{a0} + h_{a1} p^s + \cdots + h_{a(m-1)} p^{(m-1)s}$ be chosen so that each $h_{al} \leqq h_l$ and

$$\sum_{l=0}^{m-1} h_{al} = p^s - 1.$$

Then let $h_b = h_{b0} + h_{b1} p^s + \cdots + h_{b(m-1)} p^{(m-1)s}$ with $h_{bl} = h_l - h_{al}$. Then it follows directly that with this h_a and h_b the lemma is true.

Q.E.D.

LEMMA 10.8. *$w_s(h) \leqq r$ if and only if*

$$\min_{0 \leqq l < s} W_{p^s}(hq^l) < (r + 1)(p^s - 1)$$

Proof. Suppose that $w_s(h) = t$. Then, by definition of s-weight, the following holds:

$$h = h_0 + h_1 + h_2 + \cdots + h_t \tag{10.54}$$

with

a. $h_0 \geqq 0$ and $h_i > 0$ for $1 \leqq i \leqq t$.
b. h_i is a multiple of $p^s - 1$ for $1 \leqq i \leqq t$.
c. In radix-p^s arithmetic, the sum of Equation 10.54 has no carries.
d. There is no sum in Equation 10.54 satisfying (*a*), (*b*), and (*c*) with a larger value of t.

By Lemma 10.7, it follows that $W_{p^s}(h_0) < p^s - 1$ and $W_{p^s}(h_i) = p^s - 1$ for $1 \leqq i \leqq t$. Otherwise, a component h_i could be partitioned and a sum violating (*d*) could be formed. Also, it follows from (*c*) that

$$\begin{aligned} W_{p^s}(h) &= W_{p^s}(h_0) + W_{p^s}(h_1) + \cdots + W_{p^s}(h_t) \\ &= W_{p_s}(h_0) + t(p^s - 1), \end{aligned} \tag{10.55}$$

and

$$t(p^s - 1) \leqq W_{p^s}(h) < (t + 1)(p^s - 1). \tag{10.56}$$

Thus, if $w_s(h) \leqq r$, then $W_{p^s}(h) < (r + 1)(p^s - 1)$, and certainly

$$\min_{0 \leqq l < s} W_{p^s}(hq^l) < (r + 1)(p^s - 1).$$

Now assume that $\min_{0 \leqq l < s} W_{p^s}(hp^l) < (r + 1)(p^s - 1)$ and that $w_s(h) = t$. Then, for $1 \leqq i \leqq t$, $W_{p^s}(h_i p^l)$ is divisible by $p^s - 1$. Let $W_{p^s}(h_i p^l) = k_i(p^s - 1)$. Then, because of (*c*),

$$\begin{aligned} W_{p^s}(hp^l) &= W_{p^s}(h_0 p^l) + W_{p^s}(h_1 p^l) + \cdots + W_{p^s}(h_t p^l) \\ &= W_{p^s}(h_0 p^l) + (p^s - 1)\sum_{i=1}^{t} k_i \geqq t(p^s - 1) \end{aligned} \tag{10.57}$$

It follows that if $W_{p^s}(hp^l) < (r + 1)(p^s - 1)$, then $w_s(h) = t \leqq r$. Q.E.D.

The theorem now follows directly from Lemma 10.8.

Now the question arises, is the Euclidean Geometry code defined by Theorem 10.4 or 10.15 really the largest code that has all the Euclidean flats of dimension $r + 1$ or greater in its null space? For the case treated so far, with symbols from a prime field, Delsarte (1970) has shown that the polynomial code in Theorem 10.15 is generated by its minimum weight vectors, which are the flats. Thus the Euclidean Geometry code must have the entire polynomial code in its null space, and hence is maximal.

Now consider the case in which the symbols are chosen from $GF(q)$, where $q = p^{\nu}$, $\nu > 1$. The largest code which has the flats in its null space is the dual code of the code generated by the flats. This code can be characterized with the aid of the following theorem:

THEOREM 10.16. *Let* $\mathbf{v}_1, \mathbf{v}_2, \ldots, \mathbf{v}_k$ *be a set of vectors with components in* $GF(q)$, *and let* $\mathbf{v} = \sum_{i=1}^{k} \beta_i \mathbf{v}_i$, *where* $\beta_i \in GF(q^m)$, *but all the components of* $\mathbf{v}$ *are elements of* $GF(q)$. *Then there exist elements* $b_1, b_2, \ldots, b_k$ *in* $GF(q)$ *such that* $\mathbf{v} = \sum_{i=1}^{k} b_i \mathbf{v}_i$.

Proof. Let $\beta_i = b_{i0} + b_{i1}\alpha + \cdots + b_{i(m-1)}\alpha^{m-1}$, where α is an element of $GF(q^m)$. Then

$$\begin{aligned}\sum_{i=1}^{k} \beta_i \mathbf{v}_i &= \sum_{i=1}^{k} \sum_{j=0}^{m-1} b_{ij}\alpha^j \mathbf{v}_i \\ &= \sum_{i=1}^{k} b_{i0} \mathbf{v}_i + \alpha \sum_{i=1}^{k} b_{i1} \mathbf{v}_i + \cdots + \alpha^{m-1} \sum_{i=1}^{k} b_{i(m-1)} \mathbf{v}_i \\ &= \mathbf{v}\end{aligned}$$

Since the components of $\mathbf{v}$ are in $GF(q)$, it follows that

$$\sum_{i=1}^{k} b_{ij} \mathbf{v}_i = \mathbf{0} \quad \text{if } 1 \leqq j \leqq m-1,$$

and

$$\sum_{i=1}^{k} b_{i0} \mathbf{v}_i = \mathbf{v}$$

which is the required result. Q.E.D.

Let C_1 denote the code generated by the Euclidean flats of dimension $r + 1$ over $GF(q)$ and C_2 denote the code generated by the same flats, but over $GF(p)$. By Theorem 10.16, a linearly independent set of vectors over $GF(q)$ is linearly independent over $GF(p)$ and conversely. Thus a basis of C_2 can serve as a basis of C_1. The generator polynomial for a code is the greatest common divisor of any set of basis polynomials, and thus C_2 and C_1 have the same generator polynomial. Thus the (maximal) Euclidean Geometry code over $GF(q)$ has the same generator polynomial as the (maximal) Euclidean Geometry code over $GF(p)$, which in turn is characterized by Theorem 10.4 or 10.15. It can be shown that if the generator polynomial $g(X)$ has coefficients in $GF(p)$ but the code symbols are taken from $GF(p^{\nu})$, this is equivalent to ν-fold interleaving of the code generated by $g(X)$ over $GF(p)$.

Now consider Projective Geometry codes with symbols from $GF(p)$.

THEOREM 10.17. *The Projective Geometry code of order r is the dual code of the polynomial code with parameter* $\mu = (m - r - 1)(p^s - 1)$.

This follows directly from Theorems 10.6 and 10.14 and Lemma 10.8. Note that Corollary 10.2 assures independently that the vectors corresponding to the projective subspaces of dimension r are in the polynomial code.

Again the question arises whether or not this code is the largest that contains all the projective subspaces of dimension r or greater in its null space. If the symbols are taken from $GF(p)$, this question is answered affirmatively by Delsarte, Goethals, and MacWilliam (1970), Delsarte (1970), and Kasami and Lin (1971).

For the case in which the symbols are chosen from $GF(p^v)$, $v > 1$, an argument exactly analogous to that given for Euclidean Geometry codes shows that the generator polynomial for the (maximal) PG code of length n and order r over $GF(p^v)$ is the same as the generator polynomial of the length n and order r over $GF(p)$. Thus again, the codes over $GF(p^v)$ are equivalent to codes over $GF(p)$ interleaved to degree v.

Notes

Reed's procedure for decoding Muller's codes was the first use of majority-logic decoding. Prange applied a version of Reed's decoding procedure to cyclic codes and showed that several specific codes could be majority-logic decoded. Yale (1958) and Zierler showed that the binary maximum-length sequence codes are majority-logic decodable. Interestingly, the codes considered by all of these investigations turn out to be special cases of finite geometry codes.

Gallager's (1963) low-density codes are decoded with a procedure closely related to majority-logic decoding. Massey (1963) proved that all binary BCH codes of length 15 or less are majority-logic decodable. Much of the material of Section 10.1 is based on his work.

Rudolph (1967) was the first to apply finite geometries to the construction of majority-logic decodable codes, and in this sense, most of the results presented in this chapter are outgrowths of his work.

Mathematical techniques for analyzing finite geometry codes were developed by Kasami, Lin, and Peterson (1968*a*; 1968*b*) ,Weldon (1967; 1968*a*), Graham and MacWilliams (1966), Goethals and Delsarte (1968), and Chow (1968). The problem of determining the number of information symbols in finite geometry codes has been worked on by these investigators and MacWilliams and Mann (1967) and Smith (1967).

The generalized Reed-Muller codes are due to Kasami, Lin, and Peterson (1968*b*). Work on generalized Reed-Muller codes has also been done by Delsarte, Goethals, and MacWilliams (1970). Much of the original work on polynomial codes was done by Kasami and Lin.

Problems

10.1. Prove that the dual of an order-μ generalized Reed-Muller code is an order-$(m-\mu-1)$ generalized Reed-Muller code.

10.2. Construct a majority-logic decoder for the binary (15, 7) EG code.

10.3. Construct a majority-logic decoder for the binary (21, 12) PG code.

10.4. Determine the roots of $g(X)$ for the order-0 EG code of length 63 associated with EG(3, 2^2). Verify that it has $d_{BCH}=23$, $d_{ML}=21$, and $k=13$.

10.5. Prove that the dual of an EG code is a subcode of an EG code and so is majority-logic decodable.

10.6. Relate the cyclic maximum-length sequence codes (Section 8.5) to a class of majority-logic-decodable codes and prove that these codes can be L-step decoded.

10.7. Show that the product of a binary (7, 3) PG code with itself can be 1-step decoded.

10.8. Generalize the result of Problem 10.7 and prove that the product of two L-step decodable codes with minimum distances d_1 and d_2 can be L-step decoded and that all patterns of $((d_1d_2-1)/2)$ or fewer errors are correctable.

10.9. Generalize the result of Problem 10.8 to the case where one of the factor codes is L-step decodable.

10.10. After doing Problem 10.9, consider the product of two L-step decodable codes. Is the product code completely orthogonalizable? Discuss.

10.11. (Massey 1963). In all of the majority-logic decoding procedures discussed in this chapter the orthogonal check sums at Step 1 are formed by taking linear combinations of the syndrome digits (Type I decoding). Since these are linear combinations of the received digits, it is possible to express the orthogonal check sums directly as linear combinations of the received digits. This procedure is referred to in the literature (Massey 1963) as Type II decoding. Design a Type II decoder for the (21, 12) code of Problem 10.3.

10.12. Compare the complexity of Type I and Type II decoders for L-step decodable codes.

11 Burst-Error-Correcting Cyclic Codes

A burst of errors of length b will be defined to be a sequence of b error symbols, the first and last of which are nonzero. In dealing with cyclic codes it is also convenient to regard an error pattern whose nonzero symbols are confined to a total of b positions at both ends of a word as a burst. These "end-around" bursts are not distinguished from ordinary bursts in this chapter.

Good practical burst-correcting codes have been constructed both analytically and with the aid of a computer. A simply implemented decoding procedure that is applicable to all of these codes has been devised. Thus, from an engineering viewpoint, at least, the problem of designing burst-correcting codes and decoders appears to be solved.

Theorem 4.15 states that for any linear (n, k) block code, the guaranteed burst-correcting ability b obeys

$$n - k - 2b = z \geqq 0.$$

The parameter z is a measure of the inefficiency of a burst-correcting block code. For some of the codes presented in Sections 11.1 and 11.2, $z = 0$; for most others, z is only slightly larger.

11.1 Analytic Methods of Code Construction

The following theorem shows that a long cyclic code with good burst-correcting properties can be constructed by interleaving a short code.

THEOREM 11.1. *If $g(X)$ generates an (n, k) cyclic code capable of correcting all bursts of length b or less, then $g(X^i)$ generates an (ni, ki) cyclic code with burst-correcting ability bi.*

Proof. Since $g(X)$ has degree $n - k$ and divides $X^n - 1$, then $g(X^i)$ has degree $i(n - k)$ and divides $X^{ni} - 1$. All that remains is to show that the long code has burst-correcting ability bi.

The parity-check polynomial of this code is $h(X^i)$. The polynomials $h(X^i), X^i h(X^i), \ldots, X^{(n-k-1)i}h(X^i)$ form a set of $n - k$ independent parity checks on the information symbols in the positions corresponding to $X^{(n-k)i}, X^{(n-k+1)i}, \ldots, X^{(n-1)i}$. More generally, the polynomials $X^j h(X^i), X^{i+j}h(X^i), \ldots, X^{(n-k-1)i+j}h(X^i)$, $0 \leq j \leq i - 1$, form a set of $n - k$ independent parity checks on the information symbols in the positions corresponding to $X^{(n-k)i+j}$, $X^{(n-k+1)i+j}, \ldots, X^{(n-1)i+j}$. Clearly, no parity check in one of these sets checks an information symbol in another.

This suggests considering the code as a two-dimensional array of the form:

$$
\begin{array}{llll|llll}
X^{ni-1} & X^{(n-1)i-1} & \ldots & X^{(n-k+1)i-1} & X^{(n-k)i-1} & \ldots & X^{2i-1} & X^{i-1} \\
X^{ni-2} & X^{(n-1)i-2} & & & & & & \\
X^{ni-3} & & & & & & & \\
\vdots & & \vdots & & & & & \vdots \\
X^{(n-1)i+1} & & & & & & & X^{1} \\
X^{(n-1)i} & X^{(n-2)i} & \ldots & X^{(n-k)i} & X^{(n-k-1)i} & \ldots & X^{i} & X^{0} \\
 & & \text{Information} & & \text{Parity} & & &
\end{array}
\qquad (11.1)
$$

Now every row of this array is a code word in the original (n, k) code. For if $g(X^i)$ divides $a_{n-1}X^{(n-1)i+j} + a_{n-2}X^{(n-2)i+j} + \cdots + a_1 X^{i+j} + a_0 X^j$, then $g(X)$ divides $a_{n-1}X^{n-1} + a_{n-2}X^{n-2} + a_1 X + a_0$.

A burst of length bi or less can have at most b symbols in any row of the array in Equation 11.1. Since each row can correct a burst of length b or less, the code can correct all bursts of length ib or less. Q.E.D.

The technique of forming an (ni, ki) code as just explained is known as *symbol interleaving* or *interlacing*. The parameter i is referred to as the *interleaving degree.*

COROLLARY 11.1. *Interleaving a shortened cyclic (n, k) code to degree i produces a shortened cyclic (ni, ki) code whose burst-correcting ability is i times that of the original code.*

Interleaving a burst-correcting code for which $z = 0$, that is, for which b is as large as possible, always produces a code with $z = 0$. Thus, given a list of short codes with $z = 0$, it is possible by means of Theorem 11.1 to construct codes of practically any length with maximum burst-correcting ability.

Some interesting burst-correcting codes are based on the following theorem, in which $B_1(X)$ and $B_2(X)$ denote burst polynomials of degree $b - 1$ or less for which X does not divide $B_1(X)$ or $B_2(X)$.

THEOREM 11.2. (*Fire* 1959; *Melas and Gorog* 1963). *Let $g'(X)$ generate an (n', k') cyclic code. Assume that no code word in this code has the form $B_1(X) + X^j B_2(X)$, $1 \leqq j \leqq n' - 1$. Let $p(X)$ be an irreducible polynomial of degree b and exponent e such that $(p(X), g'(X)) = 1$. Then the cyclic code of length $n = n'e$ generated by $g(X) = g'(X)p(X)$ has burst-correcting ability b.*

Proof. Assume that two bursts of length b or less, $B_1(X)$ and $X^j B_2(X)$, are in the same coset relative to the (n, k) code for some j, $1 \leqq j \leqq n - 1$. Then for some polynomial $q_1(X)$

$$X^j B_2(X) + B_1(X) = q_1(X)\, g(X) = q_1(X)\, p(X)\, g'(X). \tag{11.2}$$

Now $g'(X)$ divides $X^{n'} - 1$ and consequently $X^{vn'} - 1$ for all v. Thus,

$$X^j B_2(X) = X^{j - vn'} B_2(X) + q_2(X)\, g'(X)$$

and so Equation 11.2 gives

$$X^{j - vn'} B_2(X) + B_1(X) = q_3(X)\, g'(X) \tag{11.3}$$

where v is chosen to make the degree of $X^{j-vn'}B_2(X)$ less than n'. Equation 11.3 contradicts the hypothesis that no code word in the (n', k') code generated by $g'(X)$ has the form $B_1(X) + X^j B_2(X)$, $1 \leqq j \leqq n' - 1$, unless $j - vn' = 0$ and $B_2(X) = -B_1(X)$.

Dropping the subscripts on the B's and substituting this result into Equation 11.2 gives

$$B(X)(X^{vn'} - 1) = q_3(X) g'(X) = q_4(X) p(X)$$

But by hypothesis $p(X)$ has degree b, which is at least one greater than the degree of $B(X)$. As it is irreducible $p(X)$ divides $(X^{vn'} - 1)$. But this is possible since it says that both $p(X)$ and $g'(X)$ divide $X^{vn'} - 1$. For vn' is necessarily less than n, and $X^n - 1$ is the smallest polynomial of this form divisible by $g(X) = p(X)g'(X)$. Q.E.D.

If $g'(X)$ generates a code of length n' with burst-correcting ability b, then $g(X)$ generates a code of length $n = en'$ with the same burst-correcting ability. If $g'(X)$ is chosen to be $X^{2b-1} - 1$, then the only code word in this code cannot be expressed as $B_1(X) + X^j B_2(X)$, $1 \leqq j \leqq n' - 1$. Choosing $g'(X)$ in this manner gives the Fire (1959) codes.

COROLLARY 11.2. (*Fire*). *The cyclic* $(n, n - 2b - c + 1)$ *code generated by*

$$g(X) = (X^{2b-1} - 1)p(X) \tag{11.4}$$

has burst-correcting ability b. Here $n = e(2b - 1)$, *where e is the exponent of* $p(X)$, *an irreducible polynomial of degree* $c \geq b$ *for which*

$$(p(X), X^{2b-1} - 1) = 1.$$

The proof of Theorem 11.3 does not make clear the idea behind the Fire codes. The parity checks associated with the factor $X^{2b-1} - 1$ are $2b - 1$ interlaced, evenly spaced, parity checks. Since the symbols involved in each check are spaced $2b - 1$ symbols apart, each of these parity checks will be affected by no more than one error in any burst of length $2b - 1$ or less. Thus, these parity checks give a sort of picture of the burst. Any burst of length b or less will leave at least $b - 1$ successive parity checks unaffected, and this is sufficient to tell which symbol is at the beginning of the burst. Thus, the factor $X^{2b-1} - 1$ is sufficient to determine completely the error pattern for bursts of length no greater than b. The additional information required to determine the location of the burst is provided by the factor $p(X)$.

The Fire codes require at least $3b - 1$ parity checks to correct all bursts of length b. Hence, for these codes,

$$z \geqq (n - k) - 2b = b - 1. \tag{11.5}$$

The codes developed in the next theorem or the computer-generated codes of Section 11.2 are superior to the Fire codes in most cases.

THEOREM 11.3. (Burton 1969). *Let* $p(X)$ *denote a polynomial of degree b and exponent e such that* $(p(X), X^b - 1) = 1$. *Then the* $(n, n - 2b)$ *code generated by*

$$g(X) = (X^b - 1)p(X)$$

can correct any burst of length b or less which is confined to positions $X^{ib}, X^{ib+1}, \ldots, X^{ib+b-1}$ for $0 \leqq i \leqq e - 1$. *Here*, $n = eb$.

Proof. Let $B_1(X)$ and $B_2(X)$ denote nonzero polynomials of degree $b-1$ or less. [Here, X may divide $B_i(X)$.] The theorem is proved if it can be shown that there exists no code word of the form

$$c(X) = B_1(X) + X^{ib}B_2(X) \qquad i = 1, 2, \ldots, e-1$$

If

$$B_1(X) + X^{ib}B_2(X) = q_1(X)p(X)(X^b - 1) \tag{11.6}$$

then, since $(X^{ib} - 1)B_2(X)$ is divisible by $X^b - 1$,

$$B_1(X) + B_2(X) = q_2(X)(X^b - 1).$$

But both $B_1(X)$ and $B_2(X)$ have degree less than b so it must be that $B_2(X) = -B_1(X)$. Substituting this result into Equation 11.6 gives

$$B_2(X)(X^{ib} - 1) = q_1(X)p(X)(X^b - 1).$$

Now $p(X)$ has degree b and is irreducible, so for this result to hold, $p(X)$ must divide $X^{ib} - 1$; obviously $X^b - 1$ also divides $X^{ib} - 1$. But $i < e$ and $X^{eb} - 1$ is the polynomial of lowest degree of this form which is divisible by $p(X)(X^b - 1)$. Hence, no code word of the form $B_1(X) + X^{ib}B_2(X)$ exists and every "phased" burst of length b or less is correctable. Q.E.D.

A code word in the code of Theorem 11.3 can be regarded as e b-symbol blocks. These b-tuples can be *block-interleaved* rather than *symbol-interleaved* such that all b symbols of a block are adjacent on the channel. Block interleaving the codes constructed with Theorem 11.3 to degree i produces codes with the following parameters:

$$\begin{aligned} n &= in' \\ b &= ib' - (b' - 1) \\ n - k &= 2ib' \\ z &= n - k - 2b = 2(b' - 1) \end{aligned} \tag{11.7}$$

where b' and n' are the parameters n and b of Theorem 11.3.

For large i the ratio $2b/(n-k)$ approaches unity for the Burton codes; hence, they are asymptotically optimal relative to the Reiger bound of Theorem 4.15. For even modest values of i these codes are superior to the Fire codes.

Since the Burton codes are cyclic, they can be decoded with the procedures discussed in Section 11.3.

From any (n, k) code over $GF(q^m)$, an (nm, km) code over $GF(q)$ can be derived by replacing each element of $GF(q^m)$ by its representation as an m-tuple over $GF(q)$. Such codes, especially those derived from Reed-

Solomon codes and interleaved Reed-Solomon codes, have good burst-correcting capabilities. In particular, a Reed-Solomon single-error correcting code over $GF(q^b)$ interleaved to degree i has exactly the same parameters and burst-correcting capability as the block-interleaved Burton code (Equation 11.7) with $n' = q^m - 1$, the maximum possible value. (See Problem 11.10.) Note that as a code over $GF(q^m)$ the t-error correcting Reed-Solomon code requires $2t$ check symbols and corrects, among other patterns, every burst of length t or less. Thus every Reed-Solomon code, as a code over $GF(q^m)$, is optimal with respect to the Reiger bound. It follows, as for the Burton codes, that as codes over $GF(q^m)$ they are asymptotically optimal. The multiple-burst-error correcting capability of such codes is discussed in Section 11.4.

Example. A Reed-Solomon code with symbols from $GF(2^7)$ and $t = 4$ could be used to correct all bursts of length 22 or less by coding symbols as blocks of 7 binary digits. It would require $2 \times 4 = 8$ blocks or $8 \times 7 = 56$ binary symbols as parity checks. The code length would be $7 \times (2^7 - 1) = 889$.

A Fire code to correct all bursts of length 22 or less would require $3b - 1 = 65$ binary digits as parity checks. The code length could be as great as $(2^{22} - 1) \times 43$, or approximately 160 million binary digits. On the other hand, a burst of length 8 binary digits or less could affect at most two elements of $GF(2^7)$, and thus the Reed-Solomon code could correct any two bursts of length 8 or less. It could correct as many as four bursts if each happened to lie within a single $GF(2^7)$ element.

From Equation 11.7, there exists a (3556, 3500) Burton code with $b = 22$ and $z = 12$. Note that this code has the same burst-correcting ability and number of parity checks as the Reed-Solomon code but is four times longer. It cannot correct multiple bursts, however.

BCH codes can be implemented by the methods described in Chapter 9. Alternatively, if correction of single bursts only is sufficient, the method of Section 11.3 can be used, and requires much less equipment. The additional error-correcting ability of the code can be turned to error detection (any error pattern that the code would correct, if fully utilized, it could certainly still detect) or it can be used to correct bursts beyond its guaranteed burst-correcting ability. (See Section 11.3.)

THEOREM 11.4. *If a code with minimum distance d is used to correct multiple bursts of errors, then the set of all burst patterns satisfying*

$$l + P \leq \frac{3d}{4} - 1 \tag{11.8}$$

is correctable, where P is the number of bursts and l is the total length of the bursts in a pattern.

Proof. Let $B_1(X)$ and $B_2(X)$ be two error patterns, with P_1 and P_2 bursts, respectively, of total length l_1 and l_2, respectively, and with Z_1 and Z_2 0's within the bursts, respectively. Then the weight of $B_1(X)$, denoted $w[B_1(X)]$, is $l_1 - Z_1$, and the weight of $B_2(X)$ is $l_2 - Z_2$. Assume that they are in the same coset. Then $B_1(X) - B_2(X)$ is a code word, and

$$d \leqq w[B_1(X) - B_2(X)] = l_1 + l_2 - Z_1 - Z_2 \tag{11.9}$$

If $B_1(X)$ and $B_2(X)$ are in the same coset, then $(1 + X)[B_1(X) - B_2(X)] = (1 + X)B_1(X) - (1 + X)B_2(X)$ is a code word and $(1 + X)B_1(X)$ and $(1 + X)B_2(X)$ are in the same coset. The weight of $(1 + X)B_1(X)$ does not exceed $2(P_1 + Z_1)$, and the weight of $(1 + X)B_2(X)$ does not exceed $2(P_2 + Z_2)$. Therefore,

$$d \leqq w[(1 + X)(B_1(X) - B_2(X))] \leqq 2(P_1 + P_2 + Z_1 + Z_2). \tag{11.10}$$

Adding twice Equation 11.9 to Equation 11.10 gives

$$3d \leqq 2(l_1 + l_2 + P_1 + P_2). \tag{11.11}$$

For any two bursts satisfying Equation 11.8, Equation 11.11 is not satisfied, and therefore, these bursts lie in different cosets. Thus the set of all bursts satisfying Equation 11.8 is correctable. Q.E.D.

If $P = 1$, then Theorem 11.4 states that the guaranteed burst-correcting ability of a cyclic code with minimum distance d is bounded by

$$b \geqq \frac{3d - 8}{4}$$

This result shows that a random-error-correcting code can be used to correct either random errors or bursts but not necessarily both. That is, the cosets containing correctable random-error patterns are not necessarily disjoint from those containing burst patterns. Codes for correcting both types of errors are discussed in Section 11.5.

11.2 Some Good, Computer-Generated, Burst-Correcting Codes

The codes presented in this section have been taken from lists put together by several investigators (Lucky, Salz, and Weldon 1968; Kasami 1963; Kasami and Matoba 1964; and Zetterberg 1962). For each value of efficiency, the cyclic or shortened cyclic code with the largest known ratio b/n is listed. In cases where two or more codes have the same value of b/n, the shortest is listed.

Table 11.1. Some Burst-Correcting Cyclic and Shortened Cyclic Codes. (The polynomials $g(X)$ are given in right-justified octal notation; for example, $35 = 011101 = X^4 + X^3 + X^2 + 1$.)

Code Rate $R = k/n$	(n, k)	Burst-Correcting Ability b	$z = n - k - 2b$	b/n	Generator Polynomial $g(X)$
$\frac{1}{2b+1}$	$(2b+1, 1)$	b	0	$\frac{b}{2b+1}$	$\frac{(X^{2b+1} - 1)}{X - 1}$
0.42	(7, 3)	2	0	0.286	35
0.60	(15, 9)	3	0	0.200	171
0.63	(27, 17)	5	0	0.185	2671
0.65	(34, 22)	6	0	0.176	15173
0.68	(50, 34)	8	0	0.160	224531
0.81	(67, 54)	6	1	0.090	36365
0.85	(103, 88)	7	1	0.068	114361
0.87	(63, 55)	3	2	0.048	711
0.88	(85, 75)	4	2	0.047	2651
0.91	(131, 119)	5	2	0.038	15163
0.92	(169, 155)	6	2	0.035	55725
0.93	(121, 112)	3	3	0.025	1411
0.96	(290, 277)	5	3	0.017	24711
0.98	(511, 499)	4	4	0.008	10451
0.99	(1023, 1010)	4	5	0.004	22365

Interleaving the codes of Table 11.1 permits the construction of arbitrarily long codes with the rates and values of b/n listed. Other rates can be obtained, obviously, by shortening a code with a slightly higher rate.

The long Burton codes have slightly larger burst-correcting abilities than the codes listed for $R \geqq 0.68$. (See Problem 11.4.)

11.3 Decoding

Burst-correcting cyclic codes can be decoded with an extremely simple version of the error-trapping decoder described in Section 8.9. In that section a t-error-correcting code was employed and an error pattern which had all of its t or fewer errors confined to the $n - k$ high-order positions of the code was assumed to occur. It was shown that the shifted syndrome calculated by the circuit of Figure 8.5 was identical to the $n - k$ high-order positions of the error pattern. More generally, if a correctable error pattern has all of its errors confined to the $n - k$ high-order positions, then the shifted syndrome is identical to these $n - k$ high-order error digits. This can be seen as follows.

Suppose the error polynomial has the form

$$e(X) = X^k f(X)$$

where $f(X)$ is a polynomial of degree $n - k - 1$ or less. The circuit of Figure 8.5 calculates the syndrome of X^{n-k} times the received word. In this case, then, it calculates the syndrome of $X^{n-k}e(X) = f(X) \bmod X^n - 1$. But since $f(X)$ has degree $n - k - 1$ and the generator polynomial of the code has degree $n - k$, the syndrome equals $f(X)$.

This result suggests decoding an (n, k) cyclic code with burst-correcting ability b with the circuit of Figure 11.1. (The following description assumes a binary code. The generalization to q-ary codes involves only defining suitable q-ary logic gates in Figure 11.1.) Assume that a burst of length b or less occurred. This circuit calculates a shifted version of the syndrome of the error pattern which is contained in the received word. If the burst is confined to the b high-order positions of the received word, then the b rightmost stages of the syndrome generator contain the burst, and, by the argument given in the preceding paragraph, the $n - k - b$ left most stages will contain zeros. The logical or gate detects this situation; since its output is now 0, the feedback path

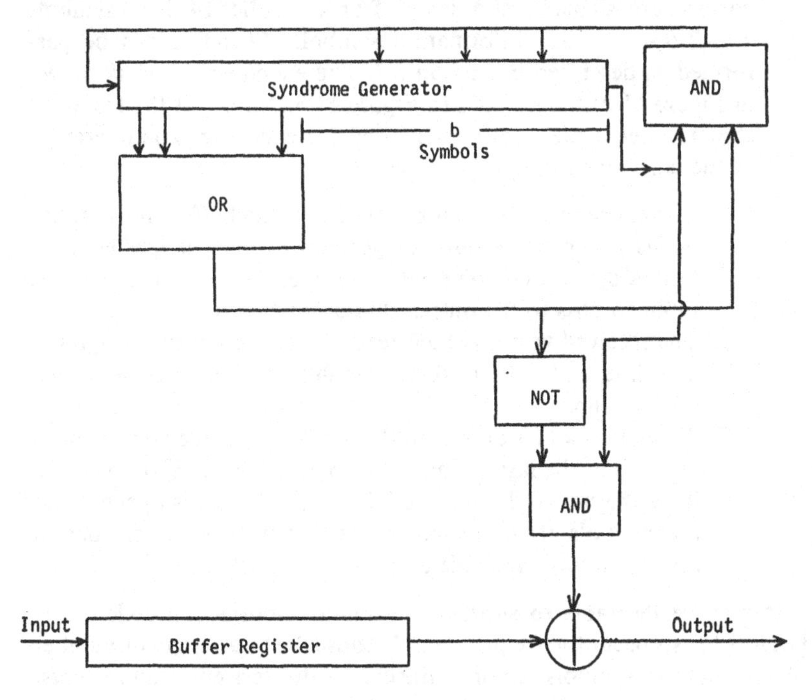

Figure 11.1. A decoder for burst-correcting cyclic codes.

in the syndrome generator is opened and the path into the binary adder is closed. Upon shifting the syndrome generator and buffer register, the syndrome, which is the error burst, is added to the received word, thereby correcting it.

Had the burst occurred elsewhere in the word, it would have been corrected in exactly the same manner. For after shifting the burst will occupy the b high-order positions of the buffer. At this time the b high-order bits of the syndrome will be identical to the burst, as before.

This decoding procedure does not correct "bursts" that occupy only the i high-order positions of the word and the $b - i$ low-order positions. Such bursts are correctable with a burst-b-correcting cyclic code, however. It is possible, even simple, to do this if a syndrome generator which does not premultiply by X^{n-k} is used. (See Problem 11.1.)

Example. The polynomial

$$g(X) = (X^5 + X^2 + 1)(X^9 + 1)$$
$$= (X^{14} + X^{11} + X^9 + X^5 + X^2 + 1)$$

generates a binary Fire code of length $n = 9(2^5 - 1) = 279$ which corrects any single burst of length 5 or less. It has 14 check symbols and $279 - 14 = 265$ information symbols. Encoding can be performed as described in Section 8.7. The encoding circuit is shown in Figure 11.2; the decoder in Figure 11.3. Note that the feedback shift register is identical to that used for encoding. The operation of the corrector follows these steps:

1. The entire received vector is read into the buffer and simultaneously into the syndrome generator which is shifted each time a symbol enters. (Gate 1 is open; that is, it allows the input to pass to the output. Gate 2 is closed.)
2. The received vector is then read out of the buffer one symbol at a time, and the shift register is shifted once for each symbol with no input.
3. As soon as all 0's appear in the first 9 stages, the error pattern must be in the last 5, and the erroneous symbols are ready to leave the buffer. Then Gate 1 is closed, Gate 2 is opened, and the symbols are corrected. If the first 9 stages never contain all 0's, an uncorrectable error has been detected.

It may be desirable to shorten a burst-error-correcting code either because bursts occur too frequently or because the total length or number of information symbols is constrained by other system requirements.

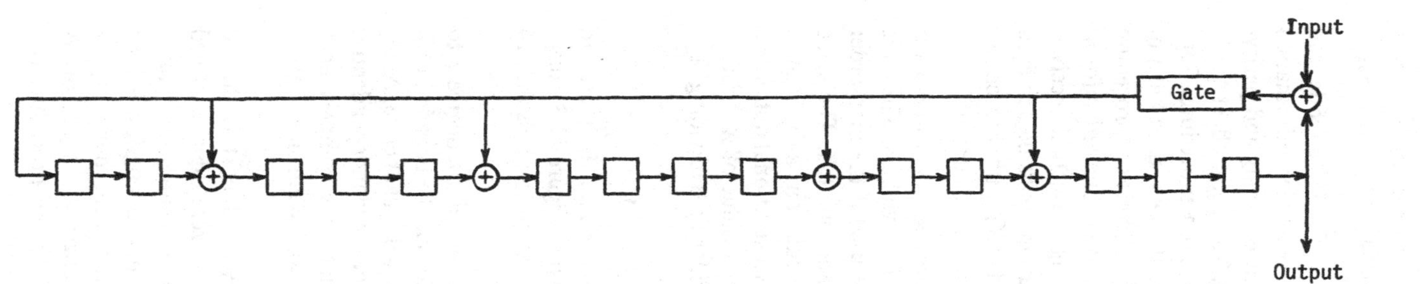

Figure 11.2. An encoder for a (279, 265) Fire code.

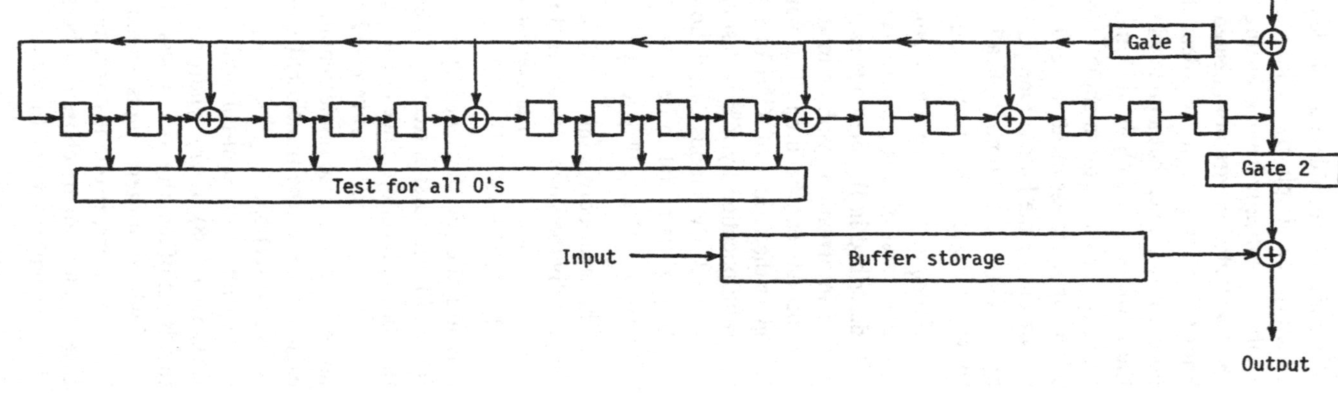

Figure 11.3. An error-correction circuit for the Fire code of Figure 11.2.

If a code of suitable natural length cannot be found, a code can be shortened simply by making some of the high-order information symbols identically 0 and omitting them. Then the encoding and parity-check calculations are not affected, since leading 0's do not affect them. Shortening does, however, affect the error-correction procedure. Suppose, for example, that a code whose natural length is n is used but s of the information symbols are omitted. Then, the correction procedure unaltered would require shifts corresponding to the s omitted information symbols, assumed to be 0's, before reading the actual received vector out of the buffer. One possible simplification could be achieved by an automatic premultiplication by $X^s \bmod g(X)$ with the circuit shown in Figure 7.8. The technique is illustrated in an example:

Example. Suppose that a binary code is required that will correct any burst of length 5 and has 200 information symbols. The code described in the previous example could be used if the high-order 65 information symbols in it are made 0 and omitted. The same encoder can be used. The parity-check calculation, as it stands, gives the residue of $X^{14}r(X)$ modulo $g(X)$. An additional automatic multiplication by X^{65} is desired; that is, the residue of $X^{79}r(X)$ is desired. By tedious calculation, the remainder after dividing X^{79} by $g(X)$ is found to be

$$X^{13} + X^{11} + X^{10} + X^9 + X^7 + X^4 + X^2 + X + 1.$$

The error-correcting circuit is shown in Figure 11.4. It is used in exactly the same manner as the circuit shown in Figure 11.3 except that here code words consist of 200 information symbols and 14 check symbols.

If a cyclic (or shortened cyclic) code is interleaved to degree i to form a longer burst-correcting code, the long code can be decoded with the above procedure since it is a cyclic (or shortened cyclic) code. Alternately, each of the i short received words can be decoded independently; however in this case implementation is somewhat more complex since each word must be transferred from the buffer and syndrome register before correction.

The *statistical burst-correction* procedure described next is due to Gallager (1968). Every syndrome has all of its nonzero digits confined to a burst of length $n - k$ or less. Thus, every coset contains an n-tuple all of whose nonzero digits are confined to a burst of length $n - k$ or less. Therefore, if one is concerned only with correcting bursts, every coset leader can be chosen to be a burst of length $n - k$ or less. A simple modification of the burst-b-correcting decoding procedure can

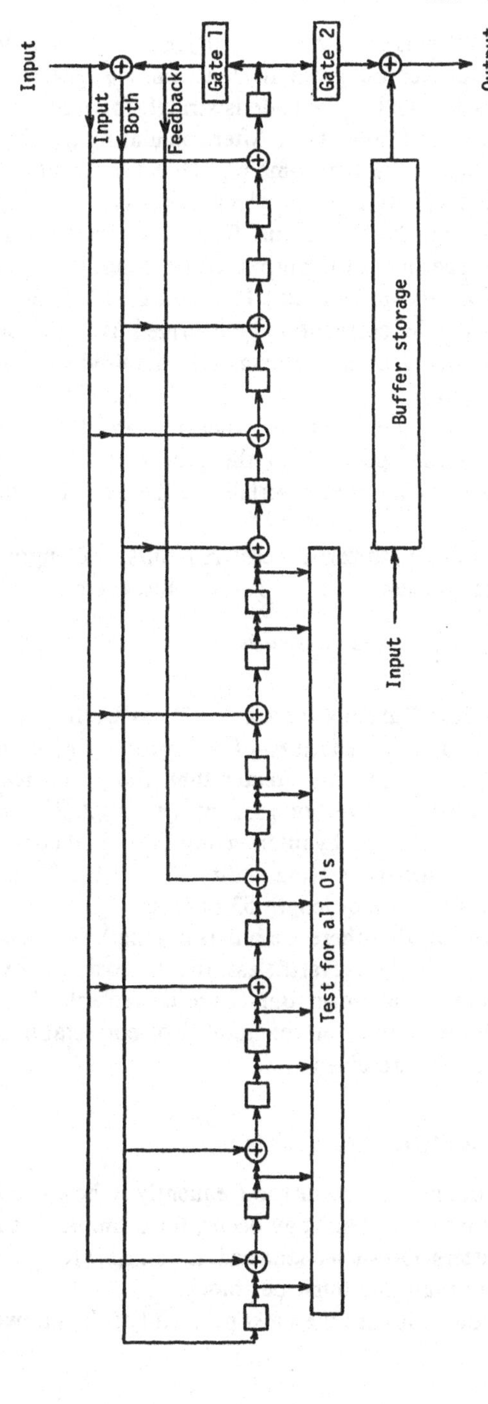

Figure 11.4. An error-correction circuit for the Fire code of Figure 11.3 shortened by 79 digits.

be used to correct all correctable bursts of length $n - k$ or less. The description of this procedure given next assumes a cyclic code; the modification for a shortened cyclic code is straightforward.

Consider the circuit of Figure 11.1. After calculating the shifted syndrome, the decoder shifts the syndrome register n times and determines L, the length of the shortest burst which appears in the syndrome register. This can be done by subtracting from $n - k$ the largest number of consecutive 0's appearing at the output of the generator. (Bursts that overlap the ends of words are ignored.) The position of the first error in this burst is recorded. The correction is performed as in the procedure described earlier. Now, however, no or-gate is required since the position of the burst is known. It is necessary merely to break the feedback connection in the syndrome generator when the first bit of the burst appears in the high-order position of the generator. Then the entire contents of the generator are added serially to the output of the buffer register.

There is one burst of length zero; there are n bursts of length one and $(n - i + 1)2^{i-2}$ bursts of length i; $2 - i - n$. Thus, there are

$$1 + n + \sum_{i=2}^{L} (n - i + 1)2^{i-2} < 2^{L+\log(n/2)} \tag{11.12}$$

bursts of length L or less. But since there are 2^{n-k} cosets, there are enough cosets to correct all bursts of length $n - k - \log(n/2)$. For k and $n - k$ large, this number is substantially greater than the guaranteed burst-correcting ability, which is overbounded by $(n - k)/2$. For example, the (150, 90) cyclic code formed by interleaving the (15, 9) code of Table 11.1 to degree 10 has burst-correcting ability 30. Yet the 2^{60} cosets are sufficient to correct all bursts of length 53 or less.

Of course, it is known that there are bursts of length $(n - k)/2 + 1$ or less which are uncorrectable. Nevertheless, the discussion above points out that a large number of longer bursts are correctable. In Gallager (1968), upper and lower bounds on the number of correctable bursts of length L, $b < L < n - k$, are given.

11.4 Multiple-Burst Correction

On some channels bursts may occur too frequently to be corrected by a single-burst-correcting code. This may occur, for example, if the bursts tend to occur in clusters. On such channels it is desirable for a code to be able to correct more than one burst per block.

The Reed-Solomon codes are the most powerful of the known classes of multiple-burst-correcting codes. Their decoding algorithm (Sections 9.4 to 9.6) is much more complex than the single-burst-correcting procedures presented in preceding paragraphs, however.

A $(q^m - 1, q^m - 1 - 2t)$ Reed-Solomon code over $GF(q^m)$ with $d = 2t + 1$ $GF(q^m)$ can be viewed as a $((q^m - 1)m, (q^m - 1 - 2t)m)$ code over $GF(q)$ which can correct any error pattern whose errors are confined to t or fewer m-symbol blocks. Since a burst of length l_i can affect at most t_i m-symbol blocks if $l_i \leqq mt_i - (m - 1)$, a t-block error correcting code can always correct a pattern of p bursts of total length l if

$$l + (m - 1)p \leqq mt \tag{11.13}$$

A t-error-correcting code interleaved to degree i is capable of correcting all single bursts of length it or less, any two bursts of length $[it/2]$ or less, . . . , or any t bursts of length i or less. This has been found to be the most practical approach to multiple burst error correction on several types of real channels. Also random-error-correcting cyclic codes have some multiple burst correcting ability; see Theorem 11.4.

11.5 Burst-Error and Random-Error Correction

If a code has random-error-correcting ability t and burst-correcting ability b and if the cosets containing the error patterns of weight t or less are disjoint from those containing the burst-error patterns (except, of course, for patterns which are both), then the code can correct both types of errors.

Several types of analytically-constructed codes have this property. Of these the most powerful are the Bose-Chaudhuri-Hocquenghem codes and, in particular, the Reed-Solomon codes.

In Section 11.1 it was pointed out that a t-error-correcting Reed-Solomon code over $GF(q^m)$ can correct all bursts of length $mt - m + 1$ when regarded as a code over $GF(q)$. Since every such burst has weight t or less [over $GF(q^m)$], the cosets containing bursts [over $GF(q)$] are disjoint from the cosets containing error patterns of weight t or less [over $GF(q)$].

In Problem 11.6, a somewhat less effective method of constructing codes for correcting bursts and random errors is discussed. Theorem 5.2 shows that product codes also have this property.

In Hsu, Kasami, and Chien (1968) several classes of computer-generated binary codes capable of burst-error and random-error correction are tabulated. Many of these codes have slightly larger values of b for a given t than the shortened Reed-Solomon codes of the same length and rate.

An (n, k) code has 2^{n-k} cosets and uses $\sum_{i=0}^{t} \binom{n}{i}$ cosets to correct all patterns of weight t or less. For even moderately large n the ratio $\sum_{i=0}^{t} \binom{n}{i} / 2^{n-k}$ is quite small for most known codes. Similarly, the fraction of the total number of cosets used to correct all bursts of length $b = (n-k)/2$ is small. Thus, a priori, there is no reason to suspect that a good random-error-correcting code should not also be able to correct fairly long bursts. The codes of Hsu, Kasami, and Chien (1968) bear this out.

Notes

The first cyclic burst-error-correcting code found was Abramson's single-error, double-adjacent-error-correcting code (Abramson 1959; Abramson and Elspas 1959). (Problem 11.9.) This was the starting point for all the other work on cyclic codes that correct single bursts. The important class of codes found by Fire (1959) resulted directly from an attempt to generalize Abramson's work. Further work has been done by Melas (1960), Reiger (1960), Kasami (1962), Elspas and Short (1962), Melas and Gorog (1963), and Burton (1969).

Most of the computer-generated cyclic and shortened cyclic codes listed in Table 11.1 were found by Kasami (1964) and Kasami and Matoba (1964).

The procedure for correcting all bursts of length $\leq b$ is due to Peterson (1961) although it is basically a refinement of Abramson's (Abramson 1959; Abramson and Elspas 1959) and Meggitt's (1960) methods. (See Section 8.9.) The procedure for correcting bursts of length greater than b and less than $n-k$ is due to Gallager.

Stone's multiple-burst-correcting codes (1963) are closely related to the Reed-Solomon codes. The latter are generally superior for correcting multiple bursts of errors, however. Theorem 11.6 is due to Stone (1961), although the version presented here follows Tavares and Shiva (1970).

Problems

11.1 Show that for every n and b there is a cyclic code of length n capable of correcting any single burst of erasures of length b or less that requires b check symbols. (Compare with Problem 4.1.)

11.2. The following elementary cyclic product code is useful for error correction. The symbols are arranged in a rectangular array as follows:

$$\begin{matrix} X_{11} & X_{22} & X_{33} & X_{44} & X_{55} \\ X_{16} & X_{21} & X_{32} & X_{43} & X_{54} \\ X_{15} & X_{26} & X_{31} & X_{42} & X_{53} \\ X_{14} & X_{25} & X_{36} & X_{41} & X_{52} \\ X_{13} & X_{24} & X_{35} & X_{46} & X_{51} \\ X_{12} & X_{23} & X_{34} & X_{45} & X_{56} \end{matrix}$$

Parity checks are satisfied as follows:

$\sum_i X_{ij} = 0$, that is, parity checks on columns

$\sum_j X_{ij} = 0$, that is, parity checks on diagonals

The symbols are transmitted row by row, left to right, top to bottom.

This can be extended to an m-column $(m+1)$-row array with $2m+1$ parity-check equations.

a. Show that there are only $2m$ independent parity-check equations.

b. Show by an elementary geometric argument that this code can correct any single burst of length b or less if $m \geqq 2b-1$.

c. Show that this is the cyclic code generated by $(X^m-1)(X^{m+1}-1)/(X-1)$, and devise a circuit for an encoder.

d. Give an algebraic proof that these codes will correct any single burst of length b or less if $m \geqq 2b-1$.

11.3. Design a decoder similar to that described in Section 11.3 which is capable of correcting bursts that overlap the ends of the received word. (Hint: Use a syndrome generator that does not premultiply by X^{n-k}.)

11.4. Show that a binary burst-correcting code with $n = 2040$, $R = 0.90$, and $b = 85$ can be constructed from the codes listed in Table 11.1. Show further that there exists a Reed-Solomon code of the same length and approximately the same rate for which $b = 97$.

11.5. Construct a Burton code with $(n-k) = 208$ and $b = 97$. Compare with the Reed-Solomon code of the previous example.

11.6. A shortened cyclic code generated by $(X^c-1)\,g_0(X)$ is known to have minimum distance $2t+2$ and burst-correcting ability b. Prove that the code can correct every random error pattern of weight t or less and every burst of length min (c, b). (Hint: Prove that any pattern of weight t or less and any burst of length min (c, b) cannot be in the same coset.)

11.7. The maximum-length-sequence binary code of length 15 is generated by 7531 (high-order first, right-justified octal notation). Show that this code in addition to being able to correct all error patterns of weight 3 or less, can also correct all bursts of length 5 or less. For the code of length 31 generated by 5 3 5 4 3 7 1 5 1, determine b assuming the code must be able to correct 7 random errors.

11.8. Verify Equations 11.12 and 11.13.

11.9. (Abramson 1959) Show that the $(2^m-1, 2^m-m-2)$ cyclic Hamming code has $b = 2$.

11.10. Let α be a root of the irreducible polynomial $p(X)$ of degree b and let C be the code with symbols from $GF(q^b)$ generated by $g(X) = (X-1)(X-\alpha^b)$. Show that if each symbol in C is replaced by its usual representation as a b-tuple over $GF(q)$, the resulting code is a Burton code.

12 Synchronization of Block Codes

In order to decode a block code the decoder must be able to distinguish between information and parity digits or, equivalently, to identify the first digit of the received word. In some channels symbols can be inserted into or deleted from a word, causing the decoder to misframe this word and subsequent ones. The problem considered in this chapter is the construction of block codes that are capable of recovering synchronization after the insertion or deletion of one or more symbols. The q-ary case is considered throughout.

Synchronization can usually be recovered by a trial-and-error approach. Misframing typically causes the received word to be substantially different from any code word. In such situations the decoder can interpret as a synchronization loss a long sequence of received words which contain an unusually large number of errors. Trying all n possible framing positions will eventually result in synchronization recovery.* While this scheme does not require the insertion of extra redundancy, a substantial number of decoding errors may occur before synchronization is recovered. In this sense the synchronization techniques presented in this chapter are superior to this trial-and-error approach.

It is considerably simpler to recover synchronization when a word has simply been misframed than it is if symbols have been added to or deleted from the word. Thus most recovery techniques operate on the

* This procedure can be very effective for convolutional codes since only n_0 synch positions are possible.

word or words following the one in which the synchronization slippage occurred, rather than directly on the corrupted word. Correction of the error patterns which result from symbol insertion or deletion, that is, *synchronization-error correction*, is quite difficult in general (Ullman 1966), and is not usually as important as *synchronization recovery*. These synchronization-error-correcting codes are not considered in this book.

It is always possible for additive errors to produce an error pattern that appears to the decoder to be the result of a synchronization slippage. After a false " synchronization," the decoder will usually recover correct framing on the next word. However, it is possible to reduce the probability of this false resynchronization by requiring that several consecutive received words give a consistent loss of synch indication before action is taken.

In a synchronous data communication system, synchronization slippages of one or a few symbols are usually more likely than larger slippages. For this reason the codes discussed in this chapter are designed to correct or detect all slippages of up to some fixed number of symbols. The problem of acquiring synchronization with no prior knowledge of correct framing, such as is encountered at the start of transmission, is not considered in detail.

In the remainder of this chapter the following convention is employed. A *synchronization loss* of s symbols occurs when the received-symbol counter loses s counts. Similarly, a *synchronization gain* occurs when the counter counts more symbols that it should.

The oldest method of recovering synchronization in a data communication system requires the use of a special synchronizing character which is inserted between code words (for example, the letter space in Morse code). It is clearly impossible to reserve one character for synchronization in a binary system, so this prefix is commonly taken to be a sequence of binary digits with a sharply peaked autocorrelation function, that is, a Barker (1953) sequence. Synchronization recovery with these sequences can be effected provided that relatively few additive errors occur in the sequence.

Rather than having a separate prefix for synchronization purposes only, it is preferable to consider synchronization and additive errors together and to construct codes that can correct them in a more unified way. Such codes are the subject of the remainder of the chapter. Three classes of codes are considered:

1. Codes that can detect or correct loss of synchronization but not additive errors.

2. Codes that can correct either loss of synchronization *or* additive errors provided both do not occur simultaneously.
3. Codes that can correct both a loss of synchronization *and* additive errors even if they occur simultaneously.

The notion of comma freedom is introduced briefly in Section 12.1; it is under this name that the most general studies of synchronization recovery have been done. For practical applications, codes related to good linear codes implement more easily, and the most attractive of these are discussed in the remaining sections.

12.1 Codes That Recover Synchronization Only

In this section it is assumed that additive errors do not occur. Also, only fixed-length block codes are considered. Codes with variable-length code words have been studied, but these lie outside the scope of this book (Gilbert and Moore 1959; Scholtz 1969).

A code is said to have *degree of comma freedom r*, if for every pair of code words $\mathbf{a} = [a_{n-1}, \ldots, a_1, a_0]$ and $\mathbf{b} = [b_{n-1}, \ldots, b_1, b_0]$, then the n-tuples $[a_{n-i-1}, \ldots, a_0, b_{n-1}, \ldots b_{n-i}]$ and $[a_{i-1}, \ldots, a_0, b_{n-1}, \ldots, b_i]$ are not code words for $0 < i \leqq r$. The code words $\mathbf{a}$ and $\mathbf{b}$ are not necessarily different. If $\mathbf{a}$ is transmitted before $\mathbf{b}$ and the decoder is attempting to decode word $\mathbf{a}$, the first of these n-tuples results from an i-symbol synchronization loss. If $r \geqq n/2$, then $r = \infty$ and the code is said to be *comma-free.*

If a code has degree of comma freedom $r < n/2$, then any synch slippage of r or fewer symbols can be detected; that is, the code has *synchronization detection capability* $r_d = r$. If $r \geqq n/2$, then any slippage can be detected.

If a code has degree of comma freedom $r < n/2$, then any synch slippage of $[r/2]$ or fewer symbols can be corrected. It is necessary only to try all alignments within $[r/2]$ symbols of the current alignment. No trial will be off by more than r symbols, and thus a code word will be found only at the correct alignment. On the other hand, if $r \geqq n/2$, the code is comma free and any synch slippage can be corrected. Let r_c denote the *synchronization recovery capability* of a code. Then

$$\begin{aligned} r_c &\geqq \left[\frac{r}{2}\right]; & r &< \frac{n}{2} \\ r_c &= \infty\ ; & r &\geqq \frac{n}{2} \end{aligned} \tag{12.1}$$

In addition it is obviously true that $r_c \leqq r$.

No cyclic shift of a code word can be another code word if a code is to be comma free. Thus, for a cyclic code or even for a linear code the degree of comma freedom is always zero. Also, the number of code words, M, in a q-ary comma-free code cannot exceed q^n/n. This result can be refined to give (Golomb, Gordon, and Welch 1958)

$$M \leqq \frac{1}{n} \sum_d u(d) q^{n/d} \tag{12.2}$$

where the sum is over all divisors d of the code length n and u is the Möbius function

$$\begin{aligned} u(d) &= 1 \quad ; \quad d = 1 \\ &= 0 \quad ; \quad d \text{ has any square factor} \\ &= (-1)^r; \quad d = p_1 p_2 \cdots p_r, \text{ where the } p_i \text{ are distinct primes.} \end{aligned}$$

Eastman (1965) has proved that the bound of Equation 12.2 is attainable for all odd values of n. The case of n even is considerably more complex, and results are still incomplete in spite of considerable effort. Scholtz (1969) has devised an algorithm for generating comma-free codes which is relatively simple to implement.

Comma-free codes as such are sensitive to additive errors. Comma-free codes with the additional capability of correcting additive errors have been investigated (Jiggs 1963), but results in this area are sparse. More powerful and useful results have been obtained by beginning with an effective additive-error-correcting code, such as a cyclic code, and then equipping it with some degree of comma freedom (Sections 12.2 and 12.3).

Cyclic codes have no comma freedom and thus are prone to undetectable synchronization errors. However, it turns out that cosets of cyclic codes are quite practical for detecting loss of synchronization and for synchronization recovery. A coset of a cyclic (n, k) code is formed by adding a fixed polynomial $P(X)$ to each code polynomial before transmission. Thus,

$$t(X) = i(X)g(X) + P(X),$$

where $g(X)$ is the generator of the cyclic code, $i(X)$ is a polynomial of degree less than k, and $P(X)$ is a fixed polynomial of degree less than n.

The additive-error-correcting ability is the same for a coset code as for the original cyclic code. If $t(X)$ is transmitted and $r(X) = t(X) + e(X)$ is received, then at the receiver the first step performed is to subtract $P(X)$ from the received polynomial $r(X)$. The result is just $i(X)\,g(X) + e(X)$, and correction can be accomplished by whatever method will work for the original cyclic code, because this is simply the sum of a cyclic code word and an error pattern.

Now suppose $t(X)$ is transmitted, and the channel causes an r-symbol synch loss and an additive error pattern $e(X)$. The received polynomial then is

$$r(X) = X^r t(X) + e(X) + \delta_1(X) - X^n \delta_2(X) \tag{12.3}$$

where $\delta_1(X)$ is the high-order portion of the subsequent word that appears as the last r symbols of $r(X)$, and $\delta_2(X)$ is the high-order r symbols of $t(X)$ that are lost. Since $\delta_1(X)$ and $\delta_2(X)$ are not known to the decoder, and since $X^n \equiv 1$ for a cyclic code of length n, Equation 12.3 can be written as

$$r(X) = X^r t(X) + e(X) + \delta(X) \tag{12.4}$$

where

$$\delta(X) = \delta_1(X) - \delta_2(X)$$

and where $\delta(X)$ has degree less than r and has unknown coefficients.

Similarly, if there is a synch gain,

$$r(X) = X^{-r} t(X) + e(X) + X^{n-r} \delta_1(X) - X^{-r} \delta_2(X) \tag{12.5}$$

where $\delta_1(X)$ is the low-order part of the preceding code word, which appears at the beginning of the received message, and $\delta_2(X)$ is the low-order part of $t(X)$, which is lost. This can be rewritten

$$r(X) = X^{-r} t(X) + e(X) + X^{-r} \delta(X) \tag{12.6}$$

where

$$\delta(X) = \delta_1(X) - \delta_2(X)$$

and again $\delta(X)$ has degree less than r and has unknown coefficients. Equations 12.4 and 12.6 differ in the sign of r but are otherwise very similar. It is therefore natural to denote the amount of gain or loss by r, using positive values for loss, negative values for gain.

Now consider synchronization error detection in the absence of additive errors. The first step in decoding is to subtract the polynomial $P(X)$ from the received word; this yields, in the case of synch loss,

$$(X^r - 1)P(X) + X^r i(X)\, g(X) + \delta(X) \tag{12.7}$$

A synch slippage of r bits is detectable if and only if the pattern $(X^r - 1)$ $P(X) + \delta(X)$ is not a cyclic code word for all choices of $\delta(X)$. But if $r \geqq n - k$, there always exists some $\delta(X)$ such that $(X^r - 1)P(X) + \delta(X)$ is divisible by $g(X)$. Thus, if $n \leqq 2k$, then there exist undetectable slippages of $n - k$ or more bits. The argument for synch gain is analogous.

THEOREM 12.1. *For any coset cyclic code with $n \leqq 2k$, the degree of comma freedom is bounded by*

$$r \leqq n - k - 1 \tag{12.8}$$

and this bound is satisfied with equality by the coset code specified by $P(X) = 1$.

Proof. Equation 12.8 follows directly from the argument just given. If $P(X) = 1$, Expression 12.7 cannot be divisible by $g(X)$ for $1 \leqq r \leqq n - k - 1$, because the degree of $\delta(X)$ is at most $r - 1$. Q.E.D.

This theorem and the definition of a comma-free code can be combined to give the following result.

COROLLARY 12.1. *Any (n, k) cyclic code has a comma-free coset if and only if $k < n/2$.*

Theorem 12.1 has another interesting corollary:

COROLLARY 12.2 *Any (n, k) cyclic code has a coset for which*

$$r_c \geqq \left[\frac{n-k-1}{2}\right]; \qquad k \geqq n/2$$
$$= \infty; \qquad k < n/2$$

Equation 12.2 shows that roughly $\log_q n$ redundant digits are necessary to assure comma freedom, and in many cases this number is also sufficient (Eastman 1965). Corollary 12.1 states, on the other hand, that $n/2$ redundant digits are necessary and sufficient for comma freedom if a coset code is used. It appears that a high price in redundancy must be paid for the convenience and simplicity of using a coset code.

The following theorem guarantees that the inequality of Corollary 12.2 can never hold.

THEOREM 12.2. *The synchronization recovery capability of a coset code derived from an (n, k) cyclic code is bounded by*

$$r_c \leqq \left[\frac{n-k-1}{2}\right]; \qquad k \geqq n/2 \tag{12.9}$$

and is unbounded for $k < n/2$.

Proof. A synch loss of r_L symbols occurs when $i_1(X)\,g(X) + P(X)$ is transmitted; after subtracting $P(X)$, the received word has the form

$$X^{r_L}i_1(X)\,g(X) + (X^{r_L} - 1)\,P(X) + \delta(X),$$

where $\delta(X)$ is an unknown polynomial of degree less than than r_L. Similarly, for an $(r_G - 1)$-symbol gain the result is

$$X^{-r_G}i_2(X)\,g(X) + (X^{-r_G} - 1)P(X) + X^{-r_G}\gamma(X).$$

Now if, for all choices of $P(X)$, these two results are equal for some choice of $i_1(X)$, $i_2(X) \neq i_1(X)$, $\delta(X)$, and $\gamma(X)$, then synchronization recovery cannot occur.

Multiplying these two results by X^{r_G} and subtracting the latter from the former give

$$C(X) = (X^{r_L+r_G}i_1(X) - i_2(X))\,g(X) + (X^{r_L+r_G} - 1)P(X) + X^{r_G}\,\delta(X) - \gamma(X).$$

Now if $r_L + r_G > n - k$, the degree of $X^{r_G}\delta(X) - \gamma(X)$ is at least $n - k$, and $\delta(X)$ and $\gamma(X)$ can be selected to make $g(X)$ divide $C(X)$. Let

$$C(X) = g(X)g_1(X)$$

Then $g_1(X) = X^{r_L+r_G}i_1(X) - i_2(X) + g_2(X)$ for some $g_2(X)$. Now if $k \geqq n/2$, then $h(X) = (X^n - 1)/g(X)$ will divide $g_1(X)$ for some choice of $i_1(X)$ and $i_2(X)$. Since $g(X)h(X) = 0$, the polynomial $C(X) = 0$. Thus, in this case $r_L + r_G \leqq n - k - 1$.

If $k < n/2$, however, there is no choice of $i_1(X)$ and $i_2(X)$ for which $h(X)$ divides $g_1(X)$. This can also be seen from Corollary 12.2, which states that there is no upper bound on r_c for $k < n/2$. Q.E.D.

The codes discussed previously in this section correct synch slippages by trying all alignments within r_c positions of the initial alignment. It may be desirable, especially when long codes are used, to avoid this search and to calculate the correct synch position directly. The following theorem shows that this is possible, even simple, and that very little synch recovery capability is lost by so restricting the decoder.

THEOREM 12.3. *Let $g(x)$ generate an (n, k) cyclic code and let $P(X)$ be a polynomial of degree $s \geqq 1$ which is not divisible by X. Then the coset generated by $g(X)$ and containing $X^{-1}P(X)$ has*

$$r_c = \left[\frac{n - k - s - 1}{2}\right]$$

Proof. The proof simply demonstrates a method of determining uniquely the amount of slip. After subtracting $X^{-1}P(X)$ from the received message, the decoder multiplies by X^{r_c+1} and divides by $g(X)$. The following argument shows that the amount of slip can be determined easily from the result.

Let us examine the case of synch loss first. By Equation 12.4, with $t(x)=i(x)g(x)+x^{-1}P(x)$ and $e(x)=0$,

$$X^{r_c+1}[r(X) - X^{-1}P(X)] \\ = X^{r+r_c+1}i(X)\, g(X) + (X^r - 1)X^{r_c}P(X) + X^{r_c+1}\,\delta(X) \quad (12.10)$$

The highest degree occurring in the second term is $r + r_c + s$ and the lowest is r_c, and these actually occur with nonzero coefficients. The highest degree occurring in the last term is less than $r + r_c + 1$ and the lowest is no less than $r_c + 1$. Since $r + r_c + s \leqq 2r_c + s < n - k$, dividing Equation 12.10 by $g(X)$ leaves the last two terms as remainder. Note that the amount of slip r can be determined by subtracting $r_c + s$ from the highest degree occurring in the remainder.

Next, consider the case of synch gain. Then, by Equation 12.6,

$$X^{r_c+1}[r(X) - X^{-1}P(X)] \\ = X^{-r+r_c+1}i(X)\, g(X) + (X^{-r} - 1)X^{r_c}P(X) + X^{r_c+1-r}\,\delta(X). \quad (12.11)$$

The highest degree occurring in the second term is $r_c + s$ and the lowest is $r_c - r$, and these occur with nonzero coefficients. The highest degree occurring in the last term is less than $r_c + 1$ and the lowest is no lower than $r_c + 1 - r$. Since $r_c + s < n - k$, the remainder after dividing by $g(X)$ is just the last two terms. This case can be distinguished from synch loss by the fact that the lowest degree occurring here is less than r_c, which is impossible with synch loss. Similarly, the highest degree occurring with synch loss is greater than $r_c + s$, which is impossible with synch gain. Finally, the amount of synch gain can be found by subtracting the degree of the lowest nonzero term from r_c. Thus, all cases can be distinguished by examining this form of the syndrome.

Q.E.D.

The obvious best choice for synch recovery in the absence of errors is $P(X) = X + 1$; then $s = 1$ and $r_c = [(n - k - 2)/2]$. For a given value of s, one more parity-check symbol is required than is indicated by the bound in Theorem 12.2. Corollary 12.2 assures that the bound can be met by a search procedure. On the other hand, the implementation suggested in the proof of Theorem 12.3 is extremely simple.

12.2 Codes That Recover Synchronization or Correct Additive Errors

There are several known methods of using a coset code for correction of additive errors and for synch recovery, which guarantee that synch recovery will be possible in any received word that contains no additive errors. This requires that two received messages corresponding to two different synch errors, to two different correctable random-error patterns, or one to a synch error and the other to a random-error pattern lie in different cosets.

Cyclic Burst-Correcting Coset Codes (*Tong 1968c*).
Let $g(X)$ generate a cyclic (n, k) code which is used to correct all bursts of length b or less and no other additive error patterns. If $P(X)$ specifies a coset of this code and if a synchronization loss of r bits occurs, the received word is (See Equation 12.7)

$$(X^r - 1)P(X) + X^r c(X) + \delta(X) \tag{12.12}$$

where $c(X)$ is the transmitted code word and $\delta(X)$ is a polynomial of degree $r - 1$ or less with unknown coefficients. This assumes no additive errors occur.

Now if $P(X)$ is chosen as

$$P(X) = X^{n-1} + 1$$

then the syndrome of the received word in Equation 12.12 is the residue of

$$[X^{r-1} - 1 + X^r - X^{n-1} + \delta(X)] \bmod g(x).$$

Now this is the syndrome of an "end-around" burst of length $r + 2$ with errors in positions X^r and X^{n-1}. If $b \geqq r + 2$, then this is a coset leader. Had an r-bit synchronization gain occurred, the syndrome would again be an "end-around" burst of length $r + 2$ but with errors in positions X^0 and X^{n-r-1}.

Since these end-around "bursts" are not as likely as ordinary bursts, their cosets can be used for synch recovery. The recovery rule is:

If an end-around burst of length $r + 2$ with errors in positions X^r and X^{n-1} is found, there was an r-bit synch loss.

If an end-around burst of length $r + 2$ with errors in positions X^0 and X^{n-r-1} is found, there was an r-bit synch gain.

THEOREM 12.4. *Let $g(X)$ generate an (n, k) cyclic code with burst-correcting ability b. If this code is used only to correct bursts of length b or less, then the coset code specified by $P(X) = X^{n-1} + 1$ has the ability to recover from a synch loss or gain of $r_c = b - 2$ or fewer symbols.*

The Reiger bound of Theorem 4.15 states that for burst-correcting block codes

$$b \leqq \frac{n-k}{2}$$

For many good cyclic burst-correcting codes, b is equal or near $(n - k)/2$. Thus, these codes are nearly optimal for synch recovery, in light of Theorem 12.2.

Cyclic Random-Error-Correcting Codes (*Tong 1966*).
The next two theorems show that certain BCH coset codes have synchronization recovery capability.

THEOREM 12.7. *Assume that $g(X) = g_1(X)P(X)$ generates a cyclic (n, k) code of minimum distance at least $2t + 1$ and $P(X)$ generates a cyclic code of minimum distance d_1, and $g_1(X)$ has at least one root of order n. Then, for the coset code containing $X^{-1}P(X)$, no coset corresponding to a synch gain or loss of r symbols is the same as a coset corresponding to a different gain or loss, or the same as a coset corresponding to t or fewer errors, provided $|r| < d_1 - t$ and $|r| < s/2$, where s is the degree of $g_1(X)$.*

Proof. That no cosets corresponding to different gain or loss are equal follows from Theorem 12.3. Let $r_1(X)$ correspond to a synch loss of r symbols and $r_2(X)$ correspond to a pattern of t or fewer errors. Then they are in the same coset only if $r_2(X) - r_1(X)$ is divisible by $g(X)$. But, by Equation 12.4

$$\begin{aligned} r_2(X) - r_1(X) &= t_2(X) + e(X) - X^r t_1(X) - \delta(X) \\ &= [i_2(X) - X^r i_1(X)]\, g(X) + (X^r - 1)X^{-1}P(X) \\ &\quad + e(X) - \delta(X) \end{aligned}$$

Since the hypotheses imply that $e(X) - \delta(X)$ has weight less than d_1, $e(X) - \delta(X)$ cannot be divisible by $P(X)$, let alone $g(X)$, unless it is zero. In that case, $r_2(X) - r_1(X)$ is divisible by $g(X)$ only if $(X^r - 1)P(X)$ is, or equivalently, if $X^r - 1$ is divisible by $g_1(X)$. The restriction on $g_1(X)$ rules this out, and hence $r_2(X) - r_1(X)$ cannot be divisible by $g(X)$. The proof for synch gain is similar. Q.E.D.

Example. Let $g(X)$ generate the binary (127, 36) 15-error correcting BCH code, and $P(X)$ generate the (127, 57) 11-error correcting BCH code. The polynomial $g_1(X)$ has degree $s = 21$ and satisfies the hypotheses of Theorem 12.5. Then $d_1 - t = 2 \cdot 11 + 1 - 15 = 8$, and $[s/2] = 10$. It follows from Theorem 12.5 that for the (127, 36) code, the coset with the generator of the (127, 57) code as $P(X)$ allows correction of every combination of 15 errors or synch recovery of up to 7 symbols of gain or loss, provided that synch loss and random errors do not occur together.

A possible correction procedure is to check for synch error as described following Theorem 12.3. If the syndrome has the wrong form, then the random-error-correction procedure is used. It could be done in the opposite sequence also.

A similar result follows as a corollary to Theorem 12.6 of Section 12.3. Since the result belongs in this section, it is stated here:

COROLLARY 12.3. *Let $P(X)$ generate an (n, k) cyclic t-error-correcting code and let $g_1(X)$ be a divisor of $X^n - 1$ with at least one root of order n. Then the coset containing $P(X)$ of the code generated by $g(X) = P(X)g_1(X)$ can recover synch loss or gain of up to t symbols if no additive errors occur, or correct up to t additive errors if no synch error has occurred.*

Example. Let $g(X)$ generate the binary (127, 36) 15-error-correcting BCH code and $P(X)$ generate the (127, 43) 14-error-correcting code. The hypotheses of the corollary are satisfied. The coset specified by $P(X)$ is a different coset of the same cyclic code than was considered in the previous example. In this case the corollary assures correction of up to 14 additive errors or a synch gain or loss of up to 14 symbols. A correction procedure is described in the proof of Theorem 12.6.

Shortened Cyclic Random-Error-Correcting Codes (*Tong 1966*).
If a cyclic code of random-error-correcting ability t is shortened by at least $2r_c + 1$ bits where $r_c = [t/2]$, then there exists a coset of this code for which the synchronization recovery capability is at least r_c. One choice for the synchronizing polynomial $P(X)$ for this coset is the residue of X^n mod $g(X)$, the generator of the code.

Let $i(X)g(X)$ denote a code word in an (n, k) shortened cyclic code. Let l denote the length of the original cyclic code. Then the transmitted coset code word is

$$t(X) = i(X)g(X) + P(X).$$

It is desired to choose $P(X)$ so that the coset code has synchronization recovery ability r_c. If an r-bit synchronization loss occurs where $r \leqq r_c$, the received word is

$$r(X) = X^r i(X)g(X) + X^r P(X) + \delta_1(X) + X^n \delta_2(X)$$

where the $\delta_i(X)$ are polynomials of degree $r - 1$ or less with unknown coefficients. The decoder subtracts $P(X)$ from this word and calculates the syndrome.

$$\{r(X) + P(X)\} = \{(X^r + 1)P(X) + \delta_1(X) + X^n \delta_2(X)\} \quad (12.13)$$

where $\{X\}$ denotes the residue class (coset) of X mod $g(X)$. Now if $P(X)$ is chosen to be the residue of X^n mod $g(X)$, then

$$\{(X^r + 1)P(X) + \delta_1(X) + X^n \delta_2(X)\} = \{X^{n+r} + \delta_3(X) + X^n \delta_4(X)\} \quad (12.14)$$

where $r + n < l$. Since the weight of $X^{n+r} + \delta_3(X) + X^n \delta_4(X)$ is at most $2r + 1$, this polynomial is a coset leader provided $r \leqq r_c = [t/2]$, where t is the error-correcting ability of the code. Since $n + r < l$, this polynomial must contain a term of degree $n + r$. Since this digit was not transmitted, an attempt to correct an error in position X^{n+r} can be interpreted as an r-bit synchronization loss.

If an r-bit synchronization gain occurs where $r \leqq r_c$, the syndrome is

$$\{r(X) + P(X)\} = \{X^n + X^{-r} \delta_5(X) + X^{n-r} \delta_6(X) \quad (12.15)$$

Since the weight of this polynomial is at most $2r + 1 \leqq t$, it too must be a coset leader. Thus, a synchronization gain is detected when the decoder attempts to correct the untransmitted digit X^n.

If, in addition to detecting a synchronization slippage, it is possible to determine the direction of the slippage, the synchronization recovery capability of the code is doubled. To do this it is necessary that the cosets for synch loss be disjoint from those for synch gain. But

$$\{X^{n+r} + \delta_3(X) + X^n \delta_4(X)\} \neq \{X^n + X^{-r} \delta_5(X) + X^{n-r} \delta_6(X)\},$$

because each polynomial has weight $\leqq t$ and they are not identical if $l - n \geqq 2r + 1$.

To summarize, if an $r \leqq [t/2]$-symbol synch loss occurs, the decoder receives an error indication in position X^{n+r}. Synch can be recovered immediately. If an $r \leqq [t/2]$-symbol synch gain occurs, the decoder receives an error indication in position X^n. To recover synch it admits the next symbol to the decoder and recalculates the syndrome. It repeats this process until a synch gain is no longer indicated. At this point synchronization has been recovered.

If $P(X)$ is chosen as X^{l-1}, an argument similar to that just given shows that the roles of synch loss and gain are interchanged. If $P(X)$ is chosen as $X^n + X^{l-1}$, then both losses and gains can be recovered in one step, but here $r_c \leqq [(t-1)/2]$.

It has been assumed that the received word is (additive) error-free. This is not quite necessary. If a slippage of r bits occurs, at most $2r + 1$ errors are introduced, so $t - 2r - 1$ additive errors can be corrected. With diminishing probability, patterns of higher weight can also be corrected.

This technique has the advantage that it is very easily implemented and requires no redundancy beyond that already present in the code.

12.3 Codes that Recover Synchronization and Correct Additive Errors

The desirability of correcting both additive errors and synch in the same word is obvious; the cost is added redundancy. The number of cosets required is so much greater that the number of check symbols required is roughly the sum of the number required for correction of the additive errors and the number required for synch recovery in the absence of additive errors. (See Problem 12.1.) Three easily implemented methods of coding which require approximately this number of check symbols are described in this section.

Coset Codes for Synch Recovery in the Presence of Errors

The following theorem shows that cosets of cyclic codes can be used for synch recovery even when random errors occur:

THEOREM 12.6. *Let $P(X)$ generate a cyclic t-error-correcting (n, k) code and let $g_1(X)$ be a divisor of $X^n - 1$ which has at least one root of order n. Then the coset containing $P(X)$ of the code generated by $g(X) = g_1(X)P(X)$ can simultaneously recover from a synch loss or gain of $r \leqq t$ symbols and correct any combination of $t - r$ additive errors.*

Proof. The proof consists of describing a correction procedure that is assured of success. Let $i(X)g(X)$ be the original cyclic code polynomial, and then the transmitted polynomial would be $i(X)g(X) + P(X)$. According to Equations 12.3 and 12.5, if an r-symbol synch loss and an additive error pattern $e(X)$ occur, the received polynomial is, after $P(X)$ is subtracted,

$$r(X) - P(X) = X^r i(X)g(X) + (X^r - 1)P(X) + e(X) + \delta(X) \quad (12.16)$$

Since, by hypothesis, the weight of $e(X) + \delta(X)$ does not exceed $(t - r) + r = t$, $e(X) + \delta(X)$ is a coset leader in the code generated by $P(X)$, and $e(X) + \delta(X)$ can be found by applying error correction for the code generated by $P(X)$ to the received polynomial of $r(X)$. The result after this correction step is

$$X^r i(X)g(X) + (X^r - 1)P(X). \qquad (12.17)$$

Next, divide by $P(X)$, and add 1. The result is

$$X^r i(X)g_1(X) + X^r. \qquad (12.18)$$

Let α be a root of $g_1(X)$ that has order n. Substituting α in Expression 12.18 gives α^r as a result, making it possible to determine r. With knowledge of r, it is possible to subtract $(X^r - 1)P(X)$ from Expression 12.17 and shift the result cyclically r places to obtain $i(X)g(X)$, the original code polynomial. At the same time it has been determined that there was a synch loss of r symbols. The case of synch gain is similar — at the last stage the resulting value for r will be slightly less than n, or equivalently, negative, and thus synch gain is distinguished from synch loss. Q.E.D.

A corollary to this theorem follows Theorem 12.5.

Example. Let $g(X)$ generate the binary (127, 36) 15-error correcting BCH code, and $P(X)$ generate the (127, 43) 14-error correcting BCH code. The hypotheses of the theorem are satisfied, and the code is capable of simultaneously recovering from an $r \leqq 14$ symbol synch loss or gain and correcting 14-r additive errors by the procedure outlined in the proof of the theorem.

Extended Cyclic Codes

Bose and Caldwell (1967) have defined an *extended** cyclic code as follows. Every code word $c(X)$ in the cyclic (n', k') code generated by $g_a(X)$ has the form

$$c(X) = i(X)g_a(X) \qquad (12.19)$$

where $i(X)$ is a polynomial of degree less than k'. To impart synchronization recovery ability to the code, the polynomial $i(X)$ is restricted to have the form

$$i(X) = i'(X)g_s(X) + 1 \qquad (12.20)$$

*Note that here the meaning of "extended" differs from that of earlier usage. For example, see Section 8.4.

That is, only a subset of the set of code words in the code generated by $g_a(X)$ is employed. The polynomial $g_s(X)$ has degree j and exponent m and divides $h_a(X)$ where $h_a(X) = (X^{n'} - 1)/g_a(X)$. The polynomial $i'(X)$ is an arbitrary polynomial of degree less than $k' - j$.

Now an extended cyclic code word is formed for transmission as follows. Let $m \leqq n$ and let

$$c_{n-1}, \ldots, c_{n-[(m-1)/2]}, \ldots, c_{[(m-1)/2]}, \ldots, c_1, c_0$$

denote the coefficients of $c(X)$. The corresponding coefficients of the extended word are

$$\overbrace{c_{[(m-1)/2]-1}, \ldots, c_1, c_0,}^{\text{Prefix}} c_{n-1}, \ldots, c_{n-[(m-1)/2]}, \ldots,$$

$$c_{[(m-1)/2]}, \ldots, c_1, c_0, \underbrace{c_{n-1}, \ldots, c_{n-[(m-1)/2]}}_{\text{Suffix}}$$

That is, the low-order $[(m-1)/2]$ symbols of $c(X)$ are used as a prefix and the high-order $[(m-1)/2]$ symbols as a suffix to form a code word in the extended cyclic code. These symbols, which are really additional parity checks, are appended to the word so that a synchronization slippage of $s \leqq [(m-1)/2$ symbols merely transforms the center of the code word $c(X)$, into a cyclically shifted version of itself, $X^s c(X)$. Therefore, even if such a slippage occurs, the additive-error-correcting ability of the code generated by $g_a(X)$ is not impaired.

More precisely, if an error pattern $e(X)$ correctable with the cyclic code generated by $g_a(X)$ is added to the cyclic code word $X^s c(X)$, the received n-tuple is

$$r(X) = X^s c(X) + e(X)$$

Note that a synchronization loss corresponds to a positive value of s. But since $X^s c(X)$ is just a code word in the cyclic code generated by $g_a(X)$ and since $e(X)$ is, by hypothesis, correctable, the decoder can determine the code word $X^s c(X)$. But, by Equations 12.15 and 12.16,

$$X^s c(X) = g_a(X)[X^s i'(X) g_s(X) + X^s] \tag{12.21}$$

Dividing this result by the known polynomial $g_a(X)$ yields the residue of $[X^s i'(X) g_s(X) + X^s] \bmod h_a(X)$. But since $g_s(X)$ divides $h_a(X)$, the remainder obtained by dividing this residue by $g_s(X)$ is congruent to

$X^s \bmod g_s(X)$ and is referred to as the *synchronization syndrome.* For $-[(m-1/2] \leqq s \leqq [(m-1)/2]$, no two of these syndromes are identical, because this would imply that $g_s(X)$ divides $X^i - 1, i < m$, and, by hypothesis, it does not. Thus, the decoder can determine s. With s known, it is a straightforward matter to determine $i'(X)$, and this completes the decoding process. Despite its apparent complexity, this procedure can be implemented in a rather straightforward manner.

The restriction made earlier that the high-and-low-direction synchronization-error-correcting ability be the same it not necessary. If slippage in one direction is more likely to occur than in the other, greater correcting ability can be provided where it is needed.

THEOREM 12.7. *Let $g_a(X)$ be the generator polynomial of a cyclic (n', k') code. The $(n' + 2r, k' - j)$ extended cyclic code constructed earlier can correct all synchronization slippages of r or fewer symbols and, simultaneously, any error pattern correctable with the original cyclic code.*

Another Technique for Error Correction and Synch Recovery

Several other methods of constructing codes for correcting synchronization slippages have been proposed. With the exception of the technique described here (Mandlebaum 1969), these codes do not appear to be as efficient as extended cyclic codes.

Suppose the $2r_c + 1$ high-order information digits of an additive-error-correcting cyclic code are restricted to be

$$\underbrace{00\cdots0}_{r_c+1}\underbrace{11\cdots1}_{r_c}$$

where the highest-order digit is on the left. The symbols 0 and 1 are elements of $GF(q)$. A framing slippage of r_c or fewer symbols will always produce a cyclic shift of the transmitted code word. Thus, any correctable additive-error pattern can be corrected despite a synch stoppage. The location of the first $2r_c + 1$ symbols of the corrected word uniquely specify correct framing. Hence, the code has synch recovery capability r_c.

The code produced with this technique is an $(n, k - 2r_c - 1)$ code. For very low values of r_c, these codes are slightly better than the extended cyclic codes; for higher values, the reverse is true. The coset codes described in this section require greater redundancy but correct larger synch loss or gain in the absence of errors, and more errors in the absence of synch loss or gain.

Notes

There are many topics that are usually considered under the name "synchronization." In this chapter we have addressed only the problem of recovering block or word synchronization using codes closely related to additive-error-correcting block codes.

Comma-free codes were first studied by Golomb, Gordon, and Welch (1958). Their work was stimulated by research on the transfer of genetic information (Crick, Griffith, and Orgel 1957), which apparently uses a form of comma-free code. Several investigators (Jiggs 1963) have considered the problem of correcting additive errors in addition to resynchronization with comma-free codes.

Coset codes were proposed for synchronization purposes by Stiffler (1965), who proved versions of Theorems 12.1 and 12.2. These codes were also studied by Levy (1968), Frey (1965), and Tong (1968*c*; 1966), among others. Much of the material in Sections 12.2 and 12.3 is due to Tong.

The extended cyclic codes of Section 12.3 were devised by Bose and Caldwell (1967) and Weldon (1968*b*). A modification of these codes called subset codes has been proposed by Tavares and Fukuda (1970*b*). These codes appear to be competitive with coset codes for synchronization recovery.

The problem of constructing codes to correct synchronization errors — as opposed to merely recovering correct framing — has been studied by Ullman (1966). He devised a class of codes capable of correcting error patterns caused by the insertion or deletion of one digit, but the cost in terms of redundancy is high.

Problems

12.1. Show that for a coset code of a binary cyclic code, the set of all code vectors resulting from synch loss of r bits fall in 2^r cosets, and similarly for synch gain.

12.2. Calculate the Hamming-type bounds on the number of parity-check symbols needed for coset codes of cyclic codes for the following cases, by bounding the number of cosets needed:

a. Synch recovery in the absence of additive errors.
b. Additive error correction or synch recovery.
c. Simultaneous synch recovery and additive error correction.

12.3. Compute the syndrome associated with a 1-bit synch gain and loss in the example in Section 12.2.

12.4. Compare the two techniques of Section 12.2 by constructing binary random-error-correcting codes with the following parameters:

Cyclic Code	Number of Random Errors Corrected	Synch Recovery Capability, r_c
(15, 7)	2	1
		2
		3
(63, 45)	3	1
		3
		5
		10

12.5. (Tavares and Fukuda) Consider an (n, k) coset cyclic code with minimum distance d. If this code is used only to correct $e \leqq [(d-1)/2]$ errors, then its synch recovery capability is

$$r_c = \min\left\{\left[\frac{d-4e-3}{2}\right], \left[\frac{n-e-2}{2(e+1)}\right]\right\}$$

and synch can be recovered in the presence of e or fewer errors. Compare codes of this type with the codes of Section 12.3.

13 Random-Error-Correcting Convolutional Codes

It has proved difficult to apply well-developed branches of mathematics to the construction and decoding of convolutional codes. Nevertheless, interesting and useful codes have been found, and the prospect is that more will be discovered in the future.

In this and the succeeding chapter, binary codes are emphasized. Sections 13.1 and 13.2 apply to all convolutional codes, including the burst-correcting codes of Chapter 14.

13.1 Encoding and Syndrome Calculation

Figure 13.1 depicts an encoder for a general (mn_0, mk_0) convolutional code. The encoder accepts k_0 information symbols (elements of $GF(q)$) at its input and produces $n_0 > k_0$ code symbols at its outputs. These output symbols are linear combinations over $GF(q)$ of the input symbols in the preceding m blocks. This encoder processes data in parallel form; if serial data is required, a conversion may be necessary.

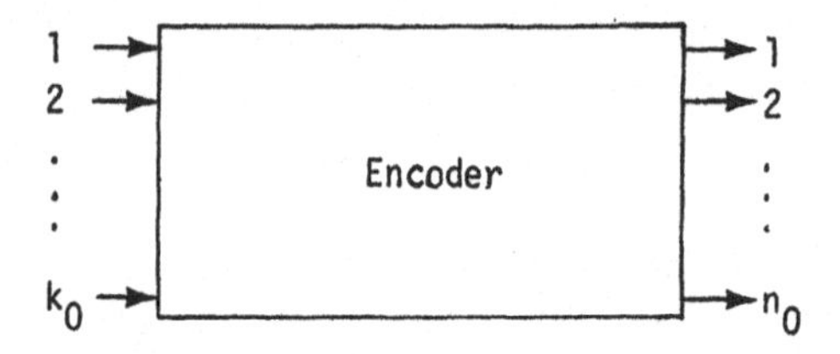

Figure 13.1. The general form of the encoder for an (n, k) convolutional code.

There are two general types of encoders for convolutional codes. The k-stage encoder shown in Figure 13.2 can be used for all codes; this is discussed below. For a systematic code, an $(n-k)$-stage encoder can be used; this is treated next.

The generator matrix for an (mn_0, mk_0) convolutional code is given in Equation 3.12.

$$\mathbf{G} = \begin{bmatrix} \mathbf{G}_0 & \mathbf{G}_1 & \dots & \mathbf{G}_{m-1} \\ & \mathbf{G}_0 & \dots & \mathbf{G}_{m-2} \\ & & \ddots & \\ & & & \mathbf{G}_0 \end{bmatrix} \tag{13.1}$$

Let $g_l(i,j)$ denote the (i,j)th element of the $k_0 \times n_0$ matrix $\mathbf{G}_l$, $l = 0, 1, \dots, m-1$ and define the (i,j)th *subgenerator polynomial*

$$g_{ij}(D) = g_0(i,j) + g_1(i,j)D + \dots + g_{m-1}(i,j)D^{m-1}$$

The quantity D is the delay operator of Chapter 7. These $k_0 n_0$ subgenerators completely specify the matrix G.

Let $m_i(D) = \sum_{l=0}^{m-1} m_{li} D^l$ denote the polynomial representation of the information sequence fed into the ith input of the encoder. Then encoding can be performed by forming the $k_0 n_0$ products.

$$m_i(D)g_{ij}(D) \qquad i = 1, 2, \dots, k_0$$
$$j = 1, 2, \dots, n_0$$

The n_0 output sequences are given by

$$c_j(D) = \sum_{i=1}^{k_0} m_i(D)g_{ij}(D) \qquad j = 1, 2, \dots, n_0$$

The jth digit of the code block at time $m-1$ is given by the coefficient of D^{m-1} or

$$\sum_{i=1}^{k_0} m_{0i}g_{m-1}(i,j) + m_{1i}g_{m-2}(i,j) + \dots + m_{(m-1)i}g_0(i,j)$$

Note that this is precisely the same as the corresponding digit in the vector product.

$$(m_{01} \dots m_{0k_0} m_{11} \dots m_{1k_0} \dots m_{(m-1)1} \dots m_{(m-1)k_0})\mathbf{G}$$

For a systematic code $\mathbf{G}_l = [\mathbf{I}_{k_0} \mathbf{P}_l]$, and so

$$g_{ij}(D) = 1 \qquad i = j$$
$$= 0 \qquad i \neq j$$

for $j \leq k_0$.

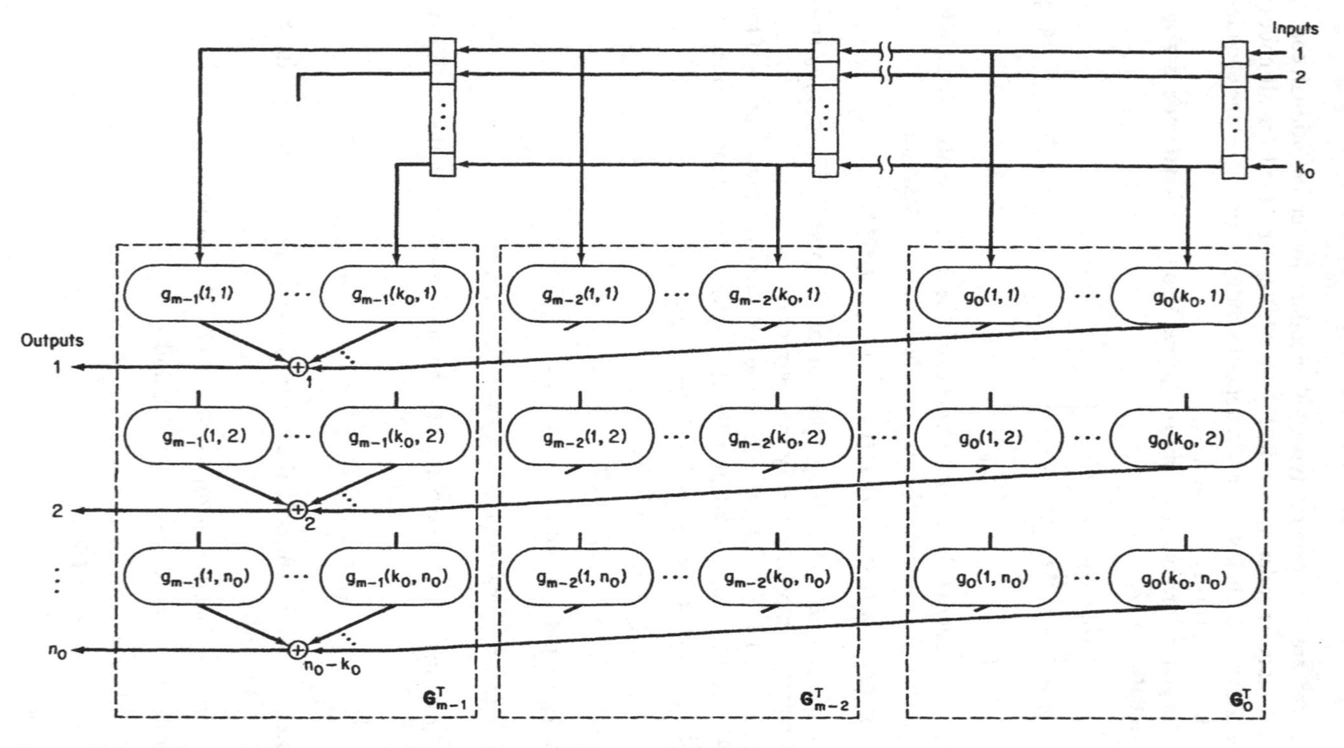

Figure 13.2. A $k = mk_0$-stage encoder for an (mn_0, mk_0) convolutional code.

Example. One single-error-correcting systematic convolutional code has $n_0 = 4$, $k_0 = 3$, and $m = 3$. Its basic parity-check matrix is

$$\mathbf{h} = [1100 \quad 1010 \quad 1111]$$

The corresponding encoder is shown in Figure 13.3a; the subgenerators are

$$g_{14}(D) = 1 + D + D^2$$

$$g_{24}(D) = 1 + D^2$$

$$g_{34}(D) = 1 + D$$

Figure 13.3b shows a version of this encoder which processes serial data. With Gate 1 open and Gate 2 closed, the k_0 digits of the $(m - 1)$th

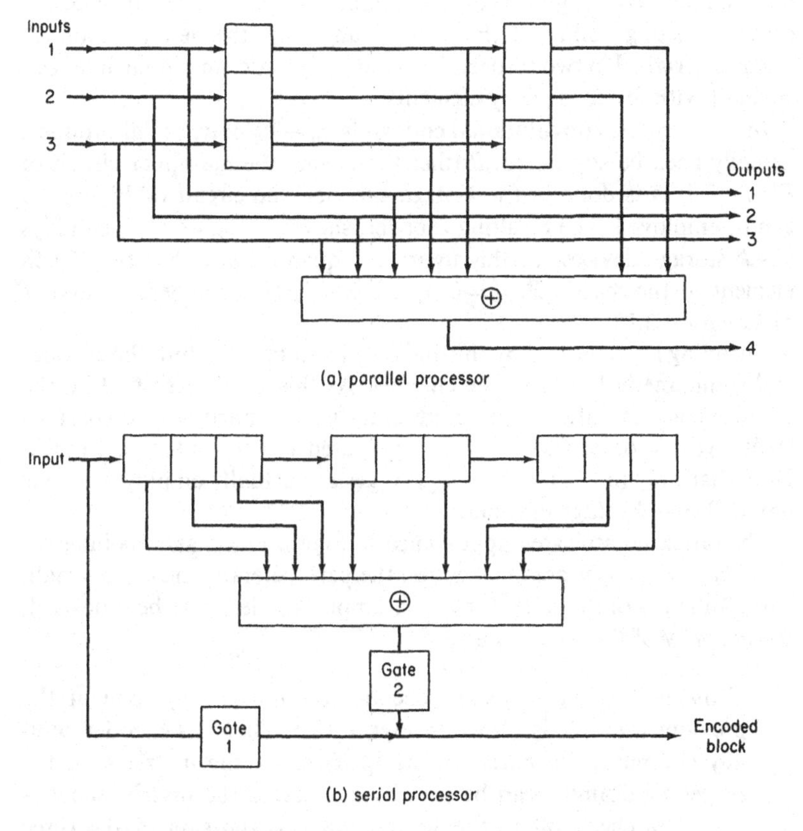

Figure 13.3. Two versions of a k-stage encoder for the (12, 9) systematic convolutional code with $g_{14}(D) = 1 + D + D^2$, $g_{24}(D) = 1 + D^2$, and $g_{34}(D) = 1 + D$.

block are shifted into the register and directly out to the channel. Then Gate 1 is closed, Gate 2 is opened, and the $n_0 - k_0$ parity checks which complete the block are read out. At this point the encoder is ready to encode the next block. This type of serial encoder can be used with any convolutional code whether in systematic form or not.

The *encoding constraint length* of a convolutional code is defined as n_0 times the number of blocks between the first and last nonzero submatrices $\mathbf{G}_l$ in Equation 3.12 (inclusive). In many cases $\mathbf{G}_{m-1} \neq \mathbf{0}$ and the encoding constraint length and decoding constraint length n are the same. It is possible, however, by elementary row operations, to transform the matrix $\mathbf{G}$ into one with a somewhat shorter encoding constraint length and which is not in echelon canonical form. (See Problem 13.12, for example.) Although this does not affect the set of code words or the error-correcting ability of the code in any way, the new code differs from the original in two respects. It is not systematic, and its encoder can be built with fewer memory elements.

In a systematic convolutional code only $n_0 - k_0$ polynomial products actually need be computed. Rather than using the multiplier circuit of Figure 7.1 as is done in the k-stage encoder, the circuit of Figure 7.3 can be employed. The resulting encoder, shown in Figure 13.4, employs $n - k$ storage devices. In this figure the quantity $p_l(i, j)$ is the (i, j)th element of the matrix $\mathbf{P}_l$, $l = 0, 1, \ldots, m-1$, of the generator matrix of Equation 3.13.

Encoding is performed by shifting a k_0-bit data block into the encoder and simultaneously out to the channel. As this block is shifted in, the entire encoder is shifted once, emitting the $n_0 - k_0$ parity bits on parallel leads. At this point the encoder is prepared to encode the next block. Note that only $(n - k) - (n_0 - k_0)$ stages are actually employed in this nominal $(n - k)$-stage encoder.

The rather complicated appearance of Figure 13.4 masks its inherent simplicity. For most practical codes, the parameters n_0 and k_0 are small. Also, for many of the codes for which simple decoders have been devised, the majority of the $p_l(i, j)$ are zero.

> *Example.* The $(n - k)$-stage encoder for the (12, 9) code of the previous example is shown in Figure 13.5. That this encoder actually computes the parity bit as specified by the matrix $\mathbf{h}$ of the preceding example can be seen by comparing the matrix and circuit. The check bit in the second block is the sum of the three information bits in this block, the first and third information bits of the previous (first) block, and the first and second information bits of the zeroth block.

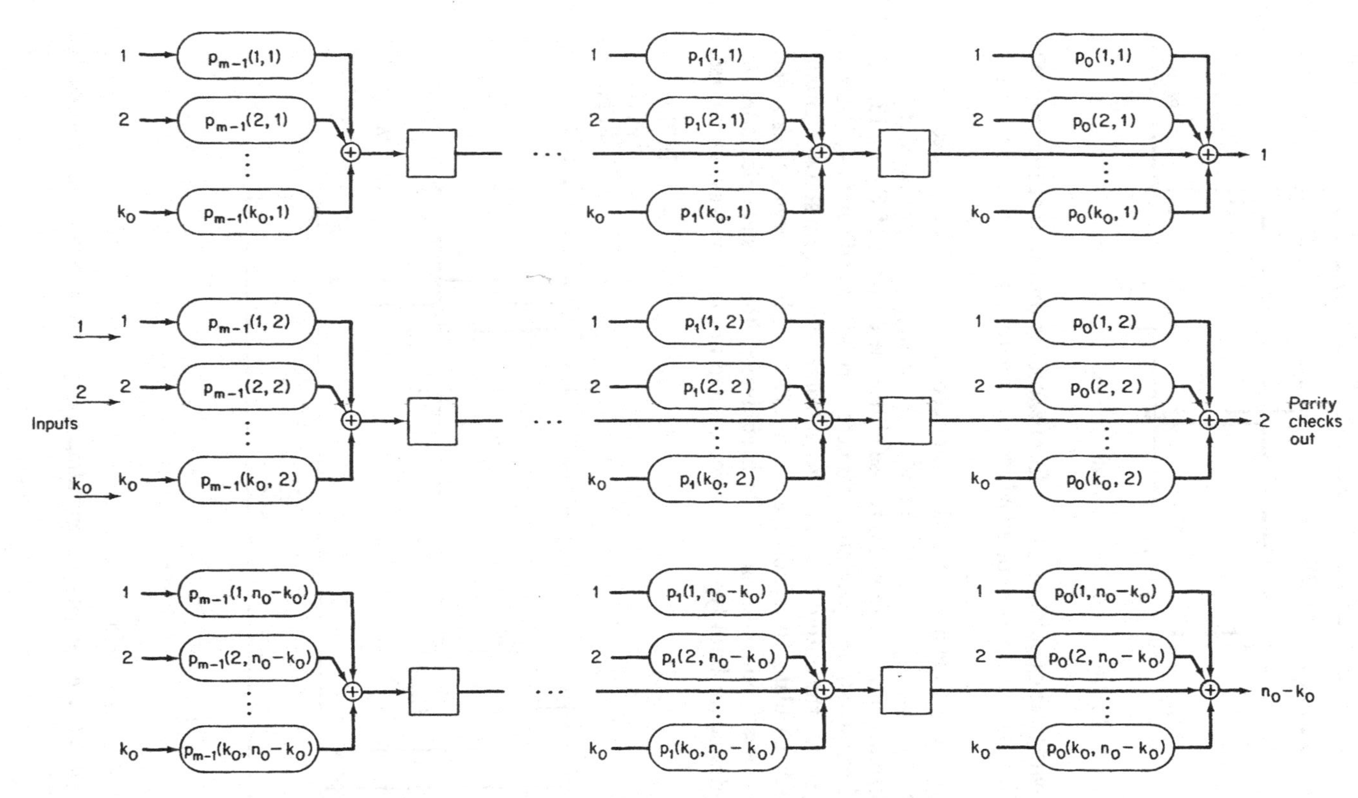

Figure 13.4. An $(n - k)$-stage encoder for an (mn_0, mk) systematic convolutional code.

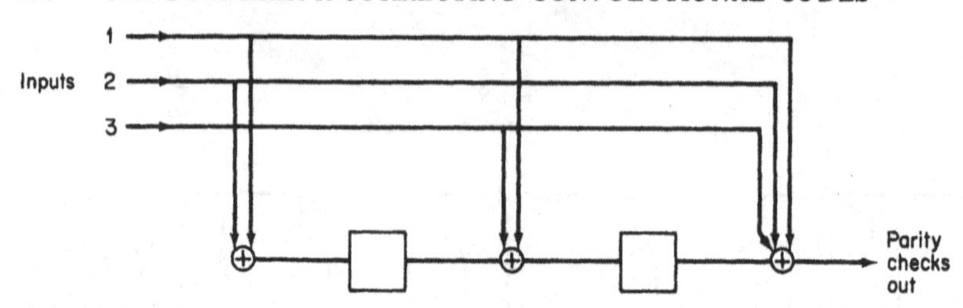

Figure 13.5. An $(n-k)$-stage encoder for the (12, 9) code.

Syndrome calculation differs from encoding only in that the received parity digits must be subtracted from the parity digits calculated on the received digits. Also, since the syndrome and the received information digits will presumably be used by the decoder, they must be stored. Thus, the syndrome is usually calculated with a k-stage register that stores the information digits. In order to use either the encoder of Figure 13.2 or 13.3 as a syndrome generator, it is necessary only to add an $(n-k)$-stage register at the output to store the syndrome. Figure 13.6 shows a circuit which calculates the syndrome for the (12, 9) code of previous examples. Since every nonsystematic code is equivalent to a systematic code, the syndrome for both types can be calculated in the same way. Of course,

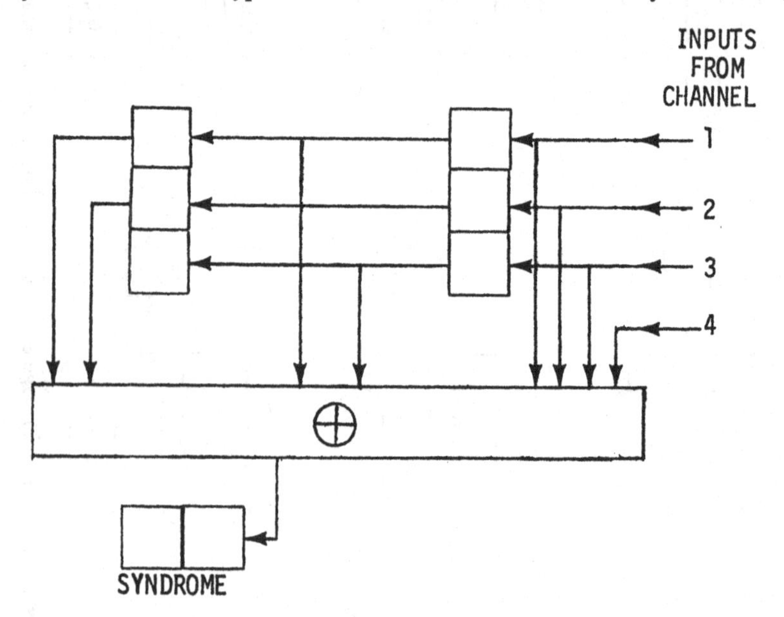

Figure 13.6. A circuit for generating the syndrome of the (12, 9) code of Figure 13.3.

the association between syndrome and error pattern will be different for the two codes but in either case an all-zero syndrome implies that a code word has been received. Errors are detected, as for block codes, by the occurence of a nonzero syndrome.

Given an (mn_0, mk_0) convolutional code capable of correcting a particular set of error patterns, it is possible to construct an $(m(n_0 - i), m(k_0 - i))$ code with the same error-correcting capabilities. This requires that each code block be *shortened* by i digits, that is, the first i information symbols in each block are always set to zero and then not transmitted.

13.2 Error Correction and Error Propagation

A general decoder for an (mn_0, mk_0) convolutional code takes the form of Figure 13.7. With Gate 1 open and Gate 2 closed, k_0 information digits are shifted into the information register. Then Gate 1 is closed and Gate 2 is opened. The encoder calculates the parity digits on the received information digits; these are subtracted from the received parity digits to form the syndrome. The logic circuit determines from the syndrome whether the oldest block of k_0 information digits stored in the information register is correct or not. If a correctable error pattern occurred, the errors in this 0th block are corrected by the logic circuit as the block is shifted out of the decoder.

At this point the errors in the 0th block are known. These errors affect the syndrome digits associated with the succeeding $m - 1$ blocks. In

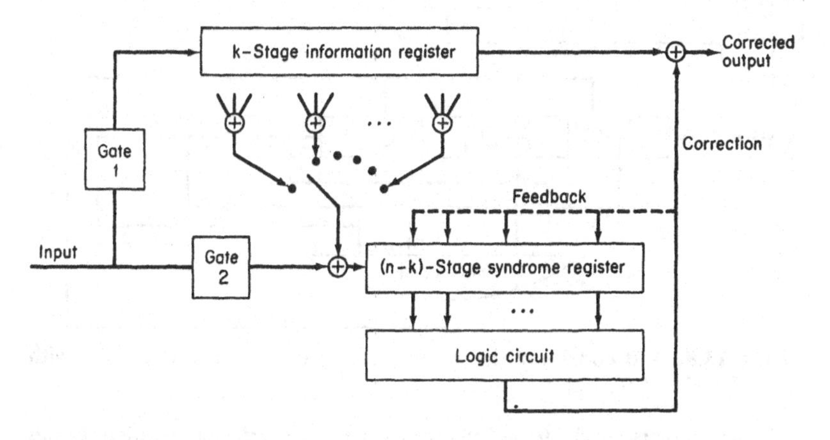

Figure 13.7. A general decoder for an (n, k) convolutional code.

order to enable the decoder to attain its full error-correcting power, the effects of these errors must be removed. This can be done by adding the dashed-line connection in Figure 13.7.

This feedback path converts the feed-forward syndrome register into a (nonlinear) feedback shift register. This can produce an effect known as *error propagation.** An uncorrectable channel error may cause the syndrome register to enter a state in which, in the absence of additional channel errors, the decoder will continue to decode incorrectly forever. The reason is that the output of the nonlinear feedback shift register with an all-zero sequence applied at its input, but with nonzero initial conditions, may be periodic.

> *Example.* A decoder for the binary double-error-correcting (12, 6) convolutional code with
>
> **h** = [10 10 10 00 00 11]
>
> is shown in Figure 13.8. (This is an example of an orthogonalizable code; see Section 13.5.) If a triple-error pattern of the form
>
> 00 01 00 01 01 00 ...
> ↑
> 0th block information bit

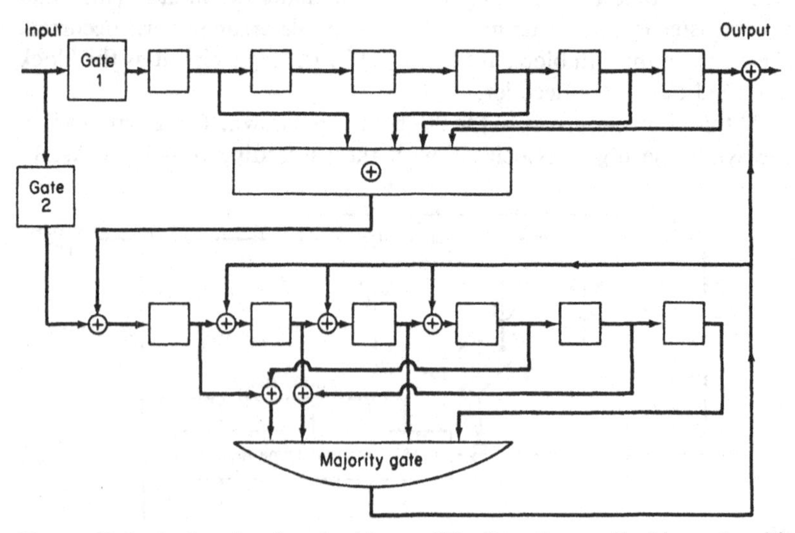

Figure 13.8. A decoder for the binary (12, 6) orthogonalizable code with $h = [1 0 1 0 1 0 0 0 0 0 1 1]$.

* Some authors use the terms infinite or catastrophic error propagation. In this book finite error propagation is not considered.

occurs, errors will propagate as long as no additional channel errors occur. For in this case the syndrome register will attain the state 011010, followed by 001101, followed by 011010, and so forth. In one state the information digit leaving the decoder is incorrectly inverted; in the other it is correct.

This error-propagation effect can be eliminated by redesigning the decoder in this example. This does not seem to be possible in general, however, and error propagation must be considered in designing error-control systems using convolutional codes.

For some of the codes discussed in this and the succeeding chapter, error propagation is not possible; for others it is. The following result specifies a sufficient condition for decoding errors not to propagate:

THEOREM 13.1. *If the effect of the (nonzero) feedback digits in a convolutional decoder is always to reduce the weight of the syndrome, error propagation cannot occur.*

Proof. Errors have occurred producing a nonzero syndrome. Error propagation will not occur if the syndrome register clears itself with a sequence of all zeros applied at its input. Suppose the syndrome digits associated with the 0th block are all zero. Then shifting the syndrome register either causes the syndrome to shift $n_0 - k_0$ digits to the right, with $n_0 - k_0$ zeros filling out the syndrome on the left end, or for its weight to be reduced by the feedback. Thus, repetitively shifting the syndrome either produces an all-zero syndrome or one whose 0th block is nonzero. If this latter situation occurs, an additional shift reduces the weight of the syndrome, regardless of the feedback. After the syndrome reaches the all-zero state, no additional decoding errors can occur.

Q.E.D.

This result will be used to show that error propagation does not occur with some practically important convolutional codes. Further results on this subject can be found in Robinson (1968) and Massey and Liu (1964). It is not strictly necessary to use this feedback information if some degradation in performance can be tolerated. It is clear that without feedback error propagation cannot occur.

Error propagation occurs for a non-systematic code with $k_0 = 1$ if the n_0 subgenerator polynomials have a common monic factor of nonzero degree. This can be seen as follows. Let $g_j(D), j = 1, 2, \ldots n_0$, denote the subgenerators and assume that

$$g_j(D) = g_0(D)g_j'(D) \qquad j = 1, 2, \ldots, n_0$$

where $g_0(D)$ is a monic polynomial of non-zero degree. Assume the all-zero word is transmitted and the n_0 received polynomials are

$$r_j(D) = g_j'(D) \tag{13.2}$$

for all j. But the same sequence is received if the original information sequence was $m(D) = [1/g_0(D)]$. Since $g_0(D)$ divides $D^n - 1$ for some n, $m(D)$ is periodic with period n. Thus in one case or the other the finite-degree error pattern of Equation 13.2 produces error propagation.

13.3 Single- and Double-Error-Correcting Codes

A class of binary convolutional codes can be constructed with parameters

$$n_0 = 2^{m-1}$$

$$k_0 = n_0 - 1$$

$$d = 3$$

for any choice of m (Wyner and Ash 1963). Choose the columns of the matrix $\mathbf{B}_0$, that is, the first n_0 columns of $\mathbf{H}$, to be the 2^{m-1} m-tuples formed by preceding each of the binary $(m-1)$ tuples by a single 1. The assignment of $(m-1)$-tuples to columns is irrelevant except that if the code is to be used in systematic form, it is necessary to assign the all-zero $(m-1)$-tuple to the n_0th column of $\mathbf{H}$ (which corresponds to a check bit). The $(m2^{m-1}, m(2^{m-1}-1))$ code specified by this matrix is capable of correcting all single errors since no two of the first n_0 columns are identical, and no other column (headed by a 0) is identical to one of the first n_0 columns (headed by a 1). These codes correspond closely to the Hamming block codes.

Example. The (12, 9) code considered in previous examples was constructed as above. Each of the first $n_0 = 2^{m-1} = 4$ columns of its parity-check matrix

$$\mathbf{H} = \begin{bmatrix} 1111 & & \\ 1010 & 1111 & \\ 1100 & 1010 & 1111 \end{bmatrix}$$

consists of a 1 followed by one of the four binary 2-tuples.

Like block codes, these codes can be shortened to provide other values of rate. This is done by setting the first i information symbols in each block equal to 0 and then not transmitting them.

The assignment of $(m-1)$-tuples to columns in the matrix $\mathbf{B}_0$ is arbitrary. However, decoding may be simplified somewhat by associating with each column the $(m-1)$-tuple that in binary notation corresponds to the number of the column within the block. The all-zero $(m-1)$-tuple is assigned to the 2^{m-1}th (parity-check) column. Then the first bit of the syndrome is a 1 if an error occurred in the 0th block and is 0 otherwise; the remaining $m-1$ bits of the syndrome give the number of the bit which is in error if an error has occurred. The implementation of the decoding process is then quite straightforward.

After a single bit error has been corrected, the syndrome, which is to be used in decoding the following block, must be modified. In this case this simply means setting the syndrome to zero after correction has been performed. Thus, by Theorem 13.1, a decoding error cannot generate additional errors in subsequent blocks and errors do not propagate.

The performance of these codes on the binary symmetric channel is considered in Frieman and Robinson (1965). The authors show that there is little difference between the performance of these codes and that of single-error-correcting (Hamming) block codes.

A class of double-error-correcting convolutional codes can be constructed as follows (Wyner 1964): From Section 9.2, for any m there exists a binary $(2^m-1, 2^m-2-2m)$ primitive BCH code with minimum distance 6. Its parity-check matrix is

$$\begin{bmatrix} 1 & 1 & \cdots & 1 & 1 \\ \alpha^{2^m-2} & \alpha^{2^m-3} & \cdots & \alpha^1 & \alpha^0 \\ \alpha^{3(2^m-2)} & \alpha^{3(2^m-3)} & \cdots & \alpha^3 & \alpha^0 \end{bmatrix} = \begin{bmatrix} \mathbf{1} \\ \mathbf{H}_1 \\ \mathbf{H}_2 \end{bmatrix}$$

where $\mathbf{H}_i$ is a binary m- by -(2^m-1) matrix and $\mathbf{1}$ is the (2^m-1)-place, all-ones row vector.

Now the $(2(2^m-1), 2(2^m-1)-2(m+1))$ convolutional code whose parity-check matrix is

$$\mathbf{H} = \begin{bmatrix} \mathbf{1} & \\ \mathbf{H}_1 & \\ \mathbf{0} & \mathbf{1} \\ \mathbf{H}_2 & \mathbf{H}_1 \end{bmatrix}$$

has $d=6$. ($\mathbf{0}$ denotes the (2^m-1)-place, all-zero row vector.) This can be seen as follows. In order for a code word with weight 5 or less to exist, some linear combination of 5 or fewer columns of $\mathbf{H}$ must be zero. At least 4 of the columns must be chosen from among the first 2^m-1 columns of $\mathbf{H}$. For the submatrix

$$\begin{bmatrix} \mathbf{1} \\ \mathbf{H}_1 \end{bmatrix}$$

is the parity-check matrix of a distance-4 Hamming code. But in order for the linear combination of the digits in the $(m+2)$th row to be zero, at least two columns must be chosen from among the last $2^m - 1$ columns of **H**. Thus, every code word has weight 6 or greater.

13.4 Self-Orthogonal Codes

These codes (Massey 1963; Robinson and Bernstein 1966) are the most extensive constructive class of convolutional codes known. Also, they can be decoded simply with majority-logic decoding. (See Chapter 10.) Unfortunately, for large values of n and k they have relatively low minimum distance.

In the following paragraphs self-orthogonal codes with $n_0 - k_0 = 1$ will be constructed. It will then be shown that the dual of an $(mn_0, m(n_0 - 1))$ self-orthogonal convolutional code is an (mn_0, m) self-orthogonal code. Codes with $n_0 - 1 > k_0 > 1$ have not yet been devised.

From Equation 3.14 the basic parity-check matrix of a binary convolutional code in systematic form with $n_0 - k_0 = 1$ is

$$\mathbf{h} = [\mathbf{P}_{m-1}^T 0 \mathbf{P}_{m-2}^T 0 \cdots \mathbf{P}_0^T 1] \tag{13.3}$$

where the $\mathbf{P}_i^T$ are k_0-place binary row matrices. In a self-orthogonal code with minimum distance d, at least $d-1$ rows of the matrix **H** are orthogonal (in the sense of Section 10.1) on each of the k_0 information digits of block zero. The matrix **h** can be specified by k_0 sets of integers chosen from the set $(0, 1, \ldots, m-1)$; the jth of these sets specifies which of the row matrices $\mathbf{P}_i^T$ have 1's in their jth positions, $1 \leqq j \leqq k_0$. That is, it specifies in which of the blocks $0, 1, \ldots, m-1$ the jth information bit is checked by the parity bit in the $(m-1)$th block.

At this point it is necessary to define what has been referred to as the *difference triangle* associated with an ordered set of integers $[0, n_1, n_2, \ldots, n_{d-2}]$, where $0 < n_1 < n_2 < \ldots < n_{d-2}$. This difference triangle consists of the set of $(d-1)(d-2)/2$ differences $n_j - n_i$ for which $j > i$. If no two of these differences are identical, the triangle is said to be *full* (Massey 1970). If the sets of differences of two difference triangles have no integer in common, the difference triangles are *disjoint*.

THEOREM 13.2. *Let $S_1, S_2, \ldots, S_{k_0}$ be the k_0 sets of integers which specify an $(mn_0, m(n_0 - 1))$ convolutional code. Let* 0 *be a member* *of every S_i. If the k_0 difference triangles associated with these sets are full and disjoint and each has $d-1$ elements, then $d-1$ of the check sums represented by the syndrome digits are orthogonal on each of the k_0 information symbols in block zero and the code has minimum distance at least d. Furthermore, m is equal to one plus the largest integer in any set.*

Proof. Since each of the sets S_i has $d-1$ elements, each of the first k_0 columns of the matrix **B** has weight $d-1$ or greater. It remains to show that the $d-1$ rows of **H** which correspond to the 1's in the ith column of **B** are orthogonal.

If two of these $d-1$ rows of **H** are not orthogonal, then they have a 1 in a common position besides zero. There are two cases to consider; this common 1 can occur in the ith digit of a block or in some other digit. In the former case this implies that there are two pairs of integers (a_i, b_i) and (c_i, d_i) in the set S_i such that their differences $(a_i - b_i)$ and $(c_i - d_i)$ are identical. Since all the difference triangles of the sets S are full, this is impossible.

Consider the second situation, in which the common 1 occurs in the jth digit of some block $j \neq i$. Let a_i and b_i denote two integers in S_i. Now if

$$a_i - a_j = b_i - b_j$$

then

$$a_i - b_i = a_j - b_j$$

and the difference triangles of the sets S_i and S_j are not disjoint. Thus, there are $d-1$ orthogonal check sums on each information digit in the block being decoded. Clearly, no code word can have weight less than d if block zero is nonzero.

The constraint length of the code in blocks is the number of blocks spanned by the sets S_i. Since block 0 is involved in each S_i, $m-1$ equals the largest integer in any S_i. Q.E.D.

COROLLARY 13.1. *A self-orthogonal code with block length n_0, with $k_0 = n_0 - 1$, and with minimum distance d has length*

$$n \geqq n_0 \left[\frac{(n_0 - 1)(d-1)(d-2)}{2} + 1\right]$$

This corollary follows from the fact that each of the $n_0 - 1$ difference triangles has $[(d-1)(d-2)]/2]$ elements and they are disjoint.

Example. A self-orthogonal code with $d = 5$ and $R = k_0/n_0 = 2/3$ is specified by 2 sets of 4 integers with the properties that no integer appears more than once among the 6 differences in either triangle and that the triangles are disjoint. The sets of integers (0, 8, 9, 12) and (0, 6, 11, 13) yield the full disjoint difference triangles:

```
  4          7
 1 3        5  2
8 9 12    6 11 13
```

The basic parity-check matrix specified by these sets is

$$\mathbf{h} = [100\ 010\ 100\ 000\ 010\ 010\ 000\ 100\ 000\ 000\ 000\ 000\ 000\ 111] \quad (13.4)$$

Note that this code has length 42, which equals n_0 times the largest integer in the difference triangles plus one.

The dual of an $(mn_0, m(n_0 - 1))$ self-orthogonal code with minimum distance d is an (mn_0, m) self-orthogonal code with minimum distance

$$\bar{d} = (n_0 - 1)(d - 1) + 1 \quad (13.5)$$

If the basic parity-check matrix of the original code is given by Equation 13.3, then for the dual code

$$\mathbf{H} = \begin{bmatrix} \mathbf{P}_0\mathbf{I} & & & \\ \mathbf{P}_1\mathbf{0} & \mathbf{P}_0\mathbf{I} & & \\ \vdots & & \ddots & \\ \mathbf{P}_{m-1}\mathbf{0} & \mathbf{P}_{m-2}\mathbf{0} & \cdots & \mathbf{P}_0\mathbf{I} \end{bmatrix} \quad (13.6)$$

where the $\mathbf{P}_i$ are $(n_0 - 1)$-bit column matrices. Now the weight of the first column of this matrix is $(n_0 - 1)(d - 1)$. If the corresponding parity-check sums are orthogonal, then Equation 13.5 holds.

Were two equations not orthogonal, then a rectangle of 1's would appear in $\mathbf{H}$ and all four of these 1's would appear in some matrix $\mathbf{P}_i$. But this is impossible because the same rectangle (rotated 90°) would appear in the parity-check matrix of the original code, implying that it was not self-orthogonal.

For these low-rate codes, Equation 13.5 and Corollary 13.1 yield the following lower bound on n:

$$n \geq n_0 \left[\frac{(\bar{d}-1)}{2} \left[\frac{\bar{d}-1}{n_0 - 1} - 1 \right] + 1 \right] \qquad (13.7)$$

Example. The sets of integers used in the preceding example can also be used to construct a (42, 14) self-orthogonal code. The basic parity-check matrix for this code is

$$\mathbf{h} = \begin{bmatrix} 000\ 100\ 000\ 000\ 100\ 100\ 000\ 000\ 000\ 000\ 000\ 000\ 000\ 110 \\ 100\ 000\ 100\ 000\ 000\ 000\ 000\ 100\ 000\ 000\ 000\ 000\ 000\ 101 \end{bmatrix} \qquad (13.8)$$

Each row of this matrix is determined by one of the two sets of integers which specify the code. For example, since the first set is [0, 8, 9, 12], the first parity bit in the 0th block checks the information bit in blocks number 0, 8, 9, and 12, as shown. The minimum distance of the code is at least 9 since there are 8 orthogonal parity-check sums on the single information digit in each block.

Theorem 13.2 reduces the problem of code construction to that of constructing disjoint, full, difference triangles. An extensive, computer-generated list of sets of integers which specify self-orthogonal codes of various rates is given in Robinson and Bernstein (1966).

Corollary 13.3 and Equation 13.7 show that self-orthogonal codes are considerably longer than the best codes for a given transmission rate and minimum distance. This is balanced to some extent by their simple decoding procedure.

For a self-orthogonal (mn_0, mk_0) code, $d-1$ of the syndrome bits are orthogonal on each of the k_0 information digits in the block being decoded. Thus, the logic circuit of Figure 13.7 can be implemented with k_0 majority gates, each of which has $d-1$ inputs.

Example. The decoder for the (42, 28) $d=5$ self-orthogonal code of the previous example is shown in Figure 13.9. Each 4-input majority gate has a 0 output when two or more 0's appear at its inputs.

Error propagation does not occur with self-orthogonal codes. For in order that a change be made in the output sequence, more than half of the orthogonal syndrome digits must be 1. Thus, the feedback always reduces the weight of the syndrome, so Theorem 13.1 applies. Robinson (1968) has shown that self-orthogonal codes can be decoded with

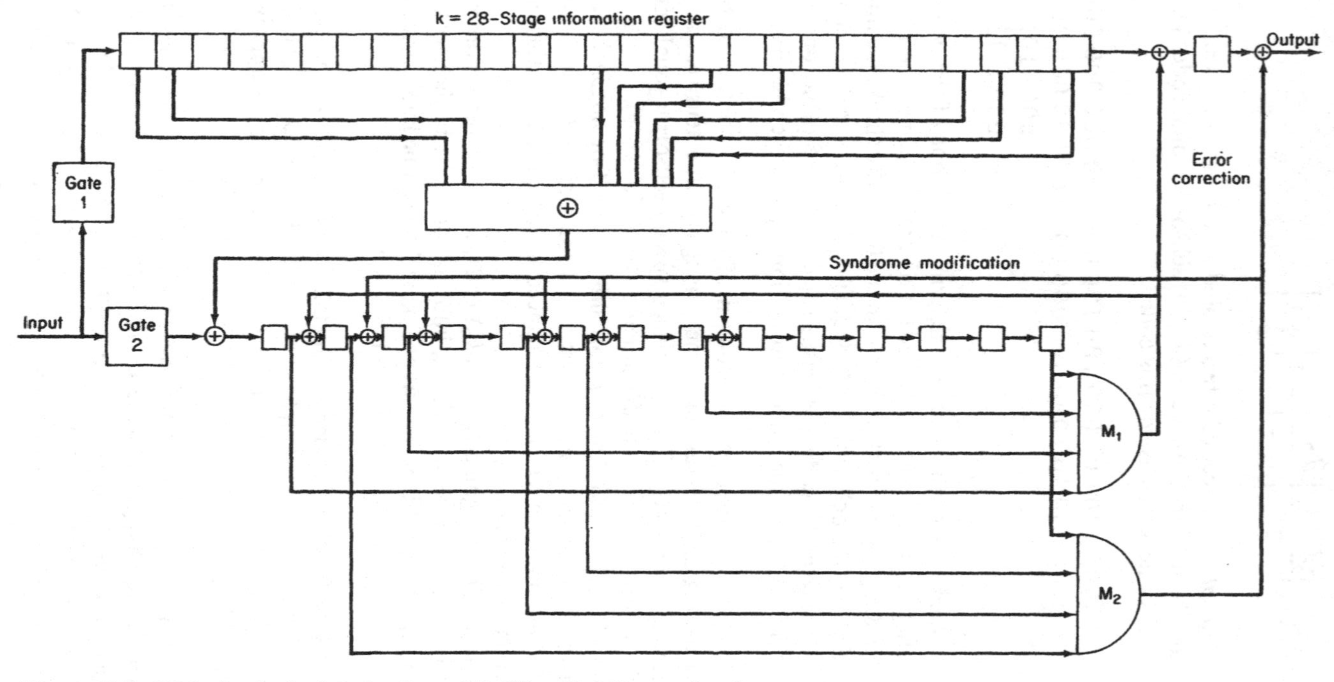

Figure 13.9. Majority-logic decoder for a (42, 28) self-orthogonal code.

definite decoding, although not without some degradation in performance.

Self-orthogonal codes can be constructed that can correct bursts of errors in addition to random errors. These "diffuse" codes are considered in Chapter 14.

13.5 Orthogonalizable Codes

These codes are more efficient random-error correctors than self-orthogonal codes, but their construction is poorly understood at present. All known codes have been constructed by an unwieldy trial-and-error procedure that seems to work only when $k_0 = 1$; binary codes with rate 1/2, 1/3, 1/5, and 1/10 are tabulated in Massey (1963); Lucky, Salz, and Weldon (1968).

Orthogonalizable codes differ from self-orthogonal codes in one important respect. In the latter, a set of $d-1$ orthogonal check sums corresponding to rows of **H** must be constructed. In an orthogonalizable code, on the other hand, the $d-1$ orthogonal check sums can correspond to rows of **H** or any linear combination thereof. Thus, the decoder for such a code with $k_0 = 1$ assumes the form of Figure 13.10; for $k_0 > 1$, additional majority gates must be added. Note that this decoder has the form of Figure 13.7 with the logic circuit composed of a set of adders followed by a majority gate.

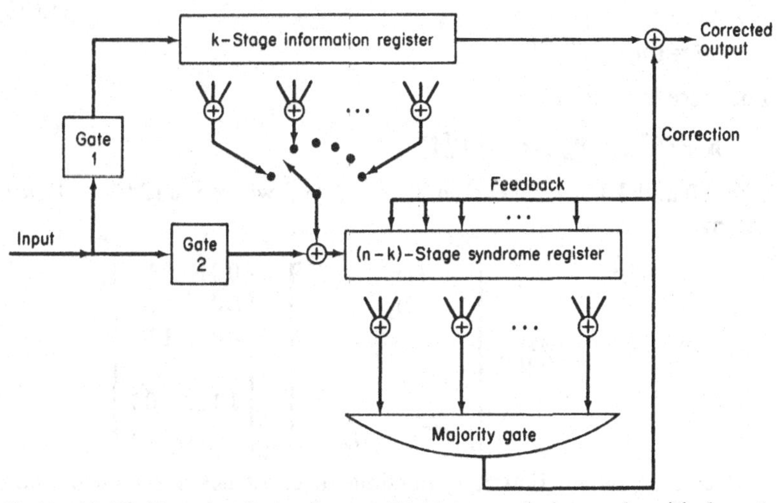

Figure 13.10. Decoder for orthogonalizable convolution code with $k_0 = 1$.

Example. The parity-check matrix of a (12, 6) orthogonalizable code with $d = 5$ is

$$\mathbf{H} = \begin{bmatrix} 11 \\ 00 & 11 \\ 00 & 00 & 11 \\ 10 & 00 & 00 & 11 \\ 10 & 10 & 00 & 00 & 11 \\ 10 & 10 & 10 & 00 & 00 & 11 \end{bmatrix} \tag{13.9}$$

The four check sums specified by the first, fourth, and fifth rows and the sum of the second and sixth rows are orthogonal on the first digit.

A decoder for this code, which employs a slightly different set of orthogonal check sums, is shown in Figure 13.8. This set of check sums was chosen to illustrate the fact that error propagation can occur with orthogonalizable codes. Since the conditions for Theorem 13.1 are not satisfied, the non-linear feedback shift register formed by the syndrome register and majority gate can produce a periodic output with an all-zero input.

The dual codes of the single-error-correcting codes of Section 13.3 are orthogonalizable. For any choice of m there exists a *uniform code* (Massey 1963) with

$$\begin{aligned} n_0 &= 2^{m-1} \\ k_0 &= 1 \\ d &= (m-1)2^{m-2} \end{aligned} \tag{13.10}$$

For these low-rate codes,

$$\mathbf{h} = [\mathbf{P}_{m-1}^T \mathbf{0}\, \mathbf{P}_{m-2}^T \mathbf{0} \cdots \mathbf{P}_0^T \mathbf{I}]$$

where $\mathbf{0}$ and $\mathbf{I}$ have dimension $2^{m-1} - 1$ and where the $(2^{m-1} - 1) \times m$ matrix

$$[\mathbf{P}_{m-1}^T \mathbf{P}_{m-2}^T \ldots \mathbf{P}_0^T] = \begin{bmatrix} (1)_2 & 1 \\ (2)_2 & 1 \\ \vdots & \\ (2^{m-1}-1)_2 & 1 \end{bmatrix} = \begin{bmatrix} 00\ldots011 \\ 00\ldots101 \\ 00\ldots111 \\ \vdots \\ 11\ldots101 \\ 11\ldots111 \end{bmatrix} \tag{13.11}$$

It can be shown that it is possible to construct $d-1$ check sums orthogonal on the information digit in the 0th block. (Massey 1963.)

Example. Let $m = 3$. The dual of the (12, 9) code of the example of Section 13.3 is a (12, 3] uniform code. Its parity-check matrix is

$$
H = \begin{bmatrix}
11 & & \\
101 & & \\
1001 & & \\
1000 & 11 & \\
0000 & 101 & \\
1000 & 1001 & \\
0000 & 1000 & 11 \\
1000 & 0000 & 101 \\
1000 & 1000 & 1001
\end{bmatrix}
\begin{array}{l}
\leftarrow \\
\leftarrow \\
\leftarrow \\
\leftarrow \\
\leftarrow \\
\leftarrow \; \oplus \\
\leftarrow \\
\leftarrow \quad \oplus \\
\leftarrow
\end{array}
$$

Rows 1, 2, 3, 4, $5 \oplus 6$, $7 \oplus 9$, and 8 are orthogonal on the information digit in block zero. Thus $d = (m + 1)(2^{m-2}) = 8$.

Theorem 13.1 does not apply to uniform codes; however, in Sullivan (1969) it is shown that error propagation is not a serious problem with these codes.

A few computer-generated orthogonalizable codes are presented in Goldman, Rowan, and Tolhurst (1969). Other than these and the hand-constructed trial-and-error codes of Massey (1963), little progress has been made on the problem of constructing good, orthogonalizable, convolutional codes.

13.6 Computer-Generated Codes

By exhaustively trying all possible subgenerator polynomials Bussgang (1965) has found all convolutional codes of rate 1/2 with $n \lesssim 32$ and rate 1/3 with $n \leqq 21$ which have maximum minimum distance. Lin and Lyne (1967) have extended the list of good convolutional codes using the following idea: Suppose an (mn_0, mk_0) convolutional code with maximum minimum distance is known. Construct an $((m+1)n_0, (m+1)k_0)$ code by appending an n_0-tuple to each subgenerator so as to minimize the number of minimum-weight code vectors. Longer codes are formed inductively in this manner. While the codes obtained by this method are not guaranteed to have maximum minimum distance, they often do, and in known cases where they do not the discrepancy is small.

Good codes with rates 1/2 and 1/3 and with $n \leqq 42$ have been devised with this approach. These and codes with $R = 1/9, 1/8, 1/7, 1/6, 1/5, 1/4$,

2/5, and 2/3 are tabulated in Lin and Lyne (1967). Forney (1968) has tabulated codes with $R = 1/2$ and $n \leq 96$. Costello (1969) describes several other algorithms for finding convolutional codes of moderate length with good distance properties.

13.7 The Viterbi Decoding Algorithm

If the number of code words in a convolutional code is reasonably small, decoding can be performed using the following method: Generate successively all q^k code words. Compare each with the received word. Decode the 0th block as the 0th block of the code word which is closest to the received word. Since q^k calculations may be required to decode n_0 bits, this maximum-likelihood systematic-search decoding procedure is limited to short codes and to codes with low rate.

Somewhat longer codes can be decoded using the following idea, due to Viterbi (1967). Consider a convolutional code with rate k_0/n_0 and basic block length n_0. Let the encoding constraint length of the code be denoted $n_e = m_e n_0$ and let $k_e = m_e k_0$ denote the number of information symbols in a constraint length. In the tree associated with the code, the k_e-tuple to be encoded determines one of q^{k_e} paths of m_e branches through the tree. Each node of the tree has q^{k_0} branches, and with each branch is associated an n_0-tuple. Let $a_0, a_1, \ldots$ denote the input information sequence; a_i is a k_0-tuple of elements of $GF(q)$. Let

$$\begin{array}{llll} \mathbf{c}_0 & = c_{00} & c_{01} & \cdots c_{0(m_e-1)} \\ \mathbf{c}_1 & = c_{10} & c_{11} & \cdots c_{1(m_e-1)} \\ & \vdots & & \\ \mathbf{c}_{q^{k_e}-1} & = c_{(q^{k_e}-1)0} & c_{(q^{k_e}-1)1} & \cdots c_{(q^{k_e}-1)(m_e-1)} \end{array}$$

denote the q^{k_e} code words of length n_e associated with the paths of the tree. The symbol c_{ij} denotes a q-ary n_0-tuple.

If the received sequence is $\mathbf{r} = r_0 r_1 \ldots$, the decoder calculates the q^{k_e} distances

$$d(\mathbf{c}_i, \mathbf{r}) = \sum_{j=0}^{m_e-1} d(c_{ij}, r_j), \qquad i = 0, 1, \ldots, q^{k_e} - 1 \tag{13.12}$$

where r_j denotes a q-ary n_0-tuple. The usual distance function is Hamming distance, although others can be used. The distances associated with the q^{k_0} paths for which the last $m_e - 1$ information blocks

$a_1, a_2, \ldots, a_{m_e-1}$ are identical are compared. The path with the smallest distance is denoted the *survivor*. This constitutes Step 1.

At Step 2 the distances between the received sequence $\mathbf{r}$ and the $q^{k_e}\, n_0(m+1)$-tuples formed by lengthening each survivor by one branch are calculated. Again, the distances associated with the q^{k_0} paths for which the last $m_e - 1$ information blocks are identical are compared and in each case the path which is closest to the received sequence is denoted the survivor.

This procedure continues with q^{k_e} calculations being performed at each step. The decoder must store the information sequences associated with the $q^{k_e-k_0}$ survivors, as well as the distances for these paths. Let m denote the number of branches which the decoder can store and let $n = mn_0$. Typically n, the decoding constraint length, will be several times larger than the encoding constraint length.

At the $(m - m_e + 1)$th step, paths of length m are being considered and the storage capacity of the decoder has been reached. Now if all $q^{k_e-k_0}$ survivors have the same information symbols in the 0th block, then the 0th block is decoded as these symbols. If all survivors do not agree, the decoder can either signal a detected error or simply guess at a_0, presumably by taking the majority vote of the survivors. After decoding, if errors have been corrected, the distance functions for the survivors must be reduced by the number of errors corrected.

The tree associated with a convolutional code is repetitive; Forney (1968) has used this fact to construct a simpler diagram called a *trellis*. The k-stage convolutional encoder of Figure 13.2 has $(m_e - 1)k_0 = k_e - k_0$ internal storage elements and hence $q^{m_e-1)k_0}$ states. Any k_0-tuple presented at the input causes this linear finite-state machine to change state and emit a particular n_0-tuple. The trellis diagram is a graphical representation of the sequence of internal states and outputs produced by all possible input sequences.

Example. The (12, 6) binary systematic convolutional code with generator matrix

$$\mathbf{G} = \begin{bmatrix} 11 & 01 & 00 & 01 & 00 & 01 \\ & 11 & 01 & 00 & 01 & 00 \\ & & 11 & 01 & 00 & 01 \\ & & & 11 & 01 & 00 \\ & & & & 11 & 01 \\ & & & & & 11 \end{bmatrix}$$

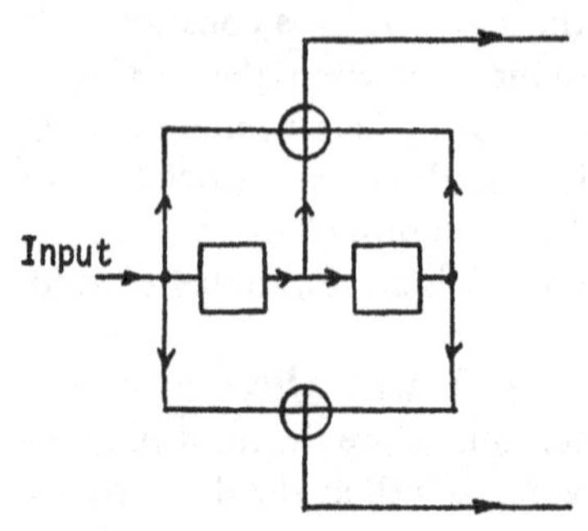

Figure 13.11. A k-stage encoder for a nonsystematic convolutional code with $g_1(D) = 1 + D + D^2$ and $g_2(D) = 1 + D^2$.

has minimum Hamming distance 5. Adding row $i + 2$ to row i, $i = 1, 2, 3, 4$, gives the matrix

$$\mathbf{G}' = \begin{bmatrix} 11 & 01 & 11 & 00 & 00 & 00 \\ & 11 & 01 & 11 & 00 & 00 \\ & & 11 & 01 & 11 & 00 \\ & & & 11 & 01 & 11 \\ & & & & 11 & 01 \\ & & & & & 11 \end{bmatrix}$$

which generates an equivalent nonsystematic code with $n_e = 6$. With $n \geqq 12$, it can correct all patterns of weight 2 using feedback decoding; with $n \leqq 10$, some double-error patterns are uncorrectable. For this code, $g_1(D) = 1 + D + D^2$ and $g_2(D) = 1 + D^2$, that is, $\mathbf{g} = 11011100\ldots$.

The encoder for this code is shown in Figure 13.11 and its trellis diagram in Figure 13.12. The encoder is initially in state 00. When a 0 is shifted into the register, the encoder changes state via the solid line; 1 causes a state change via the dashed line. The output n_0 = 2-tuple associated with each combination of input and state is displayed on the branches of the trellis.

Now suppose the all-zero sequence is transmitted and 11, 00, 00... is received. The Viterbi algorithm decodes by determining the $2^{k-k_0} = 4$ survivors at each node of the tree shown in Figure 13.13. Figure 13.14 shows the associated trellis diagram. After step 9 all surviving paths begin with 00; hence the first block is decoded correctly and the two errors are corrected.

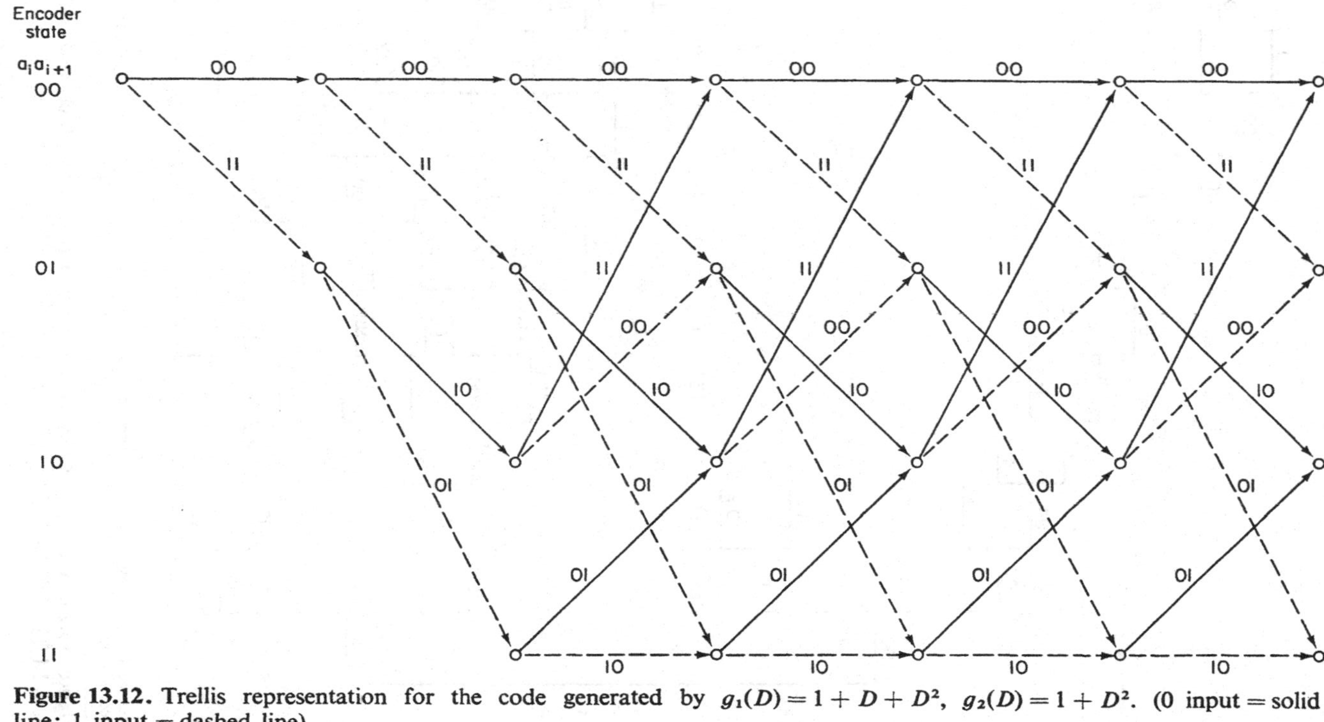

Figure 13.12. Trellis representation for the code generated by $g_1(D) = 1 + D + D^2$, $g_2(D) = 1 + D^2$. (0 input = solid line; 1 input = dashed line).

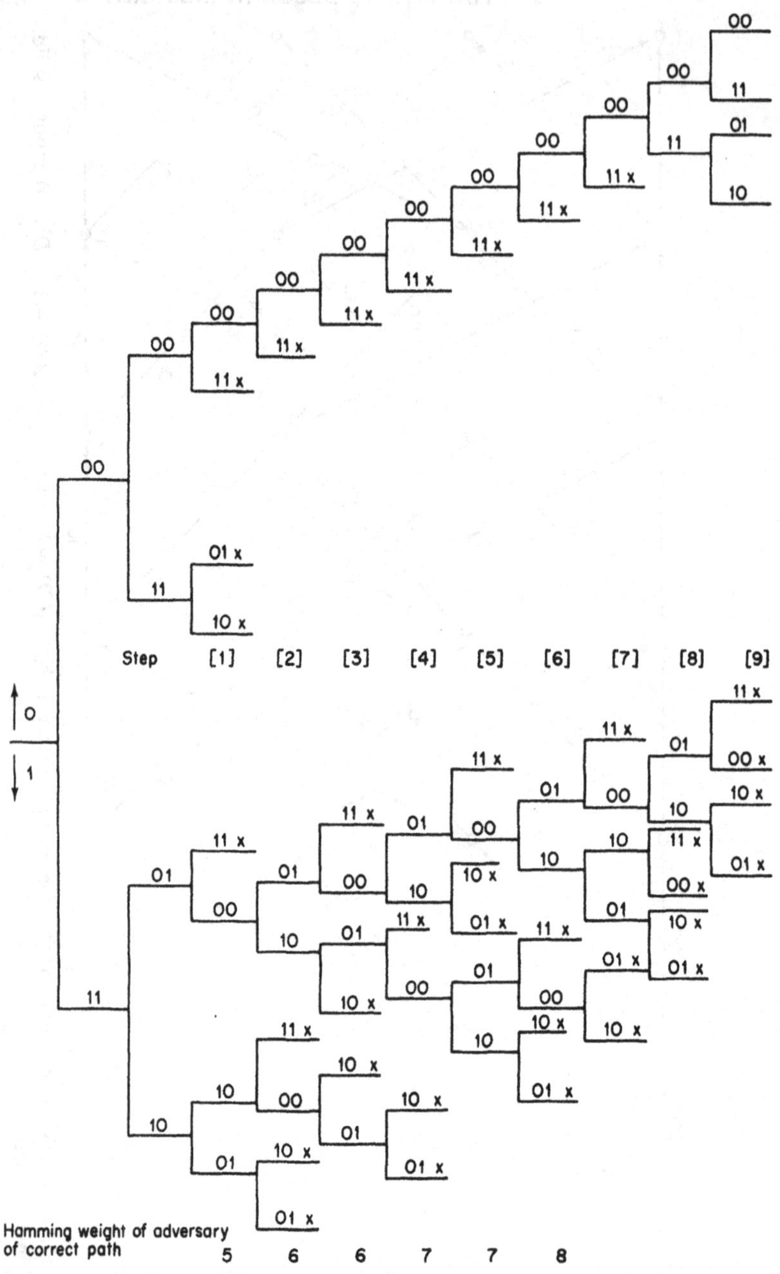

Figure 13.13. Tree traced by Viterbi decoder in correcting two errors. (g = 1 1 0 1 1 1 0 . . .)

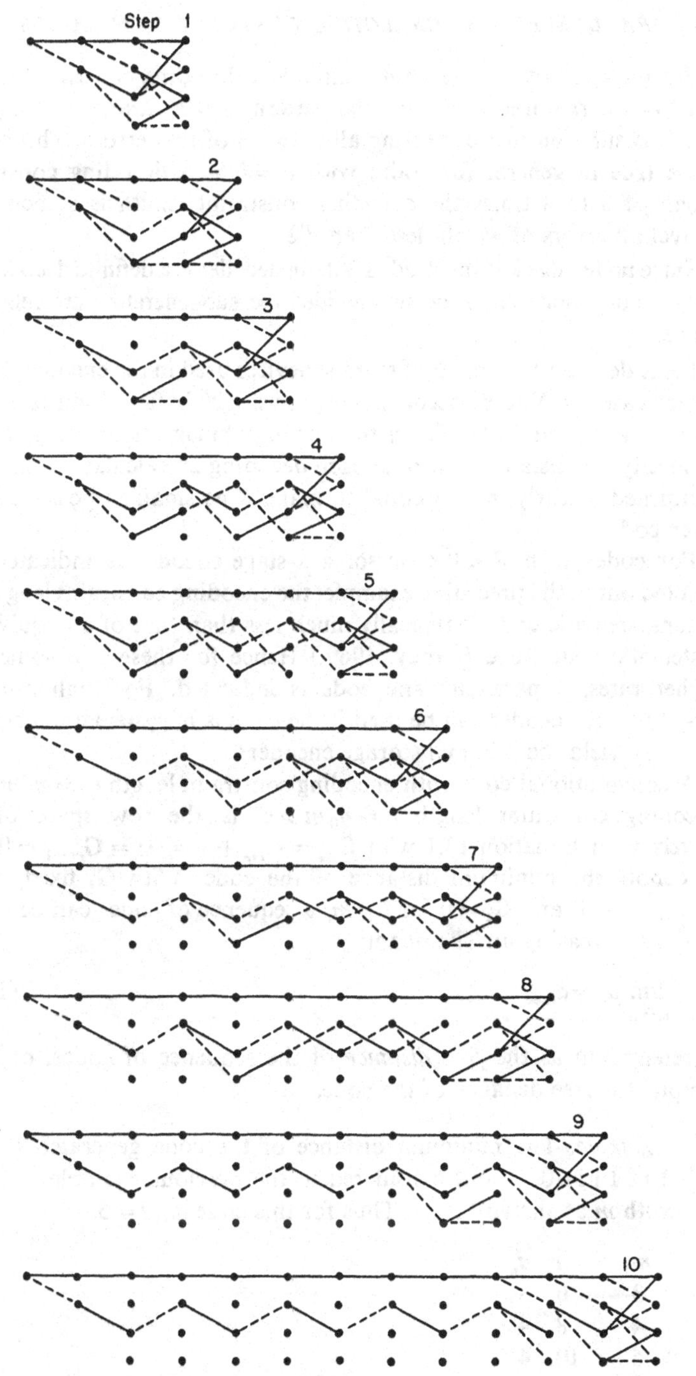

Figure 13.14. Trellis diagrams traced by Viterbi decoder correcting error pattern 11000.... g = 11011100....

For the code of the preceding example a decoding constraint length of 22 bits is required to correct the pattern 1 1 0 0 . . . . and, in fact, this length is sufficient for correcting all patterns of two errors. This seems to be true in general for codes with $R = 0.5$; a decoding constraint length of 3 to 4 times the encoding constraint length is sufficient to correct all errors of weight less than $d/2$.

Since no feedback is involved, a Viterbi decoder is a definite decoder and error propagation cannot occur provided the subgenerators are relatively prime.

Let K denote the number of storage devices used in the encoder. In the binary case the Viterbi decoder must store $K2^K$ binary digits to record the survivors, and slightly fewer than $2^K \log_2 n$ binary digits are necessary to specify the distances. Also, at each decoding 2^K calculations must be performed. Clearly it is essential to make K as small as possible for a given code.

For codes with $R < 0.5$ or so, a k-stage encoder is indicated. As pointed out in the preceding example, the encoding constraint length for a nonsystematic code is typically much less than that of an equivalent systematic code. (See Forney, 1969.) Hence for these and somewhat higher rates, a nonsystematic code is indicated. For high rates an $(n - k)$-stage encoder can be used if the code is in systematic form and this may yield the minimal storage encoder.

A convolutional code with encoding constraint length $n_e = n_0 m_e$ and decoding constraint length $n = n_0 m > n_e$ is the row space of the matrix $\mathbf{G}$ of Equation 13.1 with $\mathbf{G}_{m_e} = \mathbf{G}_{m_e} + 1 = \cdots = \mathbf{G}_{m-1} = 0$. Let d_n denote the minimum distance of the code. With $\mathbf{G}_i$ fixed, $i = 0, 1, \ldots, m_e - 1$, and $\mathbf{G}_i = 0$ for $i \geqq m_e$ a sequence of codes can be generated by increasing m. The quantity

$$\lim_{m \to \infty} d_n = d_{\text{free}} \tag{13.14}$$

is referred to as the *free distance* of the sequence of codes, or more simply, the free distance of the code.

Example. The minimum distance of the code generated by $\mathbf{g} =$ 1 1 0 1 1 1 0 0 . . . and considered in the previous example increases with m as shown below. Thus for this code $d_{\text{free}} = 5$.

m	n	d_n
3	6	3
4	8	4
5	10	4
≥ 6	≥ 12	5

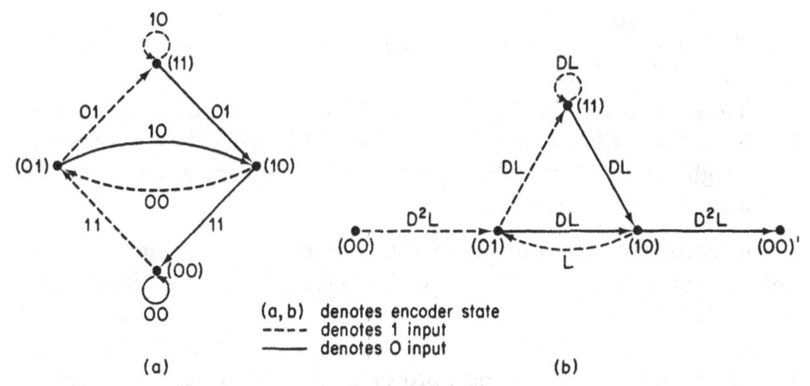

Figure 13.15. State diagram (a) and modified state diagram (b) of code generated by $\mathbf{g} = 1\,1\,0\,1\,1\,1\,0\,0 \ldots$.

Free distance is important for Viterbi decoding since the decoder complexity is only weakly dependent on decoding constraint length and the probability of error depends strongly on the free distance. Free distance, the number of code words of a given weight, and several other useful facts can be obtained quite simply from the *state diagram* of the encoder. This diagram consists of $q^{k_e - k_0}$ nodes which correspond to the encoder states and q^{k_0} directed branches emanating from each node. The q-ary k_0-tuple presented at the encoder inputs causes the encoder to emit a particular n_0-tuple and to change state. Associated with each branch of the state diagram is the corresponding output n_0-tuple and the input k_0-tuple. Figure 13.15a shows the state diagram for the code used in preceding examples.

Any nonzero code sequence corresponds to a complete circuit beginning and ending at the 0 node. Thus it is useful to split this node as shown in the modified state diagram of Figure 13.15b. Standard signal flow graph reduction techniques can then be used to determine $T(D, L)$, the transfer function of the modified flow graph. A *transfer function* $D^d L^1$ is associated with each branch, where D and L are dummy variables, d denotes the Hamming weight of the branch and the exponent of L denotes its length in branches.

Example. For the code of the preceding example,

$$T(D, L) = \frac{D^5 L^3}{1 - DL(1 + L)} = D^5 L^3 \sum_{i=0}^{\infty} (DL(1 + L))^i \qquad (13.15)$$

Setting $L = 1$ gives the *distance transfer function*

$$T(D) = \frac{D^5}{1-2D} = D^5 + 2D^6 + 4D^7 + \cdots + 2^i D^{i+5} + \cdots. \quad (13.16)$$

Thus the code has $d_{\text{free}} = 5$ and $2i$ code words of weight $i + 5$. Since the coefficient of D^5 in Equation 13.15 is L^3, the code word of weight 5 spans 3 branches. Similarly, the two code words of weight 6 span 4 and 5 branches.

The transfer function of the modified encoder state diagram can be used to calculate the probability of first error, P_{1e}, for a binary code used on the binary symmetric channel with crossover probability P. Every term $D^d L^l$ in the two-dimensional power series expansion of $T(D, L)$ corresponds to a code word of length l branches and weight d whose first non-zero symbol is in block 0.

Assume that the all-zero sequence is transmitted and consider a code word of weight d and length l. If $[(d+1)/2]$ errors occur in the d non-zero positions, incorrect decoding of the 0th block will occur. (If d is even and $d/2$ errors occur, incorrect decoding will occur with probability 0.5.) The probability of incorrect decoding into a code word of weight d is then

$$\begin{aligned} P_d &= \sum_{i=[(d+1)/2]}^{d} \binom{d}{i} P^i Q^{d-i} && d \text{ odd} \\ &= \frac{1}{2}\binom{d}{d/2} P^{d/2} Q^{d/2} + \sum_{i=[d/2]+1}^{d} \binom{d}{i} P^i Q^{d-i} && d \text{ even} \end{aligned} \quad (13.17)$$

Where the first term is omited if d is odd. Let the distance transfer function

$$T(D) = \sum_{d=d_{\text{free}}}^{\infty} t_d D^d \quad (13.18)$$

The probability of decoding the first block incorrectly is upperbounded by the sum of the probabilities of confusing this word with each non-zero code word considered independently. (This is the union bound of Equation 4.24.) That is,

$$P_{1e} < \sum_{d=d_{\text{free}}}^{\infty} t_d P_d \quad (13.19)$$

Now it can be shown (Jacobs, Viterbi, and Heller 1970) that

$$P_d < (\sqrt{4PQ})^d \quad (13.20)$$

so

$$P_{1e} \leq T(\sqrt{4PQ}) \tag{13.21}$$

Thus given the transfer function of the encoder, the evaluation of P_{1e} is straightforward. However, determining $T(D, L)$ for even moderately complex decoders is a difficult job.

13.8 Sequential Decoding

The systematic search decoding procedure described at the beginning of the preceding section requires q^k calculations to decode each block of an (n, k) convolutional code. Clearly, this procedure is applicable only to codes for which k is small. Although the Viterbi algorithm of Section 13.7 can decode longer codes, it too is limited to codes of moderate length.

Consider a memoryless channel such as the binary symmetric channel. For the overwhelming majority of paths (code words), the conditional probability that a particular code word was transmitted, given the received word, decreases exponentially with code length. If it is possible to avoid considering these improbable paths, then the average number of computations required to decode might be made manageably small even for long codes. Sequential decoding is a practical way of accomplishing this seemingly difficult feat. (Wozencraft 1957.)

The description of sequential decoding given here is intended to serve only as an introduction to the subject. The interested reader is referred to Wozencraft and Jacobs (1965) and Gallager (1968) and to their bibliographies.

Sequential decoding can be used to decode any convolutional code. In the following discussion, a binary systematic code with k_0 information bits per n_0-bit block is assumed. The encoding constraint length of the code will be $n_e = m_e n_0$. The code will be used on the binary symmetric channel with the Hamming metric; more general metrics can be employed without difficulty.

Assume that the all-zero sequence is transmitted and consider the following decoding procedure. The decoder, which can generate the code tree, examines the received n_0-tuple. It compares this n_0-tuple with the 2^{k_0} branches leaving the first node of the tree and selects the branch that is closest to the received n_0-tuple. In the absence of errors this procedure always decodes correctly.

If errors occur, the decoder will choose an incorrect branch and, even in the absence of further errors, it will not find branches that match very closely with the received n_0-tuples. This decoder "corrects" errors steadily for some time and thus decodes into a low-probability code word.

A more reasonable approach for the decoder to take is to assume that just before it began "correcting" errors it made a decoding error. It should then return to this point, change the suspected branch, and proceed along a new path in the tree. On a binary symmetric channel with crossover probability P, a received sequence of length n will differ from the transmitted code sequence in nP positions, on the average. Most other code sequences will differ in roughly $n/2$ positions. Thus the decoder will have little trouble distinguishing the correct path provided the error sequence does not contain too many errors.

However, the decoder may have to search through an enormous number of paths before the correct one is found. Fortunately the number of paths examined can be substantially reduced by searching the tree cleverly. Also, if the decoder input and output bit streams are buffered, a fairly large number of paths can be searched occasionally.

Let l denote the number of the branch presently being decoded; let $d(l)$ denote the total distance between the l-branch path being followed by the decoder and the ln_0-bit received sequence. Consider the *tilted distance function*

$$t(l) = d(l) - n_0 lP'$$

where $P < P' < 1/2$.

For the correct path, $d(l)$ will be approximately equal to $n_0 lP$ and $t(l)$ will be negative. For nearly all incorrect paths, $d(l) \approx (n_0 l)/2$, and $t(l)$ is positive. The behavior of $t(l)$ is typified in Figure 13.16. The decoder computes $t(l)$ for the path it is following; when this metric exceeds a discard threshold T, the decoder backs up to the nearest unexplored path for which $t(l) \leqq T$ and begins tracing a new path.

A procedure known as the *Fano algorithm* (Fano 1963) for discarding improbable paths and searching new ones is illustrated by the flow chart of Figure 13.17. Basically the decoder decreases the threshold by a fixed quantity Δ when it can and proceeds to the next node. If all branches from a given node exceed the threshold, the decoder retreats by one node and takes the next most probable untried branch. If all branches have been tried and rejected at that node, the decoder retreats again, increasing the threshold if necessary. The integer Δ is a design parameter that is selected to minimize the average number of branches searched by the decoder.

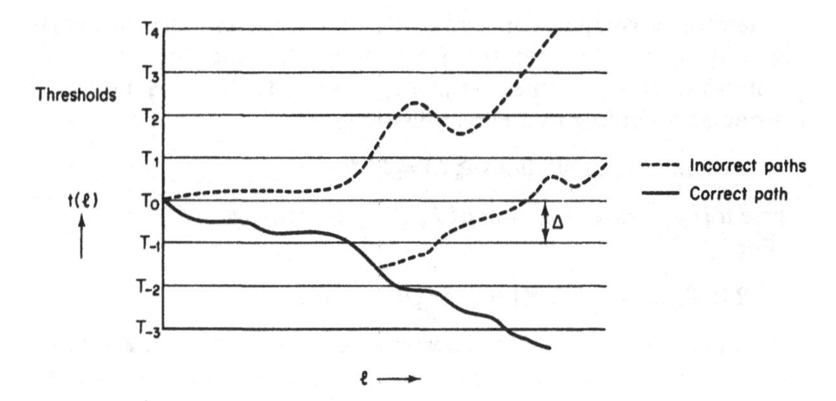

Figure 13.16. Typical behavior of tilted distance function $t(l)$.

With the Fano algorithm, no branch is ever examined twice with the same threshold; hence, the decoder cannot be trapped in a loop. Nevertheless, following the occurrence of an unusually large number of errors the decoder will be required to search through an excessively large number of branches.

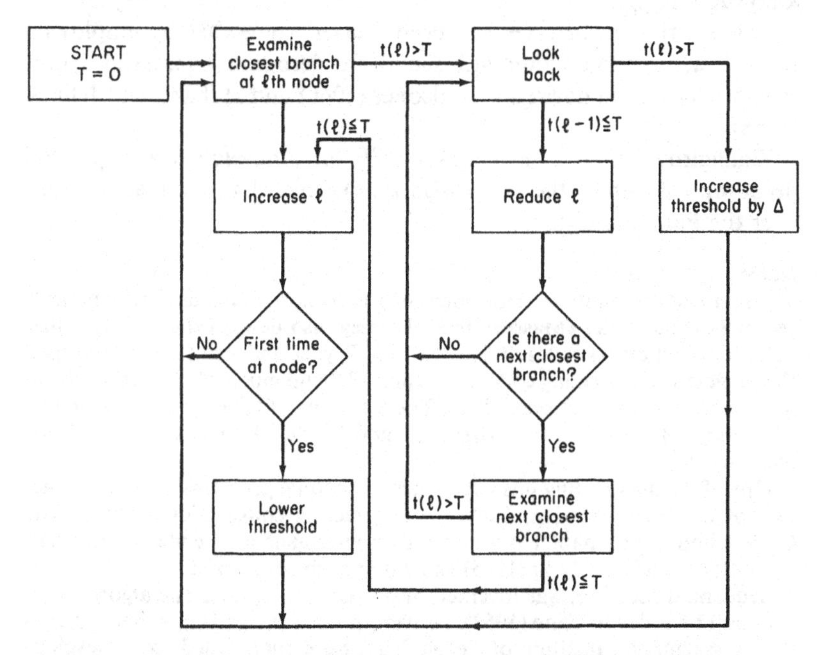

Figure 13.17. Flow chart of the Fano sequential decoding algorithm.

The variable computation load on the decoder necessitates the buffering of its input and output. It has been shown that the number of computations (that is, branches examined) required to decode a branch is distributed according to a Pareto distribution

$$Pr(\text{number computations} \geqq L) = L^{-\alpha}$$

where α is a positive function of P, R, and Δ (Savage 1966*b*).

For

$$R \geqq R_{\text{comp}} = 1 - \log(1 + \sqrt{4PQ}),$$

the mean of this distribution increases exponentially with n_e. For lower rates, the mean is bounded from above by a constant and so is effectively independent of n_e. The amount of computation required in this latter case is highly variable, however, and even with a substantial buffer, the probability of buffer overflow is considerably larger than the probability of undetected error. Since buffer overflows are always recognized by the decoder, the decoding errors they cause can always be detected.

The probability of undetected error for the Fano algorithm is ordinarily negligibly small for a practical decoder, provided it is operated at a rate $R < R_{\text{comp}}$.

This restriction on rates has been relaxed somewhat by employing block codes in conjunction with sequential decoding. Successful hybrid schemes have been devised by Falconer (1966) and Huband and Jelinck (1968).

Zigangirov (1966) and Jelinek (1969) have developed a sequential decoding algorithm (the *stack algorithm*) which has some advantages over the Fano algorithm.

Notes

The first class of multiple-error-correcting convolutional codes was Massey's self-orthogonal codes (Massey 1963). Massey also devised the orthogonalizable (trial-and-error) codes of Section 13.5. Wyner and Ash (1963) developed the single-error-correcting codes of Section 13.3 and much of the mathematical framework for convolutional codes. The k and $(n - k)$-stage encoding circuits of Section 13.1 are due to Wozencraft and Reiffen 1961 and Massey 1963, respectively.

One of the outstanding unsolved algebraic coding problems is the construction of a class of good multiple-error-correcting convolutional codes. The Gilbert bound of Chapter 4 and the computer-generated codes of Lin and Lyne (1967) and Bussgang (1965) show that such codes exist.

Sequential decoding was invented by Wozencraft (1957). The algorithm of Section 13.8 is due to Fano (1963). Numerous other researchers, primarily from the Massachusetts Institute of Technology, have contributed to its development. Several sequential decoders have been built, and with the rapidly decreasing cost of digital hardware, it seems likely that this very powerful technique will become more widely used. Its major limitation appears to be its sensitivity to clusters of errors, and this tends to limit its use to channels that closely approximate a memoryless channel.

The Viterbi (1967) algorithm of Section 13.7, like sequential decoding, uses a decoding constraint length n which is considerably larger than the encoding constraint length n_e. For this algorithm the amount of computation is more closely tied to n_e than to n, while the probability of erroneous decoding is roughly proportional to $2^{-n\,E(R)}$, where $E(R)$ is the usual error exponent. This has led to the use of a new error exponent derived as follows:

$$P_e \approx 2^{-n\,E(R)} = 2^{-n_e[nE(R)/n_e]}$$

By maximizing the ratio n/n_e, the quantity $nE(R)/n_e$ can be made considerably larger than the corresponding block-code error exponent, especially for rates near capacity. The presentation of the Viterbi algorithm of Section 13.7 follows Jacobs, Viterbi and Heller (1970).

Problems

13.1. Compare the transmission rate of a shortened Hamming code and a single-error-correcting convolutional code of approximately the same length.

13.2. The technique employed in Section 13.3 to construct double-error-correcting codes generalizes. Using the parity-check matrix of a (31, 10) BCH code with $d = 12$, construct a (62, 22) convolutional code with $d = 8$.

13.3. Devise a decoder for the double-error-correcting codes of Section 13.3.

13.4. Attempt to construct a systematic, orthogonalizable, convolutional code with $n_0 = 3$, $k_0 = 2$, and $d = 5$ whose length is less than that of the (42, 28) self-orthogonal code used as an example in Section 13.4. This problem illustrates the difficulties inherent in extending trial-and-error construction procedures to rates greater than one-half.

13.5. Construct the tree for the (12, 3) uniform convolution code of Section 13.5. Verify that for this code $d = 8$. The adjective uniform describes the unique weight distribution of the code words in the incorrect subset (lower half of the tree).

13.6. Determine the orthogonal equations necessary to decode a uniform code with $m = 4$.

13.7. The concept of effective constraint length, denoted n_{eff}, has been used in determining the probability of first error for self-orthogonal and orthogonalizable convolutional codes. Define n_{eff} as the number of digits involved in decoding the n_0 digits of block 0. Show that for a t-error-correcting code used on a BSC with crossover probability P, the probability of first error is

$$P_{1e} = \sum_{i=t+1}^{n_{eff}} \binom{n_{eff}}{i} P^i Q^{n_{eff}-i}$$

13.8. The generator matrix of any nonsystematic code with $k_0 = n_0 - k_0 = 1$ can be arranged by column permutations to give a matrix of the form

$$\mathbf{G} = (\mathbf{P}_1 \quad \mathbf{P}_2)$$

The $m \times m$ matrices $\mathbf{P}_i$ have the form

$$\begin{bmatrix} 1 & p_2 & p_3 & \cdots & p_m \\ & 1 & p_2 & \ddots & \vdots \\ & & \ddots & \ddots & p_3 \\ & 0 & & \ddots & p_2 \\ & & & & 1 \end{bmatrix} \tag{13.22}$$

where the p_i are arbitrary q-ary digits. Determine a parity-check matrix for this code. Under what condition will $\mathbf{H}$ have the form

$$\mathbf{H} = [\mathbf{P}_3^T \quad \mathbf{P}_4^T]$$

where $\mathbf{P}_3$ and $\mathbf{P}_4$ have the form of Equation 13.22?

13.9. The binary (12, 6) code whose generator matrix is

$$\mathbf{G} = \begin{bmatrix} 11 & 00 & 00 & 01 & 01 & 01 \\ & 11 & 00 & 00 & 01 & 01 \\ & & 11 & 00 & 00 & 01 \\ & & & 11 & 00 & 00 \\ & & & & 11 & 00 \\ & & & & & 11 \end{bmatrix}$$

has encoding constraint length 12. If the decoding constraint length is also chosen to be 12, the code has minimum distance 5. (See Section 13.5.)

By means of elementary row operations, construct a nonsystematic version of this code with an encoding constraint length of 8. If the decoding constraint length of the code is now reduced to 8, can all error patterns of weight 2 still be corrected?

13.10. a. Construct the modified state diagram for a convolutional code with $k_0 = n_0 - k_0 = 1$ and with $g_1(D) = 1 + D + D^2 + D^4$ and $g_2(D) = 1 + D^3 + D^4$.

b. Determine the transfer function $T(D, L)$ and d_{free}.

13.11. (McEliece and Rumsey, 1968) Let $g(X)$ generate a binary cyclic code of length n with minimum distance d; let $\bar{d}$ denote the minimum distance of the dual code generated by $h(X) = X^n - 1/g(X)$. Show that the systematic $R = 1/2$ convolutional code with $g_1(D) = 1$ and $g_2(D) = g(D)$ has

$$d_{free} \geq \min [d + 1, \bar{d} + 2]$$

13.12. Use the result of the preceding problem and the existence of the (23, 12) Golay code to construct a 4-error-correcting convolutional code.

14 Burst-Correcting Convolutional Codes

In this chapter several classes of convolutional codes for correcting single bursts of errors and combinations of bursts and random errors are presented.

14.1 Some Definitions

An (mn_0, mk_0) convolutional code is said to have *Type-B2 burst-correcting ability* $b_2 = rn_0$, if all bursts of length b_2 which are confined to r consecutive blocks are correctable but at least one burst of length $(r+1)n_0$ is uncorrectable. The *burst-correcting ability* b of a code with Type-B2 burst-correcting ability b_2 is bounded by

$$b_2 + (n_0 - 1) \geqq b \geqq b_2 - (n_0 - 1). \tag{14.1}$$

This upper bound on b and the upper bound on b_2 given by Theorem 4.18 yield the result given in Theorem 4.19:

$$b \leqq \frac{(m-1)(n_0 - k_0)}{\left[1 + \frac{k_0}{n_0}\right]} + n_0 - 1 \tag{14.2}$$

The codes constructed in subsequent sections approach this bound very closely, especially for large m and b.

Consider a code with burst-correcting ability b decoded with a particular decoder. A burst of length $l < b$ is correctable provided it is followed by a suitable number of correct digits. The smallest such number is the guard space required for the burst. The largest guard space required for any correctable burst is the *guard space of the code.* It will be seen that the guard space of a code is a function of how the code is decoded.

In general it is desirable to minimize guard space, since channel errors during this period may cause incorrect decoding. For any (n, k) code the guard space g is bounded by

$$g \leqq n - 1. \tag{14.3}$$

For several types of codes

$$g = n - b \tag{14.4}$$

and for practical decoders g cannot be appreciably smaller than $n - b$.

The basic idea behind all burst-correcting convolutional codes is that the digits involved in the decoding of a particular digit are spread in time so that only one, or at most a few, can be affected by a single burst of errors. The simplest way of accomplishing this spreading is by *interleaving.* With this technique the data stream is effectively broken into i independent streams; the parameter i is referred to as the *interleaving degree.*

There are two basic ways of interleaving a convolutional code. With *symbol interleaving* the 1st, $(i + 1)$th, $(2i + 1)$th, ... symbols are encoded independently of all other digits. With *block interleaving* the n_0-bit blocks separated by i blocks form an independent data stream. If $b < n_0$ for the basic code, block interleaving cannot be used. However, the codes developed in sections 14.2 and 14.4 generally have $b = n_0$ so this is not a serious restriction. In addition, block interleaving appears to have some implementation advantages over symbol interleaving. For these reasons only block interleaving is considered in this chapter. (See Problems 14.3 and 14.4.)

Interleaving an (n, k) block code with burst-correcting ability b to degree i produces an (ni, ki) block code with burst-correcting ability bi. Block interleaving an (mn_0, mk_0) convolutional code with burst-correcting ability b, on the other hand, produces an $(mn_0(i - 1) + n_0, mk_0(i - 1) + k_0)$ code with burst-correcting ability bi. This follows from the definition of constraint length. (See Problems 14.1 and 14.2.) Interleaving an optimal Type-B2 convolutional code, that is, one that meets the bound of Theorem 4.18, always produces a code that is also optimal in this sense. (See Problem 14.4.)

The parity-check and generator matrices of an interleaved code are related in a simple way to the corresponding matrices for the basic code.

Example. The parity-check matrix

$$\mathbf{H}_1 = \begin{bmatrix} 01 & & & \\ 10 & 01 & & \\ 10 & 10 & 01 & \\ 00 & 10 & 10 & 01 \end{bmatrix}$$

specifies a binary (8, 4) code with $b = 2$. Interleaving to degree 2 creates a (14, 7) code with $b = 4$; its parity-check matrix is

$$\mathbf{H}_2 = \begin{bmatrix} 01 & & & & & & \\ 00 & 01 & & & & & \\ 10 & 00 & 01 & & & & \\ 00 & 10 & 00 & 01 & & & \\ 10 & 00 & 10 & 00 & 01 & & \\ 00 & 10 & 00 & 10 & 00 & 01 & \\ 00 & 00 & 10 & 00 & 10 & 00 & 01 \end{bmatrix}$$

Encoders for these two codes are shown in Figures 14.1 and 14.2. Since code rate is clearly unaffected by interleaving, arbitrarily long, nearly optimal burst-correcting convolutional codes can be formed from the codes of Sections 14.2 and 14.4 for practically all values of code rate.

If a code has $b > n_0$, there are at least two fundamentally different ways in which a decoder can be built. The simplest method, conceptually at least, is to decode block-by-block as with random-error-correcting codes. A second method involves correcting the entire burst as soon as the start of the burst is detected in the 0th block. Both procedures can be used to decode the codes of Section 14.2 and will be explained there.

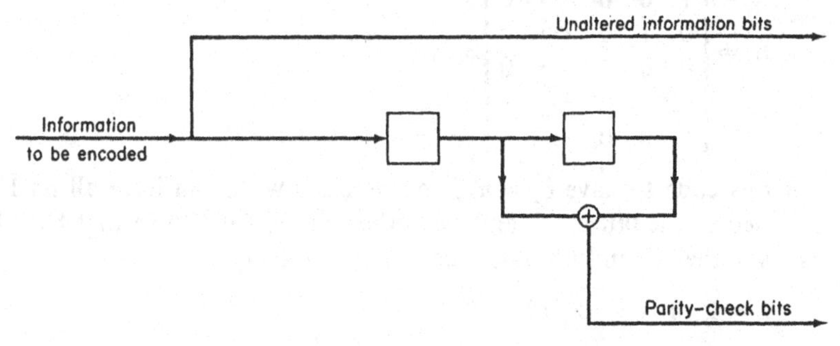

Figure 14.1. Encoder for the (8, 4) convolutional code with $h = [00\ 10\ 10\ 01]$.

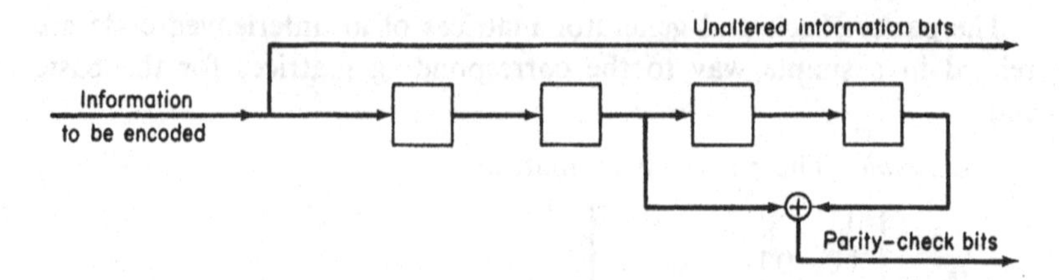

Figure 14.2. Encoder for the (8, 4) convolutional code of Figure 14.1 interleaved to degree 2.

14.2 Berlekamp-Preparata-Massey Codes

The binary codes presented in this section have one parity digit per block (Berlekamp 1964*b*; Preparata 1964; Massey 1965*a*). (Codes with $R < 1/2$ are discussed in Section 14.4.) The basic codes have Type-B2 burst-correcting ability $b_2 = n_0$. Codes with large values of burst-correcting ability can be constructed by interleaving.

In the case of $n_0 = 2$ and 3, the computer-generated codes of Problem 14.5 have the same length as the corresponding BPM codes and yet have $b - n_0$; thus, they are slightly superior to the BPM codes. These codes apparently do not generalize to other rates, however.

There exists a basic $(2n_0^2, 2n_0^2 - 2n_0)$ BPM code with Type-B2 burst-correcting ability n_0 for any choice of n_0. The parity-check matrix of such a code is of the form

$$\mathbf{H} = [\mathbf{B}_0 \mathbf{B}_1 \mathbf{B}_2 \cdots \mathbf{B}_{2n_0-1}] \tag{14.5}$$

where $\mathbf{B}_i$ is a down-shifted truncated version of $\mathbf{B}_{i-1}$; that is,

$$\mathbf{B}_i = \begin{bmatrix} 0 & 0 & 0 & \cdots & 0 \\ 1 & 0 & 0 & \cdots & 0 \\ 0 & 1 & 0 & \cdots & 0 \\ 0 & 0 & 1 & \cdots & 0 \\ & & & \ddots & \vdots \\ 0 & 0 & 0 & \cdots 1 & 0 \end{bmatrix} \mathbf{B}_{i-1}.$$

For this code to have $b_2 = n_0$, no nonzero word can have all its 1's confined to the 0th block and one other block. An n-tuple that has all its 1's in the 0th and ith blocks can be represented as

$$\mathbf{E} = \mathbf{E}_0 \mathbf{0}\mathbf{0}\mathbf{0} \cdots \mathbf{E}_i \mathbf{0}\mathbf{0} \cdots \mathbf{0}$$

where $\mathbf{E}_0 \neq 0$. Then, if $\mathbf{B}_0$ can be chosen so that $\mathbf{E}\mathbf{H}^T$ is nonzero for all choices of $\mathbf{E}_0 \neq \mathbf{0}$, $\mathbf{E}_i$, and i, then the code has $b_2 = n_0$. In order for this to occur, it must be that

$$\mathbf{E}_0 \mathbf{E}_i [\mathbf{B}_0 B_i]^T \neq \mathbf{0}; \qquad 1 \leqq i \leqq 2n_0 - 1 \tag{14.6}$$

Now for $n_0 \leqq i \leqq 2n_0 - 1$, the upper right quadrant of $[\mathbf{B}_0 \mathbf{B}_i]$ is the all-zero matrix of order n_0. Thus, choosing the upper half of $\mathbf{B}_0$ to be any nonsingular matrix guarantees that Equation 14.6 holds for $n_0 \leqq i \leqq 2n_0 - 1$. Decoding is simplified if this is chosen to be the identity matrix of order n_0, denoted $\mathbf{I}_{n_0}$.

For $1 \leqq i \leqq n_0 - 1$, Equation 14.6 holds provided the matrices $[\mathbf{B}_0 \mathbf{B}_i]$ are simultaneously nonsingular. Elementary row operations can reduce this matrix to the form

$$\begin{bmatrix} \mathbf{I}_{n0} & \mathbf{X}_i \\ \mathbf{0} & \mathbf{Y}_i \end{bmatrix}$$

and so $[\mathbf{B}_0 \mathbf{B}_i]$ is nonsingular if and only if $\mathbf{Y}_i$ is nonsingular.

The lower half of $\mathbf{B}_0$ can initially be taken to be

$$\begin{bmatrix} 0 & \cdots & & 0 & 0 & 0 \\ 0 & \cdots & & & & A \\ 0 & & & & C & B \\ 0 & & & F & E & D \\ 0 & & J & I & H & G \end{bmatrix} \tag{14.7}$$

where blank spaces in the matrix denote zeros. The letters represent binary variables that will be specified to make Equation 14.6 hold. Then the matrices $\mathbf{Y}_i$ can be represented in terms of these variables.

Example. For $n_0 = 4$,

$$\mathbf{Y}_1 = \begin{bmatrix} 0 & 0 & 0 & 1 \\ 0 & 0 & A & 0 \\ 0 & C & B & A \\ F & E & (D+C) & B \end{bmatrix} \qquad \mathbf{Y}_2 = \begin{bmatrix} 0 & 0 & 1 & 0 \\ 0 & A & 0 & 1 \\ C & B & 0 & 0 \\ E & D & 0 & A \end{bmatrix}$$

$$\mathbf{Y}_3 = \begin{bmatrix} 0 & 1 & 0 & 0 \\ A & 0 & 1 & 0 \\ B & 0 & 0 & 1 \\ D & 0 & 0 & 0 \end{bmatrix}$$

It is possible to choose the binary variables $A, B, C, \ldots$ in alphabetical order so as to make nonsingular all the square submatrices whose upper right corner forms the upper right corner of one of the $\mathbf{Y}_i$. This is possible because: (1) Each letter occurs on the minor diagonal of exactly one $\mathbf{Y}_i$; (2) Every other element in the submatrix of which it is the lower left corner has been previously determined; and (3) The cofactor of this entry is nonzero by a previous contruction or because it is an identity matrix. (See Berlekamp (1964*b*) for additional details.)

Example (cont'd). In the case of $n_0 = 4$, the successive matrices that are made nonsingular by specifying one of the letter variables are

$$\begin{bmatrix} 0 & 1 \\ A & 0 \end{bmatrix} \text{(choose } A = 1\text{)} \qquad \begin{bmatrix} 0 & 1 & 0 \\ A & 0 & 1 \\ B & 0 & 0 \end{bmatrix} \text{(choose } B = 1\text{)}$$

$$\begin{bmatrix} 0 & 0 & 1 \\ 0 & A & 0 \\ C & B & A \end{bmatrix} \text{(choose } C = 1\text{)}$$

Then choose $D = 1$ to make $\mathbf{Y}_3$ nonsingular, $E = 1$ to make $\mathbf{Y}_2$ nonsingular, and $F = 1$ to make $\mathbf{Y}_1$ nonsingular.

Clearly, the values of the letter variables are independent of n_0. The first few variables have the value

$$\begin{matrix} & & & & & A \\ & & & & C & B \\ & & & F & E & D \\ & & J & I & H & G \\ & O & N & M & L & K \\ U & T & S & R & Q & P \end{matrix} \quad = \quad \begin{matrix} & & & & & 1 \\ & & & & 1 & 1 \\ & & & 1 & 1 & 1 \\ & & 1 & 0 & 1 & 1 \\ & 1 & 0 & 0 & 1 & 1 \\ 1 & 0 & 0 & 0 & 1 & 1 \end{matrix} \tag{14.8}$$

Note that with these choices for the letters, the Berlekamp-Preparata-Massey (BPM) codes are systematic but that the parity digit in each block is transmitted before the information symbols of the block. The usual encoding and syndrome calculating circuits must be modified to take this difference into account. Figure 14.3 shows an $(n - k)$-stage encoder for the (32, 24) BPM code with $n_0 = 4$.

The codes with $k_0 = n_0 - 1$ constructed in this way meet the bound on b_2 of Theorem 4.17 with equality. Codes with $k_0 < n_0 - 1$ can be constructed using similar techniques (Preparata 1964) or by using the following idea: Given an $(m_1 n_{01}, m_1 k_{01})$ code and an $(m_2 n_{02}, m_2 k_{02})$ code capable of correcting bursts of lengths b_1 and b_2, respectively, a third code with $n_{03} = n_{01} + n_{02}$, $k_{03} = k_{01} + k_{02}$, $b_3 = b_1 + b_2$, and $m_3 = \max(m_1, m_2)$ can be constructed simply by interleaving single blocks from the two original codes. This artifice permits the construction of codes for which neither k_0 nor $n_0 - k_0$ is equal to one.

The basic BPM codes can be decoded as follows: Assume that a single

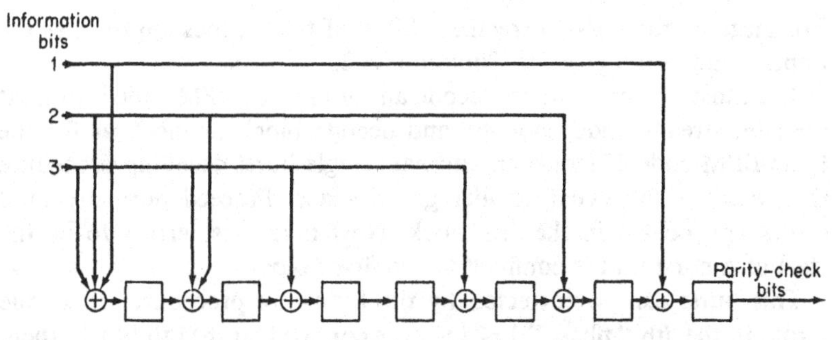

Figure 14.3. An $(n - k)$-stage encoder for a (32, 24) BPM code. The parity-check bit is transmitted first, followed by information bits 1, 2, and 3.

burst has occurred in the 0th block. Because the upper half of the matrix $\mathbf{B}_0$ was chosen to be the identity matrix, the first n_0 bits of the syndrome are identical to the error pattern that was added to the 0th block. The only additional information required to decode a block, therefore, is whether the burst occurred in the 0th block or somewhere else.

If the burst occured in the 0th block, then the second half of the syndrome must be

$$\mathbf{s}_2 = \mathbf{E}_0[\mathbf{B}_{02}]^T \tag{14.9}$$

where $\mathbf{E}_0$ denotes the burst, $\mathbf{B}_{02}$ denotes the lower half of the matrix $\mathbf{B}_0$, and $\mathbf{s}_2$ is the second half of the syndrome. In other words, since the first half of the syndrome ($\mathbf{s}_1$) is identical to $\mathbf{E}_0$, if

$$\mathbf{s}_2 + \mathbf{s}_1[\mathbf{B}_{02}]^T = \mathbf{0} \tag{14.10}$$

the burst occurred in the 0th block; otherwise, it did not.

Equation 14.10 represents n_0 linear equations involving the syndrome bits; each equation can be implemented with a single multiple-input modulo-2 adder. Then one n_0-input AND gate is sufficient to determine whether or not Equation 14.10 is satisfied.

Interleaving a basic BPM code to degree i produces a code with the following parameters:

$$\begin{aligned} m &= (2n_0 - 1)i + 1 \\ n &= mn_0 = (2n_0 - 1)n_0 i + n_0 \\ k &= mk_0 \\ b_2 &= in_0 \\ b &= b_2 - (n_0 - 1) = n_0(i - 1) + 1 \\ g &= n - 1 \quad \text{or} \quad n - b_2 \text{ (see below)} \end{aligned} \tag{14.11}$$

For large m, the burst-correcting ability of these codes approaches the upper bound on b given in Equation 14.2.

The most obvious way to decode an interleaved BPM code is to treat the i bit streams independently and decode block by block as for the basic BPM code. There is an alternate single-burst decoding procedure that yields a somewhat smaller guard space. Proceed normally until errors are located in the 0th block. Now take these errors to be the start of a burst that is confined to the first i blocks.

This burst can be corrected by the following procedure: If all the errors in the jth "phase" $1 \leqq j \leqq i$ are confined to the 0th block, then, since $\mathbf{B}_0 = \mathbf{I}_{n_0}$, the first n_0 bits of the syndrome for this phase are identical to the error digits in block zero. Thus, correction can be accomplished simply by adding the first n_0 bits of the syndrome to the 0th block for all i phases. The last $n_0 - 1$ bits of the syndrome are unused for $2 \leqq j \leqq i$.

The guard space required for an interleaved BPM code with the parameters given in Equation 14.11 is $n - 1$ bits when the i bit streams are decoded independently. When the code is decoded using this single-burst-correction procedure, $g = n - b_2$. Thus, on channels in which only infrequent long bursts of errors occur and a short guard space is important, the decoding procedure just described has advantages. However on more realistic channels, multiple bursts and combinations of bursts and isolated "random" errors can occur, and here decoding the i bits streams independently is probably better.

The decoding circuits for these two procedures are almost identical. (See Problems 14.7 and 14.9.) Also, error propagation does not occur in either decoder since the syndrome is set to zero after correction.

14.3 Iwadare Codes

The burst-correcting codes presented in this section (Iwadare 1968*b*) are defined for $k_0 = n_0 - 1$. They appear to be somewhat simpler to implement than the BPM codes of the same rate and burst-correcting ability, although their required guard space is slightly larger.

The basic Iwadare code has:

$$\begin{aligned} m &= \frac{n_0(n_0 - 1)}{2} + (2n_0 - 1) \\ k_0 &= n_0 - 1 \\ b &= n_0 \\ g &= n - 1 \end{aligned} \tag{14.12}$$

for any choice of $n_0 \geqq 2$. Note that these basic codes, unlike the basic BPM codes, correct all bursts of length n_0 regardless of phase.

The parity-check matrix of the code is specified by the matrix $\mathbf{B}_0$, where

$$
\mathbf{B}_0 = \left[\begin{array}{ll}
\overset{\longleftarrow n_0 \longrightarrow}{0\ \ldots 0001} & \uparrow \\
0\ \ldots 0000 & n_0 \\
\cdot\ \ \cdot\ \ \cdot & \\
00\ldots 0000 & \downarrow \\
0\ \ldots 0010 & \uparrow\, 2 \\
0\ \ldots 0010 & \downarrow \\
0\ \ldots 0100 & \uparrow \\
0\ \ldots 0000 & 3 \\
0\ \ldots 0100 & \downarrow \\
\vdots \qquad \vdots & \\
01\ldots 0000 & \\
10\ldots 0000 & \uparrow \\
00\ldots 0000 & n_0 \\
\vdots & \\
10\ldots 0000 & \downarrow
\end{array}\right] \tag{14.13}
$$

The jth column of $\mathbf{B}_0$, $1 \leqq j \leqq n_0 - 1$, has 1's only in positions

$$n_0 + \left[\frac{(n_0 - j)(n_0 - j + 1)}{2}\right]$$

and

$$n_0 + \left[\frac{(n_0 - j)(n_0 - j + 1)}{2}\right] + n_0 - j.$$

Example. Let $n_0 = 3$. Then

$$
\mathbf{H} = \left[\begin{array}{llllllll}
001 & & & & & & & \\
000 & 001 & & & & & & \\
000 & & 001 & & & & & \\
010 & & & 001 & & & & \\
010 & 010 & & & 001 & & & \\
100 & 010 & 010 & & & 001 & & \\
000 & 100 & 010 & 010 & & & 001 & \\
100 & & 100 & 010 & 010 & & & 001
\end{array}\right] \tag{14.14}
$$

is the parity-check matrix of a (24, 16) Iwadare code with burst-correcting ability $b = 3$. As usual, blanks represent 0's.

The decoding procedure for the Iwadare codes differs fundamentally from all decoding techniques discussed previously in that the $n_0 - 1$ information symbols in a given block are decoded at different times. In particular, the $(n_0 - 1)$th symbol is decoded after $n_0 + 2$ blocks are received, the $(n_0 - 2)$th symbol after $n_0 + 2 + 3$ blocks, ..., the first symbol after $m = n_0 + 2 + 3 + \cdots + n_0$ blocks. Thus, decoding is accomplished in $n_0 - 1$ steps.

Example (cont'd). The Iwadare code with $n_0 = 3$ has two information symbols per block. The second of these is decoded after 5 blocks are received using the two orthogonal check sums (rows 4 and 5) of the dotted submatrix of Equation 14.14. The effects of correctable errors in this second information digit can be removed before the first information digit is corrected. As a result, the matrix that is used to decode this first digit is

$$\begin{bmatrix} 001 & & & & & & & \\ 000 & 001 & & & & & & \\ 000 & & 001 & & & & & \\ 000 & & & 001 & & & & \\ 000 & & & & 001 & & & \\ 100 & & & & & 001 & & \\ 000 & 100 & & 010 & & & 001 & \\ 100 & & 100 & 010 & 010 & & & 001 \end{bmatrix} \tag{14.15}$$

The decoder for this code is shown in Figure 14.4. Note that only two of the eight syndrome bits are actually used for correction. In general, only $n_0 - 1$ syndrome digits are needed for correction.

To see that the Iwadare code actually has burst-correcting ability $b = n_0$, it is only necessary to observe in the general matrix of the form of Equation 14.15 that (1) There are two orthogonal check sums for each information bit; (2) Because of the structure of **H**, no burst of length n_0 or less can cause an AND gate (Figure 14.4) to operate at the wrong time. Note that one of the two equations always has weight two and that in order for a burst to incorrectly affect this equation and the second one, it must have length $n_0 + 1$ or greater.

The guard space required for the Iwadare codes is $n - 1$ bits. This

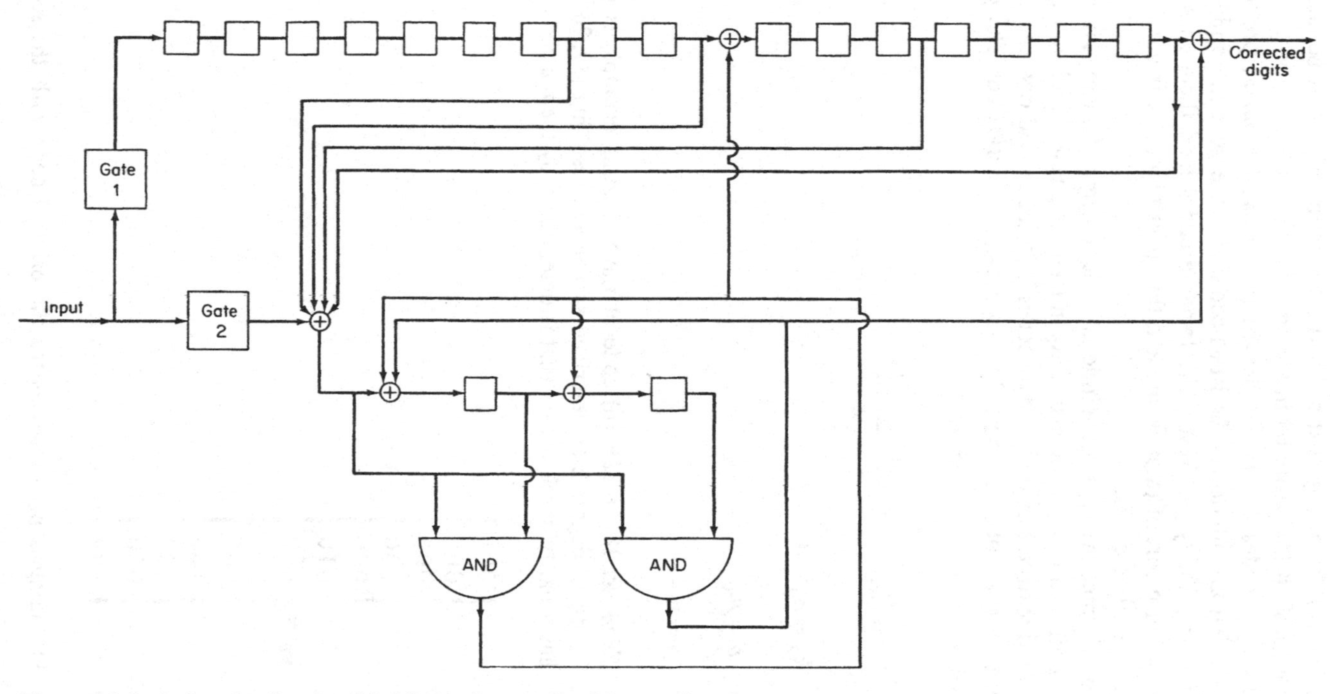

Figure 14.4. A decoder for the (24, 16) Iwadare code with $n_0 = b = 3$.

can be seen by noting that the first information digit will be decoded erroneously if the parity bit in the $(m-1)$th block is in error.

Iwadare codes can be interleaved in the usual manner, producing codes that are inferior to the BPM codes with the same rate and burst-correcting ability. However, the Iwadare codes lend themselves to a nonuniform sort of interleaving and this gives them certain advantages over the BPM codes.

Block interleaving a convolutional code to degree i involves inserting $i-1$ all-zero rows in the matrix $\mathbf{B}_0$ immediately below each row of the original matrix. For the Iwadare codes only the second row and all the nonzero rows of $\mathbf{B}_0$ except the last must be interleaved. The codes produced in this manner have

$$\begin{aligned} m &= (2n_0 - 1)i + \frac{n_0(n_0-1)}{2} \\ k_0 &= n_0 - 1 \\ b &= in_0 \\ g &= n - 1. \end{aligned} \tag{14.16}$$

Example. If the (24, 16) code of the preceding example is interleaved to degree 2 as described earlier, the resulting (39, 26) code has a parity-check matrix that is determined by the matrix

$$\mathbf{B}_0 = \begin{bmatrix} 001 \\ 000 \\ 000 \\ 000 \\ 000 \\ 010 \\ 000 \\ 010 \\ 000 \\ 100 \\ 000 \\ 000 \\ 100 \end{bmatrix}$$

Decoding is performed as for the original code with the second

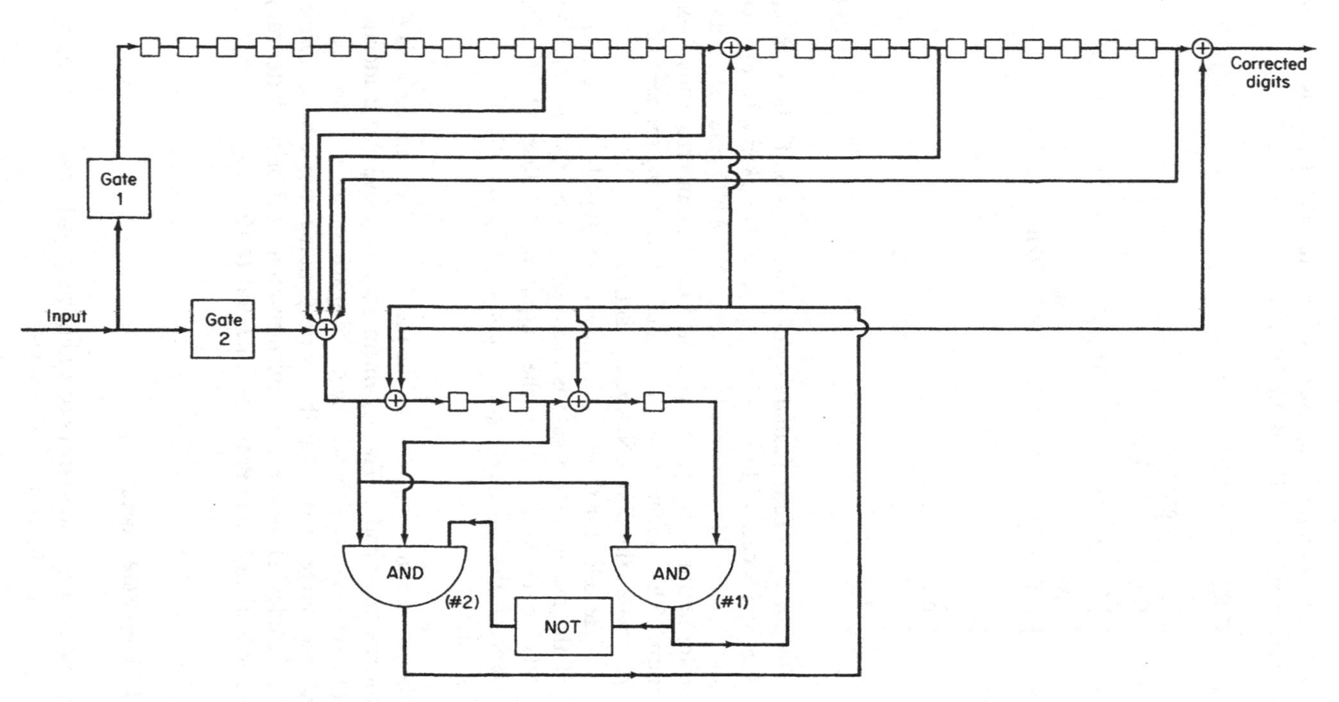

Figure 14.5. A decoder for the (39, 26) Iwadare code with $b = 6$.

information digit being corrected before the first. Thus, the matrix corresponding to Equation 14.15 is

$$
\mathbf{H} = \left[\begin{array}{ccccccccccccc}
001 \\
000 & 001 \\
000 & & 001 \\
000 & & & 001 \\
000 & & & & 001 \\
000 & & & & & 001 \\
000 & & & & & & 001 \\
000 & & & & & & & 001 \\
000 & & & & & & & & 001 \\
100 & & & & & & & & & 001 \\
000 & 100 & & & & 010 & & & & & 001 \\
000 & & 100 & & & & 010 & & & & & 001 \\
100 & & & 100 & & 010 & & 010 & & & & & 001 \\
* & * & & & & & & & & & & &
\end{array}\right] \tag{14.17}
$$

The burst-correcting capability of this code is 6. If a burst of length 4, 5, or 6 occurs with errors in the positions marked with an asterisk, this burst will be corrected. However, the AND gate for the second information digit will be activated causing an erroneous "correction." This difficulty can be avoided by inhibiting this second AND gate when the first AND gate is activated.

A decoder for this code is shown in Figure 14.5. The inhibition of the second AND gate is accomplished by the use of a single NOT gate connected to the output of the first AND gate. In general, the kth AND gate is inhibited by the jth AND gate for $j < k$.

The guard space required for the interleaved Iwadare codes is $n - 1$, as for the basic codes. The argument used to prove this is identical to that used earlier. In general, the guard space for the Iwadare decoder is somewhat larger than for the corresponding single-burst-correcting BPM decoder. However, the implementation cost of the latter may be somewhat higher. (See Problems 14.7 and 14.10.)

14.4 Low-Rate Codes

The best known burst-error-correcting codes with rate $1/n_0$, $n_0 = 3, 4, 5, \ldots$, have the following parameters:

$$m = 3$$

$$n = n_0 m = 3n_0$$

$$b = \left[\frac{n-1}{2}\right] = n_0 + \left[\frac{n_0 - 1}{2}\right] \tag{14.18}$$

$$k_0 = 1$$

$$g = n - 1$$

The matrix $\mathbf{B}_0$ for these codes has the form

$$\mathbf{B}_0 = \begin{bmatrix} \mathbf{a} & \mathbf{I}_{n_0-1} \\ \mathbf{b} & \mathbf{0}_{n_0-1} \\ \mathbf{c} & \mathbf{0}_{n_0-1} \end{bmatrix} \tag{14.19}$$

where $\mathbf{a}$ is the all-zero column $(n_0 - 1)$-tuple, $\mathbf{b}$ is the column $(n_0 - 1)$-tuple consisting of all 0's except for a single 1 in position $[n_0/2]$, and $\mathbf{c}$ is all 0's except for a single 1 in position $n_0 - 1$.

Example. A (9, 3) burst-error-correcting convolutional code with $n_0 = 3$, $k_0 = 1$, $b = 4$, and $m = 3$ is specified by the matrix

$$\mathbf{B}_0 = \begin{bmatrix} 010 \\ 001 \\ 100 \\ 000 \\ 000 \\ 100 \end{bmatrix}$$

To see that $b = [(n-1)/2]$ for a code of this type, it is only necessary to show that there exists no code word with a nonzero first block all of whose 1's are confined to two bursts of length $[(n-1)/2] = n_0 + [(n_0 - 1)/2]$. If the first block is nonzero, the information digit in that block is a 1. Consequently, the $(1 + [n_0/2])$th bit of the second block and the last bit of the third block must also be 1's, and indeed the code word does not consist of two or fewer bursts. Since the burst-correcting ability for these codes meets the upper bound of Equation 4.68 with equality, they are optimal burst correctors.

Decoding is straightforward for these codes. If a burst of length b or less occurs and the information bit in the first block is erroneous, the two parity checks on this bit will fail. Otherwise, one or both of these checks will be satisfied. If the information bit in the second block is also in error, it will be corrected in an identical fashion after the first block has been shifted out of the decoder. Theorem 13.1 shows that error propagation does not occur with these codes.

Interleaving the codes whose parameters are given by Equation 14.18 gives a class of codes for which

$$\begin{aligned} m &= 2i + 1 \\ n &= n_0 m \\ b &= \left\lceil \frac{n-1}{2} \right\rceil = i n_0 + \left\lceil \frac{n_0 - 1}{2} \right\rceil \\ k_0 &= 1 \\ g &= n - 1 \end{aligned} \tag{4.20}$$

for any choice of n_0 and interleaving degree i. Note that these codes are also optimal in the sense that they meet the bound of Equation 4.68 with equality.

14.5 Codes for Correcting Bursts and Random Errors

The convolutional codes presented in this section are designed to correct error patterns that have neither low weight nor all errors confined to a single burst. There are basically three techniques:

1. Interleaving a short random-error-correcting code.
2. Constructing a code with some burst and some random-error-correcting capability.
3. "Adaptive" decoding in which the decoder attempts to determine the type of error pattern that has occurred and correct accordingly.

Block interleaving a convolutional code with random-error-correcting capability t to degree i produces a longer convolutional code which can correct all bursts of length $[t/n_0]i$ or less, all error patterns of weight t or less, and many error patterns of weight somewhat greater than t. Among the last are patterns that can be classified as multiple bursts. (Problem 14.12.)

On many types of real channels interleaving is the most practical means of attaining a low probability of error. Although an interleaved code has low relatively minimum distance and guaranteed burst-correcting ability, these two measures of code performance are often extremely crude. An interleaved code succeeds because it corrects many patterns beyond its guaranteed capabilities.

The self-orthogonal codes of Section 13.4 have random-error-correcting capability t and burst-correcting ability that typically is only slightly larger than t. The Iwadare burst-correcting codes of the preceding section are a type of self-orthogonal code with large burst-correcting ability but for which $t = 1$. *Diffuse* self-orthogonal codes lie somewhere in between these two types of codes.

Consider a t-error-correcting self-orthogonal convolutional code. If this code has the properties that for all j, (1) no burst of length b or less that begins on or before the jth information symbol in block zero can affect more than $t - 1$ of the syndrome bits used to decode the symbol and, (2) no burst of length b or less that begins anywhere else can affect more than t of these bits, then the code is capable of correcting all bursts of length b or less.

Example. The self-orthogonal (20, 10) code with parity-check matrix

$$\mathbf{H} = \begin{bmatrix} 11 \\ 00 & 11 \\ 00 & 00 & 11 \\ 10 & 00 & 00 & 11 \\ 00 & 10 & 00 & 00 & 11 \\ 00 & 00 & 10 & 00 & 00 & 11 \\ 00 & 00 & 00 & 10 & 00 & 00 & 11 \\ 10 & 00 & 00 & 00 & 10 & 00 & 00 & 11 \\ 00 & 10 & 00 & 00 & 00 & 10 & 00 & 00 & 11 \\ 10 & 00 & 10 & 00 & 00 & 00 & 10 & 00 & 00 & 11 \end{bmatrix}$$

has $t = 2$ and $b = 4$ when decoded with majority-logic decoding. The 4 equations orthogonal on the information digit in the 0th block meet conditions 1 and 2.

There exists a (14, 7) self-orthogonal code with $t = b = 2$. The burst-correcting ability of the diffuse code has been purchased at the price of an increase in constraint length.

The problem of designing diffuse self-orthogonal codes is considered in Tong (1968a) and Iwadare (1968*b*). The computer-aided techniques described by these authors are similar to the methods used to construct the self-orthogonal random-error-correcting codes of Section 13.4 (Robinson and Bernstein 1966). It is also possible to design orthogonalizable diffuse codes (Iwadare 1968*b*), although these are even less well understood at present than the codes discussed in this section. (See Problem 14.13, for example.)

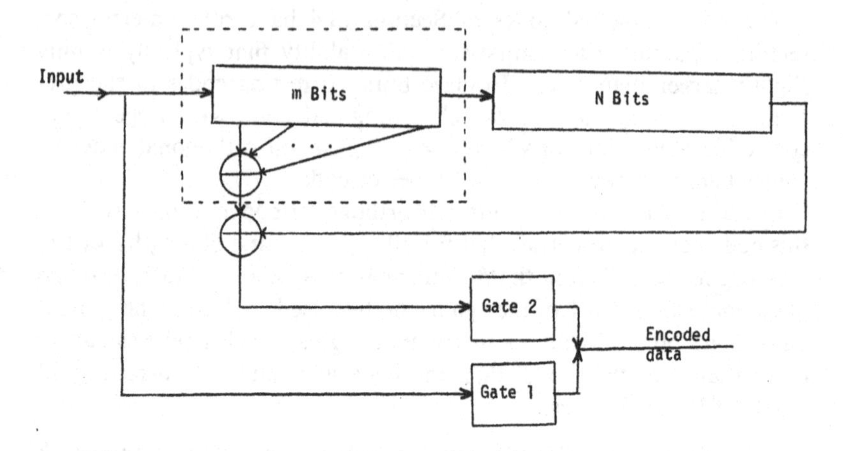

Figure 14.6. A k-stage encoder for the Gallager adaptive convolutional coding scheme.

Another attractively simple method of handling bursts and random errors with convolutional codes has been proposed by R. G. Gallager and is described by Kohlenberg and Forney (1968). This "adaptive" decoding procedure has also been applied to block codes (Tong 1968*b*; Frey 1967). The explanation below assumes a coding system with $k_0 = n_0 - 1 = 1$. The generalization to other rates is straightforward.

In Figure 14.6, the portion of the circuit inside the dashed box is an encoder for a random-error-correcting code with error-correcting ability t. Before the parity bit for the $(N + m - 1)$th block is transmitted, the information bit from the 0th block is added to it. In practical situations, $N >> m$.

If only random errors occur and the basic code can correct them, then the effect of errors in prior information bits can be removed before the 0th block is decoded (see Figure 14.7). This is the normal mode of operation.

If a long, dense, burst of errors occurs, the correction capability of the basic code will be exceeded. This basic code is designed so that only a small fraction of its cosets are used for random-error correction. Thus, with high probability an error will be detected before M erroneous decodings have occurred, that is, before erroneous digits have left the decoder.

At this point the decoder assumes that it has detected the start of a burst of length 2N or less, half of which lies in the information register.

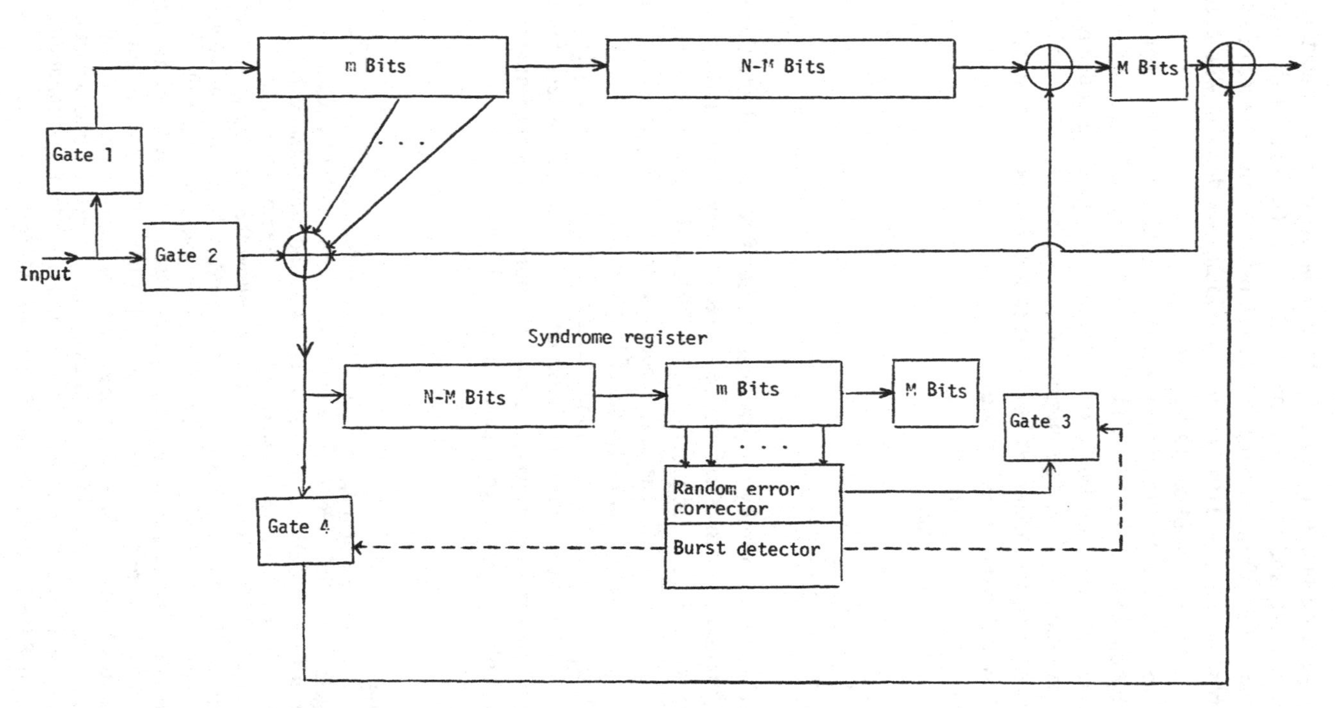

Figure 14.7 A decoder for the Gallager adaptive convolutional coding scheme.

Gate 4 is opened and gate 3 is closed (via the dashed connections in Figure 14.7), and the syndrome bit from the $(N+m-1)$th block is added to the information digit in the 0th block. In the absence of errors in blocks $N+m-1$ to $N+m-1+[b/2]$, the decoder will correct any detected burst of length $b \leqq 2N$.

The end of the burst can be detected in the same way as its beginning — by the burst-detector circuit. When a number of blocks have been decoded for which the syndrome contains all zeros, the decoder returns to the random mode. The number of blocks, like *m*, *N*, *M*, and *t*, are design parameters that must be chosen to suit the channel characteristics and overall system requirements.

With this coding scheme, the ratio of the maximum burst-correcting ability to guard space, is

$$\frac{b}{g} = \frac{2N}{2N+m}$$

which is close to unity for practical values of N and m. Note that not all bursts of length $\leqq 2N$ can be corrected, however. The best codes with $R = 0.5$ discussed previously, the BPM codes, can be decoded with $b/g \approx in_0/2in_0 = 0.5$. The latter codes are optimal (Equation 4.67) if it is necessary to correct *all* bursts of length *b*.

With Gallager's scheme some bursts of length considerably less than *b* are uncorrectable. With a suitable choice of code parameters this may not be important, however, and may be more than compensated for by the doubling in effective burst-correcting ability.

Notes

The first burst-correcting convolutional (recurrent codes) were devised by Hagelbarger (1959; 1960). These codes were also studied by Kilmer (1959). Wyner and Ash (1963) defined Type B2 codes and proved the bound given in Equation 14.1. Their results were used by Berlekamp and Preparata to construct the codes of Section 14.2; Massey devised the decoding procedure for the basic BPM codes. Iwadare extended the work of Hagelbarger and Peterson (Peterson 1961, Chapter 12) and developed the codes of Section 14.3. Diffuse codes were first devised by Massey and are described by Kohlenberg (1965). Recently Iwadare (1968*b*) and Tong (1968*b*) have attacked the problem of constructing these codes with some success. Gallager's scheme, described in Section 14.5, appears well suited to channels with dense bursts separated by low-noise periods; for some other channels an interleaved random-error-correcting code or a diffuse code seems to have advantages.

Problems

14.1. Compare the ratio b/n for the best burst-correcting convolutional and block codes with $b = 1000$ and $R = 1/3$. Explain.

14.2. Although it is not usually done, one can define "constraint length" for block codes as well as for convolutional codes. Let n_c denote the largest number of bits spanned by the bits involved in decoding any information digit of a code word.

Consider the block code produced by interleaving the (3,1) cyclic code generated by $X^2 + X + 1$ to degree 1000. Assume that subcode words are decoded independently. Compare the ratio b/n_c for this code to the similar ratios in Problem 14.1.

Explain.

14.3. Show that symbol interleaving an (mn_0, mk_0) convolutional code yields a code with block length in_0, ik_0 information symbols per block, and m blocks per constraint length. Show that block interleaving produces a code with block length n_0, k_0 information symbols per block, and $(m-1)i+1$ blocks per constraint length. Discuss from the point of view of implementation.

14.4. Given a convolutional code with $b_2 = n_0$, where b_2 meets the bound of Theorem 4.18 with equality, prove that block interleaving always produces a code which also meets this bound. Compare symbol interleaving.

14.5. (Berlekamp 1964*b*). Demonstrate that the (8, 4) code for which

$$\mathbf{B}_0 = \begin{bmatrix} 01 \\ 00 \\ 10 \\ 10 \end{bmatrix}$$

has $b = 2$. Also show that the (18, 12) code for which

$$\mathbf{B}_0 = \begin{bmatrix} 101 \\ 100 \\ 100 \\ 010 \\ 000 \\ 010 \end{bmatrix}$$

has $b = 3$. (These two codes were discovered by searching through all matrices of the given sizes.)

14.6. Construct decoders for the two codes of the preceding problem; use the ideas presented in Section 14.3. Modify the circuit for the (8, 4) code to decode when the code is interleaved to degree 10.

14.7. Construct a decoder for the BPM code with $n_0 = 4$ interleaved to degree i. Decode the i bit streams independently.

14.8. Show that the number of storage devices required for a BPM decoder of the types considered in Problems 14.7 and 14.8 is $i[n_0(2n_0 - 1) - 1)]$.

14.9. Construct a single-burst-correcting decoder for the code of Problem 14.7. (See Section 14.2.) Compare with the decoder of Problem 14.7.

14.10. Show that the number of storage devices employed by the Iwadare decoder (Section 14.3) is

$$(n_0 - 1)\left((2n_0 - 1)i + \frac{n_0(n_0 - 1)}{2}\right) + i + n_0 - 2.$$

Compare with the results of Problem 14.8.

14.11. Demonstrate that error propagation does not occur with Iwadare codes.

14.12. Consider an (mn_0, mk_0) convolutional code that can correct all error patterns of weight $t = rn_0$ or less. If the code is block interleaved to degree i, it can correct all single bursts of length ri or less. Make some definite statements about the ability of this code to correct multiple bursts.

14.13. Construct four orthogonal equations for the (18, 9) convolutional code for which

$$\mathbf{B}_0 = \begin{bmatrix} 100100011 \\ 100000000 \end{bmatrix}^T$$

Select these equations so that $b = 4$. Compare with the self-orthogonal diffuse code used as an example in Section 14.5.

14.14. Determine the effective constraint length for the (18, 9) code of Problem 14.13 and the (20, 10) self-orthogonal code discussed in Section 14.5. (See Problem 13.10.) For which code is the probability of a first error lower when used on the BSC?

14.15. Compare the maximum and average guard space requirements of block and convolutional codes with $R = \frac{1}{2}$. Discuss.

15 Arithmetic Codes

The codes presented in this chapter differ from all those previously treated in that all operations are ordinary arithmetic. These codes are practical: They can be used for data transmission with encoding and operations performed by a general-purpose computer or they can be used to check the operation of an adder. There is an interesting similarity in structure to cyclic codes.

15.1 Definition of Arithmetic Error and Distance

Numbers will be assumed to be represented as a polynomial in a radix-r system:

$$N = N_{n-1}r^{n-1} + N_{n-2}r^{n-2} + \cdots + N_1 + N_0 \tag{15.1}$$

where $0 \leqq N < r^n$ and where $0 \leqq N_i < r$. The number is written $N_{n-1} N_{n-2} \cdots N_1 N_0$. The important cases are the binary system, $r = 2$, and the decimal system, $r = 10$. The number of digits, n, is the code length.

Example. The binary number

$$11010 = 1 \times 2^4 + 1 \times 2^3 + 0 \times 2^2 + 1 \times 2 + 0 \times 1$$

which adds up to 26. The decimal number 382 means $3 \times 10^2 + 8 \times 10 + 2$.

The *arithmetic weight* of a number N is the minimum number of nonzero terms in an expression of the number in the form

$$N = a_n r^n + a_{n-1} r^{n-1} + \cdots + a_0 \tag{15.2}$$

where the a_i may be negative or positive but are less than r in absolute value. An expression for N involving terms of degree $n + 1$ or larger must have more nonzero terms than the weight of N. (See Problem 15.4.) The *arithmetic distance* between two numbers N_1 and N_2 is the weight of the difference $N_1 - N_2$. If a number N_1 is transmitted and $N_2 \neq N_1$ is received, and if the distance between N_1 and N_2 is d, then a d-fold error is said to have occurred. Thus, the occurrence of a d-fold error in a number N_1 is equivalent to adding to N_1 a number of weight d. Note that with these definitions distance depends upon the choice of radix-r.

It is easy to show as with Hamming distance, an arithmetic distance at least d between every pair of coded numbers is necessary and sufficient for detecting all $(d - 1)$-fold or smaller errors. For correcting any combination of t or fewer errors, minimum distance $2t + 1$ is necessary and sufficient, and more generally, correction of any combination of t or fewer errors and simultaneous detection of d or fewer errors requires minimum distance $t + d + 1$.

Example. For the case $r = 2$, the distance between 171 and 203 is 1, because $171 - 203 = -32 \equiv 2^5$. The distance between 17 and 32 is 2: $17 - 32 = -15 \equiv +2^0 - 2^4$. For the decimal case, 1296 and 1183 are at distance 2, because $1296 - 1193 \equiv 1 \times 10^2 + 3 \times 10^0$. The distance between 1296 and 1305 is 1, even though they differ in three digits, because $1296 - 1305 = -9 \times 10^0$

Arithmetic distance is mathematically more tractable than Hamming distance in the present context. It also matches more closely the types of errors that may occur in an arithmetic computer system. Clearly, if a single digit is in error, this is a single error; and if t digits are altered, this is at most a t-fold error. Thus, a system capable of correcting all t-fold or smaller errors in this sense corrects all numbers in which no more than t digits are altered. In an adder, however, a single error in one digit may cause several digits to be in error because of the influence of carries. Also, a carry failure may affect several digits. Such failures are still counted as single errors with this definition of distance!

It is not difficult to design a parallel binary adder for a computer in such a way that a single component failure in the adder will affect directly not more than one sum digit or one carry. A code that can correct all single arithmetic errors would be capable of correcting for any single component failure in such an adder, even though carry propagation might cause several digits in the result to be incorrect.

15.2 Properties of Arithmetic Weight for the Binary Case

Now let us assume $r = 2$. While the weight of a number is well-defined and unique, an expression of the type given in Equation 15.2 is not always unique. For example, $3 = 2 + 1 = 4 - 1$, and thus, the weight of 3 is 2, but there are two different expressions that achieve the minimum of two nonzero terms. There is, however, a canonical form for every number which has the minimum number of terms:

THEOREM 15.1. *For every number N there is a unique representation of the form*

$$N = a_n 2^n + a_{n-1} 2^{n-1} + \cdots + a_0$$

in which $a_i = \pm 1$ *or* 0, *and in which no two successive* a_i *are both nonzero. This representation has the minimum number of nonzero terms.*

Proof. First, the existence of a representation of this type with a minimum number of nonzero terms will be demonstrated, and then the uniqueness will be demonstrated. Let

$$N = b_n 2^n + b_{n-1} 2^{n-1} + \cdots + b_0. \tag{15.3}$$

If there exist two successive nonzero b_i, let the pair with the smallest i be $b_{i+1}2^{i+1} + b_i 2^i$. If $b_i = -b_{i+1}$, then $b_{i+1}2^{i+1} + b_i 2^i = b_{i+1}2^i$ and the resulting expression has fewer ones. If $b_i = b_{i+1}$, then $b_{i+1}2^{i+1} + b_i 2^i = b_{i+1}2^{i+2} - b_i 2^i$. If this substitution is made in Equation 15.3, the coefficient of 2^{i+1} will become zero. The term $b_{i+1}2^{i+2}$ can be combined with the existing term $b_{i+2}2^{i+2}$. If b_{i+2} is zero, the new expression has the same number of terms as the old. If $b_{i+2} = -b_{i+1}$, these terms cancel and there are fewer terms. If $b_{i+2} = b_{i+1}$, then combined they become $b_{i+2}2^{i+2} + b_{i+1}2^{i+2} = b_{i+1}2^{i+3}$, and the coefficient of 2^{i+2} becomes zero, while the $b_{i+1}2^{i+3}$ must be combined with the term $b_{i+3}2^{i+3}$. The "carry" may propagate to the highest-order term, but each time a carry occurs, the number of nonzero terms decreases. Thus, the resulting expression has the same general form (Equation 15.3), and has no more nonzero terms than the original expression, and has no two successive nonzero terms of degree less than $i + 2$.

If this process is repeated, an expression will result that has no two successive nonzero terms, and no more nonzero terms than the original expression. The process will certainly terminate because each step leaves at least two more terms in the low-order part which has no pair of successive nonzero terms, and there is at each step no more terms in all than the initial number, which was certainly finite.

If the original expression used had a minimum number of terms, the number of terms can decrease no more, and so the final expression must have exactly the same number of terms. Since every number certainly has an expression of the form in Equation 15.2 with a minimum number of terms, it follows that every number has an expression of that same type with a minimum number of terms and no two successive nonzero terms.

It remains to be shown that the expression is unique. First, note that in an expression of the type in Equation 15.2 with all coefficients ± 1 or 0, if the leading coefficient is $+1$, the smallest value of N could occur if all other coefficients are -1, and in that case

$$N_{\min} = 2^n - 2^{n-1} - 2^{n-2} - \cdots - 1 = 1.$$

Similarly, if the leading coefficient is -1, the largest value N could have would be -1. Thus, an expression with $a_n \neq 0$ can be zero if and only if all coefficients are zero.

Now define

$$N_1 = a_n 2^n + a_{n-1} 2^{n-1} + \cdots + a_0$$

$$N_2 = b_n 2^n + b_{n-1} 2^{n-1} + \cdots + b_0$$

and suppose that no two successive coefficients in either expression are nonzero, and that for at least one i, $a_i \neq b_i$. Then

$$N_2 - N_1 = (b_n - a_n)2^n + (b_{n-1} - a_{n-1})2^{n-1} + \cdots + (b_0 - a_0).$$

Then, if $a_i \neq b_i$, there are two cases: either $a_i = -b_i$ or one of them is zero. In the latter case, the expression for $N_2 - N_1$ has a nonzero term $(b_i - a_i)2^i$, since a carry from the $(i-1)$th position is impossible. In the former case, the term $2b_i 2^i = b_i 2^{i+1}$ results. But since neither the expression for N_1 or for N_2 has a pair of successive nonzero terms, $b_{i+1} = a_{i+1} = 0$ and the term $b_i 2^{i+1}$ remains in the expression for $N_2 - N_1$. If all pairs of terms $a_i 2^i$ and $b_i 2^i$ are combined in this manner, the resulting expression has the form in Equation 15.2. Not all coefficients are 0, and therefore $N_1 - N_2 \neq 0$, so that two distinct expressions give unequal numbers. Q.E.D.

This proof shows how to express any number in the canonical form and thus determine the arithmetic weight. Thus, 431 is, in binary notation, 110101111 or

$$\begin{aligned}431 &= \ 2^8+2^7+0+2^5+0+2^3+2^2+2+1\\ &= \ 2^8+2^7+0+2^5+2^4+0+0+0-1\\ &= \ 2^8+2^7+2^6+0-2^4+0+0+0-1\\ &= 2^9+0+0-2^6+0-2^4+0+0+0-1\end{aligned}$$

and the arithmetic weight is 4, since there are 4 nonzero terms in the final expression.

The arithmetic weights of the first few numbers is as follows:

1	2	3	4	5	6	7	8	9	10	11	12	13	14	15	16
1	1	2	1	2	2	2	1	2	2	3	2	3	2	2	1

17	18	19	20	21	22	23	24	25	26	27	28	29	30	31	32
2	2	3	2	3	3	3	2	3	3	3	2	3	2	2	1

The following pattern can be observed (Chiang and Reed 1970): Starting from any number $2^i + 1$ up to $2^i + 2^{i-1}$, the weights are just one greater than the weights of 1 through 2^{i-1}. Starting from $2^i + 2^{i-1} + 1$ and going on to 2^{i+1}, the weights are the same as for the 2^{i-1} numbers $2^i + 2^{i-1} - 1$, $2^i + 2^{i-1} - 2, \ldots, 2^i$. Theorems that demonstrate this are stated as Problems 15.2 and 15.3. These theorems enable one to write the weights of successive integers without ever expressing the integers in a binary expansion and, in fact, with very trivial calculations.

15.3 The Arithmetic Codes

Now consider a code in which the coded form of the number N is the n-digit radix-r representation of AN, where A is a constant. Note that

$$AN_1 + AN_2 = A(N_1 + N_2) \tag{15.4}$$

so that the coded form for the sum of two numbers is the sum of the coded numbers. Therefore, coded numbers can be added in an ordinary adder. Since the sum is properly coded, it may be checked or corrected.

If A has the radix r as a factor, then every coded number AN also has the radix r as a factor. In a radix-r representation, then, the lowest-order digit would always be 0 and would be useless. Similarly, if A and r are not relatively prime, certain digits are impossible in the low-order position. This is undesirable, and therefore, it will be assumed that A and r are relatively prime.

The analogy with cyclic codes is interesting. In an AN code a number is a code number — the coded form of some number — if and only if the number is a multiple of A and in the accepted range of numbers. A polynomial is a code vector in the cyclic code generated by $g(X)$ if and only if it is a multiple of $g(X)$ of degree less than n. Other similarities appear in the theory that follows.

In the next sections, codes analogous to cyclic Hamming codes, maximal-length-sequence codes, and Fire codes are presented. No one has yet found codes analogous to BCH codes or any other important class of cyclic codes, however.

For any number A, such that $(r, A) = 1$, there exists a smallest n such that $r^n - 1$ is divisible by A. If n is taken as the number of digits in a code word, then every cyclic shift of a code word is also a code word, for a cyclic shift of

$$N = a_{n-1}r^{n-1} + a_{n-2}r^{n-2} + \cdots + a_0$$

gives

$$a_{n-2}r^{n-1} + a_{n-3}r^{n-2} + \cdots + a_0 \cdot r + a_{n-1} = rN - a_{n-1}(r^n - 1)$$

which is divisible by A. First, as in the case of cyclic codes, taking the code length greater than n makes $r^n - 1$ a code word, giving minimum distance 2. Therefore, the code length should be either n, the choice analogous to cyclic codes, or some smaller number giving codes analogous to shortened cyclic codes.

The number of digits required to represent N in a radix-r system is the smallest integer greater than $\log_r N$. The number of digits required to represent AN is the smallest integer equal to or greater than $\log_r AN = N + \log_r A$. The quantity $\log_r A$ will be called the redundancy for the code; the number of redundant digits actually required will differ by less than 1 from $\log_r A$.

> *Example.* In a $29N$ code with $r = 2$, the redundancy is $\log_2 29 = 4.8$ bits. All numbers less than $2^9 = 512$ can be expressed in terms of 9 binary digits. To express $29N$ for all N less than 2^9 in binary form, 14 digits are required. Thus, 5 redundant digits are actually required.
>
> In a $3N$ code with $r = 2$, the redundancy is $\log_2 = 3 = 1.6$ bits. If a $3N$ code is used for binary representation of a decimal digit, then $N < 10$. To represent all numbers less than 10 in binary form, 4 binary digits are needed. Only 5 binary digits are required to represent $3N$ in binary form, and thus only 1 redundant binary digit is actually required.

Single-error detection requires that the minimum distance between coded numbers be 2, that is, that no two coded numbers be a distance 1 apart. Thus, for all permissible N_1 and N_2,

$$AN_1 - AN_2 = A(N_1 - N_2) \neq br^j \tag{15.5}$$

where $0 < b < r$. This can be assured by choosing A to be relatively prime to r and greater than r. The choice $A = r + 1$ will always work. A $3N$ code will detect any single error in a binary representation, and $11N$ will detect any single error in a decimal representation. Thus, single-error detection requires a fixed amount of redundancy for any given radix, no matter how large the numbers N may be. The redundancy required is $\log_r (r + 1)$, and this means that never fewer than 1 nor more than 2 extra digits will be required. This corresponds to the fact that a single parity symbol will detect single errors in ordinary linear codes, no matter how long the code is.

THEOREM 15.2. *An AN code can correct all combinations of t errors if and only if all numbers of weight t or less have distinct residues modulo A.*

Proof. Suppose two distinct numbers N_1 and N_2, each of weight t or less, have equal residues. Then $N_1 - N_2$ has residue zero; that is, it is a multiple of A and hence a code word. But $N_1 - N_2$ has weight at most $2t$, so the code cannot correct all t-fold errors. On the other hand, suppose the code has minimum weight $2t + 1$. Then, if N_1 and N_2 are distinct numbers of weight t or less, they must have distinct residues, for otherwise $N_1 - N_2$ would be a code word of weight less than $2t + 1$.

Q.E.D.

Codes with minimum distance greater than 2 can best be described in terms of a number $M_r(A, d)$ defined to be the smallest number whose product with A has weight less than d in a radix-r representation.

THEOREM 15.3. *For any choice of A and r, if N is restricted either to the range $0 \leqq N < M_r(A, d)$ or to $-\frac{1}{2}M_r(A, d-1) \leqq N < \frac{1}{2}M_r(A, d)$, the AN code has minimum distance at least d.*

Proof. If N_1 and N_2 are both within either range, $N_1 - N_2 < M_r(A, d)$ and $AN_1 - AN_2 < AM_r(A, d)$; and therefore, by the definition of $M_r(A, d)$, $AN_1 - AN_2$ has weight greater than $d - 1$. Q.E.D.

With the exception of Theorems 15.4 and 15.7 that follow, there is no way known of determining $M_r(A, d)$ except by exhaustive computation. Some values are listed in Table 15.1 for the cases of most interest, $r = 2$ and $d = 3$ or 4.

Table 15.1. Some Binary *AN* Codes

Distance-3 Codes		Distance-4 Codes			
A	$M_2(A, 3)$	A	$M_2(A, 4)$	$AM_2(A, 4)$	
11	3	43	3	2^7	+1
13	5	51	5	2^8	−1
19	27	89	23	2^{11}	−1
23	89	105	39	2^{12}	−1
29	565	153	215	$2^{15}+2^7$	−1
37	7085	185	1417	2^{18}	+1
47	178481	267	15709	2^{22}	−1
53	1266205	351	23905	$2^{23}+2^{11}$	−1
59	9099507	353	25249	$2^{23}+2^{19}$	+1
61	17602325	357	46995	2^{24}	−1
67	128207979	393	181433	$2^{26}+2^{22}$	+1
71	483939977	547	245131	$2^{27}-2^{17}$	+1
79	6958934353	555	123818877	2^{36}	−1
83	26494256091	737	5967134431	$2^{42}-2^{28}$	−1
101	5099523830125	801	10981392159	$2^{43}+2^{21}$	−1
103	11350134113449				

15.4 Perfect, Arithmetic, Single-Error-Correcting Codes

THEOREM 15.4 (*Brown* 1960). *If A is an odd prime and if 2 is a primitive element in the field of integers mod A,*

$$M_2(A, 3) = \frac{2^{(A-1)/2} + 1}{A}. \tag{15.6a}$$

If -2, but not 2, is primitive mod A,

$$M_2(A, 3) = \frac{2^{(A-1)/2} - 1}{A}. \tag{15.6b}$$

Conversely, if Equation 15.6a *holds, then A is prime and* 2 *is a primitive element mod A, while if Equation* 15.6b *holds, A is prime and -2, but not 2, is primitive mod A.*

Proof. If A is prime, then $2^{A-1} - 1 = (2^{(A-1)/2} + 1)(2^{(A-1)/2} - 1) = 0$ mod A, and if 2 is primitive, $2^{(A-1)/2} \neq 1$, so that $2^{(A-1)/2} + 1 = 0$, or $2^{(A-1)/2} = -1$. Then the residues mod A of the weight-1 errors 1, 2, $2^2, \ldots, 2^{(A-3)/2}, 2^{(A-1)/2} = -1, -2, \ldots, -2^{(A-3)/2}$ are distinct. Then, by Theorem 15.2, Equation 15.6a holds.

If -2 is primitive and A prime, then $1, 2, 2^2, \ldots, 2^{(A-3)/2}$ must be distinct since their squares are. Also, none is equal to -1, for if $2^j = -1$

mod A for some $j \leqq (A-3)/2$, then $2^{2j} = 1 = (-2)^{2j}$ mod A for some $2j \leqq A-3$, which is impossible if -2 is primitive. Again, $(2^{(A-1)/2} - 1)(2^{(A-1)/2} + 1) = 0 \bmod A$. If $(A-1)/2$ is even, $(2^{(A-1)/2} - 1)(2^{(A-1)/2} + 1) = 0 \bmod A$. If $(A-1)/2$ is even, $2^{(A-1)/2} = (-2)^{(A-1)/2} \neq 1$; hence, $2^{(A-1)/2} = -1$. Then, 2 is primitive, and Equation 15.6a applies. If, on the other hand, -2 is primitive and 2 is not, then $(A-1)/2$ must be odd. Then, $2^{(A-1)/2} - 1 = 0$, and the residues of the weight-1 errors $1, -2, 2^2, \ldots, 2^{(A-3)/2}, -1, +2, -2^2, \ldots, -2^{(A-3)/2}$ are distinct. By Theorem 15.2, Equation 15.6b holds.

Conversely, Theorem 15.2 implies that if Equation 15.6a or Equation 15.6b holds, all the residues mod A must be congruent to $\pm 2^i$, and A must be odd. Then 2, and therefore all the residues mod A, are relatively prime to A, so that A must be prime. Then the residues mod A form a field. The order of 2 is at least $(A-1)/2$, since the smaller powers of 2 have distinct residues. But the order of 2 must divide $A-1$, so it must be either $A-1$ or $(A-1)/2$. The same is true of -2. By Theorem 6.20, there is a primitive element a. If the orders of both 2 and -2 are $(A-1)/2$, then $\pm 2^j$ is always an even power of a. This is impossible. Therefore, either 2 or -2 must have order $A-1$, that is, be primitive. Q.E.D.

The codes given by Theorem 15.4 are analogous to Hamming perfect single-error-correcting codes. A code to be used with numbers in the range $0 \leqq N < 2^n$ (or $-2^{n-1} \leqq N < 2^{n-1}$) must be able to distinguish each of $2n$ possible errors and a correct coded number or $2n+1$ possibilities in all. Theorem 15.2 states that each of these $2n+1$ possibilities corresponds to a different residue, and thus $A \geqq 2n+1$. Theorem 15.4 states necessary and sufficient conditions for the equality to hold. Note the analogy with cyclic codes. In an AN code, not only must A be prime but 2 must be a primitive element. For a binary cyclic Hamming code, the generator polynomial $g(X)$ must not only be irreducible but its roots must be primitive.

All the distance-3 codes listed in Table 15.1 are of the type described in Theorem 15.4.

15.5 Arithmetic Codes with Large Minimum Distance

Let A be a prime number for which 2 is a primitive element. Then $2^{A-1} - 1$ is divisible by A. Let

$$B = \frac{2^{A-1} - 1}{A}$$

and consider the BN code. The natural number of digits to use is $n = A - 1$. This gives a cyclic-type arithmetic code. The code has $(2^n - 1)/B = A$ code numbers, which must consist of zero and the $A - 1$ cyclic shifts of the $n = (A - 1)$-digit representation of B.

The following Theorems 15.5 and 15.6 give the weight structure of this code:

THEOREM 15.5. *In the binary expression*

$$lB = b_{n-1}2^{n-1} + b_{n-2}2^{n-2} + \cdots + b_0, \qquad 0 \leq l < A$$

$$b_i = (l2^{n-i} \bmod A) \bmod 2.$$

Proof.

$$\frac{lB}{2^i} = \frac{l2^n - l}{A2^i} = \frac{l2^{n-i}}{A} - \frac{l}{A2^i}$$

$$= \left(\frac{l2^{n-i} - (l2^{n-i} \bmod A)}{A}\right) + \left(\frac{l2^{n-i} \bmod A}{A} - \frac{l}{A2^i}\right)$$

$$= (b_{n-1}2^{n-i-1} + b_{n-2}2^{n-i-2} + \cdots + b_i)$$

$$+ b_{i-1}2^{-1} + \cdots + b_0 2^{-i}.$$

Equating the integer part of both sides and multiplying both sides by A give

$$l2^{n-i} - (l2^{n-i} \bmod A) = A(b_{n-1}2^{n-i-1} + b_{n-2}2^{n-i-2} + \cdots + b_i).$$

Finally, taking residues mod 2 gives

$$-(l2^{n-i} \bmod A) \bmod 2 = (A \bmod 2)(b_i)$$

or, since A is odd,

$$(l2^{n-i} \bmod A) \bmod 2 = b_i$$

Q.E.D.

COROLLARY 15.1. *In the binary expression for B,* half the digits are 0's and half are 1's.

Proof. Since 2 is primitive mod A, the residues of 2^i mod A, $1 \leq i \leq n - 1$, give all the integers between 1 and $A - 1$. Since half of these are even, half odd, half the b_i are 1's and half 0's. Q.E.D.

THEOREM 15.6. *Let A be a prime > 3 which has 2 as a primitive element, and $B = (2^{A-1} - 1)/A$. The arithmetic weight of each code number in the BN code is $(A - 1)/3$ or $(A + 1)/3$, whichever is an* *integer. This is also the arithmetic distance between each pair of code numbers, and the minimum Hamming distance.*

Proof. Consider the case in which $(A-1)/3$ is an integer, and let

$$B = b_0 + b_1 2 + b_2 2^2 + \cdots + b_{n-1}2^{n-1}$$
$$3B = c_0 + c_1 2 + c_2 2^2 + \cdots + c_{n-1}2^{n-1}.$$

Then

$$2B = (c_0 - b_0) + (c_1 - b_1)2 + \cdots + (c_{n-1} - b_{n-1})2^{n-1} \qquad (15.7)$$

and in this expression, the coefficients $c_i - b_i$ are either ± 1 or 0. In particular, $c_i - b_i$ is 0, by Theorem 15.5, if and only if $2^i \bmod A$ and $(3 \cdot 2^i) \bmod A$ are both even or both odd. If $(2^i \bmod A) < A/3$, then $(3 \cdot 2^i) \bmod A = 3 \cdot (2^i \bmod A)$, and $(3 \cdot 2^i) \bmod A$ is even if and only if $2^i \bmod A$ is. If $A/3 \leqq (2^i \bmod A) < 2A/3$, then $(3 \cdot 2^i) \bmod A = 3 \cdot (2^i \bmod A) - A$, and if $2^i \bmod A$ is even, $(3 \cdot 2^i) \bmod A$ is odd and vice versa. If $2A/3 \leqq (2^i \bmod A) < A$, then $(3 \cdot 2^i) \bmod A = 3 \cdot (2^i \bmod A) - 2A$, and again either $2^i \bmod A$ and $(3 \cdot 2^i) \bmod A$ are both even or both odd. Thus, nonzero terms occur in Expression 15.7 for those i for which $A/3 \leqq 2^i \bmod A < 2A/3$. But since 2 is assumed primitive mod A, all the integers between 1 and $A-1$ occur as residues of $2^i \bmod A$. If $A-1$ is divisible by 3, then there are $(A-1)/3$ such residues. If $A-1$ is not divisible by 3, then since A isn't either, $A+1$ must be, and in that case the number of integers between $A/3$ and $2A/3$ is $(A+1)/3$. Thus, in Expression 15.7 there are $(A-1)/3$ or $(A+1)/3$ nonzero terms.

Now suppose $b_i - c_i$ is not 0. Then $2^i \bmod A$ is between $A/3$ and $2A/3$. It follows that $2^{i+1} \bmod A$ is between $2A/3$ and A if $2^i \bmod A$ is between $A/3$ and $A/2$, and $2^{i+1} \bmod A$ is between 1 and $A/3$ if $2^i \bmod A$ is between $A/2$ and $2A/3$. In either case, by the arguments in the preceding paragraph, $b_{i+1} - c_{i+1} = 0$. Thus, Expression 15.7 does not have two successive nonzero terms. By Theorem 15.1, the number of nonzero terms in this expression is the arithmetic weight of $2B$.

Every code word can be obtained by cyclically shifting the binary representation for $2B$. Consider the code word obtained by shifting $2B$ left cyclically i places. It can also be obtained by shifting B and $3B$ left cyclically i places and subtracting, and the resulting expression will be the shifted version of the canonical form for $2B$ given in Expression 15.7. Therefore, every code word has the same arithmetic weight, $(A-1)/3$ or $(A+1)/3$. Finally, Hamming distance is never less than arithmetic distance, so the Hamming distance is at least $(A-1)/3$ or $(A+1)/3$. But this is exactly the Hamming distance between B and $3B$, so it is the minimum distance for the code. Q.E.D.

These codes are dual codes of the single-error-correcting codes in the first part of Theorem 15.4. The question arises, what about the case in which -2 but not 2 is a primitive root mod A? The answer is, there is a code generated by $B = (2^{A-1} - 1)/A$, and theorems analogous to 15.5 and 15.6 can be proved, using the following lemma.

LEMMA 15.1. *Any integer N can be expressed uniquely in the form*

$$N = a_n(-2)^n + a_{n-1}(-2)^{n-1} + \cdots + a_0 \qquad (15.8)$$

where a_i is 0 or 1.

Proof. Add $2 + 2^3 + 2^5 + \cdots + 2^l$ to N, where $2^l > N$. Expand the sum in binary, and finally subtract $2 + 2^3 + 2^5 + \cdots + 2^l$ from the result, term by term. The desired expression results. Its uniqueness follows directly from the uniqueness of the ordinary binary expansion.

Using Expression 15.8, it can be shown, by the same method as used in proving Theorem 15.5, that the coefficients in Expression 15.8 are given by the equation

$$a_i = [(-2)^{n-i} \bmod A] \bmod 2$$

and then Theorem 15.6 and its proof follow directly for this case also.

For arithmetic codes, a burst error of length b may be defined as an error pattern $e = l2^i$, where $2^{b-1} < l < 2^b$ and l is odd. The following theorem gives the analog of the Fire codes and is of interest primarily as an example of the analogy:

THEOREM 15.7. *If A' is a prime and 2 is primitive mod A', then the arithmetic code generated by $A'(2^c - 1)$ of length n equal to the least common multiple of c and $A' - 1$ is capable of correcting any single burst of length b if $2b \leq c$ and $A' > 2^b$.*

Since it is rather lengthy and straightforward, the proof is omitted here. Some other similar extensions are included in Chien 1964*a*.

15.6 Self-Complementing $AN + B$ Codes

For some purposes it is desirable that the code for the complement of a number be the complement of the code for that number (Brown 1960). If the numbers to be coded have a base b, then the complement of N is defined to be $b - 1 - N$. If the coded numbers are represented as n-digit numbers with radix-r, then the complement of AN is $r^n - 1 - AN$.

The requirement that the code of the complement of a number be the complement of the coded number is

$$r^n - 1 - (AN + B) = A(b - 1 - N) + B. \tag{15.9}$$

This equation can be solved for B:

$$B = \frac{[r^n - 1 - A(b - 1)]}{2}. \tag{15.10}$$

A self-complementing code is possible if and only if Equation 15.10 yields an integral value for B.

An $AN + B$ code has the same distance properties as the corresponding AN code, because $(AN_1 + B) - (AN_2 + B) = AN_1 - AN_2$.

Example. Suppose that a binary $AN + B$ single-error-correcting self-complementing code for decimal digits is required. Table 15.1 shows that the smallest value of A yielding an AN code with $M_2(A, 3) \geqq 10$ is $A = 19$. For this code the largest coded number will be at least $19 \times 9 = 171$, and so will require at least $n = 8$ binary digits. Equation 15.9 yields $B = 42$, and since $19 \times 9 + 42 = 223 < 2^8$, this code is possible. The coded form of the digits is as follows:

0	00101010	5	10001001
1	00111101	6	10011100
2	01010000	7	10101111
3	01100011	8	11000010
4	01110110	9	11010101.

Three other codes, $23N + 24$, $25N + 15$, and $27N + 6$, also meet the basic requirements with an 8-binary-digit code (Brown 1960).

15.7 Implementing AN and $AN + B$ Codes

If a computer is available, the obvious way to encode for an $AN + B$ code is simply to multiply the uncoded number N by A and add B. To decode, one simply subtracts B from the received coded number and divides by A. A nonzero remainder indicates that an error occurred; the value of the remainder is characteristic of the error number, which is the difference between the received coded number and the most likely transmitted code number (see Theorem 15.2 and Problem 15.1). Table look-up, with a table that lists the appropriate error number for each possible remainder, would usually be the most expedient way to handle error correction in a computer.

Error correction for the "lossless" AN codes described in Theorem

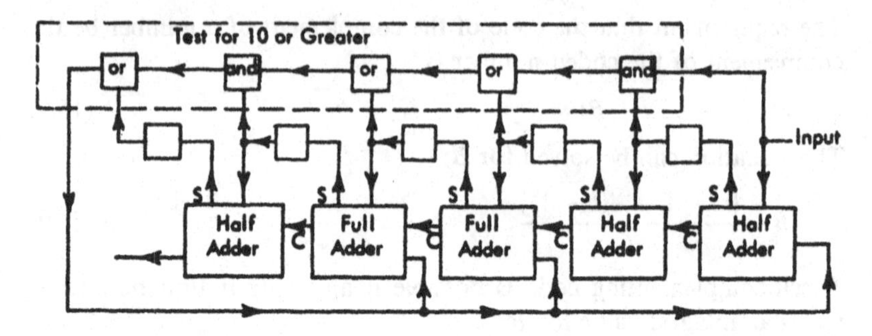

Figure 15.1. A shift register with shift multiplying by 2 modulo 19.

15.3 can be implemented in a manner analogous to that described for cyclic Hamming codes in Section 8.7. The first step is to design a shift register that multiplies by 2 mod A upon shifting. Such a device for $A = 19$ is shown in Figure 15.1. If shifting would result in shift-register contents as great as 19, that is, if the shift-register contents are 10 or greater or 9 with a 1 as input, then 19 should be subtracted from the shift-register contents at the same time that shifting is done. Subtracting 19 is the same as adding $32 - 19 = 13$ in a 5-digit binary adder. If the "test for 10 or greater" gives a 1 as its output, then 13, which is 0 1 1 0 1 in binary, is added into the register as it is shifted.

The residue of a number mod 19 can be found by shifting the number, represented in binary, into this shift register, high-order digits first, until the lowest order digit enters the register. The residue remains in the shift register.

Correction can be accomplished by shifting the register with no input until $+1$ or -1 (which appears as $19 - 1 = 18$, or in binary 1 0 0 1 0) appears in the shift register, and keeping track of the number of shifts required. If the error occurs in the jth order digit, the error is $\pm 2^j$. Since 2 is primitive modulo 19, $2^9 = -1$, and therefore if an error $+2^j$ occurs, -1 appears in the shift register after $9 - j$ shifts; while if the error is -2^j, then $+1$ appears in the shift register after $9 - j$ shifts. Thus, the error position can be determined from the number of shifts, and whether the error was $+2^j$ or -2^j determines whether $+1$ or -1 shows up first in the shift register. The details of the circuit can be organized as for cyclic Hamming codes or cyclic burst-error-correcting codes, but with a serial adder and subtractor for adding or subtracting the correction. Note also that, by Theorem 15.5, if the shift register in Figure 15.1 is shifted over and over with nonzero contents but no input, the successive low-order digits are repetitions of the digits of $B = (2^n - 1)/A$.

15.8 Separate Adder and Checker

It is often desirable to have the coded words in a checking system consist of unaltered information digits with check symbols, as they do in systematic linear codes. If such a system is used for checking an adder, it is also desirable that the adder and the equipment that processes check symbols be completely independent to avoid the possibility that the failure of a single component might affect both the sum and the check symbol in such a way that an error is undetected or not properly corrected. In this section it is shown that if the adder and checker are independent, the check symbol for a number must be either a duplicate of the number (possibly differently coded) or, for some b, the mod b residue of the number in some code. Furthermore, it is shown that to every AN code there corresponds a mod A code with the same minimum distance and essentially the same redundancy.

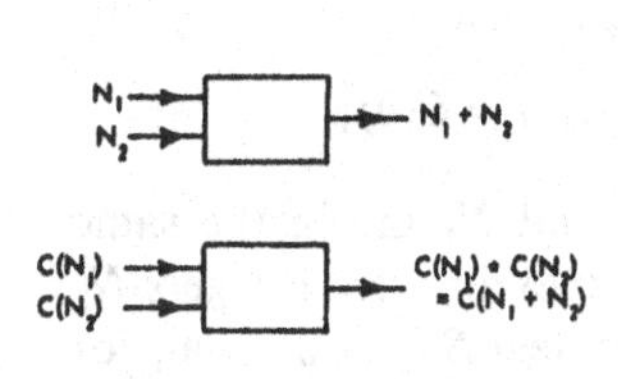

Figure 15.2. A system with separate adder and checker.

Consider the system shown in Figure 15.2, in which $C(N)$ designates the check symbol associated with N and the asterisk (*) denotes the operation done by the checker. It is required that the output of the checker be consistent with the output of the adder; that is,

$$C(N_1) * C(N_2) = C(N_1 + N_2) \quad (15.11)$$

This constraint on the code restricts it to a very special type.

THEOREM 15.8. *If there are fewer check symbols than integers in the permissible range of integers, and if the check symbols* $C(N)$ *satisfy Equation 15.11, then* $C(N)$ *must be the residue of* N *mod* b *in a coded form, where* b *is the number of distinct check symbols, and* * *is addition mod* b.

Proof. Let S denote the set of all integers N that have the same check symbol as zero; that is, $C(N) = C(0)$. The first step in the proof is to show that S is an ideal in the ring of integers. By definition, zero is in S. Note that $C(0) = C(0 + 0) = C(0) * C(0)$, and therefore, $C(0) * C(0) * \cdots * C(0) = C(0)$, no matter how many factors appear on the left. Thus, if a is in S, then $Na = a + \cdots + a$ is in S, for

$$\begin{aligned} C(Na) &= C(a + a + \cdots + a) = C(a) * C(a) * \cdots * C(a) \\ &= C(0) * C(0) * \cdots * C(0) = C(0). \end{aligned}$$

Also, if a is in S,

$$C(-a) = C(0 - a) = C(0) * C(-a) = C(a) * C(-a)$$
$$= C(a - a) = C(0)$$

and therefore $-a$ is in S also. Thus, S is an ideal.

Next, note that $C(N_1) = C(N_2)$ if and only if N_1 and N_2 are in the same residue class of S. This is shown as follows:

$$C(N_2) = C(N_1) * C(N_2 - N_1)$$

If N_1 and N_2 are in the same residue class, $N_2 - N_1$ is in S and $C(N_2 - N_1) = C(0)$.

$$C(N_2) = C(N_1) * C(0) = C(N_1 + 0) = C(N_1).$$

On the other hand, if $C(N_1) = C(N_2)$, then

$$C(N_2 - N_1) = C(N_2) * C(-N_1) = C(N_1) * C(-N_1)$$
$$= C(N_1 - N_1) = C(0);$$

therefore, $N_2 - N_1$ is in the ideal S, and N_2 and N_1 are in the same residue class of S. Note that this means that if two different integers N_1 and N_2 have the same check symbol, then the ideal S is nontrivial, for then $C(0) = C(N_1 - N_2)$, and thus the ideal contains more than just the number zero.

By Theorem 6.2, S is a principal ideal; that is, it consists of all multiples of some integer b. The residue classes are residue classes mod b. Thus, there is a one-to-one correspondence between residue classes and check symbols. For every j, $0 \leqq j < b$, consider $C(j)$ to be the code for the residue class containing j; that is, define $C(j) = j$. Then $i * j = C(i) * C(j) = C(i + j) = i + j \bmod b$, and thus the checking operation is addition mod b. Q.E.D.

If there are as many check symbols as numbers, each number has a distinct check symbol, and the checker is equivalent to a duplicate adder.

Next, consider an AN code with certain distance properties in a radix-r system. Let m be the smallest integer equal to or greater than $\log_r A$. Then every integer less than A can be expressed as an m-digit number with radix r. Consider the code in which the check symbol $C(n)$ for N is the residue of $-r^m N \bmod A$:

$$-r^m N = Aq + C(N).$$

Then the number formed by adding $C(N)$ to r^mN is

$$r^mN + C(N) = -Aq$$

which is a multiple of A, and therefore is a code number in the AN code. But $r^mN + C(N)$ as a radix-r number has the digits of N as its high-order digits and the digits of $C(N)$ as its low-order digits. Thus, the distance between two words, each consisting of a number and its check symbol, is at least the minimum distance of the AN code. In particular, single-error detection can always be accomplished by taking $C(N)$ as the residue of $-r^2N \bmod r+1$, and the values of A given in Table 15.1 can be used to form single-error-correcting and single-error-correcting, double-error-detecting check-symbol codes.

These codes are of the type specified by Theorem 15.4, with the radix-r representation of the residue of $-r^mj$ taken as the code for j. It is interesting also to note the analogy with the encoding method for cyclic codes described in Section 8.7.

Notes

Arithmetic codes appeared first in a short paper by Diamond (1955) and important early work was done by Brown (1960). The idea behind Theorem 15.1 is due to Reitwiesner (1960), and the pattern in the weights of successive integers was noted and proved by Chiang and Reed (1970). The large-distance arithmetic codes of Section 15.5 were found independently by Barrows (1966) and Mandelbaum (1967). The short proof of the distance properties given here is due to Tsao-Wu and Chang (1969). Theorem 15.8 is taken from Peterson 1958*a*. Analogous results for logical rather than arithmetic operations have been found by Elias (1958) and Peterson and Rabin (1959). Codes with residue-class check symbols have been proposed by Garner (1958). The distance-3 codes in Table 15.1 were found by Brown (1960), and the distance-4 codes were found by John Selfridge.

Problems

15.1. Show that arithmetic distance is a metric.

15.2. (Chien). Show that if $2^n \leqq l < 2^n + 2^{n-1}$ then $\omega(l) = 1 + \omega(l - 2^n)$, where $\omega(l)$ denotes the arithmetic weight of l.

15.3. Show that if $2^n + 2^{n-1} \leqq l < 2^{n+1}$, $\omega(l) = \omega(2^{n+1} - l)$.

15.4. Prove that if the representation for N, $0 \leqq N \leqq r^n - 1$, employs a term of degree $n+1$ or greater, then another representation can be found that will have fewer terms and maximum degree n.

Appendix A Inequalities Involving Binomial Coefficients

This appendix contains some inequalities useful in estimating expressions containing binomial coefficients. The material is taken from class notes for an information theory seminar given by C. E. Shannon at the Massachusetts Institute of Technology in 1956.

Let

$$G = \frac{1}{\sqrt{2\pi n\lambda\mu}} \lambda^{-\lambda n}\mu^{-\mu n} \tag{A.1}$$

Then

$$G \exp - \left(\frac{1}{12\lambda n} + \frac{1}{12\mu n}\right) < \binom{n}{\lambda n} < G \tag{A.2}$$

and

$$\frac{1}{2}\sqrt{\pi}\, G \leqq \binom{n}{\lambda n} \tag{A.3}$$

where $\mu = 1 - \lambda$ and neither λ nor μ is 0.

These two inequalities can be proved using the Stirling approximation:

$$n! \cong (2\pi)^{1/2} n^{n+(1/2)} e^{-n} \exp\left(\frac{1}{12n} - \frac{1}{360n^3} + \cdots\right) \tag{A.4}$$

It is known (Feller 1950) that $n!$ is underestimated if no terms of the series are taken; $n!$ is overestimated if only the $1/12n$ term is taken; and so forth. An overestimate of $\binom{n}{\lambda n} = n!/(\lambda n)!\,(\mu n)!$ is obtained by using Equation A.4 as an underestimate of $(\lambda n)!$ and $(\mu n)!$ and the same expression with the term $(-1/360n^3)$ omitted as an overestimate for the numerator. This gives

$$\frac{n!}{(\lambda n)!\,(\mu n)!}$$
$$< \frac{1}{\sqrt{2\pi n \lambda \mu}}\,\frac{1}{\lambda^{\lambda n}\mu^{\mu n}}\exp\left[\frac{1}{12n} - \frac{1}{12\lambda n} - \frac{1}{12\mu n} + \frac{1}{360(\lambda n)^3} + \frac{1}{360(\mu n)^3}\right]$$

The expression is symmetric in λ and μ. Suppose that $\lambda \geqq \mu$. Then

$$\frac{1}{360(\lambda n)^3} \leqq \frac{1}{360(\mu n)^3} \leqq \frac{1}{360\mu n}$$

and

$$\frac{1}{12n} < \frac{1}{12\lambda n}$$

Thus

$$\frac{1}{12n} - \frac{1}{12\lambda n} - \frac{1}{12\mu n} + \frac{1}{360(\lambda n)^3} + \frac{1}{360(\mu n)^3}$$
$$\leqq \frac{1}{12n} - \frac{1}{12\lambda n} - \frac{1}{12\mu n} + \frac{1}{180\mu n} < 0$$

This proves the upper bound, Inequality A.2. The lower bound is found similarly by using Equation A.4 with one term in the series as an upper bound for the denominator and with no terms in the series as a lower bound for the numerator $n!$.

The other lower bound, Inequality A.3, follows from Inequality A.2 unless both λn and μn are less than 3, since then $(1/12\lambda n) + (1/12\mu n)$ is less than $(1/12) + (1/36) = (1/9)$ and $\exp(-1/9) > (1/2)\sqrt{\pi}$. For the four cases in which λn and μn are both less than 3, the result is easily verified. The case $\lambda n = 1$, $\mu n = 1$ gives equality.

The "tail" of a binomial distribution can be estimated by the following formulas:

$$\binom{n}{\lambda n} P^{\lambda n} Q^{\mu n} < \sum_{i=\lambda n}^{n} \binom{n}{i} P^{i} Q^{n-i}$$
$$< \frac{\lambda Q}{\lambda - P}\binom{n}{\lambda n} P^{\lambda n} Q^{\mu n} \qquad \text{provided } \lambda > P \tag{A.5}$$

where $Q = 1 - P$. Also,

$$\sum_{i=\lambda n}^{n} \binom{n}{i} P^i Q^{n-i} \leq \lambda^{-\lambda n} \mu^{-\mu n} P^{\lambda n} Q^{\mu n} \qquad \text{provided } \lambda > P \tag{A.6}$$

Letting $P = Q = \frac{1}{2}$ and multiplying both sides by 2^n give

$$\binom{n}{\lambda n} < \sum_{i=\lambda n}^{n} \binom{n}{i} < \frac{\lambda}{2\lambda - 1} \binom{n}{\lambda n} \qquad \text{provided } \lambda > \tfrac{1}{2} \tag{A.7}$$

and

$$\sum_{i=\lambda n}^{n} \binom{n}{i} \leq \lambda^{-\lambda n} \mu^{-\mu n} \qquad \text{provided } \lambda > \tfrac{1}{2} \tag{A.8}$$

The lower bound in Inequality A.5 is obvious. The upper bound is found by overbounding the sum by a geometric series. (See Feller 1950.) The bound, Inequality A.6, is a special case of the Chernoff inequality (1952). For more precise, more general results see Feller (1943).

A sum of the form

$$\sum_{i=0}^{m} \binom{n}{i} a^i$$

can be estimated by letting $P = 1/(a + 1)$, $Q = a/(a + 1)$ and noting that

$$\begin{aligned}\sum_{i=0}^{\lambda m} \binom{n}{i} a^i &= (a + 1)^n \sum_{i=0}^{m} \binom{n}{i} P^{n-i} Q^i \\ &= (a + 1)^n \sum_{i=n-m+1}^{n} \binom{n}{i} P^i Q^{n-i}\end{aligned} \tag{A.9}$$

Each of the Inequalities A.4 to A.7 consists of some factors not strongly dependent on m and a factor $\binom{n}{\lambda n}$ or $\binom{n}{\lambda n} P^{\lambda n} Q^{\mu n}$. The binomial coefficient $\binom{n}{\lambda n}$ can be estimated using Equation A.1 and Inequalities A.2 and A.3, and the dominant factor in these expressions is $\lambda^{-\lambda n} \mu^{-\mu n}$. In calculations with large values of n, the following forms are useful:

$$\frac{1}{n} \log (\lambda^{-\lambda n} \mu^{-\mu n}) = -\lambda \log \lambda - \mu \log \mu = H(\lambda) \tag{A.10}$$

where the *entropy functions*

$$H(x) = -x \log x - (1 - x) \log (1 - x) \tag{A.11}$$

and

$$\begin{aligned}-\frac{1}{n} \log (\lambda^{-\lambda n} \mu^{-\mu n} P^{\lambda n} Q^{\mu n} &= -H(\lambda) - \lambda \log P - \mu \log Q \\ &= -H(\lambda) + H(P) + (P - \lambda) \log P \\ &\quad + (\mu - Q) \log Q\end{aligned}$$

But $\mu - Q = -(P - \lambda)$, and $dH(x)/dx = H'(x) = \log(1 - x)/x$, and therefore

$$-\frac{1}{n}\log(\lambda^{-\lambda n}\mu^{-\mu n}P^{\lambda n}Q^{\mu n}) = E(\lambda, P) \tag{A.12}$$

where

$$E(\lambda, P) = H(P) + (\lambda - P)H'(P) - H(\lambda) \tag{A.13}$$

This expression can be given an interesting geometrical interpretation as shown in Figure A.1.

Equations A.10 to A.13 hold regardless of the base of the logarithms, provided only that the same base is used in all equations. A short table calculated with common (base 10) logarithms is given in Appendix B. Longer tables, which use base 2 logarithms, are given in Dolansky and Dolansky (1952) Fano 1961.

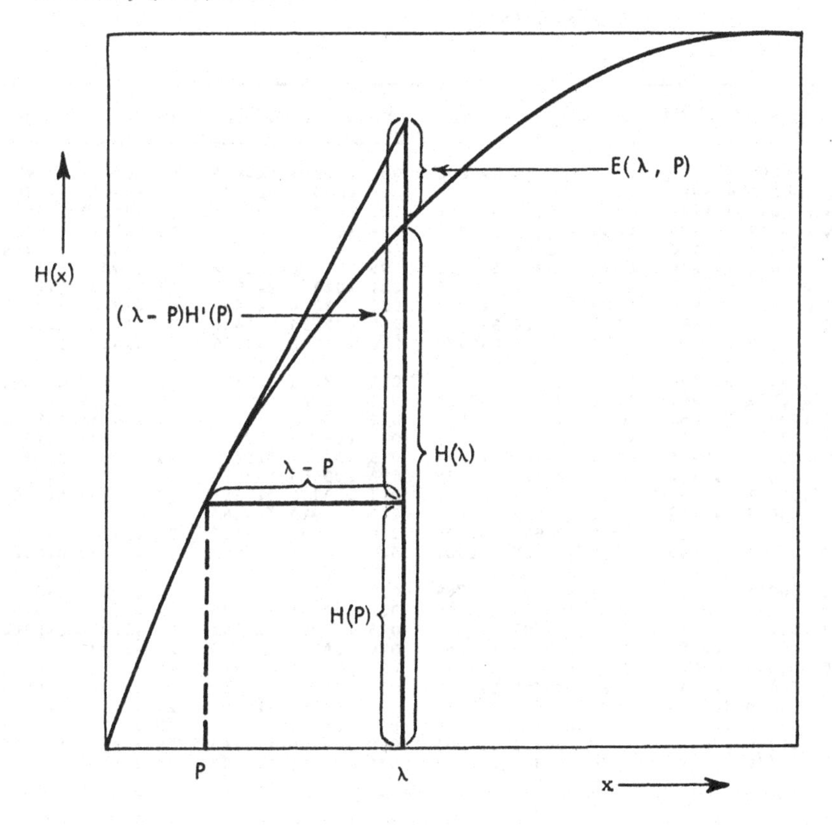

Figure A.1. Geometrical interpretation of $E(\lambda, P)$.

Appendix B Short Table of the Entropy Function (Base 10) and its First Derivative

P	H	dH(X)/dX	P	H	dH(X)/dX	P	H	dH(X)/dX	P	H	dH(X)/d
00001	.00005	5.0000	0001	.00044	4.0000	001	.00343	2.9996	01	.02432	1.9956
00002	.00010	4.6990	0002	.00083	3.6989	002	.00627	2.6981	02	.04258	1.6902
00003	.00015	4.5229	0003	.00119	3.5227	003	.00887	2.5216	03	.05852	1.5097
00004	.00019	4.3979	0004	.00153	3.3978	004	.01133	2.3962	04	.07294	1.3802
00005	.00024	4.3010	0005	.00187	3.3008	005	.01367	2.2989	05	.08621	1.2788
00006	.00028	4.2218	0006	.00219	3.2216	006	.01593	2.2192	06	.09857	1.1950
00007	.00032	4.1549	0007	.00251	3.1546	007	.01811	2.1519	07	.11015	1.1234
00008	.00036	4.0969	0008	.00282	3.0966	008	.02024	2.0934	08	.12107	1.0607
00009	.00040	4.0457	0009	.00313	3.0454	009	.02230	2.0418	09	.13139	1.0048
00010	.00044	4.0000	0010	.00343	2.9996	010	.02432	1.9956	10	.14118	0.9542
00011	.00048	3.9586	0011	.00373	2.9581	011	.02630	1.9538	11	.15049	0.9080
00012	.00052	3.9208	0012	.00403	2.9203	012	.02823	1.9156	12	.15935	0.8653
00013	.00056	3.8860	0013	.00432	2.8855	013	.03013	1.8804	13	.16781	0.8256
00014	.00060	3.8538	0014	.00460	2.8533	014	.03199	1.8477	14	.17587	0.7884
00015	.00064	3.8238	0015	.00489	2.8233	015	.03382	1.8173	15	.18358	0.7533
00016	.00068	3.7958	0016	.00517	2.7952	016	.03563	1.7889	16	.19095	0.7202
00017	.00071	3.7695	0017	.00545	2.7688	017	.03740	1.7621	17	.19799	0.6886
00018	.00075	3.7447	0018	.00572	2.7439	018	.03915	1.7368	18	.20472	0.6585
00019	.00079	3.7212	0019	.00599	2.7204	019	.04088	1.7129	19	.21116	0.6297
00020	.00083	3.6989	0020	.00627	2.6981	020	.04258	1.6902	20	.21732	0.6021
00021	.00086	3.6777	0021	.00653	2.6769	021	.04426	1.6686	21	.22321	0.5754
00022	.00090	3.6575	0022	.00680	2.6566	022	.04592	1.6479	22	.22883	0.5497
00023	.00094	3.6382	0023	.00707	2.6373	023	.04755	1.6282	23	.23420	0.5248
00024	.00097	3.6197	0024	.00733	2.6187	024	.04917	1.6092	24	.23933	0.5006
00025	.00101	3.6020	0025	.00759	2.6010	025	.05077	1.5911	25	.24422	0.4771
00026	.00105	3.5849	0026	.00785	2.5839	026	.05235	1.5736	26	.24888	0.4543
00027	.00108	3.5685	0027	.00811	2.5675	027	.05392	1.5567	27	.25331	0.4320
00028	.00112	3.5527	0028	.00836	2.5516	028	.05547	1.5405	28	.25752	0.4102
00029	.00115	3.5375	0029	.00862	2.5363	029	.05700	1.5248	29	.26151	0.3889
00030	.00119	3.5227	0030	.00887	2.5216	030	.05852	1.5097	30	.26530	0.3680

P	*H*	*dH(X)/dX*	*P*	*H*	*dH(X)/dX*	*P*	*H*	*dH(X)/dX*	*P*	*H*	*dH(X)/dX*
00031	.00122	3.5085	0031	.00912	2.5073	031	.06002	1.4950	31	.26887	0.3475
00032	.00126	3.4947	0032	.00937	2.4935	032	.06151	1.4807	32	.27225	0.3274
00033	.00129	3.4813	0033	.00962	2.4801	033	.06298	1.4669	33	.27542	0.3076
00034	.00133	3.4684	0034	.00987	2.4670	034	.06444	1.4535	34	.27840	0.2881
00035	.00136	3.4558	0035	.01011	2.4544	035	.06589	1.4405	35	.28118	0.2688
00036	.00140	3.4435	0036	.01036	2.4421	036	.06732	1.4278	36	.28378	0.2499
00037	.00143	3.4316	0037	.01060	2.4302	037	.06874	1.4154	37	.28618	0.2311
00038	.00146	3.4201	0038	.01084	2.4186	038	.07015	1.4034	38	.28840	0.2126
00039	.00150	3.4088	0039	.01109	2.4072	039	.07155	1.3917	39	.29043	0.1943
00040	.00153	3.3978	0040	.01133	2.3962	040	.07294	1.3802	40	.29229	0.1761
00041	.00157	3.3870	0041	.01156	2.3854	041	.07431	1.3690	41	.29396	0.1581
00042	.00160	3.3766	0042	.01180	2.3749	042	.07568	1.3581	42	.29545	0.1402
00043	.00163	3.3663	0043	.01204	2.3647	043	.07703	1.3474	43	.29676	0.1224
00044	.00167	3.3564	0044	.01228	2.3546	044	.07837	1.3370	44	.29790	0.1047
00045	.00170	3.3466	0045	.01251	2.3448	045	.07970	1.3268	45	.29885	0.0872
00046	.00173	3.3370	0046	.01274	2.3352	046	.08102	1.3168	46	.29964	0.0696
00047	.00177	3.3277	0047	.01298	2.3259	047	.08234	1.3070	47	.30025	0.0522
00048	.00180	3.3186	0048	.01321	2.3167	048	.08364	1.2974	48	.30068	0.0348
00049	.00183	3.3096	0049	.01344	2.3077	049	.08493	1.2880	49	.30094	0.0174
00050	.00187	3.3008	0050	.01367	2.2989	050	.08621	1.2788	50	.30103	0.0000
00051	.00190	3.2922	0051	.01390	2.2902	051	.08749	1.2697			
00052	.00193	3.2838	0052	.01413	2.2817	052	.08875	1.2608			
00053	.00197	3.2755	0053	.01436	2.2734	053	.09001	1.2521			
00054	.00200	3.2674	0054	.01458	2.2653	054	.09126	1.2435			
00055	.00203	3.2594	0055	.01481	2.2572	055	.09250	1.2351			
00056	.00206	3.2516	0056	.01504	2.2494	056	.09373	1.2268			
00057	.00210	3.2439	0057	.01526	2.2416	057	.09495	1.2186			
00058	.00213	3.2363	0058	.01548	2.2340	058	.09617	1.2106			
00059	.00216	3.2289	0059	.01571	2.2266	059	.09737	1.2027			
00060	.00219	3.2216	0060	.01593	2.2192	060	.09857	1.1950			

Appendix C Tables of Irreducible Polynomials over $GF(2)$

From Table C.2 all irreducible polynomials of degree 16 or less over $GF(2)$ can be found, and certain of their properties and relations among them are given. A primitive polynomial with a minimum number of nonzero coefficients and polynomials belonging to all possible exponents are given for each degree 17 through 34.

Polynomials are given in an octal representation. Each digit in the table represents three binary digits according to the following code:

0	000	2	010	4	100	6	110
1	001	3	011	5	101	7	111

The binary digits then are the coefficients of the polynomial, with the high-order coefficients at the left. For example, 3525 is listed as a tenth-degree polynomial. The binary equivalent of 3525 is 0 1 1 1 0 1 0 1 0 1 0 1, and the corresponding polynomial is $X^{10} + X^9 + X^8 + X^6 + X^4 + X^2 + 1$.

The reciprocal polynomial of an irreducible polynomial is also irreducible, and the reciprocal polynomial of a primitive polynomial is primitive. Of any pair consisting of a polynomial and its reciprocal polynomial, only one is listed in the table. Each entry that is followed by a letter in the table is an irreducible polynomial of the indicated degree. For degree 2 through 16, these polynomials along with their reciprocal polynomials comprise all irreducible polynomials of that degree.

The letters following the octal representation give the following information:

A, B, C, D	Not primitive.
E, F, G, H	Primitive.
A, B, E, F	The roots are linearly dependent.
C, D, G, H	The roots are linearly independent.
A, C, E, G	The roots of the reciprocal polynomial are linearly dependent.
B, D, F, H	The roots of the reciprocal polynomial are linearly independent.

The other numbers in the table tell the relation between the polynomials. For each degree, a primitive polynomial with a minimum number of nonzero coefficients was chosen, and this polynomial is the first in the table of polynomials of this degree. Let α denote one of its roots. Then the entry following j in the table is the minimum polynomial of α^j. The polynomials are included for each j unless for some $i < j$ either α^i and α^j are roots of the same irreducible polynomial or α^i and α^{-j} are roots of the same polynomial. The minimum polynomial of α^j is included even if it has smaller degree than is indicated for that section of the table; such polynomials are not followed by a letter in the table.

Examples. The primitive polynomial (103), or $X^6 + X + 1 = p(X)$ is the first entry in the table of sixth-degree irreducible polynomials. If α designates a root of $p(X)$, then α^3 is a root of (127) and α^5 is a root of (147). The minimum polynomial of α^9 is $(015) = X^3 + X^2 + 1$, and is of degree 3 rather than 6.

There is no entry corresponding to α^{17}. The other roots of the minimum polynomial of α^{17} are α^{34}, $\alpha^{68} = \alpha^5$, α^{10}, α^{20}, and α^{40}. Thus the minimum polynomial of α^{17} is the same as the minimum polynomial of α^5, or (147). There is no entry corresponding to α^{13}. The other roots of the minimum polynomial $p_{13}(X)$ of α^{13} are α^{26}, α^{52}, $\alpha^{104} = \alpha^{41}$, $\alpha^{82} = \alpha^{19}$, and α^{38}. None of these is listed. The roots of the reciprocal polynomial $p_{13}^*(X)$ of $p_{13}(X)$ are $\alpha^{-13} = \alpha^{50}$, $\alpha^{-26} = \alpha^{37}$, $\alpha^{-52} = \alpha^{11}$, $\alpha^{-41} = \alpha^{22}$, $\alpha^{-19} = \alpha^{44}$ and $\alpha^{-38} = \alpha^{25}$. The minimum polynomial of α^{11} is listed as (155) or $X^6 + X^5 + X^3 + X^2 + 1$. The minimum polynomial of α^{13} is the reciprocal polynomial of this, or $p_{13}(X) = X^6 + X^4 + X^3 + X + 1$:

The exponent to which a polynomial belongs can be found as follows: If α is a primitive element of $GF(2^m)$, then the order e of α^j is

$$e = \frac{(2^m - 1)}{\text{GCD}(2^m - 1, j)}$$

and e is also the exponent to which the minimum function of α^j belongs. Thus, for example, in $GF(2^{10})$, α^{55} has order 93, since

$$93 = \frac{1023}{\text{GCD}(1023, 55)} = \frac{1023}{11}$$

Thus the polynomial (3453) belongs to 93. In this regard Table C.1 is useful.

Marsh (1957) has published a table of all irreducible polynomials of degree 19 or less over $GF(2)$. In Table C.2 the polynomials are arranged in lexicographical order; this is the most convenient form for determining whether or not a given polynomial is irreducible.

For degree 19 or less, the minimum-weight polynomials given in this table were found in Marsh's tables. For degree 19 through 34, the minimum-weight polynomial was found by a trial-and-error process in which each polynomial of weight 3, then 5, was tested. The following procedure was used to test whether a polynomial $f(X)$ of degree m is primitive:

Table C.1. Factorization of $2^m - 1$ into Primes.

$2^3 - 1 = 7$	$2^{19} - 1 = 524287$
$2^4 - 1 = 3 \times 5$	$2^{20} - 1 = 3 \times 5 \times 5 \times 11 \times 31 \times 41$
$2^5 - 1 = 31$	$2^{21} - 1 = 7 \times 7 \times 127 \times 337$
$2^6 - 1 = 3 \times 3 \times 7$	$2^{22} - 1 = 3 \times 23 \times 89 \times 683$
$2^7 - 1 = 127$	$2^{23} - 1 = 47 \times 178481$
$2^8 - 1 = 3 \times 5 \times 17$	$2^{24} - 1 = 3 \times 3 \times 5 \times 7 \times 13 \times 17 \times 241$
$2^9 - 1 = 7 \times 73$	$2^{25} - 1 = 31 \times 601 \times 1801$
$2^{10} - 1 = 3 \times 11 \times 31$	$2^{26} - 1 = 3 \times 2731 \times 8191$
$2^{11} - 1 = 23 \times 89$	$2^{27} - 1 = 7 \times 73 \times 262657$
$2^{12} - 1 = 3 \times 3 \times 5 \times 7 \times 13$	$2^{28} - 1 = 3 \times 5 \times 29 \times 43 \times 113 \times 127$
$2^{13} - 1 = 8191$	$2^{29} - 1 = 233 \times 1103 \times 2089$
$2^{14} - 1 = 3 \times 43 \times 127$	$2^{30} - 1 = 3 \times 3 \times 7 \times 11 \times 31 \times 151 \times 331$
$2^{15} - 1 = 7 \times 31 \times 151$	$2^{31} - 1 = 2147483647$
$2^{16} - 1 = 3 \times 5 \times 17 \times 257$	$2^{32} - 1 = 3 \times 5 \times 17 \times 257 \times 65537$
$2^{17} - 1 = 131071$	$2^{33} - 1 = 7 \times 23 \times 89 \times 599479$
$2^{18} - 1 = 3 \times 3 \times 3 \times 7 \times 19 \times 73$	$2^{34} - 1 = 3 \times 43691 \times 131071$

1. The residues of 1, X, X^2, X^4, ..., $X^{2^{m-1}}$ are formed modulo $f(X)$.
2. These are multiplied and reduced modulo $f(X)$ to form the residue of X^{2^m-1}. If the result is not 1, the polynomial is rejected. If the result is 1, the test is continued.
3. For each factor r of $2^m - 1$, the residue of X^r is formed by multiplying together an appropriate combination of the residues formed in Step 1. If none of these is 1, the polynomial is primitive.

Each other polynomial in the table was found by solving for the dependence relations among its roots by the method illustrated at the end of Section 8.1.

Table C.2. Irreducible Polynomials of Degree ≤ 34 over $GF(2)$.

DEGREE 2	1 7H				
DEGREE 3	1 13F				
DEGREE 4	1 23F	3 37D	5 07		
DEGREE 5	1 45E	3 75G	5 67H		
DEGREE 6	1 103F	3 127B	5 147H	7 111A	9 015
11 155E	21 007				
DEGREE 7	1 211E	3 217E	5 235E	7 367H	9 277E
11 325G	13 203F	19 313H	21 345G		
DEGREE 8	1 435E	3 567B	5 763D	7 551E	9 675C
11 747H	13 453F	15 727D	17 023	19 545E	21 613D
23 543F	25 433B	27 477B	37 537F	43 703H	45 471A
51 037	85 007				
DEGREE 9	1 1021E	3 1131E	5 1461G	7 1231A	9 1423G
11 1055E	13 1167F	15 1541E	17 1333F	19 1605G	21 1027A
23 1751E	25 1743H	27 1617H	29 1553H	35 1401C	37 1157F
39 1715E	41 1563H	43 1713H	45 1175E	51 1725G	53 1225E
55 1275E	73 0013	75 1773G	77 1511C	83 1425G	85 1267E
DEGREE 10	1 2011E	3 2017B	5 2415E	7 3771G	9 2257B
11 2065A	13 2157F	15 2653B	17 3515G	19 2773F	21 3753D
23 2033F	25 2443F	27 3573D	29 2461E	31 3043D	33 0075C
35 3023H	37 3543F	39 2107B	41 2745E	43 2431E	45 3061C
47 3177H	49 3525G	51 2547B	53 2617F	55 3453D	57 3121C
59 3471G	69 2701A	71 3323H	73 3507H	75 2437B	77 2413B
83 3623H	85 2707E	87 2311A	89 2327F	91 3265G	93 3777D
99 0067	101 2055E	103 3575G	105 3607C	107 3171G	109 2047F
147 2355A	149 3025G	155 2251A	165 0051	171 3315C	173 3337H
179 3211G	341 0007				
DEGREE 11	1 4005E	3 4445E	5 4215E	7 4055E	9 6015G
11 7413H	13 4143F	15 4563F	17 4053F	19 5023F	21 5623F
23 4757B	25 4577F	27 6233H	29 6673H	31 7237H	33 7335G
35 4505E	37 5337F	39 5263F	41 5361E	43 5171E	45 6637H
47 7173H	49 5711E	51 5221E	53 6307H	55 6211G	57 5747F
59 4533F	61 4341E	67 6711G	69 6777D	71 7715G	73 6343H
75 6227H	77 6263H	79 5235E	81 7431G	83 6455G	85 5247F
87 5265E	89 5343B	91 4767F	93 5607F	99 4603F	101 6561G
103 7107H	105 7041G	107 4251E	109 5675E	111 4173F	113 4707F
115 7311C	117 5463F	119 5755E	137 6675G	139 7655G	141 5531E
147 7243H	149 7621G	151 7161G	153 4731E	155 4451E	157 6557H
163 7745G	165 7317H	167 5205E	169 4565E	171 6765G	173 7535G
179 4653F	181 5411E	183 5545E	185 7565G	199 6543H	201 5613F
203 6013H	205 7647H	211 6507H	213 6037H	215 7363H	217 7201G
219 7273H	293 7723H	299 4303B	301 5007F	307 7555G	309 4261E
331 6447H	333 5141E	339 7461G	341 5253F		
DEGREE 12	1 10123F	3 12133B	5 10115A	7 12153B	9 11765A
11 15647E	13 12513B	15 13077B	17 16533H	19 16047H	21 10065A
23 11015E	25 13377B	27 14405A	29 14127H	31 17673H	33 13311A
35 10377B	37 13565E	39 13321A	41 15341G	43 15053H	45 15173C
47 15621E	49 17703C	51 10355A	53 15321G	55 10201A	57 12331A
59 11417E	61 13505E	63 10761A	65 00141	67 13275E	69 16663C
71 11471E	73 16237E	75 16267D	77 15115C	79 12515E	81 17545C
83 12255E	85 11673B	87 17361A	89 11271E	91 10011A	93 14755C
95 17705A	97 17121G	99 17323D	101 14227H	103 12117E	105 13617A
107 14135G	109 14711G	111 15415C	113 13131E	115 13223A	117 16475C
119 14315C	121 16521E	123 13475A	133 11433B	135 10571A	137 15437G
139 12067F	141 13571A	143 12111A	145 16535C	147 17657D	149 12147F
151 14717F	153 13517B	155 14241C	157 14675G	163 10663F	165 10621A

Table C.2. Irreducible Polynomials of Degree ≤34 over *GF*(2).

DEGREE 12--CONTINUED					
167 16115G	169 16547C	171 10213B	173 12247E	175 16757D	177 16017C
179 17675E	181 10151E	183 14111A	185 14037A	187 14613H	189 13535A
195 00165	197 11441E	199 10321E	201 14067D	203 13157B	205 14513D
207 10603A	209 11067F	211 14433F	213 16457D	215 10653B	217 13563B
219 11657B	221 17513C	227 12753F	229 13431E	231 10167B	233 11313F
235 11411A	237 13737B	239 13425E	273 00023	275 14601C	277 16021G
279 16137D	281 17025G	283 15723F	285 17141A	291 15775A	293 11477F
295 11463B	297 17073C	299 16401C	301 12315A	307 14221E	309 11763B
311 12705E	313 14357F	315 17777D	325 00163	327 17233D	329 11637B
331 16407F	333 11703A	339 16003C	341 11561E	343 12673B	345 14537D
347 17711G	349 13701E	355 10467B	357 15347C	359 11075E	361 16363F
363 11045A	365 11265A	371 14043D	397 12727F	403 14373D	405 13003B
407 17057G	409 10437F	411 10077B	421 14271G	423 14313D	425 14155C
427 10245A	429 11073B	435 10743B	437 12623F	439 12007F	441 15353D
455 00111	585 00013	587 14545G	589 16311G	595 13413A	597 12265A
603 14411C	613 15413H	619 17147F	661 10605E	683 10737F	685 16355C
691 15701G	693 12345A	715 00133	717 16571C	819 00037	1365 00007
DEGREE 13	1 20033F	3 23261E	5 24623F	7 23517F	9 30741G
11 21643F	13 30171G	15 21277F	17 27777F	19 35051G	21 34723H
23 34047H	25 32535G	27 31425G	29 37505G	31 36515G	33 26077F
35 35673H	37 20635E	39 33763H	41 25745E	43 36575G	45 26653F
47 21133F	49 22441E	51 30417H	53 32517H	55 37335G	57 25327F
59 23231E	61 25511E	63 26533F	65 33343H	67 33727H	69 27271E
71 25017F	73 26041E	75 21103F	77 27263F	79 24513F	81 32311G
83 31743H	85 24037F	87 30711G	89 32641G	91 24657F	93 32437H
95 20213F	97 25633F	99 31303H	101 22525E	103 34627H	105 25775E
107 21607F	109 25363F	111 27217F	113 33741G	115 37611G	117 23077F
119 21263F	121 31011G	123 27051E	125 35477H	131 34151G	133 27405E
135 34641G	137 32445G	139 36375G	141 22675E	143 36073H	145 35121G
147 36501G	149 33057H	151 36403H	153 35567H	155 23167F	157 36217H
159 22233F	161 32333H	163 24703F	165 33163H	167 32757H	169 23761E
171 24031E	173 30025G	175 37145G	177 31327H	179 27221E	181 25577F
183 22203F	185 37437H	187 27537F	189 31035G	195 24763F	197 20245E
199 20503F	201 20761E	203 25555E	205 30357H	207 33037H	209 34401G
211 32715G	213 21447F	215 27421E	217 20363F	219 33501G	221 20425E
223 32347H	225 20677F	227 22307F	229 33441G	231 33643H	233 24165E
235 27427F	237 24601E	239 36721G	241 34363H	243 21673F	245 32167H
247 21661E	265 33357H	267 26341E	269 31653H	271 37511G	273 23003F
275 22657F	277 25035E	279 23267F	281 34005G	283 34555G	285 24205E
291 26611E	293 32671G	295 25245E	297 31407H	299 33471G	301 22613F
303 35645G	305 32371G	307 34517H	309 26225E	311 35561G	313 25663F
315 24043F	317 30643H	323 20157F	325 37151G	327 24667F	329 33325G
331 32467H	333 30667H	335 22631E	337 26617F	339 20275E	341 36625G
343 20341E	345 37527H	347 31333H	349 31071G	355 23353F	357 26243F
359 21453F	361 36015G	363 36667H	365 34767H	367 34341G	369 34547H
371 35465G	373 24421E	375 23563F	377 36037H	391 31267H	393 27133F
395 30705G	397 30465G	399 35315G	401 32231G	403 32207H	405 26101E
407 22567F	409 21755E	411 22455E	413 33705G	419 37621G	421 21405E
423 30117H	425 23021E	427 21525E	429 36465G	431 33013H	433 27531E
435 24675E	437 33133H	439 34261G	441 33405G	443 34655G	453 32173H
455 33455G	457 35165G	459 22705E	461 37123H	463 27111E	465 35455G
467 31457H	469 23055E	471 30777H	473 37653H	475 24325E	477 31251G
547 35163H	549 33433H	551 37243H	553 27515E	555 32137H	557 26743F
563 30277H	565 20627F	567 35057H	569 24315E	571 24727F	581 30331G
583 34273H	585 23207F	587 31113H	589 36023H	595 27373F	597 20737F
599 36235G	601 21575E	603 26215E	605 21211E	611 20311E	613 34003H
615 34027H	617 20065E	619 22051E	621 22127F	627 23621E	629 24465E
651 26457F	653 31201G	659 34035G	661 27227F	663 22561E	665 21615E
667 22013F	669 23365E	675 26213F	677 26775E	679 32635G	681 33631G
683 32743H	685 31767H	691 34413H	693 22037F	695 30651G	697 26565E
711 22141E	713 22471E	715 35271G	717 37445G	723 22717F	725 26505E
727 24411E	729 24575E	731 23707F	733 25173F	739 21367F	741 25161E
743 24147F	793 36307H	795 24417F	805 20237F	807 36771G	809 37327H
811 27735E	813 31223H	819 36373H	821 33121G	823 32751G	825 33523H

Table C.2. Irreducible Polynomials of Degree ≤34 over *GF*(2).

DEGREE 13--CONTINUED

839	26415E	841	23737F	843	25425E	845	34603H	851	31047H	853	37305G
855	21315E	857	35777H	859	32725G	869	20571E	871	30301G	873	34757H
875	21067F	877	25151E	1171	27513F	1173	33721G	1179	34775G	1189	23571E
1195	27411E	1197	20457F	1203	21557F	1205	30177H	1227	26347F	1229	27477F
1235	34243H	1237	27235E	1323	25175E	1325	31231G	1331	31131G	1333	25503F
1355	33045G	1357	24253F	1363	35351G	1365	26053F				

DEGREE 14

		1	42103F	3	40547B	5	43333E	7	51761E	9	54055A
11	40503F	13	77141G	15	47645A	17	62677G	19	44103F	21	46425A
23	45145E	25	76303G	27	62603D	29	64457G	31	57231E	33	52737B
35	64167F	37	60153F	39	62115C	41	55753F	43	72427D	45	64715A
47	70423H	49	47153F	51	67653D	53	53255E	55	41753F	57	74247D
59	40725E	61	42667F	63	65301A	65	67517H	67	45653F	69	72501C
71	67425G	73	42163F	75	73757D	77	45555E	79	74561G	81	60523B
83	53705E	85	40123E	87	41403B	89	56625E	91	70311E	93	75547C
95	45627F	97	67335G	99	56733A	101	53253F	103	66411E	105	57745A
107	65551G	109	43017F	111	62125A	113	71073E	115	67333H	117	70677C
119	52215E	121	44177F	123	70535C	125	46327F	127	71747D	129	00203
131	61335G	133	43161E	135	46047B	137	60645G	139	40317F	141	47727A
143	65001G	145	54335E	147	76175C	149	65153H	151	50351E	153	42711A
155	41625E	157	44435E	159	41163A	161	47667F	163	41441E	165	54175A
167	45713F	169	75267H	171	72051C	173	64223H	175	42337F	177	51275A
179	65155E	181	63015E	183	57521A	185	67173H	187	50661E	189	41735A
191	50645E	193	72433F	195	47043B	197	65133H	199	53543F	201	62431A
203	42777F	205	47203F	207	46605A	209	64377H	211	73725G	213	43611A
215	42301A	217	51145E	219	44307B	221	73647H	223	74427H	225	53747A
227	45511E	229	42637F	231	63117D	233	40363E	235	75201G	237	63155C
239	72717G	241	56557F	243	75363D	245	70553F	247	66675G	249	55501A
251	60263H	261	53043B	263	75303F	265	74315E	267	66031A	269	62505G
271	60057H	273	54473A	275	60253F	277	45671E	279	71525C	281	61443E
283	64635G	285	64475C	287	67401G	289	44203F	291	50343A	293	77747H
295	54101E	297	65645A	299	41177F	301	65661A	303	42361A	305	43047F
307	45563F	309	50717A	311	53233E	313	67101G	315	62251C	317	64251E
323	40635E	325	46113E	327	44367B	329	40665E	331	63331G	333	71545C
335	73107H	337	42727F	339	43775A	341	65667E	343	61677H	345	53525A
347	52723F	349	42323F	351	41433B	353	43173E	355	46305E	357	45663B
359	71315E	361	44031E	363	73457B	365	52577E	367	52621E	369	40063B
371	52027F	373	45201E	375	77001C	377	45737E	379	64035G	381	52225A
387	00253	389	60765G	391	66545G	393	71323A	395	62767G	397	73137H
399	40145A	401	63265G	403	47551E	405	71711C	407	40353F	409	76055G
411	70065C	413	73527F	415	67201G	417	43723B	419	61251E	421	47357F
423	62261C	425	50575E	427	61267H	429	40511A	431	71721G	433	65121G
435	61053D	437	45371E	439	54627E	441	77703A	443	65057H	445	76225E
451	73071G	453	52553B	455	60025E	457	60471G	459	53513B	461	67303H
463	42763F	465	52261A	467	53657F	469	75443F	471	67267D	473	53373B
475	65165E	477	44037B	479	54737F	481	61175E	483	65031A	485	51707E
487	57627F	489	57251A	491	44073F	493	45761E	495	63463C	529	65277F
531	55247B	533	56171E	535	63513H	537	43377B	539	45641E	541	63227H
547	54243F	549	62055C	551	53061E	553	46321E	555	51431A	557	71147H
559	64053D	561	41551A	563	75521E	565	46701E	567	53763B	569	56463F
571	77057G	573	41105A	579	41171A	581	41307F	583	70425E	585	74117D
587	50135E	589	67737H	591	47615A	593	53057F	595	55103F	597	54443B
599	53051E	601	61555G	603	64157D	605	57407F	611	64653F	613	65513H
615	73603D	617	47525E	619	55165E	621	64215C	623	76377H	625	57365E
627	50557B	629	45725E	631	71301G	633	56465A	635	51745A	645	00217
647	47233F	649	53015E	651	53361A	653	46215E	655	50613E	657	77211C
659	46565E	661	44141E	663	55771A	665	71263G	667	41315E	669	62225C
675	51565A	677	76267H	679	62467H	681	64003C	683	71645G	685	76223G
687	52627A	689	70665G	691	45773F	693	64033D	695	45533E	697	50007F
699	45257B	701	45311E	707	44023F	709	72153G	711	60117D	713	46617E
715	70461G	717	47513B	719	65575E	721	56435E	723	67157C	725	71403G
727	46107F	729	65007A	731	50667B	733	55331E	739	52017F	741	51317B
743	66163F	745	70767G	747	70215C	749	76401G	751	63043H	753	63753D
755	43317F	781	77031G	783	45617B	785	52603F	787	57503F	789	63667D
791	75761G	793	60075G	795	72307B	797	51633F	803	57475E	805	61533G

Table C.2. Irreducible Polynomials of Degree ≤34 over *GF*(2).

DEGREE 14--CONTINUED

807 60561C	809 53575E	811 62027H	813 64633C	815 67123F	817 43445A
819 73655C	821 54003F	823 62347F	825 63271C	827 71337F	837 57715A
839 54635E	841 46505E	843 64407C	845 57017E	847 54751E	849 42417A
851 57033F	853 54077F	855 42567B	857 50455E	859 62533H	861 42411A
867 74133D	869 72441G	871 43577F	873 52353B	875 55325E	877 67527G
879 75605C	881 52467F	883 61757F	885 66105C	887 51261E	889 62723D
903 00375	905 63537H	907 52457E	909 44735A	911 62413H	913 51671E
915 41001A	917 70773H	919 56031E	921 60227D	923 71345G	925 46125E
931 40655E	933 44221A	935 55323F	937 76005E	939 55435A	941 42531E
943 62671E	945 74277D	947 64617G	949 52137F	951 56637B	953 47753F
955 46773F	1093 72155G	1095 56067A	1097 63007E	1099 47111E	1101 54021A
1107 44523B	1109 54257F	1111 63567H	1113 43215A	1115 73665G	1117 45335E
1123 44147E	1125 62731C	1127 41657F	1129 77235G	1131 65643B	1133 51055E
1139 47637F	1141 40071E	1143 47771A	1161 00271	1163 57541E	1165 57107F
1171 61621G	1173 51511A	1175 57201E	1177 70251G	1179 43633B	1181 53315E
1187 44343F	1189 55705E	1191 40413B	1193 64641E	1195 44567E	1197 46451A
1203 60241C	1205 65705E	1207 71117H	1209 66703D	1211 53477F	1221 45355A
1223 74531G	1225 74607H	1227 71763C	1229 76707H	1235 60235G	1237 47673F
1239 54321A	1241 75571G	1243 77515G	1245 57611A	1251 55643B	1253 46175E
1255 74357H	1257 70267D	1259 46461E	1301 77345G	1303 51243F	1305 76151C
1307 56061E	1309 66427G	1315 54517F	1317 72465C	1319 50733F	1321 74045G
1323 71057D	1325 73143F	1331 51231E	1333 70201C	1335 77631C	1337 64021G
1351 72643H	1353 41777B	1355 71675G	1357 63073H	1363 47537E	1365 61261A
1367 65227H	1369 55073F	1371 77727B	1373 61363H	1379 43701E	1381 65147H
1383 52267B	1385 63153F	1387 72337G	1389 56607A	1395 40371A	1397 42721A
1419 00211	1421 75273F	1427 73555G	1429 67225G	1431 76617C	1433 74711E
1435 50325E	1437 70713C	1443 72513D	1445 57737F	1447 61333G	1449 40327A
1451 55111E	1453 40633F	1459 61641G	1461 65315C	1463 43647F	1465 67621G
1479 62745C	1481 41755E	1483 65727F	1485 74263D	1587 41573B	1589 55631E
1591 66405A	1593 60121C	1607 71615E	1609 77615G	1611 41447B	1613 46437F
1619 70633H	1621 65615G	1623 64605C	1625 55075E	1627 73151G	1637 75033H
1639 57327F	1641 66277D	1643 56007F	1645 55703F	1651 77277D	1677 00345
1683 57743A	1685 42645E	1687 50045E	1689 74255C	1691 53623E	1701 50477B
1703 52071E	1705 61237H	1707 67533B	1709 55417F	1715 45173E	1717 61461G
1719 43731A	1721 56717E	1735 54041E	1737 44613A	1739 70341G	1741 52065E
1747 56345E	1749 44441A	1751 76663H	1753 50777F	1755 70443D	2341 55471E
2347 53727F	2349 65637C	2355 57143B	2357 44741E	2379 67627D	2381 77177G
2387 51213E	2389 70273H	2395 62101G	2405 50241E	2411 65263H	2413 41241A
2451 00357	2453 76047H	2459 75723F	2469 73145C	2475 61377D	2477 41357F
2643 56421A	2645 76213H	2667 64213D	2709 00313	2731 41235E	2733 67605C
2739 44537B	2741 76505G	2763 65375C	2765 50721E	2771 75517H	2861 65357G
2867 47121E	5461 00007				

DEGREE 15	1 100003F	3 102043F	5 110013F	7 125253B
9 102067F	11 104307F	13 100317F	15 177775E	17 103451E
19 110075E	21 127701A	23 102061E	25 114725E	27 103251E
29 163005G	31 103437A	33 112611E	35 137733B	37 120265E
39 117423F	41 106341E	43 161007H	45 174003E	47 113337E
49 125263B	51 126007E	53 105257E	55 114467E	57 177207G
59 147047F	61 111511E	63 127635A	65 114633E	67 133663F
69 102171E	71 170465G	73 131427E	75 161615E	77 136143A
79 115155E	81 123067F	83 102561E	85 170057H	87 125235E
89 173117E	91 125747B	93 124677B	95 134531E	97 125507F
99 171737G	101 152417F	103 142305G	105 146255C	107 120043F
109 136173F	111 122231E	113 164705G	115 177757F	117 146637E
119 177535C	121 102643F	123 103145E	125 112751E	127 151537G
129 115135E	131 137067E	133 122707A	135 174443E	137 100541E
139 112273F	141 145573F	143 114273F	145 124511E	147 122563B
149 140703F	151 101361A	153 103125E	155 150451C	157 147303G
159 123023F	161 103751A	163 154463H	165 177541G	167 101561E
169 144473G	171 162375G	173 131013F	175 117767A	177 160521G
179 164727G	181 102367E	183 147363F	185 132367E	187 172431E
189 133627B	191 156333E	193 114505E	195 176561G	197 152235G
199 127143F	201 176133E	203 123075A	205 173357G	207 117143E
209 144461E	211 151447G	213 173661E	215 151043F	217 142327B

Table C.2. Irreducible Polynomials of Degree ≤34 over *GF*(2).

DEGREE 15--CONTINUED

219 166775E	221 153143G	223 172213F	225 105213E	227 156053H
229 156745G	231 170623B	233 140373G	235 152361G	237 142157H
239 117633F	241 103605E	243 116361E	245 137523A	247 101705E
249 116135E	251 102337E	253 173515G	259 136321A	261 120447F
263 117511E	265 115141E	267 173613F	269 131735E	271 114225E
273 121125A	275 136577F	277 113227E	279 114533B	281 166151E
283 112231E	285 165033E	287 120177B	289 117547F	291 126051E
293 111335E	295 177101G	297 143703G	299 106047E	301 137427B
303 110427F	305 131211E	307 110037F	309 160511G	311 153731G
313 144275G	315 151513C	317 133775E	319 134447E	321 127347E
323 163767H	325 110717E	327 175001E	329 100377A	331 125121E
333 136237F	335 132103F	337 171035G	339 132651E	341 134105A
343 100261A	345 170227H	347 101233F	349 100445E	351 144707G
353 165355E	355 150243H	357 163353C	359 114041E	361 113025E
363 104447F	365 143301G	367 165011G	369 137361E	371 117201A
373 141655G	375 160113G	377 106715E	379 140575E	381 112123E
387 140733F	389 124243E	391 116073E	393 147321E	395 123721E
397 150225G	399 134741A	401 157111G	403 134411A	405 172317G
407 153327E	409 140573H	411 113625E	413 101673B	415 170543F
417 176735E	419 115307F	421 141635E	423 157241G	425 153005E
427 167051A	429 177175G	431 146331G	433 166541G	435 102513F
437 123121E	439 162463G	441 134037B	443 174571E	445 123433F
447 150167H	449 175465E	451 113255E	453 137325A	455 123045A
457 133571E	459 135215E	461 110221E	463 157435E	465 121437A
467 177707G	469 143501C	471 161667F	473 157427G	475 150671G
477 112407F	479 165563E	481 112053E	483 135363B	485 130617F
487 125613F	489 114713F	491 165113G	493 143733G	495 162155E
497 135017B	499 126753F	501 137765E	503 106577E	521 112113F
523 105555E	525 153425C	527 115313A	529 105761E	531 132165E
533 176147H	535 114621E	537 135751E	539 152763C	541 124757F
543 112245E	545 123221E	547 141757G	549 160547F	551 101331E
553 156065C	555 156725G	557 113373E	559 137643F	561 156237G
563 141151G	565 126015E	567 171335C	569 146717H	571 130305E
573 121355E	579 166021G	581 145361C	583 134325E	585 157155E
587 124647E	589 163761C	591 114457E	593 155243G	595 153137D
597 137253F	599 151551G	601 113645E	603 150305G	605 163745G
607 165473F	609 113057B	611 160173H	613 177663F	615 161117H
617 144115E	619 156635G	621 150633H	623 115061A	625 143253H
627 165451G	629 160305E	631 146025E	633 106751E	635 132625E
637 160553D	643 123561E	645 116637F	647 111423E	649 117107E
651 166761C	653 153555G	655 132127F	657 112333E	659 135267F
661 146727H	663 132753F	665 143343A	667 131705E	669 141005E
671 113147F	673 125323F	675 123235E	677 103653F	679 173025C
681 120661E	683 154545G	685 133553F	687 132001E	689 153773G
691 175241G	693 160237B	695 171131E	697 172415E	699 145111G
701 122603F	707 170507C	709 160757G	711 171207G	713 147553B
715 112365E	717 146111E	719 122003F	721 121273B	723 122005E
725 135401E	727 102441E	729 175515G	731 132507E	733 130223F
735 142713C	737 102615E	739 105713F	741 134241E	743 173643F
745 163617G	747 175043E	749 132051A	751 104217F	753 115523F
755 120247B	757 164447H	759 173667F	761 137051E	775 104073B
777 177065C	779 117071E	781 115537E	783 135201E	785 146643F
787 113465E	789 152263G	791 177617D	793 104755E	795 147415G
797 126001E	799 170307F	801 174425E	803 112475E	805 173263C
807 176643H	809 130303F	811 125471E	813 173711G	815 165547E
817 163723G	819 116075A	821 150677G	823 175227G	825 166407H
827 152447H	829 126205E	835 120557E	837 160335A	839 125543E
841 144377H	843 100713E	845 121251E	847 141123D	849 174517F
851 106251E	853 116277F	855 106611E	857 174563H	859 140023H
861 132037A	863 147767G	865 164531G	867 155065E	869 146263F
871 160401G	873 102057F	875 146133C	877 117021E	879 147003F
881 127723F	883 120471E	885 162455G	887 130627F	889 152135C
891 157057H	901 162153F	903 151755C	905 170277H	907 165633H
909 173105E	911 102507F	913 176037H	915 171627G	917 162171C
919 130745E	921 177517H	923 114327F	925 127167F	927 133113E

Table C.2. Irreducible Polynomials of Degree ≤34 over $GF(2)$.

DEGREE 15--CONTINUED

929	160461E	931	117137B	933	134323F	935	123361E	937	105237F
939	166737F	941	147571G	943	127743F	945	116351A	947	157315E
949	162645G	951	162403G	953	105335E	955	124767E	957	175301E
963	134755E	965	116645E	967	143307G	969	124125E	971	155261G
973	104163A	975	167753F	977	127423F	979	115667F	981	140171E
983	133041E	985	156767H	987	116037A	989	142267G	991	130635E
1057	000057	1059	104427F	1061	113075E	1063	162133H	1065	120717F
1067	144713F	1069	121605E	1071	122225A	1073	134657E	1075	130125E
1077	177621G	1079	110741E	1081	136745E	1083	152531G	1085	115455A
1091	161235G	1093	144137G	1095	140675E	1097	145277G	1099	114303B
1101	101507E	1103	115271E	1105	151735E	1107	157205G	1109	114011E
1111	171125E	1113	147071A	1115	134721E	1117	122123F	1123	104735E
1125	133011E	1127	162337A	1129	105261E	1131	101427E	1133	156563F
1135	103663E	1137	146043H	1139	151403H	1141	100157A	1143	163653E
1145	105413F	1147	143651C	1157	156157E	1159	102463F	1161	151025G
1163	176657H	1165	166425G	1167	103617E	1169	160021A	1171	161277H
1173	165565G	1175	152153F	1177	111243E	1179	165655G	1181	134165E
1187	171467H	1189	150161E	1191	122011E	1193	125403F	1195	170007H
1197	167765C	1199	103415E	1201	137703E	1203	111563F	1205	147305G
1207	156257F	1209	175177B	1211	141317B	1213	177467H	1219	140421G
1221	127071E	1223	142457F	1225	122021A	1227	146771E	1229	110211E
1231	134567F	1233	156321G	1235	114335E	1237	111603E	1239	121275A
1241	110103E	1243	127161E	1245	163273H	1251	144533F	1253	173135C
1255	155445E	1257	140441E	1259	103761E	1261	173523F	1263	167307F
1265	127457F	1267	102205A	1269	112251E	1291	106311E	1293	141633F
1295	135151A	1297	106641E	1299	102265E	1301	164453G	1303	163071G
1305	111641E	1307	134403E	1309	102667A	1315	177055E	1317	115373F
1319	150231G	1321	175651G	1323	160377B	1325	136063E	1327	101073F
1329	165303G	1331	116675E	1333	140221A	1335	100201E	1337	103223B
1339	105415E	1341	122445E	1347	143631E	1349	137441E	1351	104421A
1353	154023H	1355	127225E	1357	176427H	1359	151265C	1361	150215E
1363	144225G	1365	115205A	1367	123307E	1369	133437E	1371	166653E
1373	101515E	1379	126023B	1381	166553H	1383	172701E	1385	140271G
1387	121143E	1389	111577E	1391	132747E	1393	143057C	1395	111137B
1397	127401E	1399	150317E	1401	177731G	1415	155335G	1417	123057F
1419	117715E	1421	162657B	1423	171745G	1425	130527F	1427	144467G
1429	115045E	1431	177115G	1433	155751G	1435	103767A	1437	115127E
1443	176741E	1445	141475G	1447	112553E	1449	154307D	1451	105621E
1453	170051G	1455	147707F	1457	160445A	1459	161031E	1461	131405E
1463	164121A	1465	111003F	1467	167331E	1469	165311G	1475	157405G
1477	140557A	1479	156655G	1481	164561G	1483	114231E	1485	106407F
1487	111033F	1489	172123G	1491	146667D	1493	143523G	1495	170765G
1497	105725E	1499	132155E	1501	150261G	1507	122517E	1509	107567E
1511	166267E	1561	153461C	1563	166011G	1565	133445E	1571	156365G
1573	176111G	1575	137331A	1577	165407G	1579	106445E	1581	145551C
1583	124341E	1585	127215E	1587	135005E	1589	117731A	1591	110141E
1593	152345G	1595	164441G	1605	172621G	1607	143567G	1609	153443H
1611	146203E	1613	120417F	1615	103553F	1617	110567A	1619	126067F
1621	140747F	1623	107037F	1625	135503E	1627	126735E	1629	172445G
1635	117131E	1637	105173F	1639	105071E	1641	174167G	1643	114745A
1645	133407A	1647	136215E	1649	153113H	1651	141321E	1653	132523F
1655	136335E	1657	167255E	1671	146301G	1673	131265A	1675	120133F
1677	157557E	1679	107711E	1681	174751E	1683	133257F	1685	151217G
1687	144653C	1689	176203H	1691	155213H	1693	135207F	1699	131367F
1701	146543C	1703	130033F	1705	166311A	1707	150213G	1709	143227F
1711	176013G	1713	147751G	1715	131543B	1717	131111E	1719	111267F
1721	144151G	1723	110433F	1733	171173F	1735	116367F	1737	115421E
1739	112223F	1741	111635E	1743	157165C	1745	135223F	1747	106143F
1749	176015G	1751	142461G	1753	154233E	1755	114677F	1757	103363A
1763	150327F	1765	126325E	1767	126105A	1769	111713F	1771	172303B
1773	170763G	1775	124175E	1777	176357F	1807	164667E	1809	136611E
1811	163123E	1813	151037D	1815	121431E	1817	110165E	1819	172005G
1821	104265E	1827	154763A	1829	152703D	1831	163555G	1833	135021E
1835	124071E	1837	164247H	1839	166113H	1841	101625A	1843	145427H
1845	106633F	1847	155437E	1849	174633H	1851	161657H	1861	174605G

Table C.2. Irreducible Polynomials of Degree ≤ 34 over $GF(2)$.

DEGREE 15--CONTINUED

1863	136701E	1865	144425E	1867	126747F	1869	157441C	1871	167015E
1873	142737H	1875	152301E	1877	131727E	1879	120221E	1881	102147E
1883	106457B	1885	152253H	1891	157645A	1893	141541G	1895	170325E
1897	141677C	1899	102733E	1901	135443F	1903	124251E	1905	150731G
1907	127137F	1909	100347F	1911	130415A	2185	147161G	2187	154247F
2189	161205G	2195	101313E	2197	175203F	2199	154507G	2201	121055A
2203	113061E	2205	170211C	2211	102763E	2213	167367H	2215	106503F
2217	133641E	2219	160175C	2221	161061E	2227	103035E	2229	173037F
2231	130737F	2233	166137C	2235	130017F	2245	122213F	2247	144577D
2249	117027F	2251	106273F	2253	107217F	2259	146373F	2261	153445C
2263	145727D	2265	121451A	2267	146607F	2269	113543F	2275	161013A
2277	177131G	2279	112633E	2281	137545E	2283	140227F	2285	112377F
2323	123163F	2325	100725A	2327	162315G	2329	155027G	2331	173551C
2333	132357F	2339	141231E	2341	117457F	2343	143403H	2345	124005A
2347	137601E	2349	143271G	2355	143727F	2357	107447F	2359	136401A
2361	157711G	2363	170337E	2373	166257D	2375	131733E	2377	176453H
2379	116057F	2381	156773H	2387	114371A	2389	155505G	2391	100641E
2393	151573E	2395	106713F	2397	177751G	2403	175601G	2405	177563G
2407	155175G	2409	170367G	2411	132015E	2413	126375E	2419	170433F
2421	151747G	2443	173153B	2445	111505E	2451	127243F	2453	107323F
2455	106745E	2457	165327B	2459	153577H	2461	150341G	2467	155737H
2469	150005G	2471	146007A	2473	146155E	2475	117655E	2477	101023E
2483	126227F	2485	173163B	2487	103175E	2489	105143F	2491	174743G
2501	101433F	2503	155757H	2505	121017F	2507	100425E	2509	126657E
2515	172363H	2517	120463E	2519	154561G	2601	126771E	2603	156161E
2605	147725G	2611	177527D	2613	121641E	2615	111365E	2617	125057E
2631	142611G	2633	110435E	2635	104575A	2637	164313G	2643	126163E
2645	112347F	2647	126155E	2649	131667F	2651	141365G	2653	116307B
2659	143531E	2661	141445E	2663	104141E	2665	167001G	2667	110343A
2669	111047F	2675	107121E	2677	106125E	2699	167203G	2701	175337F
2707	165201G	2709	106767B	2711	152351G	2713	144731G	2715	161043G
2717	113171E	2723	133533A	2725	175405G	2727	177231G	2729	127653E
2731	165535G	2733	114701E	2739	146177H	2741	121327E	2743	132277F
2745	153175G	2759	155407A	2761	145433H	2763	167463H	2765	104263A
2771	127437F	2773	176255E	2775	134435E	2777	124335E	2779	143373D
2781	170501G	2787	126711E	2789	103257E	2791	120601E	2793	155773B
2839	134255E	2841	103737F	2843	164001G	2845	161147F	2851	135565E
2853	110573E	2855	175711E	2857	116631E	2859	131623E	2861	155725G
2867	154537F	2869	114347B	2871	140755G	2873	113515E	2887	120155E
2889	160137E	2891	163647B	2893	121725E	2899	157255G	2901	141401G
2903	141125G	2905	107337A	2907	117125E	2909	144603H	2915	147635E
2917	154331G	2919	115607A	2921	154411E	2923	154155E	2925	122275E
2931	136457F	2957	126433F	2963	154515E	2965	150371G	2967	173331E
2969	146753E	2971	132741E	2973	145477H	3171	000073	3173	124115E
3175	127365E	3177	107645E	3179	117443F	3181	163335E	3187	115675E
3213	131651A	3219	170523H	3221	167313H	3223	137127F	3225	140205E
3227	102357B	3237	163365G	3239	172027H	3241	131165A	3243	162241E
3245	142223G	3251	164155G	3253	176753H	3255	152433B	3257	125271E
3271	177377G	3273	100647E	3275	121101E	3277	142751E	3283	115721A
3285	144437G	3287	177443H	3289	101613F	3291	142633H	3301	156527H
3355	165725E	3365	110405E	3367	107675A	3369	115133E	3371	101551E
3373	133213E	3379	155621C	3381	114363A	3383	161253F	3385	160413F
3399	127077E	3401	136213E	3403	171115E	3405	121553E	3411	140007G
3413	116601E	3415	147437H	3417	100223E	3419	126643E	3429	133231E
3431	162037H	3433	141027E	3435	125255E	3437	166275A	3475	171621G
3477	107373E	3479	125337A	3481	110255E	3483	114611E	3493	114055A
3495	110501E	3497	104111E	3499	146375G	3501	126557F	3507	125361A
3509	121617F	3511	103333F	3513	103053E	3527	171371E	4681	000013
4683	133261A	4685	123735E	4691	142175G	4693	131645E	4699	167637G
4709	155303H	4715	160215G	4717	163275G	4755	124053F	4757	133201E
4763	141115G	4773	161105E	4779	100021E	4781	116567B	4787	145675G
4789	123471E	4811	137613F	4813	105701E	4819	121305E	4821	146705E
4907	124621A	4909	122443E	4915	123537E	4917	124317F	4939	106677E
4941	160723H	4947	131601E	4949	113405A	4955	155517G	5285	000045
5291	155707H	5293	134277F	5299	140513C	5301	111041A	5323	127273F

Table C.2. Irreducible Polynomials of Degree ≤ 34 over *GF*(2).

DEGREE 15--CONTINUED

5325	117243F	5331	141707H	5333	134205E	5419	107417F	5421	122401E
5427	170037E	5429	107127E	5451	161465E	5453	171027C	5459	174707H
5461	145453E								

DEGREE	16	1	210013F	3	215435A	5	227215A	7	234313F
9	225657B	11	233303F	13	307107H	15	311513D	17	336523D
19	307527H	21	363501C	23	306357H	25	353573D	27	357333D
29	201735E	31	272201E	33	310327D	35	304341C	37	242413F
39	327721C	41	270155E	43	302157H	45	374111C	47	210205E
49	305667H	51	237403B	53	236107F	55	212113B	57	314061C
59	271055E	61	313371G	63	333575C	65	267313B	67	311405G
69	323527D	71	346355G	73	350513H	75	237421A	77	203213F
79	233503F	81	261105A	83	306221G	85	267075A	87	235063B
89	244461E	91	204015E	93	327421C	95	226455A	97	202301E
99	351641C	101	376311G	103	201637F	105	365705C	107	352125G
109	273435E	111	202545A	113	243575E	115	251645A	117	277535A
119	327277D	121	250723F	123	340047D	125	274761A	127	226135E
129	357047D	131	214443F	133	277213F	135	315633D	137	300205G
139	367737H	141	230535A	143	342567H	145	265157B	147	371771C
149	217137F	151	262367F	153	301663D	155	370565C	157	201045E
159	304731C	161	303657H	163	212653F	165	245351A	167	347433H
169	260237F	171	311651C	173	256005E	175	206353B	177	362053D
179	352603H	181	310017H	183	333013D	185	256415A	187	376175C
189	243513B	191	312301G	193	260475E	195	347211C	197	215345E
199	201551E	201	362555C	203	333643H	205	304261C	207	230541A
209	250311E	211	333117H	213	274317B	215	301425C	217	247353F
219	254601A	221	212063B	223	207661E	225	317171C	227	214215E
229	322661G	231	274635A	233	326035G	235	200215A	237	324127D
239	230653F	241	342105G	243	305471C	245	242437B	247	363637H
249	330561C	251	211473F	253	266663F	255	361617D	257	000717
259	255517F	261	344733D	263	311155G	265	340207D	267	273211A
269	366421G	271	221257F	273	207753B	275	226315A	277	250017F
279	243111A	281	242225E	283	204703F	285	323563D	287	230451E
289	323341C	291	271725A	293	353263H	295	306575C	297	271251A
299	335227H	301	213375E	303	340333D	305	232013B	307	312405G
309	233017B	311	266701E	313	262351E	315	324141C	317	365221G
319	213651E	321	200365A	323	215613B	325	207221A	327	323077D
329	274627F	331	302335G	333	251211A	335	262421A	337	360667H
339	223133B	341	356255G	343	337553H	345	215015A	347	221213F
349	276531E	351	325413D	353	362737H	355	240171A	357	241173B
359	274353F	361	222563F	363	231753B	365	227065A	367	217451E
369	254471A	371	356221G	373	235275E	375	372075C	377	357527H
379	241341E	381	335263D	383	311515G	385	202155A	387	254241A
389	370137H	391	300405C	393	227157B	395	237733B	397	207717F
399	303375C	401	257051E	403	245367F	405	324631C	407	274621E
409	211101E	411	324755C	413	326261G	415	236555A	417	341343D
419	220625E	421	332745G	423	374163D	425	264255A	427	234015E
429	206635A	431	320731G	433	243631E	435	325757D	437	241677F
439	217473F	441	366373D	443	230355E	445	301653D	447	264433B
449	302321G	451	333323H	453	344045C	455	317163D	457	265401E
459	325033D	461	341667H	463	276645E	465	346725C	467	301535G
469	342325G	471	202265A	473	247617F	475	325475C	477	343213D
479	237351E	481	341741G	483	361353D	485	260665A	487	276727F
489	273141A	491	233743F	493	252023B	495	272423B	497	265617F
499	273015E	501	267421A	503	351353H	505	377171C	507	317357D
517	202703F	519	241245A	521	356057H	523	217633F	525	277215A
527	257643B	529	267507F	531	311661C	533	235145E	535	202411A
537	205003B	539	366155G	541	212115E	543	375437D	545	354377D
547	236511E	549	277745A	551	241251E	553	211571E	555	245733B
557	362633H	559	201031E	561	371643D	563	340311G	565	200751A
567	232211A	569	341345G	571	374721G	573	310745C	575	227063B
577	271161E	579	322367D	581	375213H	583	330073H	585	273007B
587	341147H	589	371427H	591	200451A	593	251741E	595	345267D
597	205143B	599	212355E	601	252623F	603	331627D	605	241175A
607	355507H	609	261177B	611	317203H	613	361541G	615	363211C

Table C.2. Irreducible Polynomials of Degree ≤ 34 over $GF(2)$.

DEGREE 16--CONTINUED

617 366345G	619 337521G	621 362745C	623 366171G	625 204227B
627 222473B	629 233725A	631 346101G	633 261253B	635 354723D
637 262073F	643 206603F	645 317531C	647 215343F	649 311203H
651 221245A	653 324747H	655 301065C	657 223561A	659 232643F
661 363271G	663 253723B	665 260145A	667 337071G	669 273361A
671 224611E	673 267615E	675 377373D	677 316431G	679 237337F
681 214143B	683 272071E	685 364225C	687 230371A	689 240675E
691 306643H	693 366537D	695 233521A	697 325173D	699 241647B
701 244333F	703 311733H	705 222123B	707 234777F	709 304535G
711 202141A	713 256461E	715 374343D	717 341061C	719 375761G
721 323175G	723 236041A	725 260725A	727 222017F	729 352077D
731 231253B	733 330233H	735 210447B	737 324073H	739 306015G
741 316757D	743 302115G	745 322031C	747 226255A	749 351225G
751 344623H	753 211125A	755 337017D	757 302063H	759 375223D
761 303361G	763 313751G	765 366557D	771 000573	773 326137H
775 256553B	777 223463B	779 302577H	781 234667F	783 225405A
785 201717B	787 230257F	789 357617D	791 367333H	793 346243H
795 272445A	797 325723H	799 311103D	801 310267D	803 330177H
805 302635C	807 372301C	809 246613F	811 264507F	813 341043D
815 275357B	817 301101G	819 262135A	821 350403H	823 367033H
825 301347D	827 201607F	829 202607F	831 212737B	833 232315A
835 201367B	837 222003B	839 223121E	841 200475E	843 221151A
845 316261C	847 245265E	849 226447B	851 234155E	853 305235G
855 222267B	857 335105G	859 227475E	861 362577D	863 224671E
865 356471C	867 223255A	869 301213H	871 321453H	873 341645C
875 350277D	877 240315E	879 220343B	881 343503H	883 366673H
885 337063D	887 225733F	889 221101E	891 343547D	893 231265E
899 315737H	901 300733D	903 270403B	905 271347B	907 356741G
909 260775A	911 204343F	913 225051E	915 332655C	917 276241E
919 244251E	921 311165C	923 201771E	925 305263D	927 337547D
929 234545E	931 261141E	933 374765C	935 335205C	937 303463H
939 356233D	941 256243F	943 373053H	945 204025A	947 346467H
949 256653F	951 310671C	953 274757F	955 247275A	957 277047B
959 332663H	961 367231G	963 233035A	965 355155C	967 352653H
969 213625A	971 320225G	973 323547H	975 276031A	977 213253F
979 226073F	981 201153B	983 373363H	985 352123D	987 367065C
989 301451G	991 262233F	993 373553D	995 270253B	997 263737F
999 214267B	1001 217237F	1003 257507B	1005 365501C	1007 205535E
1041 343055C	1043 344651G	1045 211245A	1047 306573D	1049 264001E
1051 343655G	1053 201515A	1055 370743D	1057 313415G	1059 307713D
1061 320445G	1063 222425E	1065 243043B	1067 214371E	1069 370321G
1071 265231A	1073 365405G	1075 305301C	1077 364355C	1079 312615G
1081 300155G	1083 333177D	1085 341703D	1091 370275G	1093 267205E
1095 325731C	1097 376443H	1099 332033H	1101 266167B	1103 326461G
1105 244547B	1107 212647B	1109 322171G	1111 206257F	1113 277641A
1115 310517D	1117 312247H	1119 365307D	1121 310437H	1123 344513H
1125 302167D	1127 337245G	1129 247743F	1131 275141A	1133 216607F
1135 317567D	1137 255355A	1139 353153D	1141 222633F	1143 254543B
1145 211377B	1147 243135E	1149 377147D	1155 253207B	1157 337311G
1159 272175E	1161 222541A	1163 226367F	1165 324433D	1167 360623D
1169 315713H	1171 337503H	1173 326065C	1175 207307B	1177 232045E
1179 337517D	1181 353733H	1183 372435G	1185 333515C	1187 213523F
1189 200535E	1191 261263B	1193 273073F	1195 264463B	1197 347463D
1199 364201G	1201 240411E	1203 274167B	1205 362715C	1207 253603B
1209 262615A	1211 360141G	1213 315571G	1219 303045G	1221 362161C
1223 301407H	1225 251705A	1227 215615A	1229 316505G	1231 373237H
1233 214317B	1235 370541C	1237 313437H	1239 275651A	1241 361701C
1243 214663F	1245 313407D	1247 216313F	1249 271655E	1251 265663B
1253 376415G	1255 213325A	1257 355771C	1259 306235G	1261 214157F
1263 256401A	1265 272627B	1267 216777F	1269 313627D	1271 206173F
1273 361521G	1275 333733D	1285 000433	1287 264637B	1289 326317H
1291 276441E	1293 273253B	1295 341037D	1297 326715G	1299 216007B
1301 217041E	1303 222237F	1305 224107B	1307 202277F	1309 256063B
1311 240323B	1313 260655E	1315 266671A	1317 273765A	1319 377755G
1321 264037F	1323 370611C	1325 300643D	1327 335675G	1329 350057D

Table C.2. Irreducible Polynomials of Degree ≤34 over *GF*(2).

DEGREE 16--CONTINUED

1331	353531G	1333	303367H	1335	331751C	1337	335127H	1339	354413H
1341	314651C	1347	372705C	1349	346047H	1351	325647H	1353	255113B
1355	277341A	1357	252657F	1359	226075A	1361	353025G	1363	340065G
1365	375517D	1367	334347H	1369	225575E	1371	324711C	1373	245025E
1375	371227D	1377	225551A	1379	343145G	1381	242167F	1383	243411A
1385	247027B	1387	230365E	1389	321165C	1391	254515E	1393	367671G
1395	242115A	1397	220217F	1399	361563H	1401	301553D	1403	352365G
1405	204351A	1411	263047B	1413	261551A	1415	375627D	1417	205273F
1419	227577B	1421	331353H	1423	200677F	1425	205237B	1427	317441G
1429	377405G	1431	205335A	1433	213631E	1435	263003B	1437	330543D
1439	243375E	1441	303013H	1443	255655A	1445	203207B	1447	245255E
1449	353045C	1451	353135G	1453	215007F	1455	302131C	1457	205423F
1459	331577H	1461	327471C	1463	245313F	1465	245247B	1467	323715C
1469	255527F	1475	256311A	1477	333755G	1479	247377B	1481	224725E
1483	355403H	1485	315407D	1487	262471E	1489	324523H	1491	302737D
1493	374471G	1495	207675A	1497	330343D	1499	330023H	1501	261765E
1503	376451C	1505	237271A	1507	265553F	1509	251325A	1511	203303F
1513	374277D	1515	374573D	1517	250737F	1519	266745E	1521	342177D
1523	255505E	1549	241317F	1551	277347B	1553	255653F	1555	224655A
1557	246455A	1559	277565E	1561	367743H	1563	240233B	1565	307563D
1567	277053F	1569	254651A	1571	213075E	1573	263407F	1575	307533D
1577	275247F	1579	202753F	1581	256517B	1583	323113H	1585	216551A
1587	371051C	1589	254551E	1591	302257H	1593	342001C	1595	252313B
1597	316145G	1603	272207F	1605	253317B	1607	223043F	1609	355513H
1611	210233B	1613	277663F	1615	335645C	1617	355147D	1619	225573F
1621	366057H	1623	243217B	1625	337225C	1627	354503H	1629	337577D
1631	364445G	1633	370145G	1635	216177B	1637	330673H	1639	271341E
1641	317373D	1643	334555G	1645	255751A	1647	312411C	1649	212423B
1651	354047H	1653	241767B	1655	351157D	1657	342721G	1659	214053B
1669	267221E	1671	307541C	1673	334533H	1675	323145C	1677	211767B
1679	236423F	1681	325275G	1683	372057D	1685	327373D	1687	277505E
1689	272713B	1691	317361G	1693	347361G	1695	220433B	1697	354231G
1699	216477F	1701	311337D	1703	220741E	1705	324015C	1707	264271A
1709	231361E	1711	254323F	1713	302505C	1715	245417B	1717	212137B
1719	360721C	1721	217671E	1723	301021G	1725	321573D	1731	363525C
1733	272267F	1735	263401A	1737	215545A	1739	204141E	1741	276117F
1743	322515C	1745	213165A	1747	244425E	1749	212065A	1751	300135C
1753	277145E	1755	332415C	1757	360545G	1759	376475G	1761	252015A
1763	261455E	1765	333525C	1767	346335C	1769	310215G	1771	210435E
1773	201557B	1775	201373B	1777	210733F	1779	204235A	1781	203603F
1783	201155E	1785	214461A	1799	000703	1801	244035E	1803	261117B
1805	271563B	1807	242305E	1809	225735A	1811	240741E	1813	232435E
1815	262253B	1817	227647F	1819	352577D	1821	215171A	1823	343011G
1825	375333D	1827	313647D	1829	226117F	1831	326571G	1833	341523D
1835	341117D	1837	235151E	1839	344435C	1841	351021G	1843	330523H
1845	321507D	1847	347111G	1849	355323H	1851	367701C	1853	322643D
1859	341337H	1861	312471G	1863	307521C	1865	321735C	1867	303435G
1869	344203D	1871	202463F	1873	262645E	1875	233215A	1877	256353F
1879	344153H	1881	330235C	1883	247511E	1885	354415C	1887	316365C
1889	322111G	1891	314507H	1893	251765A	1895	226613B	1897	346145G
1899	333061C	1901	327337H	1903	225523F	1905	221173B	1907	205745E
1909	273235E	1911	371625C	1913	274571E	1915	227353B	1925	253215A
1927	331333H	1929	273703B	1931	270557F	1933	370467H	1935	350763D
1937	335717H	1939	211123F	1941	207163B	1943	322601G	1945	265101A
1947	377623D	1949	234675E	1951	200627F	1953	344615C	1955	372351C
1957	300025G	1959	216455A	1961	215411E	1963	333221G	1965	320151C
1967	277707F	1969	201435E	1971	333265C	1973	343335G	1975	300557D
1977	305567D	1979	355735G	1981	240477F	2115	331173D	2117	272425E
2119	234711E	2121	361707D	2123	213067F	2125	262271A	2127	363543D
2129	241757F	2131	326423H	2133	253125A	2135	342643D	2137	321433H
2139	251271A	2141	346173H	2147	211305E	2149	361371G	2151	246721A
2153	356561G	2155	222715A	2157	315225C	2159	361055C	2161	323055G
2163	214773B	2165	271215A	2167	266347F	2169	301321C	2171	232405E
2181	323157D	2183	324661G	2185	215233B	2187	215103B	2189	310003H
2191	311427H	2193	351701C	2195	365051C	2197	335477H	2199	227311A

Table C.2. Irreducible Polynomials of Degree ≤ 34 over $GF(2)$.

DEGREE 16--CONTINUED

2201 337027H	2203 303417H	2205 202721A	2211 201165A	2213 227107F
2215 203365A	2217 306373D	2219 211213F	2221 326533H	2223 344357D
2225 361437D	2227 312357D	2229 340577D	2231 254513F	2233 345363H
2235 232177B	2237 303067H	2243 310107H	2245 342421C	2247 255541A
2249 311763H	2251 323627H	2253 220037B	2255 300741C	2257 335513H
2259 206655A	2261 374255C	2263 341233H	2265 227627B	2267 260413F
2269 337647H	2275 312763D	2277 334137D	2279 270127F	2281 320055G
2283 347265C	2285 272161A	2287 336013H	2289 310443D	2291 233715E
2293 233251E	2295 374477D	2313 000771	2315 251037B	2317 271137F
2319 253123B	2321 235533F	2323 217161E	2325 256335A	2327 210177F
2329 256731A	2331 334423D	2333 271621E	2339 234037F	2341 356031G
2343 364761C	2345 332461C	2347 215127F	2349 374735C	2351 303661G
2353 341121G	2355 221603B	2357 274077F	2359 365573H	2361 356613D
2363 272215A	2365 364617D	2371 267233F	2373 366265C	2375 306405C
2377 315017H	2379 271677B	2381 345431G	2383 346365G	2385 303255C
2387 372217H	2389 200077F	2391 222443B	2393 255267F	2395 307633D
2397 346757D	2403 357451C	2405 307413D	2407 320365G	2409 205757B
2411 335405G	2413 254717F	2415 344277D	2417 215211E	2419 244737F
2421 331145C	2423 227305E	2425 364553D	2427 215135A	2437 277131E
2439 255017B	2441 374515G	2443 362363H	2445 347477D	2447 201241E
2449 370115G	2451 336675C	2453 253521E	2455 202045A	2457 364563D
2459 367527H	2461 200457F	2467 236461E	2469 356631C	2471 254643F
2473 236547F	2475 307775C	2477 353001G	2479 312507H	2481 222605A
2483 312073H	2485 260473B	2487 275435A	2489 200071E	2491 200275E
2493 264673B	2499 310527D	2501 277355E	2503 276265E	2505 235475A
2507 366733H	2509 311061G	2511 323363D	2513 314615G	2515 204567B
2517 335515C	2519 320407H	2521 257345E	2523 211327B	2525 306667D
2531 354071G	2533 233161A	2535 370371C	2537 301605G	2539 252455E
2581 314613H	2583 321247D	2585 254373B	2587 332231G	2589 350007D
2595 271547B	2597 332157H	2599 317307H	2601 303203D	2603 306645G
2605 351731C	2607 305255C	2609 356625G	2611 243771E	2613 266761A
2615 364577D	2617 301737H	2619 251675A	2621 275367F	2627 207733F
2629 371607H	2631 277327B	2633 325437H	2635 316451C	2637 343473D
2639 250267F	2641 352101G	2643 207747B	2645 251403B	2647 245057F
2649 357225C	2651 245155E	2653 344337H	2659 242017F	2661 343415C
2663 224413F	2665 363343D	2667 361635C	2669 221027B	2671 335661G
2673 214125A	2675 215575A	2677 224161E	2679 345101C	2681 314013H
2695 263425A	2697 336623D	2699 375715G	2701 247113F	2703 301365C
2705 211223B	2707 201345E	2709 351533D	2711 244745E	2713 261163F
2715 356515C	2717 302415G	2723 363455G	2725 363477D	2727 312253D
2729 337457H	2731 246515E	2733 227713B	2735 370125C	2737 313151C
2739 371007D	2741 277461E	2743 253053F	2745 243753B	2747 352363H
2749 270263F	2755 253017B	2757 256737B	2759 336615G	2761 225315E
2763 342135C	2765 273623B	2767 367161G	2769 237013B	2771 250565A
2773 306227H	2775 350523D	2777 212641E	2779 324513H	2781 202765A
2787 350351C	2789 264111E	2791 366147H	2793 300575C	2795 217635A
2797 371253H	2799 312255C	2801 252203F	2803 336007H	2805 254465A
2827 000453	2829 302151C	2831 345223H	2833 311375G	2835 215121A
2837 231651E	2839 375751C	2841 262721A	2843 222535E	2845 327323D
2851 315157H	2853 363227D	2855 371025C	2857 232561E	2859 363557D
2861 355763H	2863 312001G	2865 220747B	2867 317271G	2869 217527F
2871 324001C	2873 204013B	2875 351413D	2877 255363B	2883 361027D
2885 376347D	2887 363657H	2889 320437D	2891 320317H	2893 241161E
2895 225557B	2897 354175G	2899 237127F	2901 216241A	2903 353265G
2905 330051C	2907 263461A	2909 224305E	2915 335135C	2917 304655G
2919 237765A	2921 254727F	2923 323267H	2925 310257D	2927 332017H
2929 224035E	2931 264721A	2933 221047F	2935 346231C	2937 336545C
2951 365455G	2953 243163F	2955 202013B	2957 334213H	2959 232233F
2961 344171C	2963 320775G	2965 276463B	2967 314447D	2969 251447F
2971 236407F	2973 353711C	2979 333345C	2981 375713H	2983 257253F
2985 371551C	2987 334565G	2989 373017H	2991 366763D	2993 263641E
2995 205621A	2997 207631A	2999 345145G	3001 247461E	3003 243667B
3005 237651A	3011 371105G	3013 253055E	3015 312075C	3017 306675G
3019 373335G	3021 207613B	3023 271671E	3121 235505E	3123 220253B
3125 333171C	3127 240631E	3129 227737B	3131 311171G	3141 337571C

Table C.2. Irreducible Polynomials of Degree ≤34 over *GF*(2).

DEGREE 16--CONTINUED

3143	253237F	3145	222215A	3147	316401C	3149	343071G	3151	205305E
3153	220163B	3155	202375A	3157	354565G	3159	207227B	3161	317631G
3163	216545E	3165	362243D	3171	332363D	3173	305163H	3175	344025C
3177	320461C	3179	373407D	3181	254637F	3183	240255A	3185	357641C
3187	363057H	3189	334041C	3191	204373F	3193	240235E	3207	350325C
3209	264427F	3211	305721G	3213	301167D	3215	313577D	3217	207247F
3219	317675C	3221	256577F	3223	220233F	3225	340175C	3227	273513F
3229	370647H	3235	376055C	3237	335343D	3239	332751G	3241	340115G
3243	302267D	3245	272353B	3247	270217B	3249	260027B	3251	364473H
3253	202735E	3255	245277B	3257	206225E	3259	344023H	3269	202551E
3271	306313H	3273	345257D	3275	345677D	3277	347023H	3279	355525C
3281	241005A	3283	243337F	3285	220543B	3287	234537F	3289	230415E
3291	356177D	3293	233321E	3299	206035E	3301	277257F	3303	350705C
3305	367347D	3307	223075E	3309	260011A	3311	272021E	3313	335375G
3315	272535A	3341	000551	3343	225177F	3345	355233D	3347	242243F
3349	252661A	3351	316671C	3353	221123F	3355	300645C	3357	304161C
3363	355067D	3365	217547B	3367	240763F	3369	207441A	3371	343401G
3373	265347F	3375	343225C	3377	206151E	3379	371631G	3381	216755A
3383	344227D	3385	351611C	3387	230773B	3397	300367H	3399	254735A
3401	370151G	3403	244377F	3405	340605C	3407	316123H	3409	346415G
3411	204007B	3413	226163F	3415	350453D	3417	203175A	3419	340565G
3421	363103H	3427	212321E	3429	217353B	3431	313671G	3433	257325E
3435	226567B	3437	277035E	3439	305345G	3441	230333B	3443	271451E
3445	233571A	3447	363255C	3449	250131E	3463	366331G	3465	252755A
3467	263767F	3469	214377F	3471	213463B	3473	310633H	3475	232031A
3477	304503D	3479	340731G	3481	376125G	3483	324025C	3485	306551C
3491	231075E	3493	300453H	3495	227251A	3497	325167H	3499	346527H
3501	366117D	3503	215727F	3505	327163D	3507	323461C	3509	214251E
3511	327777H	3513	215447B	3515	240343B	3525	266461A	3527	225073F
3529	354767H	3531	332275C	3533	220075E	3535	302517D	3537	217423B
3539	266611E	3541	335061G	3543	210075A	3545	220573B	3547	302555G
3549	327727D	3555	243067B	3613	345251G	3619	245337F	3621	257453B
3623	237373F	3625	334371C	3627	355263D	3629	226741E	3631	204613F
3633	375225C	3635	203173B	3637	255125E	3639	304353D	3641	257675E
3643	354773H	3653	302033H	3655	204253B	3657	361445C	3659	205723F
3661	375555G	3663	305615C	3665	375653D	3667	252447F	3669	302445C
3671	230047F	3673	302451G	3675	206621A	3677	267227F	3683	211201E
3685	350435C	3687	377301C	3689	275747B	3691	271257F	3693	336307D
3695	241267B	3697	327623H	3699	216023B	3701	234337F	3703	355645G
3721	212033F	3723	360235C	3725	203311A	3727	237645E	3729	217563B
3731	262747F	3733	377465G	3735	332725C	3737	213727F	3739	355727H
3741	242161A	3747	343063D	3749	350031G	3751	231471E	3753	310113D
3755	242745A	3757	314531C	3759	343633D	3761	250407F	3763	344543H
3765	277065A	3767	206243F	3769	220607F	3771	223233B	3781	301033H
3783	232247B	3785	363367D	3787	271633F	3789	242321A	3791	346517D
3793	237435E	3795	337745C	3797	222377F	3799	360427H	3801	247707B
3803	226153F	3805	334603D	3811	334767H	3813	244021A	3815	254133B
3817	231057F	3819	340475C	3821	266635E	3823	324463H	3825	275675A
3855	000471	4369	000023	4371	207177B	4373	217565E	4375	214467B
4377	205317B	4379	311121G	4381	250201E	4387	254045E	4389	270271A
4391	375041G	4393	237103F	4395	267441A	4397	224173F	4403	252227B
4405	310653D	4407	237501A	4409	306043H	4411	317545G	4421	264727F
4423	304757H	4425	276573B	4427	332677H	4429	254211E	4435	310723D
4437	233327B	4439	241773F	4441	224707F	4443	356435C	4445	227611A
4451	234111E	4453	200517F	4455	311045C	4457	332707H	4459	323671G
4461	367267D	4467	235603B	4469	267135E	4471	367571C	4489	375113H
4491	231313B	4493	244077F	4499	373125G	4501	233231E	4503	323365C
4505	371557D	4507	222231E	4509	351577D	4515	327117D	4517	316767H
4519	351757H	4521	333625C	4523	352231G	4525	364715C	4531	322301G
4533	274347B	4535	345107D	4537	235167F	4539	320423D	4549	377351G
4551	235473B	4553	322351G	4555	365301C	4557	372421C	4563	232277B
4565	354123D	4567	231165E	4569	220771A	4571	215507F	4645	334437D
4647	251153B	4649	321523H	4651	263273F	4653	314435C	4659	213111A
4661	272633F	4663	317645G	4665	342153D	4667	322147H	4677	321255C
4679	277723F	4681	330271G	4683	340273D	4685	353447D	4691	253305E

Table C.2. Irreducible Polynomials of Degree ≤34 over *GF*(2).

```
DEGREE 16--CONTINUED
  4693 340431G  4695 300247D  4697 272647F  4699 250641E  4701 321771C
  4707 224457B  4709 305343D  4711 354505G  4713 250377B  4715 232637B
  4717 330741G  4723 311465G  4725 317765C  4747 206723F  4749 211521A
  4755 270573B  4757 371203H  4759 347277H  4761 374567D  4763 226343F
  4765 231221A  4771 267177F  4773 365433D  4775 334401C  4777 373677D
  4779 232441A  4781 241413F  4787 221527F  4789 204471E  4791 357511C
  4793 357173H  4795 307457D  4805 263745A  4807 375603H  4809 322165C
  4811 363623D  4813 367767H  4819 261545E  4821 321537D  4823 201561E
  4825 364321C  4827 212131A  4829 306711G  4835 235237B  4837 352677H
  4839 316053D  4841 216523F  4843 245717F  4845 267755A  4883 000543
  4885 241207B  4887 215777B  4889 371623H  4891 313167H  4893 300515C
  4899 366471C  4901 352655G  4903 311705G  4905 275177B  4907 337137H
  4909 255737F  4915 211527B  4917 352275C  4919 245711E  4921 372447H
  4923 357321C  4933 301571G  4935 202543B  4937 360067H  4939 276323F
  4941 312477D  4947 244107B  4949 345443H  4951 213233F  4953 236371A
  4955 344507D  4957 361505G  4963 231235E  4965 260757B  4967 245023F
  4969 366447H  4971 220265A  4973 265653F  4979 376663H  4981 235273B
  5003 365753H  5005 340751C  5011 302605G  5013 316475C  5015 345053D
  5017 335447H  5019 265275A  5021 260167F  5027 255707F  5029 226373F
  5031 230005A  5033 243703F  5035 363433D  5037 304327D  5203 202051E
  5205 345611C  5207 373065G  5209 333551G  5211 234501A  5213 346751G
  5219 353073D  5221 230303F  5223 317703D  5225 211107B  5227 233355E
  5229 200617B  5235 252315A  5237 203761E  5259 332201C  5261 211363F
  5267 313743H  5269 372727H  5271 350471C  5273 347247H  5275 230145A
  5277 341727D  5283 254753B  5285 265003B  5287 255425A  5289 305153D
  5291 362113H  5293 261217F  5299 236443F  5301 275753B  5303 322375G
  5305 203773B  5319 200767B  5321 234217B  5323 232513F  5325 234601A
  5331 237205A  5333 246753F  5335 364757D  5337 235257B  5339 212257F
  5341 216427F  5347 246551E  5349 203577B  5351 201643F  5353 302021G
  5355 232531A  5397 000567   5399 356433H  5401 254453F  5403 263027B
  5405 372211C  5411 302751G  5413 370257H  5415 364627D  5417 210117F
  5419 367257H  5421 222451A  5427 347323D  5429 342501G  5431 233033F
  5433 264705A  5447 254615E  5449 242635E  5451 311031C  5453 250555E
  5459 315757H  5461 206745E  5463 230173B  5465 263201A  5467 312703H
  5469 232907B  5475 334665C  5477 216351E  5479 340363H  5481 306271C
  5483 221743F  5485 375511C  5491 356717D  5493 272663B  5515 375707D
  5517 216127B  5523 264051A  5525 360755C  5527 310503H  5529 230743B
  5531 204657F  5533 360177H  5539 302541G  5541 241443B  5543 354517H
  5545 262507B  5547 211553B  5549 246747F  5555 307251C  5557 225411E
  5559 226007B  5561 304137H  5575 266363B  5577 261613B  5579 347441G
  5581 223531E  5587 332125G  5677 263431E  5683 235125E  5685 301035C
  5687 271317F  5689 201615E  5703 242173B  5705 223763B  5707 273031E
  5709 367053D  5715 374331C  5717 261227F  5719 220121E  5721 235611A
  5723 273127F  5725 275463B  5731 226171E  5733 372241C  5735 250663B
  5737 217173F  5739 356343D  5741 223705E  5747 215657F  5773 252513F
  5779 244773F  5781 217305A  5783 236715E  5785 253251A  5787 306177D
  5789 334215G  5795 337775C  5797 205341A  5799 345021C  5801 227017F
  5803 216141E  5805 267607B  5811 263503B  5813 353315G  5815 365367D
  5817 201323B  5831 355755C  5833 371177H  5835 321235C  5837 221223F
  5843 206363F  5845 334451C  5847 362317D  5849 273645E  5851 374361G
  5853 236665A  5859 235743B  5861 242633F  5863 273075E  5865 326553D
  5911 000435   5913 255021A  5915 230267B  5917 210763F  5923 321717H
  5925 325617D  5927 363007H  5929 203571E  5931 343725C  5933 220045A
  5939 231433F  5941 304457H  5943 247553B  5945 257023B  6343 377645G
  6345 220551A  6347 325303H  6349 306747H  6355 377241C  6357 372433D
  6359 230731E  6361 322405G  6363 362731C  6373 247527F  6375 352527D
  6425 000637   6427 341575G  6437 376677H  6439 204337F  6441 234241A
  6443 257255A  6445 301767D  6451 333075G  6453 213765A  6455 271207B
  6457 243441E  6471 315641C  6473 241577F  6475 330255C  6477 360733D
  6483 216513B  6485 352303D  6487 210711E  6489 210241A  6491 254075E
  6501 365325C  6503 336763H  6505 373547D  6507 304115C  6509 331617H
  6515 221425A  6541 223755E  6547 256621E  6549 210471A  6551 377203H
  6553 222527F  6555 215061A  6565 366625C  6567 376563D  6569 262227F
  6571 253653F  6573 377375C  6579 262015A  6581 241113F  6583 216537F
  6585 326647D  6599 270133F  6601 340521G  6603 230445A  6709 370713H
```

Table C.2. Irreducible Polynomials of Degree ≤34 over *GF*(2).

DEGREE 16--CONTINUED

6711	375261C	6713	242371E	6727	345425G	6729	363411C	6731	275661E
6733	372545G	6739	341711G	6741	223155A	6743	250353F	6745	251435A
6747	356417D	6757	352457H	6759	377537D	6761	342575G	6763	373773H
6765	301145C	6803	343565G	6805	232661A	6807	237211A	6809	330307H
6811	335025G	6821	353427H	6823	251543F	6825	325327D	6827	224505E
6829	252765E	6835	273421A	6837	350601C	6839	324657H	6841	270235E
6855	303075C	6857	315065G	6859	245165E	6861	217275A	6867	352137D
6869	277457F	6871	326701G	6873	304017D	6875	244365A	6885	321613D
6939	000643	6949	212371E	6951	360253D	6953	305051C	6955	361063D
6957	275343B	6963	355465C	6965	240367B	6967	242767F	6969	267625A
6983	272225E	6985	234117B	6987	264073B	6989	304633H	6995	304713D
6997	315467H	6999	355331C	7001	263161E	7003	314057H	7013	357145G
7015	277563B	7017	352437D	7019	217317F	7021	267601A	9363	342631C
9365	316027D	9371	255161E	9381	267357B	9387	307143D	9389	365345G
9395	245043B	9397	236503F	9419	257067F	9421	200641E	9427	235011E
9429	245147B	9435	300403D	9509	000515	9515	322315C	9517	261153F
9523	276277F	9525	225361A	9547	354407H	9549	262433B	9555	244611A
9557	221505E	9563	241201E	9573	235731A	9579	276057B	9581	335203H
9619	314777H	9621	256055A	9627	312545C	9637	223203F	9643	347127H
9645	322717D	9651	260541A	9805	310751C	9811	304773H	9813	335601C
9819	201263B	9829	262453F	9835	265757B	9877	260243B	9883	217603F
9893	372323H	9899	273433F	9901	360463H	9907	365637H	9909	263071A
10571	320157H	10573	204645E	10579	314043H	10581	366135C	10603	360515G
10645	241125A	10667	264323F	10837	317515G	10923	247167B	10925	312537D
10931	211737B	10933	362553H	10955	275221A	10957	323305G	10963	265773F
10965	220411A	11051	000537	11053	242341E	11059	240747F	11061	343555C
11083	204325E	11085	253401A	11443	254331E	11469	234133B	11475	340407D
11565	000727	13107	000037	21845	000007				

DEGREE	17	1	400011E	3	400017F	5	400431E	7	525251E
9	410117F	11	400731E	13	411335E	15	444257F	17	600013H
19	403555E	21	525327F	23	411077F	25	404525E	27	401523F
29	466273F	31	642015G	33	446613F	35	527427F	37	414347F
39	414443F	41	501353F	43	445141E	45	663013H	47	414663F
49	535013F	51	610215G	53	403063F	55	530765E	57	460377F
59	626653H	61	405473F	63	504671E	65	771353H	67	444611E
69	422273F	71	442571E	73	612537H	75	572325E	77	564225E
79	561175E	81	447773F	83	470337F	85	640635G	87	646775G
89	532617F	91	537773F	93	510473F	95	413651E	97	514573F
99	601335G	101	606155G	103	540041E	105	525535E	107	714303H
109	506741E	111	514045E	113	750413H	115	642433H	117	551757F
119	735207H	121	662527H	123	530645E	125	431601E	127	775325G
129	671075G	131	443043F	133	607115G	135	432265E	137	454067F
139	402545E	141	547163F	143	742377H	145	430161E	147	504505E
149	461331E	151	454433F	153	724003H	155	562467F	157	774563H
159	430053F	161	557517F	163	652243H	165	455655E	167	727113H
169	521367F	171	743537H	173	424443F	175	421215E	177	655241G
179	424107F	181	675215G	183	541625E	185	771231G	187	734703H
189	470147F	191	413557F	193	424761E	195	656765G	197	756341G
199	722571G	201	600657H	203	554347F	205	543457F	207	414115E
209	674557H	211	630043H	213	734763H	215	402253F	217	542447F
219	706353H	221	751471G	223	636031G	225	755535G	227	771451G
229	435251E	231	620071G	233	752045G	235	742003H	237	717553H
239	734727H	241	740227H	243	633051G	245	676521G	247	567321E
249	705503H	251	763237H	253	544613E	255	524057F	257	774503H
259	477743F	261	477633F	263	755723H	265	447503F	267	411347F
269	417611E	271	404121E	273	521531E	275	611073H	277	432625E
279	501275E	281	446417F	283	671763H	285	455647F	287	575245E
289	476601E	291	437631E	293	404607F	295	466457F	297	652563H
299	461471E	301	531071E	303	772047H	305	477225E	307	457601E
309	667401G	311	625321G	313	510071E	315	573213F	317	755547H
319	472617F	321	511337F	323	511373F	325	603777H	327	424505E
329	504641E	331	425601E	333	466055E	335	565765E	337	545603F
339	603205G	341	512211E	343	715147H	345	541211E	347	565171E
349	465521E	351	640407H	353	655007H	355	555477F	357	575535E

Table C.2. Irreducible Polynomials of Degree ≤ 34 over $GF(2)$.

DEGREE 18	1 1000201E	3 1010301A	5 1002241E
7 1000377B	9 1200205A	11 1703601G	13 1025711E
15 1015721A	17 1115701E	19 1023141A	21 1070477B
27 1223215A	63 1313133B	63 1313133B	63 1313133B
189 1623075C	57 1160435A	57 1160435A	171 1626367D
57 1160435A	171 1626367D	171 1626367D	133 1300565A
399 1514245C	399 1514245C	1197 1052465A	399 1514245C
1197 1052465A	1197 1052465A	73 1642365C	219 1252555A
219 1252555A	657 1253607A	219 1252555A	657 1253607A
657 1253607A	1971 1334325A	511 1231145A	1533 1055321A
1533 1055321A	4599 1341035A	1533 1055321A	4599 1341035A
4599 1341035A	13797 1777777D	1387 1011011A	9709 1001001A

DEGREE 19	1 2000047F	3 2020471E	5 2013211E
7 2570103F	9 2561427F	11 2227023F	13 2001711E
15 2331067F	17 3146455G	19 3610353H	21 2766447F

DEGREE 20	1 4000011E	3 4000017B	5 4200031A
7 4001051E	9 4040217B	11 4030071A	13 4004515E
15 4221037B	17 6000031G	19 4442235E	21 4103307B
25 4307165A	75 4266075A	33 4036267B	55 4346037B
165 5145217B	55 4346037B	165 5145217B	275 6027135C
825 6044073D	31 4034755A	93 4627377B	155 4367471A
465 5057137B	155 4367471A	465 5057137B	775 6505453D
2325 4504241A	341 4510031A	1023 7552557D	1705 6406005C
5115 5327265A	1705 6406005C	5115 5327265A	8525 5746331A
25575 6647133D	41 4027577B	123 4761757B	205 5541427A
615 7113055C	205 5541427A	615 7113055C	451 7544237D
1353 7602777D	2255 5017111A	6765 5521623B	2255 5017111A
6765 5521623B	1271 7050457D	3813 4345543B	6355 6130725C
19065 7164555C	6355 6130725C	19065 7164555C	13981 4100001A
41943 4102041A			

DEGREE 21	1 10000005E	3 10040205E	5 10020045E
7 11111115A	9 10040315E	11 10000635E	13 10103075E
15 10050335E	17 10002135E	19 17000075G	21 14600067D
49 11105347A	127 10225077A	889 11166743A	889 11166743A
6223 17155161C	337 10264425A	2359 16260075C	2359 16260075C
42799 10040001A			

DEGREE 22	1 20000003F	3 20100403B	5 20001043F
7 22222223F	9 20100453B	11 25200127F	13 20401207F
15 20110517B	17 20430607F	19 20070217F	21 31400147D
23 20005611A	69 20465307B	89 20603715A	267 24146477B
2047 22404051A	6141 36544657D	683 34230073D	15709 21774413B
60787 34603145C			

DEGREE 23	1 40000041E	3 40404041E	5 40000063F
7 40010061E	9 50000241E	11 40220151E	13 40006341E
15 40405463F	17 40103271E	19 41224445E	21 40435651E
47 44636045A	178481 43073357B		

DEGREE 24

	1 100000207F	3 100205645A
5 100305143B	7 100315361A	9 102746675A
11 125245661E	13 113646571A	15 112432273B
17 140775753D	19 113763063E	21 116636645A
45 170736335C	63 164260065C	35 113206017A
105 151255377B	105 151255377B	315 105404647B
39 156267123C	39 156267123C	117 131307443B
65 150051747D	195 132365525A	195 132365525A
585 157653375C	91 160503563D	273 137240727A
273 137240727A	819 144534331C	455 165330327D
1365 103446341A	1365 103446341A	4095 120652605A
51 155212435A	51 155212435A	153 130633327B
85 141720423C	255 172634307C	255 172634307C

Table C.2. Irreducible Polynomials of Degree ≤34 over *GF*(2).

DEGREE 24--CONTINUED			
	765 146537231C	119 123426525A	357 105732145A
	357 105732145A	1071 133125511A	595 155513755A
	1785 121720647B	1785 121720647B	5355 102474621A
	221 100466513A	663 100006161A	663 100006161A
	1989 101312015A	1105 126751351A	3315 104313243A
	3315 104313243A	9945 116055567A	1547 156652045C
	4641 124430435A	4641 124430435A	13923 112630407A
	7735 127617123A	23205 133033563B	23205 133033563B
	69615 161676707A	241 174317125C	723 171224435C
	723 171224435C	2169 154423127D	1205 132001371A
	3615 145363733B	3615 145363733B	10845 155353415A
	1687 165365701C	5061 106342635A	5061 106342635A
	15183 100605077B	8435 133567111A	25305 161276343B
	25305 161276343B	75915 100140053B	3133 101332157B
	9399 131342727B	9399 131342727B	28197 162047171C
	15665 112155405A	46995 164117115C	46995 164117115C
	140985 124055647B	21931 110001101A	109655 100011011A
DEGREE 25		1 200000011E	3 200000017F
	5 204000051E	7 200010031E	9 200402017F
	11 252001251E	13 201014171E	15 204204057F
	17 200005535E	19 200014731E	21 201015517F
	31 200523477B	601 353551603D	18631 277267355A
	1801 341573647D	55831 253566335A	
DEGREE 26		1 400000107F	3 401007131A
	5 430216473F	7 402365755E	9 410004563B
	11 426225667F	13 510664323F	15 475477275A
	17 473167545E	19 411335571E	21 433315447B
	2731 656536753D	8191 614326143D	24573 600777003D
DEGREE 27		1 1000000047E	3 1001007071E
	5 1020024171E	7 1004462703B	9 1102210617E
	11 1250025757F	13 1257242631E	15 1020560103F
	17 1112225171E	19 1037530241E	21 1006524347B
	73 1215076703A	511 1745602367D	
DEGREE 28		1 2000000011E	3 2000000017B
	5 2040000411A	7 2104210431E	9 2002004017B
	11 2000025051E	13 2020006031E	15 2040410417B
	17 2002502115E	19 2001601071E	21 2104213577A
	29 2010141305A	87 2010073021A	145 2112310701A
	435 2256267705A	43 2043450123B	129 2232610673B
	215 3417321145C	645 2507013341A	1247 2036150345A
	3741 2742450341A	6235 2052124143B	18705 2307251163B
	113 2065561561A	339 2550100465A	565 3662526717D
	1695 3655737253B	3277 2752435573B	9831 3521653421A
	4859 2313475717B	14577 3513705403A	24295 2517460277B
	72885 2037216263B	140911 2336561121A	422733 3043320155A
	127 2243345037B	381 3540233367A	635 3664406015C
	1905 3757051033D	3683 2322031441A	11049 3157336171C
	18415 2226143443B	55245 3033453267C	5461 3305002225C
	16383 2273447351A	27305 3061505731C	81915 3052445243D
	158369 3533324373D	475107 2337253731A	791845 2145723745A
	2375535 2330160331A	14351 3316136351C	43053 2374475053A
	71755 3175417143A	215265 3514237073C	416179 2755450655A
	1248537 3657555473D	617093 3614772157D	1851279 3572445367D
	3085465 3706175715C	9256395 3777777777D	
DEGREE 29		1 4000000005E	3 4004004005E
	5 4000010205E	7 4010000045E	9 4400000045E
	11 4002200115E	13 4001040115E	15 4004204435E
	17 4100060435E	19 4040003075E	21 4004064275E
	233 4125377665A	1103 4663771561A	256999 7260572607D
	2089 6202672631C	486737 6276417701C	2304167 4334123375A

Table C.2. Irreducible Polynomials of Degree ≤34 over *GF*(2).

DEGREE 30		1	10040000007F	3	10045207405A
5	10104264207F	7	17254401747D	9	10466404155A
11	10421106467B	13	10115131333F	15	12531150265A
17	11326212703F	19	10343244533E	21	14340746005C
63	15671207425A	33	10617013661A	33	10617013661A
99	10231077101A	77	10347066511A	231	12551521353B
231	12551521353B	693	12363365205A	31	10537567431A
93	13104273407B	93	13104273407B	279	17565561725C
217	13063776443B	651	14475010377C	651	14475010377C
1953	16217747517D	341	15312176137D	1023	13005472403B
1023	13005472403B	3069	15027200513D	2387	17327131755A
7161	17273014127A	7161	17273014127A	21483	15222475661C
151	11732145645A	453	15642307235C	453	15642307235C
1359	13137001367A	1057	17576155211A	3171	14046056527C
3171	14046056527C	9513	15362114071A	1661	16275156545A
4983	11747625331A	4983	11747625331A	14949	14262504223C
11627	12305126253B	34881	11274077671A	34881	11274077671A
104643	16671210137D	4681	11346765601A	14043	15727555211C
14043	15727555211C	42129	11154174627A	32767	14271111643D
98301	17313775157D	98301	17313775157D	294903	17667776677D
51491	15116464137C	154473	10170400463B	154473	10170400463B
463419	13637044253B	360437	13726766575A	1081311	14437537423D
1081311	14437537423D	3243933	17657537277D	331	13214207735A
993	15100727503B	993	15100727503B	2979	11115104367B
2317	10737311047B	6951	12374572221A	6951	12374572221A
20853	11567732701A	3641	14707036127B	10923	16076273661C
10923	16076273661C	25487	10403615303A	76461	10221305567A
76461	10221305567A	10261	16150525151C	30783	10363607103A
30783	10363607103A	92349	12553152637A	71827	14221266525C
215481	17473760245C	215481	17473760245C	646443	17070134445A
112871	12527647623A	338613	12670030647A	338613	12670030647A
790097	12105065527A	2370291	10545323161A	2370291	10545323161A
49981	10400014607B	149943	10502035235A	149943	10502035235A
449829	12240170427B	349867	10101010111A	549791	11303560025A
1649373	15735076321C	1649373	15735076321C	3848537	11010100111A
1549411	12135356633B	4648233	11274767701A	4648233	11274767701A
13944699	16471647235C	10845877	11000100011A		
DEGREE 31		1	20000000011E	3	20000000017E
5	20000020411E	7	21042104211E	9	20010010017E
11	20005000251E	13	20004100071E	15	20202040217E
17	20000200435E	19	20060140231E	21	21042107357E
DEGREE 32		1	40020000007F	3	40001114005A
5	50521021747B	7	40460216667F	9	40220536125A
11	40035532523F	13	42003247143F	15	42644424505A
17	44165166133B	19	41760427607F	21	56032357221A
51	73274317525C	85	55255004227B	255	60537314115C
257	52213142567B	771	46633742135A	1285	53046115123B
3855	47254550703B	4369	45052437233B	13107	71265756301C
21845	65636126613D	65535	57410204175A		
DEGREE 33		1	100000020001E	3	100020024001E
5	104000420001E	7	100000260001A	9	100020224401E
11	111100021111E	13	100000031463F	15	104020466001E
17	100502430041E	19	100601431001E	21	100034327001A
23	100021260105A	161	107167672771A	89	100123140475A
623	124155341567B	2047	142560223461C	14329	150052442055C
599479	125725100311A	13788017	101534661265A	53353631	107753475213B
DEGREE 34		1	201000000007F	3	201051003005A
5	201472024107F	7	377000007527H	9	203123311035A
11	225213433257F	13	227712240037F	15	213753015051A
17	251132516577F	19	211636220473F	21	377235535321C
43691	327304565547D	131071	331706543633D	393213	226405640551A

Appendix D List of Binary Cyclic Codes of Odd Length

In this table the length (*n*), number of information symbols (*k*), the true minimum distance (*d*), the minimum distance guaranteed by the BCH bound (d_{BCH}) and the exponents of the roots of the generator polynomial are tabulated for all binary cyclic codes of odd length less than or equal to 65. All (*n*, *n*) and (*n*, 1) codes are omitted. This table was compiled by Chen (1969).

* Denotes code which has larger k than BCH code with same d.

n	k	d	d_{BCH}	Roots of Gen. Poly.
7	4	3	3	1,
7	3	4	4	0, 1
9	3	3	3	1,
9	2	6	6	0, 1
15	11	3	3	1,
15	10	4	4	0, 1,
15	9	3	3	1, 5,
15	9	4	3	3, 5,
15	8	4	4	0, 1, 5,
15	8	4	3	0, 3, 5,
15	7	3	3	1, 7,
15	7	5	5	1, 3,
15	6	6	6	0, 1, 3,
15	6	6	6	0, 1, 7,
15	5	3	3	1, 5, 7,
15	5	7	7	1, 3, 5,
15	4	6	6	0, 1, 5, 7,
15	4	8	8	0, 1, 3, 5,
15	3	5	5	1, 3, 7,
15	2	10	10	0, 1, 3, 7,
17	9	5	4	1,
17	8	6	6	0, 1,
21	16	3	3	7, 3,
21	15	3	3	1,
21	15	4	3	0, 7, 3,
21	14	4	4	0, 1,
21	13	3	3	7, 1,
21	13	4	3	7, 9, 3,
21	12	3	3	9, 1,
21	12	4	3	0, 7, 9, 3,
21	12	4	4	0, 7, 1,
21	12	5	5	3, 1,
21	11	4	4	0, 9, 1,
21	11	6	6	0, 3, 1,
21	10	4	4	7, 9, 1,
21	10	5	5	7, 3, 1,
21	9	3	3	5, 1,
21	9	4	4	0, 7, 9, 1,
21	9	6	5	9, 3, 1,
21	9	8	6	0, 7, 3, 1,
21	8	6	6	0, 9, 3, 1,
21	8	6	6	0, 5, 1,
21	7	3	3	7, 5, 1,
21	7	8	5	7, 9, 3, 1,
21	6	6	6	0, 7, 5, 1,
21	6	7	7	3, 5, 1,
21	6	8	6	0, 7, 9, 3, 1,
21	5	10	10	0, 3, 5, 1,
21	4	9	9	7, 3, 5, 1,
21	3	7	7	9, 3, 5, 1,
21	3	12	12	0, 7, 3, 5, 1,
21	2	14	14	0, 9, 3, 5, 1,

n	k	d	d_{BCH}	Roots of Gen. Poly.
23	12	7	5	1,
23	11	8	6	0, 1,
25	5	5	5	1,
25	4	10	10	0, 1,
27	9	3	3	1,
27	7	6	6	1, 9,
27	8	6	6	0, 1,
27	6	6	6	0, 1, 9,
27	3	9	9	1, 3,
27	2	18	18	0, 1, 3,
31	26	3	3	1,
31	25	4	4	0, 1,
31	21	5	5	1, 3,
31	21	5	4	1, 5,
31	21	5	3	1, 15,
31	20	6	6	0, 1, 3,
31	20	6	4	0, 1, 5,
31	20	6	4	0, 1, 7,
31	16	5	5	1, 5,11,
31	16	6	6	1, 3, 7,
31	16	7	7	1, 3, 5,
31	16	7	5	1, 5, 7,
31	15	6	6	0, 1, 3, 7,
31	15	8	8	0, 1, 3, 5,
31	15	8	5	0, 1, 5, 7,
31	15	8	8	0, 1, 5,11,
31	11	11	11	1, 3, 5, 7,
31	11	11	7	1, 3, 5,11,
31	11	11	7	1, 3, 7,15,
31	10	12	12	0, 1, 3, 5, 7,
31	10	12	10	0, 1, 3, 5,11,
31	10	12	10	0, 1, 3, 7,15,
31	6	15	15	1, 3, 5, 7,11,
31	5	16	16	0, 1, 3, 5, 7,11,
33	23	3	3	1,
33	22	6	6	0, 1,
33	21	3	3	1,11,
33	21	4	3	3,11,
33	20	4	3	0, 3,11,
33	20	6	6	0, 1,11,
33	13	3	3	1, 5,
33	13	10	5	1, 3,
33	12	6	6	0, 1, 5,
33	12	10	10	0, 1, 3,
33	11	3	3	1, 5,11,
33	11	11	8	1, 3,11,

n	k	d	d_{BCH}	Roots of Gen. Poly.
33	10	6	6	0, 1, 5,11,
33	10	12	10	0, 1, 3,11,
33	3	11	11	1, 3, 5,
33	2	22	22	0, 1, 3, 5,
35	28	4	3	5, 7,
35	27	4	3	0, 5, 7,
35	25	4	3	5, 7,15,
35	24	4	3	0, 5, 7,15,
35	23	3	3	1,
35	22	4	4	0, 1,
35	20	3	3	1,15,
35	20	6	5	1, 5,
35	19	4	4	1, 7,
35	19	4	4	0, 1,15,
35	19	6	5	0, 1, 5,
35	18	4	4	0, 1, 7,
35	17	6	5	1, 5,15,
35	16	4	4	1, 7,15,
35	16	6	5	0, 1, 5,15,
35	16	7	6	1, 5, 7,
35	15	4	4	0, 1, 7,15,
35	15	8	6	0, 1, 5, 7,
35	13	8	6	1, 5, 7,15,
35	12	8	6	0, 1, 5, 7,15,
35	11	5	5	1, 3,
35	10	10	10	0, 1, 3,
35	8	7	7	1, 3, 5,
35	7	5	5	1, 3, 7,
35	7	14	12	0, 1, 3, 5,
35	6	10	10	0, 1, 3, 7,
35	5	7	7	1, 3, 5,15,
35	4	14	14	0, 1, 3, 5,15,
35	4	15	15	1, 3, 5, 7,
35	3	20	20	0, 1, 3, 5, 7,
39	27	3	3	1,
39	26	6	4	0, 1,
39	25	3	3	1,13,
39	25	4	3	3,13,
39	24	4	3	0, 3,13,
39	24	6	4	0, 1,13,
39	15	3	3	1, 7,
39	15	10	7	1, 3,
39	14	6	6	0, 1, 7,
39	14	10	8	0, 1, 3,
39	13	3	3	1, 7,13,
39	13	12	7	1, 3,13,
39	12	6	6	0, 1, 7,13,
39	12	12	8	0, 1, 3,13,
39	3	13	13	1, 3, 7,

n	k	d	d_{BCH}	Roots of Gen. Poly.
39	2	26	26	0, 1, 3, 7,
41	21	9	6	1,
41	20	10	6	0, 1,
43	29	6	4	1,
43	28	6	6	0, 1,
43	15	13	7	1, 3,
43	14	14	14	0, 1, 3,
45	35	4	3	5, 9,
45	35	4	3	5, 3,
45	34	4	3	0, 5, 9,
45	34	4	3	0, 5, 3,
45	33	3	3	1,
45	33	4	3	5, 9,15,
45	32	4	3	0, 5, 9, 15,
45	32	4	4	0, 1,
45	31	4	3	5, 9, 3,
45	31	4	3	5, 3,21,
45	31	4	4	15, 1,
45	30	4	3	0, 5, 9, 3,
45	30	4	3	0, 5, 3,21,
45	30	4	4	0,15, 1,
45	29	4	3	5, 9,15, 3,
45	29	5	5	9, 1,
45	29	5	5	3, 1,
45	29	5	5	21, 1,
45	28	4	3	0, 5, 9,15, 3,
45	28	6	5	0, 9, 1,
45	28	6	6	0, 3, 1,
45	28	6	5	0,21, 1,
45	27	3	3	5, 1,
45	27	4	3	5, 9, 3,21,
45	27	6	6	9,15, 1,
45	27	6	5	15, 3, 1,
45	27	6	6	15,21, 1,
45	26	4	3	0, 5, 9, 3,21,
45	26	4	4	0, 5, 1,
45	26	6	6	0, 9,15, 1,
45	26	6	6	0,15, 3, 1,
45	26	6	6	0,15,21, 1,
45	25	4	3	5, 9,15, 3,21,
45	25	4	4	5,15, 1,
45	25	5	5	9, 3, 1,
45	25	5	5	9,21, 1,
45	25	5	5	3,21, 1,
45	24	4	3	0, 5, 9,15, 3,21,
45	24	4	4	0, 5,15, 1,
45	24	6	6	0, 9, 3, 1,
45	24	6	5	0, 9,21, 1,

n	k	d	d_{BCH}	Roots of Gen. Poly.
45	24	6	6	0, 3,21, 1,
45	23	6	6	5, 9, 1,
45	23	6	6	9,15, 3, 1,
45	23	6	6	9,15,21, 1,
45	23	6	6	15, 3,21, 1,
45	23	7	7	5, 3, 1,
45	23	7	6	5,21, 1,
45	22	6	6	0, 5, 9, 1,
45	22	6	6	0, 9,15, 3, 1,
45	22	6	6	0, 9,15,21, 1,
45	22	6	6	0,15, 3,21, 1,
45	22	8	8	0, 5, 3, 1,
45	22	8	6	0, 5,21, 1,
45	21	3	3	1, 7,
45	21	5	5	9, 3,21, 1,
45	21	8	7	5, 9,15, 1,
45	21	8	7	5,15, 3, 1,
45	21	8	7	5,15,21, 1,
45	20	6	6	0, 9, 3,21, 1,
45	20	6	6	0, 1, 7,
45	20	8	7	0, 5, 9,15, 1,
45	20	8	8	0, 5,15, 3, 1,
45	20	8	7	0, 5,15,21, 1,
45	19	6	6	9,15, 3,21, 1,
45	19	6	6	15, 1, 7,
45	19	7	7	5, 9, 3, 1,
45	19	7	7	5, 9,21, 1,
45	19	7	7	5, 3,21, 1,
45	18	6	6	0, 9,15, 3,21, 1,
45	18	6	6	0,15, 1, 7,
45	18	8	8	0, 5, 9, 3, 1,
45	18	8	7	0, 5, 9,21, 1,
45	18	8	8	0, 5, 3,21, 1,
45	17	5	5	9, 1, 7,
45	17	5	5	3, 1, 7,
45	17	8	7	5, 9,15, 3, 1,
45	17	8	8	5, 9,15,21, 1,
45	17	8	7	5,15, 3,21, 1,
45	16	6	6	0, 9, 1, 7,
45	16	8	8	0, 5, 9,15, 3, 1,
45	16	8	8	0, 5, 9,15,21, 1,
45	16	8	8	0, 5,15, 3,21, 1,
45	16	10	8	0, 3, 1, 7,
45	15	3	3	5, 1, 7,
45	15	7	7	5, 9, 3,21, 1,
45	15	9	8	15, 3, 1, 7,
45	15	10	8	9,15, 1, 7,
45	14	6	6	0, 5, 1, 7,
45	14	8	8	0, 5, 9, 3,21, 1,
45	14	10	8	0, 9,15, 1, 7,
45	14	10	8	0,15, 3, 1, 7,

n	k	d	d_{BCH}	Roots of Gen. Poly.
45	13	5	5	9, 3, 1, 7,
45	13	5	5	3,21, 1, 7,
45	13	6	6	5,15, 1, 7,
45	13	8	8	5, 9,15, 3,21, 1,
45	12	6	6	0, 5,15, 1, 7,
45	12	8	8	0, 5, 9,15, 3,21, 1,
45	12	10	8	0, 9, 3, 1, 7,
45	12	10	10	0, 3,21, 1, 7,
45	11	6	6	5, 9, 1, 7,
45	11	9	9	5, 3, 1, 7,
45	11	9	8	15, 3,21, 1, 7,
45	11	10	10	9,15, 3, 1, 7,
45	10	6	6	0, 5, 9, 1, 7,
45	10	10	10	0, 9,15, 3, 1, 7,
45	10	10	10	0,15, 3,21, 1, 7,
45	10	12	12	0, 5, 3, 1, 7,
45	9	5	5	9, 3,21, 1, 7,
45	9	9	9	5,15, 3, 1, 7,
45	9	12	9	5, 9,15, 1, 7,
45	8	10	10	0, 9, 3,21, 1, 7,
45	8	12	9	0, 5, 9,15, 1, 7,
45	8	12	12	0, 5,15, 3, 1, 7,
45	7	9	9	5, 3,21, 1, 7,
45	7	10	10	9,15, 3,21, 1, 7,
45	7	15	15	5, 9, 3, 1, 7,
45	6	10	10	0, 9,15, 3,21, 1, 7,
45	6	18	18	0, 5, 9, 3, 1, 7,
45	6	18	18	0, 5, 3,21, 1, 7,
45	5	9	9	5,15, 3,21, 1, 7,
45	5	21	21	5, 9,15, 3, 1, 7,
45	4	18	18	0, 5,15, 3,21, 1, 7,
45	4	24	24	0, 5, 9,15, 3, 1, 7,
45	3	15	15	5, 9, 3,21, 1, 7,
45	2	30	30	0, 5, 9, 3,21, 1, 7,
47	24	11	5	1,
47	23	12	6	0, 1,
49	28	3	3	1,
49	27	4	4	0, 1,
49	25	4	4	1, 7,
49	25	4	4	1,21,
49	24	4	4	0, 1, 7,
49	24	4	4	0, 1,21,
49	22	4	4	1, 7,21,
49	21	4	4	0, 1, 7,21,
49	7	7	7	1, 3,
49	6	14	14	0, 1, 3,
49	4	21	21	1, 3, 7,
49	3	28	28	0, 1, 3, 7,

n	k	d	d_{BCH}	Roots of Gen. Poly.
51	43	3	3	1,
51	42	4	4	0, 1,
51	41	3	3	17, 1,
51	41	4	3	17, 3,
51	40	4	3	0,17, 3,
51	40	4	4	0,17, 1,
51	35	3	3	1, 5,
51	35	3	3	1,19,
51	35	5	5	3, 1,
51	35	5	4	9, 1,
51	34	6	6	0, 3, 1,
51	34	6	4	0, 9, 1,
51	34	6	4	0, 1, 5,
51	34	6	6	0, 1,19,
51	33	3	3	17, 1, 5,
51	33	3	3	17, 1,19,
51	33	4	3	17, 3, 9,
51	33	6	5	17, 3, 1,
51	33	6	5	17, 9, 1,
51	32	4	3	0,17, 3, 9,
51	32	6	6	0,17, 3, 1,
51	32	6	5	0,17, 9, 1,
51	32	6	4	0,17, 1, 5,
51	32	6	6	0,17, 1,19,
51	27	3	3	1, 5,19,
51	27	5	4	9, 1,19,
51	27	8	5	3, 9, 1,
51	27	9	9	3, 1, 5,
51	27	9	5	9, 1, 5,
51	27	9	5	3, 1,19,
51	26	6	6	0, 9, 1,19,
51	26	6	6	0, 1, 5,19,
51	26	8	6	0, 3, 9, 1,
51	26	10	10	0, 3, 1, 5,
51	26	10	6	0, 9, 1, 5,
51	26	10	10	0, 3, 1,19,
51	25	3	3	17, 1, 5,19,
51	25	6	6	17, 9, 1,19,
51	25	8	5	17, 3, 9, 1,
51	25	10	9	17, 3, 1, 5,
51	25	10	7	17, 9, 1, 5,
51	25	10	5	17, 3, 1,19,
51	24	6	6	0,17, 9, 1,19,
51	24	6	6	0,17, 1, 5,19,
51	24	8	6	0,17, 3, 9, 1,
51	24	10	10	0,17, 3, 1, 5,
51	24	10	7	0,17, 9, 1, 5,
51	24	10	10	0,17, 3, 1,19,
51	19	3	3	1, 5,19,11,
51	19	9	9	3, 1, 5,19,
51	19	10	6	3, 9, 1,19,

n	k	d	d_{BCH}	Roots of Gen. Poly.
51	19	10	9	9, 1, 5,19,
51	19	14	11	3, 9, 1, 5,
51	18	6	6	0, 1, 5,19,11,
51	18	10	10	0, 3, 9, 1,19,
51	18	10	10	0, 9, 1, 5,19,
51	18	14	12	0, 3, 9, 1, 5,
51	18	14	14	0, 3, 1, 5,19,
51	17	3	3	17, 1, 5, 19, 11,
51	17	12	6	17, 3, 9, 1,19,
51	17	14	9	17, 3, 1, 5,19,
51	17	14	10	17, 9, 1, 5,19,
51	17	16	11	17, 3, 9, 1, 5,
51	16	6	6	0,17, 1, 5,19,11,
51	16	12	10	0,17, 3, 9, 1,19,
51	16	14	14	0,17, 3, 1, 5,19,
51	16	14	10	0,17, 9, 1, 5,19,
51	16	16	12	0,17, 3, 9, 1, 5,
51	11	15	9	3, 1, 5,19,11,
51	11	15	9	9, 1, 5,19,11,
51	11	17	17	3, 9, 1, 5,19,
51	10	18	18	0, 3, 9, 1, 5,19,
51	10	18	18	0, 3, 1, 5,19,11,
51	10	18	18	0, 9, 1, 5,19,11,
51	9	15	12	17, 3, 1, 5,19,11,
51	9	15	12	17, 9, 1, 5,19,11,
51	9	19	19	17, 3, 9, 1, 5,19,
51	8	18	18	0,17, 3, 1, 5,19,11,
51	8	18	18	0,17, 9, 1, 5,19,11,
51	8	24	20	0,17, 3, 9, 1, 5,19,
51	3	17	17	3, 9, 1, 5,19,11,
51	2	34	34	0, 3, 9, 1, 5,19,11,
55	41	4	3	5,11,
55	40	4	3	0, 5,11,
55	35	5	4	1,
55	34	8	4	0, 1,
55	31	5	5	1,11,
55	30	10	5	0, 1,11,
55	25	11	7	1, 5,
55	24	12	7	0, 1, 5,
55	21	15	8	1, 5,11,
55	20	16	8	0, 1, 5,11,
55	15	5	5	1, 3,
55	14	10	10	0, 1, 3,
55	11	5	5	1, 3,11,
55	10	10	10	0, 1, 3,11,
55	5	11	11	1, 3, 5,
55	4	22	22	0, 1, 3, 5,
57	39	3	3	1,
57	38	6	6	0, 1,

n	k	d	d_{BCH}	Roots of Gen. Poly.
57	37	3	3	1,19,
57	37	4	3	3,19,
57	36	4	3	0, 3,19,
57	36	6	6	0, 1, 19,
57	21	3	3	1, 5,
57	21	14	6	1, 3,
57	20	6	6	0, 1, 5,
57	20	14	10	0, 1, 3,
57	19	3	3	1, 5,19,
57	19	16	9	1, 3,19,
57	18	6	6	0, 1, 5,19,
57	18	16	10	0, 1, 3, 19,
57	3	19	19	1, 3, 5,
57	2	38	38	0, 1, 3, 5,

n	k	d	d_{BCH}	Roots of Gen. Poly.
63	57	3	3	1,
63	56	4	4	0, 1,
63	55	3	3	21, 1,
63	54	3	3	9, 1,
63	54	3	3	7, 9,
63	54	4	4	0,21, 1,
63	54	4	3	27, 1,
63	53	4	4	0,27, 1,
63	53	4	4	0, 9, 1,
63	53	4	3	0, 7, 9,
63	52	4	3	21,27, 1,
63	52	4	3	21, 9, 1,
63	52	4	3	21 , 7, 9,
63	51	3	3	1,31,
63	51	3	3	7, 1,
63	51	3	3	15, 1,
63	51	3	3	7,15,
63	51	3	3	1, 5,
63	51	3	3	1,11,
63	51	4	4	0,21,27, 1,
63	51	4	4	0,21, 9, 1,
63	51	4	3	27, 9, 1,
63	51	4	3	7,27, 9,
63	51	4	3	0,21, 7, 9,
63	51	5	5	3, 1,
63	50	4	4	0, 7, 1,
63	50	4	4	0,27, 9, 1,
63	50	4	4	0,15, 1,
63	50	6	6	0, 3, 1,
63	50	4	3	0, 7,15,
63	50	4	3	0, 7,27, 9,
63	50	4	4	0, 1, 5,
63	50	4	4	0, 1,11,
63	50	6	6	0, 1,31,
63	49	4	3	21, 7, 1,
63	49	4	3	21,27, 9, 1,
63	49	4	3	21,15, 1,
63	49	4	3	21, 7,15,
63	49	4	3	21, 7,27, 9,
63	49	4	4	21, 1,11,
63	49	5	3	21, 1,31,
63	49	5	5	21, 3, 1,
63	49	5	4	21, 1, 5,
63	48	3	3	9,15, 1,
63	48	3	3	7, 9,15,
63	48	3	3	9, 1,11,
63	48	4	4	0,21, 7, 1,
63	48	4	4	7, 9, 1,
63	48	4	4	0,21,27, 9, 1,
63	48	4	4	0,21,15, 1,

n	k	d	d_{BCH}	Roots of Gen. Poly.
63	48	4	3	0,21, 7,15,
63	48	4	3	7, 9, 3,
63	48	4	3	0,21, 7,27, 9,
63	48	4	4	27, 1, 5,
63	48	4	4	0,21, 1,11,
63	48	5	4	7,27, 1,
63	48	5	5	27, 3, 1,
63	48	5	5	9, 3, 1,
63	48	5	4	9, 1, 5,
63	48	5	5	27, 1,11,
63	48	6	6	0,21, 1,31,
63	48	6	4	9, 1,31,
63	48	6	3	27,15, 1,
63	48	6	6	0,21, 3, 1,
63	48	6	4	0,21, 1, 5,
63	47	4	4	0, 7, 9, 1,
63	47	4	4	0, 9,15, 1,
63	47	4	3	0, 7, 9,15,
63	47	4	3	0, 7, 9, 3,
63	47	4	4	0,27, 1, 5,
63	47	4	4	0, 9, 1,11,
63	47	6	6	0, 9, 1,31,
63	47	6	4	0, 7,27, 1,
63	47	6	4	0,27,15, 1,
63	47	6	6	0,27, 3, 1,
63	47	6	6	0, 9, 3, 1,
63	47	6	4	0, 9, 1, 5,
63	47	6	5	0,27, 1,11,
63	46	4	4	21, 7, 9, 1,
63	46	4	3	21, 9,15, 1,
63	46	4	3	21, 7, 9,15,
63	46	4	3	21, 7, 9, 3,
63	46	4	4	21, 9, 1,11,
63	46	5	5	21, 9, 3, 1,
63	46	6	4	21, 9, 1,31,
63	46	6	4	21, 7,27, 1,
63	46	6	3	21,27,15, 1,
63	46	6	5	21,27, 3, 1,
63	46	6	4	21,27, 1, 5,
63	46	6	6	21,27, 1,11,
63	46	7*	4	21, 9, 1, 5,
63	45	3	3	1, 5,11,
63	45	3	3	1, 5,31,
63	45	3	3	1, 5,23,
63	45	3	3	1,11,23,
63	45	3	3	7, 1,31,
63	45	3	3	7, 1, 5,
63	45	3	3	7, 1,11,
63	45	3	3	15, 1,11,
63	45	4	4	0,21, 7, 9, 1,
63	45	4	4	7,15, 1,

n	k	d	d_{BCH}	Roots of Gen. Poly.
63	45	4	4	0,21, 9,15, 1,
63	45	4	3	7,15, 3,
63	45	4	3	0,21, 7, 9,15,
63	45	4	3	7,27, 9, 3,
63	45	4	3	0,21, 7, 9, 3,
63	45	4	4	0,21, 9, 1,11,
63	45	5	5	7, 3, 1,
63	45	5	5	15, 3, 1,
63	45	5	5	15, 1, 5,
63	45	5	5	3, 1,11,
63	45	6	6	0,21, 9, 1,31,
63	45	6	4	27, 9, 1,31,
63	45	6	4	0,21, 7,27, 1,
63	45	6	4	7,27, 9, 1,
63	45	6	4	0,21,27,15, 1,
63	45	6	3	27, 9,15, 1,
63	45	6	6	0,21,27, 3, 1,
63	45	6	6	0,21, 9, 3, 1,
63	45	6	5	27, 9, 3, 1,
63	45	6	4	0,21,27, 1, 5,
63	45	6	4	27, 9, 1, 5,
63	45	6	6	0,21,27, 1,11,
63	45	6	5	27, 9, 1,11,
63	45	7	5	15, 1,31,
63	45	7	7	3, 1, 5,
63	45	8*	4	0,21, 9, 1, 5,
63	44	4	4	0, 1,11,23,
63	44	4	4	0, 7,15, 1,
63	44	4	3	0, 7,15, 3,
63	44	4	3	0, 7,27, 9, 3,
63	44	4	4	0, 7, 1,11,
63	44	4	4	0,15, 1,11,
63	44	6	4	0, 1, 5,11,
63	44	6	6	0, 1, 5,31,
63	44	6	6	0, 1, 5,23,
63	44	6	6	0, 7, 1,31,
63	44	6	6	0,27, 9, 1,31,
63	44	6	4	0, 7,27, 9, 1,
63	44	6	4	0,27, 9,15, 1,
63	44	6	6	0, 7, 3, 1,
63	44	6	6	0,27, 9, 3, 1,
63	44	6	6	0,15, 3, 1,
63	44	6	4	0, 7, 1, 5,
63	44	6	4	0,27, 9, 1, 5,
63	44	6	6	0,15, 1, 5,
63	44	6	5	0,27, 9, 1,11,
63	44	6	6	0, 3, 1,11,
63	44	8	8	0,15, 1,31,
63	44	8	8	0, 3, 1, 5,
63	43	4	4	21, 7, 1,11,
63	43	4	4	21,15, 1,11,

n	k	d	d_{BCH}	Roots of Gen. Poly.
63	43	4	4	21, 1,11,23,
63	43	4	4	21, 7,15, 1,
63	43	4	3	21, 7,15, 3,
63	43	4	3	21, 7,27, 9, 3,
63	43	5	5	21,15, 3, 1,
63	43	6	4	21, 7, 1, 5,
63	43	6	6	21,27, 9, 1,11,
63	43	6	6	21, 3, 1,11,
63	43	6	4	21, 1, 5,11,
63	43	6	5	21, 1, 5,31,
63	43	6	5	21, 1, 5,23,
63	43	6	3	21, 7, 1,31,
63	43	6	4	21,27, 9, 1,31,
63	43	6	3	21,27, 9,15, 1,
63	43	6	5	21, 7, 3, 1,
63	43	6	5	21,27, 9, 3, 1,
63	43	7	4	21,27, 9, 1, 5,
63	43	7	5	21,15, 1, 5,
63	43	7	7	21, 3, 1, 5,
63	43	7	5	21,15, 1,31,
63	43	8	4	21, 7,27, 9, 1,
63	42	3	3	9,15, 1,11,
63	42	3	3	9, 1,11,23,
63	42	4	4	0,21, 7, 1,11,
63	42	4	4	7, 9, 1,11,
63	42	4	4	0,21,15, 1,11,
63	42	4	4	0,21, 1,11,23,
63	42	4	4	0,21, 7,15, 1,
63	42	4	4	7, 9,15, 1,
63	42	4	3	0,21, 7,15, 3,
63	42	4	3	7,27,15, 3,
63	42	4	3	0,21, 7,27, 9, 3,
63	42	5	5	9,15, 1, 5,
63	42	5	5	7,27, 1,11,
63	42	5	5	27, 3, 1,11,
63	42	5	5	27, 1,11,23,
63	42	5	5	7,27, 3, 1,
63	42	6	4	0,21, 7, 1, 5,
63	42	6	5	7,27, 1, 5,
63	42	6	5	7, 9, 1, 5,
63	42	6	5	27,15, 1, 5,
63	42	6	6	0,21,27, 9, 1,11,
63	42	6	5	27,15, 1,11,
63	42	6	6	0,21, 3, 1,11,
63	42	6	5	9, 3, 1,11,
63	42	6	4	0,21, 1, 5,11,
63	42	6	6	27, 1, 5,11,
63	42	6	5	9, 1, 5,11,
63	42	6	6	0,21, 1, 5,31,
63	42	6	4	27, 1, 5,31,
63	42	6	5	9, 1, 5,31,

n	k	d	d_{BCH}	Roots of Gen. Poly.
63	42	6	6	0,21, 1, 5,23,
63	42	6	5	27, 1, 5,23,
63	42	6	4	9, 1, 5,23,
63	42	6	6	0,21, 7, 1,31,
63	42	6	5	7, 9, 1,31,
63	42	6	6	0,21,27, 9, 1,31,
63	42	6	5	7,27,15, 1,
63	42	6	4	0,21,27, 9,15, 1,
63	42	6	6	0,21, 7, 3, 1,
63	42	6	5	7, 9, 3, 1,
63	42	6	6	0,21,27, 9, 3, 1,
63	42	6	6	0,21,15, 3, 1,
63	42	6	5	27,15, 3, 1,
63	42	6	5	9,15, 3, 1,
63	42	7	7	27, 3, 1, 5,
63	42	7	7	9, 3, 1, 5,
63	42	7	5	9, 3, 1,31,
63	42	7	5	9,15, 1,31,
63	42	8	4	0,21,27, 9, 1, 5,
63	42	8	6	0,21,15, 1, 5,
63	42	8	8	0,21, 3, 1, 5,
63	42	8	8	0,21,15, 1,31,
63	42	8	4	0,21, 7,27, 9, 1,
63	41	4	4	0, 7, 9, 1,11,
63	41	4	4	0, 9,15, 1,11,
63	41	4	4	0, 9, 1,11,23,
63	41	4	4	0, 7, 9,15, 1,
63	41	4	3	0, 7,27,15, 3,
63	41	6	5	0, 7,27, 1, 5,
63	41	6	5	0, 7, 9, 1, 5,
63	41	6	6	0,27,15, 1, 5,
63	41	6	6	0, 9,15, 1, 5,
63	41	6	5	0, 7,27, 1,11,
63	41	6	5	0,27,15, 1,11,
63	41	6	6	0,27, 3, 1,11,
63	41	6	6	0, 9, 3, 1,11,
63	41	6	6	0,27, 1, 5,11,
63	41	6	5	0, 9, 1, 5,11,
63	41	6	6	0,27, 1, 5,31,
63	41	6	6	0, 9, 1, 5,31,
63	41	6	6	0,27, 1, 5,23,
63	41	6	6	0, 9, 1, 5,23,
63	41	6	5	0,27, 1,11,23,
63	41	6	6	0, 7, 9, 1,31,
63	41	6	5	0, 7,27,15, 1,
63	41	6	6	0, 7,27, 3, 1,
63	41	6	6	0, 7, 9, 3, 1,
63	41	6	6	0,27,15, 3, 1,
63	41	6	6	0, 9,15, 3, 1,
63	41	8	8	0,27, 3, 1, 5,
63	41	8	8	0, 9, 3, 1, 5,

n	k	d	d_{BCH}	Roots of Gen. Poly.
63	41	8	8	0, 9, 3, 1,31,
63	41	8	8	0, 9,15, 1,31,
63	40	4	4	21, 7, 9, 1,11,
63	40	4	4	21, 9,15, 1,11,
63	40	4	4	21, 9, 1,11,23,
63	40	4	4	21, 7, 9,15, 1,
63	40	4	3	21, 7,27,15, 3,
63	40	6	6	21,27,15, 1,11,
63	40	6	6	21,27, 3, 1,11,
63	40	6	6	21, 9, 3, 1,11,
63	40	6	6	21,27, 1,11,23,
63	40	6	5	21,27,15, 3, 1,
63	40	6	5	21, 9,15, 3, 1,
63	40	7	7	21, 9, 3, 1, 5,
63	40	7	6	21, 9, 1, 5,31,
63	40	8	5	21, 7,27, 1, 5,
63	40	8	5	21, 7, 9, 1, 5,
63	40	8	5	21,27,15, 1, 5,
63	40	8	5	21, 9,15, 1, 5,
63	40	8	7	21,27, 3, 1, 5,
63	40	8	6	21, 7,27, 1,11,
63	40	8	7	21,27, 1, 5,11,
63	40	8	5	21, 9, 1, 5,11,
63	40	8	5	21,27, 1, 5,31,
63	40	8	7	21,27, 1, 5,23,
63	40	8	5	21, 9, 1, 5,23,
63	40	8	5	21, 7, 9, 1,31,
63	40	8	5	21, 9, 3, 1,31,
63	40	8	5	21, 9,15, 1,31,
63	40	8	5	21, 7,27,15, 1,
63	40	8	5	21, 7,27, 3, 1,
63	40	8	5	21, 7, 9, 3, 1,
63	39	3	3	1, 5,11,31,
63	39	3	3	1, 5,11,23,
63	39	3	3	1, 5,31,23,
63	39	3	3	7, 1, 5,11,
63	39	3	3	7, 1, 5,31,
63	39	3	3	7, 1, 5,23,
63	39	3	3	7, 1,11,23,
63	39	3	3	15, 1,11,23,
63	39	4	4	0,21, 7, 9, 1,11,
63	39	4	4	7,15, 1,11,
63	39	4	4	0,21, 9,15, 1,11,
63	39	4	4	0,21, 9, 1,11,23,
63	39	4	4	0,21, 7, 9,15, 1,
63	39	4	3	0,21, 7,27,15, 3,
63	39	4	3	7,27, 9,15, 3,
63	39	5	5	7, 3, 1,11,
63	39	5	5	3, 1,11,23,
63	39	6	5	7,27, 9, 1, 5,
63	39	6	5	7,15, 1, 5,

n	k	d	d_{BCH}	Roots of Gen. Poly.
63	39	6	5	27, 9,15, 1, 5,
63	39	6	5	7,27, 9, 1,11,
63	39	6	6	0,21,27,15, 1,11,
63	39	6	5	27, 9,15, 1,11,
63	39	6	6	0,21,27, 3, 1,11,
63	39	6	6	0,21, 9, 3, 1,11,
63	39	6	5	27, 9, 3, 1,11,
63	39	6	5	15, 3, 1,11,
63	39	6	6	27, 9, 1, 5,11,
63	39	6	5	27, 9, 1, 5,31,
63	39	6	5	27, 9, 1, 5,23,
63	39	6	6	0,21,27, 1,11,23,
63	39	6	5	27, 9, 1,11,23,
63	39	6	5	7,27, 9, 1,31,
63	39	6	5	7,27, 9,15, 1,
63	39	6	5	7,27, 9, 3, 1,
63	39	6	6	0,21,27,15, 3, 1,
63	39	6	6	0,21, 9,15, 3, 1,
63	39	6	5	27, 9,15, 3, 1,
63	39	7	7	27, 9, 3, 1, 5,
63	39	7	7	15, 3, 1, 5,
63	39	7	7	15, 1, 5,11,
63	39	7	7	3, 1, 5,11,
63	39	7	5	15, 1, 5,31,
63	39	7	7	3, 1, 5,31,
63	39	7	5	15, 1, 5,23,
63	39	7	7	3, 1, 5,23,
63	39	7	5	27, 9, 3, 1,31,
63	39	7	5	15, 3, 1,31,
63	39	8	5	0,21, 7,27, 1, 5,
63	39	8	5	0,21, 7, 9, 1, 5,
63	39	8	6	0,21,27,15, 1, 5,
63	39	8	6	0,21, 9,15, 1, 5,
63	39	8	8	0,21,27, 3, 1, 5,
63	39	8	8	0,21, 9, 3, 1, 5,
63	39	8	6	0,21, 7,27, 1,11,
63	39	8	7	0,21,27, 1, 5,11,
63	39	8	5	0,21, 9, 1, 5,11,
63	39	8	6	0,21,27, 1, 5,31,
63	39	8	6	0,21, 9, 1, 5,31,
63	39	8	7	0,21,27, 1, 5,23,
63	39	8	6	0,21, 9, 1, 5,23,
63	39	8	6	0,21, 7, 9, 1,31,
63	39	8	8	0,21, 9, 3, 1,31,
63	39	8	5	7,15, 1,31,
63	39	8	8	0,21, 9,15, 1,31,
63	39	8	5	0,21, 7,27,15, 1,
63	39	8	6	0,21, 7,27, 3, 1,
63	39	8	6	0,21, 7, 9, 3, 1,
63	39	8	5	7,15, 3, 1,
63	39	9	9	7, 3, 1, 5,

n	k	d	d_{BCH}	Roots of Gen. Poly.
63	38	4	4	0, 7,15, 1,11,
63	38	4	4	0, 7, 1,11,23,
63	38	4	4	0,15, 1,11,23,
63	38	4	3	0, 7,27, 9,15, 3,
63	38	6	5	0, 7,27, 9, 1, 5,
63	38	6	6	0, 7,15, 1, 5,
63	38	6	6	0,27, 9,15, 1, 5,
63	38	6	5	0, 7,27, 9, 1,11,
63	38	6	5	0,27, 9,15, 1,11,
63	38	6	6	0,27, 9, 3, 1,11,
63	38	6	6	0,15, 3, 1,11,
63	38	6	6	0, 1, 5,11,31,
63	38	6	6	0, 1, 5,11,23,
63	38	6	6	0, 1, 5,31,23,
63	38	6	4	0, 7, 1, 5,11,
63	38	6	6	0,27, 9, 1, 5,11,
63	38	6	6	0, 7, 1, 5,31,
63	38	6	6	0,27, 9, 1, 5,31,
63	38	6	6	0, 7, 1, 5,23,
63	38	6	6	0,27, 9, 1, 5,23,
63	38	6	5	0,27, 9, 1,11,23,
63	38	6	6	0, 3, 1,11,23,
63	38	6	6	0, 7,27, 9, 1,31,
63	38	6	5	0, 7,27, 9,15, 1,
63	38	6	6	0, 7,27, 9, 3, 1,
63	38	6	6	0,27, 9,15, 3, 1,
63	38	8	8	0,27, 9, 3, 1, 5,
63	38	8	8	0,15, 3, 1, 5,
63	38	8	6	0, 7, 3, 1,11,
63	38	8	8	0,15, 1, 5,11,
63	38	8	8	0, 3, 1, 5,11,
63	38	8	8	0,15, 1, 5,31,
63	38	8	8	0,15, 1, 5,23,
63	38	8	8	0, 3, 1, 5,23,
63	38	8	8	0,27, 9, 3, 1,31,
63	38	8	8	0, 7,15, 1,31,
63	38	8	6	0, 7,15, 3, 1,
63	38	10	10	0, 7, 3, 1, 5,
63	38	10	10	0, 3, 1, 5,31,
63	38	10	10	0,15, 3, 1,31,
63	37	4	4	21, 7,15, 1,11,
63	37	4	4	21, 7, 1,11,23,
63	37	4	4	21,15, 1,11,23,
63	37	4	3	21, 7,27, 9,15, 3,
63	37	6	6	21,27, 9,15, 1,11,
63	37	6	6	21,27, 9, 3, 1,11,
63	37	6	6	21,15, 3, 1,11,
63	37	6	5	21, 1, 5,11,31,
63	37	6	5	21, 1, 5,11,23,
63	37	6	6	21, 1, 5,31,23,
63	37	6	4	21, 7, 1, 5,11,

n	k	d	d_{BCH}	Roots of Gen. Poly.
63	37	6	5	21, 7, 1, 5,31,
63	37	6	5	21, 7, 1, 5,23,
63	37	6	6	21,27, 9, 1,11,23,
63	37	6	6	21, 3, 1,11,23,
63	37	6	5	21,27, 9,15, 3, 1,
63	37	7	7	21,15, 1, 5,11,
63	37	7	7	21, 3, 1, 5,11,
63	37	7	7	21, 3, 1, 5,31,
63	37	7	7	21, 3, 1, 5,23,
63	37	7	5	21,15, 3, 1,31,
63	37	8	5	21, 7,27, 9, 1, 5,
63	37	8	5	21,27, 9,15, 1, 5,
63	37	8	7	21,27, 9, 3, 1, 5,
63	37	8	7	21,15, 3, 1, 5,
63	37	8	6	21, 7,27, 9, 1,11,
63	37	8	6	21, 7, 3, 1,11,
63	37	8	7	21,27, 9, 1, 5,11,
63	37	8	7	21,15, 1, 5,31,
63	37	8	7	21,27, 9, 1, 5,23,
63	37	8	5	21, 7,27, 9, 1,31,
63	37	8	5	21, 7,27, 9,15, 1,
63	37	8	5	21, 7,27, 9, 3, 1,
63	37	8	5	21, 7,15, 3, 1,
63	37	9	5	21, 7,15, 1, 5,
63	37	9	9	21, 7, 3, 1, 5,
63	37	9	6	21,27, 9, 1, 5,31,
63	37	9	5	21,15, 1, 5,23,
63	37	9	5	21, 7,15, 1,31,
63	37	10	5	21,27, 9, 3, 1,31,
63	36	3	3	9,15, 1,11,23,
63	36	4	4	0,21, 7,15, 1,11,
63	36	4	4	7, 9,15, 1,11,
63	36	4	4	0,21, 7, 1,11,23,
63	36	4	4	7, 9, 1,11,23,
63	36	4	4	0,21,15, 1,11,23,
63	36	4	3	0,21, 7,27, 9,15, 3,
63	36	5	5	7,27, 3, 1,11,
63	36	5	5	7,27, 1,11,23,
63	36	5	5	27, 3, 1,11,23,
63	36	6	6	7,27,15, 1, 5,
63	36	6	6	7, 9,15, 1, 5,
63	36	6	6	0,21,27, 9,15, 1,11,
63	36	6	6	0,21,27, 9, 3, 1,11,
63	36	6	6	0,21,15, 3, 1,11,
63	36	6	5	27,15, 3, 1,11,
63	36	6	5	9,15, 3, 1,11,
63	36	6	6	0,21, 1, 5,11,31,
63	36	6	6	27, 1, 5,11,31,
63	36	6	6	9, 1, 5,11,31,
63	36	6	6	0,21, 1, 5,11,23,
63	36	6	6	27, 1, 5,11,23,

n	k	d	d_{BCH}	Roots of Gen. Poly.
63	36	6	5	9, 1, 5, 11, 23,
63	36	6	6	0, 21, 1, 5, 31, 23,
63	36	6	5	9, 1, 5, 31, 23,
63	36	6	4	0, 21, 7, 1, 5, 11,
63	36	6	6	7, 27, 1, 5, 11,
63	36	6	6	7, 9, 1, 5, 11,
63	36	6	6	0, 21, 7, 1, 5, 31,
63	36	6	5	7, 27, 1, 5, 31,
63	36	6	5	7, 9, 1, 5, 31,
63	36	6	6	0, 21, 7, 1, 5, 23,
63	36	6	6	7, 27, 1, 5, 23,
63	36	6	5	7, 9, 1, 5, 23,
63	36	6	6	0, 21, 27, 9, 1, 11, 23,
63	36	6	5	27, 15, 1, 11, 23,
63	36	6	6	0, 21, 3, 1, 11, 23,
63	36	6	5	9, 3, 1, 11, 23,
63	36	6	6	0, 21, 27, 9, 15, 3, 1,
63	36	7	7	27, 15, 3, 1, 5,
63	36	7	7	9, 15, 3, 1, 5,
63	36	7	7	27, 15, 1, 5, 11,
63	36	7	7	9, 15, 1, 5, 11,
63	36	7	7	27, 3, 1, 5, 11,
63	36	7	7	9, 3, 1, 5, 11,
63	36	7	5	27, 15, 1, 5, 31,
63	36	7	5	9, 15, 1, 5, 31,
63	36	7	7	27, 3, 1, 5, 31,
63	36	7	7	9, 3, 1, 5, 31,
63	36	7	6	27, 15, 1, 5, 23,
63	36	7	5	9, 15, 1, 5, 23,
63	36	7	7	27, 3, 1, 5, 23,
63	36	7	7	9, 3, 1, 5, 23,
63	36	7	5	27, 15, 3, 1, 31,
63	36	8	5	0, 21, 7, 27, 9, 1, 5,
63	36	8	6	0, 21, 27, 9, 15, 1, 5,
63	36	8	8	0, 21, 27, 9, 3, 1, 5,
63	36	8	8	0, 21, 15, 3, 1, 5,
63	36	8	6	0, 21, 7, 27, 9, 1, 11,
63	36	8	5	7, 27, 15, 1, 11,
63	36	8	6	0, 21, 7, 3, 1, 11,
63	36	8	5	7, 9, 3, 1, 11,
63	36	8	7	0, 21, 27, 9, 1, 5, 11,
63	36	8	8	0, 21, 15, 1, 5, 31,
63	36	8	7	0, 21, 27, 9, 1, 5, 23,
63	36	8	6	0, 21, 7, 27, 9, 1, 31,
63	36	8	5	0, 21, 7, 27, 9, 15, 1,
63	36	8	6	0, 21, 7, 27, 9, 3, 1,
63	36	8	6	0, 21, 7, 15, 3, 1,
63	36	8	5	7, 27, 15, 3, 1,
63	36	8	5	7, 9, 15, 3, 1,
63	36	9	9	7, 27, 3, 1, 5,
63	36	9	5	7, 9, 3, 1, 31,

n	k	d	d_{BCH}	Roots of Gen. Poly.
63	36	9	6	7, 9,15, 1,31,
63	36	10	6	0,21, 7,15, 1, 5,
63	36	10	10	0,21, 7, 3, 1, 5,
63	36	10	8	0,21,15, 1, 5,11,
63	36	10	8	0,21, 3, 1, 5,11,
63	36	10	6	0,21,27, 9, 1, 5,31,
63	36	10	10	0,21, 3, 1, 5,31,
63	36	10	8	0,21,15, 1, 5,23,
63	36	10	8	0,21, 3, 1, 5,23,
63	36	10	8	0,21,27, 9, 3, 1,31,
63	36	10	8	0,21, 7,15, 1,31,
63	36	10	10	0,21,15, 3, 1,31,
63	36	11	11	7, 9, 3, 1, 5,
63	35	4	4	0, 7, 9,15, 1,11,
63	35	4	4	0, 7, 9, 1,11,23,
63	35	4	4	0, 9,15, 1,11,23,
63	35	6	6	0, 7,27,15, 1, 5,
63	35	6	6	0, 7, 9,15, 1, 5,
63	35	6	6	0,27,15, 3, 1,11,
63	35	6	6	0, 9,15, 3, 1,11,
63	35	6	6	0,27, 1, 5,11,31,
63	35	6	6	0, 9, 1, 5,11,31,
63	35	6	6	0,27, 1, 5,11,23,
63	35	6	6	0, 9, 1, 5,11,23,
63	35	6	6	0, 9, 1, 5,31,23,
63	35	6	6	0, 7,27, 1, 5,11,
63	35	6	6	0, 7, 9, 1, 5,11,
63	35	6	6	0, 7,27, 1, 5,31,
63	35	6	6	0, 7, 9, 1, 5,31,
63	35	6	6	0, 7,27, 1, 5,23,
63	35	6	6	0, 7, 9, 1, 5,23,
63	35	6	5	0, 7,27, 1,11,23,
63	35	6	5	0,27,15, 1,11,23,
63	35	6	6	0,27, 3, 1,11,23,
63	35	6	6	0, 9, 3, 1,11,23,
63	35	8	8	0,27,15, 3, 1, 5,
63	35	8	8	0, 9,15, 3, 1, 5,
63	35	8	5	0, 7,27,15, 1,11,
63	35	8	6	0, 7,27, 3, 1,11,
63	35	8	6	0, 7, 9, 3, 1,11,
63	35	8	8	0,27,15, 1, 5,11,
63	35	8	8	0, 9,15, 1, 5,11,
63	35	8	8	0,27, 3, 1, 5,11,
63	35	8	8	0, 9, 3, 1, 5,11,
63	35	8	8	0,27,15, 1, 5,31,
63	35	8	8	0, 9,15, 1, 5,31,
63	35	8	8	0,27,15, 1, 5,23,
63	35	8	8	0, 9,15, 1, 5,23,
63	35	8	8	0,27, 3, 1, 5,23,
63	35	8	8	0, 9, 3, 1, 5,23,
63	35	8	6	0, 7,27,15, 3, 1,

n	k	d	d_{BCH}	Roots of Gen. Poly.
63	35	8	6	0, 7, 9,15, 3, 1,
63	35	10	10	0, 7,27, 3, 1, 5,
63	35	10	10	0,27, 3, 1, 5,31,
63	35	10	8	0, 7, 9, 3, 1,31,
63	35	10	8	0, 7, 9,15, 1,31,
63	35	10	10	0,27,15, 3, 1,31,
63	35	12	12	0, 7, 9, 3, 1, 5,
63	35	12	10	0, 9, 3, 1, 5,31,
63	34	4	4	21, 7, 9, 1,11,23,
63	34	4	4	21, 9,15, 1,11,23,
63	34	4	4	21, 7, 9,15, 1,11,
63	34	6	6	21,27,15, 1,11,23,
63	34	6	6	21,27, 3, 1,11,23,
63	34	6	6	21, 9, 3, 1,11,23,
63	34	6	6	21,27,15, 3, 1,11,
63	34	6	6	21, 9,15, 3, 1,11,
63	34	8	6	21, 7,27, 1,11,23,
63	34	8	5	21, 7,27,15, 3, 1,
63	34	8	5	21, 7, 9,15, 3, 1,
63	34	8	7	21,27,15, 3, 1, 5,
63	34	8	7	21, 9,15, 3, 1, 5,
63	34	8	6	21, 7,27,15, 1,11,
63	34	8	6	21, 7,27, 3, 1,11,
63	34	8	6	21, 7, 9, 3, 1,11,
63	34	9	8	21,27, 1, 5,11,31,
63	34	9	7	21, 9, 1, 5,11,31,
63	34	9	7	21,27, 1, 5,11,23,
63	34	9	5	21, 9, 1, 5,11,23,
63	34	9	8	21, 9, 1, 5,31,23,
63	34	9	7	21, 7,27, 1, 5,11,
63	34	9	6	21, 7, 9, 1, 5,11,
63	34	9	7	21, 9,15, 1, 5,11,
63	34	9	5	21, 7,27, 1, 5,31,
63	34	9	6	21, 7, 9, 1, 5,31,
63	34	9	7	21,27, 3, 1, 5,31,
63	34	9	7	21, 7,27, 1, 5,23,
63	34	9	5	21, 7, 9, 1, 5,23,
63	34	9	7	21,27,15, 1, 5,23,
63	34	9	5	21, 9,15, 1, 5,23,
63	34	9	8	21,27, 3, 1, 5,23,
63	34	9	5	21,27,15, 3, 1,31,
63	34	10	8	21,27, 3, 1, 5,11,
63	34	10	7	21,27,15, 1, 5,31,
63	34	10	7	21, 9,15, 1, 5,31,
63	34	10	5	21, 7, 9, 3, 1,31,
63	34	10	6	21, 7,27,15, 1, 5,
63	34	10	6	21, 7, 9,15, 1, 5,
63	34	10	9	21, 7,27, 3, 1, 5,
63	34	11	7	21,27,15, 1, 5,11,
63	34	11	7	21, 9, 3, 1, 5,11,
63	34	11	7	21, 9, 3, 1, 5,31,

n	k	d	d_{BCH}	Roots of Gen. Poly.
63	34	11	7	21, 9, 3, 1, 5,23,
63	34	11	6	21, 7, 9,15, 1,31,
63	34	11	11	21, 7, 9, 3, 1, 5,
63	33	3	3	1, 5,11,31,23,
63	33	3	3	7, 1, 5,11,31,
63	33	3	3	7, 1, 5,11,23,
63	33	3	3	7, 1, 5,31,23,
63	33	4	4	0,21, 7, 9,15, 1,11,
63	33	4	4	0,21, 7, 9, 1,11,23,
63	33	4	4	7,15, 1,11,23,
63	33	4	4	0,21, 9,15, 1,11,23,
63	33	5	5	7, 3, 1,11,23,
63	33	6	5	27, 9, 3, 1,11,23,
63	33	6	5	15, 3, 1,11,23,
63	33	6	6	7,27, 9,15, 1, 5,
63	33	6	6	0,21,27,15, 3, 1,11,
63	33	6	6	0,21, 9,15, 3, 1,11,
63	33	6	5	27, 9,15, 3, 1,11,
63	33	6	6	27, 9, 1, 5,11,23,
63	33	6	6	27, 9, 1, 5,11,31,
63	33	6	5	27, 9, 1, 5,31,23,
63	33	6	6	7,27, 9, 1, 5,11,
63	33	6	5	7,27, 9, 1, 5,31,
63	33	6	6	7,27, 9, 1, 5,23,
63	33	6	5	7,27, 9, 1,11,23,
63	33	6	6	0,21,27,15, 1,11,23,
63	33	6	5	27, 9,15, 1,11,23,
63	33	6	6	0,21,27, 3, 1,11,23,
63	33	6	6	0,21, 9, 3, 1,11,23,
63	33	7	5	27, 9,15, 3, 1,31,
63	33	7	7	27, 9,15, 3, 1, 5,
63	33	7	7	15, 1, 5,11,31,
63	33	7	7	3, 1, 5,11,31,
63	33	7	7	15, 1, 5,11,23,
63	33	7	7	3, 1, 5,11,23,
63	33	7	7	15, 1, 5,31,23,
63	33	7	7	27, 9,15, 1, 5,11,
63	33	7	7	27, 9, 3, 1, 5,11,
63	33	7	7	15, 3, 1, 5,11,
63	33	7	5	27, 9,15, 1, 5,31,
63	33	7	7	27, 9, 3, 1, 5,31,
63	33	7	7	15, 3, 1, 5,31,
63	33	7	6	27, 9,15, 1, 5,23,
63	33	7	7	27, 9, 3, 1, 5,23,
63	33	7	7	15, 3, 1, 5,23,
63	33	8	6	0,21, 7,27,15, 3, 1,
63	33	8	6	0,21, 7, 9,15, 3, 1,
63	33	8	5	7,27, 9,15, 3, 1,
63	33	8	8	0,21,27,15, 3, 1, 5,
63	33	8	8	0,21, 9,15, 3, 1, 5,
63	33	8	6	0,21, 7,27,15, 1,11,

n	k	d	d_{BCH}	Roots of Gen. Poly.
63	33	8	5	7,27, 9,15, 1,11,
63	33	8	6	0,21, 7,27, 3, 1,11,
63	33	8	6	0,21, 7, 9, 3, 1,11,
63	33	8	5	7,27, 9, 3, 1,11,
63	33	8	5	7,15, 3, 1,11,
63	33	8	6	0,21, 7,27, 1,11,23,
63	33	9	6	7,27, 9, 3, 1,31,
63	33	9	6	7,15, 3, 1,31,
63	33	9	9	7,15, 3, 1, 5,
63	33	9	9	7,15, 1, 5,11,
63	33	9	9	7, 3, 1, 5,11,
63	33	9	5	7,15, 1, 5,31,
63	33	9	9	7, 3, 1, 5,31,
63	33	9	6	7,15, 1, 5,23,
63	33	9	9	7, 3, 1, 5,23,
63	33	10	8	0,21, 7, 9, 3, 1,31,
63	33	10	10	0,21,27,15, 3, 1,31,
63	33	10	6	0,21, 7,27,15, 1, 5,
63	33	10	6	0,21, 7, 9,15, 1, 5,
63	33	10	10	0,21, 7,27, 3, 1, 5,
63	33	10	8	0,21,27, 1, 5,11,31,
63	33	10	7	0,21, 9, 1, 5,11,31,
63	33	10	7	0,21,27, 1, 5,11,23,
63	33	10	6	0,21, 9, 1, 5,11,23,
63	33	10	8	0,21, 9, 1, 5,31,23,
63	33	10	7	0,21, 7,27, 1, 5,11,
63	33	10	8	0,21, 9,15, 1, 5,11,
63	33	10	8	0,21,27, 3, 1, 5,11,
63	33	10	6	0,21, 7, 9, 1, 5,31,
63	33	10	8	0,21,27,15, 1, 5,31,
63	33	10	8	0,21, 9,15, 1, 5,31,
63	33	10	10	0,21,27, 3, 1, 5,31,
63	33	10	7	0,21, 7,27, 1, 5,23,
63	33	10	8	0,21, 9,15, 1, 5,23,
63	33	10	8	0,21,27, 3, 1, 5,23,
63	33	11	11	7,27, 9, 3, 1, 5,
63	33	12	8	0,21, 7, 9,15, 1,31,
63	33	12	12	0,21, 7, 9, 3, 1, 5,
63	33	12	6	0,21, 7, 9, 1, 5,11,
63	33	12	8	0,21,27,15, 1, 5,11,
63	33	12	8	0,21, 9, 3, 1, 5,11,
63	33	12	6	0,21, 7,27, 1, 5,31,
63	33	12	10	0,21, 9, 3, 1, 5,31,
63	33	12	6	0,21, 7, 9, 1, 5,23,
63	33	12	8	0,21,27,15, 1, 5,23,
63	33	12	8	0,21, 9, 3, 1, 5,23,
63	32	4	4	0, 7,15, 1,11,23,
63	32	6	6	0, 1, 5,11,31,23,
63	32	6	6	0, 7, 1, 5,11,31,
63	32	6	6	0,27, 9, 1, 5,11,31,
63	32	6	6	0, 7, 1, 5,11,23,

n	k	d	d_{BCH}	Roots of Gen. Poly.
63	32	6	6	0,27, 9, 1, 5,11,23,
63	32	6	6	0, 7, 1, 5,31,23,
63	32	6	6	0,27, 9, 1, 5,31,23,
63	32	6	6	0, 7,27, 9, 1, 5,11,
63	32	6	6	0, 7,27, 9, 1, 5,31,
63	32	6	6	0, 7,27, 9, 1, 5,23,
63	32	6	5	0, 7,27, 9, 1,11,23,
63	32	6	5	0,27, 9,15, 1,11,23,
63	32	6	6	0,27, 9, 3, 1,11,23,
63	32	6	6	0,15, 3, 1,11,23,
63	32	6	6	0, 7,27, 9,15, 1, 5,
63	32	6	6	0,27, 9,15, 3, 1,11,
63	32	8	8	0,15, 1, 5,11,31,
63	32	8	8	0,27, 9,15, 1, 5,11,
63	32	8	8	0,27, 9, 3, 1, 5,11,
63	32	8	8	0,27, 9,15, 1, 5,31,
63	32	8	8	0,27, 9,15, 1, 5,23,
63	32	8	8	0,27, 9, 3, 1, 5,23,
63	32	8	6	0, 7, 3, 1,11,23,
63	32	8	6	0, 7,27, 9,15, 3, 1,
63	32	8	8	0,27, 9,15, 3, 1, 5,
63	32	8	5	0, 7,27, 9,15, 1,11,
63	32	8	6	0, 7,27, 9, 3, 1,11,
63	32	8	6	0, 7,15, 3, 1,11,
63	32	10	10	0, 3, 1, 5,11,31,
63	32	10	10	0,15, 1, 5,11,23,
63	32	10	8	0, 3, 1, 5,11,23,
63	32	10	10	0,15, 1, 5,31,23,
63	32	10	10	0, 7, 3, 1, 5,11,
63	32	10	8	0, 7,15, 1, 5,31,
63	32	10	8	0, 7,15, 1, 5,23,
63	32	10	10	0, 7, 3, 1, 5,23,
63	32	10	10	0,15, 3, 1, 5,23,
63	32	10	8	0, 7,27, 9, 3, 1,31,
63	32	10	10	0, 7,15, 3, 1,31,
63	32	10	10	0,27, 9,15, 3, 1,31,
63	32	10	10	0, 7,15, 3, 1, 5,
63	32	12	10	0, 7,15, 1, 5,11,
63	32	12	8	0,15, 3, 1, 5,11,
63	32	12	12	0, 7, 3, 1, 5,31,
63	32	12	10	0,27, 9, 3, 1, 5,31,
63	32	12	12	0,15, 3, 1, 5,31,
63	32	12	12	0, 7,27, 9, 3, 1, 5,
63	31	4	4	21, 7,15, 1,11,23,
63	31	6	6	21, 1, 5,11,31,23,
63	31	6	5	21, 7, 1, 5,11,31,
63	31	6	5	21, 7, 1, 5,11,23,
63	31	6	6	21, 7, 1, 5,31,23,
63	31	6	6	21,27, 9,15, 1,11,23,
63	31	6	6	21,27, 9, 3, 1,11,23,
63	31	6	6	21,15, 3, 1,11,23,

n	k	d	d_{BCH}	Roots of Gen. Poly.
63	31	6	6	21,27, 9,15, 3, 1,11,
63	31	7	7	21, 3, 1, 5,11,31,
63	31	8	6	21, 7,27, 9, 1,11,23,
63	31	8	6	21, 7, 3, 1,11,23,
63	31	8	5	21, 7,27, 9,15, 3, 1,
63	31	8	7	21,27, 9,15, 3, 1, 5,
63	31	8	6	21, 7,27, 9,15, 1,11,
63	31	8	6	21, 7,27, 9, 3, 1,11,
63	31	8	6	21, 7,15, 3, 1,11,
63	31	9	7	21,15, 1, 5,11,31,
63	31	9	7	21,15, 1, 5,11,23,
63	31	9	7	21, 3, 1, 5,11,23,
63	31	9	9	21,15, 1, 5,31,23,
63	31	9	9	21, 7,15, 1, 5,11,
63	31	9	9	21, 7, 3, 1, 5,11,
63	31	9	7	21,15, 3, 1, 5,11,
63	31	9	7	21, 7,15, 1, 5,31,
63	31	9	9	21, 7, 3, 1, 5,31,
63	31	9	7	21,15, 3, 1, 5,31,
63	31	9	6	21, 7,15, 1, 5,23,
63	31	9	9	21, 7, 3, 1, 5,23,
63	31	9	7	21,15, 3, 1, 5,23,
63	31	9	6	21, 7,15, 3, 1,31,
63	31	9	9	21, 7,15, 3, 1, 5,
63	31	10	8	21,27, 9, 1, 5,11,31,
63	31	10	7	21,27, 9,15, 1, 5,31,
63	31	10	5	21,27, 9,15, 3, 1,31,
63	31	10	6	21, 7,27, 9,15, 1, 5,
63	31	11	6	21, 7,27, 9, 3, 1,31,
63	31	11	11	21, 7,27, 9, 3, 1, 5,
63	31	12	7	21,27, 9, 1, 5,11,23,
63	31	12	8	21,27, 9, 1, 5,31,23,
63	31	12	7	21, 7,27, 9, 1, 5,11,
63	31	12	7	21,27, 9,15, 1, 5,11,
63	31	12	8	21,27, 9, 3, 1, 5,11,
63	31	12	6	21, 7,27, 9, 1, 5,31,
63	31	12	7	21,27, 9, 3, 1, 5,31,
63	31	12	7	21, 7,27, 9, 1, 5,23,
63	31	12	7	21,27, 9,15, 1, 5,23,
63	31	12	8	21,27, 9, 3, 1, 5,23,
63	30	4	4	0,21, 7,15, 1,11,23,
63	30	4	4	7, 9,15, 1,11,23,
63	30	5	5	7,27, 3, 1,11,23,
63	30	6	6	0,21, 1, 5,11,31,23,
63	30	6	6	27, 1, 5,11,31,23,
63	30	6	6	9, 1, 5,11,31,23,
63	30	6	6	0,21, 7, 1, 5,11,31,
63	30	6	6	7,27, 1, 5,11,31,
63	30	6	6	7, 9, 1, 5,11,31,
63	30	6	6	0,21, 7, 1, 5,11,23,
63	30	6	6	7,27, 1, 5,11,23,

n	k	d	d_{BCH}	Roots of Gen. Poly.
63	30	6	6	7, 9, 1, 5,11,23,
63	30	6	6	0,21, 7, 1, 5,31,23,
63	30	6	6	7, 9, 1, 5,31,23,
63	30	6	6	0,21,27, 9,15, 1,11,23,
63	30	6	6	0,21,27, 9, 3, 1,11,23,
63	30	6	6	0,21,15, 3, 1,11,23,
63	30	6	5	27,15, 3, 1,11,23,
63	30	6	5	9,15, 3, 1,11,23,
63	30	6	6	0,21,27, 9,15, 3, 1,11,
63	30	7	7	27,15, 1, 5,11,31,
63	30	7	7	9,15, 1, 5,11,31,
63	30	7	7	27, 3, 1, 5,11,31,
63	30	7	7	9, 3, 1, 5,11,31,
63	30	7	7	27,15, 1, 5,11,23,
63	30	7	7	9,15, 1, 5,11,23,
63	30	7	7	27, 3, 1, 5,11,23,
63	30	7	7	9, 3, 1, 5,11,23,
63	30	7	7	9, 3, 1, 5,31,23,
63	30	7	7	9,15, 1, 5,31,23,
63	30	7	7	27,15, 3, 1, 5,11,
63	30	7	7	9,15, 3, 1, 5,11,
63	30	7	7	27,15, 3, 1, 5,31,
63	30	7	7	9,15, 3, 1, 5,31,
63	30	7	7	27,15, 3, 1, 5,23,
63	30	7	7	9,15, 3, 1, 5,23,
63	30	8	6	0,21, 7,27, 9, 1,11,23,
63	30	8	5	7,27,15, 1,11,23,
63	30	8	6	0,21, 7, 3, 1,11,23,
63	30	8	5	7, 9, 3, 1,11,23,
63	30	8	6	0,21, 7,27, 9,15, 3, 1,
63	30	8	8	0,21,27, 9,15, 3, 1, 5,
63	30	8	6	0,21, 7,27, 9,15, 1,11,
63	30	8	6	0,21, 7,27, 9, 3, 1,11,
63	30	8	6	0,21, 7,15, 3, 1,11,
63	30	8	5	7,27,15, 3, 1,11,
63	30	8	5	7, 9,15, 3, 1,11,
63	30	9	9	7, 9,15, 1, 5,11,
63	30	9	9	7,27, 3, 1, 5,11,
63	30	9	6	7, 9,15, 1, 5,31,
63	30	9	9	7,27, 3, 1, 5,31,
63	30	9	6	7, 9,15, 1, 5,23,
63	30	9	9	7,27, 3, 1, 5,23,
63	30	10	8	0,21,27, 9, 1, 5,11,31,
63	30	10	8	0,21,15, 1, 5,11,31,
63	30	10	10	0,21, 3, 1, 5,11,31,
63	30	10	10	0,21,15, 1, 5,11,23,
63	30	10	8	0,21, 3, 1, 5,11,23,
63	30	10	10	0,21,15, 1, 5,31,23,
63	30	10	10	0,21, 7, 3, 1, 5,11,
63	30	10	8	0,21, 7,15, 1, 5,31,
63	30	10	8	0,21,27, 9,15, 1, 5,31,

n	k	d	d_{BCH}	Roots of Gen. Poly.
63	30	10	7	7,27,15, 1, 5,23,
63	30	10	10	0,21, 7, 3, 1, 5,23,
63	30	10	10	0,21,15, 3, 1, 5,23,
63	30	10	10	0,21, 7,15, 3, 1,31,
63	30	10	6	7,27,15, 3, 1,31,
63	30	10	10	0,21,27, 9,15, 3, 1,31,
63	30	10	6	0,21, 7,27, 9,15, 1, 5,
63	30	10	10	0,21, 7,15, 3, 1, 5,
63	30	10	9	7,27,15, 3, 1, 5,
63	30	11	6	7,27,15, 1, 5,31,
63	30	11	11	7, 9, 3, 1, 5,31,
63	30	11	11	7, 9, 3, 1, 5,23,
63	30	11	11	7, 9,15, 3, 1, 5,
63	30	12	7	0,21,27, 9, 1, 5,11,23,
63	30	12	8	0,21,27, 9, 1, 5,31,23,
63	30	12	7	0,21, 7,27, 9, 1, 5,11,
63	30	12	10	0,21, 7,15, 1, 5,11,
63	30	12	8	0,21,27, 9,15, 1, 5,11,
63	30	12	8	0,21,27, 9, 3, 1, 5,11,
63	30	12	8	0,21,15, 3, 1, 5,11,
63	30	12	6	0,21, 7,27, 9, 1, 5,31,
63	30	12	12	0,21, 7, 3, 1, 5,31,
63	30	12	10	0,21,27, 9, 3, 1, 5,31,
63	30	12	12	0,21,15, 3, 1, 5,31,
63	30	12	7	0,21, 7,27, 9, 1, 5,23,
63	30	12	8	0,21, 7,15, 1, 5,23,
63	30	12	8	0,21,27, 9,15, 1, 5,23,
63	30	12	8	0,21,27, 9, 3, 1, 5,23,
63	30	12	8	0,21, 7,27, 9, 3, 1,31,
63	30	12	12	0,21, 7,27, 9, 3, 1, 5,
63	30	13	11	7,27,15, 1, 5,11,
63	30	13	13	7, 9, 3, 1, 5,11,
63	29	4	4	0, 7, 9,15, 1,11,23,
63	29	6	6	0,27, 1, 5,11,31,23,
63	29	6	6	0, 9, 1, 5,11,31,23,
63	29	6	6	0, 7,27, 1, 5,11,31,
63	29	6	6	0, 7, 9, 1, 5,11,31,
63	29	6	6	0, 7,27, 1, 5,11,23,
63	29	6	6	0, 7, 9, 1, 5,11,23,
63	29	6	6	0, 7, 9, 1, 5,31,23,
63	29	6	6	0,27,15, 3, 1,11,23,
63	29	6	6	0, 9,15, 3, 1,11,23,
63	29	8	8	0,27,15, 1, 5,11,31,
63	29	8	8	0, 9,15, 1, 5,11,31,
63	29	8	6	0, 7,27,15, 3, 1,11,
63	29	8	6	0, 7, 9,15, 3, 1,11,
63	29	8	5	0, 7,27,15, 1,11,23,
63	29	8	6	0, 7,27, 3, 1,11,23,
63	29	8	6	0, 7, 9, 3, 1,11,23,
63	29	10	10	0,27, 3, 1, 5,11,31,
63	29	10	10	0, 9,15, 1, 5,11,23,

n	k	d	d_{BCH}	Roots of Gen. Poly.
63	29	10	8	0,27, 3, 1, 5,11,23,
63	29	10	10	0, 7,27,15, 3, 1, 5,
63	29	10	10	0, 9,15, 1, 5,31,23,
63	29	10	8	0, 7,27,15, 1, 5,23,
63	29	10	10	0, 7,27, 3, 1, 5,23,
63	29	10	10	0,27,15, 3, 1, 5,23,
63	29	10	10	0, 7,27,15, 3, 1,31,
63	29	12	10	0, 9, 3, 1, 5,11,31,
63	29	12	10	0,27,15, 1, 5,11,23,
63	29	12	8	0, 9, 3, 1, 5,11,23,
63	29	12	12	0, 7, 9,15, 3, 1, 5,
63	29	12	10	0, 9, 3, 1, 5,31,23,
63	29	12	10	0, 7, 9,15, 1, 5,11,
63	29	12	10	0, 7,27, 3, 1, 5,11,
63	29	12	8	0,27,15, 3, 1, 5,11,
63	29	12	8	0, 9,15, 3, 1, 5,11,
63	29	12	8	0, 7,27,15, 1, 5,31,
63	29	12	8	0, 7, 9,15, 1, 5,31,
63	29	12	12	0, 7,27, 3, 1, 5,31,
63	29	12	12	0,27,15, 3, 1, 5,31,
63	29	12	8	0, 7, 9,15, 1, 5,23,
63	29	12	12	0, 7, 9, 3, 1, 5,23,
63	29	12	10	0, 9,15, 3, 1, 5,23,
63	29	14	12	0, 7,27,15, 1, 5,11,
63	29	14	14	0, 7, 9, 3, 1, 5,11,
63	29	14	14	0, 7, 9, 3, 1, 5,31,
63	29	14	12	0, 9,15, 3, 1, 5,31,
63	28	4	4	21, 7, 9,15, 1,11,23,
63	28	6	6	21,27,15, 3, 1,11,23,
63	28	6	6	21, 9,15, 3, 1,11,23,
63	28	8	6	21, 7,27,15, 3, 1,11,
63	28	8	6	21, 7, 9,15, 3, 1,11,
63	28	8	6	21, 7,27,15, 1,11,23,
63	28	8	6	21, 7,27, 3, 1,11,23,
63	28	8	6	21, 7, 9, 3, 1,11,23,
63	28	9	8	21,27, 1, 5,11,31,23,
63	28	9	9	21, 9, 1, 5,11,31,23,
63	28	9	8	21, 7,27, 1, 5,11,31,
63	28	9	7	21, 7, 9, 1, 5,11,31,
63	28	9	7	21, 7,27, 1, 5,11,23,
63	28	9	6	21, 7, 9, 1, 5,11,23,
63	28	9	7	21, 9,15, 1, 5,11,23,
63	28	9	8	21, 7, 9, 1, 5,31,23,
63	28	9	8	21,27,15, 3, 1, 5,23,
63	28	10	8	21, 9,15, 1, 5,11,31,
63	28	10	9	21,27, 3, 1, 5,11,31,
63	28	10	8	21,27, 3, 1, 5,11,23,
63	28	10	10	21, 9,15, 1, 5,31,23,
63	28	11	9	21, 7,27,15, 3, 1, 5,
63	28	11	11	21, 7, 9,15, 3, 1, 5,
63	28	11	7	21, 9, 3, 1, 5,11,31,

n	k	d	d_{BCH}	Roots of Gen. Poly.
63	28	11	8	21,27,15, 3, 1, 5,11,
63	28	11	7	21, 7,27,15, 1, 5,31,
63	28	11	9	21, 7,27, 3, 1, 5,31,
63	28	11	11	21, 7, 9, 3, 1, 5,31,
63	28	11	7	21,27,15, 3, 1, 5,31,
63	28	11	11	21, 7, 9, 3, 1, 5,23,
63	28	11	6	21, 7,27,15, 3, 1,31,
63	28	12	7	21,27,15, 1, 5,11,23,
63	28	12	7	21, 9, 3, 1, 5,11,23,
63	28	12	9	21, 7, 9,15, 1, 5,11,
63	28	12	10	21, 7,27, 3, 1, 5,11,
63	28	12	7	21, 9,15, 3, 1, 5,11,
63	28	12	7	21, 7, 9,15, 1, 5,31,
63	28	12	6	21, 7, 9,15, 1, 5,23,
63	28	12	10	21, 7,27, 3, 1, 5,23,
63	28	12	7	21, 9,15, 3, 1, 5,23,
63	28	13	8	21,27,15, 1, 5,11,31,
63	28	13	11	21, 9, 3, 1, 5,31,23,
63	28	13	7	21, 9,15, 3, 1, 5,31,
63	28	14	7	21, 7,27,15, 1, 5,23,
63	28	15*	11	21, 7,27,15, 1, 5,11,
63	28	15*	13	21, 7, 9, 3, 1, 5,11,
63	27	3	3	1, 5,11,31,23,13,
63	27	3	3	7, 1, 5,11,31,23,
63	27	4	4	0,21, 7, 9,15, 1,11,23,
63	27	6	6	27, 9, 1, 5,11,31,23,
63	27	6	6	7,27, 9, 1, 5,11,31,
63	27	6	6	7,27, 9, 1, 5,11,23,
63	27	6	6	7,27, 9, 1, 5,31,23,
63	27	6	6	0,21,27,15, 3, 1,11,23,
63	27	6	6	0,21, 9,15, 3, 1,11,23,
63	27	6	5	27, 9,15, 3, 1,11,23,
63	27	7	7	15, 1, 5,11,31,23,
63	27	7	7	3, 1, 5,11,31,23,
63	27	7	7	27, 9,15, 1, 5,11,31,
63	27	7	7	27, 9, 3, 1, 5,11,31,
63	27	7	7	15, 3, 1, 5,11,31,
63	27	7	7	27, 9,15, 1, 5,11,23,
63	27	7	7	27, 9, 3, 1, 5,11,23,
63	27	7	7	15, 3, 1, 5,11,23,
63	27	7	7	27, 9, 3, 1, 5,31,23,
63	27	7	7	15, 3, 1, 5,31,23,
63	27	7	7	27, 9,15, 3, 1, 5,11,
63	27	7	7	27, 9,15, 3, 1, 5,31,
63	27	7	7	27, 9,15, 3, 1, 5,23,
63	27	8	6	0,21, 7,27,15, 3, 1,11,
63	27	8	6	0,21, 7, 9,15, 3, 1,11,
63	27	8	5	7,27, 9,15, 3, 1,11,
63	27	8	6	0,21, 7,27,15, 1,11,23,
63	27	8	5	7,27, 9,15, 1,11,23,
63	27	8	6	0,21, 7,27, 3, 1,11,23,

n	k	d	d_{BCH}	Roots of Gen. Poly.
63	27	8	6	0,21, 7, 9, 3, 1,11,23,
63	27	8	5	7,27, 9, 3, 1,11,23,
63	27	8	5	7,15, 3, 1,11,23,
63	27	9	9	7,15, 1, 5,11,31,
63	27	9	9	7, 3, 1, 5,11,31,
63	27	9	9	7,15, 1, 5,11,23,
63	27	9	9	7, 3, 1, 5,11,23,
63	27	9	9	7,15, 1, 5,31,23,
63	27	9	9	7,15, 3, 1, 5,11,
63	27	9	9	7,15, 3, 1, 5,31,
63	27	9	9	7,15, 3, 1, 5,23,
63	27	10	8	0,21,27, 1, 5,11,31,23,
63	27	10	9	0,21, 9, 1, 5,11,31,23,
63	27	10	8	0,21, 9,15, 1, 5,11,31,
63	27	10	10	0,21,27, 3, 1, 5,11,31,
63	27	10	7	0,21, 7,27, 1, 5,11,23,
63	27	10	10	0,21, 9,15, 1, 5,11,23,
63	27	10	8	0,21,27, 3, 1, 5,11,23,
63	27	10	10	0,21, 9,15, 1, 5,31,23,
63	27	12	10	0,21, 7,27,15, 3, 1, 5,
63	27	12	12	0,21, 7, 9,15, 3, 1, 5,
63	27	12	11	7,27, 9,15, 3, 1, 5,
63	27	12	8	0,21, 7,27, 1, 5,11,31,
63	27	12	7	0,21, 7, 9, 1, 5,11,31,
63	27	12	10	0,21, 9, 3, 1, 5,11,31,
63	27	12	6	0,21, 7, 9, 1, 5,11,23,
63	27	12	10	0,21,27,15, 1, 5,11,23,
63	27	12	8	0,21, 9, 3, 1, 5,11,23,
63	27	12	8	0,21, 7, 9, 1, 5,31,23,
63	27	12	10	0,21, 7, 9,15, 1, 5,11,
63	27	12	10	0,21, 7,27, 3, 1, 5,11,
63	27	12	8	0,21,27,15, 3, 1, 5,11,
63	27	12	8	0,21, 9,15, 3, 1, 5,11,
63	27	12	8	0,21, 7,27,15, 1, 5,31,
63	27	12	8	0,21, 7, 9,15, 1, 5,31,
63	27	12	6	7,27, 9,15, 1, 5,31,
63	27	12	12	0,21, 7,27, 3, 1, 5,31,
63	27	12	8	0,21, 7, 9,15, 1, 5,23,
63	27	12	10	0,21, 7,27, 3, 1, 5,23,
63	27	12	12	0,21, 7, 9, 3, 1, 5,23,
63	27	12	11	7,27, 9, 3, 1, 5,23,
63	27	12	10	0,21,27,15, 3, 1, 5,23,
63	27	12	10	0,21, 9,15, 3, 1, 5,23,
63	27	12	10	0,21, 7,27,15, 3, 1,31,
63	27	12	6	7,27, 9,15, 3, 1,31,
63	27	13	11	7,27, 9,15, 1, 5,11,
63	27	13	13	7,27, 9, 3, 1, 5,11,
63	27	13	11	7,27, 9, 3, 1, 5,31,
63	27	13	7	7,27, 9,15, 1, 5,23,
63	27	14	8	0,21,27,15, 1, 5,11,31,
63	27	14	11	0,21, 9, 3, 1, 5,31,23,

n	k	d	d_{BCH}	Roots of Gen. Poly.
63	27	14	14	0,21, 7, 9, 3, 1, 5,31,
63	27	14	12	0,21,27,15, 3, 1, 5,31,
63	27	14	12	0,21, 9,15, 3, 1, 5,31,
63	27	14	8	0,21, 7,27,15, 1, 5,23,
63	27	16*	12	0,21, 7,27,15, 1, 5,11,
63	27	16*	14	0,21, 7, 9, 3, 1, 5,11,
63	26	6	6	0, 1, 5,11,31,23,13,
63	26	6	6	0, 7, 1, 5,11,31,23,
63	26	6	6	0,27, 9, 1, 5,11,31,23,
63	26	6	6	0, 7,27, 9, 1, 5,11,31,
63	26	6	6	0, 7,27, 9, 1, 5,11,23,
63	26	6	6	0, 7,27, 9, 1, 5,31,23,
63	26	6	6	0,27, 9,15, 3, 1,11,23,
63	26	8	6	0, 7,27, 9,15, 3, 1,11,
63	26	8	8	0,27, 9,15, 1, 5,11,31,
63	26	8	5	0, 7,27, 9,15, 1,11,23,
63	26	8	6	0, 7,27, 9, 3, 1,11,23,
63	26	8	6	0, 7,15, 3, 1,11,23,
63	26	10	10	0,15, 1, 5,11,31,23,
63	26	10	10	0, 3, 1, 5,11,31,23,
63	26	10	10	0, 7,15, 3, 1, 5,23,
63	26	12	12	0, 7,27, 9,15, 3, 1, 5,
63	26	12	10	0, 7,15, 1, 5,11,31,
63	26	12	12	0, 7, 3, 1, 5,11,31,
63	26	12	10	0,27, 9, 3, 1, 5,11,31,
63	26	12	12	0,15, 3, 1, 5,11,31,
63	26	12	12	0, 7,15, 1, 5,11,23,
63	26	12	10	0,27, 9,15, 1, 5,11,23,
63	26	12	10	0, 7, 3, 1, 5,11,23,
63	26	12	8	0,27, 9, 3, 1, 5,11,23,
63	26	12	12	0, 7,15, 1, 5,31,23,
63	26	12	8	0,27, 9,15, 3, 1, 5,11,
63	26	12	8	0, 7,27, 9,15, 1, 5,31,
63	26	12	12	0, 7,27, 9, 3, 1, 5,23,
63	26	12	10	0,27, 9,15, 3, 1, 5,23,
63	26	12	10	0, 7,27, 9,15, 3, 1,31,
63	26	14	12	0,15, 3, 1, 5,11,23,
63	26	14	10	0,27, 9, 3, 1, 5,31,23,
63	26	14	14	0,15, 3, 1, 5,31,23,
63	26	14	12	0, 7,27, 9,15, 1, 5,11,
63	26	14	14	0, 7,27, 9, 3, 1, 5,11,
63	26	14	10	0, 7,15, 3, 1, 5,11,
63	26	14	14	0, 7,27, 9, 3, 1, 5,31,
63	26	14	14	0, 7,15, 3, 1, 5,31,
63	26	14	12	0,27, 9,15, 3, 1, 5,31,
63	26	14	8	0, 7,27, 9,15, 1, 5,23,
63	25	6	6	21, 1, 5,11,31,23,13,
63	25	6	6	21, 7, 1, 5,11,31,23,
63	25	6	6	21,27, 9,15, 3, 1,11,23,
63	25	8	6	21, 7,27, 9,15, 3, 1,11,
63	25	8	6	21, 7,27, 9,15, 1,11,23,

n	k	d	d_{BCH}	Roots of Gen. Poly.
63	25	8	6	21, 7,27, 9, 3, 1,11,23,
63	25	8	6	21, 7,15, 3, 1,11,23,
63	25	9	9	21,15, 1, 5,11,31,23,
63	25	9	9	21, 3, 1, 5,11,31,23,
63	25	9	9	21, 7,15, 1, 5,11,31,
63	25	9	9	21, 7, 3, 1, 5,11,31,
63	25	9	7	21,15, 3, 1, 5,11,31,
63	25	9	9	21, 7,15, 1, 5,11,23,
63	25	9	9	21, 7, 3, 1, 5,11,23,
63	25	9	7	21,15, 3, 1, 5,11,23,
63	25	9	9	21, 7,15, 1, 5,31,23,
63	25	9	9	21,15, 3, 1, 5,31,23,
63	25	9	9	21, 7,15, 3, 1, 5,11,
63	25	9	9	21, 7,15, 3, 1, 5,31,
63	25	9	9	21, 7,15, 3, 1, 5,23,
63	25	12	11	21, 7,27, 9,15, 3, 1, 5,
63	25	12	9	21,27, 9, 1, 5,11,31,23,
63	25	12	8	21, 7,27, 9, 1, 5,11,31,
63	25	12	9	21,27, 9, 3, 1, 5,11,31,
63	25	12	7	21, 7,27, 9, 1, 5,11,23,
63	25	12	7	21,27, 9,15, 1, 5,11,23,
63	25	12	8	21,27, 9, 3, 1, 5,11,23,
63	25	12	8	21, 7,27, 9, 1, 5,31,23,
63	25	12	8	21,27, 9,15, 3, 1, 5,11,
63	25	12	7	21, 7,27, 9,15, 1, 5,31,
63	25	12	11	21, 7,27, 9, 3, 1, 5,23,
63	25	12	8	21,27, 9,15, 3, 1, 5,23,
63	25	12	6	21, 7,27, 9,15, 3, 1,31,
63	25	13	8	21,27, 9,15, 1, 5,11,31,
63	25	14	12	21,27, 9, 3, 1, 5,31,23,
63	25	14*	7	21,27, 9,15, 3, 1, 5,31,
63	25	15*	11	21, 7,27, 9,15, 1, 5,11,
63	25	15*	13	21, 7,27, 9, 3, 1, 5,11,
63	25	15*	11	21, 7,27, 9, 3, 1, 5,31,
63	25	15*	7	21, 7,27, 9,15, 1, 5,23,
63	24	6	6	0,21, 1, 5,11,31,23,13,
63	24	6	6	9, 1, 5,11,31,23,13,
63	24	6	6	0,21, 7, 1, 5,11,31,23,
63	24	6	6	7,27, 1, 5,11,31,23,
63	24	6	6	7, 9, 1, 5,11,31,23,
63	24	6	6	0,21,27, 9,15, 3, 1,11,23,
63	24	7	7	27,15, 1, 5,11,31,23,
63	24	7	7	9,15, 1, 5,11,31,23,
63	24	7	7	27, 3, 1, 5,11,31,23,
63	24	7	7	9, 3, 1, 5,11,31,23,
63	24	7	7	27,15, 3, 1, 5,11,31,
63	24	7	7	9,15, 3, 1, 5,11,31,
63	24	7	7	27,15, 3, 1, 5,11,23,
63	24	7	7	9,15, 3, 1, 5,11,23,
63	24	7	7	27,15, 3, 1, 5,31,23,
63	24	8	6	0,21, 7,27, 9,15, 3, 1,11,

n	k	d	d_{BCH}	Roots of Gen. Poly.
63	24	8	6	0,21, 7,27, 9,15, 1,11,23,
63	24	8	6	0,21, 7,27, 9, 3, 1,11,23,
63	24	8	6	0,21, 7,15, 3, 1,11,23,
63	24	8	5	7,27,15, 3, 1,11,23,
63	24	8	5	7, 9,15, 3, 1,11,23,
63	24	9	9	7, 9,15, 1, 5,11,31,
63	24	9	9	7,27, 3, 1, 5,11,31,
63	24	9	9	7, 9,15, 1, 5,11,23,
63	24	9	9	7,27, 3, 1, 5,11,23,
63	24	9	9	7, 9,15, 1, 5,31,23,
63	24	10	10	0,21,15, 1, 5,11,31,23,
63	24	10	10	0,21, 3, 1, 5,11,31,23,
63	24	10	10	7,27,15, 3, 1, 5,23,
63	24	11	9	7,27,15, 3, 1, 5,31,
63	24	12	12	0,21, 7,27, 9,15, 3, 1, 5,
63	24	12	9	0,21,27, 9, 1, 5,11,31,23,
63	24	12	8	0,21, 7,27, 9, 1, 5,11,31,
63	24	12	10	0,21, 7,15, 1, 5,11,31,
63	24	12	12	0,21, 7, 3, 1, 5,11,31,
63	24	12	10	0,21,27, 9, 3, 1, 5,11,31,
63	24	12	12	0,21,15, 3, 1, 5,11,31,
63	24	12	7	0,21, 7,27, 9, 1, 5,11,23,
63	24	12	12	0,21, 7,15, 1, 5,11,23,
63	24	12	10	0,21,27, 9,15, 1, 5,11,23,
63	24	12	10	0,21, 7, 3, 1, 5,11,23,
63	24	12	8	0,21,27, 9, 3, 1, 5,11,23,
63	24	12	8	0,21, 7,27, 9, 1, 5,31,23,
63	24	12	12	0,21, 7,15, 1, 5,31,23,
63	24	12	8	0,21,27, 9,15, 3, 1, 5,11,
63	24	12	8	0,21, 7,27, 9,15, 1, 5,31,
63	24	12	12	0,21, 7,27, 9, 3, 1, 5,23,
63	24	12	10	0,21,27, 9,15, 3, 1, 5,23,
63	24	12	10	0,21, 7,27, 9,15, 3, 1,31,
63	24	13	11	7,27,15, 1, 5,11,23,
63	24	13	13	7, 9, 3, 1, 5,11,23,
63	24	13	11	7,27,15, 3, 1, 5,11,
63	24	14	8	0,21,27, 9,15, 1, 5,11,31,
63	24	14	12	0,21,15, 3, 1, 5,11,23,
63	24	14	12	0,21,27, 9, 3, 1, 5,31,23,
63	24	14	14	0,21,15, 3, 1, 5,31,23,
63	24	14	10	0,21, 7,15, 3, 1, 5,11,
63	24	14	13	7, 9,15, 3, 1, 5,11,
63	24	14	14	0,21, 7,15, 3, 1, 5,31,
63	24	14	12	0,21,27, 9,15, 3, 1, 5,31,
63	24	14	10	0,21, 7,15, 3, 1, 5,23,
63	24	15	15	7,27,15, 1, 5,11,31,
63	24	15	13	7, 9, 3, 1, 5,11,31,
63	24	15	11	7, 9, 3, 1, 5,31,23,
63	24	15	11	7, 9,15, 3, 1, 5,31,
63	24	15	11	7, 9,15, 3, 1, 5,23,
63	24	16*	12	0,21, 7,27, 9,15, 1, 5,11,

n	k	d	d_{BCH}	Roots of Gen. Poly.
63	24	16*	14	0, 21, 7, 27, 9, 3, 1, 5, 11,
63	24	16*	14	0, 21, 7, 27, 9, 3, 1, 5, 31,
63	24	16*	8	0, 21, 7, 27, 9, 15, 1, 5, 23,
63	23	6	6	0, 9, 1, 5, 11, 31, 23, 13,
63	23	6	6	0, 7, 27, 1, 5, 11, 31, 23,
63	23	6	6	0, 7, 9, 1, 5, 11, 31, 23,
63	23	8	6	0, 7, 27, 15, 3, 1, 11, 23,
63	23	8	6	0, 7, 9, 15, 3, 1, 11, 23,
63	23	10	10	0, 9, 15, 1, 5, 11, 31, 23,
63	23	10	10	0, 27, 3, 1, 5, 11, 31, 23,
63	23	10	10	0, 7, 27, 15, 3, 1, 5, 23,
63	23	12	10	0, 7, 9, 15, 1, 5, 11, 31,
63	23	12	12	0, 7, 27, 3, 1, 5, 11, 31,
63	23	12	12	0, 7, 9, 15, 1, 5, 11, 23,
63	23	12	10	0, 7, 27, 3, 1, 5, 11, 23,
63	23	12	12	0, 7, 9, 15, 1, 5, 31, 23,
63	23	14	10	0, 27, 15, 1, 5, 11, 31, 23,
63	23	14	10	0, 9, 3, 1, 5, 11, 31, 23,
63	23	14	12	0, 27, 15, 3, 1, 5, 11, 31,
63	23	14	12	0, 9, 15, 3, 1, 5, 11, 31,
63	23	14	14	0, 7, 27, 15, 1, 5, 11, 23,
63	23	14	14	0, 7, 9, 3, 1, 5, 11, 23,
63	23	14	12	0, 27, 15, 3, 1, 5, 11, 23,
63	23	14	12	0, 9, 15, 3, 1, 5, 11, 23,
63	23	14	14	0, 27, 15, 3, 1, 5, 31, 23,
63	23	14	14	0, 7, 9, 15, 3, 1, 5, 11,
63	23	16	16	0, 7, 27, 15, 1, 5, 11, 31,
63	23	16	16	0, 7, 9, 3, 1, 5, 11, 31,
63	23	16	14	0, 7, 9, 3, 1, 5, 31, 23,
63	23	16	12	0, 7, 27, 15, 3, 1, 5, 11,
63	23	16	14	0, 7, 27, 15, 3, 1, 5, 31,
63	23	16	16	0, 7, 9, 15, 3, 1, 5, 31,
63	23	16	12	0, 7, 9, 15, 3, 1, 5, 23,
63	22	8	6	21, 7, 27, 15, 3, 1, 11, 23,
63	22	8	6	21, 7, 9, 15, 3, 1, 11, 23,
63	22	9	9	21, 9, 1, 5, 11, 31, 23, 13,
63	22	9	8	21, 7, 27, 1, 5, 11, 31, 23,
63	22	9	9	21, 7, 9, 1, 5, 11, 31, 23,
63	22	10	10	21, 9, 15, 1, 5, 11, 31, 23,
63	22	10	10	21, 27, 3, 1, 5, 11, 31, 23,
63	22	11	9	21, 7, 27, 15, 3, 1, 5, 31,
63	22	12	10	21, 7, 9, 15, 1, 5, 11, 31,
63	22	12	11	21, 7, 27, 3, 1, 5, 11, 31,
63	22	12	9	21, 7, 9, 15, 1, 5, 11, 23,
63	22	12	10	21, 7, 27, 3, 1, 5, 11, 23,
63	22	12	12	21, 7, 9, 15, 1, 5, 31, 23,
63	22	14	11	21, 27, 15, 1, 5, 11, 31, 23,
63	22	14	12	21, 9, 3, 1, 5, 11, 31, 23,
63	22	14	9	21, 27, 15, 3, 1, 5, 11, 31,
63	22	14	8	21, 9, 15, 3, 1, 5, 11, 31,
63	22	14	8	21, 27, 15, 3, 1, 5, 11, 23,

n	k	d	d_{BCH}	Roots of Gen. Poly.
63	22	14	7	21, 9,15, 3, 1, 5,11,23,
63	22	14	11	21,27,15, 3, 1, 5,31,23,
63	22	15	15	21, 7,27,15, 1, 5,11,31,
63	22	15	13	21, 7, 9, 3, 1, 5,11,31,
63	22	15	11	21, 7,27,15, 1, 5,11,23,
63	22	15	13	21, 7, 9, 3, 1, 5,11,23,
63	22	15	11	21, 7, 9, 3, 1, 5,31,23,
63	22	15	11	21, 7,27,15, 3, 1, 5,11,
63	22	15	13	21, 7, 9,15, 3, 1, 5,11,
63	22	15	11	21, 7, 9,15, 3, 1, 5,31,
63	22	15	11	21, 7, 9,15, 3, 1, 5,23,
63	22	16	11	21, 7,27,15, 3, 1, 5,23,
63	21	3	3	7, 1, 5,11,31,23,13,
63	21	6	6	27, 9, 1, 5,11,31,23,13,
63	21	6	6	7,27, 9, 1, 5,11,31,23,
63	21	7	7	15, 1, 5,11,31,23,13,
63	21	7	7	27, 9,15, 1, 5,11,31,23,
63	21	7	7	27, 9, 3, 1, 5,11,31,23,
63	21	7	7	15, 3, 1, 5,11,31,23,
63	21	7	7	27, 9,15, 3, 1, 5,11,31,
63	21	7	7	27, 9,15, 3, 1, 5,11,23,
63	21	7	7	27, 9,15, 3, 1, 5,31,23,
63	21	8	6	0,21, 7,27,15, 3, 1,11,23,
63	21	8	6	0,21, 7, 9,15, 3, 1,11,23,
63	21	8	5	7,27, 9,15, 3, 1,11,23,
63	21	9	9	7,15, 1, 5,11,31,23,
63	21	9	9	7, 3, 1, 5,11,31,23,
63	21	9	9	7,15, 3, 1, 5,11,31,
63	21	9	9	7,15, 3, 1, 5,11,23,
63	21	9	9	7,15, 3, 1, 5,31,23,
63	21	10	9	0,21, 9, 1, 5,11,31,23,13,
63	21	10	10	0,21, 9,15, 1, 5,11,31,23,
63	21	10	10	0,21,27, 3, 1, 5,11,31,23,
63	21	12	8	0,21, 7,27, 1, 5,11,31,23,
63	21	12	9	0,21, 7, 9, 1, 5,11,31,23,
63	21	12	10	0,21, 7, 9,15, 1, 5,11,31,
63	21	12	12	0,21, 7,27, 3, 1, 5,11,31,
63	21	12	12	0,21, 7, 9,15, 1, 5,11,23,
63	21	12	10	0,21, 7,27, 3, 1, 5,11,23,
63	21	12	12	0,21, 7, 9,15, 1, 5,31,23,
63	21	13	11	7,27, 9,15, 1, 5,11,23,
63	21	14	11	0,21,27,15, 1, 5,11,31,23,
63	21	14	12	0,21, 9, 3, 1, 5,11,31,23,
63	21	14	12	0,21,27,15, 3, 1, 5,11,31,
63	21	14	12	0,21, 9,15, 3, 1, 5,11,31,
63	21	14	13	7,27, 9, 3, 1, 5,11,23,
63	21	14	12	0,21,27,15, 3, 1, 5,11,23,
63	21	14	12	0,21, 9,15, 3, 1, 5,11,23,
63	21	14	14	0,21,27,15, 3, 1, 5,31,23,
63	21	15	15	7,27, 9,15, 1, 5,11,31,
63	21	16	16	0,21, 7,27,15, 1, 5,11,31,

n	k	d	d_{BCH}	Roots of Gen. Poly.
63	21	16	16	0,21, 7, 9, 3, 1, 5,11,31,
63	21	16	13	7,27, 9, 3, 1, 5,11,31,
63	21	16	14	0,21, 7,27,15, 1, 5,11,23,
63	21	16	14	0,21, 7, 9, 3, 1, 5,11,23,
63	21	16	14	0,21, 7, 9, 3, 1, 5,31,23,
63	21	16	11	7,27, 9, 3, 1, 5,31,23,
63	21	16	12	0,21, 7,27,15, 3, 1, 5,11,
63	21	16	14	0,21, 7, 9,15, 3, 1, 5,11,
63	21	16	13	7,27, 9,15, 3, 1, 5,11,
63	21	16	14	0,21, 7,27,15, 3, 1, 5,31,
63	21	16	16	0,21, 7, 9,15, 3, 1, 5,31,
63	21	16	11	7,27, 9,15, 3, 1, 5,31,
63	21	16	11	0,21, 7,27,15, 3, 1, 5,23,
63	21	17*	11	7,27, 9,15, 3, 1, 5,23,
63	21	18*	12	0,21, 7, 9,15, 3, 1, 5,23,
63	20	6	6	0, 7, 1, 5,11,31,23,13,
63	20	6	6	0,27, 9, 1, 5,11,31,23,13,
63	20	6	6	0, 7,27, 9, 1, 5,11,31,23,
63	20	8	6	0, 7,27, 9,15, 3, 1,11,23,
63	20	10	10	0,15, 1, 5,11,31,23,13,
63	20	12	12	0, 7,15, 1, 5,11,31,23,
63	20	12	12	0, 7, 3, 1, 5,11,31,23,
63	20	14	10	0,27, 9,15, 1, 5,11,31,23,
63	20	14	10	0,27, 9, 3, 1, 5,11,31,23,
63	20	14	14	0,15, 3, 1, 5,11,31,23,
63	20	14	12	0,27, 9,15, 3, 1, 5,11,31,
63	20	14	14	0, 7,27, 9, 3, 1, 5,11,23,
63	20	14	12	0,27, 9,15, 3, 1, 5,11,23,
63	20	14	14	0,27, 9,15, 3, 1, 5,31,23,
63	20	16	16	0, 7,27, 9,15, 1, 5,11,31,
63	20	16	16	0, 7,27, 9, 3, 1, 5,11,31,
63	20	16	14	0, 7,15, 3, 1, 5,11,31,
63	20	16	14	0, 7,27, 9,15, 1, 5,11,23,
63	20	16	14	0, 7,15, 3, 1, 5,11,23,
63	20	16	14	0, 7,27, 9, 3, 1, 5,31,23,
63	20	16	14	0, 7,27, 9,15, 3, 1, 5,11,
63	20	16	16	0, 7,27, 9,15, 3, 1, 5,31,
63	20	18	18	0, 7,15, 3, 1, 5,31,23,
63	20	18	12	0, 7,27, 9,15, 3, 1, 5,23,
63	19	6	6	21, 7, 1, 5,11,31,23,13,
63	19	8	6	21, 7,27, 9,15, 3, 1,11,23,
63	19	9	9	21,15, 1, 5,11,31,23,13,
63	19	9	9	21, 7,15, 1, 5,11,31,23,
63	19	9	9	21, 7, 3, 1, 5,11,31,23,
63	19	9	9	21,15, 3, 1, 5,11,31,23,
63	19	9	9	21, 7,15, 3, 1, 5,11,31,
63	19	9	9	21, 7,15, 3, 1, 5,11,23,
63	19	9	9	21, 7,15, 3, 1, 5,31,23,
63	19	12	9	21,27, 9, 1, 5,11,31,23,13,
63	19	12	9	21, 7,27, 9, 1, 5,11,31,23,
63	19	14	12	21,27, 9,15, 1, 5,11,31,23,

n.	k	d	d_{BCH}	Roots of Gen. Poly.
63	19	14	13	21,27, 9, 3, 1, 5,11,31,23,
63	19	14	9	21,27, 9,15, 3, 1, 5,11,31,
63	19	14	8	21,27, 9,15, 3, 1, 5,11,23,
63	19	14	12	21,27, 9,15, 3, 1, 5,31,23,
63	19	15	15	21, 7,27, 9,15, 1, 5,11,31,
63	19	16	13	21, 7,27, 9, 3, 1, 5,11,31,
63	19	16	11	21, 7,27, 9,15, 1, 5,11,23,
63	19	16	13	21, 7,27, 9, 3, 1, 5,11,23,
63	19	16	13	21, 7,27, 9,15, 3, 1, 5,11,
63	19	16	11	21, 7,27, 9,15, 3, 1, 5,31,
63	19	18	11	21, 7,27, 9,15, 3, 1, 5,23,
63	19	19*	14	21, 7,27, 9, 3, 1, 5,31,23,
63	18	6	6	0,21, 7, 1, 5,11,31,23,13,
63	18	6	6	7, 9, 1, 5,11,31,23,13,
63	18	7	7	9, 3, 1, 5,11,31,23,13,
63	18	7	7	9,15, 1, 5,11,31,23,13,
63	18	7	7	27,15, 3, 1, 5,11,31,23,
63	18	7	7	9,15, 3, 1, 5,11,31,23,
63	18	8	6	0,21, 7,27, 9,15, 3, 1,11,23,
63	18	9	9	7, 9,15, 1, 5,11,31,23,
63	18	9	9	7,27, 3, 1, 5,11,31,23,
63	18	10	10	0,21,15, 1, 5,11,31,23,13,
63	18	12	9	0,21,27, 9, 1, 5,11,31,23,13,
63	18	12	9	0,21, 7,27, 9, 1, 5,11,31,23,
63	18	12	12	0,21, 7,15, 1, 5,11,31,23,
63	18	12	12	0,21, 7, 3, 1, 5,11,31,23,
63	18	14	12	0,21,27, 9,15, 1, 5,11,31,23,
63	18	14	13	0,21,27, 9, 3, 1, 5,11,31,23,
63	18	14	14	0,21,15, 3, 1, 5,11,31,23,
63	18	14	12	0,21,27, 9,15, 3, 1, 5,11,31,
63	18	14	12	0,21,27, 9,15, 3, 1, 5,11,23,
63	18	14	14	0,21,27, 9,15, 3, 1, 5,31,23,
63	18	15	15	7,27,15, 1, 5,11,31,23,
63	18	15	15	7, 9, 3, 1, 5,11,31,23,
63	18	15	13	7, 9,15, 3, 1, 5,11,31,
63	18	16	16	0,21, 7,27, 9,15, 1, 5,11,31,
63	18	16	16	0,21, 7,27, 9, 3, 1, 5,11,31,
63	18	16	14	0,21, 7,27, 9,15, 1, 5,11,23,
63	18	16	14	0,21, 7,27, 9, 3, 1, 5,11,23,
63	18	16	14	0,21, 7,27, 9,15, 3, 1, 5,11,
63	18	16	16	0,21, 7,27, 9,15, 3, 1, 5,31,
63	18	17	11	7,27,15, 3, 1, 5,11,23,
63	18	17	13	7, 9,15, 3, 1, 5,11,23,
63	18	18	14	0,21, 7,15, 3, 1, 5,11,31,
63	18	18	14	0,21, 7,15, 3, 1, 5,11,23,
63	18	18	18	0,21, 7,15, 3, 1, 5,31,23,
63	18	18	12	0,21, 7,27, 9,15, 3, 1, 5,23,
63	18	19	11	7,27,15, 3, 1, 5,31,23,
63	18	20	14	0,21, 7,27, 9, 3, 1, 5,31,23,
63	18	21	21	7,27,15, 3, 1, 5,11,31,
63	17	6	6	0, 7, 9, 1, 5,11,31,23,13,

n	k	d	d_{BCH}	Roots of Gen. Poly.
63	17	10	10	0, 9,15, 1, 5,11,31,23,13,
63	17	12	12	0, 7, 9,15, 1, 5,11,31,23,
63	17	12	12	0, 7,27, 3, 1, 5,11,31,23,
63	17	14	10	0, 9, 3, 1, 5,11,31,23,13,
63	17	14	14	0,27,15, 3, 1, 5,11,31,23,
63	17	14	14	0, 9,15, 3, 1, 5,11,31,23,
63	17	16	16	0, 7, 9, 3, 1, 5,11,31,23,
63	17	18	18	0, 7,27,15, 1, 5,11,31,23,
63	17	18	18	0, 7, 9,15, 3, 1, 5,11,31,
63	17	18	16	0, 7,27,15, 3, 1, 5,11,23,
63	17	18	14	0, 7, 9,15, 3, 1, 5,11,23,
63	17	20	20	0, 7,27,15, 3, 1, 5,31,23,
63	17	22	22	0, 7,27,15, 3, 1, 5,11,31,
63	16	9	9	21, 7, 9, 1, 5,11,31,23,13,
63	16	10	10	21, 9,15, 1, 5,11,31,23,13,
63	16	12	12	21, 7, 9,15, 1, 5,11,31,23,
63	16	12	12	21, 7,27, 3, 1, 5,11,31,23,
63	16	14	12	21, 9, 3, 1, 5,11,31,23,13,
63	16	14	11	21,27,15, 3, 1, 5,11,31,23,
63	16	14	13	21, 9,15, 3, 1, 5,11,31,23,
63	16	15	15	21, 7,27,15, 1, 5,11,31,23,
63	16	15	15	21, 7, 9, 3, 1, 5,11,31,23,
63	16	15	13	21, 7, 9,15, 3, 1, 5,11,31,
63	16	19	11	21, 7,27,15, 3, 1, 5,11,23,
63	16	19	13	21, 7,27,15, 3, 1, 5,31,23,
63	16	20	13	21, 7, 9,15, 3, 1, 5,11,23,
63	16	23	23	21, 7,27,15, 3, 1, 5,11,31,
63	15	6	6	7,27, 9, 1, 5,11,31,23,13,
63	15	7	7	27, 9, 3, 1, 5,11,31,23,13,
63	15	7	7	15, 3, 1, 5,11,31,23,13,
63	15	7	7	27, 9,15, 3, 1, 5,11,31,23,
63	15	9	9	7,15, 1, 5,11,31,23,13,
63	15	9	9	7,15, 3, 1, 5,11,31,23,
63	15	10	10	0,21, 9,15, 1, 5,11,31,23,13,
63	15	12	9	0,21, 7, 9, 1, 5,11,31,23,13,
63	15	12	12	0,21, 7, 9,15, 1, 5,11,31,23,
63	15	12	12	0,21, 7,27, 3, 1, 5,11,31,23,
63	15	14	12	0,21, 9, 3, 1, 5,11,31,23,13,
63	15	14	14	0,21,27,15, 3, 1, 5,11,31,23,
63	15	14	14	0,21, 9,15, 3, 1, 5,11,31,23,
63	15	16	16	0,21, 7, 9, 3, 1, 5,11,31,23,
63	15	17	13	7,27, 9,15, 3, 1, 5,11,23,
63	15	18	15	7,27, 9,15, 1, 5,11,31,23,
63	15	18	15	7,27, 9, 3, 1, 5,11,31,23,
63	15	19	11	7,27, 9,15, 3, 1, 5,31,23,
63	15	20	18	0,21, 7, 9,15, 3, 1, 5,11,31,
63	15	20	16	0,21, 7,27,15, 3, 1, 5,11,23,
63	15	20	14	0,21, 7, 9,15, 3, 1, 5,11,23,
63	15	21	21	7,27, 9,15, 3, 1, 5,11,31,
63	15	22	20	0,21, 7,27,15, 3, 1, 5,31,23,
63	15	24	18	0,21, 7,27,15, 1, 5,11,31,23,

n	k	d	d_{BCH}	Roots of Gen. Poly.
63	15	24	24	0,21, 7,27,15, 3, 1, 5,11,31,
63	14	6	6	0, 7,27, 9, 1, 5,11,31,23,13,
63	14	12	12	0, 7,15, 1, 5,11,31,23,13,
63	14	14	10	0,27, 9, 3, 1, 5,11,31,23,13,
63	14	14	14	0,15, 3, 1, 5,11,31,23,13,
63	14	14	14	0,27, 9,15, 3, 1, 5,11,31,23,
63	14	18	18	0, 7,27, 9,15, 1, 5,11,31,23,
63	14	18	16	0, 7,27, 9, 3, 1, 5,11,31,23,
63	14	18	18	0, 7,15, 3, 1, 5,11,31,23,
63	14	18	16	0, 7,27, 9,15, 3, 1, 5,11,23,
63	14	22	22	0, 7,27, 9,15, 3, 1, 5,11,31,
63	14	22	22	0, 7,27, 9,15, 3, 1, 5,31,23,
63	13	9	9	21, 7,15, 1, 5,11,31,23,13,
63	13	9	9	21,15, 3, 1, 5,11,31,23,13,
63	13	9	9	21, 7,15, 3, 1, 5,11,31,23,
63	13	12	9	21, 7,27, 9, 1, 5,11,31,23,13,
63	13	14	13	21,27, 9, 3, 1, 5,11,31,23,13,
63	13	14	14	21,27, 9,15, 3, 1, 5,11,31,23,
63	13	20	13	21, 7,27, 9,15, 3, 1, 5,11,23,
63	13	23	15	21, 7,27, 9, 3, 1, 5,11,31,23,
63	13	23	23	21, 7,27, 9,15, 3, 1, 5,11,31,
63	13	24	15	21, 7,27, 9,15, 1, 5,11,31,23,
63	13	24	15	21, 7,27, 9,15, 3, 1, 5,31,23,
63	12	7	7	27,15, 3, 1, 5,11,31,23,13,
63	12	9	9	7, 9,15, 1, 5,11,31,23,13,
63	12	12	9	0,21, 7,27, 9, 1, 5,11,31,23,13,
63	12	12	12	0,21, 7,15, 1, 5,11,31,23,13,
63	12	14	13	0,21,27, 9, 3, 1, 5,11,31,23,13,
63	12	14	14	0,21,15, 3, 1, 5,11,31,23,13,
63	12	14	14	0,21,27, 9,15, 3, 1, 5,11,31,23,
63	12	15	15	7, 9, 3, 1, 5,11,31,23,13,
63	12	18	18	0,21, 7,15, 3, 1, 5,11,31,23,
63	12	20	16	0,21, 7,27, 9,15, 3, 1, 5,11,23,
63	12	21	21	7,27,15, 3, 1, 5,11,31,23,
63	12	21	21	7, 9,15, 3, 1, 5,11,31,23,
63	12	24	18	0,21, 7,27, 9,15, 1, 5,11,31,23,
63	12	24	16	0,21, 7,27, 9, 3, 1, 5,11,31,23,
63	12	24	24	0,21, 7,27, 9,15, 3, 1, 5,11,31,
63	12	24	22	0,21, 7,27., 9,15, 3, 1, 5,31,23,
63	11	12	12	0, 7, 9,15, 1, 5,11,31,23,13,
63	11	14	14	0,27,15, 3, 1, 5,11,31,23,13,
63	11	18	18	0, 7, 9, 3, 1, 5,11,31,23,13,
63	11	22	22	0, 7, 9,15, 3, 1, 5,11,31,23,
63	11	26	26	0, 7,27,15, 3, 1, 5,11,31,23,
63	10	12	12	21, 7, 9,15, 1, 5,11,31,23,13,
63	10	14	13	21,27,15, 3, 1, 5,11,31,23,13,
63	10	15	15	21, 7, 9, 3, 1, 5,11,31,23,13,
63	10	23	23	21, 7,27,15, 3, 1, 5,11,31,23,
63	10	27	27	21, 7, 9,15, 3, 1, 5,11,31,23,
63	9	7	7	27, 9,15, 3, 1, 5,11,31,23,13,
63	9	9	9	7,15, 3, 1, 5,11,31,23,13,

n	k	d	d_{BCH}	Roots of Gen. Poly.
63	9	12	12	0,21, 7, 9,15, 1, 5,11,31,23,13,
63	9	14	14	0,21,27,15, 3, 1, 5,11,31,23,13,
63	9	18	15	7,27, 9, 3, 1, 5,11,31,23,13,
63	9	21	21	7,27, 9,15, 3, 1, 5,11,31,23,
63	9	24	18	0,21, 7, 9, 3, 1, 5,11,31,23,13,
63	9	28	28	0,21, 7,27,15, 3, 1, 5,11,31,23,
63	9	28	28	0,21, 7, 9,15, 3, 1, 5,11,31,23,
63	8	14	14	0,27, 9,15, 3, 1, 5,11,31,23,13,
63	8	18	18	0, 7,27, 9, 3, 1, 5,11,31,23,13,
63	8	18	18	0, 7,15, 3, 1, 5,11,31,23,13,
63	8	26	26	0, 7,27, 9,15, 3, 1, 5,11,31,23,
63	7	9	9	21, 7,15, 3, 1, 5,11,31,23,13,
63	7	14	14	21,27, 9,15, 3, 1, 5,11,31,23,13,
63	7	24	15	21, 7,27, 9, 3, 1, 5,11,31,23,13,
63	7	31	31	21, 7,27, 9,15, 3, 1, 5,11,31,23,
63	6	14	14	0,21,27, 9,15, 3, 1, 5,11,31,23,13,
63	6	18	18	0,21, 7,15, 3, 1, 5,11,31,23,13,
63	6	21	21	7,27,15, 3, 1, 5,11,31,23,13,
63	6	24	18	0,21, 7,27, 9, 3, 1, 5,11,31,23,13,
63	6	32	32	0,21, 7,27, 9,15, 3, 1, 5,11,31,23,
63	5	30	30	0, 7,27,15, 3, 1, 5,11,31,23,13,
63	4	27	27	21, 7,27,15, 3, 1, 5,11,31,23,13,
63	3	21	21	7,27, 9,15, 3, 1, 5,11,31,23,13,
63	3	36	36	0,21, 7,27,15, 3, 1, 5,11,31,23,13,
63	2	42	42	0, 7,27, 9,15, 3, 1, 5,11,31,23,13,

n	k	d	d_{BCH}	Roots of Gen. Poly.
65	53	5	4	1,
65	52	6	6	0, 1,
65	49	4	3	13, 5,
65	49	5	4	13, 1,
65	48	4	3	0,13, 5,
65	48	6	6	0,13, 1,
65	41	5	5	1, 3,
65	41	5	5	1, 7,
65	41	8	6	5, 1,
65	40	8	6	0, 5, 1,
65	40	8	6	0, 1, 7,
65	40	10	10	0, 1, 3,
65	37	5	5	13, 1, 3,
65	37	5	5	13, 1, 7,
65	37	8	6	13, 5, 1,
65	36	8	6	0,13, 5, 1,
65	36	10	10	0,13, 1, 3,
65	36	10	6	0,13, 1, 7,
65	29	5	5	1, 3, 7,
65	29	12	8	5, 1, 7,
65	29	13	7	5, 1, 3,
65	28	10	10	0, 1, 3, 7,
65	28	12	8	0, 5, 1, 7,
65	28	14	14	0, 5, 1, 3,
65	25	5	5	13, 1, 3, 7,
65	25	13	10	13, 5, 1, 7,
65	25	15	7	13, 5, 1, 3,
65	24	10	10	0,13, 1, 3, 7,
65	24	16	14	0,13, 5, 1, 3,
65	24	16	10	0,13, 5, 1, 7,
65	17	5	5	1, 3, 7,11,
65	17	13	11	5, 1, 3, 7,
65	16	10	10	0, 1, 3, 7,11,
65	16	22	22	0, 5, 1, 3, 7,
65	13	5	5	13, 1, 3, 7,11,
65	13	25	16	13, 5, 1, 3, 7,
65	12	26	22	0,13, 5, 1, 3, 7,
65	12	10	10	0,13, 1, 3, 7,11,
65	5	13	13	5, 1, 3, 7,11,
65	4	26	26	0, 5, 1, 3, 7,11,

Selected Bibliography

Abramson, N. 1959. "A Class of Systematic Codes for Non-Independent Errors." *IRE Trans., IT-5,* 150–157.

———. 1960*a*. "A Note on Single Error Correcting Binary Codes." *IRE Trans., IT-6,* 502–503.

———. 1960*b*. "Error Correcting Codes from Linear Sequential Networks." Presented at the Fourth London Symposium on Information Theory, August, 1960.

———. 1963. *Information Theory and Coding*. New York: McGraw-Hill Book Company, Inc.

———. 1968. "Cascade Decoding of Cyclic Product Codes." *IEEE Trans., Com-16,* 398–402.

Abramson, N. M., and B. Elspas. 1959. "Double-Error-Correcting Coders and Decoders for Non-Independent Binary Errors." Presented at the UNESCO Information Processing Conference in Paris, 1959.

Albert, A. A. 1956. *Fundamental Concepts of Higher Algebra*. Chicago, Ill: University of Chicago Press.

Alter, R. 1968. "On the Non-Existence of Close-Packed Double Hamming Error-Correcting Codes on $q = 7$ Symbols." *J. of Computer and System Sciences*.

Assmus, E. F., and H. F. Mattson, Jr. 1962. *Cyclic Codes*. Air Force Cambridge Research Laboratories Summary Scientific Report.

Assmus, E. F., H. F. Mattson, and R. Turyn. 1965. *Cyclic Codes*. Scientific Report, AFCRL-65-322, Air Force Cambridge Research Labs, Bedford, Mass.

———. 1966. *Cyclic Codes*. Final Report Contract No. AF19(604)-8516, Air Force Cambridge Research Laboratories.

Bahl, L., and R. T. Chien. 1969. "A Class of Multiple Burst-Error Correcting Codes." Paper presented at the IEEE Symposium in Information Theory, Ellenville, N.Y.

Barker, R. H. 1953. "Group Synchronizing of Binary Digital Systems." In *Communication Theory*, ed. W. Jackson, New York: Academic Press.

Barrows, J. T., Jr. 1966. *A New Method for Constructing Multiple Error Correcting Linear Residue Codes*. Coordinated Science Lab., Univ. of Illinois, Report R-277.

Bennett, W. R., and J. R. Davey. 1965. *Data Transmission*. New York: McGraw-Hill Book Company, Inc.

Berger, T. 1970. Private communication.

Berlekamp, E. R. 1964*a*. *Block Coding with Noiseless Feedback*. Ph.D. Thesis Department of Electrical Engineering, Massachusetts Institute of Technology, Cambridge.

———. 1964*b*. "Note on Recurrent Codes." *IEEE Trans., IT-10*, 257–259.

———. 1965. "On Decoding Binary Bose-Chaudhuri-Hocquenghem Codes." *IEEE Trans., IT-11*,577–580.

———. 1968*a*. "Negacyclic Codes for the Lee Metric." *Proceedings of the Conference on Combinatorial Mathematics and Its Applications*. Chapel Hill, N.C.: University of North Carolina Press.

———. 1968*b*. *Algebraic Coding Theory*. New York: McGraw-Hill Book Company.

Birdsall, T. G., and M. P. Ristenbatt. 1958. *Introduction to Linear Shift-Register Generated Sequences*. EDG Technical Report No. 90, University of Michigan Research Institute.

Birkhoff, G., and S. Mac Lane. 1941. *A Survey of Modern Algebra*. New York: The Macmillan Co.

Blum, R. A., and A. D. Weiss. 1960. *Further Results in Error-Correcting Codes*. S.M. Thesis, Department of Electrical Engineering, M.I.T., Cambridge, Mass.

Blumenthal L. M. 1961. *A Modern View of Geometry*. San Francisco: W. H. Freeman.

Bose. R. C. 1939. "On the Construction of Balanced Incomplete Block Designs." *Ann. Eugenics, 9*, 353–399.

Bose, R. C., and J. G. Caldwell. 1967. "Synchronizable Error-Correcting Codes." *Inf. and Control. 10*, 616–630.

Bose, R. C., and R. R. Kuebler, Jr. 1958. *On the Construction of a Class of Error Correcting Binary Signaling Codes*. Technical Report, University of North Carolina, Chapel Hill, N.C. (May, 1958).

Bose, R. C., and D. K. Ray-Chaudhuri. 1960*a*. "On a Class of Error Correcting Binary Group Codes." *Inf. and Control, 3*, 68–79.

———. 1960*b*. "Further Results on Error Correcting Binary Group Codes." *Inf. and Control, 3*, 279–290.

Bose, R. C., and S. S. Shrikhande. 1959. "A Note on a Result in the Theory of Code Construction." *Inf. and Control, 2*, 183–194.

Bredeson, J. G., and S. L. Hakimi. 1967. "Decoding of Graph Theoretic Codes." *IEEE Trans., IT-14*, No. 2, 348–349.

Brown, D. T. 1960. "Error Detecting and Correcting Binary Codes for Arithmetic Operations." *IRE Trans., EC-9*, 333–337.

Brown, D. T., and W. W. Peterson. 1961. "Cyclic Codes for Error Detection." *Proc. IRE, 49*, 228–235.

Burton, H. O. 1969. "A Class of Asymptotically Optimal Burst-Correcting Block Codes." Presented at International Communications Conference, Boulder, Col.

———. 1970. "Inversionless Decoding of Binary BCH Codes or Berlekamp's Algorithm Revised," paper in preparation.

Burton, H. O., and E. J. Weldon, Jr. 1965. "Cyclic Product Codes." *IEEE Trans., IT-11*, 433–439.

Bussgang, J. J. 1965. "Some Properties of Binary Convolutional Code Generators." *IEEE Trans., IT-11*, 90–100.

Calabi, L., and H. G. Haefeli. 1959. "A Class of Binary Systematic Codes Correcting Errors at Random and in Bursts." *IRE Trans., IT-5*, Special Supplement, 79–94.

Calabi, L., and E. Myrvaagnes. 1964. "On the Minimal Weight of Binary Group Codes." *IEEE Trans., IT-10*, 385–387.

Carmichael, R. D. 1937. *Introduction to the Theory of Groups of Finite Order*. Boston: Ginn & Company.

Chen, C. L. 1969. *Some Results on Algebraically Structured Error-Correcting Codes.* Ph.D. Dissertation, University of Hawaii.

Chen, C. L., and S. Lin. 1969. "Further Results on Polynomial Codes." *Information and Control, 15,* 38–60.

Chen, C. L., W. W. Peterson, and E. J. Weldon, Jr. 1969. "Some Results on Quasi-cyclic Codes." *Information and Control, 15,* 407–423.

Chernoff, H. 1952. "A Measure of Asymptotic Efficiency for Tests of a Hypothesis Based on the Sum of Observations." *Ann. Math. Stat., 23,* 493–507.

Chiang, A. C. L., and I. S. Reed. 1970. "Arithmetic Norms and Bounds of the Arithmetic AN Codes." *IEEE Trans.. IT-16,* 470–476.

Chien, R. T. 1959. "Orthogonal Matrices, Error-Correcting Codes and Load-Sharing Matrix Switches." *IRE Trans., EC-*8, Correspondence, 400.

———. 1964*a*. "Linear Residue Codes for Burst-Error-Correction." *IEEE Trans., IT-10,* no. 2, 127–133.

———. 1964*b*. "Cyclic Decoding Procedures for Bose-Chaudhuri-Hocquenghem Codes." *IEEE Trans., IT-10,* 357–363.

Chien, R. T., B. D. Cunningham, and I. B. Oldham. 1969. "Hybrid Methods for Finding Roots of a Polynomial — With Application to BCH Decoding." *IEEE Trans., IT-15,* no. 2, 329–334.

Chien, R. T. and W. D. Frazer. 1966. "An Application of Coding Theory to Document Retrieval," *IEEE Trans., IT-12,* 2, 92–96.

Chow, D. 1968. "On Threshold Decoding of Cyclic Codes", *Inf. and Cont., 13,* 471–483.

Cocke, J. 1959. "Lossless Symbol Coding with Nonprimes." *IRE Trans., IT-*5, 33–34.

Cohen, E. L. 1964. "A Note on Perfect Double Error-Correcting Codes on q Symbols", *Inf. and Cont., 1,* 381–384.

Constantine, G. 1958. "A Load-Sharing Matrix Switch." *IBM J. Research Develop., 2,* 204–211.

Corr, F. P. 1961. "Multiple Burst Detection." *Proc. IRE, 49,* 1337.

Corr, F. P., and E. Gorog. 1963. "Les Codes Capables d'Assurer une Sécurité contre les Erreurs dans la Transmission de Données." *Onde Elec.* (France), *43,* 117–27.

Costello, D. J., Jr. 1969. "A Construction Technique for Random-Error-Correcting Convolutional Codes." *IEEE Trans., IT-15,* no. 5, 631–636.

Crick, H. C., J. S. Griffith, and L. E. Orgel. 1957. "Codes Without Commas." *Proc. Nat. Acad. Sci., 43,* 416–421.

Delsarte, 1969. "A Geometric Approach to a Class of Cyclic Codes," *J. Comb. Th.,* 6, 340–359.

———. 1970. "On Cyclic Codes that are Invariant under the General Linear Group," *IEEE Trans., IT-16,* 760–769.

Delsarte, P., J. M. Goethals, and J. MacWilliams. 1970. "On GRM and Related Codes." *Information and Control,* 403–442.

Diamond, J. M. 1955. "Checking for Digital Computers." *Proc. IRE,* 43, 487–488.

Dolansky, L., and Marie P. Dolansky. 1952. *Table of* log_2 $(1/p)$, p *log,* $(1/p)$ and $p\ log_2(1/p) + (1-p)\ log_2[1/(1-p)]$. Research Laboratory of Electronics Technical Report 227, M.I.T., Cambridge, Mass.

Dwork, B. M., and R. M. Heller. 1959. "Results of a Geometric Approach to the Theory and Construction of Non-Binary, Multiple Error and Failure Correcting Codes." *IRE National Convention Record,* Part 4, 123–129.

Eastman, W. L. 1965. "On the Construction of Comma-Free Codes." *IEEE Trans., IT-11,* no. 4, 263–266.

Elias, P. 1954. "Error-Free Coding." *IRE Trans., PGIT-4*, 29–37.
———. 1955. "Coding for Noisy Channels." *IRE Convention Record*, Part 4, 37–46.
———. 1956. "Coding for Two Noisy Channels." In *Information Theory*, ed., Colin Cherry. New York: Academic Press, pp. 61–74.
———. 1958. "Computation in the Presence of Noise." *IBM J. Research Develop., 2*, 346–353.
———. Unpublished notes.
Elspas, B. 1959. "The Theory of Autonomous Linaer Sequential Networks." *IRE Trans., CT-6*, 45–60.
———. 1960. "A Note on *P*-nary Adjacent-Error-Correcting Codes." *IRE Trans., IT-6*, 13–15.
———. 1962. *Design and Instrumentation of Error-Correcting Codes.* Rome Air Dev. Ctr. Tech. Rept. RADC-TDR-62-511, Rome, N.Y., ASTA DOC. 294 957.
———. 1967. "A Note on Multidimensional Coding." Presented at the IEEE International Symposium on Information Theory, San Remo, Italy (1967).
Elspas, B., and R. A. Short. 1962. "A Note on Optimum Burst-Error-Correcting Codes." *IRE Trans., IT-8*, Correspondence, 39–42.
Epstein, M. A. 1958. *Algebraic Decoding for a Binary Erasure Channel.* Research Laboratory of Electronics Report 340, M.I.T., Cambridge, Mass.

Falconer, D. 1966. "A Hybrid Sequential and Algebraic Decoding Scheme" Sc.D. thesis, Dept. of Elect. Eng., M.I.T.
Fano, R. M. 1961. *Transmission of Information.* New York: The M.I.T. Press and John Wiley & Sons, Inc.
———. 1963. "A Heuristic Discussion of Probabilistic Decoding." *IEEE Trans., IT-9*, no. 2, 64–74.
Feinstein, A. 1958. *Foundations of Information Theory.* New York: McGraw-Hill Book Company, Inc.
Feller, W. 1943. "Generalization of a Probability Limit Theorem of Cramer. *Trans. Am. Math. Soc.*, 54, 361–372.
———. 1950. *An Introduction to Probability Theory and Its Application.* John Wiley & Sons, Inc. New York.
Fire, P. 1959. *A Class of Multiple-Error-Correcting Binary Codes for Non-Independent Errors.* Sylvania Report RSL-E-2, Sylvania Reconnaissance Systems Laboratory, Mountain View, Calif.
Fitzpatrick, G. B. 1960. "Synthesis of Binary Ring Counters of Given Periods." *J.A.C.M.*, 7, 287–297.
Fontaine, A. B., and R. G. Gallager. 1960. *Error-Statistics and Coding for Binary Transmission over Telephone Circuits.* Technical Report 25G-0023, M.I.T. Lincoln Laboratory, Lexington, Mass. (October 1960).
Fontaine, A. B., and W. W. Peterson. 1958. "On Coding for the Binary Symmetric Channel." *Trans. AIEE*, 77, Part 1, *Comm. and Elec.*, 638–646.
———. 1959. "Group Code Equivalence and Optimum Codes." *IRE Trans., IT-5*, Special Supplement, 60–70 (1959).
Forney, G. D., Jr. 1965. "On Decoding BCH Codes." *IEEE Trans, IT-11*, 549–557.
———. 1966*a*. *Concatenated Codes.* Sc.D. Thesis, M.I.T., Cambridge, Mass. (1965); also M.I.T. Press Research Monograph 37 (1966).
———. 1966. "Generalized Minimum Distance Decoding," *IEEE Trans., IT-12*, 125–131.
———. 1968. "Review of Random Tree Codes." Codex Corporation Report.
———. 1969. "Algebraic Structure of Convolutional Codes." Presented at IEEE International Symposium on Information Theory, Ellenville, New York. Also published *IEEE Trans. IT-16* Nov. 1970.

Foulkes, H. O. 1956. "Theorems of Kakeya and Pólya on Power-Sums." *Math. Z.*, *65*, 345–352.
Frank, H., and M. Goldstein. 1967. "On the Rank and Error Correcting Capabilities of Some Graph Theoretic Codes." *Proc. First Princeton Conference on Information Science and Systems.*
Frazer, W. D. 1964. "A Graph Theoretic Approach to Linear Codes." *Proc. 2nd Allerton Conference on Circuits and Systems.*
Friedland, B. 1959. "Linear Modular Sequential Circuits." *IRE Trans.*, *CT-6*, 61–68.
Friedland, B., and T. E. Stern. 1959. "On Periodicity of States in Linear Modular Sequential Circuits." *IRE Trans.*, *IT-5*, Correspondence, 136–137.
Frieman, C. V., and J. P. Robinson. 1965. "A Comparison of Block and Recurrent Codes for the Correction of Independent Errors." *IEEE Trans.*, *IT-11*, 445–449.
Frey, A. H., Jr. 1965. "Message Framing and Error Control." *IEEE Trans. Military Electronic*, *Mil-9*, no. 2, 143–147.
———. 1967. "Adaptive Decoding Without Feedback." IBM Technical TR 48-67-001

Gallager, R. G. 1963. *Low-Density Parity-Check Codes*. Sc. D. Thesis, Department of Electrical Engineering, M.I.T., Cambridge, Mass. (1960) also M.I.T. Press Research Monograph 21, Cambridge, Mass.
———. 1968. *Information Theory and Reliable Communication*. New York: John Wiley & Sons.
Garner, H. L. 1958. "Generalized Parity Checking." *IRE Trans.*, *EC-7*, 207–213.
Gilbert, E. N. 1952. "A Comparison of Signalling Alphabets." *Bell System Tech. J.* *31*, 504–522.
———. 1960. "Synchronization of Binary Messages." *IEEE Trans.*, *IT-6*, 470–477.
Gilbert, E. N., and E. F. Moore. 1959. "Variable Length Binary Encodings." *Bell System Tech. J.*, *38*, 933–967.
Gleason, A. M. 1961. Unpublished notes.
———. 1968. "On the Golay Perfect Binary Code." MBLE Research Lab. Report R93. *Journal of Combinatorial Theory.*
Goethals, J. M. 1967. "Factorization of Cyclic Codes." *IEEE Trans.*, *IT-13*, 242–246.
———. 1966. "Analysis of Weight Distribution in Binary Cyclic Codes," *IEEE Trans.*, *3*, 401.
Goethals, J. M., and P. Delsarte. 1968. "On a Class of Majority-Logic Decodable Cyclic Codes." *IEEE Trans.*, *IT-14*, no. 2, 182–189.
Goethals, J. M., and J. J. Seidl. 1967. "Orthogonal Matrices with Zero Diagonal." *Canadian Journal of Mathematics*, *19*, 1101–1010.
Golay, M. J. E. 1949. "Notes on Digital Coding." *Proc. IRE*, *37*, Correspondence, 657.
———. 1954. "Binary Coding." *IRE Trans.*, *PGIT-4*, 23–28.
———. 1958. "Notes on the Penny-Weighing Problem, Lossless Symbol Coding with Nonprimes, etc." *IRE Trans.*, *IT-4*, 103–109.
Goldman, H. D., M. Kliman, and H. Smola. 1968. "The Weight Structure of Some Bose-Chaudhuri Codes." *IEEE Trans.*, *IT-14*, no. 1, 167–169.
Goldman, H. D., W. Rowan, and M. Tolhurst. 1969. "Threshold Decoding Selected Rate One-Half and One-Third Convolutional Codes." *IEEE Trans.*, *IT-15*, no. 1, 179–184.
Goldman, S. 1953. *Information Theory*. Englewood Cliffs, N.J.: Prentice-Hall, Inc.
Golomb, S. W. 1955. *Sequences with Randomness Properties*. Glenn L. Martin Co. Final Report on Contract No. W36-039SC-54-36611, Baltimore, Md.
Golomb, S. W., and B. Gordon. 1965. "Codes with Bounded Synchronization Delay." *Inf. and Cont.*, *8*, 355–372.
Golomb, S. W., B. Gordon, and L. R. Welch. 1958. "Comma-Free Codes." *Canadian J. Math.*, *10*, no. 2, 202–209.

Gore, W. C. 1969*a*. "Generalized Threshold Decoding and the Reed-Solomon Codes," *IEEE Trans.*, *IT-15*, no. 1, 78–81.

———. 1969*b*. "Generalized Threshold Decoding of Linear Codes." *IEEE Trans.*, *IT-15*, no. 5, 590–592.

Gorenstein, D., W. W. Peterson, and N. Zierler. 1960. "Two Error-Correcting Bose-Chaudhuri Codes are Quasi Perfect. *Inf. and Control*, *3*, 291–294.

Graham, R. L., and J. MacWilliams. 1966. "On the Number of Parity Checks in Difference-Set Cyclic Codes." *BSTJ*, *45*, 1045–1055.

Green, J. H., Jr., and R. L. San Soucie. 1958. "An Error-Correcting Encoder and Decoder of High Efficiency." *Proc. IRE*, *46*, 1741–1744.

Green, M. W. 1966. "Two Heuristic Techniques for Block-Code Construction." *IEEE Trans.*, *IT-12*, 273.

Greismer, J. H. 1960. "A Bound for Error Correcting Codes." *IBM J. Res. Development*, 4, 532–542.

Gross, A. J. 1963. "Augmented Bose-Chaudhuri Codes which Correct Single Bursts of Errors." *IEEE Trans.*, *IT-9*, 122.

Gschwind, H. W. 1967. *Design of Digital Computers*. New York: Springer-Verlag.

Hagelbarger, D. W. 1959. "Recurrent Codes: Easily Mechanized, Burst-Correcting, Binary Codes." *Bell System Tech. J.*, *38*, 969–984.

———. 1960. "Error Detection Using Recurrent Codes." Presented at the AIEE Winter General Meeting, February 1960.

Hakimi, S. L., and H. Frank. 1965. "Cut-set Matrices and Linear Codes." *IEEE Trans.*, *IT-11*, 457.

Hakimi, S. L., and J. G. Bredeson. 1968. "Graph Theoretic Error-Correcting Codes." *IEEE Trans.*, *IT-14*, no. 4, 584–591.

Hall, Marshall, Jr. 1967. *Combinatorial Theory*. Watham., Mass.: Blaisdell Publishing Co.

Hall, M. 1938. "An Isomorphism between Linear Recurring Sequences and Algebraic Rings." *Trans. Am. Math. Soc.*, *44*, 196–218.

Hamming, R. W. 1950. "Error Detecting and Error Correcting Codes." *Bell System Tech. J.*, *29*, 147–160.

Harmuth, H. F. 1960. "Orthogonal Codes." *Proc. Inst. of Elec. Engrs.* (British), *107*, Part C, Monograph 369E, 242–248.

Hartmanis, J. 1959. "Linear Multivalued Sequential Coding Networks." *IRE Trans.*, *CT*-6, 69–74.

Hocquenghem, A. 1959. "Codes correcteurs d'erreurs." *Chiffres*, 2, 147–156.

Hoffner, C. W., and S. M. Reddy. 1970. "Circulant Bases for Cyclic Codes," *IEEE Trans.*, *IT-16*, No. 4, 511–512.

Honda, N. 1956. "The Sequential Error-Correcting Code." *Sci. Repts. Tôhoku Univ.*, Series B, *8*, no. 3.

Horstein, M. 1960. *Sequential Transmission of Digital Information with Feedback*. Sc.D. Thesis, Department of Electrical Engineering, M.I.T., Cambridge, Mass.

Hsu, H. T., T. Kasami, and R. T. Chien. 1968. "Error-Correcting Codes for a Compound Channel." *IEEE Trans.*, *IT-14*, No. 1, 135–138.

Huband, F. L., and F. Jelinek. 1968. "Practical Sequential Decoding and a Simple Hybrid Scheme." *Proceedings Hawaii Int. Conf. on System Sciences*.

Huffman, D. A. 1956*a*. "The Synthesis of Linear Sequential Coding Networks." In *Information Theory*. ed. Colin Cherry, New York: Academic Press. pp. 77–95.

———. 1956*b*. "A Linear Circuit Viewpoint on Error-Correcting Codes." *IRE Trans.*, *IT-2*, 20–28.

———. 1964. "A Graph Theoretic Formulation of Binary Group Codes." Summaries of papers presented at ICMCI, part 3.

Iwadare, Y. 1968*a*. "On Type-B1 Burst-Error-Correcting Convolutional Codes." *IEEE Trans.*, *IT-14*, No. 4, 577–584.

———. 1968*b*. "Burst and Random Error Correction by Means of Threshold Decoding." Nippon Electric Co., Technical Report.

Jacobs, I. M., A. J. Viterbi, and J. A. Heller. 1970. "Convolutional Codes." Notes for Linkabit Corporation Seminar.

Jelinek, F. 1969. "A Fast Sequential Decoding Algorithm Using a Stack." *IBM J. Res. Dev., 13*, 675–685.

Jiggs, B. H. 1963. "Recent Results on Comma-Free-Codes." *Canad. J. Math.*, 15, 178–187.

Johnson, S. M. 1962. "A New Upper Bound for Error-Correcting Codes." *IEEE Trans., IT-8*, 203–207.

———. 1963. "Improved Asymptotic Bounds for Error-Correcting Codes." *IEEE Trans., IT-9*, 198–205.

Joshi, D. D. 1958. "A Note on Upper Bounds for Minimum Distance Codes." *Information and Control, 1*, 289–295.

Julin, D. 1965. "Two Improved Block Codes." *IEEE Trans., IT-11*, 459.

Karlin, M. 1969. "New Binary Coding Results by Circulants." *IEEE Trans., IT-15*, no. 1, part I, 81–92.

Kasami, T. 1960. "Systematic Codes Using Binary Shift Register Sequences." *J. Info. Processing Soc. Japan, 1*, 198–200.

———. 1961. "A Topological Approach to Construction of Group Codes." *J. Inst. Elec. Commun. Engrs.* (Japan), *44*.

———. 1962. "Cyclic Codes for Burst-Error-Correction." *J. Inst. Elec. Commun. Engrs.* (Japan), *45*, 9–15.

———. 1963. "Optimum Shortened Cyclic Codes for Burst-Error-Correction." *IEEE Trans., IT-9*, 105–09.

———. 1964. "A Decoding Procedure for Multiple Error-Correcting Cyclic Codes." *IEEE Trans., IT-10*, 134–139.

———. 1968. "Some Lower Bounds in the Minimum Weight of Cyclic Codes of Composite Length." *IEEE Trans., IT–14*, No. 6, 814–817.

Kasami, T and S. Lin. 1971. "On Majority Logic Decoding for the Duals of Primitive Polynomial Codes." *IEEE Trans., IT-17*, to appear.

Kasami, T., S. Lin, and W. W. Peterson. 1966. *Some Results on Cyclic Codes Which are Invariant Under the Affine Group.* Air Force Cambridge Research Lab. Report. Also "On the Minimum Weights of BCH Codes," *J. Inst. Elect. Communication Engr.* (Japan), *50*, 1617–1622. (1967).

———. 1968*a*. "New Generalizations of the Reed-Muller Codes-Part I: Primitive Codes." *IEEE Trans., IT-14*, no. 2, 189–199.

———. 1968*b*. "Polynomial Codes." *IEEE Trans., IT-14*, no. 6, 807–814.

Kasami, T., and S. Matoba, 1964. "Some Efficient Shortened Cyclic Codes for Burst-Error-Correction." *IEEE Trans., IT-10*, 252–53.

Kasami, T., and N. Tokura. 1969. "Some Remarks on BCH Bounds and Minimum Weights of Binary Primitive BCH Codes." *IEEE Trans., IT-15*, 408–413.

Kautz, W. H. 1959. *A Class of Multiple-Error-Correcting Codes for Data Transmission and Recording.* Stanford Research Institute Technical Report 5 (SRI Project 2124), Palo Alto, Calif., August, 1959).

Kelly, J. L. 1960. "A Class of Codes for Signaling on a Noisy Continuous Channel." *IRE Trans., IT-6*, 22–24.

Kilmer, W. L. 1959. *Some Results on Linear-Recurrent Binary Burst-Correcting Codes.* Montana State College Electronics Research Laboratory Project No. 6795–102, Technical Report No. 3, Bozeman, Montana, January, 1959.

Kilmer, W. L. 1960. *Linear-Recurrent Binary Error-Correcting Codes for Memoryless Channels.* Montana State College Electronics Research Laboratory Project No. 6795–102, Technical Report No. 4, Bozeman, Montana (January 1960). Part of these results were presented at the IRE Convention, March, 1960.

Kiyasu, Zen'ichi. 1953. *Research and Development Data*. no. 4, Electrical Communication Laboratory, Nippon Tele. Corp. Tokyo.

Kohlenberg, A. 1965. "Random and Burst Error Control." *Proceedings of the First IEEE Annual Communications Convention*, 55–66.

Kohlenberg, A., and G. D. Forney, Jr., 1968. "Convolutional Coding for Channels with Memory." *IEEE Trans.*, *IT-14*, no. 5, 618–626.

Lebow, I.L., et al. 1963. "Application of Sequential Decoding." *IEEE Trans.*, *IT-9*, 124–126.

Lee, C. Y. 1958. "Some Properties of Nonbinary Error-Correcting Codes." *IRE Trans.*, *IT-4*, 77–82.

Levy, J. E. 1968. "Self Synchronizing Codes Derived from Binary Cyclic Codes." *IEEE Trans.*, *IT-12*, 286–291.

Lin, S. 1967. "Some Codes Which Are Invariant Under a Transitive Permutation Group and Their Connection with Balanced Incomplete Block Designs." *Proceedings of the Conference on Combinatorial Mathematics and Its Applications*, Chapel Hill, N.C.: University of North Carolina Press.

———. 1968. "On a Class of Cyclic Codes," Proceedings of Symposium on Error Correcting Codes, at Madison, Wisconsin, Chapter 7, *Error-Correcting Codes*, H. B. Mann editor.

———. 1970. *Introduction to Error Correcting Codes*. Englewood Cliffs, N.J.: Prentice-Hall, Inc.

Lin, S., and H. Lyne. 1967. "Some Results in Convolutional Code Generators." *IEEE Trans.*, *IT-13*, 1, 134–139.

Lin, S., and E. J. Weldon, Jr. 1967. "Long BCH Codes are Bad." *Information and Control*, *11*, 445.

———. 1970. "Further Results on Cyclic Product Codes." *IEEE Trans.*, *IT-16*. 445–451.

Lloyd, S. P. 1957. "Binary Block Coding." *Bell System Tech. J.*, *36*, 517–535.

Lucas, M. E. 1878. "Sur les congruences des nombres eulériens et des coefficients différentials des fonctions trigonometriques, suivant un module premier." *Bull. Soc. Math. France*, *6*, 49–54.

Lucky, R. W., J. Salz, and E. J. Weldon, Jr. 1968. *Principles of Data Communication*. New York: McGraw-Hill Book Company.

MacDonald, J. E. 1958. *Constructive Coding Methods for the Binary Symmetric Independent Data Transmission Channel*. M.S. Thesis, Department of Electrical Engineering, Syracuse University, Syracuse, N.Y.

———. 1960. "Design Method for Maximum Minimum-Distance Error-Correcting Codes." *IBM J. Research Develop.*, *4*, 43–57.

MacDuffee, C. C., 1943. *Vectors and Matrices*. Ithaca, N.Y.: Mathematical Association of America.

MacWilliams, F. J. 1963*a*. "A Theorem on the Distribution of Weights in a Systematic Code." *Bell System Tech. J.*, *42*, 79–94.

———. 1963*b*. *Quadratic Residue Alphabets and How to Decode Them*. Bell Telephone Laboratories Memorandum.

———. 1964. "Permutation Decoding of Systematic Codes." *Bell System Tech. J.*, *43*, 485–505.

MacWilliams, F. J., and H. B. Mann. *1967. On the p-Rank of the Design Matrix of a Difference Set*. MRC Technical Summary, Report No. 803, Mathematics Research Center, United States Army, University of Wisconsin.

Mandelbaum, D. 1967. "Arithmetic Codes with Large Distance." *IEEE Trans.*, *IT-13*, no. 2, 237–242.

———. 1968. "A Note on Synchronizable Error-Correcting Codes." technical report.

Mann, H. B. 1949. *Analysis and Design of Experiments*. New York: Dover.

———. 1963. "On the Number of Information Symbols in Bose-Chaudhuri Codes." *Information and Control, 5,* 153–165.

Mann, H. B., editor. 1968. *Error Correcting Codes.* Proceedings of a Symposium organized by the Mathematics Research Center, U.S. Army, University of Wisconsin, New York: John Wiley & Sons, Inc.

Marcus, M. P. 1959. "Doubling the Efficiency of the Load-Sharing Matrix Switch." *IBM J. Research Develop., 3,* 194–196.

Marsh, R. W. 1957. *Table of Irreducible Polynomials Over GF(2) Through Degree 19.* NSA, Washington, D.C.

Massey, J. L. 1963. *Threshold Decoding,* M.I.T. Press Research Monograph 20, Cambridge, Mass: The M.I.T. Press.

———. 1964. "Survey of Residue Coding for Arithmetic Errors." *International Computation Center Bulletin,* Rome, Italy, UNESCO.

———. 1965*a*. "Implementation of Burst-Correcting Convolutional Codes." *IEEE Trans., IT-11,* 416–422.

———. 1965*b*. "Step-by-Step Decoding of the Bose-Chaudhuri-Hocquenghem Codes." *IEEE Trans., OT-11,* 580–585.

———. 1966. "Uniform Codes." *IEEE Trans., IT-12,*132–135.

———. 1968. "Advances in Threshold Decoding." *Advances in Communications Systems.* A. V. Balakrishnan, Ed. New York: Academic Press, Inc., vol. 2.

———. 1969. "Shift Register Synthesis and BCH Decoding." *IEEE Trans., IT-15,* no. 1, 122–127.

Massey, J. L., and R. W. Liu. 1964. "Application of Lyapunov's Direct Method to the Error-propagation Effect in Convolutional Codes." *IEEE Trans., IT-10,* 248–250.

Mattson, H. F., and G. Solomon. 1961. "A New Treatment of Bose Chaudhuri Codes." *J. Soc. Indus. Appl. Math., 9,* 4, 654–669.

McCluskey, E. J., Jr., 1959. "Error-Correcting Codes—A Linear Programming Approach." *Bell Sytsem Tech. J., 38,* 1485–1512.

———. 1965. *Introduction to the Theory of Switching Circuits.* New York: McGraw-Hill Book Company.

McEliece, R., and H. Rumsey. 1968. "Capabilities of Convolutional Codes." Jet Propulsion Lab SPS 37–50, *III.*

Meggitt, J. E. 1960. "Error Correcting Codes for Correcting Bursts of Errors." *IBM J. Research Develop., 4,* 329–334.

Melas, C. M. 1960. "A New Group of Codes for Correction of Dependent-Errors in Data Transmission." *IBM J. Research Develop., 4,* 58–65.

———. 1960*b*. "A Cyclic Code for Double Error Correction." *IBM J. Research Develop., 4,* 364–366.

Melas, C. M., and E. Gorog. 1963. "A Note on Extending Certain Codes to Correct Error Bursts in Longer Messages." *IBM J. Res. Develop., 7,* 151–152.

Mitani, N. 1951. "On the Transmission of Numbers in a Sequential Computer." Delivered at the National Convention of the Institute of Electrical Communication Engineers of Japan, November, 1951.

Mitchell, M. E. 1962. "Simple Decoders and Correlators for Cyclic Error-Correcting Codes." *IRE Trans., CS-10,* 284–291.

Mitchell, M. E., et al. 1961. *Coding and Decoding Operations Research.* G. E. Advanced Electronics Final Report on Contract AF 19(604)–6183, Air Force Cambridge Research Labs.

Muir, T., and W. H. Metzier, 1930. *A Treatise on the Theory of Determinants.* Albany, N.Y.: Dover Press. Chapter 21.

Muller, D. E. 1954. "Application of Boolean Algebra to Switching Circuit Design and Error Detection." *IRE Trans., EC-3,* 6–12.

Nordstrom, A. W., and J. P. Robinson. 1967. "An Optimum Nonlinear Code." *Information and Control, 11,* 613–616.

Omura, J. K. 1969*a*. "A Probabilistic Decoding Algorithm for Binary Group Codes." presented at IEEE International Symposium on Information Theory, also SRI Technical Report under Project 664531-226.

———. 1969*b*. "On the Viterbi Decoding Algorithm." *IEEE Trans.*, *IT-15*, 1, 177–179.

Pele, R. L. 1969. "Some Remarks on the Vector Subspaces of Cyclic Galois Extensions." *Acta Mathematica*, *20*, 237–240.

Peterson, W. W. 1958*a*. "On Checking an Adder." *IBM J. Research Develop.*, *2*, 166–168.

———. 1958*b*. "An Experimental Study of a Binary Code." *Trans. AIEE*, *77*, Part 1, *Comm. and Elec.*, 388–392.

———. 1960*a*. "Encoding and Error-Correction Procedures for the Bose-Chaudhuri Codes." *IRE Trans.*, *IT-6*, 459–470.

———. 1960*b*. "Binary Coding for Error Control." *Proc. National Electronics Conference*, *16*, 15–21.

———. 1961. *Error-Correcting Codes*. Cambridge, Mass: The M.I.T. Press.

———. 1967. "On the Weight Structure and Symmetry of BCH Codes." *Journal of the Institute of Electrical Communication Engineers*, Japan, *50*, 1183–1190.

Peterson, W. W., and E. Prange. 1964. "Symmetry Properties of Some Extended Cyclic Codes." Summaries of Papers presented at ICMCI, Tokyo, Japan.

Peterson, W. W., and M. O. Rabin. 1959. "On Codes for Checking Logical Operations." *IBM J. Research Develop.*, *3*, 163–168.

Pierce, J. N. 1967. "Limit Distributions of the Minimum Distance of Random Linear Codes." *IEEE Trans.*, *IT-13*, no. 4, 595–600.

Pless, V. 1963. "Power Moment Identities on Weight Distributions in Error Correcting Codes." *Information and Control*, *6*, 147–152.

———. 1964. *Weight Distribution of the Quadratic Residue (71, 35) Code*. AFCRL Report 64-597, Air Force Cambridge Research Labs.

———. 1968. "On the Uniqueness of the Golay Codes." *J. Comb. Th.*, *5*, 215–229.

Plotkin, M. 1960. "Binary Codes with Specified Minimum Distance." *IRE Trans.*, *IT-6*, 445–450 (1960). Also Research Division Report 51-20, University of Pennsylvania, January, 1951.

Prange, E. 1957. *Cyclic Error-Correcting Codes in Two Symbols*. AFCRC-TN-57-103, Air Force Cambridge Research Center, Cambridge, Mass., Sept. 1957.

———. 1958. *Some Cyclic Error-Correcting Codes with Simple Decoding Algorithms*. AFCRC-TN-58-156, Air Force Cambridge Research Center, Bedford, Mass., April 1958.

———. 1959. *The Use of Coset Equivalence in the Analysis and Decoding of Group Codes*. AFCRC-TR-59-164, Air Force Cambridge Research Center, Cambridge, Mass., June 1959.

Preparata, F. P. 1964. "Systematic Construction of Optimal Linear Recurrent Codes for Burst Error Correction." *Caclolo*, *2*, 1–7.

———. 1968. "A Class of Optimum Nonlinear Double Error Correcting Codes." *Inf. and Cont.*, *13*, 378–400.

Reddy, S. M., and J. P. Robinson. 1970. "Random Error and Burst Error Correction by Iterated Codes." to appear, *IEEE Trans on Information Theory.*

Reed, I. S. 1954. "A Class of Multiple-Error-Correcting Codes and the Decoding Scheme." *IRE Trans.*, *PGIT-4*, 38–49.

Reed, I. S., and G. Solomon. 1960. "Polynomial Codes over Certain Finite Fields." *J. Soc. Indust. Appl. Math.*, *8*, 300–304.

Reiffen, B. 1960. *Sequential Encoding and Decoding for the Discrete Memoryless Channel*. Ph.D. Thesis, Department of Electrical Engineering, M.I.T., Cambridge, Mass.

Reiger, S. H. 1960. "Codes for the Correction of 'Clustered' Errors." *IRE Trans., IT-6*, 16–21.
Reitweisner, G. H. 1960. "Binary Arithmetic." *Advances in Computers*, Vol. 1, ed. F. L. Alt., New York: Academic Press.
Richards, R. K. 1955. *Arithmetic Operations in Digital Computers*. New York: D. Van Nostrand Company, Inc.
Riordan, J. 1958. *An Introduction to Combinatorial Analysis*. New York: John Wiley & Sons, Inc.
Robinson, J. P. 1965. "An Upper Bound on the Minimum Distance of a Convolutional Code." *IEEE Trans., IT-11*, no. 4.
———. 1967. "Improved Gilbert Bound for Convolutional Codes." *IEEE Trans., IT-13*, no. 2, 333–335.
———. 1968. "Error Propagation and Definite Decoding of Convolutional Codes." *IEEE Trans., IT-14*, no. 1, 121–128.
Robinson, J. P., and A. J. Bernstein. 1966. "A Class of Recurrent Codes with Limited Error Propagation." *IEEE Trans, IT-13*, 106–113.
Rudolph, L. D. 1967. "A Class of Majority-Logic Decodable Codes." *IEEE Trans., IT—13*, no. 2, 305–307.
———. 1969. "Threshold Decoding of Cyclic Codes." *IEEE Trans., IT-15*, no. 3, 414–418.
Rudolph, L. D., and M. E. Mitchell. 1964. "Implementation of Decoders for Cyclic Codes." *IEEE Trans., IT-10*, no. 3, 259–260.

Sacks, G. E. 1958. "Multiple Error Correction by Means of Parity Checks." *IRE Trans., IT-4*, 145–147.
Savage, J. E. 1966*a*. "Sequential Decoding — The Computation Problem." *Bell System Tech. J., 45*, 149–175.
———. *1966b*. "The Distribution of the Sequential Decoding Computation Time." *IEEE Trans., IT-12*, 143–147.
———. 1969. "The Complexity of Finite State Decoders." Presented at International Symposium on Information Theory, Ellenville, New York.
Schalkwijk, J. P. M., and T. Kailath. 1966. "A Coding Scheme for Additive Noise Channels with Feedback." *IEEE Trans., IT-12*, 172–189.
Scholtz, R. A. 1966. "Codes with Synchronization Capability." *IEEE Trans., IT-12*, no. 2, 135–142.
———. 1969. "Maximal and Variable Word-Length Comma-Free Codes." *IEEE Trans,. IT-15*, no. 2, 300–306.
Shannon, C. E. 1957. "Certain Results in Coding Theory for Noisy Channels." *Inf. and Control, 1*, 6–25.
———. 1959. "Probability of Error for Optimal Codes in a Gaussian Channel." *Bell System Tech. J., 38*, 611–656.
Shannon, C. E., R. G. Gallager, and E. R. Berlekamp. 1967. "Lower Bounds to Error Probability for Coding on Discrete Memoryless Channels." *Inf. and Control, 10*, 65–103, 522–552.
Shannon, C. E., and W. Weaver. 1949. *Mathematical Theory of Communication*. Urbana: University of Illinois Press.
Shapiro, H. S., and D. L. Slotnick. 1959. "On the Mathematical Theory of Error-Correcting Codes." *IBM J. Research Develop., 3*, 25–34.
Shiva, S. G. S., and G. Sequin. 1970. "Synchronizable Error Correcting Binary Codes." *IEEE Trans. IT-16*, 241–242.
Singleton, R. C. 1964. "Maximum Distance q-nary Codes." *IEEE Trans., IT-10*, 116–118.
Slepian, D. 1956*a*. "A Class of Binary Signaling Alphabets." *Bell System Tech. J., 35*, 203–234.

———. 1956*b*. "A Note on Two Binary Signaling Alphabets." *IRE Trans.*, *IT-2*, 84–86.

———. 1960. "Some Further Theory of Group Codes." *Bell System Tech. J.*, *39*, 1219–1252.

———. 1968. "Group Codes for the Gaussian Channel." *Bell System Tech. J.*, *47*, 575.

Sloane, N. J. A. 1970. "A New Family of Single-Error Correcting Codes," presented at *IEEE* International Symposium on Information Theory, Noordwijk, Netherlands.

Smith, K. J. C., 1967. "Majority Decodable Codes Derived from Finite Geometries." Institute of Statistics Mimeo Series No. 561, University of North Carolina, Chapel Hill, N.C.

———. 1969. "On the p-rank of the Incidence Matrix of Points and Hyperplanes in a Finite Projective Geometry." *J. Comb. Th.*, *7*, 122–129.

Solomon, G. 1968. "Self-Synchronizing Reed-Solomon Codes." *IEEE Trans.*, *IT-14*, no. 4, 608–609.

Solomon, G., and J. J. Stiffler. 1965. "Algebraically Punctured Cyclic Codes." *Inf. and Control*, *8*, 170–179.

Spence, E. 1967. "A New Class of Hadamard Matrices." *Glasgow Journal.*, *8*, 59–62.

Stern, T. E., and B. Friedland. 1959. "Application of Modular Sequential Circuits to Single-Error-Correcting *P-N*ary Codes." *IRE Trans.*, *IT-5*, 114–123.

Stiffler, J. J. 1965. "Comma-Free Error-Correcting Codes." *IEEE Trans.*, *IT-11*, 107–112.

———. 1962. "Synchronization of Telemetry Codes." *IEEE Trans.*, Space Electronics and Telemetry, *SET-18*, 112–117.

Stone, J. J. 1961. "Multiple Burst Error Correction." *Inf. and Control*, *4*, 324–331.

———. 1963. "Multiple-Burst Error Correction with the Chinese Remainder Theorem." *J. Soc. Indus. Appl. Math.*, *11*, no. 1, 74–81.

Sullivan, D. D. 1967. "A Fundamental Inequality Between the Probabilities of Binary Subgroups and Cosets." *IEEE Trans.*, *IT-13*, 91–95.

———. 1969. "Error Propagation Properties of Uniform Codes." *IEEE Trans.*, *IT-15*, no. 1, 152–160.

Takahasi, H., and E. Goto. 1959. "Application of Error-Correcting Codes to Multi-Way Switching." Presented at the UNESCO Information Processing Conference in Paris, 1959.

Tavares, S. E., and M. Fukada. 1969*a*. "Matrix Approach to Synchronization Recovery for Binary Cyclic Codes." *IEEE Trans.*, *IT-15*, 93–101.

———. 1969*b*. "Synchronization of Cyclic Codes in the Presence of Burst Errors." *Inf. and Control*, *14*, 423–441.

———. 1970*a*. "Further Results on the Synchronization of Binary Cyclic Codes." to appear *IEEE Trans.*, *IT-16*, 238–241.

———. 1970*b*. "Synchronization of a Class of Codes Derived from Cyclic Codes." *Inf. and Control*, *16*, 153–166.

Tavares, S. E., and S. G. S. Shiva. 1970. "Detecting and Correcting Multiple Bursts for Binary Cyclic Codes." *IEEE Trans.*, *IT-16*, 643–644.

Tokura, N., K. Taniguchi, and T. Kasami. 1967. "A Search Procedure for Finding Optimum Group Codes for the Binary Symmetric Channel." *IEEE Trans.*, *IT-13*, no. 4, 587–595.

Tong, S. Y. 1966. "Synchronization Recovery Techniques for Binary Cyclic Codes." *Bell System Tech. J.*, *45*, 561–596.

———. 1968*a*. "Systematic Construction of Self-Orthogonal Diffuse Codes." Bell Telephone Laboratories Technical Memorandum, Holmdel, N.J.

———. 1968*b*. "Burst Trapping Techniques for a Compound Channel." Bell Telephone Laboratories Technical Memorandum, Holmdel, N.J.

———. 1968*c*. *Correction of Synchronization Errors with Burst-Error Correcting Cyclic Codes*. Bell Laboratories Tech. Memo.

Townsend, R. L., and E. J. Weldon, Jr. 1967. "Self-orthogonal Quasi-cyclic Codes." *IEEE Trans.*, *IT-13*, 183–195.

Trench, W. F. 1964. "An Algorithm for the Inversion of Finite Toeplitz Matrices." *J. Soc. Indust. Appl. Math.*, *12*, no. 3, 515–522.

Tsao-Wu, N. T., and S. H. Chang. 1969. "On the Evaluation of Minimum Distance of Binary Arithmetic Cyclic Codes." *IEEE Trans.*, *IT,15*, no. 5, 628–631.

Ullman, J. D. 1966. "Near Optimal, Single Synchronization Error-Correcting Code." *IEEE Trans.*, *IT-12*, 418–425.

Ulrich, W. 1957. "Non-Binary Error Correction Codes." *Bell System Tech. J.*, *36*, 1341–1388.

van der Waerden, B. L. 1949. *Modern Algebra*. (2 Volumes), translated by F. Blum and T. J. Benac. New York: Frederick Ungar Publishing Co.

Varsharmov, R. R. 1957. "Estimate of the Number of Signals in Error Correcting Codes." Doklady A.N.S.S.S.R., *117, no. 5*, 739–741.

Veblen, O., and J. W. Young. 1910. *Projective Geometry*, Vols. I and III. New York: Blaisdel Publishers.

Viterbi, A. J. 1967. "Error Bounds for Convolutional Codes and an Asymptotically Optimum Decoding Algorithm." *IEEE Trans.*, *IT-13*, 260–269.

Viterbi, A. J., and J. P. Odenwalder 1969. "Further Results on Optimal Decoding of Convolutional Codes." *IEEE Trans.*, *IT-15*, 6, 732–734.

Wagner, T. J. 1965. "A Remark Concerning the Minimum Distance of Binary Group Codes." *IEEE Trans.*, *IT-11*, 458.

———. 1966*a*. "A Remark Concerning the Existence of Binary Quasi-Perfect Codes." *IEEE Trans.*, *IT-12*, 401.

———. 1966*b*. "A Search Technique for Quasi-Perfect Codes." *Inf. and Cont.*, *9*, 94–99.

———. 1967. "Some Additional Quasi-Perfect Codes." *Inf. and Cont.*, *10*, 334.

Wallis, J. 1969*a*. "A Note of a Class of Hadamard Matrices." *Journal of Combinatorial Theory*, *6*, 222–223.

———. 1969*b*. "A Class of Hadamard Matrices." *Journal of Combinatorial Theory*, *6*, 40–49.

Wax, N. 1959. "On Upper Bounds for Error Detecting and Error Correcting Codes of Finite Length." *IRE Trans.*, *IT-5*, 168–174.

Weldon, E. J., Jr. 1963. *Asymptotic Error Coding Bounds for the Binary Symmetric Channel with Feedback*. Ph.D. Thesis, University of Florida.

———. 1966. "Difference-Set Cyclic Codes." *Bell Systems Tech. J.*, *45*, 1045–1055.

———. 1967. "Euclidean Geometry Cyclic Codes." *Proceedings of Symposium of Combinatorial Mathematics* at the University of North Carolina, Chapel Hill, N.C.

———. 1968*a*. "New Generalizations of the Reed-Muller Codes-Part II: Non-Primitive Codes." *IEEE Trans.*, *IT-14*, no. 2, 199–206.

———. 1968*b*. "A Note on Synchronization Recovery with Extended Cyclic Codes." *Inf. and Control.*, *13*, no. 4, 354–356.

———. 1971. "Decoding Binary Block Codes on Q-ary Output Channels." to appear *IEEE Trans.*, *IT-17*.

Wells, W. I. 1960. *Decoding of Group Codes for Binary Symmetric Channels*. M.I.T. Laboratory Reports 22G-0029, Lexington, Mass., March, 1960.

White, G. S. 1953. "Coded Decimal Number Systems for Digital Computers." *Proc. IRE*, *41*, 1450–1452.

Wolf, J. K. 1967. "Decoding of BCH Codes and Prony's Method for Curve Fitting." *IEEE Trans.*, *IT-13*, no. 4, 608.

Wozencraft, J. M. 1957. "Sequential Decoding for Reliable Communication." *1957 National IRE Convention Record*, *5*, Part 2, 11–25 (1957); also M.I.T. Research Laboratory of Electronics Report 325, Cambridge, Mass., 1957.
Wozencraft, J. M., and M. Horstein. 1960. "Coding for Two-Way Channels." Presented at the Fourth London Symposium on Information Theory, August 1960.
Wozencraft, J. M., and I. M. Jacobs, 1965. *Principles of Communication Engineering*. New York: John Wiley & Sons, Inc.
Wozencraft, J. M., and B. Reiffen. 1961. *Sequential Decoding*. New York: The Technology Press and John Wiley & Sons, Inc.
Wyner, A. D. and R. B. Ash. 1963. "Analysis of Recurrent Codes." *IEEE Trans.*, *IT-9*, 143–156.
Wyner, A. D. 1964. *Double Error Correcting Error Control Through Coding*. Vol. 2, Report No. AD-609-467, Dept. of Commerce Clearinghouse for Scientific and Technical Information, Springfield, Va.

Yale, R. B. 1958. *Error Correcting Codes and Linear Recurring Sequences*. Lincoln Laboratory Report 34-77, Lincoln Laboratory, M.I.T.
Young, F. H. 1958. "Analysis of Shift Register Counters." *J.A.C.M.*, *5*, 385–388.

Zaremba, S. K. 1952. "Covering Problems Concerning Abelian Groups." *J. London Math. Soc.*, *27*, 242–246.
Zetterberg, L. H. 1962. "Cyclic Codes for Irreducible Polynomials for Correction of Multiple Errors." *IEEE Trans.*, *IT-8*, 13–21.
Zierler, N. 1955. *Several Binary-Sequence Generators*. M.I.T. Lincoln Laboratory Technical Report 95, Lexington, Mass, September, 1955.
———. 1958. *On a Variation of the First Order Reed-Muller Codes*. M.I.T. Lincoln Laboratory Group Report 34-80, Lexington, Mass., October, 1958.
———. 1959. "Linear Sequences." *J. Soc. Indust. Appl. Math.*, *7*, 31–48.
———. 1960*a*. "On Decoding Linear Error-Correcting Codes-I." *IRE Trans.*, *IT-6*, 450–459.
———. 1960*b*. "On Decoding Linear Error-Correcting Codes-II." presented at the Fourth London Symposium on Information Theory, August, 1960; also M.I.T. Lincoln Laboratory Group Report 55-G-0025, Lexington, Mass. April, 1960.
———. 1960*c*. *A Class of Cyclic Linear Error-Correcting Codes in p^m Symbols*. M.I.T. Lincoln Laboratory Group Report 55-19, Lexington, Mass., January, 1960.
Zigangirov, K. S. 1966. "Some Sequential Decoding Procedures," *Problemy Peredachi Informatsii*, *2*, 13–25.

Index

9 780262 527316

Printed in the United States
By Bookmasters